THE BRITISH ALMSHOUSE

new perspectives on philanthropy *ca* 1400-1914

edited by

NIGEL GOOSE

HELEN CAFFREY

and

ANNE LANGLEY

FACHRS
FAMILY & COMMUNITY HISTORICAL RESEARCH SOCIETY

FACHRS Publications
Milton Keynes

Published by

FACHRS Publications
Family & Community Historical Research Society Ltd
Pilcot House, Pilcot, Dogmersfield, Hook, Hants RG27 8SY

ISBN: 978-0-9548180-2-9

Front Cover Illustration
Nicholas Chamberlain's Hospital at Bedworth in Warwickshire, founded 1715, rebuilt 1840,
Photograph © Anne Langley 2015

Back Cover Illustration
Portrait of Mary Sandford deposited at Gloucester Archives
(GA ref P81MI 1/6) and reproduced courtesy of St James' Parochial
Church Council, Chipping Campden

Cover design and typesetting
Angela Blaydon Publishing Limited
2 Elm Close, Ripley, Surrey GU23 6LE

Set in Times New Roman 10pt
Printed on paper from sustainable sources

FSC
www.fsc.org
MIX
Paper from
responsible sources
FSC® C020438

Printed by Hobbs the Printers Ltd, Totton, Hants. SO40 3WX
www.hobbs.uk.com

CONTENTS

LIST OF ILLUSTRATIONS

LIST OF FIGURES

COLOUR PLATES

LIST OF TABLES

LIST OF MAPS

FAMILY AND COMMUNITY HISTORICAL RESEARCH SOCIETY (FACHRS)

FACHRS was created for the alumni of a popular Open University course on 'Family and Community History'. It now has members throughout Great Britain: experienced historians who can undertake local research; their results are then combined to produce national conclusions grounded in local expertise. FACHRS adopts projects that stand in need of further research, where a team of volunteers can provide a large amount of work and local knowledge, under the academic guidance of an expert in the field. Without this support, projects such as the present one would take decades to complete, because they stand wholly beyond the capacity of individual researchers. The British tradition of historical research relies chiefly upon individual efforts rather than research teams so that the FACHRS model offers an interesting and productive alternative. Major previous FACHRS projects have included work on the Swing riots and the early history of allotments, both of which resulted in books similar to this current volume: *Swing Unmasked: the agricultural riots of 1830-1832 and their wider implications* and *Breaking New Ground: Nineteenth-century Allotments from local sources*. A project on School Logbooks led to a series of academic articles and a current project is researching the local effects of the First World War. Mini projects on topics such as railway staff, bank managers and school-teachers, have proved very popular with members. A refereed journal, newsletter, website (www.fachrs.com) annual conference and other activities ensure a thriving community of people interested in researching local history.

ACKNOWLEDGEMENTS

FACHRS is very grateful to the Aurelius Trust for a generous grant to support the publishing of this book. We would also like to thank the Economic History Society for grants to support the research, Professor Goose, Helen Caffrey and Anne Langley for their guidance and editorial skills, Anne Langley for coordinating the project, Angela Blaydon for professional editing (with assistance from Neil Blaydon) and the Almshouse Association for helpful information. Above all we would like to congratulate all the researchers (listed below) who devoted their time and enthusiasm to the work. Some devoted individuals worked on more than one county and teams contributed behind the scenes to research in London, Oxfordshire, St Albans, Staffordshire and Warwickshire. Other people sadly had to drop out of the project for personal reasons and we wish them well.

RESEARCHERS

Cheryl Bailey	Sarah Hare	Anne Prudames
Caroline Barron	Cecile Hunt	Adrienne Rosen
Val Batt-Rawden	Enid Hunt	The late Robert Ruegg
Angela Blaydon	Elspeth Johnson	Pam Sambrook
Christine Bloxham	Joyce Kirk	Michael Saxby
Ann Clark	Sue Lambert	Malcolm Scott
Gwyneth Craze	Anne Langley	Christine Seal
Linda Crust	Paul Leaver	The late Richard Seal
Janet Cumner	Clive Leivers	Adrian Shatford
Michael Drake	John Loosley	Su Shatford
Anne Earl	Carmen Mangion	Sue Smith
Stef Eastoe	Di Mehew	Derek Spruce
Judith Ellis	Denise Neilson	Kate Thompson
Stella Evans	Jean Orpin	Maeve Twisleton-Mellor
Elizabeth Fathi	Valerie Pattenden	Chris Watson
Mike Fitzgerald	Michael Pearson	Sylvia Watts
Jackie Gore	Maggie Penton	Pauline White
Noel Grimmet	Sylvia Pinches	Brita Wood

INTRODUCTION

Anne Langley

This project was launched at a conference of the Family and Community Historical Research Society (FACHRS) in 2006 when Professor Nigel Goose gave a talk on 'Poverty, Old Age and Gender in 19th-century England: the case of Hertfordshire'. The Society agreed to manage the project under the academic guidance of Professor Goose, with Dr Anne Langley coordinating it. Members of FACHRS and the Local Population Studies Society (LPSS) were invited to join the project and other enthusiasts were recruited later. The aim was to investigate the provision of almshouses in England, Wales and Scotland.

The start date was originally set at 1400 as it was felt that earlier foundations had already been well researched. The end date of 1914 was intended to respect the confidentiality of living people and to make the project more manageable. During the research phase it became obvious that clear-cut start and end dates were not possible – some almshouses had an important history before 1400, and 20th-century developments could hardly be ignored. Thus, although the main period of study still remained 1400-1914, researchers were able to look back and forward where relevant.

A briefing pack was produced plus a template for data entry that was trialled, modified and then demonstrated to researchers at a briefing meeting held in St Albans. A report of the briefing was sent to all researchers together with useful background information. Helen Caffrey joined the editorial team as a special adviser on the architecture of almshouses. Further briefing meetings were held in 2007 (addressed by Professor Richard Smith, Dr Ian Archer and Helen Caffrey) and 2009 (addressed by Professor Marjorie McIntosh and Professor Nigel Goose).

Data was collected over several years – and indeed continues today in an effort to fill gaps in the coverage. Material has been received from over fifty people covering most English counties and several London boroughs, plus examples from Scotland and Wales. Researchers found that there was considerable interest in their work; as a result they have produced academic articles and given talks on their findings to local, national and international audiences. Exhibitions have been mounted, including one at the University Library in Cambridge. Work has started on a gazetteer that is intended to provide access to the collected information via the World Wide Web and it is hoped that this will provide a valuable stimulus for further research because the data collected so far is by no means comprehensive. The other main outcome of the project is this book, which covers a wide geographical area and presents material about important aspects of almshouses.

It has taken longer than intended to produce this volume partly because of the wealth of material available, which made it difficult to finish the collection phase of the project (indeed some researchers are still enthusiastically making new discoveries). It also became clear that there were gaps in the material that needed to be filled (for example, very early almshouses, regional almshouses and gardens) and a few chapters were therefore commissioned. Finally there were changes and difficulties in the personal lives of those leading and taking part in the project (retirement, accident, illness and bereavement). Overall, however, the project has benefitted from the longer timescale and we believe that as a result this book is stronger and more comprehensive.

PART ONE

Almshouses: History, Buildings and Community

CHAPTER 1
THE CHRONOLOGY AND GEOGRAPHY OF ALMSHOUSE FOUNDATION IN ENGLAND

Nigel Goose

INTRODUCTION

Having spent a large part of my academic career researching issues surrounding poverty and social structure – in urban contexts in the early modern period and in rural contexts in the 19th century – it occurred to me in 2005 that there was a major omission in the literature, particularly from *circa* 1500 through to the present day; academic studies of English almshouses, either in particular or in general, were extremely rare. For the academic, it seemed, almshouses were only of interest to the medievalist, and from 1500 they were assigned to the periphery of the various systems of welfare, undeserving of academic interest in their own right. Even the very best studies of poverty and poor relief in early modern England have very little to say about almshouses, and imply decline in significance after their medieval heyday.[1] For the modern period, almshouses have been even more completely ignored.[2] It was this lack of academic attention to an institution that still retains a distinct physical presence, reflected in popular studies of, as well as in the form of a vibrant Almshouse Association in the early 21st century, which led to my approach to the Family and Community Historical Research Society in 2006 and, in due course, to the publication of this collection of essays. This project has stimulated enormous interest in the English almshouse and a new recognition of its historical significance. It has also led to the discovery (or rediscovery) and analysis of hitherto largely ignored historical sources, and has helped to create an agenda in terms of the various facets of the lives of almsmen and women that are reflected in the various chapters printed below. This, introductory, chapter will present an overview in terms of the chronology and geography of almshouse foundation as presently understood, to provide some context for the more detailed and specific chapters that follow, and will provide a brief introduction to those chapters, both local and thematic.

THE ORIGINS OF THE ENGLISH ALMSHOUSE

Almshouses originated in early medieval England as places that provided care for the sick poor, usually attached to a monastery. Their original focus on travellers or monks was extended in the 12th and 13th centuries to include lay people who were sick or feeble, usually housed in separate establishments administered by the monks and lay brethren. Specific care was provided for lepers in distinct institutions called lazar houses, some 250 of which were founded in the early medieval period. Hospitals were also established by non-monastic benefactors—the crown, clergymen, the aristocracy and gentry, urban livery companies and guilds or individual merchants.[3] These are the diverse origins of the modern almshouse, resulting in a confusing array of terminology in the medieval period: spitalhouses, bedehouses, Godshouses, and a range of other descriptors are used, as well as the terms hospital and almshouse. Many were multi-purpose, and had not yet evolved into the residences for the (usually) elderly poor that is characteristic of the modern almshouse. That evolution took place in the later 15th century, when English parishes started to play a fuller role in the relief of the poor, and parish fraternities increasingly accumulated stocks of land or animals, gave doles to the poor and sometimes established almshouses too.[4]

McIntosh's research reveals an upsurge of foundations after 1465 in the eight more southern or Midland counties of Berkshire, Cambridgeshire, Essex, Hertfordshire, Leicestershire, Middlesex, Nottinghamshire and Suffolk, reflecting the growing wealth of this broad region identified by Schofield and Sheail. Elsewhere, however, the trend was remarkably flat.[5] Nevertheless, late medieval England witnessed an accumulating stock of almshouses, while after *circa* 1450 the almshouse emerged in its modern form, specifically intended to provide accommodation for local elderly people who had fallen into poverty on account of age or ill-health. Lay provision gradually assumed greater importance, while lazar houses were changing into general hospitals for the poor and infirm, a trend that hastened in the 15th century as the disease declined.[6] As we approach the early modern era, therefore, there was already a mixed economy of welfare, comprising religious, private and local community provision with as yet little direct intervention from the central state.

EARLY MODERN ENGLAND

Two central events occurred in the 16th century to fundamentally alter this state of affairs, the first being the Reformation and associated Dissolution of the Monasteries and Chantries. Monasteries were swept away in 1536 and 1539, while in 1545 and 1547 the crown confiscated the property of chantries, and some hospitals and religious fraternities.[7] Between 1536 and 1549, McIntosh has estimated, 260 hospitals and endowed almshouses were closed, representing at least half of the existing institutions.[8] While the old historiographical orthodoxy focused upon the failings of the pre-Reformation monastic system of welfare, recent research has significantly modified this view, to re-emphasise the gaping hole in welfare provision the Dissolution produced.[9] Into that breach stepped new private donors, and the Tudor state.

The establishment of the Elizabethan or 'Old' Poor Law is the second key event of the 16th century, and represents the construction of the first national framework for welfare policy. Legislation to deal with sturdy beggars and vagabonds in the 1530s was supplemented with concern for the impotent poor from 1547, while in 1572 provision was made for regular collections and the appointment of overseers of the poor. The codifying statutes of 1598 and 1601 brought previous legislation together, created a clearer administrative hierarchy and provided greater powers of enforcement. Based upon the parish, the system centred upon the levying of a property-based poor rate, the provision of work for the impotent poor, the apprenticing of children and punishment of vagrants. Local churchwardens and overseers of the poor (two or four per parish) were to be responsible to two Justices of the Peace, who were to receive their accounts and to play a supervisory role, while local officers were given the power to distrain the goods of those refusing to pay.[10]

While England was far from alone in passing legislation in the early modern period for statutory poor relief financed from taxation, it stood out in respect of the extent to which that legislation was put into practice, the precise timing of widespread implementation being the only fundamental issue remaining to be resolved, and which remains the subject of debate and disagreement.[11]

Developments in philanthropy in the early modern period also remain open to debate, both through lack of research and the intransigence of available resources. Casual almsgiving, in the street or at the farm or manor gate, is impossible to measure. Some traditional forms of casual giving clearly declined across the early modern period but, for Ben-Amos, in the long term giving and support 'proliferated, diversified and survived'.[12] It remains, however, largely unquantifiable. Formal charitable giving is easier to trace. Sums were often left to the poor by will, either as a one-off payment or through an endowment. This form of charity formed the basis of Jordan's monumental *Philanthropy in England*, which employed will bequests plus identifiable lifetime endowments in ten English 'counties', 1480-1660.[13] It has been argued that Jordan exaggerated the rise in philanthropy in the later 16th and early 17th century because he failed to take account of either inflation or the growth of population. Hence there is little doubt that he was wrong to conclude that the period witnessed a 'veritable revolution... in which men's aspirations for their own generation and those to come had undergone an almost complete metamorphosis', to quote just one of a number of enthusiastic eulogies that can be found in his book.[14] Nevertheless, it has also been pointed out that charitable giving by endowment is cumulative, because endowments are not immediately used up but last as long as the trustees or other managers ensure the funds remain intact, and hence they accrete over time. Indeed, Jordan calculated that as much as 82 per cent of the total sum given for charitable uses in the period 1480-1660 took the form of capital, and would hence produce a long-term return.[15] When Jordan's figures are reworked to take account of this, the results reveal a fourfold increase in the sum available for poor relief in the 1650s compared with the 1540s, and a twofold increase in per capita terms.[16]

Almshouse endowment formed part of this. The latest figures produce by McIntosh, which come with a range of caveats, indicate that a total of 1,005 almshouses operated *at some point* between 1350 and 1599. After the mass closure of the 1530s and 1540s numbers started to recover once again, to peak in the late 16th century, with 479 institutions continuing in operation at the very end of that century — a number that still remains below the total achieved in the 1520s.[17] If we estimate that almshouses on average offered accommodation for 8-10 inhabitants, then at full capacity in the late 16th century there were places available for some 3,800-4,800 almspeople. According to the latest published estimates from the Cambridge Group for the History of Population and Social Structure, the population in 1601 was 4,161,784, of which 7.56 per cent were aged 60 plus.[18] If we assume that this was the group 'at risk' of needing almshouse accommodation, then at the end of the 16th century we can tentatively estimate that almshouses provided accommodation for between 1.22 per cent and 1.52 per cent of the relevant age group.[19]

As we move into the 17th century, it becomes possible for the first time to estimate the relative contributions of philanthropy and formal poor relief, as Slack has done by comparing a Board of Trade return dated 1696 — which calculated a national sum of £400,000 per annum collected in poor rates in England and Wales — with a figure of about £100,000 from charity in the 1650s calculated from Jordan's data. If by the mid 17th century there may still have been a balance between philanthropy and public relief, by the end of the century, Slack argues, taxation may have been providing three times as much in relief as did private charity.[20] Local evidence from the town of Colchester supports the view that by the end of the 17th century the relief of the poor had become largely the remit of corporation-sponsored relief rather than the province of private philanthropy.[21] That said, it is clear that there was substantial local variation in the availability of charitable funds in general, and almshouses in particular. For Colchester itself its 18th-century local historian Philip Morant expressed astonishment that 'in so ancient, large and considerable town as Colchester, there should appear so small, and so very few public Gifts and Benefactions'.[22] Almshouses, of course, were both a highly visible and an expensive form of charitable giving. In Colchester, if it were not for the endowment of six almshouses in St Giles' parish by John Winnocke in 1679, endowed with £41 per annum from his property in St Peter's, total charitable bequests in the late 17th century would have been far less impressive than they were.[23] Jordan calculated that 13.45 per cent of the total charitable and social relief given between 1480 and 1660 was spent on founding almshouses, ranging from a meagre 2.04 per cent in Lancashire to an impressive 25.24 per cent in Somerset. In his ten sample 'counties' containing 3,033 parishes, he found that 387 permanently endowed almshouses had been established, and a further seventy-one without a stock for maintenance.[24] Even if we disregard these seventy-one as unlikely to have survived for long, 12.75 per cent of English parishes benefited in this way, and may have accommodated between 1.80 per cent and 2.24 per cent of those aged 60 plus. However, charitable provision for the poor varied markedly from one parish to the next, regardless of the existence or otherwise of a formal poor rate.

Data collected by Archer provides further indication of the local benefits that might accrue. From an estimate of the number of almshouse places available in seventeen diverse English communities between 1589 and 1710, allied to estimates of their population sizes and the proportion aged over 60, he has calculated that between 3 per cent and 23 per cent of their elderly populations could have been accommodated in almshouses.[25] Remembering that Jordan's data suggests that 87.25 per cent of the 10,000 or so English parishes had no dedicated almshouse at all, the degree to which the early modern poor could call upon the almshouse as a component of the mixed economy of welfare was variable in the extreme.

MODERN ENGLAND, 1800-2000

The 18th century witnessed an enormous rise in the amount of money devoted to formal, state-sponsored poor relief, total expenditure increasing by a factor of ten and per capita expenditure by a factor of six. Making allowance for inflation reduces these increases considerably, though expenditure per head of the population expressed in terms of the price of wheat still quadrupled between 1696 and 1802-3.[26] But the same century also witnessed a renewed growth of charitable giving, and a change in its form. Now the new associational (or 'voluntary') charities raised funds by subscription, communally celebrating both the giver and the gift, and providing a more powerful mechanism to fund substantial projects. Religion, humanitarianism and social aspiration fuelled these endeavours, with further impetus coming from the evangelical revival of the late 18th and early 19th centuries. Endowed charities continued, but during the 18th century, it has been argued, these were overtaken by subscription-based voluntary societies.[27] The development of this new form of philanthropy makes it even harder to quantify total charitable bequests. The Gilbert Returns of 1786-88 showed that the annual income of charities for the poor amounted to almost £260,000, a figure little more than one-eighth of that paid annually in formal poor relief.[28] The return, however, has many omissions, includes only parochial charities and completely ignores the associated charities that had by now become so important.[29] It would be little more than a guess to estimate the relative value of public to private provision at this date, but given the prominence of associated philanthropy in towns, and the growing burden of poor relief in the English shires, it is at least possible that charity had become, once again, the senior partner in many urban centres, while the formal poor law dominated in the countryside.

When we move into the mid Victorian era, however, it is highly likely that private charity had by now regained the upper hand. The Brougham Commission, which conducted a county-by-county enquiry published between 1819 and 1840, revealed endowments with a total annual yield of £1,209,397 for England and Wales, a figure almost five times that reported in the Gilbert Returns fifty years earlier.[30] In 1840 total poor relief expenditure stood at just over £4.5 million, so if we allow for omissions from the Brougham reports, and also for the fact that associated philanthropy – funded by subscription rather than by personal gift – was probably by now producing a far higher annual income than were endowments, it is possible that philanthropy had overhauled formal poor relief by the start of Queen Victoria's reign.[31] Thirty years later there can be little doubt that this was the case. A further survey of the value of charitable endowments in England and Wales published in 1877 recorded a total of £2,198,464, approaching double the total declared thirty-three years before, despite the fact that the mid Victorian period saw the continued growth of associated philanthropy relative to charitable endowment.[32] State expenditure by 1870 amounted to £7.7 million, which compares with a contemporary estimate of charitable relief *in London alone* of between £5-7.5 million.[33] As Prochaska has written, 'If the first half of the nineteenth century saw philanthropy ascendant, the second half witnessed its triumph'.[34]

In the 20th century charity remained central to welfare provision, even if by now there were signs of a convergence between public and private provision, and the introduction of old age pensions in 1908 marked a symbolic break which presaged the eventual subordination of voluntarism to public welfare. The late 19th and early 20th centuries, indeed, saw some impressive new developments, such as the Durham and Northumberland Mineworkers Associations and the establishment of Whiteley Village in Surrey, which provided housing and a range of social and welfare facilities on a 230 acre estate for 350 pensioners, catering for the needs of the dependent elderly as well as for those in good health, as it does down to this day.[35] As early as 1934 Elizabeth Macadam, a leading social worker, published *The New Philanthropy*, accepting the subordination of the voluntary sector to the state.[36] While this judgement may have been premature, she did accurately predict the long-term direction of events, and the subordination of voluntarism to state provision was emphatically underwritten by the chain of reforms that constituted the emergence of the welfare state in the aftermath of World War Two. The voluntary sector did not, however, evaporate, as many commentators in 1948 had predicted.[37] Indeed, into the 21st century it has retained great diversity and a tenacity in identifying new needs as well as in satisfying old ones, which is reflected in the continued vitality of the almshouse movement to the present day. In 1943 a Nuffield Foundation study discovered nearly 1,500 almshouse charities accommodating over 22,000 people and, despite predictions of the withering away of the voluntary sector, the number of charities registered by the Charity Commission has in fact continued to grow, and that growth accelerated from the 1970s. Almshouses shared in this growth, until by 1999 the UK Almshouse Association represented the interests of 1,748 member charities, managing 2,599 groups of almshouses, providing accommodation for 31,421 residents — a growth of 43 per cent in the number of almshouse residents since 1943.[38] Recent information, taken from the Almshouse Association website, suggests a current figure of 1,800 separate almshouse charities, running 2,600 groups of almshouses, constituting over 30,000 almshouse dwellings, and providing accommodation for 36,000 individuals — a further growth of roughly 4,500, or 15 per cent, since 1999.[39]

THE GEOGRAPHY OF ALMSHOUSE PROVISION

The foregoing discussion shows how difficult it remains to faithfully reconstruct social welfare provision, and the continued problem of assessing the charitable component into the 19th century. No detailed attention has been paid to date, however, to the *Digests of Endowed Charities* that were published among the parliamentary papers from 1867 forward. These supplemented the Brougham Commission reports with evidence of those charities that had been omitted from the earlier survey, and those established since, and form a remarkable — and largely untapped — source for study of the purposes, geography and progress of charitable endowments in early- and mid-Victorian England. These returns, of course, reflected the accumulated endowment of almshouses across several centuries, and thus tell us as much about the historical development of these institutions as they do about the state of affairs at the time of their compilation. Analysis of these returns provides the basis of Table 1.I, which presents information for all English and Welsh counties on levels of endowed charitable provision in general, and expenditure on almshouses in particular, for the years 1861-8.

The results show clearly that enormous differences existed between counties in the funds available for endowed charities in general, and for almshouses in particular. Cornwall, Lancashire and Pembrokeshire, for example, contrast spectacularly with most other counties, with Bedfordshire providing fully eighteen times as much as Cornwall per capita based upon county populations in 1861/71, and nine times as much as Lancashire, a county that had also performed poorly in Jordan's early modern analysis. Proportions spent on almshouses also varied widely, from nothing at all in three Welsh counties to 46-47 per cent in Durham, Kent, Rutland and Wiltshire, while almshouse expenditure expressed per capita of the 1861/71 population aged sixty or over ranged from nothing to 64p in Bedfordshire and £1.40 in Rutland. Overall, however, 26 per cent of the annual income of endowed charities was dedicated to the support of almshouses and their inmates, while 12 per cent of localities benefited from such provision, though again with a very wide range indeed.[40]

The per capita data in column five of Table 1.I is based upon population totals as given in the 1861 and 1871 censuses, and so provides a snapshot at one point in time. The charitable stock found in 1861-8 is the accumulations of endowments over several centuries, and the per capita totals in column five will have been influenced by the rapid population growth experienced in some counties as industrialisation proceeded, and will fail to take on board the rise in voluntary or associational charity that was such a feature of the later 18th and 19th centuries. An additional calculation is therefore offered in column ten of Table 1.I, which is based upon county population totals for 1761, a date which largely preceded these developments. The geographical variation noted above is now more muted, but remains apparent, with counties such as Cornwall, Cumberland and the North Riding of Yorkshire performing particularly poorly, and Warwickshire, Bedfordshire and Rutland performing remarkably well.

TABLE 1.I
Expenditure on endowed charities and almshouses 1861-1876: England and Wales

County	Date	Pop. 1861 or 1871	% pop. age 60+	Endowed charity per capita (£)	Almshs expend. per capita age 60+ (£)	% endowed charity on almshouses	No. localities supporting almshouses	% localities supporting almshouses	Endowed charity per capita (£) pop. base 1761
Beds	1861-63	135,287	7.68	0.18	0.64	27	15	15	0.47
Berks	1862-63	176,256	8.86	0.15	0.62	36	28	20	0.27
Bucks	1862-64	167,993	8.88	0.10	0.20	19	32	19	0.17
Cambs	1863-64	176,016	9.15	0.12	0.17	13	16	12	0.27
Ches	1862-63	505,428	6.57	0.03	0.07	16	10	5	0.11
Corn	1863-64	369,390	8.60	0.01	0.02	18	13	9	0.03
Cumb	1864-65	205,276	8.64	0.03	0.02	5	7	6	0.06
Derby	1869-70	379,394	7.39	0.05	0.14	20	29	12	0.17
Devon	1865-67	584,373	9.68	0.08	0.10	13	44	12	0.15
Dorset	1863-64	188,789	9.19	0.07	0.19	24	22	15	0.14
Durham	1869-70	685,089	5.35	0.03	0.24	47	15	17	0.15
Essex	1863-64	404,851	8.47	0.07	0.16	19	38	13	0.14
Gloucs	1864-65	485,770	8.80	0.06	0.12	18	26	11	0.37
Bristol	1869-70	182,552	7.03	0.26	0.95	25			
Hants	1869-71	514,684	8.16	0.05	0.22	39	18	8	0.14
Here	1864-66	123,712	11.84	0.13	0.32	30	18	10	0.19
Herts	1862-63	173,280	8.45	0.11	0.30	23	26	21	0.20
Hunts	1863-64	64,250	8.77	0.07	0.12	15	9	13	0.13
Kent	1861-63	733,887	7.57	0.09	0.53	46	58	18	0.28
Lancs	1865-68	2,429,440	5.28	0.02	0.05	11	17	4	0.19
Leic	1862-63	237,412	8.92	0.12	0.46	34	26	15	0.27
Lincs	1864-66	412,246	8.89	0.12	0.27	21	59	14	0.27
London cos	1865-66					54			
London pars	1875-76	74,897	7.13	1.35	2.05	11	21	20	
Westminst	1875-76	246,606	6.31	0.11	0.55	30	5	50	
Midd	1861-63	1,839,799	6.20	0.03	0.11	26	42	44	0.31
Monmouth	1863-65	174,633	6.78	0.04	0.10	17	5	7	n/a
Norfolk	1862-64	434,798	10.27	0.12	0.33	29	22	5	0.20
Northants	1870-72	243,891	8.79	0.13	0.34	23	34	13	0.25
Nthumb	1869-71	386,646	6.92	0.07	0.32	31	5	7	0.19
Notts	1869-70	319,758	8.61	0.08	0.32	36	20	10	0.27
Oxon	1869-70	177,975	9.49	0.12	0.28	23	21	10	0.21
Rutland	1863-64	21,861	10.10	0.31	1.40	46	7	21	0.42
Salop	1862-63	240,959	9.24	0.11	0.31	25	17	9	0.20
Somerset	1869-71	463,483	10.09	0.06	0.16	29	36	11	0.12
Staffs	1865-66	746,943	5.87	0.04	0.09	13	19	10	0.18
Suffolk	1871-74	348,869	10.30	0.12	0.31	26	32	9	0.24
Surrey	1861-63	831,093	6.75	0.09	0.37	29	31	21	0.42
Sussex	1862-64	363,735	8.42	0.03	0.10	25	23	17	0.12
Warks	1872-74	684,189	6.28	0.09	0.25	17	16	8	0.57
Coventry	1872-74	37,670	8.31	0.41	0.91	18			
Westm	1864-65	60,817	8.98	0.12	0.15	11	3	3	0.20
Wilts	1867-69	257,177	9.99	0.08	0.38	46	28	14	0.12
Worcs	1873-75	338,837	7.99	0.11	0.36	26	13	8	0.31
Yorks ER	1872-75	312,262	8.01	0.11	0.52	37	14	7	0.36
Yorks NR	1873-75	293,278	8.15	0.04	0.14	26	19	7	0.09
Yorks WR	1873-76	1,830,815	5.97	0.05	0.20	25	69	16	0.25
Anglesey	1872-74	51,040	11.95	0.04	0.06	19	6	10	n/a
Brecknock	1862-65	61,627	8.87	0.04	0.08	17	3	6	n/a
Cardigan	1862-65	72,245	9.96	0.01	0.00	0	0	0	n/a
Carmarthen	1862-65	111,796	9.52	0.02	0.03	14	2	5	n/a
Carnarvon	1872-74	106,121	9.23	0.02	0.06	29	5	10	n/a
Denbigh	1872-74	105,102	9.12	0.06	0.17	26	9	16	n/a
Flint	1872-74	76,312	9.12	0.02	0.01	2	1	3	n/a
Glamorgan	1862-65	317,752	5.43	0.01	0.00	0	0	0	n/a

TABLE 1.I contd

County	Date	Pop. 1861 or 1871	% pop. age 60+	Endowed charity per capita (£)	Almshs expend. per capita age 60+ (£)	% endowed charity on almshouses	No. localities supporting almshouses	% localities supporting almshouses	Endowed charity per capita (£) pop. base 1761
Merioneth	1872-74	46,598	9.81	0.02	0.05	20	3	8	n/a
Montgom	1872-74	67,623	10.65	0.02	0.00	1	3	6	n/a
Pembroke	1862-65	96,278	10.17	0.03	0.02	6	1	3	n/a
Radnor	1862-65	25,382	9.33	0.03	0.00	0	0	0	n/a
Total E & W		21,204,242	7.40	0.07	0.26	26	1061	12	n/a
England		20,066,366	7.33	0.08	0.28	27	1028	12	0.24

Sources: Census of Great Britain 1861: BPP 1863 Vol. LIII Pt. I Population Tables. England and Wales. Vol. II pt. I, Summary Tables, pp. x-xiii. Digest of Endowed Charities: BPP 1867-8 Vol. LII Pt. I (433); BPP 1867-68 Vol. LII Pt.II (433); BPP 1868-69 Vol. XLV (93). 1761 county population totals from Wrigley, 'English county populations'.

TABLE 1.II
Proportion of the elderly in almshouses in England *ca* 1520-2012

Date	No. almshouses	No. residents (8 each)	No. residents (10 each)	% of the elderly (age 60+)	
1520	617	4,936	6,170	2.32 - 2.90	England
1600	479	3,832	4,790	1.22 - 1.52	England
1660 (1)	794	6,352	7,940	1.40 - 1.75	England
1660 (2)	1,019	8,152	10,190	1.80 - 2.24	England
1870 (3)	1,336	10,688	13,360	0.71 - 0.88	England
1943	1,500	12,000		0.21	UK
2012	2,600	36,000		0.28	UK

Notes
(1) Excludes London/Middlesex, and adopts Jordan's estimate of 9,321 parishes in England
(2) Includes London/Middlesex, and adopts Wrigley and Schofield estimate of 10,000 parishes in England
(3) 30% added to no. places with an almshouse in 1870 to allow for multiple institutions in towns

Sources: 1520/1600: McIntosh, *Poor Relief.* 1660: W.K. Jordan, *Philanthropy.* 1870: BPP 1867/8-1877 (various), Digests of Endowed Charities. 1943: Nuffield Foundation, *Old People.* 2012: Almshouse Association: www.almshouses.org/

Table 1.II provides a summary of the various estimates of the proportion of the 'at risk' (sixty years and over) population able to benefit from almshouse accommodation over the past five hundred years.[41] What is clear from this data is that almshouses have only ever been able to cater for a small proportion of the 'at risk' population, although that proportion could vary widely from county to county, and from locality to locality. So while this very particular form of philanthropy could be of enormous benefit to particular individuals in particular places at particular times, it has never proved adequate to provide a welfare safety net for the elderly at any point in English history and, for the majority, residing in localities where there was no endowment, almshouses were wholly irrelevant to their welfare needs.[42] The second conclusion to be drawn from Table 1.II is that a 'whiggish' interpretation of welfare history, which sees a linear growth in state welfare paralleled by a decline in private charity, is simply wrong. After a hiatus at the Reformation, the capacity of almshouse accommodation has grown steadily over the centuries, and grew particularly rapidly in the second half of the 20th century during the heyday of the new welfare state. That said, the proportionate contribution of almshouses has fallen over time. In Victorian England that fall was largely the product of rapid national population growth, and the inability of almshouse accommodation to keep pace with that growth. During the 20th century, when the fall was most dramatic, the explanation lies in the changing national demographic profile, which saw at least a doubling of the 'at risk' population as greater longevity and a falling birth rate produced a far more elderly population.

PHILANTHROPY, ALMSHOUSES AND THE STATE

Although we might regard almshouse foundation as an archetypal form of private charity, ironically it is sometimes hard to distinguish from formal relief sponsored by local parish officers and town corporations. For the 18th and early 19th centuries, Broad has questioned the dominance of the workhouse as the preferred solution to housing the poor, and argues that before 1834 poor houses and church houses played a significant role in their support over much of England. In the five counties of Bedfordshire, Buckinghamshire, Dorset, Northamptonshire and Warwickshire in the early 19th century, he identified a total of 2,291 parish houses, and 534 charity houses.[43] It is also evident that there was a blurring between public and private provision, parish authorities frequently adopting a management role in relation to endowments that were initially entirely private. In Ashwell in Hertfordshire, for example, a building initially designated as a workhouse was effectively transformed into an orphanage in the early 18th century, while in Brill in Buckinghamshire pasture lands initially designated in a disafforestation grant in the 1630s to provide direct access for the poor were eventually brought in to form part of an integrated parish provision, let to a single tenant, and the proceeds used to provide cash payments to eligible cottagers.[44]

Similar examples can be found in Colchester, where ailing charities were subsidised in the 17th century from corporation funds. John Hunwick, merchant and bailiff, left £300 in 1594 to the mayor and bailiffs to produce an annual return of £30 for the benefit of the Colchester poor, every fifth year this sum to be divided equally between the poor of the towns of Ipswich, Maldon and Sudbury, and the money was being faithfully administered in accordance with the bequest within two years.[45] By 1637 the return had fallen to £24, and after 1643 difficulty in recovering the interest led the corporation regularly to use borough revenues to make up the arrears, by which means distributions to the poor continued into the mid 18th century.[46] Changes in the use of institutions can be found too. The hospitals of St Mary Magdalen and St Catherine's in Lexden, Colchester, both survived the Reformation. Part of St Catherine's appears to have been converted to a private house and garden by 1545, but the major part survived into the 17th century as a hospital or almshouse until its conversion to a workhouse in the 18th century.[47] In Norwich in 1687 when William Doughty endowed the hospital that still bears his name, he specified that the corporation of the city was to take over its management within six years of his death. While the building of the hospital and its transfer took a little longer than that, the transfer was eventually made, and the corporation managed not only Doughty's, but also the Great Hospital, the Boys' Hospital and the Girls' Hospital through to 1835, when the Municipal Corporations Act required the establishment of independent bodies of trustees (*see* Illustration 1.a. colour Plate I).[48]

The relationship between state welfare and private charity has become increasingly blurred in the second half of the 20th century. All the available evidence points to the growing importance of grants from statutory bodies in keeping charities afloat. The state itself, it has been suggested, has emerged as 'a major philanthropist and benefactor of the voluntary services'.[49] Of course, the benefit does not all flow in one direction, for the partnership has been a mutually advantageous one. The voluntary services provide staff (both professional and volunteer), equipment, financial resources and established expertise that saves the state money and allows it to engage in a wider range of services than it would otherwise be able to encompass. The National Assistance Act of 1948 *assumed* public-private collaboration in housing the elderly, for local authorities were empowered to provide residential accommodation for the aged by giving subsidies to voluntary agencies or by employing them as their agents on locally agreed terms. Already, during World War Two, the National Old People's Welfare Committee, founded in 1941, had obtained from the Assistance Board a supplementary allowance for old people resident in voluntary homes, allowing the number of such homes to expand and charting the pattern for the future, while a Nuffield Foundation Survey, published in 1947 as *Old People*, also assumed continued public-private cooperation. When the National Assistance Act continued the payment of supplementary allowances to almshouse residents it proved possible for many institutions to reduce residents' pensions and thus to accumulate small surpluses that could be spent on maintenance. Since 1964, for almshouse charities prepared to become Registered Social Landlords, Housing Corporation grants have been available to further assistance the process of refurbishment. 'In the rehabilitation of the almshouse' Owen writes, 'ancient charity, modern voluntary effort, and statutory stewardship have joined hands in fruitful partnership'.[50]

CONCLUSION

Almshouses and the Mixed Economy of Welfare

In the later medieval period monastic, private and community provision formed the basis of social welfare. A mixed economy of welfare in the conventional sense of a combination of public and private welfare arrived with the Elizabethan Poor Law, but the situation remained complex; poor law provision was itself highly irregular in most rural parishes well into the 17th century, while urban provision often extended beyond the confines of the formal poor rate. Private charity also stepped into the breach created by the Dissolution of the Monasteries, but there was an element of serendipity here, and even some large towns failed to make substantial provision. The public and the private could merge where local authorities rescued charities that were failing, and while some parishes excluded those in receipt of formal poor relief from additional charitable help, others did not. From the 18th century the rise of associated philanthropy created a new mechanism for providing larger scale relief schemes through public subscription, though the example of cities, such as Bristol, demonstrates how closely moral reform associations worked with local authorities in the pursuit of common ends.[51] Charitable provision grew alongside formal poor relief, while local authorities made considerable provision of accommodation for the poor, which serves to cloud identification of almshouses proper. Under the New Poor Law (1834), while expenditure per head of the population remained roughly stable over the course of the Victorian period, as did the proportion of the population receiving relief in the workhouse, the percentage in receipt of outdoor relief fell considerably, at the same time as the voluntary impulse reached its apogee.[52] In terms of almshouse provision, however, enormous variation by region, county and locality — and also by gender — needs to be factored into the equation, and a full explanation of these variations by geography and gender remains to be discovered. Coalescence between public and private can be identified from the very end of the 19th century, and while it is quite clear that the state was to become the senior partner in this relationship, the later 20th century saw both the survival and further expansion of charitable provision, almshouses included, as well as the development of the public-private relationships through tax breaks, grants, increased regulation and the receipt of a variety of benefits that effectively creates a mixed economy of welfare within the walls of every 'private' almshouse.

Throughout their history almshouses have tended to cater for the 'respectable poor', local residents who have fallen on hard times as they entered old age, rather than the indigent or disreputable poor. Furthermore, their initial ability to provide care for the sick has been lost, and since the 16th century almshouse rules have commonly insisted that residents should be capable, albeit sometimes with assistance, of maintaining an independent daily regime.[53] At no time in the past did almshouses provide for more than a small proportion of the elderly, and although an ageing population in the 20th and early 21st centuries has increased the proportion of elderly in the population, many of those over the age of sixty or sixty-five have not only better state support, but also far higher accumulated net assets, better health and fitness and continue to benefit also from the support of friends and relatives.[54] It is possible, therefore, that almshouses continue to fulfil a similar function within the mixed economy of welfare, as a safety net for those elderly poor who lack alternative accommodation and support, or as a benefit that accrued from dedication to a particular occupation, as they have done for several centuries.

The relationship between public and private provision, therefore, has never been simple and clear cut, and nor did it move inexorably in one direction over time. State provision and private philanthropy frequently interacted and overlapped in a complex variety of ways, and continues to do so today. In particular we must avoid reading history backwards — adopting a teleological or 'whiggish' interpretation of history — for there was no simple progression across the centuries from voluntarism to state welfare. We should also certainly talk in terms of mixed economies of welfare rather than a single mixed economy, but above all must appreciate one fundamental difference between the public and private sectors. For while state provision began to achieve at least a degree of national coherence from at least the late 17th century forwards, charitable provision in general, and the provision of almshouses in particular, had and retains a distinct regional and, indeed, local aspect. This, of course, has important implications for social welfare policy and strategy, but it has implications too for our historical appreciation of the mixed economy of welfare. For while we might happily extrapolate from local to national data in our attempts to gain a broad understanding of that mixed economy, our generalisations have little meaning to the actual experiences of, and opportunities available to, elderly individuals at particular places at particular times. In turn, of course, this means that almshouses require the attention of historians working at the local level if we are ever to fully understand their place in the history of the mixed economy of welfare, and the geography of philanthropy should form a central feature of the agenda of future welfare historians.

Local and Thematic Perspectives

The various essays that follow in this volume demonstrate how both local perspectives and thematic studies can help to shed light upon this sadly neglected aspect of social welfare. Following general surveys of almshouse buildings and the almshouse community by, respectively, Helen Caffrey and Anne Langley in Part One of this volume, in Part Two we turn to local studies. In Chapter 4 Derek Spruce and Steve Taylor offer a case study of the development of almshouse provision in one county, Hampshire, from medieval hospitals through the Reformation and to the emergence of the 'modern' almshouse. Inter alia they find that Winchester, for instance, is pre-eminent for pre-Reformation foundations still in existence, while many other ancient houses also continue into the 21st century. Another fifty-two almshouse foundations were established in Hampshire and the Isle of Wight in the period between 1641 and 1914. In Chapter 5, Sue Lambert examines almshouses founded in Berkshire during the 17th century, determines the identity of the founders, their occupations, and their social backgrounds. Comparing the results with W K Jordan's wider assessment of the role of different social classes in charitable giving, Lambert shows that the founders, each involved in and concerned about their local communities, regarded their almshouses as their foremost charity, and that the majority, 60 per cent, founded their almshouses during their lifetimes.

London, specifically Mile End and Whitechapel, forms the subject matter of Janet Cumner's detailed study in Chapter 6. Here, Cumner reveals the diversity of founders by looking at the sixteen almshouses that were established within two miles along the main road to the east from the City of London, through Whitechapel and Mile End, between 1623 and 1839. They ranged from the grand architect-designed hospitals, such as Bancroft's and Trinity, to small unendowed houses providing rent-free accommodation, such as Cooke's and Rowe's. Founders included wealthy merchants, livery companies, City institutions and minority religious groups. By the second half of the 19th century the expansion of London and the age of the buildings, requiring expensive maintenance, were factors contributing to decisions to move away from the area, the remnants of only two now remaining.

From London we head steadily northwards, first stopping off in Warwickshire where, in Chapter 7, Anne Langley describes the founders, buildings and administration of almshouses, explores what life was like for residents, and analyses the composition of those living there in the 19th century. She finds that although provision was *relatively* plentiful, it was very patchy across the county, failing to reflect differing population densities, and also favouring the 'respectable poor'. Finally she compares the contribution made by almshouses with that of workhouses in accommodating the elderly poor in the county during the 19th century. Workhouses, she finds, housed more of the elderly poor than almshouses, particularly later in the 19th century. The almshouses, however, provided a home for more elderly women than the workhouses, and in a few places they also housed more elderly men than the local workhouse.

A similar comparison of almshouse and workhouse provision is provided by Clive Leivers in Chapter 8. Leivers' research on Derbyshire evaluates the relative contributions of the two types of institution in the county in accommodating residents aged sixty and upwards based on an analysis of the relevant Census Enumerators Books for 1851, 1881 and 1901, similar data from four Poor Law Unions in Worcestershire being provided for comparative purposes. The findings confirm that, as in southern agricultural counties, elderly men were more likely to find accommodation in the workhouse than in almshouses and that in the workhouses they outnumbered their female counterparts.[55] Leivers also makes the point that it is important to take account of the residential and social qualifications for admission to almshouses as against workhouses.

Staying in the north, in Chapter 9 Christine Seal examines almshouse provision for seamen and their families, keelmen and aged miners, who were heavily concentrated in the North East, reflecting the local economy. She looks at the historical background and the various mechanisms through which these institutions were established, as well as the architecture of the houses, with case studies of the Trafalgar Square almshouses in Sunderland and the formation of the corporate Durham Aged Mineworkers' Homes, which were among the first of their kind in both nature and scale. Like Langley and Leivers, she makes extensive use of later 19th-century census data, offering highly detailed demographic analysis for 1881 and 1901.

Part Two closes with studies of two of the composite parts of Great Britain – Wales and Scotland. Notwithstanding the fact that, overall, Wales was very poorly endowed with almshouses – as we saw in Chapter 1 above – in Chapter 10 Sylvia Pinches finds that Anglesey foundations – in terms of founders, architecture and almspeople – were typical of the general history of such establishments nationally, highlighting the intensely local feelings that often prompted their foundation. In most cases, however, it proved difficult to distinguish a national, that is, Welsh, sentiment. The most self-consciously Welsh establishment was, perhaps ironically, the Penrhos Almshouses, which were founded by the most English of the donors. For Scotland in Chapter 11, Elspeth Johnson examines why almshouse provision never matched that in England after the Reformation, with reference to the five identified around Dundee. After the Reformation, the main difference between Scotland and England was the paucity of endowed houses in the former and the greater use by poor law authorities of outdoor relief for the poor. Scotland lacked the degree of administrative control found in England, and the church held greater sway, which resulted in a greater variety of provision. Scottish practice, in general, favoured voluntary contributions and out-relief. That almshouses never reached the numbers known in England may have been caused by factors such as this dislike of indoor relief and the Scottish attitude to unemployment, which was attributed to individual failure rather than economic circumstance.

Part Three contains thematic studies. In Chapter 12 Angela Blaydon demonstrates that rules and regulations affecting almshouse inhabitants and trustees differed greatly in extent and complexity, though they changed little over the centuries, even though more standardisation is apparent after the foundation of a permanent Charity Commission in 1853. For the trustees there were requirements of appointment, such as status or residency, and of action, such as the making of regular visits to the almshouse. For the residents there were entry criteria, such as age, sex, religion and residency, and regulations relating to their lives in the almshouse; administrative rules, such as dress or how long or often a resident could be absent; practical considerations affecting the day-to-day running of the house (security, who was responsible for repairs or for cleaning); and behavioural criteria (attendance at worship, whether they could take on outside work). Sanctions included warnings, fines and expulsion. Blaydon ends by saying that more research needs to be done to find out how strictly these rules were observed, and asks whether founders were seeking to ensure their own good reputation and entry to heaven, or truly seeking to help the less fortunate.

In Chapter 13, 'An almshouse master at bay 1836-1881', Michael Drake examines the life of the Reverend John Gower, master of the Hospital at Stoke Poges, which throws an interesting light on the problems of an under-endowed almshouse for both master and inhabitants. Gower managed to make a good living for himself and his family for nearly fifty years, despite accusations of mismanagement of funds and failure to fulfil the intentions of the founder with regard to the care of the inhabitants, and an enquiry into the management of the charity by the Charity Commissioners in 1856, which led to the replacement of the Visitors by a board of trustees. Gower's history is still something of a mystery, while it is unclear whether or not it was his personality that led to his frequent friction with pertinent authorities. Many questions remain about this interesting character, questions, Drake argues, that deserve further investigation.

Two chapters focus upon possessions. Chapter 14 investigates almspeople's possessions through a detailed analysis of the register and early inventories of the Sherborne

Almshouse in north-west Dorset, which provide a rare opportunity to glimpse the belongings of poorer older people over a period of nearly two hundred years. Ann Clark finds that during the 16th century the majority of people brought bedding and utensils into the house with them, though if they had none such items would be provided, as was clothing. By the 1710s recording of the bringing in of more luxurious things – such as furniture, storage items, money – was non-existent, and by the 1740s only bedding was being noted in the register. But did this mean, Clark asks, that new entrants generally had more possessions, or fewer, or was the change merely an administrative decision? A similar theme is discussed by Brita Wood in Chapter 15, which focuses upon the provision of almshouse clothing. From an impressive sample of ninety-two almshouses, representing nine counties plus London and Anglesey, Wood finds that only a minority ('perhaps one in four') of benefactors made any provision for the allocation of clothing, and that it was a more important provision before the 19th century, early almshouses being more likely to provide ceremonial clothing and badges. It appears to have been the decision of the founder, or subsequent benefactors, whether clothing was supplied and of what type, perhaps publicly reflecting the benefactor's generosity or as part of the desire to maintain status and respectability.

In Chapter 16 Angela Nicholls's wide-ranging study examines the material benefits of an almshouse place more broadly, to assess how well off residents really were in relation to their local communities, focusing on stipends and additional benefits such as food, fuel, rent-free accommodation and practical help, with examples drawn from the late 15th to the 19th centuries. The great variation she identifies in the material benefits associated with an almshouse place demonstrates that, while some almspeople would have achieved a reasonable standard of living in comparison with other poor people, not all almspeople would have been living comfortably or could be regarded as among the pauper elite. Chapter 17 homes in on almshouse gardens. Here Sarah Hare, with particular reference to almshouse gardens in Somerset, examines the extent to which they related to residents' day-to-day lives and reflected the wishes of benefactors, and also how they reflect the architecture of the almshouse buildings themselves. She takes a chronological route, from the 15th to the 21st century, and concludes that to the present day 'gardens are still at the centre of almshouse living'.

The status of almspeople is the subject of Judith Ellis's study in Chapter 18. Ellis examines the motives of founders in establishing almshouses, and the ways in which those motives shaped the lives of inhabitants. She uses the history of the Chipping Campden Almshouses in Gloucestershire to demonstrate the high status attributed to the residents through the centuries and argues that, although from relatively poor backgrounds, the residents enjoyed a better quality of life than similar people living in the community, with a status out of proportion to the physical benefits enjoyed. Participation in public events, entertainment by patrons, participation in public ceremonies and the portraits made of some of them during the 19th century provide more evidence of the particular status the almspeople enjoyed. Finally, Ellis expresses the hope that the views of present-day almshouse residents will be studied, to see if perceptions of their status has changed.

The last two chapters examine religiously inspired almshouses. Clive Leivers' second contribution to this volume forms Chapter 19, where he focuses upon institutions dedicated to clergy widows, again in Derbyshire. Outside the norm of almshouse provision, the three foundations found in Derbyshire had distinctive features that made them part of what Leivers sees as 'a comprehensive system for the care of the widows and children of deceased clergymen'. In this county, unlike some others, there was no age or residency restriction, which meant some widows spent much of their lives in residence, while they also received a higher income than was usual and were able to live a comfortable life, 'with their fellow residents sharing values and expectations, and supported throughout by a range of charitable provision sponsored by the Anglican church'. Finally, in Chapter 20 Carmen Mangion offers a microhistorical study of almshouses dedicated to the Catholic faith in London. Catholic benefactors, she finds, believed that the faith needs for the Catholic aged were not being met in either public institutions or charitable almshouses. Five London almshouses opened in the latter half of the 19th century to meet the needs of mostly 'deserving' Catholics. The social class of almshouse inmates varied; for they could be members of the working-class poor or middle-class people who faced financial hardship, but only St Scholastica's Retreat upheld a strict middle-class identity. Almshouses apart, the Catholic Church also provided other institutions that catered for the medical needs of the elderly. What is clear is that this form of philanthropy was an important component of the mixed economy of welfare that allowed the elderly poor to subsist in Victorian London.

Taken together, these three overviews and seventeen local and thematic studies dramatically enhance our understanding of almshouses as a component of the mixed economy of welfare in Great Britain over the last millennium. Our coverage is, of course, far from comprehensive, and many of our various conclusions remain tentative. It remains too early to draw the various threads together, but even amidst the profound diversity represented in these studies, some outlines are beginning to emerge of the various categories of institution, their chronology, their architecture, their inspiration, the discipline they imposed, their geography, the demography and social status of their residents, the benefits that accrued to them, and the place of the almshouse within the wider gamut of philanthropy and social welfare in general. Hopefully other historians will pick up the baton so effectively carried here, to cement the rightful place in the historiography of social welfare of an institution that has endured so well, and adapted so vigorously, across one thousand years of British history.

Notes

1.   Slack, P. *Poverty and policy in Tudor and Stuart England*. London, 1988, pp. 114-15 and *passim*; Hindle, S., *On the parish? The micro-politics of poor relief in rural England c. 1550-1750*. Oxford, 2004, *passim*. It should be emphasised, however, that Marjorie McIntosh's research into almshouses, which extends to 1600, was already underway prior to the start of the FACHRS project.

2.   For example, Kidd, A. *State, society and the poor in nineteenth-century England*. Basingstoke, 1999; Englander, D. *Poverty and poor law reform in 19th century Britain, 1834-1914: from Chadwick to Booth*. London, 1998; King, S. & Tomkins, A. *The poor in England 1700-1850. An economy of makeshifts*. Manchester, 2003.

3.   Clay, R.M. *English Medieval Hospitals*. London, 1909, pp. xvii-30; Godfrey, W.H. *The English Almshouse with Some Account of Its Predecessor the Medieval Hospital*. London, 1955, pp. 15-20; Howson, B. *Houses of Noble Poverty: a history of the English almshouse*. Sunbury-on-Thames, 1993, pp. 17-33; Orme, N. & Webster, M. *The English Hospital 1070-1570*. New Haven and London, 1995, pp. 15-68. The best recent general survey is Sweetinburgh, S. *The Role of the Hospital in Medieval England. Gift-giving and the Spiritual Economy*. Dublin, 2004, pp. 19-67.

4.   McIntosh, M. *Autonomy and Community. The Royal Manor of Havering, 1200-1500*. Cambridge, 1986, pp. 238-40; Rubin, M. *Charity and Community in Medieval Cambridge*. Cambridge, 1987, pp. 288-9.

5.   McIntosh, 'Local Responses to the Poor in Late Medieval and Tudor England'. *Continuity and Change*, Vol 3, 1988, pp. 217-25; Schofield, R. 'The Geographical Distribution of Wealth in England 1334-1649'. *Economic History Review*, Vol 18, 1965; Sheail, J. 'The Distribution of Taxable Population and Wealth in England During the Early Sixteenth Century'. *Transactions of the Institute of British Geographers*, Vol 5, 1972.

6.   Orme, N. & Webster, M. *The English Hospital 1070-1570*. New Haven and London, 1995, pp. 28-9; Rawcliffe, C. *Leprosy in Medieval England*. Woodbridge, 2006, chapter 6.

7.   For an accessible but authoritative modern account of the break with Rome, *see* Guy, J. *Tudor England*. Oxford, 1988, pp. 116-53.

8.   McIntosh, 1988, p. 228; McIntosh, M.K. *Poor Relief in England 1350-1600*. Cambridge, 2012, pp. 124-7.

9.   Rushton, N.S. 'Monastic Charitable Provision in Tudor England: quantifying and qualifying poor relief in the early sixteenth century'. *Continuity and Change*, Vol. 16 2001; Rushton, N.S. & Sigle-Rushton, W. 'Monastic Poor Relief in Sixteenth-century England'. *Journal of Interdisciplinary History*, Vol. 32, 2001.

10. The best account of poverty and poor relief in this period is still Slack, 1988; Hindle, 2004, provides some updating and slight modifications, though is wholly rural in its focus. A useful short summary covering a longer time period is Slack, P. *The English Poor Law*. Basingstoke, 1990.

11. Solar, P.M. 'Poor Relief and English Economic Development Before the Industrial Revolution. *Economic History Review*, XLVIII, I, 1995, p. 3; Slack, 1988, p. 170; Hindle, S. *The Birthpangs of Welfare: poor relief and parish governance in seventeenth-century Warwickshire*. Dugdale Society Occasional Paper 40, 2000; Hindle, 2004, pp. 246, 251; McIntosh, 2012. For a brief discussion of these debates, *see* Goose, N. 'Accommodating the Elderly Poor: almshouses and the mixed economy of welfare in England in the second millennium', in *'Provisions for the Elderly in North-Western Europe: almshouses around the North Sea, sixteenth-twentieth centuries'*. Special Issue *Scandinavian Economic History Review* 61, 2014, pp. 35-57.

12. Ben-Amos, I.K. *The Culture of Giving. Informal Support and Gift-Exchange in Early Modern England.* Cambridge, 2008, pp. 140-1, 378.

13. Jordan, W.K. *Philanthropy in England 1480-1660: a study of the changing pattern of English social aspirations.* New York, 1959. Jordan included the cities of London and Bristol as two of his ten 'counties'.

14. Ibid., 1959, p. 240.

15. Ibid., 1959, p. 24.

16. Bittle, W.G. & Lane, R.T. 'Inflation and Philanthropy in England: a reassessment of W.K. Jordan's data', *Economic History Review*, Vol. 29, 1976; Hadwin, J.F. 'Deflating Philanthropy' *Economic History Review*, Vol. 31, 1978. This would not hold true, of course, if there was a wholesale collapse of established charities, but there is no evidence that this was the case for endowed charities.

17. McIntosh, 2012, pp. 68-71.

18. Wrigley E.A., *et al. English Population History from Family Reconstitution 1580-1837*. Cambridge, 1997, Table A9.1.

19. These figures are slightly at variance with those offered by McIntosh, 2012, p. 75.

20. Slack, 1988, p. 171.

21. Goose, N. 'The Rise and Decline of Philanthropy in Early Modern Colchester: the unacceptable face of mercantilism?' *Social History* 31, no. 4, 2006, pp. 482-3.

22. Morant, P. *The History and Antiquities of Colchester*. Chichester, 1748, reprinted 1970, Book III, p. 1.

23. *Charity Commissioners Report for Essex*, British Parliamentary Papers (BPP), 1837-8, Vol. XXV.I, *32nd Report Part I,* pp. 536-7. On his death in 1684 he left a further £5 per annum after his wife's death to the poor of the Dutch Congregation as long as it persisted, £10 to the Dutch poor, £10 to his poor neighbours in Northstreet, and £1 for each loom that his weavers had in work for him: The National Archive (TNA): PROB 11, Cann 50; TNA: PCC will of John Winnocke, baymaker, St Peters, drawn 1684, proved 1685.

24. Jordan, 1959, pp. 27, 261-2.

25. Archer, I.W. 'Hospitals in Sixteenth- and Seventeenth-century England', in *Europäisches Spitalswesen. Institutionelle Fürsorge in Mittelalter und Früher Neuzeit: Hospital and Institutional Care in Medieval and Early Modern Europe*, M. Scheutz, *et al.* (eds) *Mitteilungen des Instituts für Österreichische Geschichtsforschung*, 51, 2008, Table 4, p. 65.

26. Slack, 1990, Table 1, p. 30.

27. Kidd, A. *State, Society and the Poor in Nineteenth-century England*. Basingstoke, 1999, p. 66.

28. Owen, D. *English Philanthropy 1660-1960*. Cambridge, MA, 1964, p. 86; Slack, 1990, p. 30.

29. Owen, 1964, p. 86; Gorsky, M. *Patterns of Philanthropy: charity and society in nineteenth-century Bristol.* Woodbridge, 1999, pp. 41-2.

30. Owen, 1964, p. 192.

31. Williams, K. *From Pauperism to Poverty*. Routledge and Kegan Paul, London, 1981, Table 4.6, p. 169.

32. BPP 1877, Vol. LXVI, *Explanatory Memoranda and Tabular Summaries of the General Digest*, Table 111.

33. Kidd, 1999, p. 67.

34. Prochaska, F.K. *The Voluntary Impulse: philanthropy in modern Britain*. London, 1988, p. 41.

35. Brown, A. *The Whiteley Homes Trust 1907-77*. Chichester, 1992; Howson, 2008, p. 71.

36. Prochaska, 1988, p. 80.

37. Ibid., p. 88; Knight, B. *Voluntary Action*. London, 1993, p. 22.

38. Bryson, J.R., McGuiness, M. & Ford, R.G. 'Chasing a "Loose and Baggy Monster": almshouses and the geography of charity', *Area*, Vol. 34, 2002, pp. 50-1.

39. URL: www.almshouses.info/, 'What are Almshouses?' accessed 13th June 2012.

40. The cities included separately in the data in Table 1.I are excluded from the foregoing discussion.

41. Sixty was the most common age at which individuals were eligible for almshouse accommodation through from the 16th to the 19th centuries, and the most common age in the Victorian period to mark the onset of 'old age': Goose, N. & Looijsteijn, H. 'Almshouses in England and the Dutch Republic Circa 1350-1800: a comparative perspective', *Journal of Social History* 45, no. 4, 2012. pp. 1056-7.

42. The 'hazardous and irregular' nature of voluntary giving has also been emphasised recently by Ben-Amos, 2008, p. 388.

43. Broad, J. 'Housing the Rural Poor in Southern England, 1650-1850', *Agricultural History Review*, Vol. 48, 2000, Table 1, p. 168.

44. Broad, J. 'Parish Economies of Welfare, 1650-1834', *Historical Journal* 42, no. 4, 1999, pp. 997-8, 1000.

45. TNA: PROB 11, 45 Dixy, PCC will, John Hunwick, merchant and bailiff, 1594; Essex Record Office (ERO): Borough Muniments, Assembly Book 1576-99 [10 November, 1595, 3 September 1596].

46. ERO: Borough Muniments, Assembly Book 1620-46, f.176v [1637]; Assembly Book 1646-66; *CC* Essex, 1937-8, p. 552; Cooper, J. (ed.) *A History of the County of Essex*, Victoria County History, (*VCH* Essex) Oxford University Press, Oxford, 1994, Vol. 9, p. 369. In 1748 Morant noted that the interest on the £300 had been distributed to 1741, although 'it is sunk in proportion to the interest of other moneys', reprinted 1970, Book III, 2.

47. Cooper, *VCH* Essex, 1994, Vol. 9, p. 308.

48. Norfolk Record Office: Case 20f/14 William Doughty's Will, 25th April 1687; N/MC 2/3 Hospital Committee minutes, April 1708-April 1720. *See also* Goose, N. & Moden, L. *A History of Doughty's Hospital Norwich, 1687-2009*. Hatfield, 2010, pp. 31-4, 60-1.

49. Owen, 1964, pp. 538-41, quote on p. 541.

50. Ibid., pp. 547-52, quote on p. 552. This is discussed more fully in Part IV of Goose & Moden, 2010. Nuffield Survey Committee, *Old People*. London, 1947.

51. Fissell, M.F. 'Charity Universal? institutions and moral reform in eighteenth-century Bristol', in *Stilling the Grumbling Hive: the responses to social and economic problems in England, 1689-1750*, Davidson, L., *et al.*, (eds), Stroud, 1992, pp. 121-44.

52. Rose, M.E. *The Relief of Poverty, 1834-1914*. Basingstoke, 1972, Appendix A, p. 50; Goose, N. 'Poverty, Old Age and Gender in Nineteenth-century England: the case of Hertfordshire', *Continuity and Change*, Vol. 20, no. 3, Table 1, p. 35.

53. The increasing frailty of almshouse residents, who are themselves becoming older as they strive to maintain independent households for as long as possible, is a problem well known to the almshouse movement in the twenty-first century.

54. For a stimulating historical account of old age that also considers the elderly in contemporary Britain, *see* Thane, P. *Old Age in English History: past experiences, present issues*, Oxford, 2000. For continued family and community support *see also* Freeman, M. & Wannell, L. 'The Family and Community Lives of Older People After the Second World War: new evidence from York', *Local Population Studies*, 2009, pp. 82, 12-29.

55. Goose, N. 2005, pp. 351-84.

CHAPTER 2
ALMSHOUSE BUILDINGS:
FORM, FUNCTION AND MEANING

Helen Caffrey

Almshouses are residential charities. Whilst a good deal more than accommodation may be involved, the bottom line is permanent, free, secure and hopefully well-maintained housing. Most almshouses are readily identifiable, despite diversity of architectural interpretation, as function tends to prevail over fashion, producing a distinctive genre. However, almshouse buildings have not followed a straightforward historical pattern of linear development. Analysis shows a variable combination of features reflecting wider national architectural trends, regional or local aspects, and individual motives. Personal choice and freedom from regulation (until more recent times) by founder and trustees account for some of the latter elements in design as they have done in selection criteria and other aspects governing the almspeople's daily life. Buildings, as the public face of the charity, may be employed as statements about the founder and about his or her role as philanthropist. As memories fade and other social changes have taken place, these statements take a little more understanding to unpick.

That is one aim of this chapter. The building itself might also convey a message about the status of elderly residents and what was appropriate for the aged poor, while in many ways affecting the daily life of the inhabitants. For the individuals who became almsmen or women, the building was their home, centre of their daily existence, providing the environment in which the greater part of that time was spent. The visible façade has attracted the most attention from illustrators and commentators, but for the resident it is number and size of rooms, facilities within and elsewhere on site, access and privacy, which impinge. Physical and documentary evidence are complementary, and sometimes the building may contradict the terms of the foundation (as in the practicalities of imposing a curfew). Investigating almshouse buildings may thus lead into the heart of almshouse living, from the perspectives of beneficiary, founder, and the wider public of the period. This chapter, including appendices, also offers the reader an introductory field guide, a route to recording, understanding and consideration of further questions about how almshouses function. There is plenty of scope as changes affect the survival of earlier features, yet this in turn will become part of the physical record of social and demographic change.

The focus of this book is on the period from the 15th through to the end of the longer 19th century. In terms of buildings this means a long span of change, continuity, modernisation and replacement. For instance, a 16th-century foundation might remain in its original building for three centuries and more, but equally it might be rebuilt a couple of times and that could include relocation. These rebuilds are particularly valuable for demonstrating changes in attitude and values — what was considered appropriate for the elderly poor and their specific requirements. Some buildings and foundations both earlier and into the mid 20th century are important here, and so their contributions are included. Otherwise the buildings discussed are those present during the period and therefore seen and experienced by contemporaries, rather than solely what was new or up to date.

A cautionary note may be added here. Writers with an architectural bias have tended to concentrate on the more visually impressive, and often more prosperous, almshouses, or focus on those seen as quaint.[1] The experience of the inhabitants is thus marginalised, and a false concept of the 'typical' may arise. For evidence to produce meaningful and reasonably reliable conclusions it needs to be quantifiable (*see* Appendix 2.2). This writer's experience in producing a county study did identify some popular errors but classification of features also indicated the extent of certain trends. The multi-regional coverage in this book has enabled some hypotheses to be tested further. Literature, especially from such 19th-century novelists as Trollope, Love Peacock, Dickens and Thackeray, is another source to portray almshouses and their residents' life style, reflecting and influencing contemporary perceptions. Disappointingly few artists in Britain have chosen to depict almshouses and almspeople, although topographical prints show rather more, albeit concentrating on the public façade, usually with a few nicely placed and well-dressed foreground figures.

BUILDING TYPES

The Long Hall

Although medieval documentary evidence shows a range of choices, including an economical use of existing rather than purpose-built structures, the long hall is a form which was particular to its time in construction, though less limited in continuing use.[2] This consisted of a central space with beds down either side and sometimes forming an additional spine down the centre, reminiscent of a modern hospital ward and a reminder of the multi-purpose nature of medieval hospitals before the elderly and the sick were accorded separate provision. At the far end of the hall and integral to it was the chapel. This was significant in terms of treatment and morale and could be a source of comfort to those making their end. This form, so far as known, ceased by the time of the Reformation in England, although examples in Italy and Germany remained little altered into the mid 20th century.[3]

The best example of a long hall, still functioning as an almshouse, is the 13th-century foundation of St Mary's, Chichester, Sussex. The six-bay building of 82ft x 45ft (24.6m x 13.5m) (now lacking two original bays) is of local flint and stone on a substantial oak frame. The sweeping tiled king-post roof dominates the building, but the accommodation is single-storey on either side of the open central area. This continues uninterrupted for 47ft (14.1m) within the chapel but narrowing to 22ft (6.6m).[4] Long halls could afford some privacy by means of individual cubicles, with space for a few personal possessions. Desirability of some personal space was accepted by the 15th century when St Mary Magdalen in Winchester had moved six of its sixteen almspeople into individual houses.[5] If action followed regulation, this was applied at St Mary's, Chichester, soon after 1528.

The next age to emphasise privacy over function for those who could afford it was the 17th century. Almshouses built for the poor may embody ideas from a higher social status. At St Mary's, earlier cubicles became individual rooms for which chimneys were cut through the roof giving each almsperson a fireplace, a benefit within a design of unavoidable heat loss. Additional adjacent buildings avoid a loss in accommodation whilst allowing units in the long hall to become two-room apartments. Other instances of the long hall are known from archaeological excavation and antiquarian records. The Reverend Lukis recorded the remains of a more modest long hall at St Anne's, Ripon, North Yorkshire, at the time of its replacement. Prior to demolition in 1869 the hall had two small rooms by the entrance for a resident priest, then male and female wards on either side which later became all female apartments.[6] Two windows were placed irregularly in each long side with a chimney stack between them. The end wall of the chapel remains *in situ* within the garden.

Centripetal Almshouses

This form does not seem to have been widely used, though actual numbers may reflect in part a limited survival due to replacement. The writer found only two examples, both late 16th century but not connected in terms of founder, within one county, and perhaps significantly neither retains its original function. These buildings merit further consideration as their internal plans embody ideas of what an almshouse should be by imposing certain habits. At Kirkthorpe, near Wakefield in West Yorkshire, Frieston Hospital has six small sleeping chambers and one slightly bigger. A large fireplace with inbuilt seating provides central shared living space. Lack of individual hearths and chimneys in the outer rooms means that this fire was used for cooking, sociability and warmth, essential in winter. The system of hierarchy and control was inherent in the role of the Senior Brother who occupied the slightly larger room overlooking the door into the building. The intention is clear, but how the Senior Brother was chosen and how enthusiastically he carried out his duties, initially including distribution of the men's pensions, is not known. Social attitudes are further shown by the inclusion of an almswoman as a beneficiary, to ensure that the old men were clean and fed, but accommodated in a separate cottage (since demolished) in the grounds. By the 19th century this had become a sought-after position, whilst male applicants declined in number or became, illegally, out-pensioners.[7]

The second centripetal example is at Beamsley, near Skipton in North Yorkshire. Building was started in 1593 for the Countess of Cumberland, and completed on her instruction by her daughter Lady Anne Clifford, who also founded almshouses on her own behalf at Appleby-in-Westmorland in Cumbria. The first phase, Beamsley A, is circular, with the roof rising from a low single storey to a central point where day light is

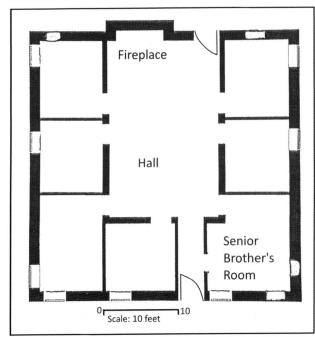

Illustration 2.a. Plan of Frieston Hospital, Kirkthorpe, West Yorkshire, built 1595, showing centripetal layout with communal living area. © *Helen Caffrey.*

admitted. The central area is set out as a chapel, through which the six almswomen would pass to reach their own personal rooms. These are wedge-shaped, and despite their dimensions of 16ft x 11ft x 6ft (4.8m x 3.3m x 1.8m), each includes a fireplace for cooking and heating, an important aspect in this exposed rural location. The Mother had a slightly larger room, containing the chest in which incoming rents were stored, and giving oversight of the doorway into the building. However the foundation was for a dozen almswomen and this structure offered no opportunity for expansion. Whatever may have been intended, the conscientious daughter added Beamsley B in the form of a simple row of one-room cottages with variable loft space. An additional front boundary wall was placed between the road and the entrance archway through the row, adorned with a foundation plaque and coat-of-arms. The Mother's authority was diminished practically by her separation from these almswomen by the long garden.[8] Lady Anne's own choice at Appleby, in which she took a close personal interest, was for a single-storey (later heightened) courtyard in local red stone about a small pebble yard.[9]

Courtyard Form

No particular date attaches to this form, although it was popular among late medieval foundations and again in the later 19th century as an architectural revival. Some writers have seen this as referencing a monastic life of devotion or an echo of an Oxford or Cambridge college, though by no means all founders had such a background. However, choice of a courtyard form was liable to have certain implications and effects. It could compactly accommodate a larger number of residents (over a dozen), especially if two-storey. The site needed to be a block rather than strip, and construction tended to be more lavish. A courtyard makes a statement: these residents are part of a community or selected enclave, and to some degree separate from the world beyond. They have a sense of security and a communal but contained quiet central space. Different interpretations of the courtyard form can affect neighbourliness and privacy, time spent in and out of doors, and the way in which the whole is perceived by the wider community. The courtyard is an important element in itself, with residents crossing it to access their individual front doors (most had no back doors) and draw water at the well usually situated here.

At Ewelme, Oxfordshire, founded in 1437, the accommodation for thirteen almsmen was on four sides of a two-storey courtyard which formed one element of a larger collegiate chantry complex.[10] Each unit was one-up, one-down, with front doors opening off the covered walkway, or cloister, or from the corner passage. At Carleton-in-Craven, North Yorkshire, Spence's Hospital was built at the end of the 17th century with a much smaller courtyard, for twelve residents, and a flight of steps at each front corner leading to a first-floor covered gallery accessing the upstairs units. Downstairs residents reach their homes from the open colonnade. The courtyard itself can only be seen, or residents able to see out, through the tall metal gates, although formerly they had the use of open space – effectively a field for cultivation – to the rear of the buildings.[11]

The increase in courtyard layouts during the mid to later 19th century may be due to an element of romantic medievalism, perhaps influenced by literature as a guide to 'what an almshouse should be'. It suggests an unexpected sense of fancy among hard-headed non-conformist textile manufacturers. Joseph Crossley, a carpet manufacturer and major employer, whose extended family was responsible for much civic building in Halifax, West Yorkshire, founded his almshouse in 1863, completed by his son in 1870, for forty-eight almspeople, men, women or couples. The design was commissioned from Roger Ives, with buildings set out on the terraced site as an asymmetric courtyard giving extensive gardens. Although the skyline is varied including tower and narrow campanile, building is essentially two storey, but inside there are small bedsits and larger units on two floors.[12] It may be compared with another almshouse, built a decade later for a similar number of inhabitants, in another northern textile city, Bradford. Superficially Bradford Tradesmen's Home is a similar courtyard layout, but here the entrance, rather than from the wide end with a view achieved by the sloping ground, is narrow, leading past the small house containing the offices for the charity's Secretary and giving a more conscious impression of a secluded enclave. The gardens enhance this, divided into individual as well as some common space. Architectural style emphasises the comparison; both are neo-Gothic, but here it is less assertive with dormers giving a cottagey feel, although in terms of social status these residents might be seen as superior, due to their former occupation and membership of the society which supported the almshouse, requiring a minimum income and permitting a companion.[13]

Courtyards offer scope to thoughtful and imaginative architects.[14] They may be large or small, urban or rural, having four sides of inward-facing houses, or three with a wall and gatehouse or other feature on the fourth side. Alternatively they may be open to public gaze with three sides only. What occupies the central space and the residents' routes across and around it are factors by which building layout directs life style: 'the material preconditions for the patterns of movement, encounter and avoidance' which form 'the material realisation – and sometimes generator – of social relationships'.[15]

The Row

This has been by far the most popular choice for almshouses, across time and place, and continues to be so. Usually a single storey, it could be built relatively cheaply on lines familiar to local builders in an urban or rural context, and could be as plain or elaborate as the founder wished or could afford. A long frontage to the road would reinforce the charity's visibility but such a terrace could also be seen to indicate a level of expenditure suitable to the beneficiaries. Such a ubiquitous form of housing lent itself to the introduction of features that confirmed its distinctive function. The only claim to similarity might come from some estate housing built by landowners interested in model dwellings and farms. In such cases the same builder could be responsible, and investigation might reveal differences in treatment of the elderly from working tenants.

One notable feature of almshouse rows is symmetry. Numbers, say half a dozen or a dozen almspeople, would be represented visually by the appropriate number of front doors and chimney stacks. This orderly façade, even where internal divisions were not so consistent, implies the importance of the message of order and regularity without individual deviation. Symmetry and unity may be emphasised by turning the two row ends gable-on to the street, with their front doors within the re-entrant angle. Some rows exploit this to produce wings, a further step towards the inward-looking enclave. The inhabitants themselves might be allocated to male or female ends of the rows, though this could depend on the trustees' need to keep the property occupied. The centre takes on special importance, architecturally and sometimes functionally. A Classical pediment, clock, niche or other detail may give dignity to a simple façade. The centre is the usual position for the building's identity to be stated on a plaque, and design is clearly ordered about this point. It also places the benefactor most literally centre stage.

Illustration 2.b. Symmetrical row with school as central feature at Mary Lowther's Hospital, Ackworth, West Yorkshire, built 1741. *Photo © Helen Caffrey.*

The Town House

This form seems to contradict some of what has been said about other diverse types. Its construction dates mainly to the 18th century, a period of fewer foundations but of prosperity and conscious civic pride in successful towns and cities. The town house resident was likely to climb stairs and traverse corridors to the front door, as in a block of flats. Inclusion of almshouses within an acceptable urban form suggests their recognition among mainstream civic amenities, even if privately funded, at a time when new models were being developed to suit specialist buildings for medical care. Occasionally the town house almshouse was just that – the former home of the donor. Dorothy Wilson left her Georgian home in York for the use of ten almswomen, as did Margaret Mason. Mary Wandesford's Old Maids' Hospital of 1743 occupies another substantial town house.[16] (*See* Chapter 19 for an illustration of town house type). But this form did not displace others, and the writer's study found none in the West Riding outside the county town.

Semis and Other Groupings

While costing more in terms of exterior maintenance, ground space and heating, semis appear from the later 19th and early 20th century. They offer a more upmarket appearance in line with contemporary bungalows.[17] Such image-changing intentions are, however, likely to be countered by the size of grouping and linear layout, in addition to the inevitable plaque. Sometimes the semis might form part of a group, for instance as visual stops to a main row, but this never became mainstream practice. The ten almshouses of the Mary Hardstaff's Homes at Carlton on the outskirts of Nottingham are set out in an arc. Two-storey Dutch gabled houses form the centre and ends of the group interspersed by bungalows and two more two-storey units. In tune with architectural taste of its time, the 1934 almshouse won a RIBA award.[18] The identity statement of the semi-detached bungalow was taken up by other charities, such as the North Eastern Railway Cottage Homes and lies beyond the period of this book.

TWENTIETH CENTURY ALMSHOUSE BUILDING

The arrival of the Old Age Pension enabled some who might have been candidates for an almshouse (where such existed) or the workhouse (numerically more likely) to pay rent for accommodation. The new local authority housing, enabled by the 1890 Housing Act and encouraged by Government subsidy from 1919, concentrated mainly on poor families, though London and some other cities did provide single-person flats, which accommodated the elderly, known as the widows' block. Local authority building for the elderly got off the ground in 1931 following the 1930 Act, which for the first time identified small houses solely for the elderly as acceptable for subsidy. Again, these developments are beyond the scope of this book, although their interaction with almshouses would repay investigation.[19] Meanwhile almshouses continued to be founded, built and appreciated, still with a distinctive identity.

One particular development, exceptional for scale of provision and method of funding as well as architecturally, is the Durham Aged Miners' Homes, founded in 1898 (*see* Chapter 9). Other almshouses for specified occupations do not necessarily show a connection to residents' previous calling beyond some occasional symbolic decoration.[20] These homes for retired mineworkers, however, have distinct features and present a subset within the almshouse genre. One of the earliest was the Joicey Aged Miners' Homes of 1906 at Houghton-le-Spring. This single-storey brick row of twelve units has the end two gable-on to the front with the roof in between extending to form a verandah supported on posts arising from a low wall. In front of this sheltered access and sitting space are gardens and to the rear small individual yards. These long streetside rows are to be found in seventy towns and villages across the coalfield. Design by any one lodge (the union branch for that pit) might be emulated by others, but not as an imposed or slavish copy.[21]

Illustration 2.c. Durham Aged Miners' Homes, Dairy Lane,
Houghton-le-Spring, County Durham, built 1926, comprising a row with
integral verandah. *Photo © Helen Caffrey.*

STYLE, MATERIALS AND DECORATION

Not surprisingly, choice of style tends to reflect the taste of the day – Tudor, Classical, neo-Gothic, Picturesque or Eclectic though rarely Arts and Crafts - tempered by funds available and sometimes more subtly by local influences.[22] Hunnyball's study of 17th-century Hertfordshire shows the gentry employing a personal classification by status, ranging from their private house through to buildings with greater public use. Almshouses came in the middle of the range, often using the same ornamental detail, such as finials or gateposts, but otherwise tending away from 'abstract stylistic concepts' to emphasise 'functional value and social associations'.[23] In this way the link with the founder was emphasised and position in the social scale demarcated.

In broad architectural terms, almshouses are a curious hybrid, incorporating elements of the polite (defined as more expensive, higher social status and part of the wider world of the period) and the vernacular (as in cottages and agricultural buildings, dependent on local resources for both materials and practice). Quality of construction and the substantial nature of almshouses (plus charitable status) accounts for their disproportionate survival in relation to other homes of the poor. Structural detail may be exploited for architectural elegance. In a straightforward row, for instance, local brick may be enhanced by stone quoins, long and short work around doors or drip moulds over windows. Above these may be decorative bargeboards or fish-scale roof tiles, while those characteristic chimney stacks also offer scope for adornment. Colour may be another form of decoration, in banded brickwork using material from more than one brickyard, or in patterning of two colours of roof tile, very visible on a low building.

Fine gradation in the use of the vernacular may be spotted where two almshouses in the same village invite comparison. At Dedham in Essex, Stephen Dunton's 1517 row of ten almshouses needed replacement by 1806. The result, at a cost of £599 5s. 6d, was still a basic row beside the street, in local brick, with the regional mansard roof. When two more units were added at both ends, these were given ridge and gable roofs; unity and balance were maintained but the vernacular is being superseded. In contrast, Mrs Barfield's Asylum for

Widows of 1834 was built as a winged row on raised ground with fretted bargeboards on gables and on the individual porches; the Picturesque has overtaken the vernacular. This may also imply the (intended) greater sophistication of these residents as almswomen might come from the big town of Colchester if vacancies were not filled by locals.[24]

Illustration 2.d. Decorative details at Mrs Barfield's Asylum for Widows, Dedham, Essex, built 1834. *Photo © Helen Caffrey.*

Where almshouses were built within model or planned villages they needed to be integrated visually yet indicative of function and status. The charming village of Milton Abbas in Dorset was the product of wholesale eviction and relocation by the landowner Joseph Damer in 1780; William Chambers and Capability Brown provided thirty-six new cottages in vernacular white-plastered cob with thatched roofs.[25] However the old settlement contained a row of almshouses built in 1674 of brick and flint banding with stone dressings and a tiled roof. These could be economically taken down and removed to the new village where they were placed opposite the church. This might be seen as a way of dealing with their very different appearance, in materials, colouring and low roofline which fails to relate to the general uniformity of Damer's creation.

In the 1860s Titus Salt built a new village for his Bradford textile workers, in a healthy location. Saltaire included an almshouse for forty-five (later twenty-two) retired workers, male, female or couples, facing onto a public green and opposite the cottage hospital.[26] Units are alternately on one or two floors, in the same stone as the rest of the village and in the Italianate style used for the mill. Within the carefully socially differentiated housing these appear closer to the public buildings or managerial level in decoration, though on an appropriately small scale.

LOCATION, BOUNDARIES AND OTHER BUILDINGS

Whilst distribution of almshouse charities nationally reflects founders rather than needs, choice of location was one of the first decisions to be made in building.[27] A landowner might allocate a site – and some in isolated spots suggest use of otherwise unproductive ground – but more often land had to be purchased. Availability, size of plot for the numbers envisaged by the foundation, and cost were clearly determining factors, especially as expenditure on land reduced the funds for construction. This was an important consideration where trustees were carrying out the founder's will and finance was finite.

However medieval choices of hospital sites were influenced by other factors. Visibility on main roads leading in and out of town was crucial for fund raising and the physical soliciting of alms on the spot. Leper hospitals or lazarhouses, some of which became almshouses when the disease receded in the later Middle Ages, were generally located at city outskirts, just outside the walls, as a compromise between public health and fund raising. The cathedral cities of Chichester and Ripon show the medieval distribution pattern for hospitals.[28] Orme attributes the growing tendency towards central sites to change in religious practice during the 15th century; as collegiate churches became fashionable, staffed by secular clergy, these might include a school and almshouse but be centrally located at the church.[29] God's House at Ewelme in Oxfordshire and Tattershall in Lincolnshire originated in conjunction with collegiate churches; in both cases the almshouses have continued, despite changes in the surrounding settlements.

Centrality may have become unquestioning habit, and post-Reformation almshouses in town and village are most often central. This ensured that even a gated enclave formed part of the local scene, both architecturally and socially, and served as encouragement to further generosity based on the acceptance of local responsibility for the (deserving) elderly without other means. Twentieth-century planning guidelines commonly state the importance in housing the elderly of access to shops and amenities, avoidance of isolation, but equally consideration of privacy and security. Almshouses have long evinced those qualities. However, population increase and industrialisation left some almshouses in districts under pressure for redevelopment and less desirable for housing. Dickens noted this when he observed: 'common-place smoky fronted London Alms-Houses with a little paved courtyard in front enclosed by iron railings, which have got snowed up, as it were, by bricks and mortar … gaps in the busy life around them, parentheses in the close and blotted texts of the streets'.[30] Canny trustees could exploit this, using high prices for sale of land to move and sometimes expand provision on new suburban sites. Recently this urban exodus has been actively pursued by Bristol Charities, an administrative amalgamation of almshouses, as distinctive central buildings are sold for their historic attraction and replacements offer more modern facilities.[31] Despite the benefits, residents' comments indicate that for some the bustle of daily life about their distinctive homes was just as important.[32]

Clustering of almshouses shows a conscious but voluntary form of zoning. This may be found across the country as in Hereford with clusters along St Owen Street and Ledbury Road on the east side of town and Whitecross Road on the west.[33] At Almondbury, West Yorkshire, there was opposition from some trustees when it was proposed that Nettleton's Almshouse should move to the opposite end of the village, away from residents' existing social networks, but this was pre-empted by a generous free gift of land in 1863. By the 1930s this was seen as the appropriate place for two new small charities, Emily Parkin's and then Houghton's.[34]

Fox Lane at the top of the town of Leyland in Lancashire has four separate almshouse properties, all dating from about the middle of the 19th century, on ground near the school, built by public subscription in 1837, where land was available but ceasing to be peripheral due to urban expansion. The Farington Almshouses arrived first, an 1849 rebuild of a 17th-century foundation, followed by another relocation and then the new Ryley Almshouses in 1887. By no means uniform, each takes the form of a short row with wings or projecting end-on gables, two with decorative black and white timbering and the recently restored Osbaldeston utilising vari-coloured brickwork. The fourth property is notable for being taller, with dormers and decorative bargeboards. This was built to rent by Susan and Mary Farington who supervised the move.[35] Known as Farington Almshouse Trust Cottages, these were let to fund the almshouses themselves, showing an interesting distinction from the homes of their poorer neighbours whom they supported.

An almshouse site is generally marked out by a substantial wall, and sometimes these have even outlasted the almshouse itself. Partly property demarcation to resist encroachment on rear greens and gardens, this also demonstrates the separate nature of the almshouse, increasing privacy and security and drawing residents closer to one another as a community. Significantly, such features have formed recent additions to listing for those almshouses with listed building status.[36] Garden, allotments, field or orchard, the grounds were an integral part of provision for the beneficiaries' mental and physical health. They might be used for sitting and strolling, for growing fruit and vegetables, sometimes for sale, and frequently included a discreet area for drying laundry. Sarah Hare suggests in Chapter 17 that even in highly regulated charities gardens offered an element of freedom.

Other buildings might be needed on the almshouse 'campus': fuel store for wood or coal; privies; sometimes a separate laundry (though this could be part of the main structure); and occasionally a well-house where the essential well or pump became an opportunity for adornment (see the cover picture). A number of almshouses, now happily connected to mains supplies, have maintained their pump, but however charming as garden features these represent physical effort for elderly shoulder muscles, while supply needed to be adequate to meet demand throughout the year. Other outbuildings are likely to be either demolished or converted to storage, for garden tools, wheelie bins or mobility scooters. A short walk may be a long hazardous one after dark, and Joseph Crossley's otherwise grateful almspeople requested lighting for the route through the grounds leading to the decently secluded privies.[37]

An almshouse that is in many ways unusual architecturally and conceptually but clearly shows these features of well, wall, garden and orchard is St Anne's Bedehouses in Lincoln.[38] Despite its name, this was founded in 1847, by Richard Waldo Sibthorp, of local landowning family but controversial personal reputation on account of his changeable religious allegiances. Due to the level of local scrutiny and an eagerness to avoid any problems attaching to his charity, the founder went by the book as regards constitution, trustees, funding and selection criteria, but perhaps needed to state their compliance overtly on site. Pugin's well-house is 'really very pretty' incorporating Sibthorp family insignia and Gothic traceried windows beneath a rose motif border and cross.[39] It is less successful practically being insufficient to shelter users during inclement weather or to encourage sociability; laundry was facilitated by two adjacent stone sinks. The next tranche of funds brought the purchase of both land for the garden and an orchard which then needed a boundary wall, constructed in diaper-patterned brickwork like the well-house. This additional cost led to deferral of the separate but onsite chapel. However, the additional ground allowed for the almswomen's private graveyard to be set out, extending the garden view from their windows.

Chapels form part of some almshouses although there is no automatic correlation with a requirement for religious affiliation or attendance within the rules. Whilst a chapel might be more likely within a surviving medieval foundation, it does not necessarily serve a large number of residents. The two sizeable communities mentioned at Halifax and Bradford incorporate chapels, but with residents' input into their manner of use. Almshouse chapels might be open for worship to the wider community, and this along with physical visibility – often requiring disproportionate finance in relation to area – may give the impression that they were frequently included. In fact they are numerically few, the writer having found them to be present at fewer than one in twelve almshouses in one county (*see* Appendix 2.2).

Less frequent again, but not unimportant where they do exist, was housing for the warden or master. Scale, quality of finish and position in relation to the almspeople's own homes state the founder's (or trustees') views on both function and social status. Hierarchy within the almspeople has already been demonstrated in the two centripetal almshouses, while more on a master's position may be found in Chapter 13. When Archbishop Holgate's Hospital at Hemsworth in West Yorkshire was rebuilt in 1858, a separate house, next door but with its own driveway from the road, gave six bedrooms and servant accommodation as well as a separate walled garden. The porter and matron (husband and wife team) lived in the gatehouse, going downstairs and across the drive between bedroom and living room, while the boardroom occupied the space above. By the later 20th century the big house was divided, with porter and matron in one half; the boardroom survives with its original furniture and fittings.[40]

AT HOME INDOORS

This is where the almsperson passed most of the time, but for which we have the least evidence. Two museums show furnished rooms; the Geffrye Museum in London (the former Ironmongers' Company's almshouses) displays an 18th- and a 19th-century almshouse room, but these are based on 'general suitability' of contents not an actual description or inventory.[41] Llanrwst's Jesus Hospital in North Wales, founded by John Wynn in 1610, offers no information on its furnished room although contents are recent in date. To furnish the home in the mind's eye, the reader is invited to use Chapter 14, remembering that the period and individual personal circumstances might give rise to different furnishing. In addition to whatever personal possessions accompanied the resident, furniture might already be part of the provision, or left by previous residents, as in rented accommodation. Essentials were a bedstead, which tended to be bulky, one or two chairs, a table and storage in the form of a chest, shelves or cupboard/dresser.

The typical almshouse, on one floor, comprised one and a half or two and a half rooms, giving either a separate living room and bedroom or a bedsit, with a scullery/pantry behind. In a bedsit, the bed might fit into an alcove and be quite unobtrusive in day time. Few such almshouses remain unaltered, but the areas most subject to changing standards have been the bathroom and kitchen (in modern terms) frequently in a lean-to at the rear. Rooms were often square or nearly so, with 10ft x 12ft (3m x 3.6m) or 12ft x 15ft (3.6m x 4.5m) as common dimensions for a single-room unit. When St Anne's at Ripon was to be rebuilt in the 1870s individual rooms were drawn up of 13ft x 12ft 6ins (3.9m x 3.75m) including the bed alcove, fireplace and cupboard, all within a back-to-back block.[42] Archbishop Holgate's Hospital, mentioned above, provided two-room units, of 8ft x10ft (2.4m x 3m) and 7ft x 15ft (2.1m x 4.5m), including the attractive but internally inconvenient pointed bays. As the rebuild neared completion the Trustees instructed the Master to 'Furnish one of the empty houses in such manner as he thinks every house ought to be fitted up, viz. the bedroom with an iron bedstead, a row of pegs and a receptacle of some kind for linen and cloths. The sitting room with a delf-case [dresser], blinds and rollers and the kitchen with a towel roller and shelves'.[43] (see Illustration 2.e. colour Plate III.)

The Durham Aged Miners' Homes were surveyed in 1980 prior to modernisation, providing an extensive body of plans from the early 20th century.[44] Most of these had a separate living room and bedroom, and were designed for couples. With a total area of 400-500 sq ft (approximately 37-46 sq m), layout varied, some even having a corridor (where the bedroom came at the front of a single-room frontage) leading from a small lobby to the kitchen/living room, then scullery beyond. This plan is that of a house, albeit small, not a bedsit, and might be seen as transitional with ideas of its period present in new building.

ARCHITECTS AND BUILDERS

The founder or the trustees, as purseholders and governors, were responsible for commissioning a new almshouse, but individual and especially internal detail may have been left largely to the architect – in practice often the builder – with instructions limited to number of units and cost. Occasionally, minute books mention a trustees' fact-finding visit to other almshouses, but without recording subsequent discussion. Who therefore made the crucial decision as to what was appropriate? How were these perceptions formed, how did they change over time, and how did they compare with local alternatives? Some illustrated resources were available, notably from 1843 in *The Builder*, an influential professional journal which disseminated good practice. Few famous architects have been commissioned to design almshouses, and those who were seem to have made little impression on the genre as a whole. Many were anonymous or were selected as 'the local firm'. The 21st century has yet to change this pattern.

The Royal Hospital, Chelsea, is exceptional as an expression of royal philanthropy designed by the leading architect of the day, catering for 412 residents as an occupational almshouse, and still retaining its original function and popularity among eligible veterans.[45] Architecturally, the buildings and layout may be studied in the context of the later 17th century and Wren's other work, but here the Hospital is considered in terms of characteristic almshouse features and its recognition of the particular needs of its client group. Charles II's foundation of 1682 demonstrated official regard for former soldiers retired due to age and disability and followed his first Hospital at Kilmainham in Ireland, though his personal financial contribution was accompanied by little enthusiasm from the Treasury. There may also have been a competitive element alongside the philanthropic, as Louis XIV had established a veterans' hospital in Paris a decade earlier. Wren's initial design of a three-storey three-sided courtyard was expanded while still under construction to cope with James II's enlarged standing army, by adding an additional, lower, 'court' on either side. The Pensioners were housed in small rooms off 200ft (61m) long corridors, an echo of the wards of the old long hall and its cubicles. These 'berths' were each 6ft x 6ft (1.8 sq m) with door and window opening onto the corridor where the resident kept a storage chest for personal belongings. The very limited personal space was perhaps a reflection of military barracks or life under canvas but gave the dignity of privacy to an otherwise communal life passed in dining hall, chapel and library as well as the extensive formal grounds. The surrounding presence of a large body of men with common background and experience may have been a positive healthy factor in terms of familiarity within a structured lifestyle for those accustomed to regulation and command.

One of Wren's successors to work at the Royal Hospital, living on site from 1807 in his capacity as Clerk of Works, was John Soane. In 1811 he was producing designs for Dulwich College, near London, to reconstruct the west wing, incorporating an art gallery. While the latter has attracted the attention of architectural historians, Soane's challenge was to integrate the gallery with the patrons' mausoleum and new accommodation for the six almswomen who were part of the original foundation by the actor Edward Alleyn. Were Soane's experience and conversations at Chelsea relevant to the plans he produced?[46] It is not clear how the two short rows of three inter-connecting rooms functioned, and residents' opinions about living beside a mausoleum within a public building were not sought. By the 1880s they had left the shared site.

Soane's distinctive style was one of those parodied by the influential AWN Pugin whose hard-hitting visual commentary on current social values compared the panopticon (Bentham's theoretical proposal for the workhouse) with the medieval monastery and charitable outreach as perceived by the recent Roman Catholic convert.[47] Yet his three almshouse projects produced disappointingly little and there is no indication that these, unlike his churches, influenced others. St John's, Alton, Staffordshire, was commissioned by his patron the Earl of Shrewsbury whose changing enthusiasms later removed the proposed almsmen from the collegiate enclave of school and church. The almshouse Pugin designed for St Joseph's, Cadogan Street, Chelsea (see Chapter 20) was subsidiary to the school and not completed, while at St Anne's Bedehouses, Lincoln, mentioned earlier, houses were built as an oddly aligned low row, incorporating a covered walk or cloisters for part, but without clear direction. The most notable feature is the very lack of symmetry, but this break from almshouse tradition was not followed elsewhere.

CHANGE AND REBUILDING

However conscientious the trustees in carrying out repairs and maintenance – and not all endowments proved adequate to this long term responsibility – there might come a point at which replacement was unavoidable. This is particularly apparent and well documented in the 19th century, with greater awareness of public health issues and the spectre of inspection and regulation by the Charity Commissioners and Sanitary Inspectorate. The latter were concerned with health standards and potential spread of diseases (a close community could be a recipe for an epidemic) while the former were concerned that charities should act in accordance with the intentions of the founder (the doctrine of cy-pres) and be financially accountable. Interpretations of intentions expressed a century or more earlier were a challenge leading to the introduction of new schemes in an attempt at bureaucratic conformity. As well as selection criteria, rules and accounting practice, buildings were affected. Comments by the Charity Commissioners on existing buildings and the changes implicit in replacement indicate what were considered to be acceptable standards, before legislation could make them mandatory.

The nature of the building is key to some of these issues. Frieston Hospital, mentioned earlier, was subject to a public enquiry in 1895. Amid a fine display of prejudice and local interests it was stated that 'the old men' were greatly irritated by the Sunday school scholars, the almshouse being used as a substitute church hall, rent-free.[48] This must have kept the almsmen confined to their unheated sleeping chambers during choir practice and other activities, contrary to the lifestyle intended by the founder. Another practice mentioned unfavourably by the Charity Commissioners on several occasions and unacceptable in new building was sharing where a charity for, say, a dozen beneficiaries, provided six units. The use of a chalk line drawn down the floor was noted as a delineation of personal space, but even if the two unhappy residents kept to their own areas, that benefit of privacy and a self-contained home was lost as was the possibility of a temporary carer staying with a sick almsperson.[49]

Not surprisingly, change in emphasis for those medieval hospitals that survived the Reformation could cause a rearrangement of space. Eastbridge at Canterbury in Kent, accommodating pilgrims to St Thomas Becket's shrine during the fourteenth century, was reformed in 1584 with a new remit to care for ten poor local almspeople and ten outpensioners. The pilgrims had slept in cubicles in the vaulted undercroft, possibly sharing during their short stay, though it is not clear whether this included the infirm and 'lying-in women' mentioned in 1342.[50] The almsmen moved above ground into the hall, and later additions were built at the back of the building as the undercroft became the coal cellar. The refectory retained its function for residents, but also became a meeting room for the wider community. More extensive alterations were needed at Lyddington, Rutland, where the former Bishop's Palace was remodelled in 1601 by Lord Burghley as the Bedehouse for twelve almsmen. Plastered oakstud partitions were inserted to provide each almsman with an individual room with his own door, window and fireplace.[51]

Among the 19th-century rebuilds are some where the Charity Commissioners apparently accepted trustees' departure from the founder's original intentions. Prior to the rebuild at Archbishop Holgate's, a new scheme was drawn up, which omitted Clause 13 of 1555; this had required the twenty male and female residents from four parishes to 'either eat their dinners together in one house being all five of them at one meal' or 'in the house where their chambers were sup together'.[52] There is no record as to how this worked originally and probably any form of communal dining had already been abandoned in the rows of the intervening rebuilds. But for some trustees, continuity was more important than opportunity for change. When the winged row of Sarah Hewley's 1700 almshouse in York was compulsorily purchased for the railway in 1840, the almspeople were moved into a new long row adjacent to their benefactor's former home.[53]

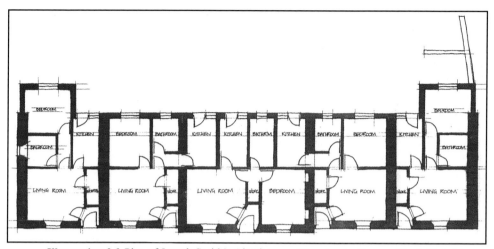

Illustration 2.f. Plan of Joseph Smith's Almshouses, Thornton-in-Craven, North Yorkshire, built 1815, drawn c. 1970. Five units and communal kitchen, modernised internally to provide individual kitchens and bathrooms.
Reproduced courtesy of the Trustees of the Smith and Crowther Almshouses.

BUILDINGS AS AN EXPRESSION OF IDEAS AND VALUES

The way in which almshouse buildings transmit ideas and values, conscious and unconscious, has been apparent throughout this chapter. In addition to a secure, rent-free home, individual design details have been shown to be integral to the residents' daily lives. Three issues are now examined: communality (the extent of independence, support and sharing); monumentality (the founder's use of the building as a personal monument); and the extent to which almshouse buildings specifically addressed the needs of the elderly, in keeping with their social status as poor but select.

COMMUNALITY

It may be hard to assess how far the residents of an almshouse saw themselves as part of a community, but this is certainly what some founders envisaged.[54] The most obvious indicator, in terms of the building, is a shared dining room, suggesting the almspeople were together two or three times a day, and that others shopped, chose the menu, cooked, served and cleared away. By and large, this happened in older and larger charities, with dining not only a means of ensuring sustenance but providing a social experience. St Cross at Winchester in Hampshire fed its almsmen in the Brethren's Hall as well as feeding 100 of the poor in the Hundred Men's Hall, from a kitchen of an appropriate size.[55] The outreach charity was discontinued but the Gaudy Dinners are still held as shared celebrations for the residents. One of Hereford's charities, the Coningsby Hospital founded in 1614, was intended for retired soldiers and mariners. Apart from such idiosyncratic regulations as parading through town as a company in red uniforms with swords, the almsmen and their 'Corporal' ate together in the dining hall. Even the menu was specified, including 'the best Shropshire cheese' and 'good and wholesome butter', with roast beef and extra beer on Sundays and holy days.[56]

Post-Reformation foundations were less likely to include communal dining, at least until the 19th century when some favoured this approach. At the Gascoigne Almshouses in

Aberford near Leeds, founded in 1844, the eight residents dined together about a large refectory table. The dining hall matched the chapel at the opposite end of the building in terms of size and formality, including the stained glass windows designed by one of the sisters. The Misses Gascoigne, joint founders in their thirties, seemed to subscribe to the dolls' house view of the almshouse, where regulation and fabric combined to control the residents' lives for the whim of the founder, as evinced through the distribution of chores and 'pocket money'.[57] This would seem to run counter to the trend for individual privacy and closer to the institutions that the almshouse was expected to surpass in dignity and respect. Communality might also be countered by separation. Some foundations were established as single sex, though many were not. Buildings might be set out or adapted to divide male from female; such seclusion would not be possible except in an institution. Gender separation was seen as important when the 14th century Almshouse and College of Sir Robert Knolles in Pontefract, West Yorkshire, was rebuilt in 1859; the earlier courtyard with its sleeping rooms and shared hall was replaced by two separate wings each with its own common room.[58]

In the 20th century the number of foundations including communal dining was declining, although some offered a common meeting space, which might include a small kitchen. Ironically the mid-century 'old folks' home' was designed around a large element of communal living in the shared sitting or day room, in tune with priorities of staff efficiency and finance. The Durham Aged Miners' Homes exemplify the debate. Initial discussions in the 1890s show the Society (a committee of miners, trade union representatives and well-disposed supporters) largely rejecting the idea of 'retirement village' or hostel. A few of the latter were built, for single retired miners, for instance at Thornley in 1915 with a dining room and reading room 'to be finished in an artistic design and all material to be of the best quality'.[59] At Murton in the mid 1930s there was to be a 'dignified and monumental' building including dining room, recreation room and a verandah giving onto the garden.[60] But both districts also built the characteristic rows of cottages. Their presence in so many pit villages located these senior citizens in a recognised position within their own existing community, where companionship and support could be balanced by independence.

Although rare and beyond the means of most philanthropists, might a self-contained village for the elderly encourage community development? Blaise Hamlet, built in 1811 by John Harford, a Quaker banker, for his retired estate staff on the edge of Bristol, consists of nine cottages about an irregular green adorned with a sundial-cum-pump. This beautiful hamlet, designed by John Nash with each house different, 'lay behind the planning and form of almost every subsequent Picturesque village'.[61] It was also isolated (though possibly serviced by the estate) and lacking shops, meeting place or any amenities. Its greatest merit may have been the relatively generous accommodation and, among almshouses, it probably comes closest to the designs advocated by T F Hunt.[62]

Very different is Whiteley Village in Surrey. This was founded by William Whiteley whose London department store was appropriately known as 'the Universal Provider'. It took six years after his death in 1907 for the trustees to purchase a suitable 'bright, cheerful and healthy spot' and building was not completed until 1921, being 'in good and substantial character and of a plain and useful design' with houses 'well lighted, ventilated and drained and so placed as to be protected as far as possible from the north and east winds'.[63] This thoughtful approach was realised in a circular layout, recalling Robert Owen's utopian vision of a planned city rather than Ebenezer Howard's garden city as currently evolving. The 300 residents were architecturally subdivided into eight sections, each designed by a different architect to avoid monotony, but under the overall charge of Walter Cave. Within the Arts and Crafts exterior the almsman or woman, or couple, inhabited the traditional room with bed alcove, scullery and larder but with the new mod cons: a gas stove (despite the ornamental tall chimneys); small bath; and WC, all indoors. Isolation was offset by the provision of a private bus service and such community facilities as hall, church, allotments, cricket ground, post office and general store. It remains exceptional among almshouses, but on account of its numbers and approach to communality it offers an interesting alternative interpretation to the Royal Hospital at Chelsea.

MONUMENTALITY

As chantry chapels and some early foundations included a requirement to pray for the souls of the founder and family, so many later ones treated them as a monument to commemorate family, long after they might otherwise be forgotten. As Dr Caleb Crowther, himself an almshouse founder, remarked in 1842 'we are indebted to the variety of the founders who hope to establish thereby a posthumous fame, which nothing else can procure for them'.[64] At least on a local level, this has generally succeeded, whether motive was originally salvation, aggrandisement or mourning. Goodall sees God's House, Ewelme, 'not simply as a memorial to the dead but as a living celebration of familial pretension and power' to be continued by successive generations.[65] Baptist Hicks' building programme still dominates Chipping Campden, Gloucestershire (*see* Chapter 18). His almshouses make a bold statement on the main street, indicating the status of the almspeople but also his family's hold over the local population, stated physically through school, church (with funerary monuments), market hall, and almshouse — a means of enforcing deference literally from the cradle to the grave.

An almshouse might, sadly, be founded as a monument to one of the younger generation whose premature death and parents' grief is recorded on a plaque. The Albert Ball Memorial Homes at Lenton, Nottingham, were founded in 1921 by Albert's father as a war memorial to the flying ace of a most practical kind.[66] The shape and layout of the building with its emblematic weather vane are intended to recall an aircraft, though this might be a disincentive to potential residents, suggesting living their latter years in a virtual tomb.

Plaques are an important feature within almshouse architecture, both as text and ornament, but more personal was a bust or full sized statue, in the grounds, in the chapel if present, or in a niche over the front door. Such figures might mean more than a name to the residents who 'met' them in going in and out, as either benevolent presence or stern reminder, reinforced by such commemorative events as a Founder's Day. The late 17th-century William Turner's Hospital at Kirkleatham, North Yorkshire, was remodelled by his great-nephew Cholmley who may have found it easier to commemorate family at the remove of a generation, showing them in their important civic and national (but not local) roles in their stained glass portraits.[67] Less commonly the residents here are represented too; these are not personal portraits, as seen in Chapter 18, but symbolic figures, placed in first floor niches of their respective male and female wings of the Hospital, showing the elderly almsperson posed in a realistic stance.

Sculpture has been revived more recently as a feature of almshouse gardens. At Trinity Hospital, Clun, Shropshire, Jemma Pearson's life-size sculpture shows two former almsmen, known from their sepia photographs, wearing uniform cloaks, as still preserved in the almshouse. Rather than expressing deference and gratitude, these two individuals are known from local tradition for having been unco-operative and giving the Warden a hard time. The sculptor had a free hand in the choice of figures, wishing to show residents relating to one another – perhaps the message is one of both companionship and independence.[68] The historical record was also consulted at St Mary's, Chichester. Helen Sinclair did not have images of individuals to work from, but chose to represent a group of five, two men and three women, as recorded on inspection in 1528 and remaining the official number of residents until new rules brought an increase to ten.[69] The figures hold hands in a circle, and if not actually dancing are certainly interacting and sharing their lives. The message might be read as both a celebration of historical continuity and the more active existence of 21st-century residents. Both these modern sculptures show beneficiaries rather than founders and significantly are placed where residents and their visitors may respond to them, rather than being on view to passers-by.

NEEDS OF THE ELDERLY

Suitability of applicants for the almshouse was assessed on a range of criteria, but one might ask: what of the suitability of the almshouse for those chosen? In comparison to issues of identity and concerns over what was fitting for the (deserving) poor, the type of building for the elderly might seem a good deal less contentious. But how much attention did design give to physical needs? While trustees' minute books discuss the cases of individuals, general principles are not stated, so the buildings must be examined for any demonstration of accepted practice. A large proportion of almshouses are single-storey thereby in accordance with modern preference to avoid the risk of falls on stairs or isolation due to lessening ability to scale them. This is also a cheap form to build where there is land available, and was a familiar 'cottage', that is working-class form of building, which may simply have persisted in charitable buildings when largely demolished elsewhere. The Chelsea Pensioners were fortunate in that Wren considerably provided the unavoidable stairs between floors with low risers; separate stairs at the south end of each wing were included as fire escapes.[70] Another point is ease of access, but steps to the front door are common even where the lie of the land and drainage make them less essential, and modern handrails indicate how frequently this may be an issue (see Illustration 2.g. colour Plate II).

Internally space might be limited, though could compare favourably with the alternatives and residents' previous experience. Housework is not always welcome. Storage space or cupboards might be provided, and fortunately a roof space reached by a loft ladder as provided at Beamsley B and its Welsh equivalent discussed in Chapter 10 were not the norm. An upstairs room open to the rafters was liable to be draughty, or 'unwholesome and imperfectly ventilated' as the Charity Commissioners observed at more than one site.[71] Next to pensions, fuel for heating and cooking and its delivery was the most likely and valuable benefit. Almshouses are notably well provided with fireplaces, those tall chimneys ensuring a decent down draft, whilst a row or courtyard reduces heat loss through limiting external walls. At Lyddington Bedehouse, the window for each house was placed opposite the hearth enabling the warden on his rounds to check on fires, whether inadequate or hazardous.[72] Some two-room almshouses had a fireplace in both rooms and when this was accompanied with free coal, as at the Durham Aged Miners' Homes, the residents must have been comfortable and cosy. The most common enemy was liable to be damp, a universal problem felt by the less active and those already suffering from work-related infirmities.

A healthy location was often mentioned as a significant element in choosing a site, although later change and industrialisation might erode this. Of the examples mentioned in this chapter, Archbishop Holgate's trustees considered a clean and adequate water supply, Joseph Crossley selected high ground above the urban smog and William Whiteley has already been quoted. But earlier founders also mention this factor, especially in connection with gardens. Lady Anne Clifford (whose mother as founder had chosen an exposed and isolated rural site) emphasised the importance of tree-lined walks.[73] Lady Hungerford at Corsham in Wiltshire provided a 'penthouse for poor people to walk in the day' — a covered way as an outdoor leisure facility when weather made a stroll to the seat at the end of the vista less attractive.[74]

As an ability to look after oneself was expected, few almshouses had specific features relating to care of the sick, at best recommending that almspeople should look after their fellows, being 'ready to care for their alms-sisters when sick and assist them in turns' as Sarah Hewley advised.[75] However Dame Sarah was also aware of the problems of living in a tight community; the almswomen should not be 'busybodies, talebearers or wander about from house to house'.[76] An area for nursing the sick was provided at Hungerford's Hospital and this job was allocated to the residents of the two nearest houses.[77] Waddington Hospital, Lancashire, was rebuilt incorporating a dispensary in the 1890s although a subscription for nursing care or a doctor on a retainer was more usual by that time.[78] Modern expectations and legislation, for instance on width of doorways and height of light switches, were unknown. Features most conducive to the health and well-being of the elderly were those of security of tenure without worry over finding the rent, the dignity of one's own home rather than feeling a burden on relatives if indeed there were any, and surrounding space, light and fresh air for those from overcrowded city environments. The almshouse also carried a bigger message to the wider community of respect due to its denizens.

FUTURE DIRECTIONS

While Goodall noted in 2001 that historians have too often 'ignored or even disdained buildings', and it might be said that architectural historians have sometimes lacked an awareness of the inhabitants, it is hoped that this book demonstrates the contrary.[79] The pivotal position of the buildings themselves has attracted notice through several county studies, and the model is in place for others to follow (see Appendix 2.1).[80] There is a lot to be done in recording buildings, and not solely their façades.

One aspect, not covered in this book, but worthy of further study, is the combined almshouse and school. The writer's pilot study found eleven in a county of nearly 120 almshouse charities.[81] Often the school outcompeted the almshouse for funds until state provision took the young elsewhere; the elderly had to wait longer for that attention. The buildings indicate interesting relationships between the two sets of beneficiaries, though in places the desire for neatness and symmetry in design seems to have ignored the practicalities of youthful noise and energy. Three other topics merit a brief mention. Some of the issues raised earlier on location and clustering suggest that links between land ownership and topography might be explored in the context of local development and the impact on the urban/rural landscape. A method of investigation, which has produced an increase in data, but also in questions, is excavation. This has tended to concentrate on medieval hospitals and their graveyards, producing valuable and sometimes unexpected insights into health and demography. But there is no archaeological justification for stopping at the arrival of the early modern period, and indeed evidence for continuity as much as change over the perceived barrier of the Reformation would be particularly welcome. The possibilities are indicated in the 2008-10 excavations at St Mary Magdalen's, Winchester, which show a post-medieval almshouse range built over the aisled hall of the previous leper hospital.[82] From the early to more recent developments: the impact of local authority provision for the elderly on almshouses and the relationship between them has yet to be fully explored.[83] Here there is no shortage of material including oral testimony for local and regional studies to assess the continuing contribution of almshouses to the wider welfare offering.

CONCLUSION

Amongst the variety of almshouse buildings, symmetry and unity of design are significant characteristics, indicative of the expected lives of the occupants. Whether set out as a row, or less frequently as a courtyard, function overrides fashion both for period and locality. Construction is generally of good quality, using both vernacular and polite features, giving rise to the distinctive almshouse genre. The façade may be a statement of founder's and residents' status behind which six or a dozen one-and-a-half or two-and-a-half room units provide the accommodation. In fewer than one in ten, communal areas may be included comprising chapel, meeting room or dining hall, but there is nearly always a garden. The almshouses are likely to be centrally located but constituting a separate enclave within the wider community. The buildings exemplify almshouse charities: independence and dignity within a caring framework.

Notes

1. Pevsner's *Buildings of England* county volumes and English Heritage's www.imagesofengland.org.uk are valuable sources but should not be taken as comprehensive.

2. Orme, N. & Webster, M. *The English Hospital 1070-1570*, New Haven, 1995, pp. 85-6.

3. Santa Maria di Scala, Siena, was a multi-purpose hospital with frescoes indicating its activities. Some of the original rooms may be seen at the hospital of the Heiligen Geist, Lübeck.

4. Green, K. 'The Hospital of St. Mary, Chichester', *Otter Memorial Papers 34*, Chichester, 2013, p. 33.

5. Orme & Webster, 1995, p. 91.

6. Pearson, E. *Ripon: some aspects of history*, Clapham, 1972, pp. 44-5.

7. Caffrey, H. *Almshouses in the West Riding of Yorkshire 1600-1900*, King's Lynn, 2006, pp. 21-3, 86.

8. Caffrey, 2006, pp. 23-5, 72.

9. Clifford, D. J. H. (ed.) *The Diaries of Lady Anne Clifford*, Stroud, 1990, p. 110, 116, 151-2, 249.

10. Goodall, J. A. A. *God's House at Ewelme: life, devotion and architecture in a fifteenth-century almshouse*, Aldershot, 2001, pp. 1-4.

11. Caffrey, 2006, pp. 38, 43, 75.

12. Bretton, R. 'Crossleys of Dean Clough', *Halifax Antiquarian Society Transactions,* i-iv, 1950-54; Caffrey, 2006, pp. 80-1.

13. Caffrey, H. 'The Almshouse Experience in the Nineteenth-century West Riding' *Yorkshire Archaeological Journal 76*, 2004, pp. 227, 230, 240.

14. Pannell, J. & Thomas, C. *Almshouses Into the Next Millennium: paternalism, partnership, progress?* Bristol, 1999, pp. 13, 19.

15. Hillier, B. & Hanson, J. *The Social Logic of Space*, Cambridge, 1984.

16. Brunskill, E. 'Some Yorkshire Almshouses', *York Georgian Society*, 1960, pp. 18-19. Hargrove, W. *A History of York*, York, 1818, pp. 289, 603.

17. King, A.D. *The Bungalow: the production of a global culture*, London, 1984, p. 249.

18. URL: www.imagesofengland.org.uk, IoE number 461963, accessed Oct. 2014.

19. Caffrey, H. 'Housing the Elderly Poor: from philanthropist to local authority', *Yorkshire Archaeological Journal,* 87, 2015, pp.170-92.

20. Almshouses for seamen especially favour such features. For example, the Fishermen's Hospital at Great Yarmouth, Norfolk, founded in 1703, displays a ship motif over the entrance, St Peter in the cupola and a herring on the weather vane.

21. Caffrey, H. 'Durham Aged Miners' Homes: unique provision for retired workers', *Journal of the Durham County Local History Society,* 80, 2015, pp. 70-103.

22. Examples of each architectural style may be seen on Images of England; Whiteley Village (discussed later) and the Sidney Hill Wesleyan Cottage Homes (Chapter 18) are in the Arts and Crafts style.

23.   Hunnyball, P.M. 'Status, Display and Dissemination: social expression and stylistic change in the architecture of seventeenth-century Hertfordshire', (unpublished D. Phil. thesis, University of Oxford, 1994).

24.   Jones, A. *A History of Dedham*, Colchester, 1907, pp. 130-7.

25.   Darley, G. *Villages of Vision*, London, 1975, pp. 12-3.

26.   Reynolds, J. *The Great Paternalist*, London, 1983, p. 278.

27.   Distribution is discussed by Nigel Goose in Chapter 1. W.K. Jordan's work (*see* Chapter 5) considered distribution during the 17th century, however availability in real terms depended not only on distance but on selection criteria and vacancies.

28.   Magilton, J., Lee, F. & Boylston, A. 'Lepers Outside the Gate', *CBA Research Report 158*, Chichester Excavations 10, 2008, pp. 48-53.

29.   Orme & Webster, 1995, p. 44.

30.   Dickens, C. *The Uncommercial Traveller*, (repr. Oxford 1964) Chapter XXIX, p. 290.

31.   Pannell & Thomas, 1999, p. 52. URL: www.bristolcharities.org.uk, accessed Oct. 2014.

32.   Jones, D. (Chief Executive of Bristol Charities), pers. com. Oct. 2007.

33.   Many of Hereford's almshouses are administered jointly by Hereford Municipal Charities whose premises are also on St Owen Street.

34.   West Yorkshire Archive Service (Kirklees): KC 643-4; Caffrey, 2006, pp. 44-5, 72.

35.   URL: www.leylandhistoricalsociety.co.uk, Fox Lane, accessed Oct. 2014.

36.   Listed building status (administered by Historic England) gives legal protection to buildings of special interest.

37.   The Trustees of Joseph Crossley's Almshouse, pers. com. 2004.

38.   Caffrey, H. 'Faith, Penitence and Charity: Pugin, Myers and Sibthorp at St Anne's Bedehouses, Lincoln', *True Principles* (Journal of the Pugin Society), vol. iv no. iv, 2014, pp. 302-17.

39.   Fowler, J. *Richard Waldo Sibthorp: a biography*, London, 1880, p. 90.

40.   Caffrey, 2006, p. 83.

41.   Curator, Geffrye Museum, pers. com. 2009.

42.   North Yorkshire County Record Office: DC/RIC ix 2/5/9, 2/5/10.

43.   West Yorkshire Archive Service, Wakefield (WYASW): C 345/1.

44.   Blackmore, Son and Co. *Durham Aged Mineworkers' Homes Association Feasibility Study*, Hull, 1980.

45.   Official Guide Book, *The Royal Hospital Chelsea*, London, 2002.

46.   Stroud, D. *Sir John Soane Architect*, London, 1984, pp. 196, 203; Ballantyne, A. 'First Principles and Ancient Errors: Soane at Dulwich', *Architectural History,* 37, 1994, pp. 98, 107.

47.   Pugin, A.W.N. *Contrasts, or, a Parallel Between the Noble Edifices of the Fourteenth and Fifteenth Century and Similar Buildings of the Present Day: shewing the present decay of taste*, Contrasted Residences of the Poor, (reprinted Leicester, 1973) p. 123.

48.   WYASW: C 547/4/1.

49.   *Charity Commissioners' Report for West Riding*, (*CC* West Riding) vol. iv, London 1897-9, p. 368.

50.   Official Guide Book, *Eastbridge Hospital: the Hospital of St Thomas the Martyr*, (undated).

51.   Woodfield, C. & Woodfield, P. *Lyddington Bedehouse*, London, 1988, p. 6.

52.   West Yorkshire Archive Service (Yorkshire Archaeological Society): DD 58.

53.   Potter, R. 2009, York, 2005, pp. 42-3, 71-2.

54.   *See* Note 52. Almshouse rules may refer to the need for residents to live on good terms with one another.

55.   McIlwain, J. *The Hospital of St Cross*, Andover, 1993.

56.   URL: www.herefordcityheritage.info, Hereford's Almshouses: Coningsby's Hospital, accessed Oct 2014.

57.   West Yorkshire Archive Service (Leeds): 1002/acc. 2379.

58.   *CC* West Riding, 1897-9, v, pp. 354-6.

59.   Durham County Record Office (DRO): D/X 832/172.

60.   DRO: D/DMA 325/1.

61.   Darley, 1975, p. 26.

62. Hunt, T. F. *Designs for Parsonage Houses, Almshouses, etc., with Examples of Gables and Other Curious Remains of Old English Architecture*, London, 1827, pp. 19-21, plates xiii, xvi.

63. URL: www.whiteleyvillage.org.uk, (repr. from Surrey County Magazine, vol. 25, no 5, May 1994), accessed Oct. 2014.

64. John Goodchild Collection, Dr. Crowther's Letter to Future Trustees, 1839.

65. Goodall, 2001, p. 3.

66. *The Lenton Listener, Albert Ball V.C.*, (repr. online URL: www.lentontimes.co.uk 2010), accessed Oct. 2014.

67. Sotheran, P. *Sir William Turner's Almshouses, Kirkleatham*, Redcar, 2008, pp. 7-8.

68. Pearson, J. pers. com. Oct. 2014.

69. Green, 2013, pp. 46, 64.

70. URL: www.chelseapensioners.org.uk, accessed Oct. 2014.

71. *CC* West Riding, 1897-9, ii, pp. 26, 37.

72. Woodfield & Woodfield, 1988, p. 6.

73. West Yorkshire Archive Service: DD 139.

74. Wiltshire County Record Office: 490/11, Plan.

75. Potts, 2005, Rules and Orders, 1707, Clause 8.

76. Ibid., Clause 11.

77. Wiltshire County Record Office: 490/11, Regulations, Clause 37.

78. Bridge, M. *Waddington Village Life in the Nineteenth Century*, Settle, 1994, pp. 144-5.

79. Goodall, 2001, p. 205.

80. Crust, L. *Lincolnshire Almshouses: nine centuries of charitable housing,* Sleaford, 2002; Watts, S. *Shropshire Almshouses*, Logaston, 2010; Caffrey, 2006.

81. Caffrey, H. 'Charity at Both Ends of Life: schools and almshouses', (unpublished conference paper Open University, 2010). Mary Lowther's Hospital, Illustration 2.b., is an example.

82. Roffey, S. 'Medieval Leper Hospitals in England: an archaeological perspective', *Medieval Archaeology*, 56, 2012, pp. 210, 215, 225.

83. See Note 19 for a first step in this direction.

APPENDIX 2.1: ALMSHOUSE DATA SHEET

Name	
Location: context, address, grid ref.	
Current use	
Date and changes	
Founder/links	
No. of units	
Materials used (whether local)	
Style	
Features	
Plan	
Garden, walls, other buildings	
Documentation	
Contacts, interview	

The central sections were expanded to use for sketches made in the field; photographs were added later. Consistent recording of details is essential to enable comparison. A thorough visual record is important in the event of later change or demolition.

APPENDIX 2.2: **FEATURES OF SURVIVING/RECORDED ALMSHOUSE BUILDINGS IN THE WEST RIDING, EXTANT 1600-1900**

Size	Small	Medium	Large	
	67	32	14	
Form	Row	Courtyard	Centripetal	Semi-detached
	39	13	2	5
Style	Classical	Gothic	Unadorned	Eclectic/other
	6	20	26	7
Communal space	Chapel	Dining/kitchen	Social, various	School
	9	3	8	8

After the terms have been defined, this example shows the sort of quantitative analysis which can be extracted from the data sheets in Appendix 2.1.

CHAPTER 3
THE ALMSHOUSE COMMUNITY

Anne Langley

INTRODUCTION

This chapter provides an overview of the almshouse community from 1400 to 1914, examining the influence of the founders and describing what it was like for those who lived and worked there. Later chapters examine in more depth related topics, such as the benefits provided for residents and the rules that governed the almshouse communities.

We need to clarify what is meant by 'the almshouse community'. The obvious community is that formed by the people living and working in the particular building or group of buildings. This small community was, however, also part of the surrounding physical community: a street, a village or a town. It could also be part of other communities — the local church, a former employer or an occupational group. Most of this chapter will examine the primary community of the almshouse itself, but it is important not to forget these other communities outside the almshouse, and indeed the families and local communities from which individual residents came and to which they still felt a connection. The Royal Hospital at Chelsea provides an example of people living in an almshouse who not only still belong to the wider military community, but also make a contribution to activities in the surrounding community on occasions, such as the Chelsea flower show (*see* Illustration 3a colour Plate IV).

FOUNDERS

Founders of almshouses had a substantial influence on the almshouse community; they had a model in mind that reflected the ideas of their time and this is one of the reasons that these communities have been slow to evolve. (It should be recognised, however, that almshouses changed more quickly during the 20th century to find a new niche within the Welfare State.) Founders ranged from large organisations to modest individuals, and their motives were also diverse, with religious or commemorative impulses as well as the obvious aims of supporting the poor and reducing the burden on the parish. An interesting example of the latter is the almshouses set up by the Aston Poor Law Union in Birmingham in 1898; clearly the guardians saw a need for such provision and believed that it would be a better solution to the needs of the elderly than the workhouse.[1] Some almshouses solicited contributions from passersby: there is a collection box built into the entrance of the 17th-century Sandes

Hospital in Kendal urging them to 'Remember the poore widows' (*see* Illustration 16.c. in Chapter 16).

Most of the early almshouses were founded by monasteries; for example, the hospitals in Hampshire described by Derek Spruce and Steve Taylor in Chapter 4. Before the Reformation, rich individuals also founded almshouses as a 'passport to paradise': residents being required to pray for the soul of the founder to assist their soul's journey after death through purgatory to heaven.[2] This practice fell out of favour and contributed to the loss of many hospitals when their associated religious foundations were abolished under the Chantry Suppression Act of 1547. Spruce and Taylor show that almost all new almshouses after the reformation were founded by lay people. Most almshouses, however, continued to have a distinctly religious atmosphere for centuries, with attendance at prayers a requirement for the residents (although those who were sick or disabled were excused from this obligation). Rules to this effect were still being made by 19th-century foundations and in some places are still observed today: Lord Leycester's Hospital in Warwick holds compulsory daily prayers in their (unheated) chapel.[3] Some almshouses were set up for particular denominations to enable old people to live in a congenial religious community and, although they did not always specify the religion of entrants, it can be assumed that most were of the relevant persuasion. One of the five Catholic almshouses in London was founded by a parish charity; later chapters examine the almshouse provision made specifically for Anglican clergy widows and Roman Catholics.

A wide range of clergymen founded almshouses, some clearly inspired by the pre-Reformation hospitals. For example, John Whitgift, Archbishop of Canterbury, founded a hospital at Croydon in 1596 and occupied a set of private rooms there at intervals until his death a few years later.[4] More modest clerical founders included the vicar of Bedworth in Warwickshire, Nicholas Chamberlain, who founded his hospital there in 1715 (*see* front cover). Clergymen often served on the board of trustees of a local almshouse *ex officio* and vestries sometimes took over responsibility for almshouses alongside their existing parish poor houses. An example of this is the Westgate Almshouses in Warwick, which were founded in the 16th century, suffered a lengthy dispute as to who should support them and eventually became part of St Mary's Almshouse charity in 1956.[5]

Some charities founded almshouses when their objectives allowed. For example, Lench's Trust in Birmingham, founded by a tanner in the 16th century, set up an almshouse in the 17th century, followed by many more during the 19th century, and is still one of the largest providers of almshouses in the country today.[6] Corporations founded almshouses where they saw the need for such provision, for example, almshouses were built in Sutton Coldfield during the 19th century by the Corporation Charity (originally founded in the reign of Henry VIII).[7] Corporations, local authorities, or parish councils – like the vestries – sometimes took over responsibility for almshouses when foundations lapsed or were in difficulties.

Other early founders of almshouses were the powerful guilds, particularly the London livery companies, some of which are described by Janet Cumner in Chapter 6. These almshouses were usually for guild members who had fallen on hard times or become too old or ill to earn a living. Guilds in many other towns and cities also provided almshouses (for example, the almshouses in Shrewsbury founded by the Drapers Company in 1444).[8] Almshouses for workers in particular occupations have a long history: the Royal Hospital at Chelsea for retired service men (and now women) is perhaps the best-known. Almshouses for clergy widows are discussed by Clive Leivers in Chapter 19 and almshouses for miners and mariners in the north-east by Christine Seal in Chapter 9. Such provision would have been an incentive to potential beneficiaries to work hard and to behave well. The mariners of Whitby were provided with a quayside hospital bearing a model ship over the entrance so the residents could still feel part of the maritime community in their retirement.[9]

A few of the gentry, rather like the guilds, provided almshouses for their servants or tenants who were no longer able to work. Thomas Hooper's almshouse at Cranborne in Dorset, for example, founded in 1660, favoured servants or labourers on his estate.[10] During the 19th century, some philanthropic employers started to make similar provision for their retired employees, such as Richard Cadbury who founded the Bourneville Almshouses at Birmingham in 1898.[11] Other almshouses, like those at Penmynydd on Anglesey, specified that relatives of the founder should be given priority for admission: 'Kindred in blood of Lewis Rogers to have first claim if they satisfy the other qualifications'.[12] Individuals, who wished to be remembered, often founded almshouses in their place of origin. The nouveaux riche founded almshouses to impress their contemporaries as well as to leave a lasting legacy. The founder's name was normally attached to the almshouse and their initials might be displayed on the building or on clothes the residents were required to wear. Alternatively the founder's emblem might be added to badges or buttons, as discussed by Brita Wood in Chapter 15. Founders were often commemorated annually with a dinner for the trustees and sometimes also the residents. Adults founded almshouses to commemorate their parents: the inscription at St Edith's Home in Warwick states that it was 'Erected ... in pious memory of her parents by Marianne Philips ... AD 1867'. Research into the almshouses of Warwickshire, however, showed that just over half of founders were childless, suggesting a particular incentive to find another way to keep their name alive in the community after their death.[13]

Individual Founders

Founders came from many walks of life, ranging from archbishops to fishmongers, and they included some interesting characters. Sir Anthony Ashley founded almshouses at Wimborne St Giles in Dorset in thanksgiving for escaping a manslaughter charge in the Star Chamber; he was famous for improving Wagenaer's sea charts in 1588, the year of the Armada.[14] Seventeenth-century founders are analysed in Sue Lambert's Chapter 5, which shows that the gentry, merchants and tradesmen founded 80 per cent of the almshouses in Berkshire during that period; one of these founders was Sir Henry Marten, a grocer's son who trained as a lawyer and rose to high office and a knighthood. In the 18th century, Francis Bancroft left money to the Drapers' company to found an almshouse and a school in London; he ordered that his body should be embalmed and displayed in the church of Great St Helens, where the almsmen and scholars were to attend once a year and afterwards enjoy a good dinner.[15] During the 19th century, philanthropic industrialists put back something into the towns and cities where they lived or worked. For example, Josiah Mason, steel pen-nib maker of Birmingham, built almshouses and an orphanage at Erdington in 1858. George Earle, builder and landowner, founded Earle's Retreat in his birthplace of Falmouth in Cornwall in 1868; he had moved to London, then Philadelphia and Indiana 'far beyond the confines of civilization' and finally returned to Falmouth to supervise the building of his almshouse.[16] In the early 20th century, Christopher Pickering, a fisherman and fishmonger, founded almshouses in Hull, Yorkshire, giving preference to people who had worked in the fishing industry or the retail trade.[17]

Women formed a substantial minority of almshouse founders, for example 36 per cent in Warwickshire. They were often widows commemorating their husbands, or daughters commemorating their parents (like St Edith's Home mentioned above). Some women, however, founded almshouses in their own right. Miss Mary Frances Maberley, daughter of the vicar of Cuckfield in Sussex, founded almshouses in 1881; interestingly, residents were appointed on condition: 'that they should be willing to receive a lodger should the Trustees desire them so to do'.[18]

ADMINISTRATION

Original trustees often included relatives of the founder, a local clergyman and other worthies, who were required to carry out the donor's intentions. As the initial trustees died they tended to be replaced with local dignitaries, thus the family connection was diluted or even lost. Most trustees took their duties seriously, as shown by the longevity of many foundations, but a few were self-interested or corrupt. The advent of the Charities Commission in the mid 19th century led to more accountability of trustees, because there were regular checks on whether the founder's wishes were being followed, but there could be considerable opposition to reform from charities unaccustomed to supervision.[19] During the 20th century, the standard of accommodation provided in almshouses (and elsewhere) improved. There is, however, tension between the desire to provide satisfactory accommodation that matches rising expectations, and the need to preserve an ancient – often listed – building. One response has been to create fewer units with better facilities within the shell of the original building.

Illustration 3.b. Boardroom at Nicholas Chamberlin's
Bedworth Hospital
Photo © Anne Langley 2009

Letters of application to almshouses can throw an interesting light on both the applicants and the admission process. Some letters came from an influential local worthy, for example, that advocating a place for a disabled man in Stratford-upon-Avon in the 17th century.[20] Other letters came from the person themselves and a particularly interesting set survives from an almshouse in Anglesey discussed in Chapter 10. A letter written by Thomas Porritt in 1840 to a trustee of Guisborough Hospital in Yorkshire states that: '[I] am now very needful indeed for I really this morning had neither a morsel of meat to eat nor money to buy anything with.' He was a 73-year-old shoemaker who affirmed his belief in the Church of England and happily he was given a place.[21] Founders or trustees often approved the candidates for admission and this process was clearly open to manipulation or even corruption. It should, however, be pointed out that many other local organisations operated on the principle of 'taking care of their own' for centuries and that equal opportunities is a relatively modern concept. One has some sympathy with the trustees; admitting a person to live in a small, close-knit community is a difficult choice and the elimination of the unsuitable or unknown could well be beneficial. Nigel Goose and Leanne Moden report that some Norwich aldermen abused their position by trading places in Doughty's Almshouse for votes in the early 19th century; after criticism from the Charity Commissioners a more transparent process of newspaper advertisement, application and interview was in place by the end of the century but they (quite reasonably) continued to give precedence to ex-employees of the almshouse.[22] It is not surprising that Dorward House of Refuge in Scotland, which forced residents to work hard, was unpopular and struggled to fill places (as discussed in Chapter 11). Most almshouses, however, were over-subscribed and Stratford-upon-Avon Corporation held a ballot for entry into the Church Street Almshouses in the early 19th century.[23]

Age limits on entry affected the community of individual almshouses. Normally there was a lower age limit (commonly sixty years of age). Dowell's Retreat in Birmingham also specified an upper age limit, only accepting people between the ages of fifty-five and seventy.[24] Exceptions were sometimes made for younger people who were disabled or particularly unfortunate and some trustees provided rooms in the almshouse to poor local families on occasions. Entrants to the Cadbury Almshouses in Birmingham were required to have an income of between £13 and £50 a year (for a single person) or £19. 10s and £60 (if married) in the late 19th century, which would have excluded both the better off and the very poor.[25] Applicants to Dowell's Retreat in Birmingham had to have two letters of recommendation from respectable householders of the parish.[26] The Parminter sisters were keen to encourage the conversion of Jews to Christianity and therefore gave preference to ex-Jewesses applying for admission to their almshouses in Exmouth, although it is not known whether they managed to find any.[27]

Rules clearly had an enormous impact on the almshouse community. They were intended to care for the residents and reduce nuisance and conflict but tended to be paternalistic – at best – and rigidly controlling at worst. We can make deductions about what the founder intended from their rules but we can never be sure how strictly the rules were enforced. Study of 19th-century censuses demonstrates that rules about age at entry and residential qualifications were sometimes broken and the rarity of expulsions suggests that rules about behaviour may also have been ignored. The 18th-century rules for Bancroft's Hospital in Middlesex give a long list of things that were forbidden: almsmen were banned from keeping a dog, pigs, rabbits or poultry; they were not allowed to take on an apprentice or sell things within the almshouse grounds; marrying without permission was banned, although existing wives were allowed to live with their husbands (however, such wives were expected to make up fires and clean the chapel and the school). The almsmen were also expected to clean their own houses and to sweep the pavement outside daily; they would be expelled for begging, theft, fornication or adultery; and needed permission for absence. The gates were locked at 9 pm in winter and 10 pm in summer.[28] Smaller almshouses fared rather better in that there was no one on site to enforce any rules set down by the founder. A detailed discussion of rules is to be found in Chapter 12.

Shocking misuse of almshouse premises was recorded at Ledbury in the 16th century, when part of St Katherine's Hospital was used to house pigs and the great hall was given over to unsuitable activities, such as bear-baiting and a fencing school.[29] Community living could cause problems, particularly with elderly people who might be suffering from dementia. In spite of the problems, however, life in an almshouse was for most residents more attractive than that outside or in the workhouse, confirming Tomkins' deductions.[30]

THE ATMOSPHERE OF THE ALMSHOUSE

Changing attitudes to almshouse residents over the centuries were reflected in the nomenclature: 'brother or sister' followed the monastic tradition of the early hospitals. 'Bedesman' described their praying (with rosary beads) for the soul of the founder and thus fell out of favour after the Reformation but the term was still in use centuries later, for example in Trollope's *The Warden*.[31] 'Inmate' (often found in 19th-century censuses) unfortunately suggests a prison or the workhouse, although it may have been more acceptable at the time. 'Almsman or woman' or 'resident' are less value-laden and are therefore being used throughout this book. Thought for early residents was shown by the delightful floral names given to individual College Almshouses in 16th-century Bury St Edmunds: Maryegold, Boradge, Flower de Luce [fleur de lys], Rose, Woodebyn and Pomegranate.[32]

Illustration 3.c. Ford's Hospital, Coventry, courtyard with residents *ca* 1900s
City series postcard in the author's possession, photographer unknown.

Buildings

One of the largest almshouses in England is the Royal Hospital at Chelsea with around 400 in-pensioners. The smallest almshouses have a couple of people living in two tiny semi-detached cottages. Clearly the community in these two extremes is very different, with a variety of experiences at almshouses of different sizes in between.

Chapter 2 describes various types of almshouse building that have a profound effect upon the atmosphere of the almshouse. A large group of residents, living in a gated quadrangle (as shown in Illustration 3.c.) clearly have a very different experience from a few individuals living in a small terraced row. The former join an established community with rules and regulations, traditions and customs, whilst the latter can please themselves in many ways. The courtyard style creates more community spirit and greater security (with the option of a porter and a locked gate) but can also lead to more control over the residents and less privacy. Communal facilities, such as a chapel, dining room, kitchen or laundry, contribute to interaction between residents. The covered pump-house at Bedworth in Warwickshire (shown on the front cover) could have led to the residents gossiping together as they collected water for drinking and washing from the pumps. Communal living fell out of favour over the centuries, with the advent of bedrooms and greater respect for privacy and individuality. It is interesting to note, however, that almshouses today are once again providing rooms for communal activities, for example, the library at Doughty's Hospital in Norwich. At the other extreme, those who lived in a small almshouse need never have spoken to their neighbours if so inclined, but even then, shared porches, lavatories, gardens and boundaries would have been a potential source of interaction (and friction) between neighbours.

Some almshouse buildings had very humble origins, such as the almshouses originally located within Bartholomew Manor, in Berkshire, which were moved into old cattle sheds in 1670. A new owner, Dr Essex Wynter, raised the roof three feet and turned them into eight cottages in 1929. He recycled shutters taken from a building in Eton College, which were carved all over with the names of boys from 1593 to 1840. These shutters now serve as inner doors to the renamed Newbury Cottages.[33] Other almshouses were judged by some to be too grand for their purpose, for example, La Providence, the French Protestant Hospital in the City of London. In 1867 a brand new building in the style of a French Chateau was built near Victoria Park in South Hackney. The Charity Commission commented that it was: 'too handsome indeed for the purpose for which it was designed, viz. the board and lodging of aged weavers and weaveresses, ordinary labourers and domestic servants'.[34]

The Royal Hospital at Chelsea provides an interesting example of an occupational almshouse with a very strong community identity. It was set up in 1682 by Charles II for army veterans in a splendid set of buildings designed by Christopher Wren (with subsequent additions and alterations by other distinguished architects). The pensioners are organised on military lines and still live in tiny wooden 'berths' that reflect the partitions provided in early monastic hospitals (*see* Illustration 3.d.). The residents, however, have access to magnificent communal rooms for sitting, dining, worship and recreation, along with cloisters, courtyards and gardens. Thus most of the pensioners' life is spent in a communal setting, with very little opportunity for personal time or possessions. Many of the fitter men are employed on voluntary work about the Hospital, wear their uniform with pride and also contribute a striking presence to activities in the wider community outside the Hospital. Out-pensioners have always outnumbered the in-pensioners and are to be found throughout England: for example, there were four Chelsea pensioners living at Lord Leycester's Hospital in Warwick in 1851, and a Chelsea out-pensioner and his wife living in Chipping Camden almshouse in 1861.[35]

Other almshouses were deliberately incorporated into a new community, for example, the Talbot Village Almshouses in Dorset, where seven almshouses were built as part of the new Talbot Village founded in 1862. Adjusting to living here was not easy for one of the inhabitants, Richard (Dicky) King who had: 'lived in an old mud cottage ... When ... he lived in the Almshouses he cooked his meals out of doors'.[36]

Illustration 3.d. A mock-up of a berth at the Royal Hospital Chelsea.
Photo 2010 © Anne Langley.

Gardens

The presence of a communal garden also provided the community of the almshouse with facilities, such as paths, seats and summerhouses, for residents to enjoy outside and gardens are discussed more fully by Sarah Hare in Chapter 17. Some almshouses provided plots of land for individual almspeople to cultivate; working on adjacent strips would have generated cooperation and no doubt friendly rivalry between the residents. Early 20th-century photographs of the Stratford-upon-Avon Church Street Almshouse garden show numbered plots with vegetables and flowers.[37] Here is an account from the granddaughter of a resident of the Woburn Almshouse: 'All those that was well enough had a little garden of coarse they had to go across the yard to the toilet and coal shed combined they kept them lock up part of the time they forgot the key and had to run for it'[*sic*].[38]

Location

Some almshouses were built in the centre of the community, particularly in villages or small towns, and this enabled active residents to go out to do their own shopping and take part in the community around them. On the other hand this setting could be rather busy and noisy for those who were frail or ill. Other almshouses were built on the edge of the community or even right out in the country. These more remote sites may have been quieter, but they prevented relatives from visiting regularly and residents from taking part in the local community. There are several examples of trustees selling off a prime central site and moving their almshouse out to a cheaper location (although cities, such as London, often spread out around these sites as they expanded); this process is described by Janet Cumner in Chapter 6.

Schools and Other Charitable Activities

Some large bequests included other foundations besides almshouses, schools being the most common. In the West Riding around 10 per cent of almshouse foundations included a school and in Warwickshire 13 per cent (the latter including the famous public school at Rugby, founded in 1567 by Lawrence Sheriff). Such schools were often adjacent to the almshouse building, no doubt disturbing the peace of elderly almshouse residents. Some schools – like that in Rugby – later moved to larger premises elsewhere, but some still operate adjacent to the almshouse. In smaller almshouses, the schoolmaster was sometimes required to act as master of the almshouse: he was on the board of trustees, kept records, enforced the rules and led prayers for the residents. He could live within the almshouse or in a schoolmaster's house nearby and sometimes his wife was also expected to help with the almshouse. In Exmouth, the four Parminter Almshouses were built around a chapel and a small school. One of the almshouse residents was required to teach in the school, though not surprisingly this proved unsatisfactory and the government closed the school in 1901 (*see* Illustration 3.e.).[39] Other less common adjacent activities include an orphanage, for example, that founded beside the Holy Saviour Almshouses at Hitchin in 1868, and a 19th-century soup kitchen set up beside the ancient Holy Jesus Hospital in Newcastle upon Tyne.[40] The former site of an almshouse could be used for other community activities: for example, a reading room was created in place of almshouses at Leatherhead in Surrey in 1885.[41]

Illustration 3.e. Tiny chapel and almshouses built in 1811, Point-in-View, Devon.
Photo © Anne Langley 2015.

Residents' Activities

The founder's day was celebrated in many almshouses by a feast for the trustees and – less often – the residents. The almshouse residents were usually required to attend church regularly, often processing there in uniform; the brethren of Lord Leycester's Hospital can be seen in a procession in Illustration 3.g. and other photographs show actors dressed up in Elizabethan costume for a pageant in 1906.[42] An interesting custom was observed in almshouses at Sherborne in the 16th century: a garland was hung up at Midsummer and the almsmen held an all-night vigil in memory of St John the Baptist (to whom the almshouses were dedicated).[43]

Visiting almshouses was a popular charitable activity in Victorian times when people from the local community might take gifts of food for the residents and sing carols for them at Christmas. Organised social activities for residents appear to be a late-19th-century development: Doughty's Hospital in Norwich provided a tea to celebrate Queen Victoria's Diamond Jubilee in 1897 followed by regular entertainments and outings in the early 20th century.[44] Some of the more active almshouse residents undertook a variety of activities including working. At Dowell's Retreat in Birmingham the rules allowed that: 'Knitting, spinning, quilting, sewing etc may be done for sale (but not for a manufactory). No bench vice or fixture or noisy work to be done.'[45] Begging could be expressly forbidden, but parish support was allowed in some cases to supplement the residents' income. There were some creative occupations: at the Talbot Village Almshouses in Dorset 'The last inhabitant of the old smuggler's cottage ... ended his days respectably in the new almshouse as a wart charmer which he charmed away by licking a finger, and rubbing the warts mumbling unknown words over them'.[46]

8. HOLTE ALMSHOUSES, ASTON LANE, ASTON, c.1926   BIRMINGHAM PUBLIC LIBRARIES

Illustration 3.f. Residents of the Holte Almshouses at Birmingham in 1926.
Reproduced with the permission of the Library of Birmingham, Birmingham Library Services
Postcard Collection, photographer unknown

Living in an Almshouse

Tomkins gives an interesting account of almshouse life from 1650-1850; she points out that almspeople experienced a wide variety of provision ranging from excellent to totally inadequate.[47] Almost all almshouses, however, conferred a high status within the local community that may well have gone some way to compensate for any deficiencies in the support provided.

Some evidence of the atmosphere within an almshouse can be obtained from the minute books and other documents that survive (though it should be remembered that these give a 'top-down' view from the trustees). A more realistic view comes from those who visited almshouses: the Gilbert Returns of 1786-8 discovered widespread problems in the administration of charities for the poor. The subsequent Brougham Reports on charities in the early 19th century recorded details of the condition of almshouses and led to the setting up of the Charity Commissioners in 1853. They had the power to challenge abuses and endeavoured to follow the principle of 'cy-pres' to ensure that the founders' intentions were followed; in practice, however, significant variations were possible in response to the changing needs of the population served by particular charities.

Photographs of almspeople often appear posed: Illustration 3.f. shows almsmen enjoying a smoke outside their homes. Direct historical evidence from almspeople themselves is hard to come by; very few letters or diaries appear to have survived although rare exceptions are mentioned by Tomkins. Another interesting account is to be found in the recollections of the daughter of an almswoman at Woburn in the 19th century:

> There was only oil lamps but while my Mother was there they had electric put in and Free of coarse, and when she died they had just started making toilets and small place to wash up whick made it much better for them ... the toilets were built in the passage[e]s ... they had there own little fire place and some of them homes had them nicely furnished and look more homely[;] there was a man to get the coal in i[f] they couldent. I meant to say they thought the old Almshouses were awful [*sic*].[48]

The following personal record from the 1930s also gives some insight: 'It is nice to rest with nothing on your mind, no rent to pay and no one to come bothering around, and you have always got someone to talk to, little bits of garden and every comfort'.[49] A contemporary account comes from a former soldier talking of the benefits of living in the Chelsea Hospital:

> We've got the club, with a bingo night. There's a bowls club. We've got our own post office and infirmary. Really this is a village. There are about 300 of us ... When you start living on your own, you think, "What if something happened to me? Who'd know?" Here, there's always somebody looking out for you. That's what I like about it. Being here makes me feel secure.[50]

Most residents must have enjoyed the peace and privacy of the almshouse, especially those who had been living in cramped conditions with their relatives. Visitors were allowed in all the almshouses (though not always to stay) but residents in the more isolated places might seldom see their family again. Residents and their families were often responsible for maintaining the cleanliness of their rooms; for example, in Streche's Almshouses at Wareham in Dorset the Town Clerk was directed to write to Churchill the Postman about the: 'dirty state of the room in the Almshouse in which his mother is living'.[51]

Illustration 3.g. Brethren of Lord Leycester's Hospital Warwick in 1939.
Reproduced with permission of The Times *and Warwickshire County Record Office, PH 143/674, photographer* The Times.

The Status of Almspeople

The status of almspeople is not easily determined and Chapter 18 explores this in more depth. There was clearly a benefit to the well-being of the individual who was part of a respected institution, particularly when they were identifiable by a uniform and located in an attractive building at the heart of the surrounding community. The pension and other benefits had more than a monetary value in conferring independence to the individual, especially in the days before universal benefits and pensions. The accommodation, however small, was sometimes shared with other relatives, who would therefore be dependent on the almsperson as benefactor and head of the household. Thus almshouses and almspeople often enjoyed a high status in the surrounding community, although this was not always reflected in the quality of the support provided, as discussed below.

SUPPORT PROVIDED

Most almshouse charities provided a modest pension and many gave free fuel too; a few residents of Doughty's Almshouse in Norwich abused their position by selling their free coal allowance.[52] Food was sometimes provided regularly or as a treat at Christmas or on the founder's day; in Woburn the Almshouses had 'a rabbit a fortnight' from the Duke's estate.[53] The sponsor of each resident had to bring hot victuals on Sundays to the Quaker Almshouses in Bridport (Dorset).[54] Angela Nicholls gives a detailed account of the benefits provided for almspeople in Chapter 16. She shows that the provision varied from mean to generous, with the average almshouse providing a tolerable, if frugal, existence to the residents. In general, they were comfortable and their standard of living compared well with what they had experienced before entering the almshouse.

Provision for the elderly that seemed adequate, even generous, in the 19th century did not meet with rising expectations in the 20th and, as a result, almshouses gradually introduced electricity, running water, indoor lavatories, bathrooms and central heating. The value of personal allowances to almshouse residents declined as a result of inflation, and provision during the 20th century was often phased out to enable residents to take advantage of new state benefits, such as the old age pension. Some almshouses now charge rent (though this may be below the going market rate) or make a maintenance charge for the provision of facilities.

Some of the older hospitals provided not only a home for the elderly, but also support for travellers (no doubt originally intended to assist pilgrims). The Hospital of St Cross gave a dole of bread and wine or beer to those who knocked at the porter's gate and the tradition continues today.[55] Other so-called 'Almshouses' for wayfarers were set up in the early modern period, although they would not fit this publication's definition of an almshouse as a home for the elderly poor so are not discussed further here.

Clothes

Some early hospitals were set up to cope with lepers, who had to wear a uniform to warn people to keep their distance and to legitimise begging. Brian Bailey suggests that the uniform worn in some almshouses was a legacy of this custom and, if this were so, early almspeople would have resented the stigma associated with such a uniform.[56] Later uniforms were associated with prison or the workhouse and this too could have caused a dislike of the compulsory garments worn in almshouses. On the other hand, the distinctive clothes may have been worn with pride (and clearly this is true of the Chelsea Pensioners' uniform). The founders' intentions were chiefly benevolent and the regular provision of clothes for poor people would have been useful when many of them had little more than the clothes they wore on entry (as described by Ann Clark in Chapter 14). A few almshouses even provided shoes, as well as clothes, regularly for the residents.[57] Brita Wood describes the provision of clothing for almshouse residents in detail in Chapter 15 and Judith Ellis discusses the relationship between clothing and the status of almspeople in Chapter 18.

Care for the Residents

Most almshouses specified that applicants should be able to care for themselves but residents inevitably deteriorated as they aged and some of the early foundations made provision for this: 'One honest poor woman about the age of 40 years, to be keeper of the said five poor men, to see them clean kept in their persons and houses, and for dressing their meat, washing them, and ministering all things necessary to them'.[58] Other foundations specified that younger residents should help cook, clean and care for older ones, and active residents could be specifically recruited for this purpose: Boveridge Almshouses at Cranborne in Dorset (founded in 1660) required that not all should be impotent or infirm: 'so that some or one might be always serviceable in case of sickness'.[59] This kind of peer support, however, generally proved unsatisfactory and paid staff were increasingly appointed. By the mid 19th century most large almshouses had a resident matron and many employed nursing staff too whilst some almshouses paid a retainer to a local doctor or apothecary. The matron was paid less than the master (if there was one) and the nurses an even smaller amount. Censuses show that a few residents had a personal housekeeper or nurse living with them, sometimes – but by no means always – a younger female relative. The master of Doughty's Hospital in Norwich was expected to visit all the residents daily and a room was set aside to act as an infirmary for residents who became seriously ill.[60]

A few almshouses made creative provision for the care of their residents. Dowell's Retreat in Birmingham had a first aid box in the 19th century: 'A small medicine chest for sudden sickness, bruises, burns, scalds etc. to be kept by the superintendant, who will send for a surgeon or physician as required'.[61] The Coningsby Hospital Chapel in Hereford had a system of speaking tubes with horn earpieces running from the reading desk to the pews to assist residents who were 'hard of hearing' but sadly these were removed during restoration at the end of the 19th century.[62]

Washing clothes, bed linen and towels could be a problem for elderly people (particularly if they were ill) and some larger almshouses provided a communal laundry or a washerwoman to assist them. St Katherine's Hospital at Ledbury in Herefordshire had a splendid 'boot bath': this was a large bath shaped like a boot into which hot water was poured for washing the residents.[63] The water must have been both cool and dirty by the time the last one used it. The Woburn Almshouses had a bath chair for the use of residents: 'There was a brick built shed for it in the yard – it was a good big woodent thing and needed a horse to pull it ... I remember someone pushing my grandmother up in it to see us about the only time and the last she came out' [sic].[64]

Illustration 3.h. Funeral procession in Rugby.
Photograph courtesy of Rugby Library Local Studies Collection, T Rug. Chu 7/2122.

Larger almshouses with nursing staff could support residents through serious illness up until death. Smaller almshouses with no nursing care relied on mutual help from residents, neighbours or relatives, and the terminally ill were likely to be sent to live with relatives, in a hospital or the workhouse. (This situation has changed during the 20th century with the advent of the National Health Service and better-organised support for the dying in their own home.) Even where there were almshouse nurses, demented residents caused disruption and could be sent to the local asylum or the workhouse. Some almshouses paid for funeral expenses but entrants to the Drapers' Almshouses in Shrewsbury had to bring with them a winding sheet and 4d. to cover the cost of their burial.[65] A few London almshouses owned their own burial ground.[66] An interesting photograph shows a funeral leaving the Lawrence Sheriff Almshouses in Rugby with mourners in black and a hearse drawn by horses with black plumes; this is not the pauper's funeral we might expect (*see* Illustration 3.h.).

RESIDENTS

Almspeople

Goose and Basten have produced a preliminary analysis of the almshouse residents found by the current project in 19th-century census returns for nine counties.[67] They found that almost all almspeople were over the age of 60, around three-quarters were female, and at least 54 per cent were widowed. Occupations were often not given, particularly for women, but the commonest occupations for male residents were agricultural labourer or labourer and those for female residents were nurse, domestic servant, servant and dressmaker. (This analysis, however, included employees and family members as well as almspeople, which means that a number of the nurses and servants were not in fact almspeople.) It can be concluded that almshouses were chiefly housing working-class people. There were some notable exceptions, such as the almshouses provided for widows of clergymen discussed in Chapter 19.

In medium-sized almshouses a trusted resident might be elevated to a leadership role (similar to that of a master). This role could include supervision of the other residents, leading prayers, paying stipends, keeping accounts and even collecting rents from associated property; in return they might have a larger pension or a bigger room.[68] At Dowell's Retreat in Birmingham one sister was paid an extra shilling a week to be doorkeeper: she was expected to show visitors around between 10 a.m. and 3 p.m.[69] Some almshouse residents were still active, working or contributing to the community: the pensioners at the Chelsea Hospital staff the gates and museum; Chapter 7 describes two almswomen at Stoneleigh caring for orphans and Chapter 19 shows at least one of the clergy widows actively engaged in local charitable activities over a long period of time.

Out-pensioners

Some of the richer almshouses supported people in their own homes and these individuals were usually excluded from taking part in the almshouse community although day-boarders paid to be fed in the medieval Sherborne Hospital.[70] A few almshouses had more out-pensioners than residents: the large number of out-pensioners supported by the Chelsea Hospital has already been mentioned and Ford's Hospital in Coventry had twenty-nine pensioners living out and just seventeen resident almswomen in 1873.[71] A study of Warwickshire almshouses in the 19th century found that around 10 per cent of almshouses regularly supported people in this way, with just over half the almspeople attached to three particular almshouses living out, often the married ones.[72] The licensed victuallers in Birmingham preferred out-pensioners to residents, presumably because they only had a small almshouse building.[73] It is often difficult to identify out-pensioners from the censuses and very little is known about them, so further research in this area would be valuable.

Employees

Residential staff might include a master, matron, nurse, cook, porter, maid and gardener. Early masters were normally ordained men who led the religious observance of the community. The master of Lord Leycester's Hospital in Warwick is required to be a retired member of the armed services; the master enjoys a beautiful private garden and in previous years had the benefit of a pineapple pit. The master of a well-endowed almshouse enjoyed a good salary, accommodation and high standing in the local community. A few masters abused their position; the most notorious case occurred during the 19th century at the Hospital of St Cross in Winchester where the absentee master lived in luxury whilst the almspeople nearly starved. Other masters were accused of such abuses with little justification: in Chapter 13 Michael Drake describes the persistent attacks on the unfortunate master of the Stoke Poges Hospital in the 19th century; Anthony Trollope's *The Warden* envisages a similar abuse of privilege inspired by real examples.[74] The master's tasks were not all grand: at Doughty's Hospital in Norwich the master was expected to take coals to the almspeople and lock up each night at 10 p.m.[75]

Matrons were often the master's wife; other matrons lived in or close by the almshouses, some with their own family too. The work of caring for the elderly was physically demanding, but the post required maturity and so the post-holders were usually middle-aged. In larger almshouses the matron could be assisted by one or more nurses who were usually young single women, sometimes a relative of one of the almspeople; training was non-existent and the pay low, but the post could include residential provision, so that they were available for crises in the night. Some nurses were excellent, but others were not: at Lady Catherine Leveson's Hospital in Warwickshire, a nurse was fined in 1724 for behaving: 'in a turbulent manner, scolding and swearing'.[76] Doughty's hospital in Norwich employed a resident washerwoman (when the task became too much for the nurses) and was unusual in setting age limits and rules to guide the behaviour of the nurses in the late 19th century; two nurses worked alternate shifts but the large turnover of staff suggests that the work was unrewarding.[77] Care for employees is not often recorded but it is reassuring to note that Doughty's Hospital provided residential places for ex-employees who were too infirm to work there any longer, regardless of their age.[78]

CONCLUSION

The almshouse community has been shaped by its foundation, history and context. The origins of almshouses in monastic hospitals can be seen in communal facilities, some of which still survive, for example, the dormitories separated by partitions at Chichester and the berths in the Royal Chelsea Hospital. The almshouse reflected the purpose for which it was set up and in the past this often generated a strong religious atmosphere. Founders included some interesting and eccentric individuals, their intentions usually set out in a will that governed the subsequent administration and rules of the almshouse. Commemorating the founder reflected the pre-Reformation requirement to pray for them and this objective was promoted by a chapel attached to some of the larger almshouses. The atmosphere of the almshouse was determined by a range of factors, including the buildings and gardens, the location and adjacent activities. Living in an almshouse ranged from a pleasant existence in grand surroundings to isolated living in a tiny room. It is interesting to note that communal activities, a feature of early almshouses that gradually fell out of favour, are increasingly being provided again. Almshouses and their residents usually had a high status in the surrounding community but this was not always reflected in the physical realities of the life provided. Support for almspeople almost always included a pension, with the addition of heating, clothing and personal care in some cases. The residents included the almspeople themselves plus employees in the larger almshouses ranging from a master and matron to a nurse and a porter. Some almshouses also had out-pensioners living in the community, either in their own home or with a friend or relative.

Attitudes to and care for the elderly have changed a great deal over the past six hundred years. Almshouse communities reflect the values of the society surrounding them, and some have led the way in physical and financial provision for the elderly. On the other hand, most almshouses displayed considerable conservatism in their rules, which were very restrictive for their residents; more recently the rules, like the almshouse buildings, have had to adapt and change to keep pace with the higher expectations and greater autonomy of older people today. Many almshouses have provided and continue to provide a pleasant haven for old people within a friendly and supportive community, and clearly almost all almshouses were preferable to destitution or the dreaded workhouse. Nowadays accommodation for the elderly elsewhere may be superior in physical terms but is much more variable in relation to the quality of the community on offer. Thus almshouses offer a good model of care for the elderly, which is of particular interest in relation to the currently ageing population of Great Britain.

Notes

1.   Images of England website URL: www.imagesofengland.org.uk, entry no. 217087, accessed 2007. These almshouses, initially called Aston Union Cottage Homes, became Fentham Road Almshouses and are now Erdington Cottage Homes.

2.   Rawcliffe, C. 'Passports to Paradise: how English medieval hospitals and almshouses kept their archives', *Archives*. Vol. 27, 2002, p. 20.

3.   Personal communication from the master, 2010.

4.   Bailey, B. *Almshouses*. London, 1988. pp. 110-12.

5.   Warwickshire County Record Office (WCRO): C.360 MOR(P), Morley, W.H. *Review of Local Charities for the Poor & the Sick for the Borough Council of Warwick*. Warwick, 1973, pp. 19-20.

6.   *Charity Commissioners' Reports for Warwickshire* (*CC* Warks.), London, 1815-35, pp. 418-441; Stephens, W.B. (ed), *Victoria County History for Warwickshire* (*VCH*, Warks), Vol. VII, London, 1964, p. 564.

7.   White, F. *History, Gazetteer and Directory of Warwickshire*, Sheffield, 1874, p. 1391.

8.   *Victoria County History for Shropshire*, Institute of Historical Research, 1973, vol.II, pp.111-114.

9.   Personal visit, 2010.

10.   *Charity Commissioners' Reports for Dorset*, London, 1818-37, p. 187.

11.   Birmingham City Archives (BCA): MS 466c/23, Trust deed, 1898.

12.   Anglesey Record Office: WPE 61/177 c. 1819. Penmynydd Hospital Rules.

13.   Langley, A. 'Warwickshire Almshouses, 1400 to 1900: affording comfortable asylums to the aged and respectable poor?' *Warwickshire History*, Vol. 14.4, 2009/10, p. 141.

14.   Cooper, A.T.P. Wimborne St Giles Church, (undated) p. 7; Stanford, G. M. 'Old Charities' in *The Dorset Year Book*, Society of Dorset Men, 1961-2, p. 80.

15.   Noorthouk, J. *A New History of London: including Westminster and Southwark*. London, 1773, p. 557.

16.   County of Cornwall Record Office: G17/6, County of Cornwall Index of Charities, 1972 [no page numbers, entry under Falmouth].

17.   *Victoria County History for the East Riding of Yorkshire*, Institute for Historical Research, London, 1969, vol. 1, p. 345.

18.   *A Short History for the 125th Anniversary*, Cuckfield, 2007, p.2.

19.   Owen, D. *English Philanthropy 1660-1960*, Cambridge MA, 1964, p. 204.

20.   Shakespeare Centre Library and Archive (SCLA): ER 1/1/62.

21.   North Riding Record Office: ZJB 7/2/63; letter from Thomas Porritt to Mr Simpson, 1840.

22.   Goose, N. & Moden, L. *A History of Doughty's Hospital Norwich, 1687-2009*. Hatfield, 2010, pp. 60-1 & 157.

23.   *CC* Warks, 1819-35, p. 47.

24.   Birmingham Library Local Studies (BLLS): LP41 14 662604, Epitome of Deeds re Dowell's Retreat, 1900.

25.   BCA: MS 466a/531, article in the *Birmingham Daily Post*, 1898.

26.   BLLS: LP41 14 662604, Epitome of Deeds re Dowell's Retreat, 1900.

27.   URL: http://en.wikipedia.org/wiki/A_La_Ronde, accessed in 2010.

28. *Charity Commission Report on City of London Livery Companies*, Vol. 4, London, 1884, pp 120-144.

29. TNA: E134/20 & 21 f. 5v, deposition of Thomas Torner.

30. Tomkins, A. 'Retirement From the Noise and Hurry of the World? The experience of almshouse life 1650-1850', Voluntary Action History Society paper (URL: www.vahs.org.uk past papers), 2008, pp. 22-4.

31. Trollope, A. *The Warden*, 1885, reissued 1998, Oxford.

32. Statham, M. (ed.), *Accounts of the Feoffees of the Town Lands of Bury St Edmunds, 1569-1622*, Woodbridge, 2003.

33. Personal communication, Val Batt-Rawden, 2000.

34. Murdoch, T. & Vigne, R. *The French Hospital in England*. Cambridge, 2009, p. 64.

35. 1851 census, HO/107/2073 fo. 220 p. 36; 1861 census, RG9/2237 fo. 89 p. 11.

36. Gillet, M. *Talbot Village: a unique village in Dorset 1850-1989*. Bournemouth, 1989, p. 19.

37. SCLA: BRR/59/27.

38. Rooke, J. *Reminiscences of Woburn by a Ninety-year-old*, Woburn, 1982, p. 16.

39. URL: http://genuki.cs.ncl.ac.uk/DEV/WithycombeRaleigh/ALaRonde, accessed Dec. 2010.

40. URL: https://en.wikipedia.org/wiki/Holy_Jesus_Hospital accessed August 2011.

41. URL: www.heritageopendays.org.uk accessed August 2011 (site no longer available)

42. WCRO: CR, 2409/8/5.

43. Hutchins, J. *History and Antiquities of Dorset*. London, 1774, p. 392.

44. Goose & Moden, p. 166.

45. BLLS: LP41 14 662604, Epitome of Deeds re Dowell's Retreat, 1900.

46. Cockburn, E. O. *The Almshouses of Dorset*. Dorchester, 1970, p. 54.

47. Tomkins, 2008.

48. Rooke, p. 15.

49. Bond's Hospital resident, 1938, cited in Cleary, J. & Orton, M. *So Long as the World Shall Endure: the 500 year history of Ford's and Bond's Hospitals*. Coventry, 1991, p. 137.

50. Lionel Osborne-Wakely quoted in Anderson, R. *The Guardian*. 4 Feb. 2006, p. 79.

51. Borough of Wareham, *Minute Book of Corporation and Almshouse*, 1869-82, pp. 125-6.

52. Goose & Moden, p. 95.

53. Rooke, p. 8.

54. Ann Clark personal communication.

55. Stone, B.J. *A Record of England National Photographic Record Association*. Stockport, 2006, p. 125.

56. Bailey, pp. 20-1.

57. For example *Doughty's Hospital in Norwich*, Goose & Moden, p. 73.

58. *CC* Warks, 1815-35, 16th-century rules for Ford's Hospital in Coventry, p. 918.

59. *CC* Dorset, 1818-1837, London, p. 186.

60. Goose & Moden, pp. 79 & 85.

61. BLLS: LP41 14 662604, Epitome of Deeds re Dowell's Retreat, 1900.

62. Bettington, E. J. *Transactions of the Woolhope Naturalists Field Club*, 1930, p. 100.

63. Sylvia Pinches, personal communication, 2012.

64. Rooke, p.16.

65. *VCH* Shropshire, Vol. ii, 1973, p. 112.

66. Bailey, p. 179.

67. Goose, N. & Basten, S. 'Almshouse Residency in 19th Century England: an interim report', *Family and Community History*, Vol. 12 i. 2009, pp. 65-76.

68. Sylvia Pinches, personal communication, 2012.

69. BLLS: LP 41 14 662604, 1900.

70. Fowler, J. *Mediaeval Sherborne*, Dorchester, 1951, p. 250.

71. White, F. & Co. *History, Gazetteer and Directory of Warwickshire*, Sheffield, 1874, p. 366.

72. The three with large numbers of out-pensioners were Ford's and Bond's Hospitals in Coventry and Oken's Almshouses in Warwick; in addition, Lady Katherine Leveson's Hospital at Temple Balsall supported

people from eligible villages in Staffordshire with a pension in their own homes, and there were a few out-pensioners at the Church Street almshouses in Stratford upon Avon. Langley, 2009/10.

73. Kelly, E.R. & Co. *Post Office Directory for Warwickshire*. London, 1882, p. xxiii.

74. Trollope, 1885.

75. Goose & Moden, p. 79.

76. Gooder, p. 61.

77. Goose & Moden, pp. 83-4.

78. Ibid., p. 157.

PART TWO

Places

CHAPTER 4
HAMPSHIRE HOSPITALS AND ALMSHOUSES
1100 TO 1640

Derek Spruce and Steve Taylor

INTRODUCTION

This Chapter presents a case study of one county covering the period from the Norman Conquest to the Civil War in order to illustrate the origins and evolution of almshouses.

Hampshire, including the Isle of Wight, was eighth in size of the thirty-nine English historic counties prior to 1888.[1] Much of the central part of the mainland county is chalk downland with areas of younger, poorer soils in the Southampton basin, including the New Forest, and in the north-east corner. The Isle of Wight has a ridge of chalk in the centre separating Eocene rocks in the north and Greensands and clays to the south. The population of Hampshire with the Isle of Wight, which was an estimated 50,000 in 1086, was concentrated along the main river valleys.[2] Winchester, the county town, site of the cathedral of a large important diocese and of the treasury of Norman kings, was located some ten miles inland where the valley of the Itchen widened out. Twynham (Christchurch) was the only town to be recorded with a market in 1086. There were a number of other small ports but during the medieval period Southampton and Portsmouth emerged as significant settlements. Small inland market towns, such as Basingstoke, Andover, Petersfield, Romsey and Newport, Isle of Wight, also emerged.[3]

HAMPSHIRE HOSPITALS AND ALMSHOUSES

Although free-standing hospitals probably existed before the Norman Conquest, the evidence for them is slim.[4] The earliest recorded institutions in the county appear in the 12th century and are described as hospitals. It is necessary to appreciate that this term had a different meaning in medieval times. Clay expressed it in the foreword to her survey of English hospitals, published 100 years ago: 'It (the hospital) was for care rather than cure: for the relief of the body, when possible, but pre-eminently for the refreshment of the soul'.[5] The English word 'almshouse' is first met in Hampshire after the Reformation and came to be associated with the care of the long-term elderly and weak. This is the way the term is defined for use in this chapter. The other words used are hospital, which is not a specific term but a general one covering a wide range of institutions that offered spiritual and physical care for the sick, travellers and aged, and leper hospital, an institution founded exclusively for the care of lepers. Lepers took part in a service, such as that in the widely-used Sarum Rite, which marked them out to live in one of Hampshire's leper or lazar houses; they were also allowed to beg within the community.[6]

Written Records

In the pre-Reformation period a major problem is that the paucity of records means that it is very likely that a number of hospitals and lazar houses went unrecorded, especially if they were small and had a short existence. Nicholas Orme and Margaret Webster state that the Will of the Bishop of Exeter in 1307 listed forty lazar houses to which he left money in Devon and Cornwall; many of these were not recorded elsewhere.[7] Unfortunately there is no similar fortuitous record for Hampshire.

An additional problem for early foundations is to determine the date they were established. The date given in the appendix to this chapter (below) is the earliest date that can be identified from written records, but this seemingly firm date can often leave uncertainties. Three examples illustrate this. First, for the important hospital of St John the Baptist in Winchester, Gommersall and Whinney considered the evidence, identified the first recorded date as 1219, and concluded that it was founded in the late 12th or early 13th century, discounting a late medieval tradition that it was founded by Bishop Beornastan who died in 934.[8] Carpenter Turner has no doubt that St Brinstan (same man, different spelling) was indeed the founder.[9] Second, the small hospital of St John the Baptist in Basingstoke is recorded as being founded about 1240 by Walter de Merton, who hailed from the town and also founded Merton College Oxford, but a search of original documents suggests that he re-founded, with additional endowments, a pre-existing small institution.[10] Third, the first recorded date for the lazar hospital near Winchester, St Mary Magdalene, is 1158 but ongoing archaeological excavations suggest a possible Anglo Saxon origin.[11] In Hampshire, as elsewhere, dates of the foundation of post-Reformation almshouses are more certain but often detailed records of their functioning are missing.

Distribution of Institutions

Map 4.i shows the distribution of pre-reformation houses across the county, that are listed in the appendix at the end of this chapter. Most towns had a hospital for lepers, usually a little away from the settlement but near the roadside so that alms could be sought and they were often dedicated to St Mary Magdalen. Examples with this dedication include one outside Andover and another a mile to the east of Winchester. Towns also often had a hospital for the care of the sick or travellers. Generally, pre-Reformation institutions, as the

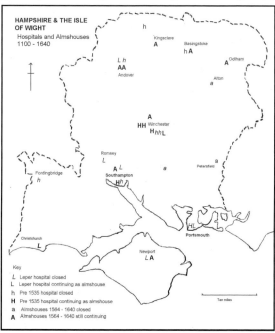

Map 4.i. Hampshire and the Isle of Wight. Map of Hospitals and Almshouses 1100-1640

appendix shows, were religious foundations, which was not surprising given that the church was the leading landowner in the county, owning approximately 25 per cent of the land plus considerable tithe income.[12]

A major role in the early institutions was catering for travellers. Orme and Webster speculate that the hospitals at Andover and Basingstoke could have been part of a chain of institutions catering for travellers from the south-west going to London, a route that persisted throughout the period covered in this chapter.[13] Travellers were also catered for at the port settlements of Southampton and Portsmouth. Both of these sites were vulnerable as they were close to the sea and were raided by the French. Early records show that St John's Hospital in Winchester offered shelter to travellers who were ill, for the relief of sick and lame soldiers, poor pilgrims and wayfaring men. The small hospital of Holy Cross at Burghclere in the north of the county was located on the road between Winchester and Oxford and catered for travellers on that important route.[14]

The distribution of new foundations over time is also of interest: Figure 4.A shows the peaks and troughs of new creations over the period under review for Hampshire. It shows the significant number of small lazar hospitals. The last one shown, at Newport on the Isle of Wight, was almost certainly functioning well before its first recorded date of 1352. The final pre-Reformation institution was the second foundation at St Cross, to be followed after a gap of 120 years by the first of the eleven small-scale almshouses founded for the local poor in the sixty years to 1624.

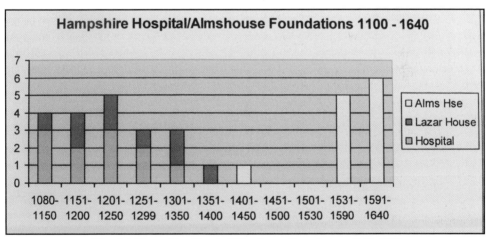

Fig. 4.A. Hampshire Hospital/Almshouse Foundations 1160-1640

It has to be recognised that the total for Hampshire is not large, so that small variations in distribution have an unduly significant visual impact on the chart (Fig. 4.A.).

Winchester ranked as one of the major towns in medieval England, its Bishopric being rated as one of the wealthiest in Europe, matching Canterbury for income.[15] One of the bishops, Henry de Blois, founded a hospital at St Cross south of the city (possibly also the leper hospital in the same city) and one of his successors, Cardinal Henry Beaufort, created a second foundation at the same site. The Bishops of Winchester lavished great sums on their own residences and this probably accounted for them not building more institutions for the poor in Hampshire, although Bishop Peter des Roches founded God's House in Portsmouth in 1215.

Hampshire Compared

The question now arises as to how typical is Hampshire when compared to England as a whole? Paucity of data makes a detailed study difficult in the pre-Reformation period. It is not possible to give a comparative estimate of the numbers of people hospitals could accommodate. Some institutions had only short life spans whilst others have continued to the present day. In view of these constraints all that could be attempted was a comparative study of the 952 foundations identified by Orme and Webster between 1180 and 1530 and the Hampshire list of twenty-one hospitals (*see* Appendix 4.1 at the end of this chapter).[16]

Figure 4.B. shows that Hampshire, when compared with the national figures, had an above-average foundation of new hospitals before the Black Death (*ca* 1350) but none after 1445, when the national figure of foundations itself was at a low level.

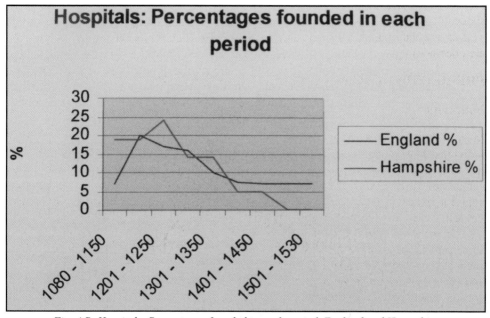

Fig. 4.B. Hospitals: Percentages founded in each period, England and Hampshire

Sixty-two per cent of pre-Reformation Hampshire hospitals were founded before 1250 compared with a national figure of 43 per cent. In Hampshire, 90 per cent were founded before the Black Death, whilst the national figure was 69 per cent. Only two (10 per cent) of hospitals were founded in Hampshire between 1350 and the Reformation, whereas 21 per cent (205) of the national total were founded as the country slowly recovered from this major population setback. All the lazar houses were founded before 1349 and those that survived responded to changed circumstances by providing accommodation for the poor by about 1500.

By 1536 the county had only 2.2 per cent of the national total of hospital foundations.[17] Although it does not compare with the number of foundations in London and the east of England, when compared with neighbouring counties it is in line with the norm for central southern England. Hampshire, with twenty-one foundations (one for every 3,760 inhabitants), compares with twenty-four in Sussex (1:4,220), twenty in Berkshire (1:2,620), seventeen in Surrey (1:3,840), and fourteen in Dorset (1:4,715); the mean for all five counties being 1:3,832. In terms of importance of individual institutions in the list of twenty-five larger non-metropolitan hospitals, there are two from Hampshire, God's House in Southampton and St Cross in Winchester.[18] Sweetinburgh, in her comparative study of Wiltshire and Warwick, notes that several hospitals had noble lay founders but these were absent in Hampshire.[19]

One final comparison that can be made is that of Winchester with other similar towns. Only six institutions were founded in Winchester but these included the two major foundations at St Cross and the civic foundation of St John's. The city's status fell as kings used their Winchester palace less often and, from a population peak in the range of 8,000 to 11,625 around the year 1300, its population was only 2,000 to 4,300 in the year 1524.[20] Hampshire was also one of the counties hardest hit by the plague years and this may account for so few foundations post 1400. Some medieval cities far outstripped Winchester in the creation of hospitals, for example, York with thirty, Norwich with seventeen and Bristol with sixteen.[21] However, this Hampshire city was comparable with other local cathedral cities, such as neighbouring Salisbury (five including Old Sarum) and Chichester (six, of which two are uncertain).

PRE-REFORMATION FOUNDATIONS

Founders

Most of the almshouses under discussion came into being as the result of the vision of an individual who decided to endow the foundation and maintenance of the institution. Many of the foundation documents have not survived but the motivation of the founders can sometimes be inferred from other evidence. Such a case is St Margaret's Wimborne, in the adjacent county of Dorset, founded originally as a leper hospital by William Fitz Parnell, himself a leper, which may have had some bearing on his choice of foundation.[22]

In medieval England the common belief was that most people after death would spend some time in Purgatory from which they would eventually be released into Heaven.[23] Time spent in Purgatory could be diminished by intercessions by the living in the form of masses and other devotions. Unsure of the link between the duration of these intercessions and the consequent beneficial reduction of time in Purgatory, wealthy people often endowed institutions designed to continue such intercessions in perpetuity.[24] This belief in Purgatory and the power of intercession to reduce time spent in it were powerful motives for people in the medieval period.

Two foundations at St Cross near Winchester, mentioned previously, were founded by wealthy bishops of high status in society. The first, around 1135, was by Bishop Henry de Blois, grandson of William the Conqueror and brother of King Stephen. The intention of the foundation is clear being for: 'Thirteen poor men, feeble and so reduced in strength that they can scarcely or not at all support themselves without other aid' plus, unusually, a generous daily meal for a hundred poor men.[25] Simple Christian charity may have been present since de Blois as a boy became a monk of the Cluniac order, famous for its teaching and example of public charity, but he also instituted it: 'for the health of the souls of myself, my predecessors and the kings of England' and the poor and devout brethren were to attend the daily services.[26] The later foundation, by Cardinal Beaufort in the middle of the 15th century, is rather clearer on these matters. Entry was reserved for thirty-five brethren and three sisters who were impoverished. Alongside this charitable intent was the requirement that they were: 'Daily to pray for Henry VI, his queen and the cardinal'.[27] Another Episcopal foundation was that of Walter de Merton, Bishop of Rochester, who added to his parents' lands in Basingstoke to endow a small hospital of St John Baptist in his home town. On his death he left 100 marks to endow a chantry chapel within the hospital to pray for his parents and himself: 'for ever'.[28]

Apart from these foundations by wealthy churchmen, there was a broad-based provision of care for travellers by most religious houses, such as Titchfield Abbey that had a guest house within their precinct. These are not enumerated here, only those who built hospitals outside their grounds being included. A 'Sisters Hospital' was built outside the city walls adjacent to St Swithun's Priory in Winchester that at one time catered for sixteen poor women cared for by nuns.[29] Hyde Abbey Hospital in Winchester also cared for the sick and poor.[30]

Apart from leading churchmen some foundations were established by wealthy citizens of the towns where the institutions were located. Gervase le Riche, a burgess and citizen of Southampton, founded God's House Hospital in that town around 1196 with further endowments from his brother and other burgesses of the town.[31] His motives are unknown but founding a religious house was a way of tying up property and minimising funds taken by the crown. Surviving early documents mention its function as being for the relief of the poor, probably on a short-term basis and as a secondary activity to its prime purpose as an Augustinian religious house.[32] Only an estimated 5 per cent of income was spend on supporting the poor. In Winchester, a leading citizen, alderman and twice Mayor, John Le Devenishe, founded St Johns around 1275: 'for the relief of sick and lame soldiers, poor pilgrims and necessitous wayfaring men'.[33]

These foundations were often much less secure in their existence than intended by their founders. Inadequate endowments, maladministration or misappropriation of funds were some of the reasons for this, at least in Hampshire. Their survival was also brought about in a variety of ways. At St Cross during the 14th century the barefaced theft of the assets by the Masters John Edington and Roger de Cloune came near to destroying the foundation and only the intervention by a new Bishop of Winchester, William of Wykeham, restored it to its original purpose. The endowments for Beaufort's foundation were purloined by his family and it ceased to function by 1492 until its re-foundation in 1887.[34] God's House in Southampton also had a chequered history until Edward III in 1343 granted custody to the provost and scholars of Queen's Hall Oxford, a change that ensured its survival until modern times.[35]

Royal intervention directing control to an Oxford College was also the route to survival for St John the Baptist, Basingstoke. In 1262, Henry III made it a royal hospital and assigned it to Merton College, whose statutes required it to maintain and encourage the hospital.[36] In 1379, Merton College started leasing the hospital rather than controlling it directly.[37] Very quickly this provided an opportunity for the warden to take all the endowment income for himself by the simple act of ensuring that the hospital had neither staff nor inmates. It was not well cared for and was ruinous by the 1780s. In the case of the identically named hospital in Winchester, the threat to its existence at the Reformation came from its chantry functions. By this time, however, it had come under the control of the civic authorities of Winchester and they were able to avoid its suppression. A wealthy citizen, Ralphe Lamb, re-endowed it in 1558 and ensured its survival to become the large almshouse charity it is today.[38]

Staff

Hospitals were commonly attached to religious houses, such as monasteries, abbeys, priories and convents. Where this was the case, the staffing of the institution was sourced from the religious brothers or sisters who were part of the order that founded and ran it, for example,

Benedictines, Augustinians and, in later medieval times, Franciscans. Otherwise staffing was very much a matter of what the founder prescribed, normally spelt out in the founding statutes.

Even where hospitals and almshouses were not run by religious orders, the senior staff were often priests. In St John's Winchester the chief administrator, the warden, was usually a priest. Beside the warden there were two other chaplains, the number of priests being an important element in the staffing of these institutions so that intercessory masses could be said frequently.[39] Other staff at St John's were not detailed but certainly included a cook. More detail is available regarding God's House in Southampton. This early 13th-century foundation consisted of the following members: a master or warden; two priests; a clerk; two or three indoor servants, such as a cook, washerwoman and dairymaid; and outdoor labourers, such as carters, ploughmen and herdsmen. This body of people had in their care up to three brothers, up to nine sisters but only three paupers, all of whom, if well enough, were expected to contribute to the work of the institution.[40] The ratio of staff to inmates in God's House may seem reasonably generous but pales by comparison with the almshouse of St Cross. As mentioned above, the original 12th-century foundation was for thirteen men. The list of staff included a master, a steward, four chaplains, thirteen clerks, seven choristers, four servers, two servants, four bakers, three brewers, one cook, one maintenance man, two grooms and three cart drivers.[41] This extensive list reflects both the considerable wealth of the founder and the nature of the institution that, although it was an almshouse, also had the capacity to carry out a complex programme of religious observance: it was a hybrid almshouse and religious institution.

Wealthily endowed, medieval hospitals and almshouses did not always attract those simply interested in altruistic involvement in caring institutions. There are many examples of individuals profiting from their positions. Indeed, it was not uncommon for the masters to be absentees holding a title with an attached income but not bothering to involve themselves in the running of the establishment. Such was the case in God's House at Southampton where the first absentee warden Bluntesdon, a favourite of the King, was appointed around 1300. Not long after this, in 1343, King Edward III granted custody of God's House to the provost and scholars of Queen's College Oxford and thereafter the provost was automatically the warden, even though living far from Southampton.[42] In this case the college acted in a conscientious way and still maintains the hospital to this day. St Cross in Winchester, probably the wealthiest foundation in Hampshire, was constantly robbed by its masters throughout the medieval period and beyond. During the 14th century there were regular disputes over the right to appoint the masters involving the King, the Bishop of Winchester and even the Pope. At various times masters were appointed, often relatives of those in power, who did not even set foot in England (Bertrand de Asserio a clerk of the diocese of Cahors) or were under age (John Edingdon) or who boldly stripped the hospital of livestock and other goods and chattels (Robert de Maidstone and others of his family). Although William of Wykeham stopped the rot, the chequered history of abuse continued until the 19th century.[43]

Residents

Many hospitals and almshouses did not specify in their statutes who was eligible for admission other than the qualification of poverty, sometimes allied with old age. Over time, however, some of them modified their criteria for entry. God's House in Southampton, whilst still catering for the poor, beggars and wayfarers, also accepted brothers who paid handsomely for the privilege of admission. In some cases these men did not reside at Southampton but were made bailiffs or stewards of various manors that were endowments of the hospital and duly resided at these locations. Accounts showed that the wardens imposed their relatives on the hospital who then received money, clothing and board.[44] St John's at Winchester specified, among others, sick and lame soldiers when it was founded in the 13th century.[45] Pilgrims and 'necessitous wayfaring men' were also catered for.[46] Like many such institutions, St John's approached the business of being a hospital with flexibility and at various times was (sometimes simultaneously) almshouse, hospital, inn and hospice.[47] Less flexibility is evident at St John the Baptist in Basingstoke. Although set up as an institution for sick folk and wayfarers, when it was later extended and re-founded between 1230 and 1240 it became primarily a retirement place for aged and infirm priests. Later still, in 1262, it was made a royal hospital to protect its foundation. Edward III in 1336 linked it to Merton College Oxford, which from 1379 leased the property to provide funds for the college.[48] This evolving discrimination in favour of people linked to the founder is also apparent at St Cross. Whereas the original foundation was simply for thirteen impoverished and impotent men, the second foundation by Cardinal Beaufort in the 15th century for thirty-five brethren and three sisters, was intended for members of Beaufort's family or those of 'gentle birth' and was described as an 'Almshouse of Noble Poverty'.[49] In order to qualify for entry people still had to have fallen on hard times through accident or disability but beyond that a social discrimination was in place.

The decline of leprosy also brought about a significant change in the type of inmate. This decline started in the 14th century and might have been linked to the Black Death but might also have been caused by a reduction in the virulence of the disease.[50] This decline is probably a significant factor in the conversion of St Mary Magdalen at Winchester from a leper hospital to an almshouse in late medieval times.[51] This also happened at Christchurch by 1646.[52]

Buildings

Most early medieval hospitals seem to have conformed to the model of an open hall or infirmary with a chapel adjacent. The chapel was located in such a way that the altar (and celebration of the Mass) could be seen by the inmates in the hall. In Hampshire there are examples of such a layout at St John's in Winchester (*see* Illustration 4.a.) and St Nicholas in Portsmouth. The configuration of buildings at other medieval foundations in Hampshire is not known except for St Cross, Winchester, which is an example of how hospitals, and almshouses in particular, evolved from the open hall to separate accommodation for each resident. The cause of this change is uncertain. It may have been the need for a more stable population better able to fulfil the founders' wishes for intercessionary prayers for their souls. Equally, it may have been a change in social attitudes about the need for more dignified, private accommodation. There is no information on the layout of the De Blois domestic building in the 12th century, but by the 15th century Beaufort's building featured separate rooms for each brother with a communal hall for dining. Today St Cross remains as a superb example of a pre-Reformation hospital with its chapel, quadrangle, communal hall, gate tower and outer court (*see* Illustration 4.c. and 4.f. colour Plate V).[53] These early buildings were all stone-built structures in contrast to the post-Reformation period where almshouses were constructed almost entirely of brick, the building material of choice for high status buildings in Hampshire after 1600.

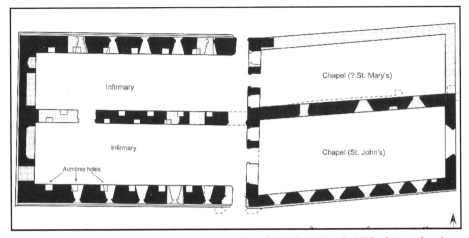

Illustration 4.a. 15th-century reconstruction of St John's Hospital Winchester showing the twin infirmaries, the slightly askew existing chapel of St John and the outline of the second chapel
(From Gomersall & Winney Hampshire Studies 2007 p.93, with permission)

Illustration 4.b. St John's House, The Broadway Winchester, showing the south wall of the ground floor of the Infirmary (13th-century) with the Assembly Room of 1769 above; beyond is the chapel, originally of *ca* 1270. Compare with Illustration 4.a.
Photo © Derek Spruce.

Illustration 4.c. St Cross, Winchester: brothers' accommodation of Beaufort's foundation in the west range. Each brother had his own accommodation of main room with chimney, bedroom, scullery with a privy to rear; occupied by de Blois brothers after *ca* 1500. *Photo © Steve Taylor.*

THE IMPACT OF THE REFORMATION

Many hospitals were attached to religious houses in medieval times and they often disappeared at the dissolution of the monasteries in the 16th century. Stand-alone hospitals and almshouses stood a better chance of survival as was the case with St Cross. John Innocent was the master when in 1535 it received a visitation from one of Thomas Cromwell's commissioners, normally the prelude to closure. However, it did survive so Innocent must have successfully argued for its exemption since it was not a monastic establishment. Ironically, Innocent later became one of Cromwell's commissioners, himself inspecting religious houses with the intent of dissolving them.[54] The survival of others is due to factors that can only be guessed at. Poor levels of endowment may have been a factor at St Mary Magdalen in Winchester. St John's in the same city also survived, but mainly due to re-foundation by a prominent local citizen and the intervention of the corporation in gaining a new charter.[55] By contrast the hospitals associated with the religious houses, the Sustain Spittal and Hyde Abbey, were both swept away. God's House in Southampton also seems to have been rebuilt at this time, its survival along with that of St John the Baptist at Basingstoke perhaps being due to their patronage by Oxford Colleges rather than religious houses.[56] It lost its chantry priest, however, as did St John's at Winchester.

Not all hospitals survived. The hospital at Fordingbridge disappeared about this time, its income having been transferred to St Cross in 1446.[57] St Nicholas at Portsmouth also ceased to function as a hospital at the Reformation although its chapel remained in use to modern times.[58] The merged hospitals of St Mary Magdalen and St John the Baptist at Andover are others that do not seem to have survived the turmoil.[59] There is, however, speculation that they provided the land for the Spital Almshouse.[60] Wilbur Jordan suggested that only four foundations survived the Reformation in Hampshire but there is evidence of six continuing beyond 1560.[61]

POST-REFORMATION ALMSHOUSES

The most obvious change in post-Reformation almshouses was their name. Beaufort used the Latin term 'Domus Eleemosynaria' or Almshouse in 1446. Only one, Christ's Hospital in Winchester, founded in 1586, used the archaic name of 'Hospital' and in other respects marks a transition between the two periods. The name includes a religious reference universally used before the reformation but rarely used after. The sale deed for the Antrobus foundation in 1624 refers to 'Hospital or almshouse', suggesting some uncertainty about the correct term or that they were interchangeable at this time.[62]

The attitude towards the poor changed during the later 16th century. As the Elizabethan poor law evolved in the second half of this century, the parish became firmly fixed as the central unit of administration. The rise in importance of this unit of government in relation to almshouse areas of benefit becomes apparent below.

Hampshire was one of the ten counties used by Jordan in his study of philanthropy in England 1480-1660 and, although his work has been criticised, his detailed comments on almshouses can shed some light.[63] Across this sample of counties, he found a huge increase in almshouse endowments between 1600 and 1630. More was given between 1610 and 1620 than for the whole period 1480 to 1600. This is reflected in Hampshire by the complete dearth of foundations between 1445 and 1564, followed by five between then and 1600. Over this whole period (1480-1660) the ten counties devoted an average of 13 per cent of their total giving to almshouse provision but in Hampshire it was only 7.55 per cent. Jordan accounts for this by saying that Hampshire, as a rural county, had a special concern for outright relief of the poor, which attracted 32 per cent of total funds – the highest of any county in the survey. He also chronicles the outpouring of wealth from London into the provinces and comments on the importance of the 1601 Charitable Trusts Act, which facilitated the creation of secure trusts for charities, for example Sir Edward More's Trust in Odiham.[64]

Founders

With one minor exception, all the post-Reformation founders were laymen and all were involved in the community in which they founded their almshouses. Although the dissolution of the monasteries saw the emergence of ennobled landowners with large estates, such as the Marquis of Winchester and the Earl of Southampton, none of them endowed almshouses in Hampshire in the 16th century. Merchants and gentry landowners provided six of the founders, with Andover Corporation creating two small almshouses, the vicar of Kingsclere founding one and Margaret Cleverly providing an unendowed almshouse in Bishops Waltham. Two merchants, Sir James Deane and Peter Symonds, who had made their fortunes in London, endowed almshouses in Basingstoke and Winchester. A third, Richard Butler, Mayor of Southampton, founded almshouses in that city. All these almshouses carried the name of their founder as a memorial to their generosity, with the exception of Christ's Hospital. Its founder Peter Symonds, however, left a very detailed will in which he set out the rules for his new institution.[65] He even set out the words of the grace, mentioning his name, to be said before meals, and all inmates had to wear a gown bearing the letters P S. Prayers for the founder's soul may not have been allowed but perpetuating the founder's memory was still an important issue.

The More (Odiham) and Symonds foundations faced challenges from relatives contesting wills and it was significant that the civic authorities in both places supported the successful attempts to protect the charities.[66]

Staff

Unlike the large staff found in pre-Reformation hospitals, which always involved a chaplain, almshouses founded after 1550 had no resident staff. This was largely because they contained small numbers of almspeople and the trusts that ran them had at most a part-time clerk. The only staff member listed was a servant woman at Christ's Hospital who looked after the four boys there. One of the 'poor old men' was appointed beadle, with 6d. a week, to see that the founder's orders were upheld. In Odiham a resident was the warden responsible for locking the gates at night.[67]

Residents

All these new creations were to serve the parishes or towns in which they were located although two, Basingstoke and Newport Isle of Wight, also included nearby parishes of importance to the founders. Many stipulated a qualifying period of time that applicants had to be resident in the area of benefit, three years in the case of Kingsclere but six years for Odiham. Three did not stipulate the sex of the residents, two were for widows, two for bachelors and two were unrecorded. At Kingsclere they were to be 'bachelors fallen on hard times through loss of income, old age, blindness or lameness'.[68] At Odiham, Sir Edward More did not stipulate the gender of appointees but had recognised similar needs to the above with the rider: 'those persons who have become reduced by misfortune from better circumstances to be entitled to preference'.[69]

It is clear that all these houses were to provide long-term, non-nursing accommodation as we would recognise it today. Although not all criteria have come down to us it is clear that patrons saw their houses providing for the 'deserving poor' and one, Edward More's at Odiham, specifically excluded those who had been in receipt of parish relief. Christ's Hospital was exceptional in another respect, for four boys between seven and seventeen years old were accommodated and apprenticed and two poor scholars supported at Oxford or Cambridge: 'to be trained to preach'.[70]

Although none of these almshouses had chapels attached to them, many, such as Odiham, were built adjacent to the parish church. A number stipulated various religious observances. Not surprisingly the Revd Browne wished his Kingsclere residents: 'to attend every service and sermon in church and to pray twice daily in own dwelling'.[71] Peter Symonds in Winchester had rather grander requirements: his six men were expected to attend twice daily at services at the nearby cathedral and process with the governors, who also carried staffs, to major festival services three times a year.[72]

Residents in five foundations were paid a stipend. At Odiham in 1623 almspeople received 1s. 6d. per week whilst at Deanes in Basingstoke seven miles away they received considerably more with 2s. 4d. a week.[73] At Kingsclere, a few miles to the north, the house was maintained by a rent charge but the income for the eight residents consisted of their equal shares from the collecting box in the church, which was opened monthly.[74] There is no information about stipends for four institutions.

Some residents of almshouses, however, received no stipend at all but were supported from the poor rate by the parish overseers; this was the case at Bishops Waltham and Smith's house at Odiham. Can these be considered as almshouses if there was no resource for sustaining the residents other than poor rate payments? Julian Smith's Almshouse was de facto a poor's house but it was not sold with the other parish houses in 1835 to fund the new Workhouse and the residents eventually received a small stipend from a Victorian philanthropist.[75] In the case of More's almshouses in Odiham, only eight of the original ten dwellings received stipends from the original endowment and the remaining two were only endowed in the 1780s by two later benefactors.[76]

Buildings

Whilst the high-status hospitals were often built of stone, by the 17th century brick was coming into widespread use in Hampshire (*see* Illustration 4.c.); all the remaining almshouses were built of brick and although some may have been thatched originally, all have tiled roofs now. Christ's Hospital, although built of brick, has large chimney stacks built of stone recycled from Hyde Abbey in Winchester.[77]

These post-Reformation institutions provided small groups of dwellings ranging from two to ten dwellings. All were separate units with their own hearths and with one exception they formed rows of terraced dwellings. Some were single-storey but a number, for example Deane's, Christ's Hospital, Antrobus and Worsley, had upper floors. None had communal rooms for dining or recreation although in some cases the latter were added later. Only one followed a courtyard plan and this is shown in Illustration 4.d.

Ilustration 4.d. Sir Edward More's Almshouses of 1623 (taken from the nearby church tower around 1885) showing courtyard form containing nine dwellings and a wash room with high front wall and gate. Note the tall brick chimneys and the large gardens. *Photo © Derek Spruce*

Some almshouses have plaques reminding passers-by of the founder and his generosity (*see* Illustration 4.e.).

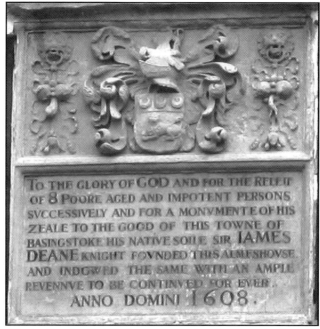

TO THE GLORY OF GOD AND FOR THE RELEIF
OF 8 POORE AGED AND IMPOTENT PERSONS
SVCCESSIVELY AND FOR A MONVMENTE OF HIS
ZEALE TO THE GOOD OF THIS TOWNE OF
BASINGSTOKE HIS NATIVE SOILE SIR JAMES
DEANE KNIGHT FOVNDED THIS ALMESHOVSE
AND INDOWED THE SAME WITH AN AMPLE
REVENNVE TO BE CONTINVED FOR EVER.
ANNO DOMINI 1608.

Illustration 4.e. Detail of commemorative plaque on the front of
Sir James Deane's almshouses in London Street, Basingstoke.
Photo © Derek Spruce.

CONCLUSION

This chapter has sought to trace the development of medieval hospitals as religious institutions with communal accommodation, through the disruption caused by the Reformation, up until the time of the Civil War. This demonstrates the early emergence of the modern concept of the almshouse with secular founders and individual accommodation.

The scale of changes can best be charted by comparisons between pre- and post-Reformation periods. The name 'hospital' was widely used before the Reformation but was replaced by the term 'almshouse' by 1640. The reasons for founding the institutions evolved over time from dealing with spiritual concerns for travellers, the unwell, especially lepers, and relatively few elderly poor to foundations that were almost entirely concerned with the latter group.

In Hampshire churchmen were very prominent in founding pre-1480 hospitals whilst after 1560 founders were almost entirely lay people, often successful merchants. No post-Reformation almshouses had chapels or resident chaplains although attendance at church was a common condition of residence. Pre-Reformation hospitals, such as God's House in Southampton and St Cross in Winchester, supported a large number of staff. In Hampshire, later almshouses in small units with residents looking after themselves in their own homes did away with the need for servants. A pattern of unpaid, often local, trustees administering these new almshouses emerged and this helped to ensure the abuses that were a feature of the earlier hospitals were lessened.

Post-Reformation almshouses as a simple row of dwellings had no communal dining area, in contrast to the hall accommodation of the earlier hospitals. Brick was the universal building material after 1600 whilst stone was used in prestigious hospitals before the 1540s.

Of the post-Reformation almshouses, all still continue except for three foundations noted in the Appendix. A further fifty-two almshouse foundations were created in Hampshire and the Isle of Wight in the period between 1641 and 1914.[78]

Notes

1. Kelly, E.R. *The Post Office Directory of Hampshire Including the Isle of Wight*. London, 1875, p. 1.

2. Welldon Finn, R. 'Hampshire', in Darby, H.C. & Campbell, E.M.J. (eds) *The Domesday Geography of South-East England*. Cambridge, 1962, pp. 310-14.

3. Hughes, M. *The Small Towns of Hampshire*. Southampton, 1976, pp. 9-10.

4. Orme, N. & Webster, M. *The English Hospital 1070-1570*. Yale, 1995, p. 19. *See also* Note 8 about St John's Hospital.

5. Clay, R. *The Mediaeval Hospitals of England*. London, 1909, pp. xvii-xviii.

6. Ibid., p. 273.

7. Orme & Webster, p. 173.

8. Gommersall, M. & Whinney, R. 'The Hospital of St John Baptist, Winchester', *Hampshire Studies*. 2007, p. 85.

9. Carpenter-Turner, B. *St John's Almshouse Charity*. Chichester, 1992, p. 2.

10. Doubleday, H.A. (ed), *The History of Hampshire and the Isle of Wight* (*VCH* Hants), Vol. II. Westminster, 1903, pp. 208-11.

11. URL: www.winchester.ac.uk/academicdepartments/archaeology/Research/MHARP/Documents/MHARPREPORT_2010%20with%20copyright%20statement.pdf accessed in April 2011.

12. URL: www3.hants.gov.uk/an_overview_of_the_hampshire_landscape-2.pdf p.31 accessed in May 2011.

13. Orme & Webster, p. 42.

14. *VCH* Hants, 1903, Vol II, pp. 200-2; Knowles, D. & Hadcock, R.N. *Medieval Religious Houses, England and Wales*. London, 1971, p. 316.

15. Darby, H.C. (ed.), *An Historical Geography of England Before 1800*. Cambridge, 1936, p. 220.

16. Orme & Webster, p. 11; [This list is largely based on Knowles & Hadcock (*see* Note 14), who give the foundation dates of institutions, pp. 312-50].

17. Knowles & Hadcock, pp. 313-39.

18. Ibid. p. 314.

19. Sweetinburgh, S. *The Role of the Hospital in Medieval England: gift-giving and the spiritual economy*. Dublin, 2004, p. 57.

20. James, T.B. *Winchester*. London, 1997, p. 88.

21. Knowles & Hadcock, pp. 312-39.

22. James, J. *Wimborne Minster: the history of a county town*. Wimborne, 1982, p. 32.

23. Roffey, S. *Chantry Chapels and Medieval Strategies for the Afterlife*. Stroud, 2008, p. 16.

24. Ibid., p. 17.

25. Hampshire Record Office (HRO): 111M94W/X1/21(i).

26. Hopewell, P. *Saint Cross England's Oldest Almshouse*. Chichester, 1995, p. 1.

27. Harriss, G.L. *Cardinal Beaufort: a study in Lancastrian ascendancy and decline*. Oxford, 1988, p. 371.

28. *VCH* Hants, 1903, Vol. II, p. 209.

29. James, p. 77.

30. Knowles & Hadcock, p. 319.

31. Kaye, J. *The Cartulary of God's House Southampton*. Vol. 1. Southampton, 1976, p. xxvi.

32. Ibid., p. xxxi.

33. Athinson, T., *Elizabethan Winchester*. London, 1963, p. 25.

34. Hopewell, pp. 45-51; Belfield, G. 'Cardinal Beaufort's Almshouse of Noble Poverty at St Cross, Winchester', *Proceedings of the Hampshire Field Club*, 38, 1982, pp. 103-111.

35. Davies, J. *A History of Southampton*. Winchester, 1883, p. 453.

36. *VCH* Hants, 1903, Vol. II, p. 209.

37. Ibid. pp. 209-10.

38. Gommersall & Whinney, pp. 89-90.

39. Carpenter-Turner, p. 12.

40. *VCH* Hants, 1903, Vol. II, p. 204

41. Hopewell, p. 5.

42. *VCH* Hants, 1903, Vol. II, pp. 203-5.

43. Ibid., pp. 194-6.

44. Prescott, E. *The English Medieval Hospital ca 1050-1640*. London, 1992, p. 29.

45. Carpenter-Turner, p. 11-12.

46. Atkinson, p. 25.

47. Carpenter-Turner, p. 7.

48 . *VCH* Hants, 1903, Vol. II, p. 209.

49. Hopewell, p. 56.

50. Magilton, J., Lee, F. & Boylston, A. *"Lepers Outside the Gate": excavations at the cemetery of the Hospital of St James and St Mary Magdalen, Chichester, 1986-87 & 1993*. Chichester, 2008, p. 11; Rawcliffe, C. *Medicine for the Soul: the life, death and resurrection of an English medieval hospital*. Stroud, 1997, pp. 11-12.

51. Roffey, S. & Marter, P. 2008, *Excavations of St Mary Magdalen Leper Hospital, Winchester: 1st Interim webreport*. URL: www.winchester.ac.uk/archaeology/Leper.htm accessed April 2011.

52. Dyson, T. *The History of Christchurch*. Bournemouth, 1954, p. 138.

53. Bullen, M., Crook, J. *et al*. *The Buildings of England: Hampshire: Winchester and The North*. New Haven & London, 2010, pp. 710-25.

54. Hopewell, pp. 72-5.

55. Gommersall & Whinney, pp. 89-90.

56. Kaye, p. lxvi.

57. Hopewell, p. 56.

58. Pevsner, N. & Lloyd, D. *The Buildings of England: Hampshire and the Isle of Wight*. Harmondsworth, 1967, p. 404.

59. Page, W. (ed). *The Victoria County History of Hampshire and the Isle of Wight*, Volume IV. London, 1911, p 356.

60. Spaul, J. *Andover an Historical Portrait*. Andover, 1977, p. 99.

61. Jordan, W.K. *Philanthropy in England 1480-1660*. London, 1959, pp. 259-63.

62. HRO: 39M74/DB8, Antrobus Bargain and Sale, 1624; Goose, N. & Moden, L. *A History of Doughty's Hospital Norwich, 1687-2009*. Hatfield, 2012, pp. 6-7, 30-32.

63. Jordan, pp. 112-3.

64. The National Archives (TNA): prob/11/141.

65. HRO: 221M85W/9, printed copy of Peter Symonds will.

66. HRO: W/B2/3 ff 54-56, Symonds; 47M81/PK74, Odiham.

67. HRO: 47M81/PK67.

68. HRO: 84M94/48/2.

69. TNA: prob/11/141.

70. HRO: 221M85W/9, Peter Symonds will.

71. HRO: 84M94/48/2.

72. HRO: 221M85W/9, Peter Symonds will.

73. Baigent, F. & Millard, J. *History of Basingstoke*. Basingstoke, 1889, p. 708.

74. HRO: 84M94/48/2.

75. HRO: 63M76/J3 p. 13, Susan Bricknell's Gift 1874, Odiham Charities.

76. *'Reports of Commissioners concerning Charities re Southampton 1819-1837'*. London, 1890.

77. Bullen, p. 688.

78. Grimmett, N. & Spruce, D. FACHRS Almshouse project results for Hampshire and the Isle of Wight, unpublished.

APPENDIX 4.1:   HAMPSHIRE AND ISLE OF WIGHT PRE-1640 MEDIEVAL HOSPITALS AND ALMSHOUSES

Town	Institution	Founded	Closed	Founder Religious/ Secular	Notes
Winchester	St Cross	1132		Rel	Bishop Henry de Bois foundation. Still in existence
Winchester	Sisters Hosp.	1148	1539	Rel	Linked to St Swithin's Priory
Burghclere	Holy Cross	1150	C16	Rel	Hosp for sick and travellers *en route* between Oxford and Winchester
Bradley	?	1150	?	Rel	Leper House; location uncertain
Winchester	St MM Hosp.	1158		Rel	Leper Hospital. Became past of St John's Winchester charity
Southampton	St M M	1173	1401	Rel	Leper H. Assets to St Denys Priory 1347
Southampton	God's House	1197		Sec	Gervase la Riche then Queens Oxford. Still in existence
Winchester	St John's	1200		Sec	Hospital. Still in existence as a large almshouse complex
Portsmouth	God's Hse or St John's Hos	1214	1540	Rel	Founder Bishop Peter de Roches for travellers, poor and sick
Alton	St MM H	1235	?		Leper Hospital; little evidence
Basingstoke	St John B	1238	1780s	Rel	Priests, 2 poor + Merton C
Andover	St John B	1247	1547	Rel	United 1340 with St Mary M.
Andover	St M M	1248	1340	Rel	Leper Hospital United 1340 with St John Baptist
Portsmouth	St MM H	1253	1340	Rel	Leper Hospital
Fordingbridge	St J Baptist	1288	1550	Rel	For poor travellers + wayfarers. Income to St Cross 1450s
Winchester	Hyde Abbey	1300	1539	Rel	Hospital especially for pilgrims
Southampton	St John	1315	?	Rel	Hospital
Romsey	St MM + St Anthony	1317	1544	Rel	Lepers and other paupers.
Christchurch	St M M	1318		Rel	Leper Hospital; later for poor
Newport IOW	St Augustine	1352	+1352	Sec	Hospital
Winchester	St Cross	1445		Rel	Beaufort's Almshouse of Noble Poverty
REFORMATION					
Southampton	Butler's AH	1564		Sec	Almshouse
Andover	Acre's	1570		Sec	Almshouse
Andover	Spittal	1586	1902	Sec	Almshouse
Kingsclere	Browne's	1586		Vicar	Almshouse
Winchester	Christ's H	1586		Sec	Almshouse; now part St John's
Basingstoke	Deane's	1609		Sec	Almshouse
Bishops Waltham	Cleverly AH	1609	1882	Sec	Unendowed AH
Newport IOW	Worsley AH	1618		Sec	Almshouse
Odiham	Julian Smith	1620		Sec	Unendowed AH; now small museum
Petersfield	Antrobus	1622	1920	Sec	Almshouse
Odiham	Edward More	1623		Sec	Now Odiham Consolidated Charity. Trebled in size 20th century

Sources: Knowles & Hadcock (*see* Note 14);
Doubleday & Page (*see* Note 10);
Grimmett & Spruce (*see* Note 78).

CHAPTER 5
SEVENTEENTH-CENTURY BERKSHIRE ALMSHOUSES[1]

Sue Lambert

INTRODUCTION

The aim of this chapter is to identify the number and locations of almshouses founded in Berkshire during the 17th century. Particular attention will be given to the identity of the founders, their occupations and their social backgrounds. These findings will then be compared with W K Jordan's wider assessment of the role of different social classes in charitable giving.[2]

The county of Berkshire had good communications by river (particularly the Thames and Kennet) and a network of roads, which facilitated both internal and external trading. The county's proximity to London was certainly advantageous both for its local economy and its social structure. Berkshire included a particularly rich agricultural area, the Vale of the White Horse, and was famous for its cloth industry, with centres for the trade at Newbury and Reading. In terms of connections with the capital, several of the founders of Berkshire almshouses described themselves as 'of London' in their wills. This would not necessarily mean that they had no links at all with Berkshire, but London was often the location of their principal residence, or was where they conducted their businesses.

DATING THE FOUNDATIONS

The most easily accessible source for establishing the foundation date of an almshouse is a plaque on the building itself. Displayed prominently on the front of the almshouse, or over the entrance, the minimum amount of information on a plaque would be the founder's name and date of the foundation. Seven of the almshouses in this study have plaques but they vary considerably in the amount of information they provide. The plaque on the almshouse at Wantage reads: 'The gift of Mr Robert Stiles of Amsterdam, merchant, who died ye October 3rd 1680. Deo et pauperibus' (*see* Illustration 5.a.).[3] One of the Reading almshouses gives more detail: 'Sr Thomas Vachell Kt. erected these Alms-houses Anno Dom. 1634 and endowed them with Forty Pounds per Annum for ever for the Maintenance of Six poor men'.[4] The plaque on the Maidenhead foundation records that: 'These Almshouses were erected and built at the sole and proper cost and charges of James Smith Esquire, Citizen and Salter of London in the year of our Lord 1659.'[5]

Foundation dates given on plaques must nevertheless be checked against documentary evidence wherever possible, whether that be the founder's will, an indenture setting up the

Illustration 5.a. Plaque at Stiles almshouse, Wantage.
Photo © John Wells

endowment, a foundation deed, or other documents held by the trustees of the charity. In the majority of cases in this study, the dates were verified. One of the two that remained was Smith's Almshouses, mentioned above, for which several additional written sources were available. In 1661 an indenture was drawn up between James Smith and twenty fellow citizens and members of the Salters' Company, who were to be the trustees, and in the same year the deeds to Norden's Farm were given to the Company, the rents from which formed the principal endowment for the charity. Smith died in 1667, so without any further written evidence of an earlier date, 1659, which is on the plaque, is taken as the foundation date. The second was Donnington Hospital, which was one of two almshouse re-foundations in Berkshire during the 17th century. A bronze plaque in the porch records details of the background of the almshouse:

> Founded in 1393 by Letters Patent of Richard II. Granted to Sir Richard Abberbury and re-established in 1601 by Letters Patent of Queen Elizabeth, granted to Charles Howard, Earl of Nottingham, under the title of the Hospital of queen Elizabeth in Donnington.[6]

At the Reformation the Hospital was seized by the Crown, the Queen conferred the lordship and manor of Donnington on Howard in 1601 and the re-foundation charter for the hospital was drawn up in 1602.

Two of the almshouse plaques were written entirely in Latin, which, by the 17th century, was quite unusual. At Wokingham, the antiquarian, Elias Ashmole, recorded the translation of one inscription as: 'Henry Lucas Esq.; among other monuments of piety and charity, did devote this Hospital to the glory of God, and comfort of the poor, for the benefit and example of posterity'.[7] At Twyford the dedication was translated as: 'To God and for the poor. Year 1640. My soul lives and will praise thee and thy judgement will aid me'.[8] Significantly, both these examples seem to display the piety of the founders, while also lauding their charitable actions.

The plaque on the almshouse in Wallingford appears straightforward and informative: 'This hospital was built and endowed for the relief of six poor people by Mr William Angier and Mary his sister A.D. 1681.'[9] The founder of the almshouse, however, was really William's brother John Angier. In his will of 1681 he left a total of £870 for the building of the almshouse and for buying land as an endowment. Angier had, however, specifically stated that his own name was not to appear:

I desire that the names only of my late dear Brother William Angier and of my sister Mrs Mary Angier (and not my own may be engraven in a Stone to that purpose at the ffront of the said Almshouse and that the same was built and endowed by them).[10]

Any information displayed on almshouse plaques clearly needs to be checked and verified.

In those almshouses established during the lifetime of the founder, it is often more difficult to find a definitive foundation date. This is the case for Harrison's, Webb's, Hall's, Coxedd's and Jemmett's Almshouses. For each of these only an approximate date, usually the date their wills were proved, has been used. Plotting the dates of almshouse foundations, using decades as intervals, reveals that the foundation dates were remarkably evenly spaced chronologically (*see* Table 5.I).

TABLE 5.I.
Almshouse foundations in Berkshire during the 17th century, by decade intervals

1600s	1610s	1620s	1630s	1640s	1650s	1660s	1670s	1680s	1690s
1602									
1609									
1611									
	c1617								
		1625							
			1634 x2						
				1640					
				1641					
				1647					
					c1653				
					1659				
						1663			
							1671		
							c1676		
								1680	
								1681	
								1687	
									c1690
									c1696

LOCATION OF THE ALMSHOUSES

Looking at the places within Berkshire where almshouses were founded, or refounded, during the 17th century (*see* Map 5.i), it is clear that they were distributed across the county. It ought to be mentioned at this point that the almshouse at Wokingham was a fortunate inclusion for the county because Henry Lucas, the founder, put aside a sum of money in his will for: 'the building founding and endowing of an Hospitall or Almshouse in the Countie of Berks or in ye Countie of Surrey.'[11] Other market towns where almshouses were founded during this period included Lambourn, Maidenhead, Newbury, New Windsor, Reading, Wantage and Wallingford. The rural locations were at Bray, Donnington, Lyford, Shrivenham and Twyford. Significantly, three of the rural almshouses were located in the country seats of, or on other land belonging to, the Berkshire gentry. A significant feature that the map does not show is the occurrence of clusters of almshouse foundations; there were three newly founded in Newbury, and no less than six in Reading, over the course of the 17th century.

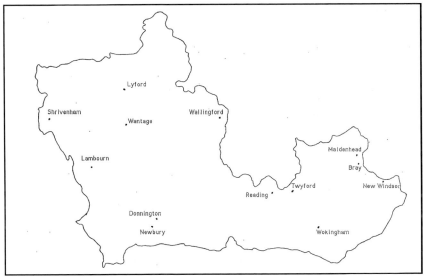

Map 5.i. Location of almshouses founded in Berkshire during the 17th century

POSTHUMOUS FOUNDATIONS

Of the total of twenty almshouse foundations in Berkshire, the majority were established during the lifetime of the benefactor: only eight almshouses were founded by will. The latter included several whose founders were well aware of their own mortality. William Goddard stated:

> And whereas my desire and purpose is in my life tyme (if it please God to prolong the same) to erect and build an Hospitall in the parish of Bray in the county of Berks for Poore people to abide and inhabite.[12]

The founder of Lucas's Hospital remarked on:

> old age full of yeares and also of Infirmityes which are the forerunners of Mortality Do as I ought dayly call to mind my dislodging, and therefore for the getting of my little house in order[13]

and he proceeded to do just that.

Richard Jeyes did not mind whether his almshouses were to be purpose built or not:

> I give and bequeath one hundred and twentie pounds of lawfull English money to build or buy fouer Almeshouses for fouer poore widows within the parish of St Maries in Reading.[14]

Thomas Pearce of Newbury left £400 to his trustees and directed them to 'buy a Convenient habitation for two poore people' and then to purchase land that would form the endowment for the charity with the remaining sum. His trustees were also charged with electing the two almsmen, paying their weekly stipend, and providing them with a gown every second year. Pearce was mindful: 'That there may for ever be a succession of trustees to take care that my Charity may not be abused'.[15]

In his will Oliver Ashcombe earmarked the location for his foundation for ten poor men or women: 'an Almshowse to be built for that purpose in the Close where the widowe Gawlton doth nowe dwell in Liford'.[16] John Hall's almshouses were in Chain Lane, Reading and he ensured that Elizabeth, his wife and executrix, was closely associated with his almshouse charity after his death. She was to elect the almsfolk, give them their yearly allowance for fuel, and their weekly stipend. On her death these functions were to pass to the Mayor, Aldermen and Burgesses of the Corporation of Reading. Hall directed that his almsfolk be: 'five poor single persons of good Reputation of the Towne of Reading aforesaid there to live and inhabit rent ffree soe long as they shall behave themselves well' and further:

> I doe desire my said wife that Thomas Green of Reading Scrivener, my brother
> in law Joseph - of Henly and my old servant Ffrancis Goodwin may be three
> of them if they think fit to accept thereof.[17]

So again this shows personal involvement by the founder in the selection of almspeople, even though the almshouse was founded by will.

The case of Robert Stiles' Almshouse is a slightly different matter because he died abroad, leaving an oral will. Apparently it was left to his nephew Joseph Haskins Stiles, who had been in partnership with his uncle as a draper in Amsterdam, to carry out Robert's last wishes. Stiles had left 'large sums in Charities' including the money used in building the almshouses in his birthplace of Wantage.[18]

LIFETIME FOUNDATIONS

Turning to those almshouses established in the founders' lifetimes, it might be anticipated that there would be more evidence of personal involvement and motive. Interestingly, the majority of these founders do go on to mention their almshouses when they write their wills: only Henry Howard, Earl of Nottingham, Sir Thomas Vachell and Sir Richard Harrison seem not to have done so.[19] However, as each of their almshouses had been founded many years prior to their deaths, and therefore were well-established, perhaps they felt no need to mention them in their wills.

There is just one line mentioning his charity in Jacob Hardrett's will. He had re-founded a hospital that had originally been established in the early 16th century, and left: 'to the ffyve poore Almesmen of my Almeshouse att Lambourne in Barkshire ffyve shillings a piece'.[20] In Newbury, Francis Coxedd's foundation was already functioning as an almshouse when he came to draw up his will. He mentioned:

> my two messuages and tenements situate, lying and being at West
> Mills...formerly purchased by me of William Harrow and now in the
> possession of my two poore Almesmen Richard Parsons and Thomas Martin.[21]

John Webb also named individuals as potential inhabitants of the almshouse, nominating his: 'ffourer poore widdowess of honest and godly life and conversation'.[22] Richard Reeve referred to the almshouse 'built by mee in Windsor' and frequently mentioned an earlier foundation deed or: 'Settlement of Almes houses' which detailed who the trustees of the charity were, the provision of a gown for the almsfolk, and probably rules and regulations or at least expectation of what he regarded as proper behaviour, the 'persons to inhabite in the said Almeshouses during their lives behaving themselves as is expressed in my Settlement'.[23] In tracing the history of his foundation Bernard Harrison seemed proud of his achievement, recalling that:

> with the consent and agreement of the Mayor and Burgesses of Reading I have att my owne costes and charges erected and built upon a parcel of their voyde ground in St Giles parish in Reading aforesaid foure small tenements and made them fitt and habitable for foure poore aged homeless and ympotent persons.[24]

Both Sir Henry Marten's and William Kendrick's almshouses were unfinished when they prepared their wills. Marten expressed his hope that soon his two sets of almshouses, at Longworth and Shrivenham, respectively, be completed.[25] Earlier in his will he had referred to 'the perfecting of those ten in Shrivenham which I am now about and purpose to finish my selfe as soon as I can conveniently yf God lend mee life'.[26] In the case of Kendrick's Almshouses, when he came to write his will a great deal of preparation had already been done but they were not yet inhabited. He left detailed instructions concerning the administration of the almshouses, qualifications for admission, and daily religious observance. For example, he stipulated that one specific, small item was to be bought for the almspeople and used on a daily basis:

> I doe will that myne executor or executors speedily after my decease shall buy provide and allow to and for the said Almsfolk a book of Common prayer to be from tyme to tyme used for the reading of prayer in the said Almshouse according to my will.[27]

Such care in setting down his intentions resulted in six of the seven sheets of his will being filled with details relating to the management of his almshouse.

FOUNDERS' OCCUPATIONS AND STATUS

We now turn attention to the founders' occupations and social status. W K Jordan's definitions of social classes have been adopted – nobility, upper gentry, lower gentry, merchants, artisans, tradesmen and professions – so that a comparison can be made between his findings and this local study. The involvement of founders in their local communities, and further charitable bequests in their wills, has also been considered here. It proved difficult at times to assign an individual benefactor to one of Jordan's classes, particularly when an occupation was not mentioned in the will, such as those who only used a title such as 'Esquire'. Of these men, those who were members of the livery companies were included with the merchants, following Jordan's practice, even though this involves an element of conjecture.

Nobility

Charles Howard, Earl of Nottingham, Baron of Effingham was the only example of the nobility amongst 17th-century Berkshire almshouse founders. Elizabeth I created him Earl in 1597, and gave him the lordship and manor of Donnington in 1601 as a reward for his services as Lord High Admiral and especially for his role in defeating the Spanish Armada.[28] Although he 'is conjectured to have rebuilt at his own expense, the hospital on its ancient site, [and] ordained rules for the government thereof' it is difficult to assess his subsequent involvement with the Hospital (*see* Illustration 5.b. colour Plate VII).[29] As Patron he was required to appoint the Master and almsmen, someone to audit the accounts yearly and, along with the Master, to settle disputes between the almsmen. All of this was stipulated in the rules and regulations that he and the then Master of the Hospital, Richard James, drew up in 1619. Howard did not mention the Hospital in his will, though he did leave four pounds a year to the poor of the parish of Leatherhead in Surrey, which was to be distributed by the overseers of the poor.[30]

Gentry

Defining the gentry is notoriously difficult.[31] Jordan divided the gentry into what he described as: 'two fairly well defined groups, the upper and the lower gentry'.[32]

Upper gentry

Defined by Jordan as 'simply the knights and their immediate families' three 17th-century Berkshire almshouse founders fit into this category.[33] Both Vachell and Harrison came from well-established Berkshire gentry families. Each included their principal manors in the opening lines of their wills: 'Sir Thomas Vachell of Coley in the County of Berks knight' and: 'Sr Richard Harrison of Hurst in the County of Berks Knt'.[34] They also both acted as justices of the peace and served as both deputy lieutenants and sheriffs of Berkshire.[35] Neither of them mentioned their almshouse foundations in their wills, and only Sir Thomas Vachell left an additional bequest, giving ten pounds to the poor of Reading 'to be distributed amongst them att the tyme of my buryall'.[36] Marten was knighted in 1616, in his will describing himself as: 'Sir Henry Marten of the city of London, Knight, Judge of his Majesties High Sheriff of Admiralty and of the Prerogative Court of Canterbury'.[37] His family background suggests a rapid rise into the ranks of the gentry, while his father was 'technically a gentleman by virtue of the lands he held in Berkshire, gained his livelihood as a London grocer'.[38] Henry Marten pursued a successful and distinguished legal career and his wealth enabled him to purchase no fewer than eight manors in Berkshire over a forty-year period.[39] As a result he 'owned one of the largest individual estates in the county'.[40] He lent Charles I £3,000 in 1639 and this resulted in great anxiety as to whether he would actually get his money back, which he expressed in his will.[41] The repayment of the loan, with interest, was due 'at Michelmas Day 1642' (his will was written in August 1641, Michaelmas is in September). In mentioning his intention to found almshouses at Longworth and completing those at Shrivenham he stated:

> And these things had I done my selfe long since yf the Kinge had not borrowed my money from mee For I did never comend any man that would putt off a good worke to his Executor that was in his owne power to doe by himselfe. Butt now things are as they are, I hope the money will be justly paid and the good worke accomplished. according to my harts desire.[42]

Sir Henry Marten clearly showed heartfelt concern over the founding of his almshouses. In a codicil to his will he also left money to both the parish and the poor of St Bartholomews, Aldgate, London and to the 'hospitalls around London viz Christs hospitall and St Bartholomews hospitall'.[43]

Lower gentry

People belonging to the lower gentry, according to W K Jordan, would have 'so described themselves in their own wills'.[44] Richard Reeve of New Windsor had, in his lifetime, lent the

Corporation of Windsor £300, the repayment of which he apportioned in his will. Two hundred pounds was to buy land: 'the rents, issues and profits thereof' to be applied in repairing his almshouses and for the 'yearly maintenance and reliefe of the Almes people'. The remaining sum due:

> I give and bequeath the said hundred pounds to the said Corporation of
> Windsor towards the finishing the New market house now in hand as a token
> of my affection and respect towards them.[45]

Reeve had earlier founded a bread charity in the town, which benefited fifty poor persons twice a year.[46]

Francis Coxedd left one shilling each to sixty poor widows of Newbury and further sums specifically for poor people of Bartholomew Street, Northbrook Street and Cheap Street in Newbury. As far as his almshouses were concerned he ensured that the maintenance of the two poor men and repairs of the almshouses were covered by the rents from endowed lands and further any 'Overplus thereof shall be employed ... for the teaching of such and so many poor children of the said town of Newbury to read or write'. Significantly he also gave money towards an earlier almshouse foundation in the town: 'I give and bequeath unto the twelve poor Almes people belonging to the Church Almeshouses of Newbury aforesaid two shillings and sixpence a piece'.[47] These almshouses were in St Nicolas churchyard and benefited twelve poor men and women.[48]

John Webb's charity was primarily to benefit one of the parishes in Reading. He not only required that his almspeople be 'ffoure poore widows of honest and godly life and conversation of the parish of Sainte Lawrence', but also established a weekly lecture to be preached by the minister in the church, and left the sum of twenty shillings to the poor of the parish on the day of his burial. In addition he left half that sum to the parishes of St Giles and St Mary's in Reading, again to be distributed on the day of his funeral. The poor of Bucklebury in Berkshire were also to receive twenty shillings and he also gave ten pounds towards the purchase of a house for the school master of the free school in Reading.[49]

Oliver Ashcombe of Lyford came from an established Berkshire gentry family, who owned the manors of Lyford and Childrey. The ten 'aged poore and impotent people' to inhabit his almshouse in Lyford were to be 'elected or chosen by my heirs' (*see* Illustration 5.c.).[50] Such a firm family involvement with an almshouse could last for years and often the trusteeship of the charity was tied to the ownership of the manor.

Henry Lucas, of London, Esq., was included in the lower gentry because family connections indicate that he came from such a background. In his will he mentioned that the estate left at his death was due to his own hard work: 'for what my father left me was snatched from me by unhappie Suits in Law during my Childhood' and he also acknowledged those relatives who had assisted him earlier in his life:

> I give to my honoured kinsman the Ladie Anne Fane the widdow of Sir George
> Fane Knight the summe of one thousand pounds in a heartie and thankfull
> acknowledgement of the many Charities I received from them both dureing the
> distresses of my life.[51]

Sir George Fane was a cousin of Henry Lucas. Trained as a lawyer, although never called to the Bar, Henry Lucas eventually became secretary to Henry Rich first Earl of Holland, Chancellor of Cambridge University. Lucas also twice served as one of the university's representatives as MP.[52] This connection with the university is apparent in Lucas' bequests: not only did he leave money for the foundation of a mathematical professorship –

subsequently held by Isaac Newton and Stephen Hawking among others – he also bequeathed his substantial book collection to the University Library. He declared in his will that these bequests were made to 'testifie my affection both to ye place and learning'. Regarding the remainder of his estate, which still amounted to about £7,000, he wrote:

> I intend to restore it to God from whose bountie I received the whole and therefore to hereby will and appoint that my Executors shall employ the same for the building founding and endowing of an Hospitall or Almeshouse ... for the reliefe of so manie poor old men and a Master ... as may be conveniently provided for.[53]

Lucas also stipulated in his will that once his executors had died the management of the hospital in Wokingham was to pass to the Master, Wardens and Company of Drapers in London. This was particularly surprising because Henry Lucas was not a member of the Company. Equally surprising was the fact that the Company was unaware of their potential role in Lucas's Hospital until many years later. The minutes of the Court of Assistants for 17 August 1675 noted their agreement to take on the trust, in consideration 'that a Charity of so great value might not be exposed to those hazards that a refusall by the Company might produce'.[54]

Illustration 5.c. Lyford Almshouse. *Photo © John Wells*

Merchants

Jordan defined merchants as those involved in wholesale trade, often members of the London livery companies.[55] Originally established as trade guilds responsible for the regulation of their specific trade, the livery companies came to dominate not only the business life of London, but its governance as well. The office of Lord Mayor of the City of London, for example, has for centuries been held by a prominent member of one of the city livery companies. So it is not surprising that those 17th-century Berkshire almshouse founders who were members of livery companies also described themselves as 'of London' in their wills, since the capital was where they conducted their business.

In his will, James Smith of London, Esq., mentioned the 'Company of Salters (whereof I am a member)'. He bequeathed £100 to the Company with the intention that the yearly income, together with any surplus from the endowment of the Maidenhead almshouse, was to be specifically used for the Master, Wardens and Assistants of the Company to travel from London to 'Visit these Almeshouses' on a yearly basis. His other bequests were varied and numerous. He left twenty-four pounds for six poor boys and girls born in Hammersmith to be apprenticed, remembered the poor people of Redditch and, like Sir Henry Marten mentioned earlier, left sums to both Christ's and Bartholomew's Hospitals in London. A further tranche of his charitable gifts was specifically for the Salters' Company: £100 was to go towards their stock; plate in the form of a 'standing Cupp and cover to it of Silver Guilt' was to be bought; and lastly money was to be used as a loan for 'two young men ffree of the said Company by ffifty Pounds a peece for ffoure yeares gratis And without any interest for the same'. James Smith was clearly heavily involved in the Company, since at his funeral he requested:

> soe many poore men As I shalbe yeares old att the tyme of my decease twenty shillings a peece to attend my Corps in Blake Gownes on the day of my funerall And my further will is that all the Almsmen of the Company of Salters ... And all the Porters usually labouring att my Shop shall be part of these poore men.[56]

Smith's funeral procession would have been an impressive sight.

Like Smith, Philip Jemmett was a member of a livery company, in his case the Brewers' Company. An entry in the Court Minutes for 5 November 1667 recorded:

> 'This day Philip Jemmitt Esq. a member of the Court and Tenant to the Company of several houses at Garlickhythe in Thames street burnt down by the late dreadful fire, being now present did move the Court to consider that his loss was very great'.[57]

It is assumed that the foundation of his twelve almshouses in Newbury was prior to the calamity of the Great Fire of London that affected his business so badly. It is known that by his will he left the almshouses in trust to his grandson Jemmett Raymond, from which time the foundation was known as Raymond's Almshouses.

In the Letters Patent founding his almshouse, William Goddard of Westminster in the County of Middlesex Esq., was referred to as: 'sometime a Citizen and Fishmonger of the City of London being in his lifetime charitably affected towards the poore'.[58]

He founded Jesus Hospital in Bray and made the Company of Fishmongers trustees and governors of the charity, attesting to: 'the special trust and confidence which I have and doe repose in the said Wardens and Commonalty of the Mistery of fishmongers of the City of

London'. According to the instructions he left in his will, the forty inhabitants of the almshouse were to consist of six men or women 'chosen of the most aged and poorest decayed persons' of the Company 'being freemen and freewomen of the said Company' and thirty-four from the parish of Bray where they were to have lived for at least twenty years. All of the 'Brethren and Sisters' as they were to be called, were to be 'of the age of fifty yeares at the least' and, furthermore, married couples 'shall not be allowed or admitted to be a Brother and a Sister of the said Hospital but either the husband or the wife the one or the other but not both'.[59]

The remaining 17th-century Berkshire almshouse founders included in this category were cloth merchants. Robert Stiles is described as 'merchant' on the plaque adorning his Wantage almshouse. A clue to how Stiles may have referred to himself can be gleaned from a will that was drawn up when he was a young man, prior to emigrating and settling in Amsterdam. It began: 'Robert Stiles of London, apprentice to Richard Cooke, of the same Citty, Draper'.[60] This document was produced as evidence when the detail of Stiles' oral will was contested by a relative. It is fair to assume that Robert Stiles completed his apprenticeship and became a Draper.

Both William Kendrick of Reading and Thomas Pearce of Newbury used the term 'Clothier' when describing themselves in their wills. During the 17th century the Berkshire woollen cloth industry declined dramatically and the cloth manufacturing towns of Newbury and Reading were particularly badly hit. In a Reading Corporation minute dated November 1623:

> all the Clothiers of this Corporacion were agayne warned to attend to shew
> causes of the decay of their trade, and whie they cannot sett the poore on worke
> as they have done, but suffer them to cry and complayne for lacke of worke.[61]

The Corporation tried corrective measures, for example, by restricting aspects of the manufacturing process – such as weaving and dressing cloth – to premises within the town. These measures were ultimately unsuccessful, due to the fact that Reading's occupational structure was changing, moving away from the textile trade and 'finding a new orientation as a processing and distributing centre for malt and grain.'[62] In 1632, William Kendrick, who by this time was mayor, reported a dire situation: 'we have seen a great failing in our town within twenty years past ... we are not sure the trade of clothing will continue'.[63] Kendrick's almshouse was founded just two years later and he stated that his:

> desire and will is that all such men as shalbe placed as Almsmen in the said
> Almshouse shalbe from and taken out of the Clothwork House in Reading
> aforesaid which is of the foundation or provision of my brother Mr John
> Kendrick late deceased.[64]

The Clothwork House, built to employ the poor in the clothing trade was only successful for a few years. Nevertheless the provision of the workhouse and the almshouse by the two Kendrick brothers meant that there was the potential for some continuity of care for a small section of the poor of Reading; this was remarkable for the time. The Kendricks were a leading Reading family, Thomas Kendrick, father of John and William had started the family cloth business. The elder son John Kendrick, who established his business in London, became a freeman of the Drapers' Company and also left numerous charitable bequests on his death. It is notable that on William Kendrick's funerary monument in St Mary's Church, Reading, his brother's good works are celebrated alongside his own.[65]

William Kendrick was very specific about the men who were to inhabit his almshouse. Not only were they to be from the Clothwork House, they:

> shalbe shearmen, weavers ... and others imployed or thereabout that work ... shierman may be preferred before any others because I know their trade is so laborious that they cannot in ould age soe well endure the labour thereof.

He went on to state that if none from the workhouse could be found then others in the clothing trade could be considered, and if none from the trade, then: 'other poor men of the said Borough of honest fame and conversation shall and maybe chosen and placed as Almsmen'.[66] By broadening out the qualifications for admission, Kendrick ensured that his almshouse continued to serve its useful purpose.

Thomas Pearce also stipulated occupational qualifications for his almsmen. Within a year of his death his trustees were to choose: 'Two poore weavers that is of the age of Sixty or thereabout. And that is free of the Company of Weavers that is of honest life and good behaviour' and further:

> when either of those shall dye My will is my aforesaid Trustees shall within one month after Elect and chuse another ffreeman that is Dyer of the said Company of Weavers that is of good conversation (And noe other trade whatsoever).[67]

The Company of Weavers in Newbury had been founded in the reign of Henry VIII and a royal charter was granted in 1601. The Company, like the Corporation of Reading, responded to the decline in the cloth industry by restricting trade: 'by their articles of agreement in 1688 they undertook not to undercut each other and not to spin yarn outside the borough'.[68] Pearce, who it is presumed was a member of the Company, also bequeathed twenty shillings to be spent by his trustees:

> the next day after the Company of Weavers shall hold their feast upon a Collation or Banquet. And fforty shillings to be disposed of by them Equally between Twenty poore weavers or poore weavers widdowes And amongst noe others And to be distributed upon the aforesaid day.[69]

It is interesting that Jordan only sub-divided the class of merchant in his volume concentrating on London; those members of the livery companies were divided into the greater and lesser merchants based on their wealth.[70] It might have been useful for him to have included some distinction between merchants within the main work, though he did include: 'retailers not of merchant rank, members of lesser companies' with his tradesman class.[71] The Newbury Company of Weavers would be regarded as a lesser company. As both Pearce and Kendrick described themselves as 'Clothier' in their wills, it was important to class them together. Considering the size of these men's almshouse foundations (Pearce's for two poor people, Kendrick's for five) it seems likely that Pearce's business in Newbury was on a smaller scale than Kendrick's in Reading.

Artisans

Jacob Hardrett was 'of the parish of St Clemente Danes without Temple Bar London, Jeweller' and in his will left – in addition to the five shillings a piece each to the almsmen in his almshouse at Lambourn – five pounds to the poore of the parish of St Clement, three pounds to the poor of the French Church in London and twenty shillings to the poor of Twickenham in the County of Middlesex.[72]

Richard Jeyes, glover, was an assistant of the Corporation of Reading, and was also involved in several capacities in the administration of St Mary's parish in the town, including churchwarden, surveyor of the highways and overseer of the poor. His four almshouses were to benefit those of St Mary's and may well have been a personal response to a need he observed within the parish. He also left four pounds to St Mary's parish, and three pounds to the other Reading parishes, St Lawrence and St Giles. Jeyes' other charitable bequests went further afield. He gave £100 each to Newbury and Wokingham in Berkshire, Henley in Oxfordshire, and Andover in Hampshire, specifically to 'be imployed for the use of the poore as a stock for ever'.[73]

Tradesmen

Included in Jordan's definition of tradesmen were shopkeepers, innkeepers and brewers, although he contended that this class was 'not notable for its charities'.[74] Nevertheless, there were two tradesmen among the founders of 17th-century Berkshire almshouses. John Angier of Wallingford, Ironmonger, listed his charity first in the list of his bequests:

> Item my desire is that the Corporation of Wallingford aforesaid whereof I am a member in some convenient time after my decease find and provide some fit place or piece of ground within the Borough of Wallingford aforesaid either held of the said Corporation or to be purchased by my Trustees hereinafter named whereupon an Almshouse may be built.[75]

Similarly 'Bernard Harrison of Reading in the countie of Berks. Beerbrewer' was a member of his town corporation.[76] Of particular significance is an entry in the corporation records of the lease to Harrison of 'the house wherein he now dwelleth, being the land of John A'Larder'. This was part of the endowment left by A'Larder for his almshouse in Reading, founded in the 15th century. Harrison was therefore to pay: 'the yearly rent of five pounds, to be paid half yearly for the use of the almsmen'.[77] So, Harrison had a personal connection with an established almshouse, and this may well have provided the motive to found his own. The only additional charitable bequest he left was: 'ten pounds in money to be distributed amongst the poore people of the town of Reading on the daye of my buriall'.[78] Jordan argued that tradesmen: 'ranked far below the merchants in wealth, prestige and civic pride'.[79] Although it is likely that they had modest wealth and prestige, both tradesmen in this study were members of their town corporations, and John Angier in particular was proud of his connections with the town and corporation of Wallingford.

Professions

John Hall of Reading, apothecary, was the sole representative of the professional class amongst 17th-century Berkshire almshouse founders. In addition to the provision of an almshouse for five poor single persons, he stipulated that after his death two tenements in Reading were to be converted into one: 'for a schoolmaster to live and inhabit'. He also directed the Mayor, Aldermen and Burgesses of Reading to choose three poor boys out of the three parishes of Reading and place them with the schoolmaster who would 'teach them to read write and cast accompt' and at the end of the year 'they shall place the said boyes out Apprentices to some handicraft Trade'.[80]

TABLE 5.II

WK Jordan's analysis of the classes contributing to all forms of charitable giving, 1480-1660, compared with those who founded 17th-century Berkshire almshouses

Class	W K Jordan's study Number of donors	% of donors	Class	17th century Berkshire almshouses Number of donors	% of donors
Crown	36	0.10			
Nobility	192	0.55	Nobility	1	5.00
Upper gentry	959	2.74	Upper gentry	3	15.00
Lower gentry	3753	10.73	Lower gentry	5	25.00
Yeomen	5144	14.71			
Husbandmen	5079	14.53			
Agricultural labourers	634	1.81			
Upper clergy	175	0.50			
Lower clergy	1561	4.46			
Merchants	3679	10.52	Merchants	6	30.00
Tradesmen	2640	7.55	Tradesmen	2	10.00
Burghers	1557	4.45			
Artisans	2089	5.97	Artisans	2	10.00
Professionals	866	2.48	Professionals	1	5.00
Unidentified	6601	18.89			

CONCLUSION

In comparing Jordan's analysis of the social classes contributing to all forms of charitable giving, 1480-1660, with those who founded 17th-century Berkshire almshouses (*see* Table 5.II) we find broadly similar results. The merchants are in the majority, closely followed by the lower gentry; the upper gentry, tradesmen and artisans are next, leaving the professions and nobility as the smallest percentage of donors. With such a small sample, though, the results can change significantly if a founder is classified in another group; for example, if Pearce were to be classed as a tradesman rather than merchant, then the balance shifts to an equal position between the merchants and lower gentry and the upper gentry and tradesmen. Even allowing for such an adjustment, what remains clear is the significant impact on almshouse foundations made by the merchants and gentry of Berkshire in the 17th century.

This study has established that a total of twenty almshouses were founded across Berkshire during the 17th century. One surprising discovery was that there were no women amongst the founders in this study. What has been revealed, though, is that the founders represented here regarded their almshouses as their foremost charity; in the majority of cases, the largest proportion of sums allocated for charitable giving was devoted to their almshouses. Any further bequests – such as money for education, apprenticeships, stock for the poor of parishes and funeral doles – were supplementary to their main charity. It was significant that the majority of these men, 60 per cent, founded their almshouses during their lifetime. They were personally involved in their charities, often naming specific individuals as potential inhabitants, and establishing mechanisms for the future trusteeship of their almshouses. Their motives included a religious impulse and civic pride. The building and endowment of almshouses was a timely, local response to the needs of the aged poor. The founders' intentions went further; each of their almshouse charities was intended to last in perpetuity, serving the local community forever.

Notes

1.   This chapter is based on work done for my thesis: Lambert, S. '17th Century Berkshire Almshouses', unpublished MPhil thesis, University of Reading, 1997. I have excluded Barker's almshouse, Hurst (trust deed dated 1682) from this chapter because the founder William Barker in his will described himself as 'of Hurst in the county of Wiltshire'. Hurst was partly in Berkshire, partly in Wiltshire.

2.   Jordan, W.K. *Philanthropy in England, 1480-1660: a study of the changing pattern of English social aspirations*, London, 1959. Berkshire was not one of the ten counties he used as a representative sample in his study; they were Buckinghamshire, Hampshire, Kent, Lancashire, Norfolk, Somerset, Worcestershire, Bristol and London (he included Middlesex in London). Jordan followed this initial study with: Jordan, W.K. *The Charities of London, 1480-1660: the aspirations and achievements of the urban society*, London, 1960; and Jordan, W.K. *The Charities of Rural England, 1480-1660: the aspirations and achievements of the rural society*, London, 1961.

3.   Stiles Almshouse, Wantage: plaque.

4.   Reproduced in Blandy, W.E.M. *History of the Reading Municipal Charities: including Allen's Charity and the Green Girl's Foundation*, Reading, 1962, between pp. 14-15.

5.   Smith's Almshouse, Maidenhead: plaque.

6.   Donnington Hospital: plaque.

7.   Ashmole, A. *The Antiquities of Berkshire Vol. I: with a large appendix of original papers, pedigrees of families in the said county, and a particular account of the castle and town of Windsor*, London, 1723, pp. xlv-vi.

8.   Finch, J. 'Twyford Almshouses', *Journal of Twyford & Ruscombe Local History Society*, Vol. 34, 1993, p.19.

9.   Wallingford Almshouse: plaque.

10.   The National Archives (TNA): PROB 11/363, Prerogative Court of Canterbury (PCC), will of John Angier, 1681.

11.   Drapers' Hall, London, Drapers' Company Records (DHL): V202/1c, notes of particulars concerning the will of Henry Lucas.

12.   London Metropolitan Archives (LMA): CLC/FE/G/057/MS10975, William Goddard's Charity.

13.   DHL: V202/1c, notes of particulars concerning the will of Henry Lucas.

14.   TNA: PROB 11/211, PCC, will of Richard Jeyes, 1647.

15.   TNA: PROB 11/337, PCC, will of Thomas Pearce, 1671.

16.   TNA: PROB 11/119, PCC, will of Oliver Ashcombe, 1611.

17.   TNA: PROB 11/438, PCC, will of John Hall, 1696.

18.   Anon.'Robert Stiles, Merchant, of Amsterdam', *Wiltshire Notes and Queries*, Dec. 1914, p. 149.

19.   Philip Jemmett's will has not been traced.

20.   TNA: PROB 11/163, PCC, will of Jacob Hardrett, 1633.

21.   TNA: PROB 11/411, PCC, will of Francis Coxedd, 1690.

22.   TNA: PROB 11/239, PCC, will of John Webb, 1653.

23.   TNA: PROB 11/393, PCC, will of Richard Reeve, 1688; the earlier Settlement document has not been traced but some details from it have been included in the *Charity Commissioners Report for Berkshire* Part 1, 1837-38; and in Tighe, R.R. & Davis, J.E. *Annals of Windsor: being a history of the castle and town with some account of Eton and places adjacent*, Vol. II, London, 1858, pp. 369-70.

24.   TNA: PROB 11/132, PCC, will of Bernard Harrison, 1617.

25.   Those at Longworth seem never to have built, those at Shrivenham are only for eight almspeople.

26.   TNA: PROB 11/187, PCC, will of Henry Marten, 1641.

27.   TNA: PROB 11/167, PCC, will of William Kendrick, 1634.

28.   Morris, W.A.D. *A History of the Parish of Shaw-cum-Donnington*, Newbury, 1969, p. 25.

29.   Gray, E.W. *History and Antiquities of Newbury and its Environs*, Speenhamland, 1839, p. 183.

30.   TNA: PROB 11/190, PCC, will of Charles Howard, 1642.

31.   *See,* for example, the first chapter in Coss, P. *The Origins of the English Gentry*, Cambridge, 2003.

32.   Jordan, 1959, p. 323.

33.   Ibid., pp. 323-4.

34. TNA: PROB 11/178, PCC, will of Thomas Vachel, 1634; TNA: PROB 11/245, PCC, will of Richard Harrison, 1654.

35. Durston, C.G. 'Berkshire and its County Gentry, 1625-1649', unpublished PhD thesis, University of Reading, 1977, pp. 72, 202.

36. TNA: PROB 11/178, PCC, will of Thomas Vachell, 1634.

37. TNA: PROB 11/187, PCC, will of Henry Marten, 1641.

38. Levack, B.P. *The Civil Lawyers in England, 1603-1641: a political study*, Oxford, 1973, p. 16.

39. Ibid., pp. 252-3.

40. Durston, C.G. 'London and the Provinces: the Association Between the Capital and the Berkshire County Gentry of the Early 17th Century', *Southern History*, Vol. 3, 1981, pp. 50-1.

41. Oxford *Dictionary of National Biography* (DNB), James S. Hart Jr 'Marten, Sir Henry (c.1561-1641)', Oxford, Sept. 2004; online edn, Jan. 2008. URL: www.oxforddnb.com/view/article/18167, accessed 12 Mar. 2010.

42. TNA: PROB 11/187, PCC, will of Henry Marten. 1641.

43. Ibid.

44. Jordan, 1959, p. 324.

45. TNA: PROB 11/393, PCC, will of Richard Reeve, 1688.

46. Tighe & Davis, Vol. II, p. 369.

47. TNA: PROB 11/411, PCC, will of Francis Coxedd, 1690.

48. Gray, p. 134.

49. TNA: PROB 11/239, PCC, will of John Webb, 1653.

50. TNA: PROB 11/119, PCC, will of Oliver Ashcombe, 1611.

51. DHL: V202/1c, notes of particulars concerning the will of Henry Lucas.

52. DNB, John Martin, 'Lucas, Henry (bap. 1587, d. 1663)', Oxford, Sept. 2004; online edn, Jan. 2008. URL: www.oxforddnb.com/view/article/17128, accessed 12 Mar. 2010.

53. DHL: V202/1c, notes of particulars concerning the will of Henry Lucas.

54. DHL: V202/1b, Court of Assistants, minutes, 17 Aug. 1675.

55. Jordan, 1959, p. 327.

56. TNA: PROB 11/325, PCC, will of James Smith, 1667. Unfortunately Smith's occupation is indecipherable.

57. Brewers' Hall, London, Brewers' Company Records, Court Minute Book, 1667.

58. LMA: CLC/FE/G/057/MS10975, office copy of letters patent.

59. LMA: CLC/FE/G/057/MS10975, office copy of William Goddard's will.

60. Anon, 'Robert Stiles, Merchant, of Amsterdam', *Wilts. Notes and Queries*, Dec. 1914, p. 147.

61. Guilding, J.M. (ed.), *Reading Records: diary of the corporation Vol. II James I to Charles I (1603/4-1629)*, London, 1895, p. 160.

62. Goose, N.R. 'Economic and Social Aspects of Provincial Towns: a comparative study of Cambridge, Colchester and Reading, *ca* 1500-1700', unpublished PhD thesis, University of Cambridge, 1984, p. 16.

63. Goose, N. 'Decay and Regeneration in 17th Century Reading: a study in a changing economy', *Southern History*, Vol. VI, 1984, p. 59.

64. TNA: PROB 11/167, PCC, will of William Kendrick, 1634.

65. Ashmole, Vol. II, pp. 345-6.

66. TNA: PROB 11/167, PCC, will of William Kendrick, 1634.

67. TNA: PROB 11/337, PCC, will of Thomas Pearce, 1671.

68. Garlick, V.F.M. *Newbury Charities and Gifts*, Newbury, 1972, p. 23.

69. TNA: PROB 11/337, PCC, will of Thomas Pearce, 1671.

70. Jordan, 1960, p. 50.

71. Jordan, 1959, p. 328.

72. TNA: PROB 11/163, PCC, will of Jacob Hardrett, 1633.

73. TNA: PROB 11/211, PCC, will of Richard Jeyes, 1647.

74. Jordan: 1959, p. 328.

75. TNA: PROB 11/363, PCC will of John Angier, 1681.

76.   TNA: PROB 11/132, PCC will of Bernard Harrison, 1617.

77.   Guilding, Vol. II, 1895, p. 5.

78.   TNA: PROB 11/132, PCC, will of Bernard Harrison, 1617.

79.   Jordan, 1959, p. 328.

80.   TNA: PROB 11/438, PCC, will of John Hall, 1696.

CHAPTER 6
MILE END AND WHITECHAPEL:
THE ALMSHOUSES ALONG THE GREAT ESSEX ROAD AND THEIR FOUNDERS

Janet Cumner

INTRODUCTION

The main road to the east from the City of London leaves via Aldgate and passes through the parishes of Whitechapel and Stepney. At the mile point is Mile End, from 1722 the site of the first gate from London on the turnpike to Shenfield, Essex and the name of a wider district. This Great Essex Road to Harwich carried commodities and produce to and from East Anglia and the east coast ports. Of particular note were the thousands of animals driven along it to City markets each year.[1] Whitechapel was an ancient parish, while Mile End was one of the eight hamlets that made up the large parish of Stepney.[2] In the 17th and 18th centuries Whitechapel was already crowded, but at Mile End only ribbon development stretched eastward beside the road, with a community of merchants and rich widows inhabiting fine houses.[3] To the rear of the roadside development was open land in both directions that was encroached upon over time to form the overcrowded neighbourhoods of the 19th-century East End.

Between 1623 and 1839 sixteen almshouses were established along less than two miles of the roadside through Whitechapel and Mile End (*see* Map 6.i and Table 6.I). The area owed its popularity with almshouse builders to a number of factors. Proximity and ease of access to the flourishing City of London allowed close regulation and monitoring of charitable establishments by various City-based bodies. Small plots of building land were much cheaper and more available in the eastern suburbs than in the crowded City or more fashionable areas to the west. Organisations looking for almshouse sites sought an 'airy and convenient place for the Alms-Folks'.[4] They were often keen that it should be prominent to passers-by so that the founder could be honoured.[5] The roadside sites in Mile End provided, initially at least, accessible, conspicuous and salubrious semi-rural locations for worthy pensioners to pass their last years. As well as City-based bodies, occupational groups, successful local residents and various religious groups made provision for the elderly poor along this road.

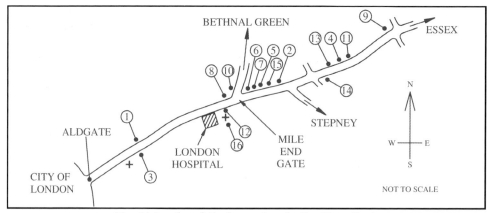

Map 6.i. Location of Almshouses along the Great Essex Road

TABLE 6.I
Almshouses along the Great Essex Road

	Almshouse	Opened	Founder	Administered by
1	Whitechapel Parish	1614	unknown	Whitechapel Vestry
2	Judge Fuller's	1623 (founded 1591)	John Fuller	Stepney Vestry
3	Meggs's	1658	William Meggs	Meggs's heirs, later Rector & Vestry of Whitechapel
4	Astill's	1665	Margaret Astill	Cripplegate parish
5	Vintners' Company	1676 (founded 1449 in the City of London)	Guy Shuldham	Vintners' Company
6	Skinners' Company	1685	Lewis Newberry	Skinners' Company
7	Trinity Hospital	1695	Captain Henry Mudd	Trinity House
8	Pemel's	1698 (founded 1681)	John Pemel	Drapers' Company
9	Cooke's & Rowe's	1706	Alice Carant, formerly Rowe, formerly Cooke	Independent trustees, later the vestry of the hamlet of Mile End Old Town
10	Captain Fisher's	1711	Robert Fisher, William Ogbourne	Trinity House
11	Bancroft's Hospital	1727	Francis Bancroft	Drapers' Company
12	Yoakley's	1789 (founded pre-1708 in Spitalfields)	Michael Yoakley	Trustees from the Quaker community
13	Spanish & Portuguese Jews' Hospital	1790 (founded 1747 in Stepney)	London congregation of Sephardi Jews	Trustees from the Sephardi community
14	German Jews' Hospital	1806	Abraham Goldsmid	Ashkenazi Jewish trustees
15	Pantin's	1823	Michael Pantin	Trustees from Brunswick Chapel
16	Female Servants'	1839	National Guardian Institution for Families and Servants	National Guardian Institution for Families and Servants

CITY LIVERY COMPANY ALMSHOUSES

Early almshouses were often set up by trade associations to cater for members no longer able to earn a living and in London the Guilds – and their successors the City Livery Companies – fulfilled this role. The wealth generated in London was enormous and charitable giving in the capital amounted to a third of the total for the country between 1480 and 1660.[6] By the terms of his will in 1421, the extremely rich merchant Richard 'Dick' Whittington made many charitable bequests including the foundation of an almshouse for thirteen men. He gave management of his establishment to the Mercers' Company of which he had been Master three times. In so doing he firmly established the idea of wealthy city men and their Livery Companies founding almshouses for the poor and this became a popular form of London philanthropy.[7]

Vintners' Almshouses

The first Company to build by the Great Essex Road were the Vintners, who replaced City almshouses lost in the Great Fire, in Mile End. Two single-storey rows, each of six houses, formed two sides of a rectangle with the main road, and a chapel, where public prayers were said twice a week, completed the layout.[8] When they were ready for occupation in 1676 the almsmen and women who were billeted in the City at the Company's expense were reluctant to move out to the suburbs and only did so when threatened with expulsion if they did not move within a fortnight. After the move, their pensions were increased to 1s. each week paid by the Company's Beadle at the Almshouses.[9]

Managing mixed-sex accommodation presented the Company with some discipline problems and by the beginning of the 18th century the occupants were exclusively female. From 1716 vacancies were announced at a meeting of the Company's Court of Assistants and filled at the next meeting about a month later. Status was the main criterion for selection with widows of the highest officers of the Company receiving substantial out-pensions while widows of Assistants and Liverymen were given precedence over those of freemen for almshouse places.[10] In spite of this, if two vacancies were filled at the same time, the Company insisted that lots be drawn to stop one of the candidates pulling rank and selecting the better room. All unsuccessful candidates were awarded about 5s.[11]

Benjamin Kenton was Master of the Vintners' Company in 1776.[12] He had made a large fortune from the successful bottling of beer for export to the warm climates of the Empire.[13] At his death in 1800 he left a charitable bequests of £2,250 to rebuild the Company's Mile End almshouses and provide additional pensions for the residents.[14] The houses were replaced in 1803 on the same site, mainly reusing old materials. Each consisted of one large room with folding doors and a bed recess with a cellar or kitchen below; it was 1859 before water closets were installed in each house.[15] The almshouses continued in use until they were bombed in World War Two and new houses were later built in Sussex; these were sold in the 1990s.[16]

Whilst a number of establishments may lay claim to being the inspiration for Titbull's Alms Houses portrayed in 1861 by Charles Dickens in *The Uncommercial Traveller*, B.W. Matz, writing in *The Dickensian* in 1905, had no doubt that it was the appearance of the Vintners' Almshouses that most closely matched Dickens's description of Titbull's:

> Titbull's Alms-Houses are in the east of London, in a great highway, in a poor, busy and thronged neighbourhood ... smoky-fronted ... with a little paved court-yard in front enclosed by iron railings, which have got snowed up, as it were, by bricks and mortar; which were once in a suburb, but are now in the densely populated town ... with a grim stone very difficult to read, let into the front of the centre house ... ornamented atop with a piece of sculptured drapery resembling Titbull's bath-towel.[17]

Matz recognised the 'bath-towel' as matching that on the stone at the front of the Vintners' Houses.[18]

Dickens's description of the area around Titbull's gives an excellent word-picture of what the roadside in Whitechapel and Mile End would have been like in the mid 19th century:

> Old iron, cough drops, artificial flowers, boiled pigs'-feet and household furniture … and saucers full of shell-fish in a green juice which I hope is natural to them when their health is good, garnish the paved sideways as you go to Titbull's ... On Saturday nights when there is a greater stir than usual … itinerant vendors of miscellaneous wares even take their stations and light up smoky lamps before the iron railings.[19]

Skinners' Almshouses

Twelve Skinners' Company Almshouses built round a courtyard nearby resulted from the will of Lewis Newbery in 1685, with each unit consisting of one room and a cellar.[20] Entrance from the road was by a wicket-gate in a high wall.[21] Also provided were a chapel with a small square garden behind and a house for a minister, who had to say prayers daily and preach a sermon on Sunday for the occupants. Over the gate were: 'the effigies of two old cripples; the one with a crutch, the other leaning on a staff; and the Skinners Arms'.[22] The Master, Wardens and Assistants of the Skinners received the £1,851 remaining in the estate after building costs.

Each almswoman originally received £5 4s. per year plus coals. By 1861 the sum had risen to £20 a year and one of the occupants, who acted as gatekeeper, received an additional £10. The chaplain and a chaplain's clerk were each paid stipends with a gardener paid £6 a year and £29 for nurses caring for the aged occupants. Over time additional bequests were made to the establishment and the Company met costs from those and its general funds. It was not until 1884 and at the direction of the Charity Commissioners that the interest on Newberry's original £1,851 was credited to the almshouse endowment rather than being absorbed into the Company's funds.[23] Although this practice may appear dubious, the costs met by the Company over the years must have far exceeded the 5 per cent interest payable on Newbery's capital sum. The almshouses continued in Mile End until 1895 when they were relocated to a site in Palmers Green.[24]

Pemel's Almshouses

John Pemel was born in Lewes, Sussex, apprenticed as a Draper in 1622 and at his death in 1681 he was an Assistant in the Drapers' Company and a Governor of St Thomas's Hospital. In his will he left £1,200 to the Company to be invested in land in order to generate income to build and endow eight almshouses: 'on a piece of ground in or near Mile-end'.[25]

The Drapers Company invested Pemel's capital for seventeen years before they had accumulated the £564 required to secure a site 'abutting the highway from Whitechapel to Bow' and build eight almshouses (see Illustration 6.a.). These opened in 1698, constructed as Pemel had decreed in a single storey row of eight dwellings with yards or gardens. Following the founder's wishes, four houses were allocated to: 'widows of mariners or seamen … living in the parish of Stepney because it hath pleased God to bless me with most part of that estate he hath given me by trading into parts beyond the seas.' The other four were for 'poor pious distressed widdows of deceased freemen of the said Company'.[26] If the women remarried they were required to leave. The occupants received £4 each year by four quarterly payments plus a supply of 'good seacoales'. Every other year £6 was spent on providing cloth gowns with a badge on the right breast showing the Company's arms; the women were required to wear these whenever they went out. The four non-Company widows were nominated by the hamlets of Stepney parish in turn. By 1851 all eight widows living in the houses still received the founder's original allowance of 6s. 8d. monthly and the Company's four widows got an additional £1. 4s. 10d. each month from general Company funds.[27]

In 1863 the Drapers wished to sell the Mile End site to Mann, Crossman & Paulin of the adjacent Albion Brewery for the sum of £1,900. The Charity Commissioners reported that the arrangement of the houses was: 'very defective, viz., one watercloset in the centre for the use of all the occupants, one receptacle for the dust, and one cistern for the supply of water, several of the inmates being too infirm to fetch the latter are much inconvenienced'. The women, echoing Dickens's comments on Titbull's, complained that the 'constant noise of the thronged road and the costermongers who are established immediately in front of the almshouses are great disadvantages'. None of the occupants objected to being relocated to new buildings next to other Company almshouses about two miles to the east in Bow. This arrangement only lasted until 1870 when all the occupants were moved to a large site in Tottenham.[28]

Illustration 6.a. Pemel's Almshouses, 1815, R.B. Schnebbelie
(reproduced courtesy of the Drapers' Company)

Bancroft's Hospital

A second larger almshouse was built by the Drapers' Company on a five acre site on the north side of the road at Mile End in 1736. Bancroft's Hospital was a foundation consisting of twenty-four (later thirty) almshouses and a school for one hundred boys. Its entire endowment came to the Company in 1727 from sixty-year-old Francis Bancroft. He had served the Lord Mayor of London in various official capacities and operated on his own account as a middleman.[29] His reputation was equivocal; according to his contemporary John Strype he was 'a common pest of the Citizens' who 'not only pillaged the Poor but likewise the Rich' by taking pay-offs from those he summoned before the City courts for trivial misdemeanours.[30]

Bancroft had never been active in the Drapers' Company, however he relied upon them to administer his will.[31] He died a bachelor and left £25,000 to the Company, the largest sum they had ever received for charitable purposes.[32] The Company built an impressively spacious quadrangle with the school, chapel, and masters' houses to the rear and the almshouses in facing rows making up the other two sides. The site also had an acre of garden, a burial ground and playgrounds for the boys.

Bancroft's will set out a detailed scheme for the management and regulation of the almshouses and the school. Only 'deserving and real poor objects ... of good life and conversation' who were members of the Company were eligible for the houses with preference being given to freemen. Wives were admitted with their husbands, but had to leave if widowed. The men dressed in buff coloured gowns and were required to attend the chapel twice a day with their wives unless unwell. Twice each year the almsmen walked into the City to hear commemorative sermons preached, after which they were rewarded with a dinner. From 1727, each year the almsmen received £8 paid quarterly and six sacks of coal with a 'bays gown' every third year. By 1853 they were being paid £30 a year plus coals with nursing or medical care as required. Almsmen who undertook additional tasks, such as the porter, chapel clerk and gatekeepers, were paid between £5 and £16 extra each year.[33]

A small committee oversaw the establishment and was required to visit 'once a year, or oftener if occasion requiring ... to inquire into the state, condition, and behaviour of the said poor men'; as well as to 'take, view, and give orders for the needful repairs of the said school and alms-houses'. The Committee was then allowed to spend up to £5 on a dinner for its members and the two schoolmasters to mark the occasion.

There were twenty-eight rules set out by the Company for the almsmen and their families to observe and breaking them often resulted in an appearance before the Visiting Committee.[34] Almsman James Luke Sedgewick, a former cork cutter aged fifty-seven, appeared on 28 May 1847 to explain why he had frequently missed the afternoon service in contravention of Rule VIII. The Committee were not satisfied with his explanation and ordered him to attend in future.[35] Mr Sedgewick was a long-term resident. He entered the Hospital with his wife, Mary, but she died in 1855, and two years later he married fifty-nine year old spinster, Sarah Davidson, who was living in Cooke's and Rowe's Almshouses just along the road. Sarah died three years later and in 1864, aged seventy-four years, Sedgewick married fifty-one-year-old widow, Mary Ann Lack. He died in 1871 at the age of eighty having lived in the Hospital for thirty years with three wives.[36]

From its records, the Drapers' Company seems to have spent far less time dealing with disciplinary problems in the large school than with bad behaviour, including drunkenness, bickering and even fighting, among the thirty almsmen and their wives. This may have influenced the decision to close the almshouses when the Hospital was demolished and the site sold in 1884. The school relocated to Woodford, Essex; the Mile End site now forms part of the campus of Queen Mary College, University of London.[37]

Fuller's Almshouses

A set of almshouses that lay back from the roadside were the result of a bequest by John Fuller in his will proved in 1592. Fuller was a lawyer and judge in the City of London. He left lands in Lincolnshire to endow two sets of almshouses: 'for the funding, sustenation &

relief, from time to time, of certain poor, needy & impotent people' consisting of twelve women in Shoreditch parish and twelve men in Stepney.[38]

Fuller's will required that the Mercers' Company manage the establishments. There is no evidence that he was a member of the Company, but he may have consulted them before the event. Whatever the case, the Mercers eventually declined to act and the two parishes finally took on responsibility. It was not until 1623, almost thirty years after Fuller's death, that three houses, each with four rooms and small gardens, were finally built at Mile End. Fifty pounds per year was paid into the charity by successive owners of Fuller's Lincolnshire lands. In spite of an order in Chancery to incorporate the charity in 1687 this was not done until 1864, when several Stepney churchwardens were appointed Trustees. Occupants were chosen by the eight Stepney hamlets, each being responsible for repairs to the rooms occupied by their nominees. The churchwarden of Christ Church in Spitalfields received the £50 each year and distributed 2s. to each pensioner every week for which duty he received £2 a year.[39] The wives of married men were admitted with their husbands and allowed to remain if widowed. In the 1851 census return eleven of the houses were occupied by widows and only one by a family with a male head.[40] By the mid 19th century the buildings were dilapidated and in 1865 new provision was made ten miles to the north east in Leytonstone, Essex and the houses were demolished.[41]

MARITIME ALMSHOUSES

For centuries London was the principal port in the kingdom and the Thames was thronged with ships trading across the world. The hamlets of the ancient parish of Stepney covered a large area stretching east along the north bank of the river from the Tower of London and included the Upper and Lower Pools of London, which in the 17th and 18th centuries, before the building of the great commercial docks, were the centres of loading and unloading activity. The area was home to large numbers of seafarers of all ranks and others from associated maritime trades who, often at great risk, supported the burgeoning power of the Royal Navy and the East India Company and the enormous national economic benefits that came as a result. Stepney parish was therefore an obvious choice for almshouses for distressed mariners, their widows and dependants and four sets were built along the roadside at Mile End to meet this need as well as others nearer the river.

Trinity Hospital

The largest of these almshouses was Trinity Hospital, built and run by the Corporation of Trinity House in 1695. At that time the organisation already had a long and illustrious history. In 1513 Henry VIII granted a charter incorporating an existing fraternity of mariners: 'so that they might regulate the pilotage of ships in the King's streams'.[42]

Known as Trinity House, the Corporation was responsible for licensing Thames pilots, keeping the river clear and, later, establishing and maintaining lighthouses and other aids to offshore navigation around the coast. By 1685 its Charter included bye-laws enforcing 'the Conversation, good Estate, wholsome Government, Maintenance and Encrease of the Navigation of this Kingdom, and of the Mariners and Seafaring Men'. In a similar fashion to the Livery Companies the governance of the Corporation was in the hands of the Trinity Court Brethren. All were originally drawn from the higher ranks of the Royal Navy, the Merchant Navy and the Government's Navy Office.[43]

The ancient Guild possessed almshouses at Deptford and had an established history of charitable giving.[44] This philanthropic tradition was maintained and wealthy seafarers made gifts and bequests to the Corporation. In addition, considerable revenue was generated from its monopolies and fines. All surplus funds were devoted to the charitable support of seafarers and their dependants, including almshouse provision and out-pensions. Trinity House operated similarly in a number of major ports (*see* Chapter 9 for details about those on the north-east coast). In London the Deptford almshouses were expanded twice in the 17th century, but the provision there did not meet demand.[45] Trinity House, therefore, made additional provision among the seafarers living in the riverside parishes on the north bank of the Thames.

In his will dated 28 May 1692, Henry Mudd, an East India ship's captain, left land in 'Milend near the Road' to Trinity House and required 'that the said Corporation shall build almshouses thereon for the use and habitacion of their poor'.[46] He left no endowment for the almshouses, but since he was a member of the Elder Brethren and Deputy Master when he died he could be confident that his wishes would be fulfilled.[47]

Illustration 6.b. The Captains' Houses, Trinity Hospital in 2011.
Photo © Janet Cumner.

Twenty-eight houses for 'decayed ship's Commanders and their widows', known as the Captains' Houses were built on Mudd's land in 1695 using the Corporation's charitable funds (*see* Illustration 6.b.). The Captains' Houses consisted of two rows of fourteen single-storey houses with semi-basements and steps up to pairs of front doors; the rows faced each other across a central grassed area. The other two sides of the quadrangle consisted of the road to the south and a substantial chapel to the north. This impressive group of buildings in the classical style is still to be found lying back from the bustling Mile End Road behind its gates. Since the 1950s the buildings have been private housing and replacement provision was made of twenty almshouses for retired mariners and their widows at Walmer in Kent.[48]

The occupants at Mile End were from the merchant service; provision for Royal Navy pensioners was made at Greenwich. There the imposing Royal Naval Hospital designed by Wren was under construction at the same time also overseen by senior Trinity House figures.[49] Trinity House issued its pensioners with blue stuff brass-buttoned gowns. In 1720 Strype reported that they each received a pension of 12s. on the first Monday of every month paid by a Corporation official who travelled to Mile End from the City.[50]

Admission was by written petition to the Trinity House Corporation.[51] These gave considerable detail of an applicant's career at sea and family circumstances. Applications came from ports all around the country. A typical applicant was Richard Kirby who had been born in Bridlington, Yorkshire in 1782, married his wife Mary in 1805 and had served at sea from 1798 until 1837. When he applied for admission to Trinity Hospital in 1846 he was living in North Shields on the Tyne. Included with his petition was an affidavit concerning an action fought with an American Privateer and another saying that the Duke of Wellington had directed him to apply; he was admitted three years later with his wife and an unmarried daughter and died at Mile End in 1861.[52]

Mudd's original site was extended to the rear and additional houses were built. At the 1851 census there were seventy-eight units for pensioners and their families. Twenty of these, known as Griggs Houses, accommodated the widows and elderly unmarried daughters of mariners, the latter officially described as 'old maids'. In 1881 three Blair sisters, all spinsters and over seventy, were living together in one of Griggs Houses. They were the daughters of William Blair, commander of *The Three Brothers,* who had gone down with his ship early in the century in the West Indies. Their mother, Barbara, had applied for help in 1809: 'being in a bad state of health and with three young children'.[53] At the 1851 census all four women were in one of the Captains' Houses. After their mother's death the daughters left and worked as dressmakers locally before returning to their former home in old age.[54]

Captain Fisher's Almshouses

In 1843 six more houses had been added to the Trinity Hospital site to replace almshouses in nearby Dog Row.[55] In 1711 Captain Robert Fisher of Whitechapel had built four almshouses, each consisting of one room and a cellar, for the widows of ships' commanders. After his death in 1715 the Corporation of Trinity House took over management and supported the occupants with £6 a year, plus £1 for fuel and a new gown every other year.[56] In 1725 William Ogbourne of West Ham built two more houses adjoining Fisher's, which were also managed by Trinity House. After 1843 the Dog Row site was used to generate income for Trinity Hospital.

Cooke's and Rowe's Almshouses

Another set of almshouses providing rooms for eight poor seamen or their widows was itself founded by a widow in memory of her seaman husband. In her will of January 1702 Alice Carant set out arrangements for the foundation of two sets of almshouses, one in the riverside parish of St Paul Shadwell and the other at Mile End. At the time of her death Alice was about forty years old, she had been married three times and her son had predeceased her. She and her last husband William Carant signed articles of agreement at their marriage, only three months before her death, under which she retained complete control of her household goods, jewellery, diamond rings and £2,000.[57] It was this sum that, after complicated reversionary bequests, was intended to finance the almshouses.[58] It is unclear how much was actually used in the project for, although both sets were built, they appear to have had no endowment.

Alice required that the almshouses carry the name of her first husband Captain James Cooke as well as her own name and title from her second marriage, Dame Alice Rowe. Cooke had been an experienced captain of impressive sailing ships trading on behalf of the East India Company to India and Java.[59] He left Gravesend on 26 August 1687 but died on board his ship the *Royall James and Mary* anchored in the Straits of Hormuz off the coast of Persia. The ship returned in September 1691 and two weeks afterwards Alice was granted probate of Cooke's will.[60] Its provisions included bequests of £50 each to the poor of the two parishes in which Alice later chose to build the almshouses known as Cooke's and Rowe's.

The establishment in Mile End consisted of four two-storey houses each with two rooms. Eight seamen's widows were nominated for the almshouse by Stepney parish. Since the houses were unendowed, they eventually became dilapidated and the hamlet of Mile End Old Town, in which they were situated, took them over in return for the right to present candidates to all eight houses. By 1881 the almshouses were ruinous and that year the site was let on a building lease and the houses demolished. From 1885 the charity paid out-pensions of 4s. a week to eight elderly seamen or their widows who had been resident in Stepney for at least five years and were not receiving poor relief.[61]

ALMSHOUSES WITH RELIGIOUS LINKS

The size and wealth of London and its position as the capital of a relatively tolerant state means that it has long been a popular destination for refugees and migrants. In the Early Modern Period, while the crowded square mile of the City of London could not accommodate large numbers of incomers, the areas immediately to its east were more sparsely populated, not controlled by City interests and therefore ripe for development. The Protestant Huguenots arriving from persecution in Catholic France in the late 17th and early 18th centuries joined native migrants to the capital in colonising much of the open land to the east. In the centuries that followed they were succeeded by Irish, Jews and Bangladeshis.[62] In the 17th century the newly developing area also provided a relatively safe location for the emerging protestant congregations who would not conform to the articles of the Established Church of England. These various groups, as well as some Anglicans, set up almshouse foundations with distinct religious characteristics in East London. A number were to be found by the roadside in Whitechapel and Mile End.

Meggs's Almshouses

Wealthy Whitechapel resident William Meggs (died 1678) was a loyal Anglican who, during the Civil War, experienced at first hand the difficulty in maintaining his faith in the face of a strongly Puritan regime. Meggs's brother James (1606-1672) and brother-in-law John Johnson were Rectors of London parishes; both were ejected from their livings in the 1640s and Meggs was imprisoned. They were only reinstated at the restoration of Charles II in 1660.[63]

In his will William Meggs stated that his family had lived in Whitechapel for at least a century; a fact worthy of note in a parish where much of the population consisted of recent migrants and transients. He had strong family ties to the City establishment as well as the Church of England. His maternal grandfather Sir Thomas Campbell was Lord Mayor of London in 1609 and

Illustration 6.c. Megg's almshouses, 1819, R.B. Schnebbelie.
Reproduced courtesy of Tower Hamlets Archives.

his uncle by marriage, Anthony Abdy, was Deputy Director of the mighty East India Company.[64]

William Meggs used his fortune generated in the City to support his faith by making the major contribution to rebuilding Whitechapel's parish church and in 1658 he built twelve one-roomed almshouses on the south side of the main road in Whitechapel (*see* Illustration 6.c.). Meggs left £1,500 to invest in land as an endowment for his almshouses; he required that occupants should not be 'sturdy idle people but Antient men and women which are fallen to decay and are fitting to be partakers of such a charitable releif as this'. Overriding requirements were that occupants should attend church and worship 'according to the customs of the Church of England'; they should be over fifty years old and unmarried or widowed.[65] The parish took over management from Meggs's heirs and, although he provided for occupants of either sex, by the 19th-century censuses all the occupants were local widows.[66]

Under the terms of the will occupants received 2s. each week and a supply of coal; this remained unchanged until at least 1773.[67] In 1819, Meggs's houses were improved and further endowed by Benjamin Goodwin, a local resident originally from Bury St Edmunds. They were operated by the parish until 1883, when the site was bought by the East London Railway Company to build a station.[68] Ten years later the Trustees built new almshouses five miles to the north-east in West Ham, which, in 2013, provided homes for the elderly in twelve sheltered housing units.[69]

Whitechapel Parish Almshouses

John Strype in 1720 recorded that across the road from Meggs's Almshouses was another set which predated them and 'belongeth to the Parish and containeth sixteen Rooms, for as many poor Widows, who have a weekly Salary paid by the Parish'.[70] These almshouses were established in 1614 and are shown on John Roque's map published in 1747, but no further records have been found.[71] On later maps the site was occupied by Whitechapel parish workhouse (built in 1768).

Pantin's Almshouses

Next to the Vintners' houses there was a charity school and a chapel run by a congregation of Calvinistic Methodists, who had moved from Spitalfields in 1808. In 1822 Michael Pantin, a blacklead pencil manufacturer, who had also relocated to Mile End from Spitalfields, left bequests totalling £1,775 to the school and congregation for general charitable purposes.[72] In 1825 his executors used the money to build a new chapel and schoolrooms on the same site and to provide almshouses in the chapel yard.[73] In 1835 the houses were described in the *Christian Penny Magazine* as: 'six gothic almshouses for female members of the congregation over 60 years of age … built by Whitechapel architect and builder James Little'.[74] Throughout the 19th-century censuses the almshouses remained an almost entirely female community, sometimes widows living alone, but often with adult unmarried daughters or other female relatives and, occasionally, young grandchildren in the household. By the 1891 census only three of the houses were occupied and ten years later there was no sign of them in the returns.[75]

Astill's Almshouses

A small set of almshouses just to the west of Bancroft's Hospital had close associations with the City of London, but with a parish rather than a Livery Company. The houses were provided for the poor of St Giles Cripplegate to commemorate Margaret Astill, a widow who lived in Lad Lane in the nearby parish of St Lawrence Jewry.[76] She had died, with her two servants, in the Great Plague of 1665 and was buried in the north aisle of her parish church with her husband Thomas (died 1636) and his first wife.[77] Thomas had been a member of the Fraternity of Innholders and left considerable sums for charitable purposes including the poor in the parish of St Giles Cripplegate.[78] The couple obviously had close ties to this parish: in 1639 Margaret set aside the income from a hundred acres in Lincolnshire for charitable causes, including £5 each year for 'the poorest, aged people of Cripplegate'. A will for Margaret has not been located and so its provisions are uncertain. Cripplegate parish records do include books recording the issue of clothing to poor girls and boys from as late as 1840 by 'Mrs. Astill's Charity'.[79] However, they make no reference to the almshouses at Mile End, so how many there were, or how long they continued to function, is unclear.

Yoakley's Almshouses

At Whitechapel the Quakers administered almshouses in Yoakley's Buildings. Michael Yoakley was born in humble circumstances in Margate, Kent in 1631 and baptised into the Church of England. His father, also Michael, moved to London and joined the recently formed Society of Friends. They believed in a personal relationship with God and living out faith by action and were much persecuted at that time for their non-conformity. Michael the Elder died in London in the Plague Year, 1665, when his death was entered in the records of the Ratcliff Monthly Meeting, which had started ten years earlier in Mile End.[80]

Michael the Younger, aged fourteen, began work as a ship's boy on the sailing hoys plying between the Kent ports and London. As his seafaring career progressed he moved to the capital where he attended the Ratcliff Monthly Meetings. In 1662 he bought property in Wentworth Street, Spitalfields and built Hope Court on part of the site. By the 1670s and 1680s he was owner and master of the ship *Hopewell* sailing to the American colonies. He traded with the east coast and in particular the colony of Pennsylvania, which had been founded by fellow British Quaker William Penn (1644-1718) as a holy experiment, designed to grant asylum to the persecuted under conditions of equality and freedom.[81] Pennsylvania expanded rapidly and Yoakley benefitted considerably from his part in meeting its growing demand for supplies from London.

In 1685 the Ratcliff Monthly Meeting minutes report Michael's marriage to Mary, widow of his friend Henry Munday and the mother of two sons. Michael died in 1708 and was interred in the Friends' burial ground in Ratcliff.[82] His will left his property to his wife and her heirs and included charitable bequests and provision for his spinster sister in her old age.[83] Mary died in 1730 and the last of her heirs in 1733 so all the property unexpectedly fell to the use of the Yoakley charity.

Yoakley's will made provision for the foundation of almshouses in Margate, but some years before his death he had also set aside three of his houses in Hope Court specifically for the occupation of nine poor aged female Friends.[84] These Spitalfields houses continued to be used until 1789 when the Trustees decided to move to houses by the roadside at Whitechapel just to the east of the London Hospital which had been built there in 1757. There were soon complaints about the state of the Whitechapel houses; they were said to be 'not well accommodated for warmth' and were expensive to maintain. Since the charity had considerable assets it was decided to build 'comfortable and distinct tenements' on the site and ten were built in 1801 at a cost of £1,050; these were Yoakley's Buildings. The almswomen were each receiving a weekly pension of 2s. 6d when they moved to Whitechapel, which had increased to 4s. when the new houses were completed in 1801 and 5s. plus coals by 1823.[85]

In 1834, with considerable funds at their disposal, the Trustees bought land at Stoke Newington, about three miles to the north-west and built ten almshouses.[86] They decided that due to their age and infirmity the existing almswomen would not be removed to Stoke Newington and the two sets of almshouses would run in tandem until they had died.[87] The only exception to this was Louisa Du Sommerard, a French woman by birth and a member of the Ratcliff and Barking Monthly Meeting. She had lived at 5 Yoakley's Buildings since 1833 but transferred to Stoke Newington where she died in 1847 aged sixty-six years.[88]

Michael Yoakley's Quaker faith and the motivation for his charitable activities are reflected in the inscription he left for his Margate almshouses:[89]

> In much weakness ye God of Might did bless
> With increase of Store
> Not to maintain Pride and Idleness
> But to relieve ye Poor.
> Such industrious poor as truly fear ye Lord
> Of a Meek,   )
> Humble, and   )   according to his Word.
> Quiet Spirit   )
> Glory to God Alone
> M. Y.[89]

The Stoke Newington houses closed in 1957, but the Margate foundation continued. In 2013, being one of the largest Quaker charities, it provided forty-five almshouses (with domiciliary care), a residential care home, respite care facilities and a state of the art training facility.[90]

Female Servants' Almshouses

In 1839 the Trustees decided to let Yoakley's Buildings and made alternative arrangements for the three remaining elderly Quaker occupants. The lease was taken by the National Guardian Institution for Families and Servants, which had been set up in 1825 by prominent Quaker minister, prison reformer and philanthropist Elizabeth Fry (1780-1845).[91] It had both commercial and charitable aims, being an agency to match servants of good character to respectable families and also providing 'succour and help' to domestic servants, so many of whom Fry felt 'had come to sorrow, in every sense, for the lack of temporary refuge and assistance'.[92] It was supported by voluntary contributions from the nobility and gentry and by subscriptions from those seeking servants.[93]

The 1851 and 1861 censuses show that the Institution continued to use Yoakley's Buildings as almshouses, this time for retired female domestic servants.[94] Almswomen were selected by ballot of those who had given donations, known as Life-Governors and subscribers, at specially convened meetings.[95] In 1847, there was a list of ten women for five vacancies. The same procedure was applied to appointing a matron in 1847, when a short list of eight was drawn up from almost thirty applicants, their names being listed in the notice of the meeting published in *The Times*.[96] The almshouses continued for thirty years until 1869 when the Treasurer of the Institution, Elizabeth Fry's eldest son John Gurney Fry (1804-1872), surrendered the lease as the 'institution was about to be dissolved'. Thereafter the Buildings were let on weekly tenancies and occupied by working families.[97]

Spanish and Portuguese Jews' Hospital

Like the Quakers, London's Jewish communities provided for vulnerable co-religionists, motivated by their beliefs exemplified in Psalms 71:9: 'Cast me not off in the time of old age; when my strength faileth, forsake me not'. The Jews had been allowed back into the country by Cromwell in 1657 for the first time since their expulsion by Edward I in 1290. The first arrivals included many affluent businessmen, who settled in the area around Bishopsgate immediately to the east of the City. They came freely and were disposed to speak English and conform to the English way of life, while not compromising their beliefs. They were Sephardic Jews, originally from Spain and Portugal, many of whom had fled the Inquisition and settled in Amsterdam. A synagogue was immediately established and the community thrived through the Restoration. In 1701 a new synagogue was built in Bevis Marks on the eastern borders of the City by a congregation known as Shaar HaShamayim (The Gate of Heaven).[98] In 1747 this body founded the Spanish and Portuguese Jews' Hospital in Stepney to cater for the congregation's sick and aged poor and lying-in women.

In 1790 new premises were built to the north of the roadside in Mile End immediately in front of the Old Velho Cemetery, the first burial ground acquired by the Jews after their resettlement.[99] It appears that Beth Holim, the old people's home, was housed in a separate building to the rear of the main hospital.[100] The mid-19th-century census returns show fourteen elderly occupants, including two married couples in 1841 and, in 1851, thirteen occupants with one couple. Ten years later there were twenty-three old people, but the number of medical patients had fallen from seven to two. The oldest inmate in 1851 was Mariah Mendoza, aged 95 years, and the number of residents born outside England fell from seven in 1841 to three in 1851 and only one in 1861, all the others having been born in areas immediately east of the City. The twenty or so occupants were cared for by a master and matron, two nurses, two servants and a washerwoman.[101] The Hospital was rebuilt in 1913 by the Mocatta family, descendants of some of the first arrivals in the 1650s. It included a two-storey row of cottages to the rear of the main building and linked to it by a veranda; these cottages housed elderly married couples.[102] Beth Holim left Mile End in 1977 and the buildings were converted to student accommodation for Queen Mary College. Still known as the 'Spanish and Portuguese Jews Home for the Aged', the foundation moved to Wembley, north London and in 2013 provided sixteen sheltered housing units and a care home for fifty-one elderly people of the Jewish faith.[103]

German Jews' Hospital

Almost opposite Beth Holim on the south side of the road was the second Jewish establishment, the German Jews' Hospital or Neveh Zedek (Abode of Righteousness). It had been founded to cater for poor Ashkenazi Jews who arrived in increasing numbers from the eighteenth century onwards in response to waves of persecution in central Europe, Poland and Russia. These arrivals spoke Yiddish and were much less inclined to assimilate into the English community than the earlier arrivals. London's Jewish population doubled between

1850 and 1880 and, by the 1901 census, there were more than 42,000 Russian and Polish Jews living in Stepney alone.[104]

The moving force behind the foundation of the Hospital was Abraham Goldsmid (1758-1810). The son of a merchant born in Amsterdam, he set up in business with his brother Benjamin (1755-1808); firstly they were merchants, then financiers. They became very powerful in the money market during the Napoleonic Wars; both made considerable fortunes and purchased impressive property in London and the country where they lived as gentlemen.[105] They were known for their public and private philanthropy and their names appeared on the subscription lists of charities of all denominations. Their charitable activities have been described as 'on a really grandiose scale' and comparable only with that of the later 'Magnificent Rothschilds'.[106]

In 1795 Abraham sent out an appeal for funding an Ashkenazi Jews' Hospital. Within a week £11,900 was raised and the total quickly reached £20,000. Interestingly, forty-one of the eighty-six subscribers were non-Jews, reflecting the circles in which the brothers moved.[107] After years of struggle with government bureaucracy, building at Mile End was completed in 1806. Although known as a hospital, there was no medical treatment; its twin aims were 'uplifting the morals and occupations of the young poor' and providing for the aged poor. Initially eighteen children were boarded and taught useful trades and a section was used to accommodate ten elderly people. Life within the institution was in accordance with strict Jewish observance. The buildings were extended in 1818 and by the censuses in 1841 and 1851 there were six male and five female elderly residents, who were outnumbered by the young trainees. By 1861 seventy-one young people were living there, but all the old people had gone.[108]

THE ALMSHOUSES IN THE NINETEENTH CENTURY

By the middle of the 19th century, development had engulfed all the once open spaces of Mile End and the almshouses were part of an 'East End' that was busy, bustling and teeming with people who were predominantly poor. The Great Essex Road, always a major thoroughfare, carried even more traffic and was lined with shops, pubs and small businesses with numerous costermongers plying their trade from barrows along the edge of the road. The almspeople's semi-rural retreat was no more.

The almshouse establishments must have made an impression on the neighbourhood, many with their chapel bells tolling regularly and their occupants venturing out on their errands, especially Pemel's ladies and the men from Bancroft's and Trinity Hospitals dressed in their impressive gowns. The 1851 census (see Table 6.II) recorded a total of 209 almspeople resident in the twelve establishments then to be found along the road. In addition there were 151 relatives living in the almspeople's households. Most of these were to be found with the men of Bancroft's and Trinity Hospitals, many of whom had their wives and children with them. Almswomen in the other establishments were most often supported by a co-resident female relative, usually, although not always, an unmarried daughter.

Only twenty-six of the almspeople had never been married, while 128 were widowed and fifty-five married; all but two of the latter group were men in the two Hospitals. The almspeople ranged in age from 40 to 95 years. Although a few younger people were admitted, by far the majority were over 60 years and the average age across all the establishments was 71 years. The almspeople's birthplaces in the census reflect the diversity of the establishments: some were born locally, but others – such as those in the Jewish Hospitals – were natives of Holland, Poland or Russia. Among the seafarers and their dependants in the Trinity Hospital there was a preponderance of those born in coastal districts of England, Scotland and the Channel Islands. A few of the old captains reflected a probable link to a previous generation of seamen, for 78-year-old James Yuit had been born 'at sea' and 77-year-old John Frith in Bermuda.

TABLE 6.II

Whitechapel/Mile End Road Almshouses 1851: Demographic Profile of occupants (based on the 1851 census returns)

Almshouse	No. of Almspeople			Resident Relatives	Marital Status of Almspeople			Age of Almspeople	
	Male	Female	Total		Married	Widowed	Single	Av. (yrs)	Range
Bancroft's	30	---	30	32	24	5	1	66	53-86
Cook's & Row's	---	7	7	2	---	7	---	65	42-74
Female Servants'	---	13	13	----	---	4	9	71	56-87
German Jews'	6	5	11	----	---	11	---	76	64-90
Judge Fuller's	1	11	12	5	1	11	---	75	63-85
Meggs's	---	12	12	3	---	11	1	73	65-86
Pantin's	---	5	5	4	---	5	---	69	56-92
Pemel's	---	6	6	1	---	5	1	70	61-81
Portuguese Jews'	3	10	13	----	1	7	5	75	40-95
Skinners'	---	12	12	----	---	12	---	66	50-79
Trinity Hospital	35	41	76	100	29	38	9	74	56-93
Vintners'	---	12	12	4	---	12	---	67	55-90
Totals	**75**	**134**	**209**	**151**	**55**	**128**	**26**	**71**	**40-95**

CONCLUSION

The large number of almshouses along less than two miles of roadside at Whitechapel and Mile End illustrate the wide variety of establishments found throughout the capital. They ranged from the grand architect-designed Hospitals, such as Bancroft's and Trinity, administered by mighty City institutions, to small unendowed houses providing rent-free accommodation, such as Cooke's and Rowe's.

The founders included those whose wealth arose from involvement with London's great overseas trading activities, whether providing bottled English beer for use throughout the Empire or sailing ships trading with the East or North America. Some were local men 'made good'; others had come from the provinces and made their fortunes in the capital. Two of the founders were women, one of whom, Dame Alice Rowe, was determined to leave a reminder of her brave seafaring first husband and possibly emphasise her status as the wife of a Baronet for good measure. Religious minorities set up modest establishments to support their most vulnerable members in an area where cheap housing provided homes for poor immigrants and native non-conforming Christians alike.

Whilst the almshouses along the road met the needs of some of the local elderly poor, much of the provision focused on meeting the needs of particular interest groups from outside the area. Many of the members of the Livery Companies or occupational groups, such as the seamen had little or no connection with the locality before they arrived as pensioners.

By the second half of the 19th century the Trustees of some almshouses began to consider moving the establishments to more salubrious areas further into the suburbs. For most, there was a requirement to invest heavily in the repair or rebuilding of old premises and so a new building in pleasant, less crowded surroundings often held great appeal. Sometimes this was coupled with a financial incentive, such as that presented to the Drapers' Company in 1863 when the Charity Commissioners agreed that the price offered for the Pemel's site by the adjacent brewery company would never be matched. Trustees sometimes took the opportunity to capitalise on the expansion of London's infrastructure, such as in 1883 when the Meggs's site was sold to a railway company.

A few establishments stayed on their old sites into the 20th century; the Vintners and Trinity Hospital left after the Second World War and the Beth Holim in 1977. In the early 21st century the private housing that was previously the Captains' Houses and the student accommodation (formerly the Beth Holim) are the only reminders of the sixteen almshouses formerly established along what is now the Mile End Road.

_____

Notes

1   Tames, R. *East End Past*, London, 2004, pp. 48-9.

2   The hamlets were: Bethnal Green, Limehouse, Mile End Old Town, Mile End New Town, Poplar, Ratcliff, Spitalfields and Wapping.

3   This community is explored in Morris, D. *Mile End Old Town 1740-1780: a social history of an early modern London suburb*, London, 2002.

4   Strype, J. *Survey of the Cities of London and Westminster*, London, 1720, App. 2, ch. 1, p. 21, URL: www.hrionline.ac.uk, accessed Sept. 2013.

5   Haslam, K. *A History of the Geffreye Almshouses*, Geffrye Museum, London, nd, p. 9.

6   Howson, B. *Houses of Noble Poverty*, 1993, p. 88.

7   URL: www.mercers.co.uk, accessed Sept. 2013.

8   Charity Commission, *City of London Livery Companies Commission Report,* Vol. 4, (London, 1884), pp. 553-6, URL: www.british-history.ac.uk, accessed Sept. 2013

9   Crawford, A. *The Vintners' Company*, London, 1977, p. 168.

10   Ibid., p. 206.

11   Morris, 2002, p. 80.

12   Webb, C. *Index of Vintners' Company Apprenticeships*, London, 2004, p. 172.

13   Crawford, pp. 210-11.

14   The National Archives (TNA): PROB11/1342, will of Benjamin Kenton, proved 1800.

15   Crawford, p. 206.

16   URL: www.vintnershall.co.uk, accessed Sept. 2013.

17   Dickens, C., *The Uncommercial Traveller*, London, 1991, pp. 306-7

18   Matz B W. 'Through Whitechapel with Dickens', *The Dickensian*, I, 9, Sept. 1905, pp. 234-89.

19   Dickens, 1991, pp. 307, 312

20   TNA: PROB11/379, will of Lewis Newbery, proved 1685.

21   Wadmore, T.F. *Some Account of the Skinners' Company*, London, 1902, pp. 225-6.

22   Strype, 1720, App.1 ch.12, p. 101, URL: www.hrionline.ac.uk/strype accessed Sept. 2013

23   *Charity Commission Report on City of London Livery Companies*, Vol. 4, London, 1884, Skinners' Charities Part 1, pp. 327-43.

24   URL: www.skinnershall.co.uk, accessed Sept. 2013.

25   TNA: PROB 11/370, will of John Pemel, proved 1681.

26   Archer-Thompson W. *Drapers' Company: history of the Company's properties and trusts,* London, 1940, pp. 148-50.

27   Drapers' Company Archives, C/13/i.

28   'Report on the Charities of the Drapers' Company: Part III', *City of London Livery Companies Commission. Report*, Volume 4, 1884, pp. 160-177. URL: www.british-history.ac.uk, accessed Sept. 2013.

29   Wing, K.R. *A History of Bancroft's School, 1737-1987*, Woodford, 1987, p. 11.

30   Strype, 1720, p. 278, URL: www.hrionline.ac.uk/strype, accessed Sept. 2013

31   Wing, 1987, p. 2.

32   TNA: PROB11/626, Will of Francis Bancroft, proved 1727.

33   'Report on the Charities of the Drapers' Company: Part I', *City of London Livery Companies Commission. Report*, Volume 4, 1884, pp. 120-144. URL: www.british-history.ac.uk, accessed Sept. 2013.

34   Ibid, pp. 178-215.

35   Drapers' Company Archives, E/MB3.

36   London Metropolitan Archives (LMA): Registers of St. Dunstan, Stepney, P/DUN/095 & 101; Censuses: 1841, HO 107/713, Book 12, fo. 10; 1851, HO107/1553, fo. 243; 1861, RG9/299, fo. 133; 1871, RG10/566, fo. 20.

37   URL: www.thedrapers.co.uk, accessed Sept. 2013.

38   TNA: PROB11/79, will of John Fuller, proved 5 May 1592.

39   Baker, T.F.T. (ed), *A History of the County of Middlesex: Volume 11*, Victoria County History, 1998, pp. 83-6, URL: www.british-history.ac.uk/report, accessed Sept. 2013.

40   1851 Census, HO107/1553, fo. 285.

41   Baker, 1998, p. 86.

42   URL: www.trinityhouse.co.uk/about_us/history/index.html, accessed Sept. 2013.

43   Tames, 2004, p. 30, Rodger, N.A.M. *The Safeguard of the Sea*, London, 2004, p. 223; Wheatley, K. *Guide to Maritime Britain*, Webb & Bower, Exeter, 1990, pp. 83-4, URL: www.portcities.org, accessed Sept. 2013.

44   Divers, D. & Jarrett, C. Excavations at the Mouth of Deptford Creek, Greenwich Reach, *Society for Post-medieval Archaeology*, London, 2004, p. 6, URL: www.ads.ahds.ac.uk/catalogue/adsdata/arch-457-1/dissemination/pdf/vol09/vol09_01/09_01_006_015.pdf, accessed Sept. 2013.

45   Ibid., pp. 7-10.

46   TNA: PROB 11/411, will of Henry Mudd, proved 1692.

47   Greenwich Industrial History, 3, 1, 2000, report of talk by Peter Gurnett on 'Trinity House' in April 1999 to The Docklands History Group, URL: www.gihs.gold.ac.uk/gihs11.html, accessed Sept. 2013.

48   URL: www.trinityhouse.co.uk, accessed Sept. 2013.

49   Ibid.

50   Strype, 1720, App. 1, ch. 12, p. 101 URL: www.hrionline.ac.uk/strype accessed Sep. 2013.

51   Copies of petitions from 1787-1854 can be consulted at London Metropolitan Archives, and copies of original documents can be ordered on URL: www.findmypast.co.uk.

52   LMA: Ms30218C, p. 264.

53   LMA: Misc. papers, MS30218c.

54   Censuses: 1851, HO107/1540 fo. 692; 1861, RG9/294 fo. 96; 1871, RG11/419 fo. 12.

55   Baker, 1998, pp. 260-3 URL: www.british-history.ac.uk/report, accessed Sept. 2013.

56   Strype, 1720, pp. 288-9, URL: www.hrionline.ac.uk/strype, accessed Sept. 2013

57   LMA: P93/DUN/269, marriage register St. Dunstan, Stepney 4 Oct. 1701

58   TNA: PROB 11/463, will of Alicia Carant, proved 1701/2.

59   Farrington, A.J. *A Biographical Index of East India Company Service Officers 1600-1834*, London, 1999, p. 169.

60   TNA: PROB 11/405, will of James Cooke, proved 1691.

61   Baker, 1998, pp. 83-6 URL: www.british-history.ac.uk/report, accessed Sept. 2013.

62   Tames, 2004, pp. 24-5.

63   Darlington, I. (ed), *Survey of London Vol 25*, London, 1955, pp. 91-4, URL: www.british-history.ac.uk/report.aspx?compid=65449, accessed Sept. 2013.

64   Thornbury, W. *Old and New London Vol. 1*, London, 1878, pp. 396-416, URL: www.british-history.ac.uk/report.aspx?compid=45053, accessed Sept. 2013; Abdy of Albyns, Essex, URL: www.cracroftspeerage.co.uk.online/content/AbdyBa1660, accessed Sept. 2013.

65   TNA: PROB11/356, will of William Meggs, proved 26 Nov 1678.

66   Censuses: 1841, HO 107/716 Bk 2; 1851, HO 107/1545 fo. 323; 1861, RG9/271 fo. 52; 1871, RG9/271 fo. 52; 1881, RG11/444 fo. 69.

67   Noorthouck, J. *A New History of London*, London, 1773, pp. 900-2.

68   Maddocks S, 'Whitechapel', Co Partnership Herald, III, 34, 1933, URL: www.mernick.org.uk/thhol/whitechapel, accessed Sept. 2013.

69   URL: www.newhamstory.com/node/1127, accessed Sept. 2013.

70   Strype, 1720, Bk. 4, p. 47, URL: www.hrionline.ac.uk, accessed Sept. 2013.

71   Cox, J. *London's East End*, London, 1994, p. 124; Rocque, J. *Plan of the Cities of London and Westminster*, London, 1747.

72   TNA: PROB11/1673, will of Michael Pantin proved 1823.

73   Lewis, S. (ed), *A Topographical Dictionary of England*, Midloe - Millfield, London, 1848, pp. 316-9.

74   *The Christian Penny Magazine*, pp. 153-4, 4 May 1835, London, Wood & Son. URL: books.google.co.uk/books?id=EiAFAAAAQAAJ, accessed Sept. 2013.

75   Censuses: 1861, RG9/297 fo 125; 1891, RG12/305 fo 8.

76   Cox, 1994, p. 128.

77   LMA: P69/LAW1, Burial Register St Lawrence Jewry, 1665.

78   TNA: PROB11/172, will of Thomas Astill, proved 1636.

79   LMA: P69/GIS/D/038. St. Giles, Cripplegate, Mrs. Astill's Charity Clothing Books

80   Tames, 2004, p. 43.

81   Oxford *Dictionary of National Biography*, URL: www.oxforddnb.com, accessed Sept. 2013.

82   Marsh, R.H. 'Presidential Address', *Journal of the Friends History Society,* Vol. 14, 4, 1917, pp. 146-8.

83   TNA: PROB11/503, will of Michael Yoakley, proved 1708.

84   Marsh, 1917, p. 148.

85   Marsh, 1917, p. 149.

86   URL: www.stokenewingtonquakers.org.uk, accessed Sept. 2013.

87   SFA: Temp. Mss.748/1/5 p. 94.

88   SFA: Temp. Mss.748/5/1, p. 12; SFA, Temp. Mss. 748/1/5 p. 190.

89   Beck, W. *Ye Yoakley Charity*, London, 1884, reissued 1894.

90   URL: www.michaelyoakley.com, accessed Sept. 2013.

91   SFA: Temp. Mss 748/1/5 p. 106; URL: www.ucl.ac.uk/bloomsbury-project/institutions, accessed Aug. 2011.

92   Pitman, E.R. Elizabeth Fry, London, 1884, p. 174, URL: www.kouroo.info/kouroo/transclusions/18/80S/84/1884_ElizabethFry.pdf, accessed Sept. 2013.

93   *The Times*, 11 Jun. 1842, p. 3, col. B.

94   Censuses: 1851, HO107/1545, fo. 241; 1861, RG9/271, fo. 21.

95   *The Times*, 25 Jun. 1847, p. 1, col. A.

96   Ibid., 11 Jun. 1842, p. 3, col. B.

97   SFA: Temp. Mss. 748/1/5, p. 136; 1881 Census, RG/10 444, fo. 23.

98   URL: www.bevismarks.org.uk, accessed Sept. 2013.

99   Lewis, 1848, pp. 313-6.

100   The first edition OS map of 1876 shows an L-shaped building labelled 'Asylum for the Aged'.

101   Censuses: 1841, HO107/713 Bk.12, fo. 18; 1851, HO107/1553, fo. 266; 1861, RG9/299, fo. 122.

102   URL: www.britishlistedbuildings.co.uk, accessed Sept. 2013.

103   URL: www.housingcare.org/housing-care/facility-info-129157, accessed Sept. 2013.

104   Gordon, I., Travers T. & Whitehead, C. London School of Economics and Political Science, London 2007, *The Impact of Recent Immigration on the London Economy.* URL: www.lse.ac.uk/geographyAndEnvironment/theimpactofrecentimmigrationonthelondoneconomy.pdf, accessed Sept. 2013.

105   Oxford *Dictionary of National Biography*, URL: www.oxforddnb.com, accessed Sept. 2013.

106   Embden, P. *The Brothers Goldsmid and the Financing of the Napoleonic Wars*, paper read to the Jewish
       Historical Society of England, 1939, pp. 234-7, URL: www.jhse.org/book/export/article/15356, accessed
       Sept. 2013.

107   The Susser Archive, ch. XV, URL: www.jewishgen.org/JCR-UK/susser/roth/chfifteen.htm, accessed Sept.
       2013.

108   Censuses: 1841, HO107/713 Bk.12; 1851, HO 107/1553 fo. 52; 1871, RG9/294, fo. 62.

CHAPTER 7
WARWICKSHIRE ALMSHOUSES: TO WHAT EXTENT WERE THEY 'AFFORDING COMFORTABLE ASYLUMS TO THE AGED AND RESPECTABLE POOR'?[1]

Anne Langley

Warwickshire has a fine heritage of almshouses in towns and villages, ranging from ancient timber-framed buildings through grand collegiate foundations to modest brick rows, many of which are listed and a few are of national importance. This chapter describes their founders, buildings and administration, exploring what life was like for residents and using censuses to analyse those living there in the 19th century. Finally it compares the contribution made by almshouses with that of workhouses in accommodating the elderly poor in Warwickshire during the 19th century.

INTRODUCTION

The county boundaries employed here were those extant in 1900 (thus including Coventry but excluding Birmingham). There was a wide range of institutions that had at some stage been called an 'almshouse' or 'hospital'. The classic almshouse was a purpose-built, endowed charity, providing a residential home and a pension for the elderly. Other so-called 'almshouses' were actually parish poor houses: ordinary cottages let rent-free to a family who might be receiving parish relief. In addition there were some curious 'almshouses', such as those intended for travellers (Butler's and Chapman's at Coleshill), apprentices (Puckering's in Warwick) or beggars (the 'Mendicity Receiving House' in Kineton).[2] This chapter concerns the thirty-four classic almshouses founded between 1400 and 1914 (*see* Appendix 7.1.), excluding the early religious hospitals, parish poor houses, and the four anomalies mentioned above.[3]

A range of primary and secondary sources has been employed including valuable primary source material that has been deposited in local archives, trade directories and the 19th-century Commissioners' Reports on Warwickshire Charities.[4] Almshouse residents were studied in the censuses of 1851 and 1881. Well-known Warwickshire almshouses (particularly the hospitals of Bond, Ford, Lady Katherine Leveson and Lord Leycester, *see* Illustration 7.a.) are mentioned in several books about almshouses.[5] Little has been published specifically about almshouses in Warwickshire, though Mary Raphael included chapters about three of them in a book published in 1927 and six have received attention in monographs.[6] Angela Nicholls's unpublished MA dissertation provides a recent discussion of almshouses in Warwickshire, with details about nineteen of them.[7]

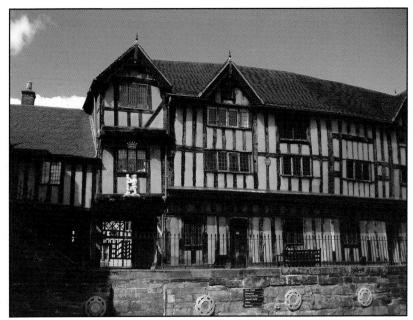

Illustration 7.a. Lord Leycester's Hospital in Warwick. *Photo © Anne Langley*

THE FOUNDATION OF ALMSHOUSES

The inspiration for almshouses lay in the hospitals set up by religious foundations to relieve the poor, sick and elderly in towns, such as Coventry and Warwick. The first recognisable almshouses (as defined here) were set up by medieval guilds to provide accommodation for members no longer able to earn a living. Accounts survive from 1417-18 concerning an almshouse provided by the Guild of the Holy Cross in Church Street, Stratford-upon-Avon, that is still in use today. Bond's Hospital was built beside the guild-supported Bablake College in Coventry in 1506.[8] The Reformation led to the closure of many hospitals and almshouses, as discussed in Chapter 1. The need for them, however, remained and five managed to survive in Warwickshire. The guilds in Stratford-upon-Avon and Warwick were suppressed but their almshouses were taken over by the respective town corporations. The Coughton Almshouses survived (even though the family was Catholic) because they were a small private charity. The two Coventry hospitals (founded by Thomas Bond and William Ford in the early 16th century) had more of a struggle, being claimed by the crown after the Reformation but later rescued by the corporation.[9] Later on several almshouses were re-founded on monastic sites or had links with early hospitals: the remains of St Michael's Hospital in Warwick, for instance, 'were appropriated as an almshouse for old women'.[10] The Lower Saltisford Almshouses nearby were founded by Sir Thomas Puckering in 1635, and supported by subsequent owners of the Priory, who clearly felt a similar responsibility to the poor of the parish as did their monastic predecessors.[11]

A few of the landed gentry, rather like the guilds, provided almshouses for their servants or tenants who were no longer able to work, an example being the Coughton Almshouses founded by Sir Robert Throckmorton in the early 16th century.[12] Similar motives could be attributed to Robert Dudley, Earl of Leicester and a favourite of Queen Elizabeth I, who founded his hospital in Warwick for old soldiers in 1571.[13] Individuals who wished to do good works and to be remembered for their benevolence also endowed almshouses. Some had made their fortune in London or elsewhere, but founded an almshouse in their place of origin, thus Thomas Newcombe, printer to Charles II, built a row of almshouses at Dunchurch in Warwickshire.[14] The nouveaux riche founded almshouses to impress their contemporaries and memorialise their names. Clothes bearing the founder's initials were worn in four almshouses (Lady Katherine Leveson's at Temple Balsall, Thomas Oken's in Warwick, Stoneleigh, and Lawrence Sheriff's in Rugby) and a fifth had the founder's emblem (Lord Leicester's bear and ragged staff) on silver buttons and badges (*see* Illustration 7.b.). Founders were often commemorated annually with a dinner for the trustees. At the Bedworth Hospital, Nicholas Chamberlain's feast became too expensive and was replaced by the distribution of buns to local schoolchildren with the result that founder's day is now known as 'Bun Day'.[15]

Illustration 7.b. Silver badge for almsmen at Lord Leycester's Hospital, Warwick.
Photo © Anne Langley

Table 7.I analyses the dates of foundation of thirty-four almshouses in Warwickshire. The 15th century figure is almost certainly an underestimate, because few records have survived, and many monastic hospitals were abolished during the Reformation. A closer examination of the data shows a fifty-year gap in almshouse foundation between 1518 and 1567, around the time of the Reformation, followed by a temporary increase. These figures confirm the findings on national almshouse foundation by Marjorie McIntosh and Angela Nicholls, who both reported an increase after the Reformation.[16] A further peak in foundation occurred during the 19th century, particularly in towns.

TABLE 7.I.
Date of foundation of Warwickshire almshouses

Date of Foundation	Number of foundations
1400-1499	1
1500-1599	9
1600-1699	7
1700-1799	4
1800-1899	11
1900-1914	2
Total	**34**

'I, having no child, do dispose of my estate to the charitable uses following' declared Nicholas Chamberlain in 1715.[17] The parental status of other founders of almshouses in Warwickshire was investigated and of the twenty-one individuals (for whom the relevant information is available) just over half were childless. It seems likely that rich but childless founders were endeavouring to keep their name alive as well as putting their fortune to good use for the benefit of future generations. Sixty-four per cent of founders were male, presumably reflecting their greater wealth and status. Female founders, however, included Lady Katherine Leveson, whose hospital was one of the largest and best-endowed in the county. She may have been inspired by family links: her great-grandmother, Lady Alice Leigh, founded the Stoneleigh Almshouses in 1576; and her grandfather, Robert Dudley Earl of Leicester, his hospital in 1585.

Table 7.II analyses the status of almshouse founders in Warwickshire. A few were founded by organisations (charities and guilds) and some by landed gentry, but two thirds were established by well-to-do commoners from a range of occupations: builder, clergyman, draper, glazier, goldsmith, grocer, lawyer, mercer, printer, schoolmaster and wool merchant.

TABLE 7.II
Classification of Warwickshire almshouse founders

Type of founder	Number of almshouses
Commoner	22
Nobility or gentry	6
Charity	4
Guild	2
Total	**34**

BUILDINGS

Early almshouses were usually timber-framed, for example, the two hospitals in Coventry. A few were built of stone (also used to clad the original timber-framed almshouses in Stoneleigh) but most were of cheaper materials. The great fire of Warwick in 1694 destroyed Oken's Almshouse in Pebble Lane, along with many other timber-framed buildings and in response to this disaster, the Oken Charity prudently built new brick almshouses adjoining those of Eyffler in Back Hills.[18] Existing buildings were sometimes turned into almshouses and the remains of St Michael's Hospital in Warwick has already been mentioned. The Lord Leycester Hospital occupied timber-framed guild premises plus an adjacent inn and had a narrow escape from the great fire that started nearby (*see* Illustration 7.a.). The original guild hall was divided by wooden partitions to make cubicles for the residents but by the 1920s this splendid room was used for washing clothes and storing coal.[19] Some founders and architects copied the work of their predecessors, for example, the original Temple Balsall Hospital was said to have been modelled on the almshouses at Stoneleigh.[20] Almshouses are often situated in the centre of the community, making an important visual contribution to the scene and many almshouse buildings in Warwickshire have been listed as of architectural significance, though sadly others have been lost, including the 18th-century Lawrence Sheriff Almshouses from a key location opposite the parish church in Rugby.[21]

The form of most almshouses was a row of individual dwellings under one roof often with shared access via porches or stairs. A few opted for a grander style with buildings set around a courtyard, for example, the hospitals at Warwick, Temple Balsall and Bedworth; Ford's hospital in Coventry was built around a narrow rectangular courtyard (*see* Illustration 7.c. colour Plate VI). The larger almshouses included other buildings besides accommodation for the elderly, such as a house for the master or matron, a chapel, a board-room and even a kitchen and dining room at the Lord Leycester Hospital.

Many of the almshouses were modified or even completely rebuilt over the years and others were demolished to make way for development or because they became dilapidated (*see* Appendix 7.1). Coventry's almshouses suffered during the Second World War when a bomb fell on Ford's Hospital, killing the matron and several inmates and destroying some almshouse records.[22] Empty rooms in the almshouse at Leamington Hastings were used for evacuees during the Second World War.[23] Former almshouse buildings have been converted for various other purposes. St Edith's Home in Warwick has an interesting history: during the 20th century it became derelict, was restored as a home for poor choirboys, turned back into a home for the elderly and now provides supported living for disabled people.[24]

Half of the Warwickshire almshouses bear an inscription, which usually commemorates the founder, but may also mention the founder's family, the architect and other details of interest. That at Mancetter records: 'These Almshouses with An Endowment of Two Thousand Pounds were the Sole Gift of James Cramer Esqr Late Citizen & Goldsmith of London And Native of this Place. Built Ann. Dom. 1728'. Sometimes the founder's initials were incorporated in the architectural design, as at the hospitals of Lord Leycester and Nicholas Chamberlain. The architecture may be plain or fancy, thus the almshouses at Knowle sport splendid buttresses between their chimney stacks and St Edith's Home in Warwick is adorned with religious statues.

Illustration 7.d. Church Street Almshouses in Stratford-upon-Avon. *Photo © Anne Langley*

Maintenance proved to be an ongoing problem, and endowments were sometimes inadequate. Some of the early 19th-century parliamentary Commissioners' reports paint a gloomy picture of dilapidated buildings that were cold and damp. Accounts for the Church Street Almshouses in Stratford-upon-Avon report on work carried out over the centuries with the pump repaired, windows glazed and locks replaced (*see* Illustration 7.d).[25] Originally, many almshouses had a communal pump or well to provide water — there is a charming pump house at Bedworth containing two pumps, one providing well-water for drinking and the other rain-water for washing. Water from the well at Temple Balsall was contaminated and caused problems throughout much of the late 19th century.[26] Modern facilities have now been introduced and things have changed a great deal since entrants to Bond's Hospital were required to bring a chamber pot with them in the 17th century![27] Inventories for almspeople are rare, but one for a carpenter in the Stoneleigh Almshouse included his work tools, his bedstead, bedding and other domestic items.[28] Wills with lists of possessions also exist for a few almshouse residents.[29] Some almshouses provided furniture: iron bedsteads in the hospital at Bedworth and stoves in the Church Street Almshouses in Stratford-upon-Avon.[30] Residents of Ford's hospital in Coventry were not allowed to leave belongings to their relatives and their possessions had to be sold to defray expenses after their death.[31]

Gardens were usually provided and smaller rows of almshouses could have individual plots at the back of each house to enable the residents to grow vegetables as shown by the purchase of beans and plants for widow Wright at Shustoke recorded in 1726.[32] The Church Street Almshouses in Stratford-upon-Avon had numbered garden plots for the residents, one of whom, Ephraim Pulley, was also renting an allotment in his nineties.[33] At the Lord Leycester Hospital in Warwick the residents each had a strip of ground to grow vegetables; this garden has now been restored and is open to the public with a gazebo, sheltered seating and other features. Larger almshouses, particularly those built around a courtyard, tended to have communal gardens managed for the residents, as can be seen at Bedworth (*see* Illustration 7.e. and front cover).

Illustration 7.e. Nicholas Chamberlain's hospital at Bedworth, 1839.[34]

ADMINISTRATION

A magnificent hall was constructed in 1840 for the trustees of the Bedworth Hospital with a minstrels' gallery and wood panelling bearing coats of arms (*see* Illustration 3.b.). Most trustees served their charity well but some were guilty of 'malfeasance'.[35] Members of founders' families could resent property being left to a charity and try to frustrate their wishes. In Coventry, Thomas Bond's grandson tried to purloin the land left to support Bond's Hospital, but the city sued him in the court of chancery and won it back.[36] In Leamington Hastings, the brother and nephew of the founder Humphrey Davis were accused of not putting poor people in his almshouse and of selling land left to support the charity, so they were sacked and new trustees appointed.[37] Coventry Corporation was accused of failing to keep proper accounts for Ford's Hospital in the 18th century.[38] In the 1850s, Berkswell parishioners complained about churchwardens spending income on new pews rather than the poor.[39] Several almshouse charities prospered as their investments became more valuable, thus Nicholas Chamberlain's land near Bedworth proved to contain coal, which funded the rebuilding and expansion of his hospital in 1840. Other almshouses, however, struggled when income from the original bequest dried up or was unable to keep pace with inflation, such as in Dunchurch, where parishioners had to contribute half the cost of rebuilding Newcombe's Almshouses in 1818.[40]

The larger almshouses had residential staff including a master, sometimes a clergyman who led the religious life of the community. The master of the Lord Leycester Hospital in Warwick received a handsome salary of £400 a year in the early 19th century.[41] He enjoyed grand quarters, a fine private garden and kept several servants. By 1881 all the larger almshouses had a matron, who might be the master's wife (as at Bedworth Hospital), and nurses were also employed to provide personal care. Matrons and nurses were paid less than the master: at Temple Balsall the master received £70 a year, the matron £40 and the nurse £22 in the 1820s.[42] Other employees of larger almshouses might include a porter, a cook and a gardener. Nineteenth-century censuses show a few residents had their own personal carer (a housekeeper or nurse) living with them.

Admission to an almshouse was usually restricted to particular groups. There was often a residential qualification, usually for the applicant to have lived locally for a number of years. Just one almshouse, Nicholas Chamberlain's, specified that entrants should have been born in Bedworth, but clearly this rule was not enforced because 19th-century censuses show a few people living in this almshouse had been born elsewhere. The age for entry, when specified, was usually over sixty, though two of the almshouses in Alcester were for those over fifty.[43] An early 17th-century letter survives from Joane Greville requesting places for Robert White of Stratford and his wife 'one that hath always lived by his labour…being derelict & lame one his hand' who 'will be always redy too pray for you' (the latter reflecting the survival of pre-Reformation ideas on the benefit of chantries).[44]

Thirty-five per cent of these Warwickshire almshouses were founded solely for women and four of these almshouses were specifically for widows.[45] Twenty-one per cent were for men while the remainder took individuals of both sexes (often including couples). Two of the 'male' almshouses accepted wives, but one would evict a widow three weeks after her husband's death.[46] Marrying would also lead to eviction from St Edith's Home in Warwick.[47] The Bleachfield Almshouse in Alcester was originally for unmarried people but by 1851 contained mostly widowers. Applicants for some almshouses, particularly the earlier foundations, had to be regular churchgoers. The first occupational almshouses were set up by medieval guilds, for example the Church Street Almshouses at Stratford-upon-Avon. The

Lord Leycester Hospital in Warwick was created for former soldiers and is still in use today by retired members of the armed services, whilst the Smallwood Almshouses in Alcester had 'A preference for poor tradesmen and their widows in reduced circumstances'.[48] The Throckmorton family gave preference to tenants or former employees for admission to their Coughton Almshouses.[49] The two Coventry hospitals favoured freemen of the city and their widows in the 19th century.[50]

Most almshouses were designed to provide a home for the elderly poor, however an entry fee of 6s. 8d. was charged for admission to the Church Street Almshouses in Stratford-upon-Avon in the 16th century, which must have excluded the very poor.[51] At that time widows of Ford's Hospital residents received a smaller pension than widowers and had to share a room (*see* Illustration 16.b.).[52] Pensions varied considerably, but a number of Warwickshire almshouses were paying a pension of around five shillings a week in the 1850s, plus free housing, which compared well with the average weekly agricultural wage of 8s. 5d. in southern counties at that time.[53] Residents of several almshouses were earning too much to be eligible for the pension introduced by Lloyd George in 1908. A few almshouses supported 'out pensioners' who lived at home.[54] Poor relief was often a contentious issue; in Warwick, women in a local almshouse were receiving poor relief in the 1580s.[55] Some almshouses, however, would not accept anyone on parish relief, for example those at Tanworth-in-Arden.[56] The residents of the Cramer Almshouses in Mancetter were forbidden to beg or ask for alms, whilst those at Shustoke were allowed to receive parish relief to supplement a pension of three guineas a year (just over a shilling a week, clearly not enough to live on).[57] Berkswell experienced an interesting policy reversal on this topic: in the 18th century, parish housing was restricted to those 'not receiving alms of the said parish', yet by 1874 the almshouse residents 'have poor relief'.[58] Analysis of the 1851 census identified thirty-five paupers living in five almshouses (13 per cent of all 1851 almshouse residents) most of whom were in the towns of Warwick and Kenilworth, with a few rural paupers at Shustoke.[59] Unfortunately paupers were not recorded as such in the 1881 census and so it is not possible to discover from this research whether any almshouse residents were receiving parish relief at this date.

Almshouse founders usually set out rules to assist the smooth running of the community: 'Se them well ordred, and no evil ruele kepte among them'.[60] Full sets of rules were found for six almshouses.[61] Foundations set up in the 19th century could have rules that were just as patronising as those from 300 years earlier, for example, those of St Edith's Home founded in Warwick in 1868.[62] Rules often concerned religious aspects of the community, thus the almspeople at the Church Street Almshouses in Stratford-upon-Avon were required in the 17th century 'to attend Prayers in the Chappell on weekdays and to church on Sundays'.[63] Church attendance was still expected — and indeed compulsory in many almshouses — until the 20th century. Misbehaviour was a perennial problem: residents of Ford's hospital would be ejected for 'haunting alehouses, making strife or other notable misdemeanors'.[64] Serious illness or dementia were also potential problems: a resident of Nicholas Chamberlain's Hospital at Bedworth became 'a dangerous lunatic' and was removed to the County Asylum where she died of exhaustion a few days later.[65]

Many almshouses provided free coal and sometimes other benefits, such as Temple Balsall Hospital that kept a cow to provide milk for residents and also supplied rather coarse bread.[67] Other charitable donors sometimes provided additional support for residents, such as beef on St Thomas' day in Bond's Hospital, Coventry.[68] As well as providing nursing care, a few almshouses appointed a doctor or apothecary. In 1776 an apothecary was paid five guineas a year to attend the residents of Lady Katherine Leveson's Hospital at Temple Balsall

Illustration 7.f. Brethren at Lord Leycester hospital in their gowns, 1900s.[66]

in Warwickshire and give them medicine and by 1850 this salary had doubled.[69] Some paid funeral expenses; in 1427-8 there is a moving record of the money expended on wax candles, a winding sheet and beer for men to watch over the corpse of an almsperson in the Church Street Almshouses in Stratford-upon-Avon.[70] Clothing for residents was provided by six of the larger almshouses, often a coat or cloak that had to be worn at all times or on specific occasions (*see* Illustration 7.f.).[71] In 1732 Sir Hugh Clopton left money to provide blue coats and gowns for residents of the Church Street Almshouses in Stratford-upon-Avon every other year, any residue being used to provide straw hats and aprons for the women.[72] It is not clear whether residents appreciated the clothes and wore them with pride, or resented being 'badged' and stigmatised as poor in the eyes of the local community.

Daily activities could also be controlled by rules. At St Edith's Home in Warwick the residents had to obtain the consent of the superintendent to be absent for more than an hour in a day, scarcely enough time to go shopping.[73] In collegiate communities the front door was locked each night, which sounds unreasonable but would have had security benefits. At the Tanworth-in-Arden Almshouses no almsperson was to be absent for more than twenty-four hours without permission, there was to be no sub-letting of rooms and sharing required permission.[74] Male relatives were banned from living at the Elborrow Almshouses in Rugby.[75] An analysis of two censuses, however, suggests that almshouse residence rules were fairly relaxed during the 19th century, when relatives, sometimes even whole families, were living with residents in 84 per cent of the Warwickshire almshouses.

Relatives living in an almshouse benefited from accommodation, but were not given a pension. The commonest relation was a spouse, followed by children and then grandchildren living with them. In Temple Balsall, Elizabeth Smith had her daughter and two grandchildren aged eleven and two living with her.[76] Visitors were found staying with the residents in a quarter of Warwickshire almshouses and a few almspeople had a servant or even a lodger living with them. The new Stoneleigh Almshouses contained a couple of young 'Warwick Union Boarders' in 1871, presumably orphans who the poor law guardians were paying the almswomen to care for (and similar provision was proposed for an almshouse at Southam that was never built).[77] In the 20th century a young couple lived in one of the old almshouses at Stoneleigh; twins were born there and the family eventually moved into one of the larger new almshouses. The father worked for Lord Leigh, which is presumably why they occupied housing originally intended for the elderly.[78]

ALMSHOUSE RESIDENTS

The length of time individuals spent in the almshouse can only be discovered by painstaking research in admission registers. This has not been possible for most Warwickshire almshouses, but 19th-century censuses show a few people living in an almshouse for at least twenty years whilst a couple of women lived in the hospital at Temple Balsall for over fifty years.[79] Most residents ended their days in the almshouse and there is a moving array of tiny crosses for almswomen in the adjacent Temple Balsall churchyard.

Details of 559 residents in thirty Warwickshire almshouses were studied in the 1851 and 1881 censuses (*see* Table 7.III).[80] The head of household and any spouse were included, but not other relatives, visitors or almshouse staff. Nearly two-thirds of almspeople were women (slightly lower than the 74 per cent found by Nigel Goose and Stuart Basten in their survey of nine other counties).[81] Ninety-three per cent of the almspeople were over sixty years of age, and many considerably older, with a few living to be over a hundred. There were exceptions, presumably for good reasons. Widow Ann Crisp at the Butlin's Almshouses in Rugby in 1851 was only thirty-six, with two daughters aged twenty and thirteen.[82] Twenty-year old Richard Cleaver and his wife Mary were removed from Berkswell to their parish of settlement (Leamington Hastings) and rather surprisingly given a room in the almshouse there.[83] Other young residents were disabled: almshouses in Stratford-upon-Avon and Warwick admitted younger people who were blind or crippled.[84] Only nine of the 559 residents were recorded as disabled, but these were concentrated in a few almshouses, suggesting considerable under-recording elsewhere. Seventy per cent of the 559 almspeople were widowed (somewhat higher than the 54 per cent found by Goose & Basten), 18 per cent were married and 10 per cent single. Overall, 76 per cent of the almspeople had been born in Warwickshire. As expected, the proportion was higher in the eleven rural almshouses: 83 per cent as opposed to 73 per cent in the nineteen urban almshouses.

TABLE 7.III
Analysis of Warwickshire almshouse residents (1851 and 1881 censuses combined)

	Gender		Age				Status				Birthplace		Occupation					Total
	Male	Female	<60	60s	70s	>79	Widow/er	Married	Single	Unknown	Warks	Other	Alms person none or unknown	Unskilled	Skilled	Tradesman	Professional	
No	202	357	41	118	268	132	392	98	57	12	427	132	291	153	90	19	6	559
%	36	64	7	21	48	24	70	18	10	2	76	24	52	28	16	3	1	100

Analysis of occupations is difficult because often none was given in the census, particularly for women; married women with no occupation recorded have therefore been classified by their husband's occupation (if known). Of the 268 people whose former occupation could be identified, over half were unskilled workers (including labourers), followed by skilled workers, then tradesmen and finally a few professionals (mostly teachers). Unsurprisingly there were more skilled workers in urban almshouses and more unskilled workers in rural almshouses. Individual almshouses often contained people from the chief local industry: needle-makers in Alcester, silk workers in Coventry and hatters in Mancetter, for example. An in-depth study of almsmen at the Lawrence Sheriff Almshouse in Rugby showed a marked shift in occupations – in 1851 all but one of the eleven almsmen had been labourers, but thirty years later they were mostly former tradesmen.[85] The exclusion of the 'undeserving poor' from almshouses also affected the situation because some admission policies favoured decayed skilled workers and trades people. The employees living in almshouses (not included in the analysis above) were largely female servants, nurses or housekeepers.

What was it like living in an almshouse? Most almshouse charities provided a modest pension and free fuel; in general residents must have enjoyed the peace and privacy of the almshouse, especially those who came from cramped conditions. Visitors were allowed in all the almshouses (though not always to stay) but residents could be very isolated in some places: an entrant to Temple Balsall asked for time to pay a last visit to her children in 1850.[86] In the 17th century, the overseers of the poor used the almswomen at Leamington Hastings as cheap labour spinning hemp and later on Widow Hewitt taught the village girls to spin.[87] Temple Balsall provided a lending library in 1852 but some residents were illiterate (or visually impaired) as the matron had to read letters to them.[88]

Community living inevitably led to problems. There are reports of a chalk line drawn down the centre of a shared room and fisticuffs in the Bedworth Almshouses.[89] Much worse was the allegation that John Johnson poisoned eight of his fellows in the hope of becoming senior brother at Bond's Hospital in Coventry (though happily the records do not confirm this).[90] Five almshouses were adjacent to schools founded by the same charity where the noise and mischief of the young must have tried the patience of the residents.[91] A few individuals were 'deprived' or fined for bad behaviour and drunkenness was mentioned occasionally in the records of Temple Balsall.[92] There was scandal at the Davies Almshouses in Leamington Hastings when Jane Man (the unmarried daughter caring for a resident) got pregnant; she was evicted in 1694, but returned ten years later to care for another resident.[93] In 1811 Widow Makepeace was expelled from the same almshouses for causing a fire in the communal kitchen.[94] In spite of the problems, however, life in Warwickshire almshouses was considerably more attractive than that in the workhouse, confirming Tomkins' deductions.[95] Individuals who deteriorated to a state where they could not cope in the almshouse might be transferred to the lunatic asylum or the workhouse.[96]

ALMSHOUSE CONTRIBUTION TO HOUSING THE ELDERLY POOR

It is important to discover the extent of the contribution made by almshouses to housing the elderly poor in Warwickshire. This is most easily studied in the 19th century, when we have reasonably reliable census information. Broad pointed out that 163 Warwickshire charity houses (including almshouses) provided over a third of local housing for the poor in the 1830s, the remainder being provided by parish poor houses; this charity housing comprised a larger proportion than in the four other counties he studied.[97] The Poor Law Amendment Act of 1834 ordered the provision of workhouses for every Union and the sale of parish houses (though the latter appears to have been ignored in many Warwickshire parishes). The importance of almshouses increased as poor houses were disposed of, but decreased again as workhouse provision expanded.

Parish poor houses are difficult to identify in the censuses but workhouses and almshouses are usually easy to find. The workhouse population over fifty-nine years of age was compared with the almshouse population in the catchment area of the Union concerned in 1851 and 1881 (*see* Table 7.IV).[98] Overall, the results show more old people living in the ten Warwickshire workhouses: 752 compared with 501 in the twenty-three related almshouses.[99] In 1851 there were slightly more old people in workhouses than in almshouses

(263 compared with 239), but by 1881 the workhouses had expanded to house almost twice as many old people as the almshouses (489 compared with 262). The overall figures conceal some interesting gender differences: there were more elderly women in almshouses than in workhouses (though this was less true by 1881). In the workhouse, on the other hand, there were more old men than old women, thus reinforcing Nigel Goose's findings of gendered spaces in Hertfordshire institutions.[100] In addition it is worth noting that in 1851 the almshouses in some Unions (particularly Foleshill, Rugby, Solihull and Warwick) were providing more places than the local workhouse for old people; by 1881, however, all the workhouses (except Foleshill) were accommodating more old people than the local almshouses.

TABLE 7.IV
Numbers of elderly people in Warwickshire almshouses and workhouses
(1851 plus 1881 censuses)

	23 Almshouses		10 Workhouses	
Census year	**Males**	**Females**	**Males**	**Females**
1851	93	146	168	95
1881	98	164	331	158
Total	191	310	499	253
All people	501		752	

CONCLUSION

The typical founder of an almshouse in Warwickshire was a self-made childless man who wished his name to survive and to do good to the poor, and thus it appears that many founders were motivated as much by self-interest as philanthropy. Warwickshire almshouse buildings cover a range of styles and periods; many are of architectural significance (and listed accordingly) and even the less well-known almshouses can include delightful details. Almshouse residents were largely female, often widowed, and a few lived there for over fifty years. A surprising number of other people lived with the designated almsperson, sometimes even whole families. Most residents were over sixty, but there were a few younger people, the result of the trustees offering a home to the poor and disadvantaged, in effect using the almshouse as a parish poor house. Residents' occupations are often unknown (particularly for women), but those recorded include retired servants, labourers, skilled workers and trades people plus a few teachers and the occasional farmer. By the end of the 19th century, there were fewer labourers in almshouses, possibly reflecting the national shift from agricultural to urban/industrial occupations. The almshouse offered sheltered housing to the elderly that was often superior to anything they had previously experienced. There were some problems within the almshouse community but most appear to have been resolved without recourse to the ultimate sanction of eviction.

Overall, Warwickshire has been well provided with almshouses, perhaps reflecting the relative prosperity of this county. We might conclude that Warwickshire almshouses had considerable success in their aim of 'affording comfortable asylums to the aged and respectable poor'.[101] They did not, however, offer comprehensive provision for the elderly. There was a very uneven distribution of almshouses, bearing little relationship to population density: for example in 1881 there was no almshouse in the town of Leamington Spa (with a population of 25,141), whilst Stoneleigh village had two sets of almshouses for a population of 1,216. Also, there were fewer places for men, and entry policies often discriminated against the 'undeserving poor'. Consequently many old people without family support faced destitution and the workhouse. A study of local workhouses showed that overall they housed more of the elderly poor than almshouses, particularly later on in the 19th century. The almshouses, however, provided a home for more elderly women than did the workhouses, and in some places they also housed more elderly men than the local workhouse. Almshouses, therefore, made a very significant contribution to housing the elderly in Warwickshire, but further research on the relative contribution of almshouses, parish poor houses and workhouses would be valuable.

Notes

1.   Pigot, J. & Co's *Directory of Warwickshire*, 1821, p. 766.

2.   *Reports of the Commissioners on Charities for Warwickshire* (*CC* Warks), 1815-35, pp. 567-8, 790-3; 1851 census HO/107/2074 fo. 43 p. 6.

3.   St John's in Coventry; St Michael's and St John's in Warwick. There were a large number of parish poor houses; those called 'almshouses' at some stage were at: Berkswell, Coleshill (Harvey's and Everett's), Coventry (West Orchard), Grandborough (Sutton's), Hathoway, Lapworth (two), Nuneaton, Sutton Coldfield (Boldmere) and Warwick (St Mary's, Upper Saltisford, Yardley's and Corporation). The last were set up after the great fire of 1694 to house twenty-eight homeless women. Berkswell built 'proper' almshouses in 1853. Stratford-upon-Avon built poor houses in Hathoway to supplement the workhouse there. It is difficult to draw a clear distinction between almshouses and parish poor houses and others might well disagree with the classification in this chapter.

4.   *CC* Warks, 1815-35.

5.   Including: Bailey, B. *Almshouses*, London, 1988; Godfrey, W. *The English Almshouse*, London, 1950; Hallet, A. *Almshouses*, Princes Risborough, 2004; Howson, B. *Houses of Noble Poverty*, Sunbury-on-Thames, 1993; Howson, B. *Almshouses: a social & architectural history*, Stroud, 2008.

6.   Raphael, M. *The Romance of English Almshouses*, London, 1926. Cleary, J. & Orton, M. *So Long as the World shall Endure: the 500 year History of Ford's and Bond's Hospitals*, Coventry, 1991; Gooder, E. *Temple Balsall from Hospitallers to a Caring Community: 1322 to modern times*, Chichester, 1999; MacFarquhar, G. *Leamington Hastings Almshouses and Poor's Plots*, Rugby, 1984; Johnstone, R. *The Thomas Huntbach Charity of the School and Almshouses*, Shustoke, 2006; *Lord Leycester Hospital Warwick*, anonymous booklet, *ca* 1995.

7.   Nicholls, A., 'The Relief of the Elderly Poor in Early Modern Almshouses: a Warwickshire case study', unpublished MA dissertation, Warwick University, 2007 (WCRO library: C 362.6 Nic).

8.   And was sometimes called 'Bablake Hospital'. Ford's Hospital was often called 'Greyfriars' because it stood in Greyfriars Lane, but had no other links to the monastic priory.

9.   Salzman, L.F. (ed.) *Victoria County History for Warwickshire* (*VCH* Warks), ii, 1908, p. 112.

10.   White, F. & Co. *History, Gazetteer and Directory of Warwickshire*, Sheffield, 1874, p. 207.

11.   *CC* Warks, pp. 823-4.

12.   *CC* Warks, p. 23.

13.   White, F. & Co., 1850, pp. 469-70.

14.   *CC* Warks, p. 709.

15.   WCRO: PH 649/72.

16.   McIntosh, M. 'Local Responses to the Poor in Later Medieval and Tudor England', *Continuity and Change*, 3 (2), 1988, pp. 221-8; Nichols, 2008, p. 19.

17.   Will of Nicholas Chamberlain, 1715, cited in the Parsonage display, Bedworth.

18.   Now Castle Hill; Bolitho, P. *Warwick's Most Famous Son*, Warwick, p. 29.

19.   Nicholls, 2008, p. 49; Raphael, 1926, p. 51.

20.   Gooder, p. 56.

21.   Aliberti, M. 'The Lawrence Sheriff Almshouses' in *Aspects of the Past III*, Rugby, 2001, p. 65-7.

22.   Bond's Hospital in Coventry was less seriously damaged; Bailey, 1988, p. 81.

23. MacFarquhar, 1984, p. 20.

24. WCRO: DR 395/19.

25. Shakespeare Centre Library and Archive (SCLA), BRU 5/2/42; 5/3/116; 5/1/96.

26. Gooder, pp. 124-6.

27. Cleary & Orton, 1991, p. 46.

28. Alcock, N. *People at Home: living in a Warwickshire village 1500-1800*, Chichester, 1993, p. 143.

29. Gooder, pp. 65-6 and Nicholls, 2008, p. 71.

30. *CC* Warks, pp. 688 and 47.

31. *CC* Warks, p. 918.

32. Johnstone, 2006, [no page numbers].

33. Langley, A., 'The Promised Land: allotments in nineteenth-century Warwickshire', *Warwickshire History*, 8, ii, 2005-6, pp. 58-65.

34. WCRO: CR 351/23, lithograph by J. Hawkins, reproduced by kind permission of Warwickshire County Record Office.

35. They were inefficient or corrupt.

36. Cleary & Orton, 1991, p. 11.

37. *CC* Warks, p. 194.

38. Cleary & Orton, 1991, pp. 68-70.

39. *CC* Warks, pp. 638-9.

40. *CC* Warks, p. 710.

41. White, 1874, p. 236.

42. *CC* Warks, p. 265.

43. *CC* Warks, pp. 7-8.

44. SCLA: ER 1/1/62.

45. Priory Almshouses in Alcester; Denton's in Kenilworth; Elborrow's and Butlin's in Rugby.

46. Aliberti, 2001, p. 64.

47. WCRO: DR 395/19/8

48. *VCH* Warks, iii, 1945, p. 21.

49. *CC* Warks, p. 23.

50. Cleary & Orton, 1991, p. 121.

51. Nicholls, 2008, p. 71.

52. Cleary & Orton, p. 45.

53. Caird, J. *English Agriculture in 1850-51*, London, 1852, p. 512.

54. The two Hospitals in Coventry and Oken's almshouses in Warwick.

55. Kemp, T. *Book of John Fisher 1580-1588*, Warwick, 1900, p. 94.

56. WCRO: CR 2044/34.

57. *CC* Warks, pp. 491, 536.

58. *CC* Warks, p. 639; White, 1874, p. 585.

59. 'Pauper' or 'receiving parish pay', but this may have been omitted by some enumerators.

60. Sir Robert Throgmorton's guidance for the Coughton almshouses set up in 1518, *CC* Warks, p. 23.

61. Sixteenth-century rules for Ford's Hospital in Coventry (note 64), 17th-century rules for Bond's Hospital in Coventry and the Church Street Almshouses in Stratford-upon-Avon (notes 27 and 63), undated rules for Lady Leveson's Hospital at Temple Balsall (Gooder, p. 60), 18th-century rules for Elborrow's almshouse in Rugby (note 75) and 19th-century rules for St Edith's Home in Warwick (note 47).

62. WCRO: DR 395/19/8.

63. Seventeenth-century rules, SCLA: BRU 15/15/106.

64. Sixteenth-century rules of Ford's Hospital in Coventry, *CC* Warks, 1815-35, p. 918.

65. WCRO: DR 225/373/1.

66. WCRO: PH 352/187/39, reproduced by kind permission of Warwickshire County Record Office.

67. *CC* Warks, 1815-35, p. 264; Gooder, 1999, p. 128.

68.   Lufkin's Charity, CC Warks, 1815-35, p. 896.

69.   Gooder, p. 63; White, 1850, p. 867.

70.   SCLA: BRT 1/3/38, 1427-8.

71.   The Hospitals in Bedworth, Warwick and Temple Balsall; Lawrence Sheriff and Oken's almshouses and those in Church Street Stratford-upon-Avon.

72.   White, 1874, p. 1246.

73.   WCRO: DR 395/19/8.

74.   WCRO: CR 2044/34.

75.   *CC* Warks, 1815-35, p. 722.

76.   1881 census, RG11/3085, fo. 28 p.12.

77.   RG10/5198 fo. 78 p.26; WCRO: DR 852/56, the almshouse at Southam was to provide a home for an orphan cared for by two of the almswomen but the funds were used for other charitable purposes.

78.   Personal communication from Shirley Ball, 2015.

79.   WCRO: DR(B) 36/5.

80.   Excluding the four almshouses founded after 1881: Knowle, Rowington, Smallwood (Alcester) and St Joseph's Homestead (Stratford).

81.   Goose, N. and Basten, S. 'Almshouse Residency in Nineteenth-century England: an interim report', *Family and Community History*, 12 i, 2009, pp. 65-76.

82.   1851 census, HO107/2069, fo. 265 p. 32.

83.   MacFarquhar, pp.10-11.

84.   Jones, J. *Family Life in Shakespeare's England, Stratford-upon-Avon 1570-1630*, Stroud, 1996, p. 93; Nicholls, 2008, p. 67.

85.   Using earlier censuses to find the almsmen's occupations, if omitted from the 1881 census.

86.   Gooder, p. 59.

87.   MacFarquhar, pp. 9 and 17.

88.   Gooder, p. 64.

89.   John Burton, personal communication, 2008.

90.   Raphael, p. 61; Cleary & Orton, p. 51.

91.   The five were: Temple Balsall, Bedworth, Shustoke, Elborrow and Laurence Sheriff in Rugby; the latter moved away from Rugby School later.

92.   WCRO: DR(B) 36/5.

93.   Nicholls, p. 77.

94.   MacFarquhar, p. 18.

95.   Tomkins, A. 'Retirement from the Noise and Hurry of the World? The experience of almshouse life 1650-1850', Voluntary Action History Society paper (www.vahs.org.uk past papers), 2008, pp. 22-4.

96.   WRCO: DR(B) 36/5; DR 947/72.

97.   Broad, J. 'Housing the Rural Poor in Southern England, 1650-1850', *The Agricultural History Review*, 48, 2000, pp. 151-70.

98.   Workhouses drawing on parishes outside the county (and the related almshouses) were excluded from this analysis.

99.   The workhouses (and related almshouses) were: Atherstone (two in Mancetter), Coventry (Bonds and Fords), Foleshill (Bedworth), Meriden (Berkswell and Shustoke), Nuneaton (none), Rugby (three in Rugby plus Dunchurch and Leamington Hastings), Solihull (Temple Balsall), Stratford-upon-Avon (two in Stratford), Southam (none) and Warwick (six in Warwick, one in Kenilworth and two in Stoneleigh).

100.   Goose, N. 'Poverty, Old Age and Gender in Nineteenth-century England: the case of Hertfordshire', *Continuity and Change*, 20, 2005, pp. 351-84.

101.   Pigot, p. 766.

102.   Farr, M. (1977) 'Nicholas Eyffeler of Warwick, glazier: executors' accounts and other documents concerning the foundation of his almshouse charity', 1592-1621 in Bearman, R. (ed.) *Miscellany*, Dugdale Society Publication, xxxi, pp. 29-110.

103.   Langley, A. 'Warwickshire Almshouses, 1400 to 1900: affording comfortable asylums to the aged and respectable poor?', *Warwickshire History*, XIV, 4, 2010, pp. 139-55.

APPENDIX 7.1:   ALMSHOUSES IN WARWICKSHIRE 1400-1900

Community	Location	Name	Founder	First year	Last year	Size	Main references
Alcester 1	Priory St	Priory	John Bridges	1659	Dem. 1950s	4	CCW pp. 7-8
Alcester 2	Bleachfield St	Bleachfield	George Ingram	1680	Dem. 1960s	4	CCW pp. 7-8
Alcester 3	Mount St	Smallwood	William Smallwood	1895	Original	6	VCH Vol. 3 p. 21
Balsall Temple	Temple Balsall	Lady Leveson's Hospital	Lady Katherine Leveson	1679	Rebuilt 1725	20 + 16	WCRO DRB 36/5
Bedworth	Hall Yard/ All Saints Sq.	Bedworth Hospital	Rev. Nicholas Chamberlain	1715	Moved 1840	18 + 22	CCW pp. 683-90
Berkswell	Church La.	Berkswell	Local Charity	1853	Original	10	CCW pp. 639-40
Coughton	Birmingham Rd	Throckmorton's	Sir Robert Throckmorton	1518	Change use > 1901	6	CCW p. 23
Coventry 1	Hill St	Bond's Hospital	Thomas Bond	1506	Original restored	10*	Cleary & Orton
Coventry 2	Greyfriars St	Ford's Hospital	William Ford	1509	Original restored	6 + 6*	Cleary & Orton
Dunchurch	The Square	Newcombe's	Thomas Newcombe	1690	Original	6	CCW pp. 709-11
Kenilworth	High St	Widows' Charity Houses	George Denton	1644	Rebuilt 1830s	3 + 1	CCW pp. 327-8
Knowle	High St	Berrow	Wm & Mary-Jane Berrow	1886	Original	4	Images of England 218347
Leamington Hastings	Village	Davis's	Humphrey Davis	1607	Original	8 + 2	CCW pp. 194-201
Mancetter 1	Mancetter Rd	Cramer's	James Cramer	1724	Original	6	CCW pp. 491-3
Mancetter 2	Mancetter Rd	Cramer's	Cramer's charity	1822	Original	5	CCW pp. 491-3
Rowington	The Avenue	Rowington	Rowington Charities	1907	Original	8 + 9	www.rowington.org
Rugby 1	Church St/ Dunchurch Rd	Lawrence Sheriff's	Lawrence Sheriff	1567	Rebuilt 1777 Moved 1961	4 + 8	CCW pp. 724-5
Rugby 2	High/Saint Johns St	Elborrow's	Richard Elborrow	1707	Moved 1885	6	CCW pp. 721-4
Rugby 3	Bridget/ Stephen St	Butlin's	Miss C. Butlin	1848	Moved 1905	6	Kelly 1876 p. 739
Shustoke	Station Rd	Huntbach's	Thomas Huntbach	1709	Original	6	Johnstone
Stoneleigh 1	The Green	Old Almshouses	Sir Thomas & Lady Alice Leigh	1576	Original	10	CCW pp. 335-7
Stoneleigh 2	The Bank	New Almshouses	Lady Margarette Leigh	1855	Change use >1957	4	White 1874 p. 839
Stratford 1	Church St	Church St	Holy Cross Guild	1427	Original	10 + 12	SCLA BRU 15/15/106
Stratford 2	Guild St	Newlands	Miss M. Newland	1857	Original	4	White 1874 p.1251
Stratford 3	St Joseph's Homestead	Albany Road	Agnes & Rose Carr-Smith	1911	Original	4	SCLA P. 87.3
Sutton Coldfield 1	Mill St	Mill Street	Corporation Charity	1825	1924	10	CCW p. 605
Sutton Coldfield 2	Walmley Rd	Walmley	Miss Francis Lingard	1863	Original	4	VCH Vol. 4 p. 245
Tanworth	Bates Lane	Whitehead	Misses Lloyd	1871	Original	4	WCRO CR 2044/34
Warwick 1	Pebble La./ Castle Hill	Oken's	Thomas Oken	1570	Moved 1696	6 + 6	Bolitho
Warwick 2	High St	Lord Leycester Hospital	Robert Dudley Earl of Leicester	1571	Original	12	LLH booklet
Warwick 3	Westgate	Westgate	Guild of Holy Trinity & St George	<1580s	Rebuilt 1888	8	CCW pp. 823-4
Warwick 4	Castle Hill	Eyffler's	Nicholas Eyffler	1591	Original	8 + 5	Farr
Warwick 5	Saltisford	Lower Saltisford	Sir Thomas Puckering	1635	Dem. 1964	4 + 2	VCH Vol. 8 p. 550
Warwick 6	Emscote	St Edith's Home	Miss Marianne Phillips	1868	Original	12	WCRO DR 395/19

Key to Appendix 1

*	Out-pensioners also supported
Bolitho	*Warwick's most famous Son* (*see* Note18)
CCW	*Commissioners' Reports on Warwickshire Charities* (*see* Note 2)
Cleary & Orton	*So long as the World shall Endure* (*see* Note 6)
Dem.	Demolished
Farr	'Nicholas Eyffeler of Warwick' (*see* Note 102)
Images of England	URL: www.imagesofengland.org.uk
Johnstone	*Thomas Huntbach Charity - Shustoke* (*see* Note 6)
Kelly	Kelly, E.R. & Co., *Post Office Directory for Warwickshire*, London, 1876
LLH booklet	*Lord Leycester Hospital Warwick*, undated
Original	Original building still stands (in 2015)
SCLA	Shakespeare Centre Library and Archive
Size	Number of original places, plus any expansion before 1900
Sutton	Sutton Coldfield
WCRO	Warwickshire County Record Office
White	*History, Gazetteer and Directory for Warwickshire*, 1874 (*see* Note 10)
VCH	*Victoria History for the County of Warwick*, London, 1945-69

ACKNOWLEDGEMENTS

I am grateful for valuable editorial advice from Nigel Goose and Helen Caffrey, and also Robert Bearman, editor of *Warwickshire History* (which published an earlier version of this chapter).[103] I also wish to thank Gillian Mason (for researching Lord Leycester hospital) and Angela Nicholls (for sharing unpublished material from her MA dissertation).

CHAPTER 8
HOUSING THE ELDERLY IN NINETEENTH-CENTURY DERBYSHIRE: A COMPARISON OF ALMSHOUSE AND WORKHOUSE PROVISION

Clive Leivers

INTRODUCTION

One of the aims of the research project undertaken under the auspices of FACHRS and LPSS was to establish the contribution made by almshouses towards the 'mixed economy of welfare'. One element of this assessment was to compare the extent of residential accommodation provided by almshouses and workhouses in the last half of the 19th century. In his survey of the populations of Hertfordshire workhouses, Goose found a 'pronounced skew towards men amongst elderly inmates' and suggested that one possible reason could be the 'relative provision of almshouse accommodation for men and women'.[1]

This chapter contributes to that assessment by evaluating the relative contributions of almshouses and workhouses in the county of Derbyshire for residents aged sixty and upwards, based on an analysis of the relevant Census Enumerators Books (CEBs) for 1851, 1881 and 1901. Similar data from four Poor Law Unions (PLUs) in Worcestershire are provided for comparative purposes.[2]

THE STUDY AREA

At the end of the 19th century there were thirty-five almshouses in Derbyshire; in the mid century there were thirty-two, with the eight new foundations between 1851 and 1901 compensating for the four almshouses that had closed during that time. Each of these undoubtedly provided a welcome place of refuge for the mostly elderly inhabitants, but it is instructive to assess the overall quantitative contribution made by these institutions to the provision of residential accommodation for the elderly.

There were nine post-1834 Poor Law Unions in Derbyshire, each with their own workhouse, at Ashbourne, Bakewell, Belper, Chapel-en-le-Frith, Chesterfield, Derby, Glossop, Hayfield and Shardlow. Six of the Unions comprised exclusively Derbyshire parishes; the other three also covered parishes in neighbouring counties: Ashbourne included fifteen parishes in Staffordshire; Hayfield included the Cheshire parish of Disley; and Shardlow included fifteen parishes in Leicestershire and Nottinghamshire. Nine Derbyshire almshouses were located in parishes served by Unions in adjacent counties: Leicestershire,

Nottinghamshire, Staffordshire and Yorkshire. So, in drawing comparisons, those Unions including non-Derbyshire parishes have been excluded, as have Chapel-en-le-Frith and Glossop, which contained no 19th-century almshouses, and Hayfield, which had only one almshouse in its area: a foundation of 1880 at New Mills. Thus the review will concentrate on the Unions of Bakewell, Belper, Chesterfield and Derby.

Bakewell covered some fifty, mainly rural, parishes within the White Peak, with its workhouse, opened in 1841, able to accommodate 200 inmates. There were two long-established almshouses in Bakewell and Cromford and a new foundation at Matlock was opened in 1898. Belper comprised thirty-five parishes to the south of Bakewell union and had an industrial character (45 per cent of the population were employed in manufacturing and 12 per cent in mining in 1851), with fair-sized towns at Alfreton, Belper, Ripley and Wirksworth.[3] The Belper Union workhouse opened in 1840 with a capacity of 300. There were five almshouses in the territory of the union, at Belper, Duffield, Holbrook, Morley and Wirksworth.

Chesterfield Union embraced 141 square miles and thirty-four parishes in the north-east of the county, with small towns at Bolsover, Clay Cross, Dronfield and Staveley; Chesterfield itself being the largest town in the county after the county town. The area was a mix of industrial villages — mainly coalmining and iron manufacture, which accounted for 20 per cent of the population — and some agricultural parishes with almost 28 per cent of the population employed in farming and breeding.[4] The Chesterfield workhouse was built in 1839 to accommodate 300 paupers. There were a couple of almshouses in the town of Chesterfield (to be merged into one new building in 1875) and other foundations at Newbold and Staveley.

Derby Union essentially comprised the five parishes of the county town and three immediately adjacent townships that were to be incorporated within the town boundaries by the end of the century. So the whole PLU area was essentially urban in nature with 56 per cent of the population engaged in manufacture and 10 per cent in domestic service.[5] The original workhouse (built 1837-8) could provide accommodation for 300 but was replaced by a larger structure in 1878. In 1851 there were four almshouses within the town but in the last decade of the century the almshouse founded by Bess of Hardwick closed, whilst one new foundation for retired lace workers was built in 1886.

A COMPARISON OF WORKHOUSE AND ALMSHOUSE POPULATIONS

Table 8.I sets out the basic data from the three decennial censuses used in this exercise. The total number of workhouse inmates increased significantly over the fifty years – from 575 in 1851 to 1,294 in 1901 – particularly in Chesterfield and Derby, with the former showing almost a fourfold increase and Derby an increase of 330 per cent. Bakewell saw only a slight increase – 27 per cent – mainly of male inmates, with Belper seeing a similar degree of growth and gender distribution.

At every point, the majority of inmates were male, with proportions ranging from a bare majority of 51 per cent in Bakewell in 1881 to 70 per cent in Belper in 1901. The proportion of over-sixties also grew over the period, rising from under a fifth in 1851 to almost a half fifty years later. In 1851 and 1881 the figures are more or less comparable to those in earlier studies; in the examples used by Hinde & Turnbull the proportions ranged between 18 per cent in Basingstoke in 1851 (very close to the Derbyshire figure of 19 per cent) and 38 per cent in Leicester in 1881 (10 per cent higher than the overall Derbyshire figure, although for the urban PLU of Derby the proportion was also above 30 per cent). The

Hertfordshire results for 1851 reported by Goose give a higher figure of 30 per cent with a sex ratio (male to female) of 236 to 100. By 1901, however, over 40 per cent of residents in all four workhouses were aged sixty and above, as was the case in Hertfordshire in 1891.[6] Analysing the over-sixty population, throughout the period there was a preponderance of elderly male inmates, particularly in Chesterfield and Belper: 90 per cent in Chesterfield in 1851 and 80 per cent in Belper in both 1881 and 1901. Apart from the position in Derby in 1851, where 54 per cent of elderly residents were male, the proportion of elderly males to females was consistently above 2:1 with about one third of the female inmates being over sixty years old.

TABLE 8.1
Age Profile of Derbyshire workhouse/almshouse inmates

	Total residents	M	F	Over 60 No	Over 60 %	Males 60+ No	Males 60+ % of total 60+	Females 60+ No	Females 60+ % of total 60+
1851									
Bakewell									
Workhouse	112	59	53	19	17.0	14	73.7	5	26.3
Almshouses	16	8	8	9	56.3	3	33.3	6	66.7
Belper									
Workhouse	206	112	94	24	11.7	15	62.5	9	37.5
Almshouses	21	13	8	18	85.7	12	66.7	6	33.3
Chesterfield									
Workhouse	95	60	35	20	21.1	18	90.0	2	10.0
Almshouses	22	4	18	17	77.3	3	17.6	14	82.4
Derby									
Workhouse	162	98	64	46	28.4	25	54.3	21	45.7
Almshouses	79	31	48	59	74.7	26	44.1	33	55.9
Total									
Workhouse	575	329	246	109	19.0	72	66.1	37	33.9
Almshouses	138	56	82	103	74.6	44	42.7	59	57.3
1881									
Bakewell									
Workhouse	112	57	55	20	17.9	14	70.0	6	30.0
Almshouses	17	7	10	11	64.7	4	36.4	7	63.6
Belper									
Workhouse	238	145	93	76	31.9	61	80.3	15	19.7
Almshouses	28	15	13	21	75.0	12	57.1	9	42.9
Chesterfield									
Workhouse	330	173	157	78	23.6	54	69.2	24	30.8
Almshouses	27	4	23	19	70.4	2	10.5	17	89.5
Derby									
Workhouse	508	291	217	157	30.9	115	73.2	42	27.8
Almshouses	83	22	61	67	80.7	19	28.4	48	71.6
Total									
Workhouse	1,188	666	522	331	27.9	244	73.7	87	26.3
Almshouses	155	48	107	118	76.1	37	31.4	81	68.6

/Table 8.1 contd on next page

TABLE 8.I (contd)

	Total residents	M	F	Over 60 No	Over 60 %	Males 60+ No	Males 60+ % of total 60+	Females 60+ No	Females 60+ % of total 60+
1901									
Bakewell									
Workhouse	142	85	57	58	40.8	38	65.5	20	34.5
Almshouses	19	6	13	17	89.5	6	35.3	11	64.7
Belper									
Workhouse	254	179	75	120	47.2	96	80.0	24	20.0
Almshouses	20	13	7	17	85.0	11	64.7	6	35.3
Chesterfield									
Workhouse	364	231	133	157	43.1	115	73.2	42	26.8
Almshouses	21	2	19	20	95.2	2	10.0	18	90.0
Derby									
Workhouse	534	330	204	256	47.9	175	68.4	81	31.6
Almshouses	79	23	56	70	88.6	22	31.4	48	68.6
Total									
Workhouse	1,294	825	469	591	45.7	424	71.7	167	28.3
Almshouses	139	44	95	124	89.2	41	33.1	83	66.9
Overall Totals									
Workhouse	3,057	1,820	1,237	1,031	33.7	740	71.8	291	28.2
Almshouses	432	148	284	345	79.9	122	35.4	223	64.6

Source: Derbyshire Census Enumerators books , The National Archives, Kew
1851	HO107	2142-4, 2147, 2149
1881	RG11	3395, 3398, 3404, 3407, 3409, 3413, 3432-3, 3446
1901	RG13	3214, 3216, 3221, 3224, 3248-9, 3262, 3288

The data for the residents of almshouses presents a more varied picture due to the various qualifications determined by the founders. Of the three institutions in Bakewell PLU, one was for single men (Bakewell), one for widows (Cromford), and Matlock provided for single women or married couples, though the great majority of residents were widows or spinsters. The emphasis on provision for women becomes more apparent in the figures for elderly residents, with two-thirds being women in all three enumerations. In Chesterfield union the only almshouse catering for men was that at Staveley, which actually took both sexes. Despite one of the three original almshouses in Chesterfield being endowed for three men or women, by the 19th century no men were in residence, so 80 per cent of residents were women, most aged over sixty.

The reverse situation applied in the area of the Belper union. Two establishments — Wirksworth and Morley — were exclusively male; the other three catered for both men and women, who at Duffield and Holbrook had to be over the age of sixty. The census data reflects this gender balance with male residents, both overall and aged sixty plus, being in the majority at every census.

Four of the almshouses in Derby provided for both men and women, including that run by the Liversage charity, which was the largest establishment in the county with over fifty residents recorded in the census returns. The other institution was one of the three almshouses in the county devoted to housing the widows of Anglican clergymen (described in more detail in Chapter 19). But here again the majority of residents were female, with overall more than two-thirds of those enumerated being women; the proportion of over-sixties was broadly similar.

A preliminary analysis of the results from the FACHRS project shows that three-quarters of almshouse residents were female, with proportions ranging from 4.8:1 in Middlesex to 1.4:1 in Norfolk.[7] The equivalent figure for the Derbyshire almshouses included in this survey is 1.89:1 although the result for almshouses in all Derbyshire PLUs comes a little higher at 2.2:1

Drawing these findings together in a comparison of workhouse and almshouse provision for the elderly, in 1851 Chesterfield saw a virtual equality in overall numbers, although as stated earlier the majority of almshouse residents were women. The censuses of 1881 and 1901 show a significant growth in the provision of male places in the workhouse, rather less marked for women, but by the end of the century twice as many aged women were housed in the workhouse than in the almshouses, while the workhouse continued to dominate provision for men.

The almshouses in the Bakewell union in both 1851 and 1881 housed virtually the same number of elderly women as did the workhouse; but in 1901, despite the opening of the new foundation at Matlock, the three almshouses contained only half the number of elderly women that were found in the workhouse. Throughout the period under review there were significantly more aged men in the workhouse than occupied almshouse places.

A similar widening of the relative differences in workhouse and almshouse provision was found in Belper. There was no marked change in the number of almshouse residents over the fifty years, but there were five times as many elderly workhouse residents in 1901 as there had been fifty years earlier - with an even greater growth in the number of elderly males.

Derby saw perhaps the greatest change in the relative provision. In 1851 the four almshouses provided more places for the over sixties than did the workhouse – even, marginally for men; half of these places were found in the Liversage Almshouses, which played an ever larger role in almshouse provision in the town for the rest of the century as additional places were provided. But with the opening of the new workhouse in 1878, almshouse provision was overshadowed and by 1901 the number of elderly workhouse residents had shown the same degree of increase as in Belper with more than seven times the number of elderly men than in 1851.

So, in broad terms, the findings confirm that, as in other areas of the country, the county's almshouses were directed more towards the provision of sheltered accommodation for elderly women and that the majority of poor elderly men had to look to the workhouse for institutional accommodation. This situation became increasingly apparent by the end of the century. In 1901 there were 424 elderly men residing in the four workhouses studied — compared to the forty found in the almshouses — and exactly half of these were in the Liversage Almshouses in Derby. For elderly women the situation was less dramatic, with 167 in the workhouses compared to seventy-seven almshouse residents.

COMPARABLE DATA FROM WORCESTERSHIRE

Table 8.II sets out the equivalent data for four Worcestershire PLUs: those centred on the county town, another major centre in Kidderminster and two more rural unions based around Martley and Pershore. There was a total of twenty-four almshouses in these PLUs: twelve in Worcester, eight in Kidderminster and two in both Pershore and Martley.

TABLE 8.II
Age Profile of Worcestershire workhouse/almshouse inmates

	Total residents	M	F	Over 60 No	Over 60 %	Males 60+ No	Males 60+ % of total 60+	Females 60+ No	Females 60+ % of total 60+
1851									
Worcester									
Workhouse	387	217	170	137	35.4	72	52.6	65	47.4
Almshouses	120	52	68	87	72.5	42	48.3	45	51.7
Pershore									
Workhouse	60	31	29	16	26.7	11	68.7	5	31.3
Almshouses	7	2	5	4	57.1	1	25.0	3	75.0
Kidderminster									
Workhouse	171	103	68	33	19.3	25	75.7	8	24.3
Almshouses	46	17	29	34	73.9	13	38.2	21	61.8
Martley									
Workhouse	120	56	64	20	16.7	13	65.0	7	35.0
Almshouses	14	5	9	1	7.1		0.0	1	100.0
Total									
Workhouse	738	407	331	206	27.9	121	58.7	85	41.3
Almshouses	187	76	111	126	67.4	56	44.5	70	55.5
1881									
Worcester									
Workhouse	267	165	102	89	33.3	59	66.3	30	33.7
Almshouses	200	77	123	155	77.5	64	41.3	91	58.7
Pershore									
Workhouse	84	44	40	26	30.9	17	65.4	9	34.6
Almshouses	29	11	18	20	68.9	7	35.0	13	65.0
Kidderminster									
Workhouse	327	201	126	95	29.1	75	78.9	20	21.1
Almshouses	55	14	41	43	78.2	12	27.9	31	72.1
Martley									
Workhouse	111	75	36	42	37.8	30	71.4	12	28.6
Almshouses	15	9	6	Nil	.0	Nil	0.0	Nil	0.0
Total									
Workhouse	789	485	304	252	33.2	181	71.8	71	28.2
Almshouses	299	111	188	218	72.9	83	38.1	135	61.9
1901									
Worcester									
Workhouse	296	179	117	199	67.2	122	61.3	77	38.7
Almshouses	148	45	103	128	86.5	41	32.1	87	67.9
Pershore									
Workhouse	66	35	31	32	48.5	21	65.6	11	34.4
Almshouses	28	12	16	19	67.9	6	31.6	13	68.4
Kidderminster									
Workhouse	358	196	162	154	43.0	94	61.0	60	39.0
Almshouses	60	13	47	50	83.3	10	20.0	40	80.0

/Table 8.II contd on next page

TABLE 8.II (contd)

	Total residents	M	F	Over 60		Males 60+		Females 60+	
				No	%	No	% of total 60+	No	% of total 60+
Martley									
Workhouse	111	71	40	51	45.9	42	82.3	9	17.7
Almshouses	18	7	11	1	5.6	1	100.0	Nil	0.0
Total									
Workhouse	831	481	350	436	52.5	279	64.0	157	36.0
Almshouses	254	77	177	198	77.9	58	29.3	140	70.7
Overall Totals									
Workhouse	2,358	1,373	985	894	37.9	581	64.9	313	35.1
Almshouses	740	264	476	542	73.2	197	36.3	345	63.7

In Worcestershire, overall numbers of workhouse residents also increased over the fifty years, but by no means to the extent evident in Derbyshire, with a rise of only 13 per cent compared to the more than doubling of Derbyshire inmates. The latter rate of increase was seen in Kidderminster workhouse, where numbers rose from 171 in 1851 to 358 fifty years later; perhaps surprisingly, overall numbers dropped in the Worcester workhouse.

As in Derbyshire, male inmates were in the majority on all occasions, except in Martley workhouse in 1851 where there were slightly more women. With residents over sixty, the Worcestershire figures again show broadly the same picture as in Derbyshire, with proportions rising from 28 per cent in 1851 to 52 per cent in 1901, both figures a few points above the Derbyshire situation. But as in other findings, it was the elderly male who was increasingly found within the workhouses, with the proportions rising from 58.7 per cent in 1851 to almost 72 per cent thirty years later before falling back to 64 per cent in 1901. In Kidderminster workhouse, three-quarters of the over-sixties were male in 1851, with this figure rising by four percentage points in 1881, before falling back to around the county average in 1901.

Figures for almshouse residency in the four Worcestershire PLU areas again reinforce the data from other counties. Women were in the majority at all three census enumerations and this preponderance increased over the fifty years. Whilst the overall female/male ratio was 1.8:1, this masks a rise from 1.5:1 in 1851 to 2.3:1 in 1901.

Overall numbers of almshouse residents rose from 187 in 1851 to 254 in 1901, with marked increases in Worcester, where the 123 female residents in 1881 outnumbered their sisters in the workhouse by twenty-one. On a smaller scale, Pershore saw a similar rate of increase from just seven almshouse residents in 1851 to four times that number in succeeding enumerations.

In comparing the number of elderly residents in the two types of establishment, whilst the numbers of female residents were relatively similar, with just seventeen more women over sixty found in the workhouses, there was a marked preponderance of elderly male workhouse residents – 279 compared to the fifty-eight almsmen. There were more almswomen in the Kidderminster area than elderly female workhouse inmates in both 1851 and 1881, as was the case in the Worcester and Pershore unions in 1881 and 1901; indeed, in 1881 there were three times as many elderly women in the Worcester almshouses than were housed in the workhouse.

DERBYSHIRE DATA RELATED TO AGE PROFILE

TABLE 8.III
Selected Derbyshire PLU populations aged 60 and over

Percentages in brackets show residents as percentage of over 60 population

	1851		1881		1901	
	M	**F**	**M**	**F**	**M**	**F**
Bakewell						
Total population	14,753	15,127	14,909	15,613	16,220	17,441
Total over 60	1,271	1,241	1,395	1,415	1,436	1,694
Percentage over 60	8.6	8.2	9.4	9.1	8.9	9.7
Resident in	14	5	14	6	38	20
Workhouse	[1.1%]	[0.4%]	[1.0%]	[0.4%]	[2.6%]	[1.2%]
Resident in	3	6	4	7	6	11
Almshouses	[0.2%]	[0.5%]	[0.3%]	[0.5%]	[0.4%]	[0.7%]
Belper*						
Total population	23,448	23,424	29,356	28,828	36,631	35,981
Total over 60	1,713	1,713	2,354	2,292	2,497	2,586
Percentage over 60	7.3	7.3	8.0	7.9	6.8	7.2
Resident in	15	9	61	15	96	24
Workhouse	[0.87%]	[0.52%]	[2.6%]	[0.65%]	[3.8%]	[0.9%]
Resident in	12	6	12	9	11	6
Almshouses	[0.7%]	[0.35%]	[0.51%]	[0.39%]	[0.44%]	[0.23%]
Chesterfield						
Total population	23,688	22,107	51,723	47,018	69,393	63,463
Total over 60	1,589	1,612	2,679	2,638	4,575	4,546
Percentage over 60	6.7	7.3	5.2	5.6	6.6	7.2
Resident in	18	2	54	24	115	42
Workhouse	[1.1%]	[0.1%]	[2.0%]	[0.9%]	[2.5%]	[0.9%]
Resident in	3	14	2	17	2	18
Almshouses	[0.2%]	[0.9%]	[0.1%]	[0.64%]	[0.04%]	[0.4%]
Derby*						
Total population	20,775	22,909	38, 681	39,950	51,802	55,025
Total over 60	1,130	1,379	1,970	2,457	2,978	3,773
Percentage over 60	5.4	6.0	5.1	6.2	5.7	6.9
Resident in	25	21	115	42	175	81
Workhouse	[2.2%]	[1.5%]	[5.8%]	[1.7%]	[5.9%]	[2.4%]
Resident in	26	33	19	48	22	48
Almshouses	[2.3%]	[2.4%]	[0.96%]	[1.95%]	[0.7%]	[1.3%]

Overall Totals		1851			1881			1901	
	Total	**M**	**F**	**Total**	**M**	**F**	**Total**	**M**	**F**
Over 60 population	11,648	5,703	5,945	17,200	8,398	8,802	24,085	11,486	12,599
Resident in Workhouses	105	72	37	331	244	87	591	424	167
Percentage in Workhouses	0.9	1.3	0.6	1.9	2.9	0.98	2.5	3.7	1.3
Resident in Almshouses	103	44	59	118	37	81	117	41	83
Percentage in Almshouses	0.9	0.8	0.99	0.07	0.4	0.9	0.5	0.3	0.66

* in 1890 one parish transferred from Belper to Derby which also gained one parish & part of another from Shardlow PLU
Source: Census Enumerators Books Derbyshire as for Table 1; population data from www.visionofbritain.org.uk

One other measure of the respective contribution made by the two types of institution in providing residential accommodation for the elderly in Derbyshire is provided in Table 8.III. This shows the number of workhouse/almshouse residents as a percentage of the total population over the age of sixty in the four Union areas. Bakewell Union had the smallest increase in population over the fifty years but the highest proportion of elderly people of both sexes throughout. The percentage of the elderly in Belper stayed roughly the same throughout the period despite a steady rise in overall population. Chesterfield Union saw almost a threefold increase in population over the fifty years due, in some measure, to an influx of workers into the industrial sector with ironworks expanding and the opening of numerous deep coal mines; the proportion of over sixties, however, changed far less dramatically, with virtually the same percentages in 1851 and 1901.[8] Derby's rise in overall population was also significant but again proportions of the elderly showed little change. However, the percentage figures for the elderly population do mask a considerable numerical change with almost a tripling of numbers for both sexes over the fifty years in Chesterfield and Derby; there was an increase of between 700 and 800 in Belper (*see* Illustration 8.a.), with Bakewell showing an increase of 150 for men and 450 for women.

The percentage of the elderly in union workhouses grew over time from less than 1 per cent in 1851 to 2.5 per cent fifty years later. This was especially the case for men – as the

earlier analysis would suggest – with the percentages rising from 1.3 per cent in 1851 to 3.7 per cent in 1901. However, these figures were markedly lower than those reported for Hertfordshire, where the overall percentages were 4.6 in 1851 and 3.09 in 1891, with the male proportions being 6.8 in 1851 and 4.89 in 1891.[9] Throughout the fifty years, Derby housed the highest proportion in its workhouse with the male percentage rising from 2.2 in 1851 to 5.5 in 1901. The provision for males in Belper showed a marked rise from 0.8 per cent in 1851 to 3.8 per cent fifty years later.

The percentage contribution made by the almshouse sector shrank since the only new establishment during this period was Matlock Almshouse (in the Bakewell Union); and despite some expansion at the Derby Liversage Almshouses this was offset by the closure of the Devonshire Almshouse.

Illustration 8.a. Entrance to Belper workhouse.
Photo © Christine Seal, 2004

CONCLUSION

This survey has broadly confirmed previous findings that elderly men were more likely to find accommodation in the workhouse than in almshouses, and that in workhouses they outnumbered their female counterparts. It has also demonstrated that this situation was not restricted to the southern agricultural counties examined in earlier research. Various reasons have been suggested for this gender imbalance: that elderly women were better able to look after themselves; that they were more useful to relatives (in, for example, caring for children and helping with household chores); and that more arduous male employment resulted in earlier and greater need for residential accommodation for men.[10]

Nigel Goose has drawn attention to the special problems faced by the aged agricultural labourer in Hertfordshire where 73 per cent of elderly male workhouse inmates in 1851 had been so employed.[11] Derbyshire had a more mixed economy than Hertfordshire and in the county as a whole the agricultural sector employed less than a quarter of the county's workforce in 1851 with the manufacturing sector accounting for 42 per cent.[12]

Even in the Ashbourne PLU area, where half of those employed worked in the agricultural sector, the agricultural labourer was not predominant among the elderly men in the workhouse. In 1851 there were only two agricultural labourers among the eight elderly male residents; in 1881 they numbered seven in a total of twenty-nine men over the age of sixty, with six other labourers of varying kinds and twelve other occupations represented.

In reviewing almshouse provision, the terms of the endowment are significant factors. Of the almshouses in this study, four were reserved for men; six for women and seven catered for both sexes. In addition, as Alannah Tompkins has pointed out, almshouse trustees could be choosier in the selection of inmates, whilst poor law officials had restricted options for dealing with the aged poor.[13] In three of the Derbyshire almshouses, the receipt of poor relief was, in fact, a bar to admission.

In assessing the contribution of almshouse provision within a particular Poor Law Union, one has to keep in mind that, in some cases, admission to almshouses did not depend on a specific residential qualification and therefore does not, as Goose & Basten point out, 'necessarily reflect the local system of welfare'.[14] The Derby Almshouses illustrate the point: Large's Hospital provided accommodation for the widows of Anglican clergymen with no apparent residential qualification. Three widows of Derbyshire clergymen were among the inmates, but all were from outside the Derby PLU area, and at an enquiry by a Charity Commissioner in 1860, one almswomen was said to be 'to all intents a non-resident, as she keeps a lodging house in London'.[15] Nor did the foundation contribute significantly towards housing the over sixties: throughout the period the majority of residents were below that age.

The almshouses founded by the Countess of Shrewsbury and Robert Wilmot similarly accepted inmates from outside the town. At the 1860 enquiry mentioned above, the then governor of Wilmots, Sir Henry Wilmot, stated: 'I name whoever I please as inmates ... They do not necessarily belong to Derby, but I think they should be connected to the family, old tenants or servants'.[16] Similarly, the Duke of Devonshire chose the people to be allocated places in the Shrewsbury Almshouse, who came from 'either old diseased servants of the Devonshires or old decayed burghers of Derby'.[17] The establishment founded by Boden and Company in 1886 catered exclusively for retired employees of the firm.

So, of the five establishments, only Liversage's was restricted to residents of the town — indeed to the specific parish of St Peter, which in 1881 contained 19 per cent of the total population in the PLU, but provided 63 per cent of the almshouse inhabitants. Such was the attraction of the facilities offered by the charity that the clerk to the PLU told the Charity

Commissioner that there was an 'influx of persons into the parish who wish to obtain a settlement, in order to become recipients of the Charity'. This was despite the Commissioner criticising the low rate of allowances paid to the inmates (then between 4s to 6s weekly), commenting that: 'Almshouses were of no use whatever if the inmates were to be no better than paupers'.[18]

This review has shown that useful information can be obtained from a broad, quantitative survey of the respective contributions made by almshouses and workhouses to the relief of the elderly. But in reviewing the contribution of almshouse provision, it is equally important to take account of the residential and social qualifications for admission. Further studies in other locations would enable a wider analysis across the differing economic and social areas of the country.

Notes

1.   Goose, N. 'Workhouse Populations in the Mid Nineteenth-century: the case of Hertfordshire', *Local Population Studies*. Vol. 62, 1999, pp. 52-67.

2.   Data kindly supplied by Christine Seal.

3.   Smith, A.D. *The Derbyshire Economy in 1851*. Derby, 1977, pp. 7-8 and 34.

4.   Ibid., pp. 8-10 and 34.

5.   Ibid., pp. 35-6.

6.   Hinde, A. & Turnbull, F. 'The Population of Two Hampshire Workhouses 1851-1861', *Local Population Studies*. Vol. 61, 1998, pp. 38-53; Goose, N. 'Poverty, Old Age and Gender in Nineteenth-century England: the case of Hertfordshire', *Continuity and Change*. Vol. 20.3, 2005, pp. 360-2.

7.   Goose, N. & Basten, S. 'Almshouse Residency in 19th Century England: an interim report', *Family and Community History*. Vol. 12.1, 2009, pp. 69-70.

8.   Riden, P. & Fowkes, D. *Bolsover: castle, town and colliery*. Chichester, 2008, pp. 101-2; Hey, D. *Derbyshire - a history*, Lancaster, 2008, p. 389.

9.   Goose, 2005, pp. 360-2.

10.   Hinde & Turnbull, 1998, p. 49; Goose, 1999, p. 60; Englander, D. *Poverty and Poor Law in 19th-century Britain 1834-1914*. London, 1998, p. 34.

11.   Goose, 2005, p. 361.

12.   Smith, p. 34.

13.   Tompkins, A. 'Almshouse Versus Workhouse: residential welfare in 18th-century Oxford', *Family and Community History*. Vol. 7.1, 2004, pp. 45-58.

14.   Goose & Basten, p. 72.

15.   *Derby Mercury*, 22 Aug. 1860.

16.   *Derby Mercury*, 29 Aug. 1860.

17.   Glover, C. & Riden, P. (eds), *William Woolley's History of Derbyshire*. Chesterfield, 1981, pp. 27-8.

18.   *Derby Mercury*, 22 Aug. 1860.

CHAPTER 9
OCCUPATIONAL ALMSHOUSES
IN NORTH-EAST ENGLAND

Christine Seal

INTRODUCTION

The study area covers the counties of Durham and Northumberland, and the almshouses in the Yorkshire ports of Whitby, Scarborough and Hull. The north-east of England had a number of almshouses for various occupations including seamen, miners, keelmen, widows of clergy and workers on large estates. In the main these were for retired workers or their widows. Almshouses for seamen and mariners dominate the north-east coastal towns, while the villages of County Durham and Northumberland started to build homes for aged miners from the end of the 19th century. There were also almshouses for the labourers on the John Eden estate at Urpeth and for the estate workers of Lord Armstrong at Rothbury. The aged miners' homes were not unique to this part of England, as the county of Yorkshire set up their own association. There are, however, no occupational almshouses in Cumberland and Westmorland, just across the Pennine Hills from the north-east. The Cumbrian counties have a coastline on three sides of this region, but the author has found no almshouses for mariners in any of the major ports on the coast there.[1]

The aim of the chapter is to examine the provision of almshouses in the north-east for the seamen and their families, the keelmen and the aged miners. The discussion will include the historical background to foundation, an analysis of the demography of almshouse residents, the architecture of the buildings, a discussion of Trinity House in the north-east, a case study of the Trafalgar Square almshouses in Sunderland, and the formation of aged miners' homes.

ECONOMY AND POPULATION OF THE NORTH-EAST

Natural resources in the north-east comprised coal, lead and iron, with agriculture concentrated in most of the northern and western areas of Northumberland. In the medieval period the economy of Newcastle, on the north bank of the river Tyne, and of Gateshead on the south bank, was based on exporting coal, wool and hides. In the 16th and 17th centuries coal mining was concentrated around Tyneside and the Washington area of Wearside, where there was easy access to ports for transportation of the coal.[2] Northumberland was a rural county at the beginning of the 19th century with the population concentrated around

Newcastle-upon-Tyne. The new railways in the 19th century, funded by coal-owning families, enabled coal mining to spread further into County Durham but this was a time of horse-drawn trains rather than locomotives. The increasing number of railroads at the collieries enabled ports on the Tyne, Wear and Tees to expand and other ports were built on the Northumberland and Durham coast. With the development of coal mining in the 19th century the population of the north-east rose greatly. From just 10,000 miners employed in 1810, by 1919 there were 223,000 coal miners, of whom 154,000 were in the Durham coalfields. The major changes occurred between 1801 and 1851 with the development of industries and railways being built. The new town centre of Newcastle was developed on the gardens of a country estate from 1835, in what is described as 'the grand classical style.'[3] In the north-east the chemical industry was started and foundries industrialised. Both sides of the Tyne saw coalmining, glassmaking and heavy industry, such as ship building and gun manufacture.[4]

TABLE 9.I
Population of north-east counties and major towns

County/Town	1801	1851	1901	% increase in population between 1801 and 1901
County Durham	149,384	390,997	1,187,361	695
Northumberland	168,078	303,568	603,119	259
Newcastle	42,560	89,156	215,328	406
Gateshead	20,466	24,805	108,024	428
Sunderland	26,304	70,576	158,877	504
South Shields	14,031	35,790	97,263	593
Hull	22,161	50,670	239,517	981
Scarborough	13,673	24,615	38,161	179
Whitby	18,217	21,592	21,743	19
Middlesborough	239	7,893	116,546	48,664

Sources: Census Reports, County York, Durham and Northumberland, 1901, Population Tables I, Vol. II, England and Wales, Divisions 10-IX; Page, W. (ed.), *Victoria County History of Durham*, London, 1907, p. 244.

In the County of Durham, the increase in population, as with Newcastle, was chiefly due to manufacturing and mining. The industrial development was late, compared to other counties, and included shipbuilding, glass manufacture, coal mining, lead mining in Weardale, Teesdale and the Derwent Valley (though this had almost died out by the 20th century), and textiles in the south of the county. Iron ore was discovered in 1837 and the Consett Iron workers established in 1841.[5]

Sunderland developed as a coal port but became well-known for shipbuilding; shipyards were to be found all down the north-east coast employing large numbers of the local population. Middlesbrough, which was just a hamlet in 1801, saw a huge increase in population as it developed into a town and coal port, largely because of Darlington businessman Joseph Pease and his Quaker colleagues.

ALMSHOUSE SAMPLE FOR THE NORTH-EAST

The north Yorkshire coastal towns have been included in this study of the north-east because they provide almshouse accommodation for mariners. Fifty-three almshouses or hospitals were found in the north-east counties, but only seven of these almshouses accommodated seamen, mariners or their widows and dependents (*see* Appendix 9.1 for a list of almshouses discussed). The earliest foundation of an occupational almshouse was the Trinity Almshouses in Newcastle, founded by Trinity House in 1584, and the latest foundation was the Aged Miners' Homes at the end of the 19th century and the beginning of the 20th century. Almshouses usually accommodated small numbers of people, such as the Wilson's Mariners' Asylum in Scarborough, where just fourteen people were provided

Illustration 9.a. Master Mariners Asylum, Tynemouth
Photo © C. Seal, 2010

with places. At the other extreme there were the Trafalgar Almshouses in Sunderland, accommodating 145 almspeople in 1881.

ALMSHOUSES FOR SEAFARERS IN THE NORTH-EAST

Tynemouth, the most northerly port on the north bank of the Tyne estuary, had just one almshouse: the Master Mariners' Asylum founded in 1829 by the Tyneside Masters as a Friendly Society to provide pensions for mariners when aged sixty or incapacitated (*see* Illustration 9.a.). The Society then built a home in North Shields for elderly master mariners and their wives, completed in 1840. The Tyne Mariners' Asylum was neo-Tudor in style and built on land given by the Duke of Northumberland; the building has a central clock tower with commemorative plaque and a statue of the Duke is found in the garden entrance at the front. By the early 20th century the society had merged with the Tyne Mariners Institute and formed the Tyne Mariners Benevolent Institution.

In Newcastle the Trinity Almshouses were built by Trinity House in 1584 and the Keelmen's Hospital dates from 1701. Tyneside keelmen were employed by the Newcastle Hostmen (a cartel of business men who formed a monopoly to control the export of coal from the River Tyne). One penny was deducted weekly from the keelmen's wages for every tide they had gone during the week to fund assistance to the men.[6] The trustees were stewards of the Hostmen's Guild. Disputes arose over the charging mechanism and from 1730 keelmen started their own Friendly Society. Disputes arose regularly with the Hostmen who ran the Hospital until 1787, when an Act of Parliament established it as a charity. The Keelmen's Hospital contained a plain brick quadrangle with the residents living 'in crowded chares' [lanes] and the south range included a central square clock tower (*see* Illustration 9.b).[7] The Hospital was taken over by Newcastle Corporation in the 1870s.[8]

Illustration 9.b. Keelmen's Hospital, south range, Newcastle *Photo © C. Seal 2010*

South Shields is the next port south of Newcastle and it contained thirty-nine cottages, called the Master Mariner Cottages, built here from 1843 for aged seamen, widows and orphans. The almshouses had Tudor detail and numbers 1-22 were set round three sides of a garden courtyard. The remainder of the almshouses, numbers 23-39, were built around 1859 with the same detail, and together with the earlier buildings now form a large square through the centre of which runs Broughton Road.[9] When analysis was made of the census for 1881 and 1901, 130 residents in these cottages were families and children, not all of whom appeared to have connections with the sea.

Sunderland was one of many ports around England burdened with discharged seamen and with many widows of lost or dead seamen. By the mid 19th century relief was required for an 'average of 800 widows, 800 orphans and other children and for 300 worn out, disabled or temporarily unemployed seamen'.[10] The seamen were supported by the Muster Roll Charity paid for by the employers of Sunderland, which provided accommodation initially at Assembly Garth in the town and, from 1840, additional accommodation was provided at Trafalgar Square Almshouses. In Bishopwearmouth, a parish of Sunderland, the Marine Institution was set up in Crowtree Lane in 1820 for widows of master mariners or their unmarried daughters. In Sunderland an Act was passed in 1747: 'An Act for the Relief and Support of maimed or disabled Seamen, and the Widows and Children of such as shall be killed, slain, or drowned in the Merchants' Service'. All ships registered at Sunderland were required to pay 6d per month for 'every sailor on board, whilst employed'. This was paid by the owners and not deducted from the sailor's wages.[11] In contrast, in Newcastle and Hull an Act of Parliament in 1742 levied 'the sum of 6d per month, to be paid out of the wages of all seamen employed in ships and vessels belonging to their respective ports.'[12] By 1827 the sum of £2,000 had been collected but this was inadequate to support the 1,800 claimants, mainly widows and dependent children.

The Seamen's Houses stand at Whitby in Yorkshire (*see* Illustration 9.c. colour Plate VIII); the front was built of brick in Jacobean style by Sir George Gilbert Scott in 1842. Further south Scarborough has two sets of almshouses. The Trinity House Almshouses in St Sepulchre Street were built in 1832 and described by Pevsner as 'purely classical'. The Wilson's Mariners' Asylum was built four years later in Castle Road one storey in height 'of red brick and gabled and dull' . Brian Bailey described them as: 'dull utilitarian buildings typical of the new industrial approach to housing the poor'.[13] In contrast, *A Topographical Dictionary of England* describes the Wilson's Mariners' Asylum as 'a beautiful range in the Elizabethan style'.[14] These were two very different opinions on the style of these almshouses. Each almshouse comprised two rooms: 'most comfortably and conveniently arranged for their poor occupants'.[15] Hull was similar to Scarborough in having several sets of almshouses for mariners. The Master Mariners' Almshouses of 1834, sadly flattened in the Second World War, were described as having thirteen bays with bays one and thirteen 'flanked by giant Doric pilasters' but the rest was plain.[16] Trinity Almshouses in Hull are described later in the discussion of Trinity House.

Only two of the almshouses discussed in this chapter, the Woodcock and Marine Institution at Sunderland, and the Wilson's Mariner's Asylum at Scarborough, were endowed by an individual. All the others were founded by a society, corporation, local lodges (Aged Miners' Homes), Trinity House or Muster Roll.

The terms of endowment were important in determining who was given an almshouse place. Admission to the almshouses was mostly determined by age, gender and residence. Elizabeth Woodcock, founder of the Marine Institution at Crowtree Road, was precise in the requirements for admittance to the Institution. They included:

- Aged over 56
- Irreproachable moral character
- Member of the Church of England
- Widow or unmarried daughter of master mariner
- Master mariner to be resident in Sunderland or Bishopwearmouth, a commander of ships belonging to port of Sunderland
- Woman resident in Sunderland or Bishopwearmouth at nomination
- Not receiving poor relief
- No income greater than £20 per annum[17]

Inhabitants were expected to conform to a level of respectability and be of irreproachable character.[18] By 1906 the Charity Commission rules required almspeople for the Marine Institution to be selected after 'investigation of the character and circumstances of the applicants ... [and] whether they have shown reasonable providence' and preference was given to those longest resident in the parish. The investigation and checking of applicants was to be carried out by the Charity Organisation Society (established in 1869) or 'other like agency'.[19] This was the only almshouse investigated to mention another agency.

THE DEMOGRAPHY OF NORTH-EAST ALMSHOUSES

This section analyses the demography of the residents of the thirteen almshouses for seamen in County Durham, Northumberland and North Yorkshire. It includes a discussion of their gender ratios, marital status, age structure and the number of resident relatives, using census data for 1851, 1881 and 1901. The analysis will concentrate on the 1881 and 1901 censuses to show the demographic profile in the late 19th century compared with that at the beginning of the 20th century. Qualitative information has been used to expand the understanding of a particular almshouse; it was not available for every almshouse, but helped to give an insight into, for example, the type of person entering the house, as the analysis of the life of Richard Tether will demonstrate in the discussion of Trinity House Almshouses below.

Table 9.II lists the almshouses for seamen and mariners in the north-east and gives the demographic profile for each almshouse in 1881. Only females were resident in one house: the Woodcock and Marine Institution. Overall, females represented 61.5 per cent of the selected almshouse population (Table 9.II) and the proportion of females over sixty was very similar (61.9 per cent). The percentage of residents over sixty in all the selected almshouses is 48 per cent, but if Keelmen and South Shields are excluded from the data then the proportion of those over sixty in the almshouses is 70 per cent.

TABLE 9.II
The demographic profile of selected almshouses for seamen and mariners in the north-east of England, 1881

	N. of almspeople			N. of almspeople over 60 years			Relatives resident	Marital status		
	Total	M	F	Total	M	F		Mar	Wid	S
Trinity, Newcastle	28	9	19	16	7	9	8	11	10	4
Tynemouth	9	3	6	5	2	3	4	3	2	4
Trafalgar Sq	145	57	88	116	46	70	25	52	72	14
Woodcock	5	0	5	3	0	3	2	0	2	2
Keelmen Hosp	178	83	95	12	8	4	106	56	14	25
South Shields	146	62	84	13	3	10	84	30	26	36
Assembly Garth	80	32	48	63	26	37	13	32	15	12
Carr Lane Mariners	52*	19	33	50	19	31	0	23	28	0
Carr Lane Master Mariners	40	9	31	36	9	27	4	14	22	4
Trinity, Scar	47	17	30	27	11	16	9	16	21	2
Wilson Asylum	20	5	15	13	4	9	4	5	11	2
Seamen Hosp, Scarborough	69	23	46	30	11	19	20	22	19	11
Whitby	90	31	59	52	20	32	18	36	28	7
TOTALS	909	350	559	436	166	270	297	300	270	123
		38.5%	61.5%		38.1%	61.9%				

*six staff not included

Table 9.III gives the demographic profile for each almshouse in 1901. Of the fourteen almshouses listed, only one was solely for females (still Woodcock). Overall, there were more females than males in most of the other houses (the exceptions being the Wilson Asylum at Scarborough and the Whitby Almshouse). For the population over sixty, females represented 55.7 per cent of the almshouse population, but at the individual house level, they outnumbered males in eleven of the fourteen almshouses.

TABLE 9.III
The demographic profile of selected almshouses in the north-east of England, 1901

	N. of almspeople			N. of almspeople over 60 years			Relatives resident	Marital status		
	Total	M	F	Total	M	F		Mar	Wid	S
Trinity, Newcastle	20	6	14	13	6	7	7	9	5	5
Tynemouth	71	27	44	27	9	18	31	29	11	12
Trafalgar Sq	150	65	85	142	64	78	5	89	53	9
Woodcock	9	0	9	8	0	8	0	0	7	2
Keelmen Hosp	175	87	88	24	16	8	115	46	20	32
South Shields	116	51	65	17	6	11	55	43	12	32
Assembly Garth	67	32	35	59	31	28	5	22	39	6
Carr Lane, Mariners	50	16	34	44	16	28	9	24	22	5
Carr Lane, Master Mariners	48	17	31	44	17	27	0	28	16	3
Trinity Almshs	24	11	13	23	10	13	0	10	14	0
Trinity, Scar	29	9	20	26	9	17	3	15	11	2
Wilson Asylum	23	14	9	22	14	8	2	16	7	2
Seamen Hosp	50	19	31	34	15	19	8	22	19	8
Whitby	83	44	39	45	21	24	21	24	27	19
TOTALS	915	398	517	528	234	294	261	377	263	137
		43.4%	56.5%		44.3%	55.7%				

Attention is drawn in Table 9.III to the Keelmen's Hospital where only twenty-four of the 175 residents were over sixty. Seventy were under eighteen and therefore not included in the marital status calculations; over two-thirds of the residents were relatives. This Hospital was clearly not a typical almshouse accommodating almspeople over sixty. The Mariner Cottages at South Shields was a further example where only seventeen of the 116 residents were over sixty years of age and again they were accommodating relatives of the almsperson. Unfortunately few records survive for this almshouse, other than architectural details, so it has been assumed that this was the intended composition of the almshouse, comprising almspeople and their families. If these two almshouses are excluded from the data, the proportion of residents over sixty in 1901 increases from 58 per cent to 78 per cent. In Trafalgar Square, only eight of the almspeople were under sixty and only a small number were single. Both Carr Lane Almshouses in Hull were dominated by female residents.

Between 1881 and 1901 the percentage of females in the almshouses declined from 61.5 per cent to 56.5 per cent. From all the almshouses in the 1881 sample, just over half the residents were female. The 1901 census sample contained two almshouses with predominately male residents. The proportion of residents in the almshouses over sixty years increased from 48 per cent in 1881 to 58 per cent in 1901 but these figures were distorted by the two almshouses housing families. If Keelmen and South Shields are excluded from the data, the proportion of residents over sixty years of age increased from 70 per cent in 1881 to 78 per cent in 1901. The percentage of almspeople over sixty years in the north-east almshouse sample is lower than that found by Clive Leivers in Derbyshire. Leivers examined the almshouses and workhouse population in the County of Derbyshire, an agricultural, mining and industrial county, particularly around the central and northern parts of the county. Derbyshire does not have the heavy industry of the north east but is the county with most similarities to the north east where an analysis of almshouse demography has been completed. The Derbyshire sample showed that 76 per cent of the almshouse population were over sixty years in 1881 and by 1901 this had risen to 89 per cent.[20]

So how does the demography of the selected north-east almshouses compare to other findings? Anne Langley found that residents of Warwickshire almshouses comprised two-thirds of women (68 per cent), while Goose and Basten, in their preliminary data set, found almost three-quarters of almshouse people were female.[21] The north-east sample is distorted by the unusual almshouse population found in two of the sample (Keelmen's Hospital and South Shields) and shows only just over half the almshouse population of the selected sample were women.

TRINITY HOUSE IN THE NORTH-EAST

Trinity House was formed in 1514 by a royal charter from Henry VIII to the Guild of the Holy Trinity, to regulate the pilotage of harbours and the erection of lighthouses on the coast. The Guild was renamed Trinity House and is responsible for the safety of shipping and the well-being of seafarers. Even before the royal charter was granted a number of almshouses for aged mariners and their families were being maintained by individual Trinity Houses.[22] In England there were only four of these hospitals, at London, Newcastle-upon-Tyne, Hull and Scarborough, of which three were in the north-east. The sailors would contribute to a fund to run the houses: 'so they knew there would be somewhere to go when they had to retire.'[23] Newcastle was the most important port in the north-east and the Society of Masters and Mariners of Newcastle was established in the town in 1492. Trinity House in Newcastle had responsibility from the Tees in the south to Holy Island off the Northumberland coast, while Trinity House at Hull's responsibility stretched from the Tees to Winterton Ness in Norfolk. At Trinity House in Hull the main revenue until 1872 came from primage (a payment on each ton of freight). This was a duty collected from the master of ships and averaged nearly £3,400 a year between 1813 and 1822. By 1876 the income per year was around £12,000.[24]

The Trinity House Newcastle Almshouses were established by the Guild of the Blessed Trinity and incorporated in 1492 and re-founded in 1584. In 1505 the Guild secured land for a peppercorn rent of a 'red rose'; this land was known as Dalton's Place in Broad Chare and was rented from Ralph Hebborn. The first charter in Newcastle permitted the Brethren to levy dues on ships trading into the River Tyne at the rate of two pence per English ship or four pence per foreign ship. Changes to the regulations resulted in the formation of the Newcastle-upon-Tyne Commission and the collection of fees by the new commission. The result was that the Fraternity of Hostmen at Newcastle and the Trinity House at Kingston upon Hull lost the income they had derived from shipping. A succession of almshouses was built and rebuilt on the site to house seafarers and their dependants in need. In the 21st century Trinity House supports the charity of the Tyne Mariners' Benevolent Institution at Tynemouth and the Sunderland Aged Merchant Seamen's Homes and Distressed Mariners Fund.[25]

The Newcastle Trinity Almshouses comprised two ranges of dwellings able to accommodate thirteen aged men and thirteen widows. It was proposed in 1505 that the Trinity House site should contain a meeting house, chapel and almshouses, but many changes were made to the site over the years. In 1791 the boardroom (also known as the Election Room) was rebuilt.[26] A plaque on the building records the rebuilding of 1787 (*see* Illustration 9.d.). According to Pevsner's guide of 1992 there was a further block of almshouses on the far side of the raised yard built about 1782, then a second larger courtyard called the Low Yard, and on the south side of this yard was 'the gable end of a modest almshouse block dated 1820'.[27] Approximately 340 brethren, the majority of them out-pensioners, were assisted by Newcastle Trinity House.[28] The out-pensioner list provides information on the type of person assisted by the House. This included Mrs Margaret Watson who was born in 1840 and had three dependent children: Joseph was born in September 1874; John in December 1877; and Cecil in June 1880. In 1887 Mrs Watson received varying amounts each quarter, ranging from £9 10s. to £11 10s. In contrast, on the next page of the ledger was the list of the widows of freemen who only received out-pensioner payments of £2 5s. per quarter.[29]

In a petition for a Newcastle Trinity Almshouse place, Ann Turnbull wrote: 'that your Petitioner is the widow of Robert Turnbull who was admitted a brother of the said house in 1766; that he was several years Master of the *Friendship* of London and others out of this port ... [the] petitioner will be 57 years of age against May next'. Her proof of eligibility came from her local church and confirmed she was the widow of Robert Turnbull 'and that she is a woman of a good character'.[30]

As with the early foundation at Newcastle, the Hospital of Trinity House in Hull was founded in 1369 and provided a refuge for retired sailors. Trinity Almshouses were rebuilt in 1753 with accommodation for thirty-two residents. By 1823 there was accommodation for thirty-four brethren and each received 7s. per week. In addition to the Trinity Almshouses in Hull there were other local almshouse charities managed by Trinity House. These included Ferrier's Hospital for ten people built in the 17th century and rebuilt in 1822; by 1823 there were twenty-one rooms and a weekly stipend of between 4s. 6d. and 10s. The available documents do not

Illustration 9.d. Almshouse plaque on wall of almshouses in inner yard at Trinity House, Newcastle *Photo © Christine Seal 2015*

explain why there was such a wide variation between the lower and higher amount paid as a stipend. Ferrier's Hospital was granted to Trinity House around the 1630s. Robinson's Almshouses were also granted to Trinity House around 1697 and housed six seamen's widows.[31] In 1834 Trinity House built the Master Mariners Almshouses in Carr Lane for forty-four residents, and the Mariners' Almshouses, also in Carr Lane, at dates between 1837 and 1857. One resident of Hull Trinity Almshouse was Captain Richard Tether. Born in 1825 he married Mary Ann Elliott in 1846; they had six children, all born in Hull but only three are listed as alive in the 1911 census. Richard's marine registry ticket says he first went to sea in March 1839 as an apprentice to the Merchant Marine East India trade, just fourteen years old. By 1858 he was a master mariner. He is said to have been Master of Trinity House Almshouse on Posterngate in Hull between 1896 and 1906, although the 1901 census only lists him as a resident of the almshouse. Richard and his wife were still living in the Trinity Almshouses in Hull at the 1911 census age eighty-six and eighty-three, respectively. Richard's wife died in 1913 and he died in 1921 but there is no mention in the family history as to whether he spent his final years in the almshouse.[32]

Trinity House Hospital in Scarborough was established in 1602 to provide a refuge for retired sailors and consisted of thirty-one dwellings for married and disabled seamen or their widows. The residents of this Hospital received just 7s. 6d. each, half of that paid in the Merchant Seamen's Hospital in the same town.[33]

TRAFALGAR SQUARE MERCHANT SEAMEN'S ALMSHOUSES

The fourteen almshouses at Church Walk in Sunderland were built by William Drysdale in 1840 and were to house aged merchant seamen and their wives and widows. The almshouses are laid out in a square with railings on one side, two storeys high with fourteen houses divided into flats. The listed building detail states there are four houses on each side, one in each corner, and three along the top, built of brick, but this makes only thirteen when the census details give fourteen houses. In the census, each house contained approximately twelve to fourteen people and was divided into separate rooms. In the 1881 census, for example, house one contained thirteen people, with eight of these listed as head of a household, four of whom were married (Table 9.IV). Apart from a grandson to resident Ann Stewart, and the wife of John Brown, all residents were over sixty years of age.

TABLE 9.IV
Residents of 1 Trafalgar Square in 1881

Name	Relationship	Marital Status	Age	Occupation	Place of Birth
Ann Stewart	Head	Widow	75		Sunderland
Stafford Stewart	g/son		17	Mariner	Sunderland
William Young	Head	Widow	81	Retired mariner	Berwick on Tweed
Margaret Thompson	Head	Widow	80		Durham
George White	Head	Married	75	Retired mariner	Sunderland
Elizabeth White	Wife	Married	69		Sunderland
Samuel Dawson	Head	Married	74	Nightwatchmen dock	Sunderland
Rhoda Dawson	Wife	Married	70		Sunderland
Richard Hunter	Head	Married	76	Ret. Ship carpenter	Sunderland
Mary Hunter	Wife	Married	78		Sunderland
John Blakelock	Head	Widow	81	Retired mariner	Sunderland
John Brown	Head	Married	66	Retired mariner	Sunderland
Elizabeth Brown	Wife	Married	50		Sunderland

Source: RG11/5000, fo.20 P.34

Each house has two windows on each floor with a centrally positioned door. In the centre of the building there was a painted plaque in high relief with a sailor and lion supporting escutcheons and maritime symbols. Under this is the inscription: 'TRAFALGAR SQUARE, ERECTED BY THE TRUSTEES OF THE MUSTER ROLL ANNO DOMINI 1840, UNDER THE 4TH AND 5TH OF WILLIAM IV' together with the names of the Trustees.[34] Above the painted plaque: 'ENGLAND EXPECTS EVERY MAN TO DO HIS DUTY'.

The demographic profile of Trafalgar Square Almshouses (Table 9.V) shows that females dominated the residents, whether as wives given residence alongside their husbands, or as widows entitled to a place in their own right. Widows outnumbered other residents (except in 1851 and 1901) ranging from 35 to 58 per cent of residents. The census year 1901 was unusual in that there was a higher percentage of married couples resident in the house. There was no change to the gender balance between 1851 and 1901, where women dominated in every census.

TABLE 9.V
The demographic profile of merchant seamen's homes (Trafalgar Square): 1851-1901

Date	N. of Almspeople			Resident Relatives	Marital Status of residents(%)			Age	
	Total	M	F		Mar	Wid	Single	Average	Range
1851	174	75	99	35	58	38	15	69	60-90
1861	155	59	96	26	39	42	10	69	60-90
1871	148	51	97	21	38	45	7	73	60-101
1881	145	57	88	25	36	50	10	73	61-87
1891	130	42	88	8	35	58	5	71	60-97
1901	150	65	85	5	59	35	6	73	60-84

Sources: 1851 HO107/2397 fo.84 p.70; 1861 RG9/3777 fo.67 p.43; 1871 RG10/5013 fo.52 p.26; 1881 RG11/5000 fo.20 p.34; 1891 RG12/4143 fo.136 p.27; 1901 RG13/4719 fo.28 p.22.

Notes: The average age and range of ages excludes all those residents aged under 60.
Wives of residents are included in the marital status numbers but not included in the resident relatives. Children under 18 have been excluded from the 'single' count.

The average age for the six census years was 71.3 years, range 69 to 73, with the lowest average age around the mid 19th century. The number of single residents decreased at the same time that the number of resident relatives decreased. Were the Trustees clamping down on family members living in the almshouses with residents? As few records survive for this house there was no way of confirming the reason for the decrease in the number of relatives. In 1867 there is reference in the Muster Roll minutes for both Trafalgar Square and its neighbouring almshouse, Assembly Garth, to an average age of seventy-one years and four months. There were thirty-four married residents, fifty-three were widowed, eighteen single and together with people living with the residents (thirty-four), this brought a total of 139 living in the almshouses.[35] The 1891 census produces some unusual data with the lowest number of residents in the almshouses but whether this was down to the census enumerator we cannot be sure. No admission registers survive for this almshouse apart from the tenancy forms signed in the mid 19th century. The tenancy forms or agreements ask the almsperson to agree that:

> I, the undersigned ... of Sunderland, in the County of Durham, a pensioner
> under the Merchant Seamen's Fund Winding-up Act ... do hereby acknowledge
> that I occupy the Room No ... in Trafalgar Square or Assembly Garth, as a
> tenant, at the Will and Pleasure of the Trustees for the time being acting in the
> Port of Sunderland ... and I agree with such Trustees that I will quit possession
> of the said Room, and deliver the Room to them, at any time on demand being
> made. Witness my hand this ... day of ... 18...[36]

There were problems with reading this compilation of tenant agreements. The agreements found were not in chronological order and had been copied from the originals (which have not been deposited with any archives). Using the records found, 193 pensioners were admitted to Trafalgar Square between 1861 and 1872, an average of seventeen new pensioners each year. During the eleven years, the proportion of men admitted was 54 per cent but this is at odds with the census findings that show more female residents in every census. It appears, therefore, that this is not a complete record of admissions between 1861 and 1872 and, if the originals could be found, it would be expected that records would show a preponderance of females admitted to the almshouses.

The surviving papers for Trafalgar Square are silent on the residential qualifications for a place in the almshouses. As Clive Leivers found in the analysis of selected Derbyshire almshouses, not all occupants had been resident in the locality or required to live in the locality as part of the conditions to gain an almshouse place.[37] Were places in Trafalgar Square restricted to those from the local area? The residents of Trafalgar Square were not required to be born in Sunderland or to be resident in Sunderland for a specific length of time. The analysis of birthplaces showed that over 60 per cent of residents in the almshouse were born in Sunderland (except in 1861) and a further 5-12 per cent were born in coastal towns in England (Table 9.VI).

TABLE 9.VI
Place of birth of merchant seamen home residents, 1851-1901

Year	% born in Sunderland	% born in ports in England
1851	61	7
1861	52	12
1871	62	5
1881	65	11
1891	71	9
1901	65	8

Under 50 per cent of residents in each census had an occupation or former occupation described in the census (Table 9.VII). The percentage of residents described as mariners, seamen or retired mariners varied between 19 and 34 per cent. In the case of widows, the most frequent reference in the occupations was to 'former mariner's widow'. No overall conclusions can be drawn on occupation as a high percentage of residents were women with no occupation given.

TABLE 9.VII
Occupations of merchant seamen home residents, 1851-1901

Year	% described with an occupation	% of residents described as mariners/seamen
1851	48	34
1861	38	30
1871	35	24
1881	39	19
1891	54	28
1901	42	26

Note: those described as 'former mariner's widow' were excluded from this analysis.

THE AGED MINERS' HOMES

Unlike the homes for seamen, which were endowed by individuals and trade associations, the homes for the aged miners were endowed by their own relief fund. The person behind the vision: 'to provide a Home for the Aged Miner and his wife as they enter upon the eventide of life', was Joseph Hopper. Joseph, born in 1856 at Windy Nook near Gateshead, was a working miner and a Methodist local preacher and went on to become a member of the Board of Guardians and other public bodies.[38] The origin of the aged miners' homes goes back to 1898 and the founding of the Durham Aged Mineworkers' Homes Association (DAMHA). The miner, once old and unable to work, had to leave his tied cottage, and for many the workhouse was the only option in old age.

Each area in County Durham and Northumberland had its association or lodge and Joseph was a member of the Felling Lodge and a delegate to the Durham Miners' Association. Joseph brought a resolution to the Northumberland and Durham Miners' Permanent Relief Fund in June 1894 that:

> The miners of the county were unable, for the most part, to make full and adequate provision for old age, and suggested that some action should be taken with a view to providing Homes for Aged Miners.[39]

When all the discussions on providing homes was taking place there were 115,361 members contributing to the Miners' Permanent Relief Fund. Joseph put forward a further resolution at a meeting in Newcastle-upon-Tyne:

> That this meeting is of opinion that whilst the four shillings per week which our aged miners receive from the Superannuation Fund is helpful it is insufficient to provide an aged couple with food, firing, shelter and clothing in a reasonable manner ... we resolve to push forward the movement for the establishment of Aged Miners' Homes ... according to the requirements and circumstances of each locality.[40]

Joseph Hopper was to become Secretary and Clerk of Works of the Durham Aged Miners' Homes Association. When he died in 1909, his friend John Oxberry continued the work.[41] Dr Wilson was the first President of DAMHA and served from 1898 until his death in 1915. Like Joseph Hopper, John Wilson had experienced pit life, worked as a sailor, but following a religious conversion, he became a Primitive Methodist and progressed in his public life as Chairman of Durham County Council, a magistrate, Member of Parliament and a union agent.[42]

The Northumberland Aged Mineworkers' Homes Association (NAMHA) was established in 1900 to help retired miners find accommodation when evicted from their miner home. Started initially by the Northumberland Miners' Association, it was supported by local cooperatives, Deputies Association and Mechanic Union branches. These branches and associations encouraged the miners to pay a little money per week to the association. The first homes built by NAMHA were at East Chevington near Broomhill in 1902 and William Cobb from the Byker area of Newcastle was the first applicant for a home at East Chevington, his name drawn out of the hat; William was married and aged 68 years.[43]

How was the purchase of land and buildings funded in County Durham? The committee of Hopper, Wallace, Ede, Johnson and Wilson were determined that it would not be compulsory to contribute to the fund. Instead they proposed a voluntary contribution of one shilling per member per year from all in the Miners' Association, which would provide a sum of approximately £3,000. The Miners' Lodges together with the Federation Board and the Deputies readily contributed to the housing fund, while donations were also received from members of the public.

Illustration 9.e. Aged Miners' Home Ebchester, County Durham. *Photo © C. Seal, 2012*

Where were the first aged miners' homes built? The building and administration of the homes was undertaken by a district committee, consisting of colliery union members. One member of the district committee represented the District on the Durham Mineworkers Association Committee. Prior to the setting up of DAMHA, the Boldon Lodge had established homes at Boldon Colliery. The Lodge rented an old mansion and two nearby cottages from the Ecclesiastical Commission, and the building was converted into tenements by the miners for the old men of the Boldon Lodge. By 1904 the Bolden Lodge had been granted a ninety-nine-year lease under the name of the 'Boldon Colliery Aged Miners' Homes Association'.[44] The second group of homes at Emmaville near Ryton was the work of a coal owner, Dr John Bell Simpson, the managing director of Stella Coal Co. Ltd, in memory of his father.[45] As the association was entering into further negotiations with the Ecclesiastical Commission to rent nine acres of land in three parts of County Durham, an opportunity to purchase the colliery village of Haswell Moor arose at a cheap price. Haswell Moor consisted of 112 houses each with a garden, all of which were freehold and in a poor state; the cost per house to purchase and repair was £25. One generous donation of £25 for a Haswell cottage arrived from the Coroner of Findon Hill in the county and his wife. Mr Graham wrote: 'we would like to feel that we have made one old couple happy by paying the cost of one of the Haswell Moor cottages, as intended to be made fit for habitation and therefore propose to subscribe £25'.[46] At the same time as the Haswell Moor homes were purchased, the Aged Miners' Association purchased a further ninety-eight houses and school buildings at Shotton for £1,300. These houses were leased to two local coal companies and the school buildings sold after three years for £850.[47]

The opening of the houses at Haswell Moor in October 1899 was conducted by the Chairman, Dr Wilson, with an inaugural address given by the Bishop of Durham, Dr Westcott. Dr Westcott said: 'that Durham was pointing the way to a solution of the problem of the Aged Miner and expressed his belief that the Scheme would be considerably extended in the County and beyond'.[48] As at HaswellMoor, the redundant colliery houses in Houghall and Shincliffe Bank Top were also converted into aged miner homes. Most of the homes consisted of one bedroom, living room/kitchen and scullery and a back garden to grow vegetables.[49] The twenty aged miner homes at Ushaw were opened in 1910 and funds to erect these single storied terraced homes were raised by the New Brancepeth, Bearpark and Ushaw Moor Lodges. Most of the homes were built in the 1920s across approximately seventy sites in County Durham. By 1924 the DAMHA had 1,000 homes, a combination of newly built and renovated ex-colliery dwellings.[50] When the Joseph Hopper Homes at Birtley were renovated in 1996, a tin box was found in the eaves of the building. One of the workmen who built the houses in 1923, John Francis Callan, had left a note saying: 'I wish the old people who shall live in these homes will always find their lives happy and gay, and may their last years be the happiest of all'.[51] John Callan senior came from Castleblayrey in County Monaghan and was the foreman in charge for builders, Charles & Co. Table 9.VIII is a selective time line of aged miner homes in County Durham and Northumberland described in the archives of the DAMHA and NAMHA.[52]

The aged miners' homes at Houghton-le-Spring were built at the end of 1926 and consisted of two rows of terraced bungalows. Plaques and foundation stones detail the local dignitaries who laid stones on 9 October 1926. The Homes Committee comprised twenty people whose names are listed on a dedication stone on the gable of the East Row homes. The homes were built from a small voluntary weekly levy from miner wages and from donations of land and materials from mine owners and other people; they were let free of charge.[53]

Each group of aged miner homes laid down their own rules for the residents to enable the smooth running of the houses and to keep the peace. For example, at the Joicey Aged Miners' Homes, the Lambton Collieries Ltd (who were responsible for these homes) required each resident to be 'of sober, respectable habits and must not be guilty of or permit any disorderly conduct'. The residents, or as the rules described them, the tenants, were required to keep the front garden 'cultivated' and in good order, and would receive sufficient coal for domestic use only. Unfortunately for the wives of the miners, they could be required to vacate an aged miners' home on the death of their husband if they were under fifty-five years of age.[54]

TABLE 9.VIII
Timeline of Aged Miner Homes in County Durham and Northumberland*

Date	Event/Homes
1896	First homes opened at Down Hill House, Boldon
1897	Ten dwellings and 106 dwellings turned into homes by Dr J B Simpson at Emmaville (Ryton) for Stella Coal Co Ltd
1898	Founding of Durham Aged Mineworkers Homes Association
1899	John Johnson Memorial Homes, Haswell Moor; 98 houses and school buildings bought at Shotton for £1,300 and leased to two coal companies; Aged Miners' Home at Rowlands Gill opened
1900	Northumberland Aged Mineworkers Homes Association founded
1902	Dr Simpson provided ten homes at Throckley, Northumberland; Broomhill Aged Miners' Home opened (NBL)
1908	Houses built at Wrekenton and named Wallace Village
1909	200 homes available for married couples
1910	Coronation Homes at Esh Winning opened
1910	475 homes available
1911	Aged Miners' Home Eldon Bank Top, Shildon opened
1912	Woodhorn Colliery homes opened (NBL)
1913	Queen Mary visits homes at Ushaw Moor, Middlestone Moor, Shincliffe
Before 1914	Sixty-five houses at Shincliffe gifted by J H Love and Ecclesiastical Commissioners; Houses at West Pelton, Tanfield Lea by Lord Joicey; six cottages at Langley Moor by North Brancepeth Coal Co plus land; Thornley Aged Miners' Homes built; Middlestone Moor and Shincliffe built
1918	Forty-eight houses at South Shields by Harton Coal Company; 16 houses at Boldon by Ecclesiastical Commission providing land; William Robinson Memorial Homes built at Hetton le Hole.
1920	Total 700 homes built to this date
1923	1,600 people housed in DAMH
1924	Aged Miners' Home Langley Park opened; Joseph Hopper Memorial Trust Homes, Birtley opened
1925	Forty houses at Watling Street, Langley Park, Chopwell, Allendale
1926	Houghton-le-Spring Aged Miners' Homes built at Dairy Lane;
nd	Fishburn Aged Miners' Homes; Byron Terrace at Seaham

* This timeline includes only some of the aged miners' homes as an example. There were many built between 1900 and the 1930s

Source: Atkinson, G., *The Miner's Heritage, a History of the Durham Aged Mineworkers' Homes Association, 1898-1998*, www.durhamhomes.org.uk/theminersheritage, pp. 28-9.

In a letter published in the village of Thornley, assistance was asked from the public to help to carry out the building of twelve aged workmen's homes. The letter went on to say that Thornley was unusual in that the colliery owners did not hold any land in the neighbourhood and as a result a great deal of money was expended in purchasing the land.[55] Dr Wilson launched the scheme in 1913 and after that date the Thornley workmen subscribed each week and raised sufficient to purchase the site. The correspondence does not indicate how long the Thornley men and villagers contributed to the fund. When the foundation stone for eight houses was laid at Randolph Colliery by Sir A F Pease, he said: 'there could be no finer work, surely, than to provide for the comfort and happiness of aged miners who had spent nearly all of their lives in daily toil in that district, and other places'.[56] Building was to start in the spring of 1914 at an estimated cost of £3,000 and comprised a terrace of single-storey bungalows. The Thornley Committee felt that all sections of the community were in sympathy with the scheme and would want to contribute. The rules for Thornley Aged Miners' Home required residents to be members of their trade unions and ex-workmen of the colliery and stated that a new employee of the colliery would be required to work for ten years before his name could be submitted for an aged miners' home.[57] Each community set its own rules and, as other aged miners' homes rules have not yet been found, it is not clear whether union membership was a countywide requirement.

CONCLUSION

Research for the FACHRS almshouse project identified fifty-three almshouses in County Durham and Northumberland, plus a further three sets of almshouses provided for the estate workers of John Eden and Lord Armstrong. Seven of the fifty-three almshouses accommodated aged seamen and mariners. In addition to these almshouses there were many aged miners' homes built in the 20th century. Only four were discussed in this chapter. This chapter has focused on the almshouses for seamen and the homes for aged miners. These differed from the other almshouses in that only two were endowed by an individual, the rest being endowed by a Society, a local Lodge or corporation.

The north-east was an area of heavy industry, of natural resources in coal, lead and iron ore and of a coastline that enabled ship-building industries and large ports to flourish. The population of the region increased substantially as a result of the development of these industries in the early 19th century, leading to pressure on provision for the elderly. What was to happen to the retired seamen, the aged miners or their widows when they were no longer able to support themselves? Of the huge number of sailors and mariners in the ports of the north-east, only 915 men and women were accommodated in almshouses in 1901, the vast majority being left to fend for themselves in old age or widowhood. This was, however, not so true for aged miners because whole villages were taken over by the DAMHA to help accommodate them and their wives. Without the initiatives described in this chapter, the only recourse was to the workhouse for aged miners, seamen and their widows unable to support themselves in old age. This is an area for further research.

The proportion of females to males in this north-east sample is low compared with other county studies. The proportion of residents over sixty in the almshouses studied (excluding two discussed below) increased from 70 per cent in 1881 to 78 per cent in 1901. The Keelmen's Hospital and the South Shields Mariners Cottages, however, did not contain the usual age group: their residents included few over sixty years old (14 per cent and 15 per cent, respectively) and there were also large numbers of relatives present in these two houses. It might be questioned whether these two almshouses should have been included in this study, because of the high number of residents under sixty and those without seafaring occupations. Both almshouses, however, had a condition of admission that they were for seafarers or their widows and therefore met the requirement as an occupational almshouse for inclusion in this study.

In building the first aged miners' homes, the Durham miners 'took a long step in the path of benevolence':

> The ultimate success of a movement like the Aged Miners' Homes Scheme lies in the willingness of the thousands of workmen about the mines to assist. Based on that, the county can be studded with homes where the aged and worn-out miner and his partner can find home comfort and warmth when the sun of their life is nearing the setting and the shadows of life's evening are gathering thick around them. No young man can measure the full meaning of such provision, but all can feel the rich mental luxury which will assuredly result from taking part in the providing.[58]

At the Joicey Homes in Thornley all applicants for an aged miners' home were required to be union members. In the 21st century the Aged Miners' Homes are assisting in the regeneration of coalfield communities; they are now open to the general public, but points are awarded for colliery service, age and years on the waiting list.[59]

This chapter has enabled a deeper understanding of not only the occupational almshouses but also the development of the Aged Miners' Homes in county Durham and Northumberland. Durham was the first County to provide homes for this category of the elderly on a large scale and it was highly unusual for any institution to provide so many homes. Northumberland and Yorkshire mineworkers started their aged miner homes shortly after County Durham. The provision of these homes was an impressive response of local organisations to the demands made by the highly specialised local economy on the working population. They provided a vital contribution to the mixed economy of welfare by providing support for elderly miners and their families.

Notes

1.   The keelmen were boatmen who worked the keels (large boats with shallow draught) by loading and transporting coal on the Rivers Tyne and Wear to waiting collier ships; URL: http://beta.charitycommission.gov.uk/charity-details/?regid=259236&subid=0, accessed 20.2.2012.

2.   McCombie, G. *Newcastle and Gateshead*. Yale University Press, New Haven, 2009, pp. 6, 16.

3.   URL: www.englandsnotheast.co.uk, accessed 20.2.2012.

4.   McCombie, pp. 6, 16.

5.   Page, W. (ed.). *Victoria County History of Durham*. Vol. 2. Archibald Constable, London, 1907, p. 275.

6.   Tyne and Wear Archives (T&WA): 418/4, Articles of the Keelmen's Hospital Society, p. 19.

7.   Pevsner, N. & Grundy, J. *The Buildings of England, Northumberland*. Penguin, London, 2nd edn, 1992, p. 477.

8.   URL: http://en.wikipedia.org/wiki/keelmen, accessed 20.2.2012.

9.   URL: http://southtyneside.info/applications/2/listedbuildings, accessed 20.1.2011.

10.   Milburn, G.E. & Miller, S.T. (eds), *Sunderland River, Town and People: a history from the 1780s*. Sunderland Borough Council, 1988, p. 76.

11.   Fordyce, W. *The History & Antiquities of the County Palatine of Durham*. Vol. 2, Nichols & Son, London, 1857, p. 457.

12.   White W. & Co. *Directory of Northumberland and Durham*. E. Baines & Son, Leeds, 1827, p. Lxxxvi.

13.   Pevsner, N. *The Buildings of England, Yorkshire: The North Riding*. Penguin Books, Harmondsworth, 1966, pp. 330, 332, 397; Bailey, B. *Almshouses*. Hale, London, 1988, p. 160.

14.   URL: www.british-history.ac.uk. *A Topographical Dictionary of England*, pp. 26-30.

15.   URL: www.ramsdale.org/scarboro.htm accessed 2.3.2011.

16.   Pevsner, N. *The Buildings of England, Yorkshire: York and the East Riding*. Penguin Books, Harmondsworth, 1972, pp. 272-3.

17.   Durham Record Office (DRO): EP/Biw446, Scheme of Endowment of the Sunderland and Bishopwearmouth Marine Institution, 1889, p. 6.

18.   Humphreys, R. *Sin, Organised Charity and the Poor Law in Victorian England*. Macmillan Basingstoke, 1995, p. 64.

19.   DRO: EP/Biw447, Charity Commission, 2 Jan. 1906.

20.   Leivers, C. 'Housing the Elderly in Nineteenth-century Derbyshire: a comparison of almshouse and workhouse provision', *Local Population Studies*, 83, 2009, pp. 59-60.

21.   Langley, A. 'Warwickshire Almshouses 1400-1914, Part II: founders, buildings and residents', *FACHRS Newsletter*, Vol. 10, February 2009, p. 9; Goose, N. and Basten, S. 'Almshouse Residency in Nineteenth-century England: an interim report', *Family and Community History*, 12, 2009, p. 69.

22.   URL: www.trinityhouse.co.uk, accessed 20.2.2012.

23.   URL: www.bbc.co.uk/northyorkshire, accessed 20.2.2012.

24. URL: www.british-history.ac.uk. Allison, K. J. (ed) *A History of the County of York East Riding*. Vol 1: the City of Kingston upon Hull, 1969, pp. 397-407.

25. URL: http://trinityhousenewcastle.org.uk/history, accessed 20.2.2012.

26. Pevsner, N. & Grundy, J. *The Buildings of England, Northumberland*. Penguin, London, 2nd edn, 1992, p. 476.

27. Pevsner, N., & Grundy, J. *Northumberland*. Penguin, London, 2nd edn., 1992, pp. 474-6.

28. URL: www.british-history.ac.uk. *A Topographical Dictionary of England*. (1848), pp. 379-89.

29. T&WA: GU/TH/9a/3.

30. T&WA: GU/TH/101/1, 1807 and GU/TH/102/1-15.

31. URL: www.british-history.ac.uk. *Victoria County History, a History of the County of York, East Riding.* Vol. 1, pp. 335-47.

32. URL: http://irenaus.net/how/ahnen12.html, accessed 20.2.2012.

33. URL: www.british-history.ac.uk. *Victoria County History, A History of the County of York, North Riding.* Vol. 2.

34. URL: www.sunderland.gov.uk/. Listed Building Entry.

35. Sunderland Local Studies Centre (SLSC), L361-TRA, Muster Roll Minutes.

36. SLSC: L362.SASS.

37. Leivers, 2009, p. 64.

38. Durham Record Office (DRO), Pamphlet, D/DMA (Sam Watson) box 38/3.

39. DRO: D/DMA 38/3, chapter 2.

40. DRO: D/DMA 38/3, chapter 3.

41. Wilson, J. *A History of the Durham Miners' Association 1870-1904*. Durham, Veitch & Sons, 1907, p. 297.

42. Atkinson, G. *The Miner's Heritage, A History of the Durham Aged Mineworkers' Homes Association, 1898-1998*. p. 37, URL: www.durhamhomes.org.uk/theminersheritage

43. URL: www3.northumberland.gov.uk/catalogue. NRO: Northumberland Archives, Catalogue description, NAMHA:NRO 08303/18

44. Atkinson (DAMHA), p. 10.

45. Ibid., p. 11.

46. Wilson, 1907, p. 298-9.

47. Atkinson (DAMHA), p.14.

48. DRO: D/DMA 38/3, Joseph Hopper, the Pioneer of the Durham Aged Mineworkers' Homes Association.

49. URL: http://ushawmoor.awardspace.info/history/aged.htm, accessed 8.2.2012.

50. Bailey, 1988, p. 190.

51. Atkinson (DAMHA), p. 43.

52. As the Aged Miner Homes (AMH) are not identified in the census of 1901, and few had been completed then, a demographic analysis of population has not been carried out.

53. URL: http://www.houghtonlespring.org.uk/articles/dedication_stones_in_houghton.htm, acessed 8.2.2012.

54. Atkinson (DAMHA), p. 42.

55. DRO: D/Ph 150/7, Thornley Aged Miners' Homes rules.

56. URL: http://ushawmoor.awardspace.info/history/aged.htm, accessed 8.2.2012.

57. DRO: D/Ph 150/6, letter Feb. 1914.

58. Speech on the opening of the first homes at Haswell Moor by Mr J Wilson in Wilson, J. *A History of the Durham Miners Association, 1870-1904*. J H Veitch & Sons, Durham, 1907, p. 301.

59. URL: www.durhamhomes.org.uk, accessed 20.2.2012.

APPENDIX 9.1:   ALMSHOUSES FOR SEAMEN AND OTHER OCCUPATIONAL GROUPS IN THE NORTH EAST (IN GEOGRAPHICAL ORDER)

Name of Almshouse	Location	No.	Who admitted	Founded	Founder
Master Mariner Asylum	Tynemouth	32	Aged mariners and their dependents	1829	Tyneside Masters
Trinity Almshouses	Newcastle	26	Aged seamen & widows	1584	Trinity House
Keelmen's Hospital	Newcastle	54	Old and sick keelmen and widows	1701	Funded by Keelmen
Master Mariner Cottages	South Shields	39 cottages	Aged seamen, widows and orphans	1843	South Shields Master Mariners Asylum & Annuity Society
Assembly Garth	Sunderland	38 rooms	Disabled sailors and seafarers' widows and children	1750	Seamen's fund administered by Custom House
Woodcock Alms/ Maritime Institution	Sunderland	10	Widows, unmarried daughters master mariners	1820	Elizabeth Woodcock
Merchant Seamen's Almshouses, Trafalgar Sq.	Sunderland	14 houses	Aged seamen, wives and widows	1840	Trustees of Muster Roll
Hartley Colliery Memorial Cottages	Blyth, NBL		Poor & elderly miners	1910	Aged Miners Association
Ushaw Aged Miners' Homes	Ushaw, County Durham	20 homes	Miners	1910	Funds raised by New Brancepeth, Bearpark and Ushaw Moor Lodges
Mariners Almshouses	Hull	40 rooms	Old, infirm and retired seamen and families	1848	Trinity House
Master Mariners Alms Houses	Hull	37	Master mariners, seamen of Hull, wives or widows	1834	Trinity House
Trinity Almshouse	Hull	32	Old, infirm and retired seamen	1753	Trinity House
Merchant Seamen's Hospital	Scarborough	36 dwellings	Aged seamen, their widows and children	1752	Shipowners of town
Trinity House	Scarborough	31 dwellings	Old and disabled mariners and families	1602	Trinity House
Wilson's Mariners' Asylum	Scarborough	14 dwellings	Distressed mariners	1837	Richard Wilson
Mariner's Hospital	Whitby	50 tenements	Merchant seamen and their families	1676	Shipowners

CHAPTER 10
ANGLESEY ALMSHOUSES

Sylvia Pinches

Anglesey is an island off the north-west coast of Wales, linked to the mainland by bridges – for a road in 1826 and a railway line in 1850. Its population in the 19th century peaked at 43,243 in 1851, declining to 34,808 in 1901, with a higher than average proportion of residents aged over 65 in the period 1881-1901 (*ca* 8 per cent compared with a national average of just under 5 per cent).[1] Although apparently remote, barricaded behind the mountains of Snowdonia and only accessible by sea for most of its history, it was in fact a staging post on an important route from England to Ireland. The port of Holyhead is only sixty-six miles from Dublin. At first, vessels from Chester called at Holyhead on the way to Ireland; from the time of Elizabeth I royal couriers, later the Royal Mail, used the road and ferry route to Holyhead. The island was open to influences from over the sea as well as by land from north Wales, midland and north-western England and even London.

'*Mônwysion*', the men of Anglesey, had long travelled on business and for education. This contact was stimulated by the Acts of Union 1536-1543, many men of the island following the lead of the great-grandfather of King Henry VIII, Owain Tudur (Tudor) of Penmynydd, to service in England. Some returned but many settled 'across the water', though still retaining links with their Anglesey families and a strong affection for their native island. This is reflected in the number of charitable bequests made by those who had left to their kinsmen and neighbours at home, present and future. These included simple distributions to the poor on the death of the donor and endowments for continued support of the needy, including the provision of almshouses. Many also sought to equip likely boys for careers in the church or in the law, both in England and at home, by funding schools and scholarships to the universities.[2] Between 1540 and 1640, 162 Anglesey students spent time at the university of Oxford, forty-four at Cambridge and forty-two at the Inns of Court in London, while others went to Dublin or even further afield.[3] The published lists of *alumni* show this pattern repeated down the centuries.

There are only four sets of almshouses in Anglesey, and one failed establishment, but they are well documented. Of those built, one is no longer an almshouse (having converted to giving pensions in 1868), one continues (although in a very impoverished condition) and two still fulfil their original purpose. Their dates of foundation cover the period *ca* 1605 to *ca* 1905 and their histories are comparable with those of almshouses elsewhere during the period. A detailed examination of the founders, the form of their foundations, their subsequent histories and the lives of the almspeople will give an opportunity to examine whether there is anything distinctively Welsh in this group of almshouses.

THE FOUNDERS

17th Century

The late 16th and early 17th centuries saw a flurry of foundations of almshouses nationally and Anglesey was no exception.[4] In the ten-year period 1609-18 four Anglesey donors were involved in trying to establish almshouses. All four of them had followed the road to England, though taking different routes to success. The men concerned also reflect Jordan's findings that many of those who made their money in London left bequests to their native places; such men particularly favoured the support of the poor and the establishment of schools.[5] Studies of Early-Modern Welshmen in London show similarities to other migrant groups down the centuries – dense networks of kinship and neighbourhood connections supporting new arrivals and at the same time helping to maintain a distinct identity.[6] Francis Hughes, Squire Beadle of Cambridge, expressed it clearly in 1666: 'As I have beene alwayes willing, soe shall I ever be ready to doe all the best and faythfullest offices I can for my friends, relatives and countrymen'.[7]

The origins and early career of Hughes' great uncle David Hughes are somewhat obscure. He was born in the parish of Llantrisant and was probably a member of the lower gentry. Whatever his precise family connections, he established himself in Norfolk and became steward of the manors of Woodrising and Whinburgh. If he was the David Hughes who had entered Gray's Inn in 1582, he may also have practiced as an attorney; he certainly became a wealthy man. Like many a childless bachelor, he turned his mind to charity. In 1603 he established a grammar school in Beaumaris, the main town and seat of local government in Anglesey. Over the next few years he bought considerable property in Anglesey with which to endow his charity.[8] By the time he came to write his will in 1609, he had decided to found an almshouse as well as the school (*see* Illustration 10.a.). He left the residue of his property to his feoffees for the school and almshouses and to provide fellowships at the University of Oxford.[9]

Illustration 10.a. The former David Hughes Grammar School, Castle
Ditch, Beaumaris
Photo © Sylvia Pinches

Even less is known of the background of Lewis Rogers of Penmynydd, until he was made free of the Company of Barber Surgeons in London on 30 June 1590.[10] He had been apprenticed to Robert Balthrop, who was Serjeant Surgeon to King Edward VI and Queen Elizabeth until his death in 1591 when he mentioned Lewis Rogers in his will.[11] Rogers was elected Warden of the Company in 1614, 1616 and 1617 and looked likely to have been Master had he not died.[12] By the time he died at East Greenwich in 1618 he had acquired considerable property in London and also had money out at interest. Rogers' friend and co-founder of the Penmynydd almshouses, Lewis Owen, was probably the grandson of Owen Tudur Fychan of Penmynydd. Lewis Owen had taken the court route, and became Serjeant of the Larder to James I.[13]

Robert Flood, as he is styled in his will (really Llwyd or Lloyd) was, through his mother, a kinsman of Lewis Owen. He was the son of Dafydd Lloyd of Henblas in the parish of Llangristiolus, a noted poet, linguist and upholder of Welsh traditions. Three of Robert's brothers entered the church but Robert was styled 'gentleman' in his will. According to Griffiths, he was secretary to the 9th Earl of Northumberland. Although the editor of the 9th Earl's household papers says that *that* Robert Flood came from Shropshire, he quotes the will of this Robert Flood, making bequests to a number of identified members of the Earl's household, including his 'bound friend', Sir Edward Francis, steward of the household and seneschal of Petworth.[14] He was probably a relatively young man at the time he died in London in 1617, as two of his brothers were still at university and their father was still alive.[15]

19th and 20th Centuries

With the founders of the mid-19th-century almshouses in Holyhead we move up the social scale, into the Anglo-Welsh aristocracy. William Owen Stanley (1802-1884) was the younger of twin brothers, sons of Sir John Stanley of Alderley in Cheshire. His paternal grandmother was Margaret Bold of Penrhos near Holyhead. William's elder twin succeeded to the title, while William inherited his grandmother's estate in Anglesey and with it a strong sense of responsibility for the local people.[16] Account books show the regular disbursement of meat and drink to the poor from Penrhos in the 1840s and 1850s.[17] As heir of Penrhos he was responsible for the distribution of part of the charity of Mrs Margaret Wynne, daughter of John Owen of Penrhos, awarding the rent of a small farm to a poor widow of Holyhead.[18] The heir of Penrhos was also trustee of Arthur Griffiths' Charity for the poor of Holyhead.[19]

In 1832 W O Stanley married Elin Williams of Bodelwyddan Castle, Flintshire, one of eight children, all proud of their Welsh heritage. Her sister, Mary, who married George Lucy of Charlecote in Warwickshire, kept a harpist.[20] Another sister, Margaret, married Sir Willoughby de Broke of Compton Verney, Warwickshire, and on being widowed retired to Anglesey and devoted herself to gardening and good works.[21] Elin and William Stanley were childless and noted for their support of many public works and charities in the town of Holyhead, including building the Sailors' Home and Reading Room (in 1871) and the Stanley Sailors Hospital (in 1872).[22] It was Elin who was the driving force behind the establishment of the almshouses.

The founder of the most recent of the almshouses had more in common with his 17th-century predecessors than with the aristocratic Stanleys. Although of a still humbler background, being the son of a shoemaker and smallholder, he too moved away to make his fortune, this time in commerce rather than the professions. John Prichard Jones (1845-1917) was born in Newborough and as a young boy was apprenticed to a draper in Caernarfon. After working in other towns in north Wales, he moved to London. In 1872 he became a buyer at Dickins, Stevens and Dickins of Regent Street, eventually becoming a partner, when the company became known as Dickins and Jones.[23]

Common Threads

All of the men under discussion maintained strong family links and an attachment to Anglesey. As well as founding almshouses, they all made other charitable gestures, either during life or through bequests. Flood and Rogers left money to be distributed to the poor after their deaths. Robert Flood's were the most modest and very typical of the period in which he lived. He directed that his executor should distribute £5 to the poor of Llangristiolus, where he had been born, 40s. to the poor of Cerrigceinwen (the adjoining parish), and 40s. to the poor of the parish where he should be buried. His other bequests were all to his family, friends and servants.[24] Lewis Rogers favoured the parish where he lived, but only if he should be buried there. Rogers also remembered his fellow Barber Surgeons, leaving:

> To the Company of the Barber Surgeons of London of which I am a brother £20 to make a cup for the hall wherein I would have engraven the words viz "The Gift of Lewis Rogers"... To and among the decayed poor of the Barber Surgeons company £100 to be put out to the best use by the Master and Wardens... Twenty pounds for the company of the Barber Surgeons to be kept at their hall if they do come to my burial and they to have their charges borne for their coming and return by water.[25]

The receipt of the £100 is recorded in the minute books of the Company of Barber Surgeons.[26] The Wardens' Accounts for 1618-19 record, 'Payed for a Cup Case for Mr Rogers Cupp *vs. vjd*'.[27] The Cup does not appear in the earliest surviving inventory of Company plate, in 1710, and may well have been sold during the 1640s.[28]

Rogers also thought of the members of Jesus College Oxford, leaving them 'ten pounds towards their maintenance as a token of my good will'.[29] His friend Lewis Owen went on to endow two scholarships in Jesus College for pupils from David Hughes' grammar school in Beaumaris, strengthening the connections between the school and the college already implicit in Hughes' foundation.[30] Prichard Jones, who had only attended a village school himself, encouraged both 'self-education' and the nascent University of Wales. He established an Institute and Reading Room as part of his almshouse complex at Newborough and gave £17,000 to University College Bangor in 1910. Prichard Jones also supported many aspects of Welsh cultural life, in Wales and in London.[31] The Stanleys, as already noted, supported many good causes, including schools. W O Stanley was also: 'a gentleman who was deeply versed in the ancient things of Celtic archaeology, as witness his numerous articles in the earlier *Arch. Camb.*'.[32]

All of these benefactors, except Prichard Jones, were childless. They all maintained family and neighbourhood links with Anglesey, supported education and had an interest in Welsh culture. It is to their almshouses that we now turn.

THE FOUNDATIONS

The Legal Provisions of the Almshouses

Charitable trusts could be created by will, by deed or, occasionally, by Act of Parliament, the most common method being by will. Of this small Anglesey sample, two almshouses were established by deed and three were set out in wills, with varying success: one, bequeathed by Robert Flood, failed entirely. Flood named no trustees specifically for his charity, appointing his brother as his executor, with his father and a cousin as overseers. The residents of his almshouses were to be appointed by 'the heirs of my father's house and the churchwardens of Llangristiolus'.[33] Whether the sale of his London property did not realise sufficient funds, or whether there was some failure on the part of his executor and heirs, it appears that his almshouses were never built. The Commissioners of Inquiry into Charities in 1833 recorded it as a 'lost' charity.[34]

The foundation of Lewis Rogers in the parish of Penmynydd would also have failed were it not for the exertions and generosity of Lewis Owen. Rogers' estate only covered his funeral expenses and personal legacies. Owen, being 'desirous in regard to his promise to see so charitable a work finished in his lifetime, though it were in part at his own proper cost', gave land on which to build the almshouses and endowed them with an income from the rectory of Eglwys Rhôs, in the county of Caernarfon. Following his death in 1623, his own will, especially the endowment of the almshouses, was disputed in the Court of Chancery and it was not until 1633 that an Order finally settled the estate and management of the charity.[35] The original trustees were Richard Owen Tudor and Hugh Williams; the Order added the incumbent and churchwardens of Penmynydd. Hugh Williams and his heirs male were to be collectors of the rents, rendering accounts yearly at Easter to the inhabitants of Penmynydd. Any disputes were to be settled by the Justices of Assize of Anglesey, to whom a pair of gloves to the value of 10s. was to be given annually.[36]

Even though the will of David Hughes gave more detailed instructions for establishing his almshouses, and his trustees included not only named individuals but also the bishop of Bangor and the mayor of Beaumaris for the time being, not all his directions were followed. He had wanted the almshouses to be built near the church in Llanerchymedd, a small market town three miles from his birthplace of Llantrisant.[37] They were, in fact, built in the parish of Llanfaes, in a part that was in the Borough of Beaumaris, though a good mile from the town itself. This is probably because the grammar school was already established in the town and the trustees had their meetings there.

There are distinctions to be made between the two almshouses established by life-time gifts. The Penrhos Almshouses established by the Stanleys in Holyhead were an old-fashioned paternalistic and private charity, built in 1859. Only in 1868 was a Charity Commission Scheme drawn up, setting them on a formal footing. The Prichard Jones Institute was a far more business-like arrangement, with a proper Trust Deed from the outset.[38] Although Elin Stanley was the moving force behind the Holyhead almshouses, the formal arrangements had to be done in the name of her husband. The Charity Commission Scheme of 28 April 1868 brought together the Penrhos Almshouses with Margaret Wynne's Charity and Arthur Griffiths's Charity, regularising the way in which Stanley had been diverting the income of these two charities to the almshouses. The sole trustee was to be the owner of 'the mansion house of Penrhos in the parish of Holyhead', although 'if a minor, incapacitated or permanently residing outside the United Kingdom or if a woman, then the bishop of Bangor to act'.[39] Although incapable of being a trustee, it was Elin Stanley who undertook the management of the almshouses, including making appointments and keeping the accounts. After her death, the administration was undertaken by Miss Jane Adearne, a relative.[40] After W O Stanley died in 1884 the solicitor wrote to her, saying:

> I mentioned to Lord Stanley that the management of the Almshouse devolved on him, and that you will have pleasure in continuing to look after them as you have done since Mrs Stanley's death, selecting proper persons for admission, and attending to the clothing of the inmates, when his lordship said he would be very glad for you to attend to those matters.[41]

The Trust Deed drawn up in 1905 to regulate the Prichard Jones Institute and Cottage Homes was a very different affair. Although, like many of the earlier foundations, it first placed management of the charity in the hands of family members (in this case the donor's two brothers), after their decease power was vested in *ex officio* Governors:

> The chairman of Newborough Parish Council (or successor council), the representative on the Anglesey County Council for the parish; the rector for the time being of St. Peter's Newborough; the ministers in charge of the various churches Protestant non-conformist now or to come; head master of the elementary school; three co-optative governors, one of whom shall always be a woman, to be elected biennially by a majority of the votes of the Governing Body as above constituted.[42]

As well as nominating Governors, the Deed made provision for a more professional daily management, with the appointment of a Librarian to oversee the Institute who must be married, his wife to act as Matron of the Cottage Homes. This contrasted with the paternalistic oversight of the Penrhos Almshouses and even more so with the earlier arrangements at Penmynydd, where one of the almsmen was appointed to see that the rules were observed. Here:

> One of the ten Almsmen, able to read distinctly and write legibly, shall be chosen President or Registrar, and shall have the largest room ... and he shall set down all particulars of any breaches of the Rules, reporting the same to the Governors, for which the President is to have a fourth of all fines over and above his share in common with the rest, and if he make default, he also shall be liable to be fined and punished.[43]

English was the language of law and governance in Wales after 1536 and so it is no surprise that the minutes and correspondence of the various trustees were in English, even when it is clear that some of the trustees were Welsh speaking. Even the petitions of the applicants were usually in English. It was a new thing when Prichard Jones stipulated that the rules for his Institute and Cottage Homes should be printed in Welsh as well as English.[44]

Malfeasance

Charges of malfeasance could be brought against trustees by legal process under the Act of Charitable Uses, 1601, but usually complaints were first addressed to the trustees by letter or petition. The main causes of dissatisfaction were the pensions or living conditions of the almspeople and the manner in which they were appointed. The officers of the beneficiary parishes often admonished the trustees about delays in appointing people, or complained that their recommendations had been ignored. In 1826 the parishioners of Llantrisant complained that the trustees of the David Hughes Charity did not furnish accounts and had not paid any surplus income to the parish for years, as set out in the will. On 30 October 1826 a meeting of the vestry, after reading the will: 'Resolved that the Revd H W Jones Rector of the Parish be requested to communicate the feelings of the Parish on these Subjects to the Trustees acting under the said Will'. Unsatisfied, the parishioners then instigated a case in Chancery.[45] Thereafter matters seem to have run smoothly. On 10 November 1868 the secretary of the trustees wrote to the parish officers:

> I request you will send me, as soon as possible a List of Poor persons who are entitled in your parish, to the benefit of this Charity, as in former years – I intend being at Llanerchymedd on Thursday the 17th of December next for the purpose of distributing the balance of the £42 10s. 3d. [illegible] on this year's accounts, so as to enable the poor people to procure some comforts for Christmas season.[46]

At Penmynydd it was the almspeople themselves who had cause for complaint. In 1784 they sent a petition to the justices concerning stoppages of their allowances. They had been told that the money withheld was to help pay for repairs to the almshouse and for the cost of their burials, but they questioned the legality of the deductions. They also believed that they should be paid quarterly, as directed in the will, not half-yearly as was the custom.[47] There was dissatisfaction again in 1849 when seven of the almsmen of Penmynydd complained that they sometimes had to wait three months for their allowances after they became due, and that consequently they had to buy food on credit and so pay more for it. They also complained about the bad state of repair of the almshouses. For these faults they blamed the Revd James Williams, who stoutly refuted the allegations in a long series of correspondence.[48]

Physical Form

All but the Prichard Jones Institute are examples of vernacular architecture using local materials. To this degree, they are distinctively Welsh, but their physical arrangement is not dissimilar from that of English almshouses of similar periods. The row was the most common form, whether single-storeyed or with second floors.[49]

Illustration 10.b. Penmynydd almshouses *Photo © Sylvia Pinches*

Penmynydd is a single-storey row, built of stone rubble with a slate roof (*see* Illustration 10.b.). The building was originally two-storey, according to the Charity Commissioners' *Report* in 1833. However, there are references to building 'lofts' (bedrooms) over the chambers in 1837.[50] The original arrangement may have been the typical vernacular style of north Wales, being one and a half storeys, with what is called a 'crog loft' under the roof. Certainly the implication is that the sleeping chamber was reached by ladder in the 1850s, for in 1859 the Revd Williams wrote to Henry Wynne Jones telling him that as he had promised John Glynn a new ladder he had better see to it at once so as to give him no grounds for non-residence.[51] In the mid 19th century a row of outhouses was provided and two privies built at the bottom of the yard.

What David Hughes wanted was a row of eight, two-storey almshouses. He said that the almshouses should be 'fit for the condition of poor impotent persons viz., to contain in length eight several rooms at the foundation under one roof and so many above parted asunder with partitions with door and chimney to each room'.[52] There was no stipulation as to building material, but stone is likely to have been used in this county, although the choice of 'partition' suggests wood-framed divisions between the rooms. What was actually built was eight single-storey dwellings with lofts and a chapel, arranged in a courtyard plan. They were described in 1867 as:

> Consisting of eight tenements and a small chapel, form three sides of a quadrangle, four other tenements belonging to Sir R B W Bulkeley, who nominates the occupants constituting the fourth side. Each tenement contains on the ground floor one room in part divided, in which the inmates generally live; and on the first floor another room or cock loft.[53]

Illustration 10.c. David Hughes Almshouses, Beaumaris.
Photo © Sylvia Pinches

The building has some pretensions to architectural sophistication (*see* Illustration 10.c.). A spate of building in and around Beaumaris at this time reflected the adoption of Renaissance detailing into Anglesey buildings.[54] The almshouses have an original segmental-headed entrance archway, which has chamfered jambs and moulded stops. Above the keystone is a label inscribed '1613 DH', with a heart in between the numerals and letters. It is similar to the date label on the grammar school (*see* Illustration 10.d.). Unfortunately, it is not possible to compare the surviving ovolo-moulded mullions of the Beaumaris court house (1614) and earlier school building with those at the almshouse, as most of the windows of the latter have been replaced by iron casements. The only original window is in the east wall of the chapel; its north reveal bears the date '1613', the initials 'RB', and a bull's head between them.

Illustration 10.d. Date stone from the David Hughes Grammar School
Photo © Sylvia Pinches

The Holyhead almshouses in plan, form and materials seem to be deliberately vernacular and modest. The plan is neither a row nor a true courtyard: the dwellings are arranged on three sides of a square, but the accommodation looks outward, doors giving onto the streets. They are built of grey-brown rubble with a paler freestone plinth, quoins and dressings and have a pitched slate roof. Although there is a finely-carved slate escutcheon on the gable facing Ty'n Pwll Road, showing the impaled arms of W O and Elin Stanley, this is not an original feature: it was reset here in the 1940s, having been removed from the so-called 'Elin's Tower' on Holyhead Mountain.[55] It would appear that the Stanleys did not intend to vaunt themselves or the family name, as the almshouses were officially known as 'The Penrhos Almshouses', after the family estate.[56]

Illustration 10.e. Penrhos Almshouses from the SE, the arms of William and Elin Stanley just visible on the gable to the right. *Photo © Sylvia Pinches*

The only one of the Anglesey almshouses known to have been designed by an architect, rather than created by a local builder, is the Prichard Jones Institute and Cottage Homes. The architect was Rowland Lloyd Jones, who was the Caernarfon County Architect and hence designed many institutional buildings, including the Workhouse in Pwllheli and the Cottage Hospital in Caernarfon. The latter was in a similar style to the Prichard Jones Institute, though with 'gothic' detailing, comprising a two-storey central block with single-storey wings, bow windows and a variety of roof levels.[57] The Prichard Jones complex is a fine example of Edwardian design in 'Elizabethan' style. The imposing two-storey Institute, with gables and central tower, is flanked by three single-storey cottages on either side, facing each other over an open green. The buildings are of Anglesey granite, with details in 'Ruabon stone', that is, red brick, and pitched slate roofs.

Illustration 10.f. Prichard Jones Institute and Cottage Homes, Newborough *Photo © Sylvia Pinches*

ALMSPEOPLE

In all cases the almspeople were to be local, either natives or long-time inhabitants of the beneficiary parishes, 'poor' and of exemplary character. Robert Flood was the least prescriptive donor, for his almspeople were simply 'to be elected for mere poverty'.[58] David Hughes appointed the residents of his almshouse in the following proportions: three from Llantrisant; two from Rhodogeidio; two from Llechcynfarwy; and one from Gwredog. He said that his trustees should appoint: '(setting aside all favour respect kindred and all partialitie) eight poor old impotent persons of honest name and such as live in the fear of God without the touch of any public or noted crime'.[59]

Lewis Rogers also stressed that those appointed should be of:

> Honest fame and conversation and have not been publicly reprehended or
> punished by lawfull authoritie for theft whoredom drunkenness or blasphemy
> at any time within the space of three years before their said election.[60]

His own kindred were to have first claim if they satisfied the other qualifications, but there is no evidence that any such ever applied. Rogers did not specify where the almspeople should come from. It seems that the detailed arrangements for the selection of the ten poor people:

> Were framed in the lifetime of the two persons Richard Owen Tudor and Hugh
> Williams, to whom Lewis Rogers had by his will committed the direction of
> his charity, and may reasonably be considered as constituting the particulars of
> the foundation as completed by Lewis Owen.[61]

Two of the ten were to be women, out of the parishes of Penmynydd, Ysceifiog, Pentraeth and Llanffinan. The Orders and Directions 'made for the better governing of the Penmynydd almshouses', drawn up in 1819, further refined the arrangements, stating that two should be from Penmynydd, three from Pentraeth, two from Llanffinan and two from Llanfihangel Ysceifiog, the tenth room alternating between the last two parishes.[62] By 1891 new rules stated that: 'if the parish, whose turn it is, has not an eligible Candidate, the Parish next on the list shall have the offer, and so on to the others in the above order'.[63]

The later foundations were little different; both restricted their benefits to single parishes and required those appointed to be of good character. The Stanleys directed that their almspeople were to be poor persons of good character who had resided in the ancient parish of Holyhead for not less than three years. They were to be not less than sixty-five years of age. There were places for twelve people, although only two of the seven original residents, appointed in 1859, were men. No more men were appointed until 1909.[64] Prichard Jones sought to 'provide Cottage residences, gardens and pensions for some deserving inhabitants of the parish of Newborough'; they had to have been resident for at least ten years. There were to be two single or widowed men and two single or widowed women and two married couples, the men to be not less than sixty years old and the women not less than fifty-five, unless the wife of a man over sixty. Strictly disbarred were: 'a) married persons with young children; b) professional paupers; c) persons convicted of felony or misdemeanour; d) persons of notoriously bad character'.[65]

The Mechanics of Application

When a vacancy occurred at the Penmynydd or Beaumaris Almshouses the respective trustees notified the parish with the right to nominate to that chamber. The following correspondence clearly sets out the procedure that was then to be followed:

> To John Jones Esq., Secretary of the Feoffees, Tynygongl, Beaumaris;
>
> Treiorwerth 8 March 1822
>
> Dear Sir,
>
> I have just heard that there is a Vacancy in the Beaumaris Almshouse to which the Parish of Llechcynfarwydd is entitled to send a pauper – the Overseer was with me this morning with a poor man who is a proper object to be recommended to the Trustees and a Petition will be drawn as soon as you have the goodness to let me know how to proceed – I have a Draft of a Petition that was once presented unsuccessfully.
>
> In the mean time I have written to Lord Bulkeley and the Bishop lest they should inadvertently make a promise to some other applicant.
>
> I am dear Sir
>
> Yours truly,
>
> H Wynne Jones [Rector]

The clerk replied:

> It seldom occurs that when a Vacancy happens in the Almshouse that there are not two or three Candidates for admission. In that Case the different persons

appear before the Trustees at their meeting & their several Claims to the benefit of the Charity Scrupulously examined & preference given to the one deemed the greatest object, age and Infirmities having their due weight. The Feoffees have never to my knowledge made promises in favour of any particular person but always prefer him whom they deem the fittest object if properly recommended & having a good Character. When the usual petition is prepared the usual way is to get the Signatures of the Minister & Churchwardens & of as many of the respectable parishioners as conveniently can be there to which with a Certificate signed by the Clergyman of the Parish is produced at the Meeting & if all is right and in conformity to the injunctions of the Founder's will an order is made for the admission and recorded upon the Books of the Charity.[66]

In the records of both charities there are a number of surviving petitions and letters of testimonial in support of applications. Most of these stress the applicant's birth or settlement in the parish, before setting out their unfortunate circumstances due to old age or incapacity, then giving a fulsome account of their good character.[67] The most unusual of the Beaumaris applications was that on behalf of Richard Jones in 1826:

We, the Rector and Parishioners of the said Parish, most humbly beg you'll recommend Richard Jones, who is a heir by birth to the said chamber – R. Jones is a son to the late Meredith Jones of Llanerchymedd, who through the influence of your honoured Father was situated in the said Alms house.[68]

As outlined above, Mrs Stanley and then Miss Adearne took personal care to select and appoint the residents of the Penrhos Almshouses. However, a notice of any vacancy and the qualifications required of candidates was to be affixed:

To or near the principal outer door or entrance gate to the almshouses and of the parish church of Holyhead for the period of fifteen days at least. Such notice shall be given in every case before the expiration of one calendar month from the occurrence of the vacancy.

The applicant had to produce 'testimonials and other evidence of his or her qualifications for the appointment'.[69] The rules at the Prichard Jones Cottage Homes did not require testimonials, but 'each applicant must apply to the Secretary for a printed form of application; this form must be carefully filled up and returned to the Secretary, and the governing body will consider the application in due course'.[70]

LIVING IN THE ALMSHOUSES

Rules and Regulations

Almshouses, perhaps more than any other form of charity, often had very strict rules about who might benefit and how the recipients should comport themselves. Despite the 300-year difference in their dates of foundation, the rules of the Anglesey almshouses have many similarities in their strictures and the punishments for infringement. All forbad drunkenness, Prichard Jones adding gambling to his prohibitions. Residents of Penmynydd were forbidden to beg. The Penmynydd and Penrhos Almshouses, 250 years apart, made it clear that residents were not to take in house guests or lodgers. However, the 19th-century census enumerators' books show that this was not strictly observed at Penmynydd, as a number of people had grandchildren living with them and, in one case in 1881, a boarder.[71]

David Hughes said that if any of the almspeople were given to drunkenness, frequenting alehouses, swearing or cursing, or absenting themselves from church on Sunday, they were to be warned on the first offence, fined a year's stipend on the second and expelled on the third.[72] At Penmynydd, too, the punishment for infringing the rules included the withholding of a quarter's pension and, as a last resort, expulsion, but only on the evidence of three witnesses presented to at least three governors.[73] The residents of the Penrhos Almshouses could also be removed for 'insobriety, insubordination, breach of rules or immoral or unbecoming conduct' or 'the Trustee may if he so think fit suspend the payment of the stipend to the Almsperson either wholly or in part during such time as he shall think fit and expedient'.[74] Although the formal rules of the Prichard Jones Institute were simple (no intoxicating liquor, no gambling and regular attendance at a place of worship):

> The governing body shall have full power to cause a resident within the Institute to be removed at any time, and his or her place to be filled up by another for any cause which in the opinion of the governing body shall be sufficient.[75]

Religious Observance

Every foundation except the Penrhos almshouses made regulations about religious observance. At Penmynydd the residents were expected to attend divine service at the parish church whenever it was held. In addition, the 'President' (almsman in authority), who had the largest room, was to 'reverently read divine prayers every morning and evening to the rest of the said ten poor persons except on such days as divine service is said in the parish church'.[76] At Beaumaris, David Hughes' will stipulated that the almspeople 'shall exercise themselves to the service of God' and they were not to be 'remiss or negligent in repairing to the church on the Sabbath days and on other times appointed for divine service'.[77] By 1832, at least, Sunday morning prayers were read in the chapel of the almshouses by the usher of the grammar school and the headmaster, an ordained minister, administered the sacrament four times a year.[78] In 1901, even though the building was no longer used as almshouses, the census enumerator recorded the chapel as: 'mission room - no service'.[79] If the residents of Penmynydd failed to attend services:

> No extream sicknesse or reasonable cause appearing, then he or she shall for the first time of offending forfeit and lose 4d. the second time 6d. the third time 12d. the fourth time 5s. the fifth time 10s. the sixth time 20s. and the seventh time to be suspended from a quarter's pension and if he or she shall offend hereinafter within the year then to be expulsed out of the almshouse at the discretion of three of the governors.[80]

By the early 19th century Anglesey, like much of Wales, had a large dissenting population. The Commissioners of Inquiry noted of Penmynydd that: 'some of the almspeople attend divine service in the parish church, and the rest frequent a chapel in the parish'.[81] In 1856 the rector wrote to the Charity Commissioners, saying that: 'with respect to the rule requiring attendance in the parish church during divine service, it would appear that its stringency has been relaxed in the tolerant spirit of the times'.[82] That toleration was not to continue. The rules were reinforced in 1876 and 1891, culminating in the expulsion of

William Jones, a nonconformist, in 1893. His cause was taken up by local people, led by Ellis Jones Griffith the Liberal MP for the county. They complained that the almshouses were intended for the poor of the parish, but they were 'administered purely for the benefit of communicants of the Anglican church'.[83] David Lloyd George raised a question in the Houses of Parliament and a Commission of Inquiry was called. A new Scheme was drafted in 1896, the rules no longer requiring attendance at church.[84]

Prichard Jones, himself a Methodist, avoided such conflicts by stipulating that: 'The charity shall be for ever unsectarian in its character and unconnected with any political party organisation'. Balance was maintained in the choice of governors, including the rector of Newborough and 'the ministers in charge of the various churches Protestant non-conformist now or to come'.[85] Even so, 'every resident within the Institute shall be required to go to a place of worship for at least one service per week if physically and mentally fit so to do'.[86]

Good Neighbours

Living in such close proximity, it is perhaps not surprising that conflicts sometimes arose between the almshouse residents. Some cases came before the magistrates, as in 1839 when John Jones the younger, shoemaker, and John Jones the elder, tailor, both of the almshouse in Beaumaris, were bound over to keep the peace for six months towards William Lewis. The 1841 census shows a William Lewis at the almshouse, but the Jones's had both left.[87] At Penmynydd in 1850 the tenants wrote, in Welsh, to one of the trustees protesting about the appointment of an anti-social new tenant: '*os daw na cheiff Dim lonyd* [if he comes we shall have no peace]'. The petition may have been successful, as certainly John Jones was not resident in 1851.[88] In contrast, although William Roberts, who applied to the Beaumaris Almshouses in 1822, was described as 'a quiet, inoffensive fellow', he was not appointed.[89]

Maintenance

Despite the requirement of the Hospitals for the Poor Act of 1597 that almshouses should have endowments with an income of at least £10, a number of benefactors continued to erect houses without providing any endowment for their upkeep, still less for the maintenance of the residents, which meant that many old and frail people lived very precariously in damp and unsuitable accommodation.[90] Even when an endowment was established, it could be eroded by inflation, especially in the case of a rent charge, as, for example, the £6 a year to each almsman at Penmynydd.[91] In 1784 the inhabitants of the almshouses petitioned the Justices of the Peace asking for an increase in their money, saying that: 'their present allowance is insufficient to keep them from want and starving because of the high cost of food'.[92] On the other hand, where the endowment took the form of property, with increasing rents the value of pensions also increased. At Beaumaris the original stipend of 12s. 6d. a quarter (just under a shilling a week) had increased to 1s. 6d. a week by 1665. It was 5s. a week in 1800 and 6s. in 1831.[93] It was up to 8s. a week by 1860, but then reduced to 6s. A new Scheme was obtained in 1869 and after that no new residents were appointed, pensions being paid instead. (The almshouse buildings were exchanged with Sir Richard Bulkeley for property adjacent to the school in Beaumaris, to allow the school to expand.) The pension was 8s. a week in 1896.[94] This was a generous amount, especially when compared with the 1s. a week paid to the residents of the Penrhos Almshouses and even the 5s. a week (7s. 6d. for a couple) at Newborough. The Beaumaris residents also received 40 lbs of beef at Christmas and a ton of coal a year, the residents of the Penrhos almshouses also being supplied with coal.[95] Even so, many residents of the almshouses had to continue working to support themselves.

Clothing

Only two of the Anglesey almshouses provided clothing. David Hughes ordered that his almsmen should receive six yards of good white frieze to make a gown at the feast of St Thomas the Apostle, and this cloth was still being supplied in the early 19th century.[96] At Holyhead, Elin Stanley decided that the almswomen should wear a version of Welsh 'national dress', although her sister, Mary Lucy, had not been impressed when she and her daughter had been forced by Lady Hall of Llanover to wear 'two frightful lintsey [*sic*] petticoats and bodies, two Welsh chimney-pot black hats with coarse mob caps' to attend the Abergavenny Eisteddfod in 1850 (*see* Illustration 10.g. colour Plate IX).[97] Lady Llanover, as she is generally known, was born Augusta Waddington and at the age of twenty-one married Benjamin Hall of Abercorn, Monmouthshire. She threw herself into her new life, learning Welsh and running her household like a medieval prince's court, complete with harpist and bard.[98] Her prize essay at the 1834 Cardiff Eisteddfod: 'On the advantages resulting from the preservation of the Welsh language and the costumes of the Principality' and a set of prints she commissioned depicting 'typical' costume, are widely credited with 'inventing' Welsh costume. Lady Llanover railed against 'false respectability which encourages forms of dress incompatible with "active employments" [and] exchanging wool packs for bales of cotton', with the resultant demands for higher wages, as well as the loss to artists of the picturesque. One of her clearly stated motives was the encouragement of the Welsh woollen industry, which was in a state of decline.[99]

Elin Stanley seems to have shared Lady Llanover's views, designing her own fabric and costume for the almswomen and having it made locally. Pasted inside the front cover of the first account book of the Penrhos Almshouse is a type-written note:

Elin Stanley's last wishes October 20 1876.

We were speaking of the endowment of the Almshouse. That must be as you think best, and I should like the Annual Clothing of Red Cloaks, Hats and Gowns to be made according to pattern; and good bedding to be secured alternate years … Your affect: Ellin.[100]

That year black gowns for mourning were supplied to the residents. Thereafter the entries refer merely to cloaks and gowns, though on the death of W O Stanley in 1884 black gowns were issued again. An invoice from the Llywenan Factory, Bodedern dated 31 December 1885 describes: '84 yards stuff at 2/6 £10 10s. Brown handwoven with dark blue stripes made at Llywenan Pandy after Mrs Stanley's design for Almshouses' (*see* Illustration 10.h.).[101] Pandy Llywenan was one of a small number of mills in Anglesey producing woollen cloth in the 19th century, most specialising in a coarse blue cloth. For a while the mill traded as 'The Anglesey Tweed Mill'. It finally closed in 1955, the last, by far, of the Anglesey mills.[102] Later entries in the accounts suggest that Evan Jones continued to supply material for gowns until the early 1890s. Then clothing and bedding was bought from D Jones, Hughes Jones and Brown & Co. The accounts for 1899-1909 are missing; in 1910 dress materials and flannels were purchased from D Jones and in 1911 from H Roberts, Boston St, Holyhead.[103] It was on the succession of the 3rd Baron, Lyulph Stanley, in 1903 that the requirement to wear the 'national' costume had been relaxed. He felt that it was 'an indignity and that they should be allowed to wear their own clothes. This "Permissiveness" was furiously opposed by cousin Jane Adearne ... she had been devoted to [William and Elin Stanley] and consequently any deviation from their custom and rules was bitterly resented by her'.[104]

Although certainly based on what was being worn in the late 18th and early 19th centuries in some areas of Wales (not unlike English rural costume of a similar period), the idea of a national dress was promoted by the land-owning and literary and artistic elite of Wales during the 1820s and 1830s, partly to encourage the local woollen industry. The widespread acceptance and wearing of a particular form of dress as a conscious expression of Welshness was undoubtedly also influenced strongly by the tourist trade. Increasing numbers of prints depicting women in 'traditional' costume were produced from the middle of the 19th century. They exaggerated 'the "quaint" tall hats and blue capes [and] finally were overtaken by the totally theatrical postcards, produced in their thousands from the late 19th century.[105] Even the Penrhos almswomen appeared on postcards, although never identified as almswomen, only as depicting 'Welsh women' or 'Welsh costume'. A photograph of the almswomen taken *ca* 1900 is pasted into the account books of the charity. This image was published as a tinted postcard by Tuck's before 1907 and was still appearing on souvenir plates in the 1980s. Other postcard companies also produced versions of this image and of other photographs of the women, all in costume around the obligatory tea-table (*see* Illustration 10.g. colour Plate IX).[106]. Further information about rules and regulations and clothing is to be found in Chapters 12 and 15.

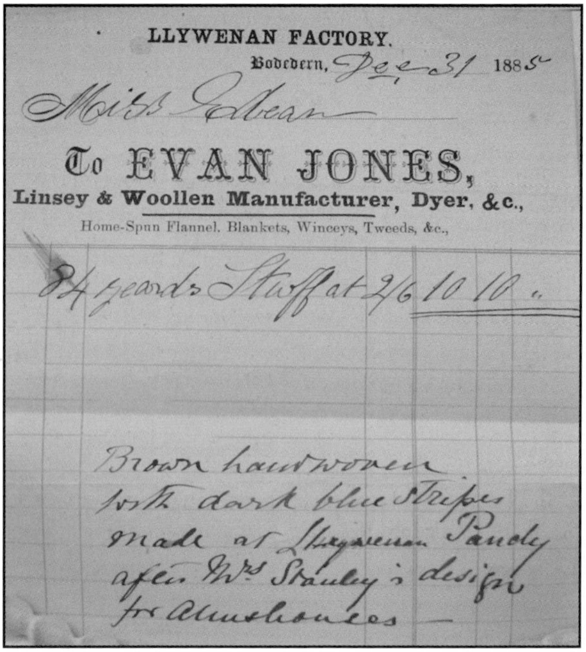
LLYWENAN FACTORY.
Bodedern, Dec 31 1885
Miss Adean
To EVAN JONES,
Linsey & Woollen Manufacturer, Dyer, &c.,
Home-Spun Flannel, Blankets, Winceys, Tweeds, &c.,
84 yards Stuff at 2/6 10 10 .
Brown handwoven with dark blue stripes made at Llywenan Pandy after Mrs Stanley's design for Almshouses —

Illustration 10.h. Invoice from the Llywenan Factory, for 'Brown handwoven with dark blue stripes made at Llywenan Pandy after Mrs Stanley's design for Almshouses'
Reproduced courtesy of Archives and Special Collections, University of Bangor, [Penrhos VII/531], 1885

CONCLUSION

This sample of almshouse foundations in Anglesey is too small to be statistically significant. However, spanning four hundred years and being generally well-documented, their history is illustrative of themes and experiences that have been identified in studies of almshouses elsewhere in Britain. Analysing their histories thematically has drawn out common threads. One of the most striking features is the intensity of local feelings that often prompted their foundation. Even so, it has been difficult to distinguish a national, that is a Welsh, sentiment, beyond that normal sense of affection for one's native place, which was shown by many other founders of charities. The periods at which these almshouses were founded also seem to reflect patterns that can be discerned in English foundations. There, a flurry of activity in the early 17th century was followed by a long period in which fewer almshouses seem to have been founded, until a revival of interest in this type of charity in the 19th century. However, emphasising the lack of new foundations has the danger of obscuring the fact that many earlier foundations (including those in Anglesey) continued to function, if not always to flourish, throughout the 18th century. A revival of interest in the foundation of almshouses during the 19th and, indeed, the 20th centuries may reflect both increasing population and greater longevity, leading to more elderly people needing care. As is to be expected, because Wales was under the same laws as England after 1536, the ways in which the almshouses were established, the procedures of their trustees and their relationships with the Charity Commissioners were the same as in England.

When the physical form of the almshouses is considered, something more distinctively Welsh can be discerned. The three earliest sets of almshouses are readily identifiable as being from North Wales because of the building materials and techniques of their construction. Yet the plan forms (a row and two quadrangles) are to be found throughout England. In the case of the Penmynydd and Beaumaris Almshouses this vernacular style probably arose because of the generally modest nature of their funding. In the case of the Penrhos almshouses, built by the Stanleys who could well have afforded something grander, it appears to be a deliberate choice. But was the decision to adhere to the local style of cottage a reflection of locality, if not nationality? It may rather have been a decision to build something that would not have been 'too grand' for the humble recipients of the charity, a sentiment sometimes expressed elsewhere. It is interesting that Prichard Jones, who otherwise very consciously promoted Welsh culture and language, chose to build in a revivalist style typical of England. His decision to have the rules of the Institute and Almshouses printed in Welsh was both an affirmation of Welshness and an acknowledgement that many local people, particularly the elderly, spoke no English. (The 1911 census shows that all the residents in the Newborough Almshouses spoke only Welsh.)[107] The controversies over nonconformity, though not confined to Wales, were certainly typical and often expressed through the medium of Welsh.

It is really only with regard to the costumes of the Penrhos almswomen that there is anything clearly 'Welsh', and here it is a self-consciously created Welshness. The initial choice of the style of clothing may have been part of a romantic re-envisioning of Welshness, in keeping with the Stanleys' sense of tradition, but by the beginning of the 20th century the costume was seen as an 'indignity' by the new trustee. There is no way of knowing what the women themselves thought. They were presumably grateful for the warmth of the flannel, but did it enhance their sense of identity, either as almswomen or as Welshwomen? The irony is, that although the women no longer wore the costume, their images on countless postcards and souvenirs throughout the 20th century has perpetuated the image of 'Welsh traditional costume' and so of Welshness.

Notes

1   All places mentioned in the text are in Anglesey unless otherwise stated. Census data from URL: www.visionofbritain.org.uk/data_theme_page.jsp?u_id=10134754&c_id=10001043&data_theme=T_POP accessed 28 Aug. 2011.

2   Carr, A. 'An Introduction to the Endowed Charities of Anglesey', *Transactions of the Anglesey Antiquarian Society* (*TAAS*), 1966, pp. 71-92.

3   Griffith, W.P. 'Welsh Students at Oxford, Cambridge and the Inns of Court *ca* 1540-1640', (unpublished PhD thesis, University of Wales, 1982), cited in Griffiths, W.P. 'Addysg a Chymdeithas ym Môn, 1540-1640' ['Learning and Community in Anglesey, 1540-1640'], *TAAS*, 1985, pp. 25-54, 34.

4   Owen, D. *English Philanthropy, 1660-1960*, Cambridge MA., 1965, p. 74.

5   Jordan, W. K. *Charities of London: the aspirations and achievements of the urban society*, London, 1960, pp. 308-9.

6   Jones, E. (ed.), *The Welsh in London, 1500-2000*, Cardiff, 2001, passim.

7   Cited in Griffith, 1985, p. 38.

8   Carr, A. 'Four Centuries of Scholarship', *TAAS*, 2004, pp. 65-76.

9   The National Archives (TNA): PROB 11/115.

10   Barbers' Company Freedom Register C/4/1 folio 27. The author is grateful to Joy Thomas, Archivist of the Barbers' Company, for this reference.

11   TNA: PROB 11/78.

12   Young, S. *Annals of the Barber-Surgeons*, London, 1890, pp. 528-32. Available online at URL: www.archive.org/details/annalsofbarbersu00youn.

13   Griffiths, J.E. *Pedigrees of Anglesey and Caernarvonshire Families*, London, 1914, p. 106.

14   Ibid., p. 122; Batho, G.R. (ed.), *Household Papers of Henry Percy, 9th Earl of Northumberland (1564-1632)*, London: Camden Series 3, vol. 93, p. xxv, 147, 153, 156, 162.

15   TNA: PROB11/129.

16   Bangor University Archives (BUA), Butterworth, G. 'The Story of Penrhos', TS, 1947, *passim* and Lubbock, A. 'The Owens and Stanleys of Penrhos: an account of its owners from 1513-1948', TS, 1972, *passim*; both in the Introduction to Penrhos Papers Catalogue.

17   BUA: Penrhos Papers, I/1319-1337.

18   Carr, pp. 76-7; *Report of the Commissioners to Inquire into the Charities of Anglesey* (*CC* Anglesey), London, 1833, p. 674.

19   *CC* Anglesey, 1833, p. 675; BUA: Penrhos Papers, I/1466-99 and IV/89-123.

20   Fairfax-Lucy, A., (ed.), *Mistress of Charlecote: the memoirs of Mary Elizabeth Lucy*, London, 1983, passim.

21   Claydon House: Verney Letters, 10/960, 10/1066.

22   Williams, R.T. (Trebor Môn), *Nodion o Gaergybi, sef cyfres a lythyrau hynafiaithol, hanesol a chofianol am Ynys Cybi*, ['Notes from Holyhead, i.e. collections and letters ancient, historical and reminiscent about Holy Island'], Bala, 1879, *passim*; Hughes, D.L. & Williams, D.M. *Holyhead: The Story of a Port*. Holyhead, 1981, p. 119.

23   Introduction to BUA: BMSS PJI.

24   TNA: PROB11/129.

25   TNA: PROB11/131.

26   Barber's Company: Court Minute Book B/1/4 pp. 319, 320.

27   Barber's Company, D/1/1 p. 182.

28   Ex info. Barber's Company archivist.

29   TNA: PROB11/131

30   W.P. Griffith, 'Addysg a Chymdeithas ym Môn, 1540-1640' ['Learning and Community in Anglesey, 1540-1640'], TAAS, 1985, pp. 25-54, 41-2.

31   URL: www.penmon.org/page83.htm accessed 17 April 2010.

32   Lloyd, J.E. & Jenkins, R.T., *Dictionary of Welsh Biography Down to 1940*, London, 1959.

33   TNA: PROB11/129.

34   *CC* Anglesey, 1833, p. 694; Jordan, 1960, p. 147.

35   *CC* Anglesey, 1833, p. 751-2; Anglesey Archives (AA): WPE 61/153.

36   National Library of Wales, Panton Papers, MS 9072E, 10 Aug. 1793; listed in TAAS, 1929, p. 51.

37   TNA: PROB11/115.

38   AA: WM/1887.

39   BUA: Penrhos, III/262.

40   BUA: Penrhos, V/862 & VI/58-81.

41   Letter 9 April 1884, loose in BUA: Penrhos, VII/531.

42   AA: WM 1887.

43   AA: WPE 61/177.

44   AA: WM 1887; Prichard Jones Institute, *Catalogue of Books and Rules of the Institute*, London, 1905.

45   CC Anglesey, 1833, pp. 727-30.

46   AA: WQSA/CHA/2/820.

47   AA: WPE 61/206.

48   AA: 61/250-1; 252-63.

49   Caffrey, H. *Almshouses in the West Riding of Yorkshire 1600-1900*, King's Lynn, 2006, pp. 27-32; Hallett, A. *Almshouses*, Princes Risborough, 2004, pp. 24-5.

50   AA: WPE, 61/224.

51   AA: WPE, 61/209.

52   TNA: PROB11/115.

53   Charity Commission Inquiry under Mr Skirrow, quoted in the *Return on the Endowed Charities of Anglesey*, London, 1897, p. 44.

54   Longley, D. 'Tudor Rose, Castle Street, Beaumaris', *TAAS*, 2010, pp. 65-84, 81.

55   Butterworth, 1947: 'transferred in recent years'.

56   BUA: Penrhos III/262.

57   Gwynedd Archives, Caernarfon Office, xm/maps/6162/71, 73.

58   TNA: PROB11/129.

59   TNA: PROB11/115.

60   AA: WPE 61/177.

61   *CC* Anglesey, 1833, p. 754.

62   AA: WPE 61/177.

63   AA: WPE 61/183.

64   BUA: Penrhos III/262; Penrhos VII/533.

65   AA: WM 1887.

66   AA: WQSA/CHA/2/789.

67   AA: WPE/61/190/1-16; WPE/61/193-196; WQA/FS/20; WQSA/CHA/2/787-98.

68   AA: WQSA/CHA/2/796.

69   BUA: Penrhos Papers, III/262.

70   AA: WM 1887.

71   TNA: RG11/5573, fo. 41.

72   TNA: PROB11/115; *CC* Anglesey, 1833, pp. 725-34.

73   AA: WPE 61/177.

74   BUA: Penrhos III/262.

75   AA: WM 1887.

76   AA: WPE 61/177.

77   TNA: PROB11/115.

78   *CC* Anglesey, 1833, p. 734.

79   TNA: RG 113/5277/fo. 12.

80   AA: WPE 61/177.

81   *CC* Anglesey, 1833, p. 756.

82   AA: WPE 61/281.

83   Williams, E.A. (trans. Gwynne Griffith, G.), *The Day before Yesterday: Anglesey in the nineteenth century*, Beaumaris, 1988, p. 270.

84   TNA: TS 18/1250.

85   AA: WM 1887.

86   Prichard Jones Institute, 1905.

87   AA: WQ/S/1839/H/46; TNA: HO 107/1363, fo. 6.

88   AA: WPE 61/208; TNA: HO107/2517, fos 80-81.

89   AA: WQSA/CHA/2/790.

90   39 Eliz. c. 5.

91   *CC* Anglesey, 1833, p. 756.

92   AA: WPE, 61/206.

93   TNA: PROB11/115; Lambeth Palace Library Charters and Miscellaneous MSS VI, 46 fo. 129r. and Lambeth Palace Library (Tenisonian), MS639, fo. 355; *CC* Anglesey, 1833, pp. 725-34.

94   *Endowed Charities*, 1897, pp. 36, 43-7.

95   AA: WM 1887; BUA: Penrhos VII/531-2.

96   *CC* Anglesey, 1833, pp. 725-34.

97   Fairfax-Lucy, pp. 95-6.

98   Draisey, D. *Women in Welsh History*, Swansea, 2004, p. 135.

99   Stevens, C. 'Welsh costume and the influence of Lady Llanover', talk given 2000, published by the National Museum of Wales on their website, URL: www.llgc.org.uk/fileadmin/fileadmin/docs_gwefan/amdanom_ni/cyfeillion/darlithoedd/cyfn_dar_CStevens_000916S.pdf, accessed 13 Dec. 2010.

100   BUA: Penrhos, VII/531.

101   Ibid.

102   Jenkins, J.G. *The Welsh Woollen Industry*, Cardiff, 1969, pp. 234-5.

103   BUA: Penrhos, VII/531-2.

104   From the memoirs of Constance Hugh Smith 1845-1918, Chester Record Office, ref. DSA, cited in BUA: Lubbock, 1972.

105   Stevens, accessed Dec. 2010.

106   BUA: Penrhos VII/531; postcards in author's possession; ex info J. Comerford.

107   RG14/34/4 accessed through www.findmypast.co.uk/ 7 August 2013.

CHAPTER 11
ALMSHOUSES IN SCOTLAND
WITH PARTICULAR REFERENCE TO
TAYSIDE AND STIRLING

Elspeth Johnson

INTRODUCTION

In Scotland, the term 'almshouse' is not common and none of the institutions described below included the term in their name; they were, however, analogous to English almshouses and therefore are referred to as almshouses in this chapter. The map below shows the location of the five Scottish almshouses located around Dundee that are included in this study. Fortuitously, when the histories of these houses are described in chronological order, each contributes an insight into the care of the aged poor in Scotland, from pre-Reformation times to the 20th century. The history of the Scottish Poor Law provides the context for this chapter, and although the houses are limited in number and geographical distribution, it is hoped that they represent, in some measure, the Scottish perspective.

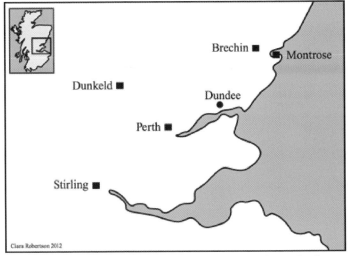

Map 11.i. Map to show location (■) of Houses in Scotland
included in this study.
Reproduced by kind permission of Ciara Robertson © 2012

In 1997 a project to identify and record medieval hospitals in Scotland was set up and funded by Historic Scotland. The outcome, following four years of field work and data collection, is a series of regional gazetteers of such sites, held by the National Monuments Office in Edinburgh.[1] Derek Hall, one of the project team, has published some of the issues to emerge from the preparation of the gazetteer, particularly in Tayside.[2] A final list of 178 medieval hospitals in Scotland was produced representing almshouses, bedehouses, poorhouses, leper hospitals, hospices for pilgrims and travellers, hospitals for the sick; and a sizeable group whose function is no longer identifiable. Standing remains of the earliest buildings are few and far between but the best surviving example of a maisondieu (almshouse) is at Brechin. Its foundation and subsequent history will be common to many religiously-endowed almshouses of the pre-Reformation era.

PRE-REFORMATION ENDOWMENTS

Brechin Maisondieu

Sir William de Brechin, grand-nephew of King William the Lion, founded the almshouse called Maisondieu in 1256. The Charter, witnessed by the Bishop of Brechin, Albin, records that William gave the mills of Brechin and other lands to God and the poor, as well as the Chapel of the Virgin Mary, in return for prayers for his soul and for those of his predecessors and successors.[3] The maisondieu was attached to the Chapel; it consisted of rooms for four old or infirm people and each was given a plot of land to tend. A precentor and two chaplains also lived in the maisondieu to care for the occupants.[4]

Illustration: 11.a. The remnant of the Chapel of the Virgin Mary and its Maisondieu, Brechin.
Photo © Elspeth Johnson

St George's Hospital, Dunkeld

Another early example of an almshouse is St George's Hospital in Dunkeld, founded in 1503 by the then Bishop of Dunkeld, George Brown. Although the original charter of mortification is not on record, the foundation was confirmed by charter in May 1587 and entered in the Privy Seal Register.[5] Such charters of mortification, common in the pre-Reformation period, required the beneficiaries to pray regularly on behalf of the deceased benefactor to atone for his sins.

Bishop Brown, with the consent of the Dean and Chapter, erected a hospital on the west side of the Cross of Dunkeld, with seven small houses for seven poor and elderly men, long time resident in Dunkeld, to be called bedesmen. The endowment was to be paid yearly from the lands of Fordeshaw and Auchagovan. This income was to provide each bedesman with a free house and two pecks of oatmeal annually (about 18 lbs), a suit of white woollen cloth and ten shillings Scots. The patronage was bestowed on the Prebendaries of Fordishaw, but as this ecclesiastical order disappeared with the Reformation it then devolved to the Commissaries of the diocese, who administered it until the 20th century.

THE POOR LAW IN SCOTLAND

Until the Reformation many hospitals, as listed in the Historic Scotland Gazetteer, were associated in some way with the church, as in the case of the Brechin Maisondieu and St George's Hospital in Dunkeld discussed above. Following the Reformation, in 1562, an Ordnance of Mary Queen of Scots' Privy Council confirmed that revenues once enjoyed by Catholic Chaplains were to be applied to the care of the helpless and disabled poor, including the elderly. This Ordnance was later ratified by charters of James VI. By 1579, following several amendments (in part modelled on the Elizabethan Poor Law) to the original 'book of discipline' of 1562, the principles of the Poor Law in Scotland had emerged and remained until 1845. They were that:

> (i) Parishes, or burgh magistrates in the towns, became the administrative unit to be responsible for 'aged and impotent' persons. Kirk sessions consisting of church elders and local magistrates collected and distributed monies to this end. The income came from a variety of church sources (including rents, pre-Reformation endowments and church collections) and from landowners (heritors) and the guildry on a voluntary basis;

> (ii) A distinction was made, when providing relief, between the deserving poor, who were entitled to aid and free medical care, the occasional poor, who had no rights but who might qualify for support – if thought deserving – and the undeserving poor: the 'stout and strong beggars, who running from place to place, make craft of their begging'.[6]

The one significant difference between the English and Scottish Laws was that English parishes were to provide work and work materials for those needing employment, whilst Scottish parishes were not. However, it was in the interpretation and implementation of the Laws that further differences emerged. Scotland, a smaller society, had little in the way of effective secular government but a strong Church.[7] The Kirk Sessions and Burgh Magistrates administered the system as they saw fit and consequently there was little uniformity. It was possible to levy a local rate on heritors and citizens, erect workhouses or assist the able-bodied unemployed, in times of need: 'but for most the law was remote. Local practice and tradition was what was understood'.[8] Scottish practice, therefore, in general favoured voluntary contributions and out relief.

THE EFFECT OF THE REFORMATION

The Reformation affected the two endowed almshouses in Brechin and Dunkeld differently.

In Brechin, the revenues that Mary Queen of Scots decreed should go to the care of the poor and helpless were considerable and described as 'a great revenue without question' by the writer of the First Statistical Account for Brechin.[9] However, a 'puppet' Bishop was appointed by the Earl of Argyll. The Bishop was empowered to sell, for his own benefit, all the revenues and properties belonging to the see, then vacant or when they should become vacant. This Bishop, Alexander Campbell, made large grants to his patron and to the Erskine family with the result that within one bishopric, the revenue became one of the smallest in Scotland.[10] The revenues to support the maisondieu were among those dispersed and it fell into disrepair. A 'hospital' under the terms of the original royal charter was eventually set up in 1608, in a pre-Reformation church property, but it was never popular. The bedesmen had to live on the premises, without their wives, and wear the prescribed 'blue gown' that approved begging. This practice of social demarcation was common and disliked by the recipients.[11] The hospital became expensive to maintain and was in disrepair by 1688.[12]

In Dunkeld, Bishop George Brown's endowment continued to support seven bedesmen until the houses were destroyed by fire, along with all related documentation, following the Battle of Killiecrankie in 1688-9. The small houses remained in a ruinous state until rebuilt in 1757, partly from public subscription but principally from an advance of £222 Sterling by Thomas Bisset, a Commissary and Patron of the Hospital. The new building is described as: 'a tenement consisting of two houses, both back and before, below and above, loan [lying] upon the area of the former hospital where its ruins lay'. One house faces the High Street and the other, in front, faces the market and village cross.[13] The 'front' house of the two houses is currently (2014) the National Trust gift shop or 'elle shop' with an iron standard gauge or elle, used to ensure market traders were using correct measures for cloth, fixed to the external wall. The coat of arms of Bishop George Brown is built into the fabric of the upper storey external wall.

Illustration 11.b. The rebuilt hospital 1757 with Bishop Brown's Coat of Arms, now the National Trust Ell Shop and Little Houses of Dunkeld *Photo © Elspeth Johnson*

A long-standing quarrel between the Bissett family and the Duke of Athol over ownership of the new 'hospital' resulted in years of neglect. A court of law decided in favour of Thomas Bissett but it was not until Patrick Bissett, grandson of Thomas, was appointed to manage the hospital fund in 1823 that outstanding rents were collected and repairs made so that the buildings were once again habitable. The bedesmen, however, never resided in the hospital Thomas Bissett had built for them. Instead the new 'hospital' contributed an income to the endowment of over £17 a year from rents.

Table 11.I below lists the bedesmen, residents of Dunkeld, who derived benefit from this charity in 1826. They numbered more than seven, perhaps because of the increased income to the foundation; subsequent lists, however, reverted to seven bedesmen.[14]

TABLE 11.I
Bedesmen of St George's Hospital, Dunkeld in 1826

Name	Trade	Where born	Age	Yrs in Dunkeld	Family	Societies	Work
Peter Dow	Labourer and Singing Master	?	76	39	alone	Old Mason's	unable
James Robertson	Cobbler	Caputh	66	49	alone	none	little
David Hair	Shoemaker	Dowally	71	60	yes	Shoemaker's	little
James Cocker	Slater	Dunkeld	77	77	yes	Old Mason's	unable
James Campbell	Sherrif	LittleDunkeld	53	23	yes	Weaver's	unable
Wm McFarlane	Shoemaker	Dunkeld	65	65	yes	Shoemaker's	works
Peter McG?	Tailor	Logierait	72	51	yes	Old Mason's	unable
? Robertson	Labourer	Logierait	76	24	yes	Chapman's	unable
Peter Conacher	Tailor	Dowally	66	50	yes	Old Mason's	unable
John Duff	Wright	Kirkmichael	79	?	yes	none	unable
Robert Munro	Labourer	?	63	?	alone	Weaver's	unable
James McFarlane	Mason	Dunkeld	67	67	alone	Old Mason's	unable
John McFarlane	Weaver and Balm maker	Logierait	36	36	alone	none	sells herring
Charles Duff	Lunatic	Dunkeld	45	45	yes	none	sent to asylum
Wm, Stewart	Tailor	Moulin	90	40+	yes	none	blind

As can be seen, most of the men were elderly and had been born in or near Dunkeld and lived there for many years. Most too were unable to work. However, it seems that the foundation was, even from this glimpse, sympathetic to need. Thus younger men, such as Charles Duff, a lunatic, James Campbell, an ex-sherrif unable to work, and John McFarlane, possibly without a regular income, were recipients. William McFarlane did work but had a large family to support, so he too benefited. It is interesting to note that several recipients were members of trade societies that would also pay a small pension. Relief, through the Hospital, included one stone, imperial weight, of oatmeal, delivered every fortnight besides occasional additional allowances until all the yearly meal was served out.[15]

Extant letters of application show that, well into the 20th century, old men of the village valued this charity. It continued until 1957, when there were only two bedesmen receiving benefit and the hospital building was taken over by the National Trust for Scotland.[16] The 'back' houses fronting the approach to the Cathedral, along with other houses in the street, were beautifully restored and are known as the Little Houses of Dunkeld, providing homes for the people of Dunkeld, but not specifically for 'aged or impotent' persons.

POST-REFORMATION ENDOWMENTS

By the end of the 16th century the Kirk Sessions of many Scottish Burghs had established
hospitals with monies recovered from the Catholic Church, according to the edicts of Mary
Queen of Scots and her son James VI. In the larger burghs, the model of the pre-Reformation
endowed hospital was adopted by Trade Incorporations and Town Councils. Examples are
the Merchants House in Glasgow, an almshouse for merchants, and the Hospital for six old
men built by Paisley Town Council in 1618. Other wealthy merchants, like Heriot, in
Edinburgh and Hutcheson in Glasgow, benefitted their communities through educational
endowments or Hospital Schools. Today very few of these buildings remain. Those in the
larger towns were often demolished to make way for more spacious workhouses as the
numbers of poor increased in the 18th and 19th centuries; those in smaller towns, like
Brechin, as we have seen, were shunned by the poor, who preferred out relief.

Cowane's Hospital, Stirling

Cowane's Hospital in Stirling was built as an almshouse, according to the legacy of John
Cowane, a prosperous Stirling merchant who died in 1633. It is described by Derek Hall as
the 'latest' medieval almshouse to be founded in Scotland.[17] It followed the precedent of the
Glasgow Merchants House in that it was founded for local merchants in straightened
circumstances. The hospital is described by Deborah Howard as one of the finest buildings
of the period and one of the best surviving examples of a medium-sized Scottish charitable
hospital or almshouse of the mid 17th century.[18] The substantial legacy of 40,000 merks
(£26,600 Scots or £2,216 sterling) was to be:

> employed on land or annual rent for building and erecting of ane Hospitall or
> Almoushous within the said Burgh to be callit in all tyme comying
> COWANE'S HOSPITALL. And for the enterteying and sustenying thereintill
> of the number of twelf decayed Gildbreither, actual Burgesses and Indwellers
> of the said Burgh.

The deed of foundation establishing the hospital is dated 13 February 1637.[19] The trust
has an almost continuous documentary record from that date, including the hospital accounts,
from which a detailed description of the building can be derived.[20] The town council was
mostly made up of guild brethren or burgesses, from whom the patrons were to be drawn.
John Cowane was a member of the guild brethren but also an active politician beyond
Stirling. He was an energetic member of the convention of local burghs and a Member of
Parliament; his business interests too were wide-ranging. He never married or had a
legitimate heir and such circumstances probably influenced him to establish the hospital,
rather than an educational endowment or gift to the church.[21]

Building was started in May 1637 but not completed until 1650. Slow progress can, in
part, be attributed to the facts, exposed in the accounts, that expenditure on the building
quickly outstripped the annual income from the foundation. There may have been labour
shortages too. In 1644 the Marquis of Montrose was in town, recruiting for his army to fight
the Covenanters, and in 1645 plague struck the burgh and hundreds died, including Patrick
Sword, the hospital master, and many of the tradesmen and labourers connected with the
building.[22] The hospital patrons had grand designs from the outset. John Mylne IV, the royal
master mason (architect) and keeper of the king's castles, palaces and defensive structures
was appointed to design the building. Many of the materials, such as dressed stone for

windows and doorways and slate for the roof, were brought in from distant quarries and some timber was imported from as far away as Norway. Skilled craftsmen were employed and the building had a positive effect on the local economy, by supplying work and attracting craftsmen as well as generating demand for local materials that could be used, and in leading the way in architectural fashion, such as slate roofing.[23]

Illustration 11.c. Cowane's Hospital and Bowling Green, Stirling
*Reproduced with kind permission of the Charity Officer of Cowan's Hospital
Maintenance Trust*

The E-shaped plan of the hospital was uncommon in Scotland at that time. There were two lateral wings and a central stair-tower projecting from the north front. Today, the building still retains much of its original appearance despite many alterations and reconstruction of the interior; and it forms a good example of a building type once found in many Scottish burghs.[24] The building originally contained three storeys, the tower being two storeys in height above the rest of the building. On the front of the tower there is a niche containing the statue of John Cowane, commonly referred to as Staneybreeks, and also attributed to architect Mylne. A local legend says that Staneybreeks comes down from the plinth each New Year's Eve to dance! The Hospital includes many Dutch-inspired features, such as crow-stepped gables, now seen as typically Scottish, and a Dutch bell hangs in the belfry. These are attributed to Mylne's association with his Dutch contemporaries but may also be a recognition, by the architect and trustees, of John Cowane's own business links with the Low Countries.[25]

The failure to install pensioners immediately after 1650 can be explained in part by the poor state of funds but also because the building was used as a hospital for soldiers by the occupying Royalist forces during the Civil War, and then as a store for local merchants. In the meantime, the practice of loans or cash grants and regular payments to out-pensioners had begun. John Buchanan, who had been a 'caretaker' of the Hospital, was given £48 in 1652 'for supplying his present necessity' and a weekly pension of £2 from 1660 until his death in 1662. In 1664 William Stewart was granted 40s. a week and provided with a suit and cloak (lined with black plaid), the breeches warmly lined, two shirts, a hat (the lower orders wore caps) and a pair of shoes. It all cost £60, which would have been a year's wages for some. Stewart was the first to be clothed at Hospital expense but his outfit was not a uniform and was not seen as degrading, unlike the blue uniforms of those receiving 'indoor' relief at Brechin Hospital and other similar refuges. Also, his pension was such that he never needed to live in the Hospital.[26] Another early beneficiary was Cowane's 'natural' son, Walter Cowane. From 1661 until his death in 1667 he was loaned sums amounting to several hundred pounds and granted a weekly pension.[27] In 1661 a payment was also made to Jean Stewart, wife of Walter Dick, a merchant, who was granted £48 to take her child to London to be 'touched' by the restored king for 'curing of the cruels': glandular, tubercular swellings in the neck, also known as the king's evil.[28]

It was not until 1671 that the Patrons decreed that the 'weekly' pensioners were, in future, to reside in the Hospital. In the original layout of the interior, the principal and upper storeys of the main block were partitioned into several rooms. An inventory of contents of the Hospital, dated August 1679 and retained in the Patrons' records, shows that there were six bedrooms, each of which could be occupied by two men; a hall, a dining room, a business room, servants' and keeper's quarters, records office and food store. This original layout can still be visualised from internal and external evidence. The inventory shows that each double bedsitter had a fire, seats, cooking equipment and a boxed bed.[29] Cleaners and washer-women were also appointed when the Hospital was occupied. These roles were often taken by the wives of the pensioners. They did not live in the Hospital with their husbands but were paid a wage and received a pension on the death of their spouses.[30] In subsequent years, cash pensions were reduced and the difference made up with oatmeal, coal and candles.[31] The rules were first mentioned in July 1676 when it was ordained that they should be displayed in every room 'that none may pretend ignorance'. A copy survives in Stirling Council Archives. Illustration 11.d. is a typescript copy from the Patrons' Archive. These rules appear severe, and may have been one reason for a drift of pensioners away from residence in the Hospital.

By 1698, after less than forty years as an almshouse, there were no pensioners living in the house. The Cowane's pension of £2 4s. a week was more than adequate to live independently. Meanwhile other groups took up an increasing proportion of funds, such as widows and sons of guildry men and those seeking crisis payments.

Shortly before 1724 the Hospital was modified according to new needs. The main block was divided into an upper hall and a lower hall and from that date the term Guildhall was regularly applied to the upper hall. Thereafter the building was used for a great variety of purposes, including school, hospital at times of epidemic, and concert hall, as well as the meeting place for the guildry. Later, in 1852, the floor between the two halls was removed and the current hall with its high roof was formed. A new three-light window was also inserted at this time, with a stained glass depiction of John Cowane.

During the mid 17th century, the Hospital Patrons had bought up lands in and around Stirling and thus boosted the disposable income of the foundation. By the 18th century the number of beneficiaries had increased so that in 1790 it was reported that there were 'above one hundred pensioners on this charity'.[32] Throughout the century the values of the pensions had been allowed to erode and the pensions of between 1s. 6d. and 2s. 6d. per week were not the near-luxury of the original pensions a century earlier. However, compared with the Kirk Session payments to paupers of 6d. a week, a Cowane's pension was still highly valued. Several changes had taken place during the century. The original wishes of Cowane were never followed, but deviations were usually instituted on sensible grounds, although without legal authority. Hence, the number of women beneficiaries continued to increase, several recipients lived outside Stirling and none lived in the hospital. Quarterly payments increased and one-off payments were still made for such things as setting up a business or emergencies, such as a funeral. Guildry members also benefitted as the differential between a Cowane's pension and other provision made such membership similar to a life assurance policy.[33]

PENALTIES FOR TRANSGRESSIONE BE ORDINARES OF COWAN ES HOSPITALL

PATRONS OF COWANE'S HOSPITAL
Scottish Charity: SC019364

First, that each persone who is absent from publict prayers in the hospitall hall they being in health the oversier to taike notice of such ane persone or persones and delate them to the masters of the said hospitall for the tyme who is to detine tua shilling scots of their weiklie mentinance for each dyats absence.

Secondlie, that each persone being in health beis absent from the church upon the Lords day both in the foir and afternoon and upon the weekdayes when their is divine service the oversier is to delate them to the masters of the said hospittall who is to detine four shilling scotes of their weiklie mentinance for each dyatts absence.

Thirdlie, He who is found guiltie of suearing banning [1] fflytting [2] or anyuther uncivill cariadge the oversier is to delate [3] him to the saids masters who are to detine six shillings eight pennies scottes of his weiklie mentinance for each fault.

Fourthlie, that if any persone sall be found to abuse or damnifie their bedcloathes or uther plenishing alloted to them in evrie chamber that they are to be punished by the Magistrats, dean of gild, Ministers, and ane tradsman Counceller.

Fyftlie, that noe persones who hes the benefite of the said hospittal sall after he is installed therein presume to mary under the paine of being extruded furth yrof (thereof).

Sixtlie, if any of the forsds (afore-said) persones installed as said is committ furnicatione (as god forbid) they are to be extruded furth of the said hospittall.

Seaventlie, that if any difference sall fall out betuixt the oversier and any of the persones in the said hospittall the Masters of the Hospitall sall make tryall yrof And report the same to the Magistrats, dean of gild, Ministers and ane tradsman Counceller are to judge the same as they sall think fitt.

Eightlie, that if ony persones in the said Hospittall sall be furth theirof at nine hours at night in the sumbertyme that they sail pay tua shilling scotes for ilk hours transgressione and for ilk nights absence six shilling.

Nynthlie, that incaice the said oversier sail be found guiltie of the breach of any of the injuctiones above wrlttln that their is to be detined of his cellarie [4] be the Masters of the said Hospittall the triple mor nor (than) what is contained in evrie article above written.

Tentile, if any of the saids persons sall not give obedience to the forsds articles bot persevear in clissobeying of the same that they are to be extruded furth of the said Hospittall.

Eleventlie, if any of the forsds persons sall be found drunk that their sail be deteined of the first end of their weiklie pensione for the first fault six shilling eight pennies, for the second ten shilling, for the thrid threttine shillings four pennies, and incaice they persevear they are to be punished at the ll-lagistrats dicreitione.

[1] abusing   [2] scolding   [3] report   [4] salary

Illustration 11.d. List of Penalties at Cowane's Hospital
Reproduced with kind permission of the Charity Officer of Cowan's Hospital Maintenance Trust

The Poor Law (Scotland) Act of 1845 established central control of poor relief for the first time, and parochial (civil) administration legally responsible for raising a local poor rate, so that those meeting poverty, sickness and hardship criteria had a right to assistance and fewer people were reliant on charities, such as Cowane's. As a result, in 1849 the Patrons decided to abandon occasional relief. However, small pensions continued to be granted throughout the 19th and into the 20th century. By 1900 the pension was 3s. per week and there were only forty-one female and fourteen male pensioners. The numbers fell throughout the 20th century and today (2014) there are none. A Housing Trust was set up in 1994 because the trust wished to revert to the initial wishes of Cowane's endowment. To this end it now concentrates on providing subsidised housing for the frail and the elderly poor. Meanwhile, plans are in progress for a 21st-century renovation of this historic building.[34]

The garden and bowling green [35]

The history of the garden is as well documented as Cowane's Hospital and its design is equally remarkable. It was first planted in 1661 to provide fruit and vegetables for the residents, with a sundial at its centre and a pleasure garden for recreation. A balustraded terrace was added in 1701. The early garden imported Dutch plants, including peach and apricot trees, and is recognised as one of the most notable remaining early Dutch-style gardens in Scotland. Like the architecture, the Dutch influence stems from Cowane's own trading interests and the architect Mylne's association with his Dutch contemporaries. Today the eastern side of the Hospital is flanked by a paved terrace and beyond this at a lower level is a bowling green. It is thought that the terrace dates from the 1660s; the bowling green is the second oldest in Scotland and dates from 1712 when it probably replaced the original kitchen garden or recreation area. The bowling green may have been another Dutch 'import' as it was a popular game there and in France by this time. The Hospital was the meeting place for the town guildry who may well have enjoyed such a facility.

The 1712 redesign was carried out by Thomas Harlow, gardener to the 6th Earl of Mar at nearby Alloa House. He bordered the bowling green with Dutch/French style triangular parterres. Unfortunately, these parterres were cut back in the late 20th century to allow the bowling green to expand, although it ceased as such shortly afterwards in 1998. The proposals for renovation of the Hospital also include the garden and bowling green.

King James VI Hospital Perth[36]

King James VI Hospital in Perth is a Category A listed early-Georgian building. James VI established the Perth foundation, initially under the regency of the Earl of Moray in 1569, the date of the first charter. A second charter was granted in 1587, when the King came of age. This charter, known as the King's Gift, 'granted to the poor members of Jesus Christ, in all time coming, abiding and residing within our said Burgh of Perth'.[37] The endowment consisted of lands, rents and annuities belonging to all monasteries, as well as chapels and altars within religious houses. The charter directed that the endowments be administered by the Kirk session on behalf of the poor, who are described as maimed and distressed persons, and included the elderly as well as orphans and fatherless children. A hospital master was to be appointed to collect the rents and other 'obligations'.[38]

As in Brechin, after the Reformation, 'if possession could have been obtained of what was formally conveyed, the poor would have had reason to be satisfied, and to rejoice together. But possession was no easy matter'.[39] Valuable lands and properties belonging to the Carmelites, the Blackfriars and the Charterhouse had been quickly sequestered at the time of the Reformation, but securing and maintaining its rightful income was a major pre-occupation of the Kirk session, and the hospital master in particular, for centuries to come.

The first Hospital master was appointed in 1577 and there has been a constant succession to the present day.[40] In 1596, the first Hospital, probably the renovation of an earlier Chapel of our Lady, was receiving old people, but by 1651 this or another building on the same site was destroyed by Cromwell's troops. It was another century before the current hospital was built. Use of the site on Blackfriars and Charterhouse lands was agreed with the town council, although a long term legal wrangle between the Kirk and the council concerning the rental income of these lands was not finally settled in favour of the hospital foundation until 1758, when the General Assembly of the Kirk intervened.[41]

The King James VI Hospital was designed by James Cree. The form is a classic H plan and is thought to include some features of the old Charterhouse that earlier stood on the site. In particular, an 'anachronistic' turnpike stair suggests that some parts of an earlier building may have been incorporated. It has recently been described as a 'pauper's palace of some magnificence'.[42]

Illustration: 11.e. King James VI Hospital, Perth
Photo reproduced with permission of Mr Graham Mackenzie, Hospital Master, 2012

It cost £1,614 10s. 7d. to build in 1749-50, the money coming partly from the foundation and also from public subscription: there is a room within the Hospital, still used for meetings, that is lined with panels identifying the subscribers and their subscriptions. Originally the Hospital housed a charity school, church, industrial school, correction house and poor house and also had community facilities for baking, brewing and laundry, as well as the meeting room and the Hospital Master's living quarters. Rosemary Mitchison comments that the plans for the Hospital, housed in the Scottish Record Office, 'show the expansive generosity then common'.[43]

The Hospital was successful for a number of years but maintaining the building became a problem and many residents were unhappy with the 'poorhouse' image. As a result, in 1814 the management decided that the residents should become out-pensioners with a pension of £12 per annum, and that the building should generate income from rents. Demand for out relief put pressure on the pension, and a half pension of £6 per annum was introduced, which quickly became the norm. In 1836, it was reported that seven pensioners received the full share and forty-nine a half-share. It appears from the report that this discrepancy had not been planned, or indeed intended, and the report advised that the number of full pensions should be increased to at least fourteen before further half-pensions were granted (the amount presumably related to need).[44] Payments were also made for medical expenses, funeral expenses and education. This arrangement continued until 1973, with more than fifty 'out-pensioners' recorded as receiving housing benefit in some years. Between 1973 and 1975, the building was refurbished with the help of the Gannochy Trust. It has been converted into twenty-one, one- or two-bedroom apartments that are much sought after.

Dorward House[45]

In 1837, on Coronation Day (and just a few years prior to the momentous changes in provision for the elderly to arise from the Poor Law (Scotland) Act of 1845), the foundation stone of Dorward House was laid in Montrose. William Dorward was a self-made business man who had never married. He continued with his business interests until his death in April 1848, at the age of 83, in order to sustain his considerable charity, including the endowment of Dorward House of Refuge.[46]

Dorward had first approached the Town Council with his proposal in February 1838, which they accepted and granted two acres of land within Stone Park, overlooking Montrose Links, for his proposed building. His will, written in January 1839, sets out the reasons for his generous gift and provides a framework for the administration of the House. The preamble reads:

> I William Dorward, merchant in Montrose, having witnessed the miseries and privations endured by the aged and infirm, who, from weakness, or other bodily distress, are unable to earn anything for their support and pay house-rent and are thus compelled to trust to the charity of the public as their only means of living; and having also witnessed the many orphans and children who have been deserted or abandoned by their parents, left to provide for their necessities by begging, which leads to idleness and vicious habits, often ending in confirmed vice; and being anxious to provide an asylum for the reception of such objects of commiseration and compassion and to aid in alleviating their sufferings, I have therefore resolved to grant the sum of ten thousand pounds sterling for the erection and endowment of a house for their reception and care...[47]

He proposed a Board of twenty-four Trustees, twelve of whom he nominated himself, a further four to be nominated by the Town Council, four by the Kirk Session and four by the heritors. The Trustees were charged with arranging the building of and completing within twelve months an institution to be called 'in all time coming, Dorward's House of Refuge for the Destitute'; in addition to receiving and caring for adults and children from Montrose, it was also to include: 'old, worn-out and decayed pauper fishermen, or their widows or orphan children belonging to the village of Ferryden'.[48]

The house with its fittings and furnishings was to cost no more than £2,000; in fact the trustees under-spent by just 2s. 9d. The house itself, built of the local red sandstone, was described as 'an elegant and commodious building' in the local press.[49] The extensive garden produced vegetables for the kitchen and included a profitable piggery and chicken coop. The original house was improved when circumstances demanded and funds allowed. In 1886, the single bathroom (there were separate toilets) was replaced by two bathrooms, one for males and one for females. In 1902, new basins for bathrooms and new toilets were installed; the next year central heating was installed, a novelty at the time.

During the ten years between the founding of the House of Refuge and his death in 1848, Dorwood continued to take an interest in the institution he had endowed and on his death a further £14,131 13s. 11d., the residue of his estate, went to the House of Refuge.

Illustration: 11.f. Dorward House, Montrose.
Photograph supplied by Brian Smith of gable-end photography

Dorward was careful to lay down a number of conditions relating to both the selection of residents and the administration of the House.[50] Firstly, in terms of eligibility, he insisted that there should be no religious discrimination; nor a distinction between legitimate or illegitimate children, suggesting an enlightened and liberal outlook. On the other hand, he stipulated that persons with mental illness, epilepsy, venereal disease, fever or infection should not be admitted, a condition that led to difficult decisions when residents became ill after entering the house. The trustees were to accept only residents who were already on the Poor's Rolls of Montrose and Craig (Ferryden) parishes and who had therefore already been through an assessment of need.

Secondly, Dorward was insistent that there should not be idleness in the House and instructed that: 'persons received into the said institution shall be employed in such useful work or labour as their age and strength of body will permit and as the Trustees or Manager shall consider most fitting and proper'.[51] The garden with its vegetables, poultry and pigs for the House, and its sale of surplus produce offered plentiful scope for labour and the elderly women were encouraged to knit garments for sale. Children were sent into employment as soon as they left school, and their meagre wages returned to the House to buy clothing and other necessities. However, it was oakum picking that set Dorward House apart and proved a disincentive to residents and prospective residents alike.[52] Oakum is the material produced when old ropes are cut up and teased out: it was used in caulking wooden ships where it was forced into the spaces between planks and covered with pitch. The picking of oakum was a monotonous, dirty and hand-breaking job, usually reserved for prison inmates as a punishment. The average price for a hundredweight of oakum was £1 4s. and in some years Dorward House was selling almost a ton, so it was a major industry within the precincts of the House. Oakum picking was introduced to Dorward House in 1840 soon after its opening, so it can be assumed that William Dorward approved of this initiative. This work quickly influenced perceptions and it was often difficult to persuade the poor, particularly the aged, to enter the House. This caused Dorward great concern and he tried to sweeten the pill by providing new Sunday clothes every second year, and increasing the stocks of tea, sugar and cordial.[53] However, the oakum work did not cease until the 1880s.

Thirdly, Dorward insisted that the House must remain completely independent of the traditional guardians of the poor – the Kirk Session, the Town Council and the heritors – despite their considerable representation on the Board. Nor was it to be known as a Poor's House. Finally, Dorward expected the parish poor funds of Montrose and Ferryden to pay £400 per annum to the upkeep of the House, in return for the admission and care of up to 100 paupers, including children. Later this arrangement was changed and the Parochial Boards, set up in 1845, paid an agreed weekly amount for each resident, according to the provisions of the new Poor Law (Scotland) Act.

These conditions for the House, set out by Dorward, meant that its provision lay uneasily alongside the needs of its residents and the framework of the new Poor Law. A Bill of Parliament in 1851 clarified some ambiguities and enabled the Trustees to act on a 'firm basis of law', firstly in relation to the disqualification of residence for those who became mentally or physically ill within the House and secondly to spend money on the education of the children. It was, however, the financial payment that Dorward had stipulated from the Parochial Boards – and after 1896, the Parish Council – that became a particular and long-lasting bone of contention. If Dorward House did not have sufficient residents, then its income and capacity to continue provision was threatened. The parish poor, however, were often reluctant to go to Dorward House, and much preferred 'out relief' or the new 'Poor's House' provision in Montrose, built in 1857 with more comfort and amenities than Dorward House.

Illustration 11.g. Extract from Admissions Register for Dorward House 1857-1900

An extract from the Admissions Register, 1857-1900, provides some insight into the residents admitted in 1881/2.[54] Seven elderly men and women, all described as 'weak' in health, and four young boys, orphaned or deserted, entered the House during the space of a year. Their length of stay varied. Patrick Littlejohn, a school teacher, was there for sixteen years until his death in March 1897. Walter Adamson Henderson, a grocer aged 41, stayed only for fifteen weeks and left to work, while Agnes Milne committed suicide after nine months residence. Only one of the adults was discharged for bad conduct – David Christie, perhaps frustrated by the strict rules, was absent without leave. Of the children, William Jolly stayed for eleven years until he was twenty-one, when he left because he was able to support himself. Another child, John Strachan, also left after ten years having obtained an apprenticeship and being able to provide for himself. The other two boys appeared to be still resident in 1900.

To fill the House and thus generate the income required to be self-sufficient, the Board of Management felt the necessity to advertise further afield when residents were not forthcoming from the local parishes. 'Boarders' was the term used for those residents taken in from other parishes – such as Monifieth some twenty miles away – that would pay the 5s 6d per week cost of maintenance. This practice continued and the proportion of boarders from other parishes grew steadily until it was more than half by 1915. The Parish Council constantly upbraided the Board of Management, suggesting the practice contravened William Dorward's original intentions of providing for the poor of Montrose and Ferryden and was therefore illegal. The Council, in turn, was particularly worried that those coming to live in Montrose were not sufficiently vetted and might not be of appropriate character. Of even more significance was the worry that if such 'boarders' stayed for longer than three years they would, thereafter, become the responsibility of Montrose Parish Council.

Matters eventually came to a head in 1920 when both parties – Montrose Parish Council and Dorward House Board of Trustees – faced expensive court action to resolve their differences. Fortunately common sense prevailed and a resolution was reached. Dorward House was allowed more flexibility in its choice of resident but with primary consideration to be granted to those described in William Dorward's Deed of Covenant. After this, paupers on the poor's roll of the local parish councils, were to be given priority, while residents from other parish councils could be accepted, as long as strict regulations regarding the length of stay had been made in advance. In return, Dorward House accepted eight parish council representatives onto its Board. It had survived almost certain bankruptcy, if a court case had ensued, but at the expense of its autonomy. William Dorward's endowment had become an anachronism as local authorities assumed the mantle of providing for the aged poor and were supported by legislation to make this provision. However, despite this, Dorward House has survived and today (2014) is a residential care home, providing for the aged and infirm as the founder intended.

After 1845, parishes in Scotland could choose to set up workhouses or poor's houses (as seen in Montrose) or to give out relief. Outside the cities and larger towns, many Scottish parishes operated what they called 'almshouses' or 'parish homes'. These were most often small establishments, consisting of cottages, or small apartments in a larger house, where residents could live as in their own home. These Scottish parish homes were not privately endowed but a product of 19th-century legislation. Similar parish houses in England, usually known as poorhouses, were provided for the poor by benefactors and parishes over a much longer period of time. Neither the Scottish parish homes nor the English poorhouses were specifically designed for the elderly and thus they fall outside the scope of this project's definition of an almshouse.

THE POOR LAW (SCOTLAND) ACT 1845

The system of relief that had been adequate in pre-industrial times was unable to cope with mass unemployment and the migration to the larger towns and cities that occurred in the 1830s and 1840s, due to a shift to heavy industry and also the influx of a largely Irish workforce. Some attributed the increase in urban populations directly to charitable funding. As early as the late 18th century it was reported that every twelfth person in Stirling received charity and the Kirk minister making the observation blamed the excess of available funding from sources, such as Cowane's endowment. Such attitudes gathered momentum, particularly among the heritors, traditionally generous voluntary contributors. In addition, the Disruption of 1843, when many dissenting congregations broke away from the Established Church to form the Free Church, significantly reduced the fund raising capability of the Kirk. The Kirk sessions, depleted in finance and with more poor people seeking relief, could no longer carry out their duties. In Brechin, according to the New Statistical account of 1833:

> From sixty to 200 paupers receive aid from the session funds. Some are weekly pensions (1s) and widows with children (1/6) per week. The funds from church collections, rents and mort cloths amount to £250-0-0. There is yet no assessment (of landowners) but it is feared if the poor and also Dissenters increase in number, that recourse must be had to it.[55]

The Poor Law (Scotland) Act of 1845 (often referred to as the New Poor Law) did just that. The new Parochial Boards were elected bodies with statutory status having powers of assessment to obtain finances to meet the needs of the poor within their parishes. Parishes could continue out relief, or build Poor Houses for the sick and destitute, and there was to be a formal assessment of applicant need. There was, for the first time, to be supervision of the system. Although the Act brought Scotland more closely in line with England, there remained a major difference in the legal entitlement of the able-bodied to relief. In Scotland 'poverty was not recognised as an economic phenomenon but rather a failure of moral purpose'.[56]

CONCLUSION

Until the mid 16th century the care of the aged and sick, outside the family and community, lay mainly with the Church in both Scotland and England. Before the Reformation most almshouses were either endowed by rich landowners or the aristocracy, such as William de Brechin, or churchmen, like Bishop George Brown of Dunkeld. The almshouses were located within, or close to, church precincts and administered by the church. The occupants earned their alms through prayer for their benefactors.

The devastation of the Reformation affected both countries similarly. The Dissolution of the Monasteries reduced church alms giving, and the confiscation of Church properties removed a massive source of income that had supported the poor. Marjorie McIntosh indicates that around 260 hospitals and endowed almshouses, about half of the total, were closed in England between 1536 and 1549. After 1550, however, there was an increase in almshouse foundation as communities and individuals sought to increase voluntary support of the poor.[57] A similar, but smaller, increase of endowments in the years immediately following the Reformation is also noted in Derek Hall's listings of medieval almshouses in central Scotland.[58]

Despite this increase in endowments, the main difference between Scotland and England following the Reformation is the paucity of endowed houses in Scotland, particularly outside the major towns and cities, and an evolving system of poor relief that favoured out-relief. A century after the Scottish Poor Law of 1579, the rural parishes were managing to care for their poor through administration of voluntary contributions by the Kirk sessions. In the burghs, the town councils and guildry, as well as the Kirk, managed poor relief on a similar basis. There was no effective legal framework and no uniformity of provision. Unlike England, the setting of a local poor rate was rarely achieved outside the cities and most rural parishes could not afford to build and keep accommodation on the basis of voluntary contributions. However, even where comfortable endowed houses were built, as in Stirling and Perth and – much later – in Montrose, a number of factors limited their success.

In rural areas where out relief was the norm, the system generally worked well, particularly when there was plentiful employment. But when times were hard, some parishes fared better than others, depending on the generosity of the heritors.[59] In the north of Scotland, the clan system provided its own support, without any legal framework, until fragmented and dispersed in the 18th century. Thereafter parishes could expect only very small incomes from church collections. Endowments were rare and family and community care prevailed until the 20th century.

Where there were endowed houses in Scotland, there were many similarities with England. Royal patronage was not confined to James VI of Scotland, who founded the magnificent Hospital in Perth. His grandson, Charles II of England, founded the Chelsea Hospital, for injured or aged soldiers unfit for military service in 1661; and his great-granddaughter, Mary, with her husband, William of Orange, founded the naval equivalent in Greenwich.[60] John Cowane, a wealthy merchant, who founded his hospital in Stirling for 'decayed guildbrether', was not alone among merchant benefactors. His foundation mirrors those of the London livery companies and trade foundations in many cities, north and south of the border.[61] Both men and women were benefactors in England. The Scottish houses in this study were all endowed by men; but in Dumfries, Mary Carruthers endowed cottages for lame or blind women.[62] As in England, it was common for endowed houses in Scotland to stipulate that residents should be from the local area.

All the endowed buildings in this study, with the exception of Brechin Maisondieu and the original Dunkeld Bedehouses, are large single buildings with the individual units, shared or communal, within the building. There are many examples of this style in England, and the familiar cottage-type almshouse is not unknown in Scotland, for example, the Mary Carruthers Cottages in Dumfries.

In three of the foundations studied, live-in accommodation was a short-term feature of the endowment. In Dunkeld the new-build homes under a single roof were never lived in by the bedesmen; Cowane's Hospital provided homes for less than forty years and King James VI Hospital for only sixty-four years. All three buildings were eventually used to raise income through rental for the endowments, the pensioners receiving a monetary sum, and/or oatmeal, in place of the accommodation. In the case of Cowane's Hospital and King James VI Hospital, residential accommodation was disliked and out relief much preferred. It may have been because of the rules required of communal living or, as in the case of King James VI Hospital, because the provision was perceived to be that of a poor's house and socially discriminating. Furthermore, the costs of up-keep and management of such buildings was high and it was apparent that more relief could be distributed to the needy through out relief.

Dorward House of Refuge and Correction continued to provide accommodation for the poor. Endowed on the eve of the Scottish Poor Law Act of 1845 and after the English Poor Law Act of 1834, it can be viewed as an anachronism in both countries because it sought to provide accommodation for which local authorities were legally responsible. This endowment seems to have been part-modelled on the English workhouses or houses of correction that also operated in the larger Scottish towns. In Montrose, the residents were to be usefully employed, but the oakum-picking regime of the first forty years of the house can be likened to workhouse or prison work of the period. The residents were not criminal but poor, and so the emphasis on degrading work most probably reflected the prevailing attitude to the able-bodied unemployed in Scotland. Here, economic unemployment was perceived to be the failure of the individual: an attitude to the poor not addressed in Scotland until well into the 20th century. Despite Dorward's best intentions, the poor of Montrose preferred either out relief or the relative comfort of the poor's house, built in 1857 from the poor relief tax, to his grand House of Refuge and Correction.

Notes

1.   Royal Commission on Ancient and Historic Monuments, Scotland, (RCAHMS): E13.1. CAT; the gazetteers were published by the Scottish Urban Archaeological Trust.

2.   Hall, D. 'Unto Yone Hospital at the Tounis End': the Scottish medieval hospital, *Tayside and Fife Archeological Journal*, 12, 2006, pp. 89-105. This paper was based mainly on Hall, D & Cachart, R. *Gazetteer of Medieval Hospital Sites in Angus, Perth and Kinross and East, West and Midlothian Council Areas* (report prepared for Historic Scotland), Scottish Urban Archaelogical Trust, Perth, 1997 (see note 1. above).

3.   Black, D. *History of Brechin to 1864*. Edinburgh, 1867, p. 16.

4.   Macpherson, E. & Fitchet, J.M. *Brechin Through the Ages*. Angus District Libraries Museum Service, [no place of publication] 1984, p. 5.

5.   Perth and Kinross Council Archive (PKCA): MS207/1 Dispositions, 1818-1902.

6.   Donachie, I. & Hewitt, G. *A Companion to Scottish History from the Reformation to the Present*. London, 1989, p. 151.

7.   Mitchison, R. *The Old Poor Law in Scotland, 1574-1845*. Edinburgh, 2000, p. 8.

8.   Donachie & Hewitt, p. 151.

9.   Sinclair, Sir John (ed.), *The Statistical Account of Scotland, 1791-1799*, Vol XIII, E.P. Publishing, Wakefield, 1976, p. 86.

10. Black, p. 39.

11. Mitchison, p. 98.

12. Black, p.43.

13. PKCA: MS207/1/2, p. 4.

14. Ibid., MS207.

15. Ibid., MS207/2/1, Mealbook records for bedesmen, 1872-1957.

16. Ibid., MS207/2/2, Private letters of application pertaining to the Bedesmen.

17. Hall, p. 90.

18. Howard, D. quoted in Benjamin Tindall, *Architects: Cowane's Hospital, Stirling, Conservation Plan: Consultation Draft*, 2011, p. 68.

19. Stirling Council Archive (SCA): S361 76HOS, Deed of Foundation.

20. Harrison J.G. *The Construction of Cowane's Hospital*, an undated draft at Cowane's Hospital, p.1. Later published as 'Building Cowane's Hospital, Stirling, 1636-50', in *Vernacular Building*, 33, 2009-2010.

21. Tindall, B. *Cowane's Hospital, Stirling, Conservation Plan: Consultation Draft*, 2011, pp. 18-9.

22. Harrison, *The Construction of Cowane's Hospital*, pp. 14-5.

23. Ibid., p. 3.

24. Howard, p. 68.

25. Tindall, pp. 20-2.

26. Harrison J.G. *History of Cowane's Hospital,* an undated draft at Cowane's Hospital, pp. 1-3.

27. Ibid., p. 20.

28. Ibid., p. 21.

29. Stirling Burgh Records, B66/25/690, Inventory of the Pleinishing in Cowane's Hospitall, Auguste 4th 1679.

30. Harrison, *History of Cowane's Hospital*, p. 9.

31. Ibid., p. 7.

32. Ibid., p. 14.

33. Ibid., p. 17.

34. I am indebted to Hazel Barton, Master and Factor of the Patrons of Cowane's Hospital, for current information.

35. Tindall, pp. 20-2. A detailed historical account of the garden was drawn up by the local branch of the National Association of Design and Fine Arts Societies (NADFAS) in 2001 and is appended to the Consultation Draft.

36. A substantial archive is held in National Archives of Scotland, NAS GD79. In addition the National Register of Archives holds a list of historical papers of the Hospital that are in private hands, NRAS 268.

37. Milne, R. *Rental Books of King James VI Hospital, Perth*, printed by Wood & Son, Perth, 1891, p. iv.

38. Ibid., p. v.

39. Ibid., pp. v and vi.

40. I am indebted to the current Hospital Master, Mr. Graham Mackenzie, for his generous assistance.

41. Milne, p. xxiv.

42. Haynes, N. *Perth and Kinross: an illustrated architectural guide*. Rutland Press, Edinburgh, 2000, p. 23.

43. Mitchison, p. 107.

44. Milne, p. xxxvii.

45. Primary Records are *in situ* at Dorward House. A list is available.

46. Watson, H. 'William Dorward Esquire', *Journal of the Tay Valley Family History Society*, June 2004, pp. 33-7.

47. Coull, W.W. & Johns, T.W. *Dorward House: an anniversary history 1838-1988*. Angus Council, [no place of publication noted] 1988, p. 9.

48. Ibid., p. 9; Ferryden was a fishing village nearby.

49. Ibid., p. 11.

50. Ibid., p. 10.

51. Ibid., p. 10.

52. Ibid., p. 14.

53. Ibid., p. 15.

54. Tay Valley Family History Association, Library, Dundee, MSS Ref.PO2D, Dorward House Admission Register, 1857-1900.

55. *The New Statistical Account of Scotland*, Vol XI, Blackwood & Sons, Edinburgh & London, 1845, pp. 129-41.

56. Donnachie & Hewitt, 1989, p. 152.

57. McIntosh, M. 'Local Responses to the Poor in Late Medieval and Tudor England' *Community and Change* 3 (2), 1988, p. 228.

58. Hall, 2006, 12, pp. 103-5.

59. Mitchison, pp. 99-100.

60. Hallett, A. *Almshouses*. Shire Publications Ltd, 2004, p. 9.

61. Ibid., pp. 13-4.

62. Ibid., p. 15.

PART THREE

Themes

CHAPTER 12
ALMSHOUSE RULES AND REGULATIONS FOR TRUSTEES AND ALMSPEOPLE WITH PARTICULAR REFERENCE TO SURREY

Angela Blaydon

INTRODUCTION

Rules and regulations controlling an almshouse reflected the wishes of the founder for a seemly community of the deserving poor and, from our point of view, have the attraction of demonstrating details of life in an almshouse community. There were selection criteria for entry to an almshouse and then rules and regulations affecting both the residents and the trustees. There were sanctions (usually fines and expulsions) for breaking the rules but it is difficult to know to what extent these rules were implemented and further research on this topic would be welcome.

This chapter will examine rules and regulations from almshouses located throughout England, with particular reference to Surrey, my own area of research. This research analysed information from 131 almshouses in twenty-two counties and references for them are listed in Appendix 12.1 at the end of the chapter.[1] Unattributed information and quotations in the text all come from the relevant references in this Appendix.

Not all almshouses have extant rules and regulations. In the county of Surrey, the existence of 126 almshouses was identified (though not all still survive and not all of the 144 parishes in the county were exhaustively researched). Of these 126 almshouses, references were located to twenty-five sets of rules and regulations, less than 20 per cent of the total number. This does not, of course, imply that the other almshouses did not have rules and regulations, but merely that they have not been preserved or possibly were never written down at all. It is worth noting that almshouses with written evidence of rules were nearly always those with an adequate endowment; this might suggest that wealthy founders were more likely to plan their legacy carefully and set out rules for their almshouse, or that endowed almshouses may have taken better care of their archives so that the rules survive. The latter is, however, not necessarily true — Andrew Windsor's Almshouses in Farnham, Surrey (founded in 1620), never had any rules, even though the author witnessed a room full of documents at the Almshouse dating back to the foundation and including registers listing every almsperson admitted since 1620.

Most of the rules and regulations were made to control the lives of almspeople within the confines of the almshouse, in order to provide a secure and pleasant life for the residents. Some rules and regulations also curbed their lives outside the boundary of the establishment so as to maintain the image and good reputation of the founder. One can only speculate as to the impact rules had on the residents but it might be inferred that only people prepared to conform would apply to live in an almshouse, and that strict rules were likely to exclude more unconventional individuals.

There was, and still is, a great variety of different rules and regulations, many of which were common to all almshouses, some were unusual, whilst others were extreme. Sometimes they were copied from one establishment to another, or used as a basis for regulation elsewhere. Some almshouses appear to have had very few rules, whilst others had extensive lists, such as those of Holy Trinity Hospital in Suffolk (founded in 1644) with forty-three different rules and regulations for the almsmen. Some rules were handsomely presented (*see* Illustration 12.a.) whilst others were not (*see* Illustration 12.b.). A fairly typical set of rules is to be found in Appendix 12.2.

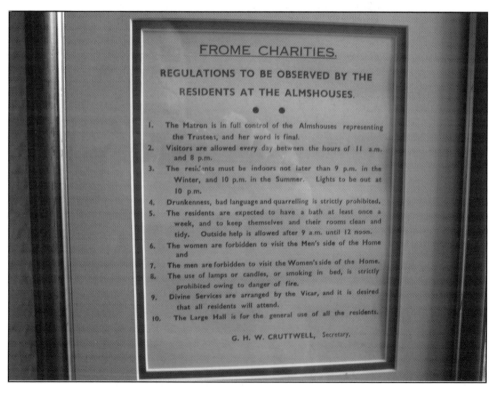

Illustration 12.a. Frome Charities Rules and Regulations
© *Sarah Hare, Somerset and reproduced by kind permission*

The establishment of the Charity Commission and the Commissioners' new Schemes from the mid 19th century promoted more standardisation of rules for residents and trustees alike. The relationship between foundation dates and the rules and regulations of almshouses has been investigated and is discussed further in the conclusion.

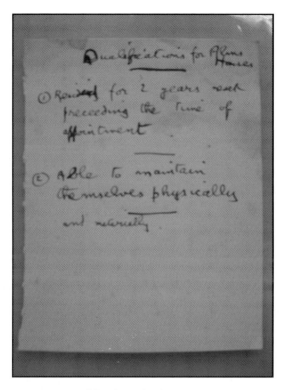

Illustration 12.b. Qualification rules for Fetcham Almshouse, Surrey
Reproduced by kind permission of Surrey History Centre ref: FET-5-19

TRUSTEES

All trusts required trustees and usually an indenture founding the almshouse would specify the selection, requirements and regulations for the trustees, aimed at the smooth running of the almshouse and administration of the endowment. Occasionally these indentures would also detail more precise requirements to be met before a person could be appointed a trustee. Regulations regarding trustees were only available from twelve establishments, so it is not possible to give a comprehensive analysis of trustees' rules.[2] These few examples do, however, suggest that regulations for trustees were as varied as those for the almspeople. For some almshouses, including all those in Surrey, no regulations whatsoever for trustees were found, whilst in other almshouses the number of trustees, a residence qualification and frequency of visits were explicitly noted. The lack of rules and regulations regarding the administration of an endowment could have serious consequences, for example at Windsor's Almshouses in Farnham, Surrey, when the death of the founder in 1625 resulted in a lengthy and costly court case to establish his unwritten wishes.[3]

Trustees were usually selected by the founder of an institution, often from friends or relatives and people of standing in the local community. The indenture would then give trustees the freedom to nominate their successors to the post. Occasionally the founder restricted who could take on the role by prescribing that at least one trustee must be the local vicar, churchwarden or schoolmaster, whilst others stated that at least one or more of the trustees must be a descendant of the family. Other rules, such as those of Feilding's

Almshouse at Ashtead in Surrey (founded in 1736), state that only 'executors of the will and their heirs and the Lord of the Manor of Ashtead and the Minister of the Parish of Ashtead' can elect almswomen.[4]

The trustees for Verney's Almshouses in Buckinghamshire (founded in 1691-4) were merely required to be 'discreet' inhabitants of the parish, meaning those holding office in a parish or well-respected members of the community. Of the ten almshouses giving information on trustees' requirements, six stated the number of trustees, ranging from three to seven, but only two stipulated that the local vicar must be one of them.

Four almshouse indentures specify visits, with Cleeton St Mary in Shropshire (founded in 1883) requiring the vicar to visit weekly. Houblon's at Richmond in Surrey (founded in 1757) required the governors to visit twice a year. Seckford's at Woodbridge in Suffolk (founded in 1587) only required official visits once every three years. At Holy Trinity, Long Melford in Suffolk (founded ca 1664), the Bishop of Norwich had to visit once every three years and on each visit receive a pair of gloves. Queen Anne's Hospital in Newport Pagnell (founded in 1280) required the governors to meet half yearly, at 'a convenient public house' in Newport Pagnell to transact all necessary business over 'a decent thrifty dinner' at 'as small expense as might be not exceeding £1 5s.'. This institution was the only one specifying that all buildings were to be insured against fire (although accounts for almshouses in some Surrey parishes show payments being made for insurance). It is possible that the insurance requirement at Queen Anne's Hospital was instigated in 1891 when brick buildings replaced the 1615 stone buildings.

Two of the almshouses specified a residency qualification for the trustees: Verney's in Middle Clayton, Buckinghamshire (founded in 1694) stated seven 'discreet' inhabitants of Middle Clayton or from within five miles; whereas Revi's of Newport Pagnell (founded in 1763) also in Buckinghamshire, only required that the governors reside in Newport Pagnell or within ten miles of the parish. One almshouse, Webb's of Capel in Surrey (founded in 1873), made being a member of the established church a requirement for a trustee; it also required that one trustee must always be of lineal descent (or husband of a lineal descendant) of Charles Webb in whose remembrance the almshouses were established.

The founder of Doughty's Hospital in Norwich stated in the Indenture of 1687 that six years after his death the executors of his will (who were also trustees of his endowment) were to convey the hospital, its lands and property to the Corporation of Norwich. It took about ten years before this was accomplished as it would appear that the trustees were reluctant to hand it over.[5]

It would seem therefore that the rules and regulations for trustees were usually not onerous, with occasional official visits required. The only rigorous diktats, from the few examples available, would seem to be those requiring the vicar of Cleeton St Mary in Shropshire to visit weekly and the chaplain of St Bartholomew's Hospital in Oxford (founded in 1128) to provide bread and beer for the almsmen. Further research in almshouse archives might reveal more details about trustees' involvement and to what extent the rules concerning them were monitored in practice.

SELECTION CRITERIA FOR ALMSPEOPLE

Applicants had to fulfil the relevant criteria to be considered for entry into the almshouse. These might include: income, residency, gender, disability, age and religion. Not all of these criteria were always stipulated, but in a number of cases they were all specified.

PLATE I. Doughty's Hospital and Garden, Norwich
(Illustration 1.a.) © *Nigel Goose 2009*

PLATE II. Stydd Almshouses near Ribchester, Lancashire, founded 1728 by John Shireburn. The unique design indicates the internal plan: three two-and-a-half room units above two, an unusual number. Stydd is in the heart of Catholic Lancashire, a tiny hamlet including both a Roman Catholic 'barn church' and the medieval chapel of St Saviour's, formerly run by the Knights Hospitallers, who also had a hospital nearby. (Illustration 2.g.) © *Helen Caffrey*

PLATE III. Gatehouse (including trustees' boardroom and porter and matron's home) at Archbishop Holgate's Hospital, Hemsworth, West Yorkshire, rebuilt 1858. (Illustration 2.e.) © *Helen Caffrey*

PLATE IV. Royal Chelsea Hospital Pensioners in Uniform
(Illustration 3.a.) © *Anne Langley 2010*

PLATE V. St Cross, Winchester showing stone row almshouses and chapel.
(Illustration 4.f.) © *Derek Spruce*

PLATE VI. Ford's
Hospital showing
timber-framed
courtyard.
(Illustration 7.c.)
© *Anne Langley 2010*

PLATE VII. Donnington Hospital showing red brick with fine Tudor chimneys.
(Illustration 5.b.) © *John Wells*

PLATE VIII. Entrance to the
Mariner's Hospital, Whitby.
(Illustration 9.c.)
© *Christine Seal 2012*

PLATE IX. The Penrhos Almswomen in their costume outside the almshouse at Holyhead, 1900s. Post-card by the Pictorial Stationery Co. Ltd in the possession of the author, Sylvia Pinches. (Illustration 10.g.) .

PLATE X. A modern-day resident of Lady Katherine Leveson's Hospital, Temple Balsall in Warwickshire, dressed as a 'Dame' in a replica costume.. (Illustration 15.d.) © *Brita Wood*

PLATE XI. Resident's garden with flowers, statue and chairs at Partis College, Bath.
(Illustration 17.g.) © *Sarah Hare*

PLATE XII. Vegetable garden at Sidney Hill Wesleyan Cottages, Somerset.
(Illustration 17.j.) © *Sarah Hare*

Martha Nobes (widow)
æt (76) Jan?? 1849

PLATE XIII. Portrait of Martha Nobes deposited at Gloucester Archives (GA ref P81 MI 1/6) and reproduced courtesy of St. James' Parochial Church Council, Chipping Campden.
(Illustration 18.b.)

Martha Nobes was aged 75 when her portrait was painted in 1849 and she died just before the 1851 census was taken. Her husband, William, was an agricultural labourer. They had six children but it appears that none were able to support her after her husband died.

Richard Cooper. (Widower)
at 77.

PLATE XIV. Portrait of Richard Cooper deposited at Gloucester Archives (GA ref P81 MI 1/6) and reproduced courtesy of St. James' Parochial Church Council, Chipping Campden.
(Illustration 18.c.)

Richard Cooper entered the almshouse in 1839, having been supported for many years on poor relief. The Vestry Minutes show him applying for (but not always getting) help in the form of an allowance, smock frocks, shoes and linen. His son Francis, aged 25, was living in the almshouse with him. Both of them are listed as agricultural labourers in the 1851 census.

The word 'poor' was used regularly in qualification criteria. Occasionally it was specified that applicants should not be in receipt of Poor Law Relief payments (mentioned by seven of the 131 almshouses with rules, just under 5 per cent). This criterion, however, seems to have been included more as a reason for expulsion if a resident was in receipt of Poor Relief than as a bar to election as a resident.[6] On the other hand, two of the 131 stipulated that the intended resident *must* be in receipt of Poor Law Relief payments (Colston's at Mortlake, originally founded 1687, and Robinson's at Walton on Thames, foundation date unknown, both in Surrey). Founders seem to have had varying ideas on the maintenance of the almspeople, with five of the almshouses insisting that residents maintained themselves (applicants to the Partis College in Somerset, founded in 1825, had to have between £20 and £30 a year) whilst four only admitted those not able to maintain themselves.

The items that entrants had to bring with them were sometimes specified: St Barthololew's Hospital in Oxford (founded in 1126) required potential almsmen to bring all their moveable goods with them; Stoke Poges (founded in 1557) required appointees to provide their own bedding; whilst Rand's in Bradford (founded in 1876) only allowed approved furniture. This topic is discussed further in Chapter 14.

Residency was a common criterion. Sixty-three, very nearly half of the almshouses, mentioned some form of residency and/or a locality. The Duchess of Marlborough's Almshouses at Bladon cum Woodstock in Oxfordshire (founded in 1798) gave the very broad qualification 'from England and Wales'. A few, such as the Great Almshouses at Burford in Oxfordshire (founded in 1457) and Pate's at Cheltenham in Gloucestershire (founded in 1574), specifically stated that the applicant must have been born in the relevant parish, with the Great Almshouses also insisting on a lifetime's residency. Length of eligible residency again varied, from two years (Holy Trinity Hospital at Long Melford in Suffolk, founded in 1573) to twenty-one years (Wyatt Almshouses at Broughton in Oxfordshire, founded in 1859). Some almshouses specified the number of individuals to be elected from specific parishes, such as Lybbe's Almshouses of Goring in Oxfordshire (founded in 1714), where '2 of Goring, 1 each of Checkendon & Whitchurch' were to be elected.

Gender was also frequently mentioned. Twenty-three of the 131 almshouses (just over 17 per cent) specified women only. Fourteen almshouses (approximately 10 per cent) specified men only, but two of those allowed them to bring their wives with them. Thirty-three almshouses (approximately 25 per cent) specified both men and women, many stating the numbers of each, whilst about half, sixty-six (50 per cent), did not mention gender at all. Thus it can be seen that three-quarters of the almshouses studied here would accept both men and women who fulfilled the relevant criteria. The evidence from this project and elsewhere (summarized by Goose and Basten) suggests a majority of places for men in early modern almshouses that was replaced, at least by the 19th-century, by a majority of places for women.[7] The greater longevity of women did, however, often lead to a preponderance of women actually living in almshouses. Where women were specified, many almshouses referred to widows, although two, Bishop Duppa's and Houblon's both at Richmond in Surrey, both specified 'unmarried' women. Many referred to the prospective residents as 'must be single' or 'unmarried', although these definitions may have included the widowed. At Snodland's Almshouses in Kent they clarified this, stating: 'Each house for a man and wife or widow or widower'. Partis College at Bath in Somerset would not admit a candidate if their mother or sister was already a resident. Bancroft's Hospital, in London, stated that any wife found to be with child was to be removed until the child was delivered, otherwise the couple would be expelled. This was presumably so that responsibility for upkeep of such a child did not fall upon the charity; it is not known whether this situation ever arose or the outcome if it did.

A few of the early foundations specified more men than women, but in some cases it is clear that these women were, in effect, employees, admitted to care for the men. An example is Holy Trinity Hospital at Long Melford in Suffolk, founded in 1573 for twelve poor unmarried men and two widows, with the proviso that: 'Two honest widows and townswomen nominated: 1 to be butler and laundress; 2 to cook and dairy woman; both to care for aged sick and impotent and both to brew and bake'.

Age was another common qualification. This varied considerably, with anything from a minimum of 40 years (Parson's in Oxford, founded in 1816) to a minimum of 60 years, mentioned by fourteen almshouses, with varying ages specified in between. Twenty-seven almshouses in all (just over 20 per cent of the 131) mentioned a specific minimum age as a qualification, whereas God's House at Ewelme in Oxfordshire (founded in 1437) merely stated 'tried and broken in age' and others referred to 'impotent' (i.e. incapable), 'decrepit' or simply 'aged'. Similar results were found by Goose and Basten in their preliminary analysis of this project's findings.[8]

The situation of the individual was referred to in various ways and often by more than one term. The most frequently mentioned, by a third of the almshouses, was 'poor' (as discussed above) whilst 7 per cent referred to 'infirm', 'lame' or 'blind'. Only three almshouses (2 per cent) specifically stated that appointees must not be ill (including God's House at Ewelme in Oxfordshire that stipulated 'not mad' as a qualification for entry). Other criteria related to the perceived character of the applicant: 'old', 'good character' and 'religious' were used by 8 per cent; and 6 per cent mentioned 'honest and impotent'. Frieston Hospital at Kirkthorpe in West Yorkshire (founded in 1595) gave a list of what they would not accept in a potential appointee: 'No idolaters, swearers, drunks, profaners'.

Religion was clearly an important criterion to founders. Bishop Duppa's and Houblon, both in Richmond, Surrey, insisted that the Lord's Prayer, the Ten Commandments and the Apostles Creed were all recited in English by the candidate prior to election. Twenty-two establishments (15 per cent of the 131 almshouses) stated that the potential resident must be a member of the Church of England.[9] Of these twenty-two, one was founded in 1375 (thus this religious criterion must be a later addition). Only one of those mentioning religion specifically stated 'not Papist' (Frieston Hospital at Kirkthorpe in West Yorkshire, founded in 1595). It seems likely that the benefactor of this almshouse, being established so soon after the Reformation, was keen to demonstrate his allegiance to Henry VIII's Church of England. Hillier's Almshouse in Surrey (founded in 1800) specified 'Protestant dissenters' as the religion of potential residents. (Catholic almshouses are discussed in Chapter 20 but it is worth noting that not all of these insisted on entrants being Roman Catholics.)

There were also occupational selection criteria: those working for a particular employer or connected with a particular industry. The Method Almshouses, at Urpeth near Chester Le Street in Durham, was founded in 1863 for labourers on the Beamish Estate or their widows. Partis College in Bath required: 'widowed gentlewomen or orphaned daughters of clergy, professionals or merchants', who must be over 50 years of age.

RULES AND REGULATIONS FOR ALMSPEOPLE

Once elected, the residents of some almshouses were subject to a number of rules and regulations, unlike the loosely controlled trustees. The rules and regulations offer an interesting insight into the daily lives of residents and can be roughly divided into three categories: administrative, practical and behavioural. The rules were reinforced by the appointment of some form of overseer to help with the smooth running of the almshouse in thirty-nine almshouses (29 per cent). This person was variously called overseer (2), matron (5), superintendent (3), chapel clerk, warden (8), master (5), visitor, mayor, porter, tutor/teacher (3), paymaster, almsperson designated (2), minister, dean and chapter, and bailiff, with two almshouses not specifying the title of this person. The overseer often lived in the almshouse or close by, except in the case of St Bartholomew's in Oxford, where the overseer was the Provost of Oriel College.

Administrative Regulations

Administrative criteria included: signing of the rules by the proposed resident and/or taking an oath to keep the rules; conspicuous display of the rules within the almshouses; and regular reading of the rules. Very few almshouse rules actually mention keeping a register (7 per cent) although it seems likely that other almshouses had some form of record. Some registers were to keep details of applicants and almspeople, whilst others just to keep a record of fines and expulsions.

Stipends were paid in many almshouses and 45.5 per cent of rules specifically mentioned a stipend: 11 per cent of these were paid annually, 2 per cent monthly, 20 per cent weekly (with 12 per cent unspecified). Only five almshouses (4 per cent) stipulated that the resident must have a means of support, three of which specified the amount ranging from £13 a year at Sidney Hill Churchill Wesleyan Almshouse in Somerset (founded in 1907) up to £40 a year at Parsons Almshouses in Oxfordshire (founded in 1816). The founders made provision in eleven almshouses (8 per cent) to expel those who, in their view, acquired sufficient funds not to require the benefit of an almshouse. Obviously 'sufficient' is subjective and varied over time and unfortunately we do not know the dates when these rules were written so no direct comparison of incomes can be made. A compromise was offered to any resident of the Elias Davey Almshouses in Croydon (founded in 1447) who inherited 3 marks (£2) or more: they had to deposit half in the common chest if they wanted to remain in the almshouse, which also required residents to bequeath all their goods to it.[10]

Some benefactors insisted that the residents wore a standard gown and sometimes a badge. Often these gowns were to be worn whenever the resident left the almshouse, so that they were identifiable, but in some instances they were to be worn at all times with stiff fines for non-compliance, or even expulsion from the Hugh Perry Almshouse at Wootton under Edge in Gloucestershire (founded in 1638). Clothing is discussed further in Chapter 15.

Some of the rules and regulations concerned sharing of accommodation or letting out of rooms. Thirty-five almshouses (over 26 per cent of the total) stated no letting of rooms; almost 21 per cent would allow sharing, but generally only with permission, and sometimes on a temporary basis whilst the almsperson was sick. Elborrow Almshouse for widows at Rugby in Warwickshire (founded in 1707) specified no male relations. Twenty almshouses (15 per cent) clearly stated that marriage was not allowed, although some would allow marriage with permission. Fifteen per cent of almshouses banned sharing under any circumstances, stating that other residents or the nurse were to tend a sick person.

Residence in the almshouse was considered desirable and some even specified the amount of time allowed outside the buildings, whether it was day or night and when permission had to be sought to be absent. We cannot know whether this was for the protection of the almsperson or so that the trustees could keep account of their whereabouts. Twenty-two almshouses allowed absence without permission, but specified the length of the absence varying from daytime only up to twenty-eight days. Twenty-one almshouses only allowed absence with permission; thirteen of these did not specify a time period, whilst the remainder allowed from one day to two months per year. Thirty-eight (over 28 per cent) of all the almshouses mentioned allowing some form of absence, be it with or without permission, whilst the three almshouses at Burford in Oxfordshire (The Great, The Lessor and Castle Almshouses, founded in 1457, 1538 and 1726, respectively) specified expulsion if permission was not sought after one week's absence. Bancroft's at Mile End in London (founded in 1735) stated: 'Any employed in the Company's service at the Hall, may be licenced to be absent during the daytime only in regard to this employment'. Elias Davey's Alms Houses at Croydon in Surrey stated: 'Not be out of sight of almshouses unless visiting church or churchyard'. Only one almshouse, St Bartholomew's Hospital in Oxford, specified a loss of stipend if absent without leave. Interestingly, the majority of almshouses in Surrey, London, Warwickshire, Yorkshire and Oxfordshire did not have any requirements regarding absence.

Practical Considerations

Most of these rules related to the smooth day-to-day running of the almshouses for the benefit of all and they can be sub-divided into those affecting security, the maintenance of the buildings and cleanliness. Forty almshouses (30 per cent) mentioned that the almspeople were responsible for all or some of: staircases and windows, their own room and personal hygiene.

Concerning security, Bancroft's Almshouse in Mile End, London (founded in 1735) specified: 'Two almsmen residing in the lodges keep the key of his respective gate and lock up'. The residents of Tooley and Smart's in Ipswich (founded in 1552) were to leave the outer door of their rooms unlocked at night for nurses to have access. Safety concerns were also shown by Smith's at St Mary Elms in Ipswich (founded in 1766) that did not allow any resident to enter the cellar without a lantern.

Another security restriction was that of a curfew: thirty almshouses (23 per cent) specifically referred to gates or doors being locked at night with two-thirds of them specifying the times, varying between summer and winter. The unfortunate almspeople of Holy Trinity at Long Melford in Suffolk (founded in 1573), were instructed that between 1 March and 1 September they must be in bed by 9 pm and rise at 7 am. The Blue House and Sidney Hill Churchill Wesleyan (founded in 1907), both in Somerset, specified lights out by 10 pm. It is, however, unlikely that these regimes could have been enforced.

Fire was a serious hazard (particularly for timber-framed buildings) and there were serious concerns about confused elderly people setting the whole place alight. The source of the risk changed over the centuries. Early almshouses were more often based on communal living: Anthony Bradshaw's at Duffield in Derbyshire (founded in 1614) specified: 'To keep one ffyre in the house to be common amongst them'. Later on almspeople were more likely to have their own fireplace. Only five almshouses gave the responsibility of sweeping chimneys to the almsperson, with one, Partis College in Bath (founded in 1825), stating this must be done twice a year. A couple of almshouses mentioned the use of fires: Huish Homes at Taunton in Somerset (founded in 1868) stated 'Not be careless of fires. No candles, oil lamps, oil stoves in the Almshouses'.[11] Barlborough Almshouses at Chesterfield in Derbyshire (founded in 1752) required 'Fires and furnaces to be put out: by 10 pm LadyDay to Michaelmas; by 9 pm Michaelmas to Lady Day'. One almshouse, Bartholomew Thomas Almshouses at Bicknoller in Somerset (founded in 1904), did not allow paraffin heaters. The

French Protestant Hospital in London (founded in 1718) ruled that no lighted candle was to be taken to the dormitories without permission of the porter and 'females not allowed footwarmers or stone hot water bottles that have to be put in the fire for fear of accident' and also 'no residents to enter the kitchen'.

Three almshouses mentioned smoking in their rules and regulations. Mickleham Almshouses near Dorking in Surrey (founded in 1845) expressly forbade smoking in any part of the almshouses and its land. The French Protestant Hospital at Bath Street in London (founded in 1718) forbade smoking in the dining rooms or courtyard. The Blue House at Frome in Somerset (founded in 1465) forbade the use of candles or lamps and specified no smoking in bed (though the latter rule must have been a later addition, since tobacco was not introduced into Europe until the 1520s).

Maintenance of the building was mentioned in some regulations, with residents expected to perform repairs, or pay for them. Sixteen (12 per cent) of the almshouses specifically stated that the almsperson was responsible for repairs, with six of the sixteen mentioning windows. Glass was an expensive item around the time of the foundation of many almshouses in the 16th and 17th centuries and so the cost of repairs would have been a serious concern. Seven founders (5 per cent) were concerned about the fabric of the buildings and specifically mentioned no defacing of brick, tile, wainscot, plaster, doors, walls, etc., with two (Seckford's Hospital in Suffolk, founded in 1587, and Fishmonger's in London, founded in 1618) insisting on immediate expulsion for any transgressions. Five sets of rules mentioned the fastening of items to the walls of the almshouses. Three categorically stated no, one only with consent, and the fifth, Bancroft's, specified: 'All such including locks, bolts and other improvements to be retained in almshouse upon death, removal or expulsion'. Any damage to the buildings, whether internal or external, would involve costs for repair should it be discovered after the departure of the tenant and the cost would then fall on the trustees to put right.

With regard to cleanliness, the main responsibility of the almspeople was in keeping the common areas of the buildings clean and tidy, with seventeen almshouses (13 per cent) specifying either general cleaning of common areas to be done on a rota system (as at Smith's Almshouses, St Mary Elms in Ipswich, founded in 1760) or the appointment of one particular almsperson. At Bancroft's (at Mile End in London, founded in 1735) one almsman had to 'sweep and keep chapel and school clean and in order, bring in coals, light fires, sweep and clean portico, stone steps, pavement' and the east gate almsman was to sweep, clean and roll gravel roads and footpaths by 10 am.[12] Bridge's Almshouse at Cirencester in Gloucestershire (founded in 1620) required 'Garden to be kept neat and free from rubbish'. Ravensworth Almshouses, at Lamesley in Durham (founded in 1835) expected friends or family to carry out duties if the almsperson was infirm. At Goring Heath Almshouses in Oxfordshire (founded in 1726) the nurse was to wind the chapel clock and at Anthony Bradshaw's at Duffield in Derbyshire (founded in 1614) the nurse was required to: 'wash chaplain's surplus in return for small beer'.[13] The latter almshouse also required the youngest almsperson to clean and dust the pews and the monument to the founder in the Church.

As well as the common areas, almspeople were expected to keep their own rooms clean and tidy, and also see to their personal hygiene. The Blue House at Frome in Somerset (founded *ca* 1465) insisted that the almspeople take a bath once a week. Tooley and Smart's Almshouse in Ipswich (founded in 1552) insisted that the almsperson take a bath at least once a fortnight.

The use of a dust hole was mentioned by seven (5 per cent) almshouses, with only Bancroft's stipulating 'all ashes, soil, dust and other waste' to be deposited. Six of these seven almshouses were in London and the seventh was in Surrey, not far from Hedger's, which had moved there from Southwark. This suggests that waste disposal was a particular problem in London. The London Almshouses (founded in 1836) stated 'no throwing out of slops, no dirt near the doors' but did not mention a particular place for the waste. Sometimes unpleasant cleaning was paid for: in 1590 Quartermain's Almshouse (or Lord William's) at Thame in Oxfordshire, founded in 1447, paid: 'To the most ancient almsman of the 5 almsmen for the time being, and in default to some other almsmen to keep clean the water course between the almshouse and the privy. 4s 0d p. A.'

Keeping animals, whether for food or as pets, was restricted in several almshouses. Animals were banned by fourteen of the almshouses: six were non-specific, a couple stipulated no dogs, whereas Wyatt's at Godalming in Surrey (founded in 1619) listed no dogs, rabbits, poultry, pigeons or swine. Bancroft's in London (founded in 1735) imposed a 5s. fine for each offence of keeping an animal on the premises. Two establishments, Cure's of Southwark in London (founded in 1584) and The Sidney Hill Churchill Wesleyan Cottage Homes in Somerset (founded in 1907), did allow a cat to be kept and one, Bartholomew Thomas Almshouses at Bicknoller in Somerset (founded in 1902), would only allow animals with permission of the Trustees.

Behavioural Criteria

The general behaviour of residents was of great concern to the majority of founders as this would reflect upon their memory and status (as discussed in Chapter 18). Behavioural criteria were imposed chiefly to ensure the peace and comfort of all residents, but religious observance – discussed a little later – may have been more for the benefit of the founder.

Seven almshouses stated that the almsperson had the responsibility to be neighbourly, live peacefully or quietly, with Frieston Hospital at Kirkthorpe in West Yorkshire (founded in 1595) enjoining their almspeople to 'live godly, charitably, gently, quietly, brotherly behave and to all men humbly and gently'. Twenty-six others merely stated that the almspeople were to help each other, either at all times or more specifically 'when ill'. Mental illness seemed to be of concern to many benefactors, presumably because this would be a burden on the trustees, and seven almshouses gave this as a reason for expulsion.

Criminal convictions of any kind were mentioned by nine of the almshouses (almost 7 per cent).[14] Hedge-breaking was considered a criminal offence at one time.[15] Seven of the nine almshouses specifically mentioned hedge-breaking: three had a zero-tolerance attitude (Fishmongers of Newington, Abbot's Hospital in Guildford and Anthony Bradshaw's Almshouses in Duffield, all founded in the 17th century), whilst two (Seckford's Hospital in Woodbridge, founded in 1587 and Michel's in Richmond, founded in 1695) gave the perpetrators two chances to reform before expulsion on the third offence.

Trade or employment was an issue on which the rules were inconsistent: some banned work (or limited the type of work allowed) whilst a few encouraged it. Some founders wished to prevent unsightly activities (such as taking in laundry) or noisy ones that would disturb the community. Others may have been concerned that their residents should remain poor and thus deserving of charity (even though residents in some almshouses needed extra money to supplement the meagre stipend paid). Of the twenty-eight (21 per cent) specifically mentioning trade and/or employment, ten (36 per cent) did not allow it, four (14 per cent) allowed it, and four only allowed it with permission. The remaining ten were more specific. Dowell's Retreat in Birmingham (founded in 1820) stated: 'Knitting, spinning, quilting, sewing, etc., for sale allowed. No noisy work allowed. Cannot go out to nurse or receive a pension in to nurse'. Bancroft's (founded in 1735) specified: 'No selling of chandlery ware, liquors, fruits, or keep any bulk or stall, public shop, put up a sign or showboard'.[16] Reynardson's at Haringay in London (founded in 1689) said: 'Not to sell spirituous liquor or other goods; nor fruit be sold at ye gate or before the wall', with Woollaston-Pauncefort Almshouses (founded in 1658), also in Haringay, merely stating 'not to use as a shop'. On the other hand, the Hospital of Stoke Poges in Buckinghamshire (founded in 1557) required: 'work in garden for profit of house or forfeit 4d'. Holloway's at Witney in Oxfordshire (founded in 1724) allowed 'labouring with their own hands for a maintenance', whilst Featherstone Bead House in West Yorkshire (founded in 1613) allowed only 'small means' for instance, child-minding and shoe repairs. Sir George Croke's Almshouse at Studley in Oxfordshire (founded in 1640) stated: 'All should do some work and not be idle to help towards their maintenance so they may eat their own bread, give to others and keep themselves when sick'.[17] Winwood Almshouses at Quainton in Buckinghamshire (founded in 1687) specified fines for 'Refusal to do honest work' with expulsion on the third refusal (this could, however, refer to work required within the almshouse, such as cleaning).

Work in the gardens or farm was mentioned by fourteen of the almshouses (11 per cent). St Bartholomew's Hospital in Oxford (founded in 1126) stated in 1128 'able bodied to work on the farm'. Anthony Bradshaws's (founded in 1614) required residents to 'keep the garden well replenished with herbes'. The three almshouses at Burford in Oxfordshire (founded in 1457, 1538, 1726) all had the same rule, namely 'Cultivate themselves or employ someone to do the work on strip of land granted to each almswoman. Cannot part with or give away this land without permission'.[18] Seckford's in Ipswich (founded in 1587) recommended digging, planting or other commendable exercise. Fourteen out of the twenty-two almshouses in Surrey for which extant rules and regulations were found, merely mentioned there was a garden or small garden with each dwelling, for which the almsperson was responsible.

Religious matters were important to many founders whose rules not only specified religious belief in entrants, but also how often the residents should pray and/or attend church. Some founders were particularly concerned about the fate of their soul after death and therefore specified that residents of their almshouse should pray for them in order to speed their journey to Heaven; unsurprisingly this was particularly true before the Reformation. Fifty-six almshouses (43 per cent) specified some form of worship for residents. The rules concerning worship varied from a simple agreement to do so, private prayers, saying grace before eating or attendance at some form of worship, to the very stringent requirement of attendance at 6 am, 9 am and 3 pm daily services (Stoke Poges in Buckinghamshire, founded in 1557) with various combinations in between. Some specified the place of worship, for example 'matron's room', 'at the Church' or 'in the chapel'. Others stipulated times to worship, such as Goring Heath Almshouses in Oxfordshire, founded in 1726, which specified daily worship in the almshouse at 10.15 am and 3 pm in winter (3.15 pm in summer) and on the Sabbath at 10.15 am and 2.15 pm. Elias Davey's Almshouse in Croydon (founded in 1447) detailed the content of the daily rituals instructing the almspeople to: 'Attend every divine service at Croydon Church with special prayers for King and founder. Also daily 3 Ave Marias, 15 Paternosters, 3 Creeds ... At least once a day gather at the tomb of the founder and pray for his soul'. Many almshouses insisted on attendance (unless unable due to proven illness or infirmity) often imposing a fine if there was no just cause for non-attendance.

SANCTIONS

The consequences of breaking rules and regulations included warnings, fines or expulsion. Uncommon sanctions existed too: Cure's, at Southwark in London (founded in 1584) not only fined its residents, but on the fourth offence the transgressor was also placed in the stocks. A resident of the French Protestant Hospital in London (founded in 1718) was 'shut up on bread and water' for begging. Of the 131 almshouses with rules, just under a third made no specific mention of sanctions; these almshouses were predominantly located in Oxfordshire and Surrey, though the reason for this is not clear.

Fines were imposed for a wide variety of transgressions, including non-attendance at worship, absence, stealing, begging, not wearing the gown outside, marrying, and breakages. The amount of the fine ranged widely, though in some cases it was not recorded. Others gave considerable detail, such as Seckford's Hospital at Woodbridge in Suffolk (founded in 1587) where fines were entered into a pensions book and any revenue used for maintenance of the almshouses and the poor of the parish.[19] Mary Warner's Almshouse at Boynton in Suffolk (founded in 1736) fined 1s. plus the weekly allowance for not sweeping the chimney and 1s for each offence of not wearing gowns in public. At Beamsley Hospital in North Yorkshire (founded in 1593) 'For wilfully breaking the rules, a fortnight's worth of offender's pension taken and given to the more virtuous of the residents and a payment to the informer', which suggests an unfortunate incentive to tale-bearing.

Most important to founders and trustees were problems that reflected badly on the almshouse, such as committing crimes, drinking, brawling, swearing, blaspheming or immoral behaviour. Anthony Bradshaw's at Duffield in Derbyshire (founded in 1614) explicitly forbade 'whoring'. The Sir William Drake Almshouse at Amersham in Buckinghamshire (founded in 1657) had a zero tolerance attitude, with immediate expulsion for all the usual offences, but also including 'incontinence'.[20] King Edward VI's Almshouse at Saffron Walden in Essex (founded in 1400, but renamed in the 16th century) included 'Be a common haunter of alehouses and evil company' and 'be Disobedient' amongst reasons for expulsion. A total of forty-one almshouses (over 30 per cent) mentioned fines and/or expulsions for these sorts of misbehaviour, whilst only sixteen fined for non-attendance at worship.

Overall, the most common reasons for expulsion were: marriage; committing crimes; infringement of the rules; misconduct; immoral conduct (adultery, fornication or incest); inheriting or having a specified amount of money or income and even not wearing the almshouse gown. A couple of almshouses (Edward's in Southwark, founded in 1717, and Elborrow's in Rugby, founded in 1707) expelled residents for non-attendance at worship. John Denham's at Egham in Surrey (founded in 1624) specified 'cursing, blaspheming, drunk, idle, wanderers, talebears, busy bodies, contentious or scandalous' as reasons for expulsion. A detailed study of the records for Doughty's Hospital in Norwich revealed interesting reasons for expulsion that included being rude to the local mayor (in 1700), attacking another resident with a jug or having 'dirty habits' (in the 19th century).[21]

Immediate expulsions were surprisingly common and not just a last resort (*see* Table 12.I). In some cases a general 'disregarding the rules' led to immediate expulsion, such as at the Boultbee Almshouses in Hampshire (founded in 1864) and Mary Giles' Almshouse, Chertsey, in Surrey (founded in 1841). Other places gave a warning, with the threat of expulsion for repeat offences.

These sanctions need to be seen in their historical context, taking into account the fact that rules were sometimes compiled or modified some time after the date of foundation. For example, Abbot's Hospital at Guildford in Surrey (founded in 1622) included witchcraft as a reason for expulsion.

TABLE 12.I
Reasons for immediate expulsion

Category	Per cent of almshouses
Drinking/brawling/swearing, etc.	24.4
Absence without permission	25
Defacing	33
Sharing	37.5
Hedge-breaking	43
Begging	44
Stealing	50

CONCLUSION

The founders put in place regulations concerning the establishment and governance of their almshouse and, not surprisingly, it is clear that regulating the almspeople was considered more important than regulating the trustees. Having provided a safe and secure dwelling place for their beneficiaries, founders then proceeded to stipulate criteria for selecting residents. Some of these criteria were designed to select local people and others to ensure the candidates were of good character, god-fearing and worthy: the deserving poor in most cases. Most almshouses were intended for the elderly (though the minimum age for entry varied considerably). Approximately three-quarters of the almshouses would accept both men and women; the longer survival of women, however, did lead to an overall preponderance of women in almshouses.

Having established that those appointed to the almshouse were suitable, the founders then endeavoured to ensure that they stayed suitable. Worship was a common theme, although the extent varied from a mere reference to being a member of the Church of England, to stipulating the exact services of divine worship to be attended and even the content of the prayers. The founders appeared to be particularly concerned with problems that reflected badly on the image of the almshouse, such as drinking and immoral behaviour. Some regulations deterred the residents from straying through a system of fines and the threat of expulsion. Some of the reasons for fines or expulsions seem strange today, but they were intended to ensure the smooth running of the almshouse. Some almspeople had to wear a kind of uniform or a badge on their outer clothing, which would advertise their identity and the benevolence of the founder (as discussed further in Chapter 15). This might be regarded as another form of control over the residents.

Although many of the rules appear regularly in some form or other in most almshouses, there were only two examples of rules mirroring each other. Firstly, the three almshouses at Burford in Oxfordshire had almost identical rules although they were founded in different centuries – 1457, 1538 and 1726, respectively – indicating that they must have been copied from one to the other. Similarly, Abbot's Hospital at Guildford in Surrey (established in 1622) had almost identical rules to Whitgift's Hospital in Croydon (founded in 1599) but with a few variations in the later foundation, presumably dictated by the archbishop's own interests. It is worth mentioning that Abbot's Hospital buildings were also based on the design of Whitgift's Hospital, although not on such a grand scale.

Perhaps the most surprising finding about almshouse rules is how little they changed over the years. Early injunctions to pray for the soul of the founder may have fallen out of favour after the Reformation, and expulsion for witchcraft was last seen in the 15th century, but in general 19th-century foundations had rules that were often as restrictive as those of the 16th century. It is important to recognise that some surviving sets of rules are undated, and others are known to have been written after the date of foundation so that it is difficult to draw firm conclusions on how rules changed over time. The restrictiveness of rules bore no obvious relationship to the date of foundation, the size of the buildings or the number of residents involved. As mentioned in the introduction to this chapter, almshouses with written rules tended to be those that were well-endowed but the reason for this is not clear. We may deduce that the extent of regulation must be credited chiefly to the beliefs and idiosyncrasies of the individual benefactors.

In conclusion, it would seem that many founders of almshouses were keen to demonstrate their own 'godliness' in the provision of safe, well-ordered accommodation for the less fortunate in their area. The numerous rules that nowadays appear strict may only be a reflection of the sort of society in which they lived when founding their establishments. It is important to point out that we do not know whether these rules were, in fact, strictly observed, and this requires further research in almshouse archives. Were the founders setting up almshouses chiefly to ensure the continuation of their good reputation and entry to heaven, or were they truly munificent in primarily trying to help their less fortunate fellow men and women?

Notes

1.   The counties with rules and regulations referenced in this chapter are: Buckinghamshire, Derbyshire, Dorset, Durham, East Suffolk, Essex, Gloucestershire, Hampshire, Kent, London, Norfolk, North Gloucestershire, Northumberland, Oxfordshire, Shropshire, Somerset, Staffordshire, Suffolk, Surrey, Warwickshire, Worcestershire and Yorkshire.

2   The twelve almshouses were: Webb's at Capel, Bishop Duppa's and Houblon's at Richmond, all in Surrey; Dowell's Retreat at Birmingham; St Edith's Home at Warwick, and Elborrow at Rugby, all in Warwickshire; Verney's at Middle Clayton, Revis's at Newport Pagnell and Winwood at Quainton, all in Buckinghamshire; Goring Heath and Sir George Croke's at Studley, both in Oxfordshire; and Doughty's at Norwich in Norfolk.

3.   Heather, P. *Andrew Windsor's Almshouses in Farnham*, Farnham, 2008.

4.   Surrey History Centre (SHC): 6703/3/1.

5.   Goose, N. & Moden, L. *A History of Doughty's Hospital Norwich, 1687-2009*, Hatfield, 2010, pp. 31-2.

6.   The almshouses using 'not in receipt of Poor Law Relief payments' as an eligibility criterion: Walton on Thames Almshouses, The Almshouses Fetcham, Mary Giles' Almshouse Chertsey, Coopers' Almshouses Egham, all in Surrey; Goring Heath Almshouses, Oxfordshire, and Goodrich's Almshouses, Prestbury, Gloucestershire.

7.   Goose, N. & Basten, S. 'Almshouse Residency in 19th-century England: an interim report', *Family and Community History*, Vol. 12 i. 2009, pp. 65-76.

8.   Ibid.

9.   The twenty-two almshouses were: Dowell's Retreat in Birmingham; Cleeton St Mary's in Shropshire; Ravenstone's Almshouses at Milton Keynes in Buckinghamshire; Barlborough Almshouses at Chesterfield in Derbyshire; Mrs Woodcock's Marine Almshouses at Bishopwearmouth in Durham; Bearpacker's Hospital at Wotton under Edge in Gloucestershire; Partis College at Bath in Somerset; Smith's Almshouses at St Mary Elms, Ipswich, in Suffolk; Snodland's Almshouses at Snodland in Kent; in Surrey: Hillier's Almshouses at Guildford, Madam de Bosset Almshouses at Petersham, and the Church Almshouses, Michel's, Bishop Duppa's and Houblon, all at Richmond; in Oxfordshire: Wyatt Almshouses at Broughton, Deddington Charity Estates at Deddington, Lady Ann Moreton's Almshouse at Kidlington, Townsend's

Almshouse at Witney, and Parson's Almshouse and Tawney's Almshouse both at Oxford; Woollaston-Pauncefort Almshouses at Haringey, London.

10. 1 mark = 13s. 4d. or two-thirds of one pound.

11. 'Taunton Town Charity, Almspersons Rules, Applicable to All Almshouses' from framed list *in situ* at the Huish Homes, Taunton, photographed by Sarah Hare with permission.

12. 'Report on the Charities of the Drapers' Company: Appendix', City of London Livery Companies Commission. Report; Volume 4, 1884, pp. 178-215. URL: www.british-history.ac.uk/report.aspx?compid=69711 Date accessed: 31 March 2009.

13. Oxford Record Office (ORO): Charity minute book of Goring Heath 1834-61, 015/1/A2/ 1-2; 'surplus' presumably referred to a surplice.

14. The nine almshouses were: Abbot's Hospital in Surrey; St Edith's Home in Warwickshire; Burford Almshouses in Shropshire; Bancroft's Almshouses in London; Verney Almshouses in Buckinghamshire; Nappers Mite Almshouses in Dorset; Seckford's Hospital in Suffolk; and Assendon and Lady Ann Moreton's Almshouses, both in Oxfordshire.

15. Taking wood for fuel from hedges. See McIntosh, M K. *Controlling Misbehavior in England, 1370-1600*, Cambridge, 2002, pp. 84 on for fuller explanation.

16. City of London Livery Companies Commission. Report; Volume 4, 1884, pp. 178-215. URL: www.british-history.ac.uk/report.aspx?compid=69711 Date accessed: 31 March 2009.

17. ORO: Croke's Almshouse Rules, 014/A/5.

18. The Great Almshouses, The Lesser/Wisdom's Almshouses, Castle's Almshouses, Burford, Oxon. The Cheatle Collection of records housed in the Tolsey Museum (a collection of transcripts). Gretton, R H. *The Burford Record*. Oxford, 1920, Archive Ref: COS BURF 352(GRE).

19. Suffolk Record Office (SRO): FB/104/L1/32. There was immediate expulsion for: being married; having or inheriting an annuity or lands of £5 or more; fornication; adultery; incest; crime; drinking or keeping of alcohol. Fines levied were: for non-attendance at worship 2d. for each offence; swearing: 2d. per offence; scolding: 6d. per offence; brawling: 1st offence - 2s. 6d, 2nd offence - 5s, 3rd offence – expulsion; absence without permission: 4d. per offence; for begging: 1st - 6d., 2nd - 12d., 3rd - 2s., further - 3s. 4d.; hedge-breaking: 1st offence - 4d., 2nd - 8d., 3rd – expulsion; defacing of any part of the almshouse – expulsion; gambling or haunting taverns: 1st - 1s., 2nd - 2s., 3rd – expulsion.

20. Presumably sexual rather than urinary incontinence.

21 Goose & Moden, pp. 42, 93-6,

22. SRO: FB 104/L1/44.

ACKNOWLEDGEMENTS

I would like to thank the following researchers on the project for their generosity in providing material to enable me to write this chapter and apologise to any whom I have inadvertently failed to mention: Cheryl Bailey, Helen Caffrey, Ann Clark, Jacqueline Cooper, Janet Cumner, Michael Drake, Mike Fitzgerald, Noel Grimmett, Sarah Hare, Sue Lambert, Anne Langley, Clive Leivers, John Loosley, the late Robert Ruegg, Pam Sambrook, Christine Seal, Susanne Shatford and Sylvia Watts. I would also like to thank Surrey History Centre for the help and forbearance of all their staff whilst researching Surrey almshouses.

APPENDIX 12.1: LIST OF ALMSHOUSES WITH RULES AND REGULATIONS.

Almshouses are sorted alphabetically firstly by County then by Almshouse Name

Almshouse County	Almshouse Name	Almshouse Location	Source/Ref.
Bucks	Hickman's Almshouses	Aylesbury	*Victoria County History of Bucks Vol 3;* 26th Charity Commissioners Report for Bucks (*CC* Bucks), BPP, 1833, xvii: 19, p. 138
Bucks	Hospital of Stoke Poges	Stoke Poges	Ibid., p. 119-20
Bucks	Oxford Lane Almshouses	Great Marlow	Ibid., p. 138
Bucks	Queen Ann's Hospital	Newport Pagnell	*CC* Bucks, 27th report, 1834, xxi, p.150
Bucks	Ravenstone Almshouses	Ravenstone, Milton Keynes	Ibid., 1834, p. 180-81.
Bucks	Revis's Almshouses	Newport Pagnell	*CC* Bucks, 1833, xvii: 19, 27th report, p. 161-2
Bucks	Seymour Almshouses	Langley	*CC* Bucks, 1833, xvii: 19, 25th report, p. 100
Bucks	Sir William Drake Almshouse	Amersham	Ibid., pp. 19-20.
Bucks	Verney Almshouses	Middle Claydon	Ibid., 19, 27th report, p. 21.
Bucks	Winwood Almshouses	Quainton	Ibid., 19, 25th report, p. 22
Derbyshire	Anthony Bradshaw's Almshouses	Duffield	Watson, W R. *The Illustrated History of Duffield*, Otley, 1986, Ch.12.
Derbyshire	Barlborough Almshouses	Barlborough, Chesterfield	Derbyshire Record Office (DeRO) D 1490 A/PF 38
Derbyshire	Ticknall Hospital	Ticknall	DeRO: D 5916/3
Dorset	Nappers Mite Almshouses	Dorchester	Dorset Record Office: D1/MJ/29
Dorset	SS John the Baptist and John the Evangelist Almshouses	Sherborne	Mayo, C H. *An Historic Guide to the Almshouse of St John the Baptist and St John the Evangelist, Sherborne.* Oxford, 1933, pp.76-7.
Durham	Coopers' Almshouses	Sedgefield	Durham Record Office (DuRO): D/Se29
Durham	Greatham Hospital	Greatham	Tyne & Wear Archives (T&WA): D/Gre103
Durham	Jane Gibson's Alms Houses	Bishopwearmouth	DuRO: EP/Biw979
Durham	Jesus Hospital	Newcastle upon Tyne	T&WA: 595/51
Durham	Method Almshouses	Upeth nr Chester Le Street	DuRO: D/X 863/1
Durham	Mrs Woodcock's Marine Alms-Houses	Bishopwearmouth	DuRO: EP/Biw445
Durham	Ravensworth Almshouses	Lamesley	DuRO: EP/Lam 12/10
Essex	King Edward VI Almshouses	Saffron Walden	Essex Record Office: *CC* Essex p. 809
Gloucs	Bearpacker's Hospital	Wotton under Edge	Gloucestershire Archives (GA): D 3469/5/177
Gloucs	Bridge's Almshouse	Cirencester	GA: P86/1 CH5
Gloucs	Earl of Gainsborough's *Almshouses*	Chipping Campden	*Charity Commissioners Report for Gloucestershire*, 1819-1837, p.141
Gloucs	Goodrich's Almshouses	Prestbury	GA: P254 CH7
Gloucs	Groves Almshouses	Tewkesbury	GA: P329/2 CH 5/1
Gloucs	Hay Cottage Homes	Cheltenham	GA: CBR C3/3/5/1/2
Gloucs	Hugh Perry Almshouse	Wotton under Edge	Personal communication, John Loosley

Gloucs	Mr Edward Richardson's, Sir Francis Russell's and Barnes' Almshouses	Tewkesbury	GA: TBR E26/1-24
Gloucs	Pate's Almshouses	Cheltenham	GA: P78/1 CH6/6
Hampshire	Boultbee Almshouses	Emery Down	Personal communication, Noel Grimmett
Hampshire	Earl of Southampton's Almshouses	Titchfield	Personal communication, Noel Grimmett
Kent	Snodland's Almshouses	Kent	www.town-talk.net/pdf/ Sep¬06/P31-P40.pdf no longer available
London	Bancroft's Hospital	Mile End	*Charity Commissioners Report on City of London Livery Companies*, Vol 4, London, HMSO, 1884. Drapers' Charities, Part 1
London	City of London Almshouses	Brixton	J Weale (ed) *London Exhibited in 1852*, p. 219
London	Cure's Almshouse	Southwark	London Metropolitan Archives: P92/SAV/1528 St. Saviour's, Southwark, Ordinances for College of the Poor
London	Edward's Almshouse	Southwark	Highmore, A. *Pietas Londinensis: the history, design and present state of the various public charities in and near London*, Phillips, London, 1810, pp. 535-537
London	Fishmongers Almshouse	Newington	Eason, A.H. *The Story of the Fishmongers' and Poulterers' Institution 1827-1927*. London, 1930
London	French Protestant Hospital	Bath Street	URL: www.frenchhospital.org.uk
London	Michael Yoakley Charity, Yoakley Buildings Quaker Almshouses	Whitechapel	Society of Friends Archive: Mss.748/5/1
London	Reynardson's Almshouses	Haringay	Haringay Archives Bruce Castle Museum: D/PT/7C/1-2
London	Woollaston-Pauncefort Almshouses	Haringay	Highgate Literary & Scientific Institution Archives: L1/SLA/43
N. Yorks	Beamsley Hospital	Beamsley	West Yorkshire Archive Service: YAS, DD139
Norfolk	Doughty's Hospital	Norwich	Goose, N. & Moden, L. *A History of Doughty's Hospital Norwich, 1687-2009*. Hatfield, 2010, p. 31
Northumberland	Jesus Hospital	Newcastle upon Tyne	T&WA: Jesus Hospital 595/51, 10 Victoria, 26th August 1846
Oxon	Assendon Almshouses	Upper Assendon *(now Stonor)*	*Charity Commissioners Report for Oxfordshire* (*CC* Oxon.), 1818-1837, p. 655
Oxon	Banbury Almshouse: Guild of the Blessed Virgin Mary	Banbury	Colin Crouch, 'Banbury charities: Historical Notes', 1882
Oxon	Bletchingdon Hospitall Houses	Bletchingdon	*CC* Oxon., 1818-1837, pp. 294-5
Oxon	Bloxham Almshouses	Bloxham	*CC* Oxon., 1818-1837, p. 384
Oxon	Castle's Almshouses	Burford	*CC* Oxon., 1818-1837, p. 446
Oxon	Charles Lister's Hospitall	Mapledurham	*CC* Oxon., 1818-1837, p. 223
Oxon	Cutler Boulter Almshouses	Oxford	*CC* Oxon., 1836. p.?
Oxon	Deddington Charity Estates	Deddington	*CC* Oxon., 1818-1837, p. 516
Oxon	Duchess of Marlborough's Almshouses	Bladon cum Woodstock	*CC* Oxon., 1818-1837, p. 500
Oxon	God's House at Ewelme	Ewelme	Goodall, J.A.A. *God's House at Ewelme*. 2001, Appendix 1

Oxon	Goring Heath Almshouses	Goring Heath	*CC* Oxon., 1818-1837, p. 333
Oxon	Holloway's Almshouses	Witney	*CC* Oxon., 1818-1837, p. 290
Oxon	Lady Ann Moreton's Almshouse	Kidlington	*CC* Oxon., 1818-1837, p. 522
Oxon	Longland's Almshouses	Henley	*CC* Oxon., 1818-37, p. 203
Oxon	Lybbe's Hospital	Goring	Oxford Record Office (ORO): L.C./1/2
Oxon	Messenger's Almshouses	Henley	*CC* Oxon., 1818-37, p. 203
Oxon	Newbury's Almshouses	Henley	*CC* Oxon., 1818-37, p. 40
Oxon	Parson's Almshouses	Oxford	*CC* Oxon., 1818-37, p. 402
Oxon	Quartermain's/Lord William's Almshouses	Thame	ORO: P/330/3/A/1
Oxon	Radcliffe's Almshouses	Steeple Aston	ORO: BNC Hurst: Steeple Aston 27-9 1664-83
Oxon	Sir George Croke's Almshouses	Studley	*CC* Oxon., 1818-37, p. 403
Oxon	St Bartholomew's Hospital	Oxford	ORO: 4495 box 11
Oxon	Stone's Almshouses	Oxford	Tiffany, M.N.E. *The History of the Rev. Mr. William Stone and his Hospital.* Oxford, 2000
Oxon	Tawney's Almshouses	Oxford	ORO: COS OXFO 361.7 stack
Oxon	The Great Almshouses	Burford	Gretton, *The Burford Record*, Oxford, 1920
Oxon	The Lesser Almshouses/ Wisdom's	Burford	Ibid.
Oxon	Townsend's Almshouses	Witney	Townley, S. (ed.) *Victoria County History for Oxfordshire* (*VCH*, Oxon.) vol. XIV, p. 165
Oxon	Wolsey's Almshouses	Oxford	Christ Church Archives: DP vi.b.l, f. 190
Oxon	Wyatt Almshouses	Broughton	*VCH*, Oxon., vol. IX p. 102
S. Yorks	Mary Bellamy's Almshouse	Rotherham	*Charity Commissioners Report for West Riding*, vol. i, p. 401.
Shropshire	Burford Almshouses	Shropshire	Shropshire Archives (SA): P50/Q/7/1
Shropshire	Cleeton St Mary Almshouses	Cleeton St Mary	SA: P48/Q/4/73
Somerset	Bartholomew Thomas Almshouses	Bicknoller	Personal communication, Sarah Hare, 2013
Somerset	Huish Homes	Taunton	Personal communication, Sarah Hare, 2013
Somerset	Mells Almshouse	Mells	Personal communication, Sarah Hare, 2013
Somerset	Partis College Almshouse	Bath	Bath Record Office: 0354/4
Somerset	Spital almshouses	West Monkton	Personal communication, Sarah Hare, 2013
Somerset	The Blue House	Frome	Personal communication, Sarah Hare, 2013
Somerset	The Sidney Hill Churchill Wesleyan Cottage Homes	Churchill	Personal communication, Sarah Hare, 2013
Staffordshire	Hospital for Widows	Newcastle under Lyme	Staffordshire Record Office: D593/B/1/13/330
Suffolk	Holy Trinity Hospital	Long Melford	Wigmore, E. *Holy Trinity Hospital, Long Melford: a 16th century almshouse*, Long Melford, 1995
Suffolk	Mary Warner's Charity	Boyton	Suffolk Record Office (SRO): FC 163/L1/3
Suffolk	Seckford's Hospital	Woodbridge	SRO: FB 104/L1/32
Suffolk	Smith's Almshouses	St Mary Elms, Ipswich	SRO: FB 104/L1/44
Suffolk	Tooley and Smart's Almshouses	Ipswich	SRO: GA 403/B/3
Surrey	Abbot's Hospital	Guildford	Taylor, B. *Abbot's Hospital Guildford.* Guildford, 1999

Surrey	Almshouses	Mickleham	Surrey History Centre (SHC): MIC22/, MIC23/
Surrey	Almshouses	Fetcham	SHC: FET5,7
Surrey	Almshouses	Walton on Thames	Personal communication, the late Robert Ruegg
Surrey	Bishop Duppa's Almshouse	Richmond	SHC: *Charity Commissioners Report for Surrey* (*CC* Surrey), 1934 p. 361
Surrey	Bishop Juxon's Almshouse	Mortlake	SHC: 2414/9/364
Surrey	Church Almshouses	Richmond	Personal communication, the late Robert Ruegg
Surrey	Cleave's Almshouses	Kingston upon Thames	Pountney, E.R. *Cleave's Almshouses 300th Anniversary*, Kingston-upon-Thames, 1969
Surrey	Colston's Almshouses	Mortlake	Personal communication, the late Robert Ruegg
Surrey	Coopers Almshouses	Egham	SHC: *CC* Surrey, 1819-1837, p.680
Surrey	Elias Davey's Alms Houses	Croydon	Lambeth Palace Library: Register of John Morton 1485-1500, Vol 1 fo. 199-202
Surrey	Hammond's Almshouse	Chertsey	SHC: *CC* Surrey, 1934 pp. 655-6
Surrey	Harman Attwood Almshouse	Warlingham	SHC: *CC* Surrey, pp. 548-60
Surrey	Hedger's Almshouse	Southwark, now Merrow	SHC: 1802/9
Surrey	Henry Bridges Almshouses	Thames Ditton	SHC: *CC* Surrey, 1824, p. 593, ref.2629/17
Surrey	Hickeys Almshouses	Richmond	SHC: QS6/1/box1
Surrey	Hilliers Almshouses	Shoreditch, then Guildford	Personal communication, the late Robert Ruegg
Surrey	Houblon Almshouses	Richmond	*Barnes and Mortlake Herald* dated 16 Dec 1911, Richmond Local Studies Library
Surrey	John Denham's Almshouse	Egham	SHC: 2118/2/5
Surrey	Knight's Almshouse	Wrecclesham	SHC: 1505/3/2; *CC* Rep. pp. 587-92
Surrey	Lovejoy's	Guildford	SHC: *CC* Surrey, p. 697
Surrey	Madam de Bosset Almshouses	Petersham	Personal communication, the late Robert Ruegg
Surrey	Mary Giles' Almshouse	London Street, Chertsey	SHC: 6200/ADD/box 77, Bundles 6 & 7
Surrey	Michel's Almshouse	Richmond	*Barnes and Mortlake Herald* dated 16 Dec 1911, Richmond Local Studies Library
Surrey	Queen Elizabeth's Almshouses	Richmond	Personal communication, the late Robert Ruegg
Surrey	Robinson's Almshouses	Walton on Thames	Personal communication, the late Robert Ruegg
Surrey	Webb's Almshouse	Capel	SHC: CAP/17/5
Surrey	Weston Green Almshouses	Thames Ditton	Personal communication, the late Robert Ruegg
Surrey	Whitgift Almshouses	Croydon	Personal Communication, Cheryl Bailey
Surrey	Windsor's Almshouse	Farnham	SHC: 8421/3-5, 1505 Box46; *CC* Surrey, pp. 587-92
Surrey	Wyatt's Almshouses	Godalming	Personal communication, the late Robert Ruegg
W. Yorks	Featherstone Bead House	Featherstone	*Charity Commissioners Report West Riding*, v, p. 146-51
W. Yorks	Frieston Hospital	Kirkthorpe	Ibid., v, pp. 720-34

W. Yorks	Rand's Almshouses	Bradford	Bradford Local Studies Library: B363.5
Warwickshire	Church St Almshouses	Stratford upon Avon	Shakespeare Centre Library & Archives: BRU 15/15/106
Warwickshire	Dowell's Retreat	Birmingham	Birmingham Library Archives: LP 41 14 662604,1900
Warwickshire	Elborrow's Almshouse	Rugby	*Charity Commissioners' Report for Warwickshire*, 1815-35, p. 722
Warwickshire	Lady Katherine Leveson's Hospital	Temple Balsall	Gooder, E. T*emple Balsall from Hospitallers to a Caring Community 1322 to modern times.* Chichester, 1999, p. 60
Warwickshire	St Edith's Home	Emscote, Warwick	Warwickshire County Record Office: DR 395/19/8

APPENDIX 12.2:   TRANSCRIPT OF A FAIRLY TYPICAL SET OF RULES AND REGULATIONS FROM SMITH'S ALMSHOUSES, ST MARY ELMS, IPSWICH, FOUNDED IN 1766.[22]

Rules to be observed by the inhabitants of St Mary at Elms Almshouses

1st   All the women are required to give strict attendance to the public prayers read in their parish church on Wednesday and Friday throughout the year and whoever is absent (unless some very good excuse be assigned and approved of by the Trustees) shall forfeit six pence of their weekly payment for every such offence.

2ndly   The poor women must attend the public service of their church upon Sundays, or they will upon the same terms be liable to the same abatement in their pay as mentioned in the former rule.

3rdly   They must prepare themselves for and receive the Holy Sacrament as often as it is administered in their parish church, and they are required and exhorted to have morning and evening prayers in the Almshouses upon the days they do not attend the public worship of God in the parish church.

4thly   If any woman or women be convicted by the evidence of two or more of the inhabitants of the said house or by the evidence of any one officer of the parish before the Trustees of contentious strife, abusive language, cursing and swearing, or any other notorious crime to the [inversion?] of that Christian Harmony and Godliness that should subsist amongst them, she or they should forfeit on shilling for the first, and second offence, and be expelled the House for the third.

5thly   All the women are required to be at home by nine o'clock in the evening in winter and by ten in the summer season – viz by nine from Michaelmass to Lady day and by ten from Lady day to Michaelmass – and no one of them shall be out of the Almshouses without leave of the Trustees.

6thly   No woman shall take any person into her rooms with her as a lodger, companion, or otherwise upon pain of expulsion – unless she is thro infirmity absolutely unable to take care of herself – and even in that case no person is to be admitted as an assistant, but such as one as shall be approved of by the Trustees.

7thly   No woman shall presume to keep any kind of shop or to sell anything whatsoever in her respective rooms upon pain of expulsion.

8thly   Each person shall keep her respective rooms and cellar clean and not deface or injure them – and they are all expected by turns to clean the common passages of the house as often as it shall be necessary. And upon a survey of the Trustees they shall be found wanting therein any person or persons that neglect to give her or their assistance shall have so much of her or their pay stopped as by the Trustees shall be thought sufficient to satisfy any person for doing that necessary work.

9thly   If it appears upon proper evidence that any woman placed in the Almshouses hath in a clear annuity or in lands, [and] hereditaments fourteen pounds per annum, or if any such annuity etc. shall be afterwards be given unto her every such woman shall forthwith be removed and another chosen in her room, or if it be known certainly that any of the elected women have husbands living, such women shall be immediately removed and others chosen.

10thly   No one of the poor women shall go abroad without leave of the Trustees or wander about and ask alms or solicit gifts of charity, without being liable to the abatement of one weeks pay for the first and second offence and to expulsion for the third.

11thly   When the glass windows are broken in any of the women's respective apartments, the money for the reparation of them shall from time to time be deducted out of the weekly payments of the inhabitants thereof

12thly   No woman must go into her respective cellar after candle light without a lantern upon pain of expulsion if there are any sorts of chips, straw, [illegible], or kindling therein that is likely to be set on fire.

27 June 1766

CHAPTER 13
AN ALMSHOUSE MASTER AT BAY:
THE LIFE OF JOHN ALEXANDER GOWER,
MASTER OF THE STOKE POGES' HOSPITAL 1836-1881

Michael Drake

INTRODUCTION

This is the story of an obscure Victorian clergyman, master of Stoke Poges' Hospital, of the people he was appointed to serve, and of the local bigwigs – some recognised nationally – he somehow offended.

Illustration 13.a. The Stoke Poges' Hospital building in 2015
Photo © Simon Drake taken by kind permission of the current owners, Nicholas and Gemma Fowler.
Since the Hospital was sold by its trustees in 1947, it has been occupied as a private house (The
Clockhouse). The former master's house is in the middle of the building, with the chapel to its left
and the almspeople's accommodation to its right

John Alexander Gower was the master of Stoke Poges' Hospital (an almshouse) from 1836-1881. He was appointed to the post by Lord Hastings of Loughborough, whose family had founded the almshouse by Act of Parliament in 1557-58, on the recommendation of Sidney Godolphin Osborne, then Vicar of Stoke Poges. It was not a rich 'living', indeed not a 'living' at all, the stipend being no more than £24 a year, sometimes paid in arrears, but it came with a fine house. Gower belonged to that growing body of Church of England clergy that, as the 19th century progressed, exceeded the ability of the Church to employ satisfactorily.[1] As a result he, and those of his fellow clergy in a similar position, were forced into 'an economy of makeshifts'. Although the term is commonly used to describe the often parlous position of the poor in 18th- and 19th-century England, I shall endeavour to demonstrate its aptness for at least one member of a wholly different social class.[2]

THE MASTER OF THE STOKE POGES' HOSPITAL

John Gower was the son of the Rev. Henry Hesketh Gower of Great Marlow, where he was born in 1804. His father does not appear to have had a living nor does he appear in the Church of England database.[3] He does appear, however, in the Buckinghamshire *Posse Comitatus* of 1798, which was rather unusual for a clergyman.[4] Gower also appears, with his title, at the baptism of several of his children in the register of the parish church of Great Marlow between 1799 and 1806.[5] He died in 1810, leaving his entire estate to his wife, noting only that those who advised her should pay attention 'particularly to the boys'.[6] John Gower went up to Oxford in the year of his father's death, although whether that was cause or effect we do not know. He went as a six-year-old chorister to Magdalen College where he continued to sing for his supper until 1820.[7] From 1817-1819 he was also a chorister at St John's College.[8] Both posts marked his entry into the 'economy of [middle class] makeshifts'. He was matriculated at Magdalen on 7 July 1821, receiving his BA in 1827, having been awarded a Class II in *Literis Humanioribus* in the Michaelmas Term of 1826.[9] This education was funded, one assumes, at least in part by his being what the *Alumni Oxoniensis* describes as a clerk at Magdalen, from 1820-27 and a chaplain from 1827-32.[10]

His income from the mastership of the Stoke Poges' Hospital was derisory. However it is possible he had a private income derived from his father and possibly his wife.[11] Furthermore, he used the accommodation provided for him at the Hospital to tutor a number of pupils. As a result we find that, according to the 1841 census, he lived in the master's house with his wife and four children aged between one and five years; a sister-in-law; five male pupils, four of whom were aged fifteen and the other fourteen; and two female servants. The almshouse had but three residents of whom two were male and one female (three fewer than the full complement, *see* below).[12] That some income came from the five pupils seems unquestionable, from his sister-in-law more doubtful. That only three alms people were present, instead of the six intended by the founder of the Hospital, might also have benefitted its master financially.[13]

By 1851, John Gower and his wife were living in the master's house with five children (this number does not include their son Hesketh, who appeared in the 1841 census); his sister-in-law, now described as a visitor and widow; six scholars between the ages of fourteen and eighteen; a governess and four female servants. There were now four almspeople, two men and two women.[14] Gower was living as one would expect a successful clergyman to do, but he could not have done so on his almshouse master's salary of £24 a year. One assumes that his pupils, and possibly the funding of only four alms people instead of six, were again major contributors to his standard of living.

According to the 1861 census, Gower had only one 'private pupil', a young man aged nineteen, but he still had three servants. The rest of the household consisted of his wife and two daughters, and a husband and wife described as visitors. There were now five alms people: three men and two women.[15]

The sister-in-law, who had appeared in the 1841 and 1851 censuses, made a reappearance in that of 1871. She, together with Gower, his wife, two unmarried daughters, a grandson and a granddaughter (both aged four years and both born in Calcutta, East Bengal – now Kolkata) and four female servants and a visitor made up the household. The almshouse now contained its full complement of six people: three men and three women.[16]

By the 1881 census Gower had lost two stalwarts of his Stoke Poges' household, namely his sister-in-law, aged 75 at her death in 1874, and his wife, who died aged 77, in September 1880.[17] Interestingly, in view of the two grandchildren born in Calcutta, Gower lost a son (Basil Henry Stephens Gower) in India (not the father of the aforesaid grandchildren), who died very suddenly in Bareilly, Oude, on 14 February, of a heart aneurism; at the time he was a captain in the 17th Bengal Cavalry.[18] There were still two unmarried daughters, a grand-niece and four servants in Gower's household.[19] Gower himself died on 26 August 1881, being described in the burial notice as: 'for 45 years chaplain of Stoke Poges Hospital'.[20] In the year he died there were three almsmen and three almswomen in the Hospital, the full complement.

Reviewing John Gower's life as the Master of Stoke Poges Hospital, one is struck by two aspects. First, his standard of living appears to have been well up to that of a parish priest with a 'good living.' Second that 'living' seems to have been the product of a number of 'makeshifts.' He took in quite a number of pupils; he provided a home for a sister-in-law, who could well have contributed to the running costs of his household; in later life he also had grandchildren and a grand-niece living with him. Now, of course, these could have been but temporary visitors. But, given that two were born in Calcutta, the presumption is that he was providing longer-term care, which could well have been paid for. As we shall see, Gower also rented out his house in the summer for four guineas a week, something that brought him into conflict with the trustees of the almshouse. All these stratagems contributed to his standard of living and all can be described as components of a middle class 'economy of makeshifts'.

THE ALMSPEOPLE OF THE STOKE POGES' HOSPITAL

According to its founder in 1557, the master of the Stoke Poges' Hospital was to be 'a priest of honest and godly conversation'. The 'four poor men' in his charge were to be 'sole or married'; the two women were to be 'sole and unmarried'. The master was to receive £10 a year, the brethren £5 and the sisters £4. They did not hang on to this very long, for when they received it (each quarter) they had to pay for their board; the master paying 2s. a week, the brothers 1s.4d and the sisters 1s. One of the brothers acted as steward for a week at a time. This was because all were to eat together in the hall of the Hospital. They were all to have a livery each year: the master's to consist of four yards at 6s. 8d. a yard, the brothers and sisters, three yards at 5s. a yard. These differential charges were carried through to the rudimentary health insurance enjoined by the founder. For into 'the common box' – a chest with three keys – were to be placed, every quarter, 2s. by the master; 20d. by each brother and 1s. by each sister: 'to be employed upon them in sickness'. Lord Hastings must have expected little call upon the contents of this box as, rather oddly, he stated that when the box contained £40 or above, then £20 should be spent on a variety of good works, from 'mending the highways', to providing for the 'marriage of poor maids'. All members of the hospital had to provide their own bedding, but only the brothers and sisters had to leave half of what they owned to the common box on death. The brothers and sisters were not to leave the parish of Stoke Poges without the permission of the master; on the other hand they were to inform the founder, his heirs or the visitors (namely the Dean of Windsor and the Provost of Eton who were to receive a pair of gloves and 6s. 8d every New Year's day), if the master was not doing his job properly. The master and his charges had to attend church daily at 6 and 9 am and at 3 pm.[21]

One assumes that for 200 years or so, matters at the Hospital continued as the founder intended. However, a dramatic change occurred in 1765. Both the original almshouse – which adjoined the Park of Stoke Poges – and part of its endowment ('pasturage for 6 cows in the Park and Congrye of Stoke Poges') turned out to be 'attended with some inconvenience' for Thomas Penn, the new lord of the manor and owner of the said park. Presumably he didn't want the cows or the almshouse (probably somewhat dilapidated by now) spoiling his view. Eighteenth-century landlords had a reputation for being somewhat fussy about matters like this. Penn, therefore, proposed to build a new hospital: 'equally as good and commodious in every respect and particular as the then existing hospital', and to provide pasture for six cows elsewhere in the parish. Not only that, Thomas Penn also agreed to pay for the Act of Parliament that was necessary to make the transaction legal.[22]

When the Commissioners of Inquiry into the charities of England and Wales came to examine the Hospital of Stoke Poges in the 1830s they remarked that at the west end was a chapel that adjoined the master's apartment, whilst the alms people, residing at the east end, enjoyed: 'on the ground floor a large kitchen, a pantry, a cellar, a larder, a wash-house and a brew-house and on the floor above six bedrooms. The whole is in good repair'.[23]

Whilst the commodious nature of the accommodation would appear to be due to the late Thomas Penn's desire to get the old almshouse and its six cows out of his sight, other changes reveal moves away from the expressed wishes of the founder. First, livery was no longer worn; the master no longer dined with the almspeople; and the late master, Mr Bold (1802-31), had 'by the direction of the visitors, separated from the rest one of the bedrooms which became vacant and which has since been considered as part of the master's apartments'.[24] Furthermore, 'the statutes respecting prayers and sermons' were neglected, and the brothers and sisters complained that, whilst the rents enjoyed by the Hospital had risen, their allowances had not. Recognising the justice of this, the then master, the Rev. Richard Moore Boultbee, had distributed a £1 extra to each of the brothers and sisters at Christmas 1831: 'having money in hand sufficient for that purpose' (this had come from the Rev. Arthur Bold's executors).[25] He also proposed that instead of the allowances of bread, meat, etc., each of the alms people should get a weekly allowance in money. According to the Commissioners inquiring into the hospital, the accounts for 1831 showed that of a total expenditure of £135 8s., some £24 15s. 6d. was paid to the baker and £12 3s. 0d. to the butcher.[26] Finally, at the time the Charity Commissioners reported on the hospital, there was a dispute between the master and his charges as to who should benefit from the proceeds of the Hospital's garden or use it for the purposes of exercise and recreation. The Commissioners appeared to side with the almspeople on this, whilst noting it would require an Act of Parliament to change anything, and that the hospital did not have the funds to do this![27]

It would seem that, although by the 1830s the Hospital of Stoke Poges had moved from its original foundation, both physically and as regards some of the wishes of its founder so far as dress and religious observance were concerned; and although the master no longer appeared to bear anything like the same relationship to the brothers and sisters of the almshouse as the founder had decreed, nevertheless there was much that remained the same.

However, a major change in the running of the Hospital, not remarked upon by the Commissioners in their 1832 report, had occurred in 1787. In that year the Hospital had ended its involvement in dairy farming. We only know about this from 1775 onwards, when the extant accounts begin, but it is clear that income from this activity was substantial. For example, in 1775 the Hospital earned 15s. 9d. from the sale of milk, £1 10s. 5d. from the sale of butter and 8s. 0d. from hay, and sold sixteen calves for £52 13s. 6d. The only other income for the hospital was rent from four sources. Out of a total income of £113 13s. 2d. (ignoring £15 19s. 7³/4d. brought forward from 1774) some 46.3% came from pastoral activities and 53.7% from rent.[28]

The hospital did have outgoings in connection with its pastoral activities. For instance, in 1775 under 'disbursements', the accounts show that £12 7s. 0d. was spent on ten calves, with prices ranging from 17s. 0d to £1 9s. 6d., the higher prices being paid in the second half of the year. On 2 January, £9 9s. 0d. was spent on a cow and calf. Seven cows were taken for 'bulling' at 1s. a time. There was also an item for straw: £1 14s. 3d. in the week from 26 August to 2 September. This may have been for the almspeople's mattresses, although it could have been used for winter bedding for the cattle. Finally, there was an item 'cows on board and hiring' amounting to £5 6s. 10d. We have then, an income of £52 13s. 6d. and an expenditure of £29 4s. 1d., making a net contribution to the hospital's finances for the year of £23 9s. 5d.[29] Pastoral activities ceased in 1787, the income derived from them being replaced, though not completely, by rent, presumably from the land previously used for those activities.

THE STORM CLOUDS GATHER

Concern at the running of the Stoke Hospital first appears to have been brought to the attention of a national audience on 5 July 1854 when a letter appeared in *The Times* from S G Osborne, the vicar who had originally recommended Gower's appointment. As the letter is central to the controversy surrounding John Gower it appears below:

> It is my wish, Sir, with your permission, to call the attention of the Charity Commissioners to an institution in which it is my belief the intentions of the founder and benefactor have for very many years been shamefully abused.
>
> A certain Lord Hastings, of Loughborough, in the year 1557, founded a "hospital" for the support of a chantry priest and four bedesmen; he endowed it with a sum then worth £50 a year, more or less. The said hospital was erected in Stoke Park ... in the Parish of Stoke Poges, near Slough ... In the year 1765, Mr. Penn the then owner of the said park, procured an act of Parliament, enabling him to pull down the building and re-erect it, where it now stands, in another part of the same parish, he at the same time securing to its use an augmented income.
>
> For some time I was the vicar of Stoke; the present master was presented to the hospital by Lord Hastings, at my request. Long previous to his appointment, and since, a good deal of discontent has existed as to the condition of the charity. A certain Mr. Depree, of Langley, a man who had risen by his own exertions from poverty to wealth, made it his business to look for

every possible source of information as to the rights of the poor people elected to the charity, and those of the master appointed to it. He, I well remember showed to me that it had for many years been shamefully abused. The successive masters had obtained ... for themselves much of what belonged by right, and by the intention of the founder, to the objects of the charity. The almshouse accommodation had been contracted to extend that of the master; and this not only as regarded the dwelling part of the building, but also as regarded the garden of the poor people and other privileges they enjoyed. The chapel in my time, existed, and a neat building it was, well adapted to its purpose, but not used for it. I myself being interested in the matter, applied to the then Dean of Windsor and Provost of Eton on the subject. I was again and again promised investigation but never obtained it.

I now challenge the attention of the Charity Commissioners to the subject. I ask as a simple matter of justice that inquiry shall be made as to the manner in which the statutes are obeyed. Are the funds carefully managed so that the intentions of the pious founder, where possible, are carried into effect? Are the number of people sustained as alms men or women the proper number? Have they the proper allowance? Has their garden, or any of it, been taken from them and added to that of the master? Has any part of their premises been contracted that the master's residence may be improved? Has the chapel been used as such, or has it until lately been used for some of the commonest purposes of life?

I may be told that there is an investigation now pending, or perhaps now complete, into this matter. I ask, if so, to what extent has it been carried – by what authority – and how far have the almspeople had their rights fairly advocated? It is a case, I believe, in which justice cannot be satisfied unless the inquiry is of a strictly official and impartial character – one which looks neither to the right or left; that is deaf to private solicitation, or private interest; that will search out to reveal, and remedy all the abuse that slack visitors and grasping masters may for the last better part of a century have perpetrated. I claim no merit in calling attention to what I do believe to be a most gross case of abuse ... My interest in the parish is now simply one whose most active, and, I trust, most useful years was there passed; who had many a true friend, and could say when he left it, he believed he did so under proof of a regard for him, and his which he is never likely to forget.

S.G. OSBORNE.[30]

It is not clear why Osborne had turned against his protégée, Gower, but he may have been keen to dissociate himself from the appointment once criticisms had been raised. John Gower replied on the following day, although his letter was not published until 11 July 1854; a bone of contention as we will see. Here it is:

Sir. – I am sure you will do me the justice to insert as speedily as possible, the following statement of facts and figures, in reply to the communication addressed to you by your correspondent in *The Times* of today. That I may not occupy your columns inconveniently, I will be as brief as possible:-

The whole income of the hospital amounts to £137 13s., and consists of the following items:-

Quitrent from the manor of Creach St. Michael	£50	0	0
Lands in the parish	75	0	0
Cottages in ditto	11	0	0
Mr. Bold's legacy	1	13	0
	£137	13	0

The income is applied in the following manner:-

Maintenance of four poor people, including their food, clothing, allowance, and firing	£58	16	0
Good Friday gifts	1	4	0
Sunday ditto	0	17	4
Fire insurance	4	8	9
Vicar's and Rector's tithe	12	9	2
Rates and taxes	7	6	8
Average medical expenses	5	8	0
Average repairs	27	7	0
Master's salary	23	0	0
Double income tax on the above, about	4	5	0
	£145	1	11

The whole subject was, I believe, investigated in 1832, under Lord Brougham's Act, is now under investigation, and I have no doubt full justice will be done to all parties; and, though grasping may consist in little as well as much, the reading public will not fail to be amused at the notion of grasping masters with an income of £23 a year, and to whom, as proved by the books of the said hospital, the institution has been constantly in debt since the year 1600 and downwards.

In reference to the treatment of the poor people, I will only add that no one will court the present Inquiry more than   Your obedient servant

JOHN ALEXANDER GOWER
The present Master of Stoke Hospital.
Stoke, Slough, Bucks, July 5.

P.S. I have not noticed the various errors in your correspondent's letter, but will merely add that the original number for which the hospital was founded was six not four. This number was, about 50 years ago, reduced to five, and a few years since to four, by the authority and under the sanction of the visitors, the funds being found inadequate for the maintenance of the greater number.[31]

Gower was not happy that his reply to Osborne had been held over by the editor of *The Times* (who was a friend of Osborne), so, on Saturday 15 July, he wrote to the *Daily News*. Its editor obliged, with all three letters appearing on Tuesday 18 July:

Slough 15 July 1854

SIR – The editor of *The Times* having done me the tardy justice of admitting into its columns, six days after date, my reply to the insinuated charges of "shameful abuse" and "grasping masters," contained in the accompanying letter of their honourable, reverend and "able" correspondent S.G.O., and having reason to believe that that delay has been a serious detriment to me personally, my only alternative is to have recourse to the columns of those periodicals whose editors, without fear or partiality, will let the accused speak for himself as promptly as the accuser. To my simple statement in reply I have only to add my assured conviction that neither at this present nor any former period has that gentleman had any proof of abuse brought before him in connection with this charity; that my accounts have been duly examined and approved by the visitors up to the year 1850; that every item of these accounts has been duly laid before the Commissioners of Inland Revenue, who have returned the tax charged thereon, and that in addition to the pending visitation, I have recently requested the commissioners of charities to send down an inspector to examine and report on the past and present condition of the institution. The honourable and reverend gentleman has, without the least intimation to myself dragged me his brother clergyman and quondam friend to the bar of public opinion, and has at the same time ingeniously contrived to call public attention to his own services and their reward. The public, sir, will know how to appreciate the self-devotion of the one and the delicacy of the other. With many apologies for troubling you at so great length.

JOHN ALEXANDER GOWER Master of the Stoke Hospital

Appended is Mr Osborne's letter and my reply; and I shall feel it an act of great courtesy on your part if you will publish them in your columns.[32]

For some reason, Gower's letter to the *Daily News* is slightly different to his letter in *The Times*. For instance it includes £1. 1s. 0d. for winding the clock (to which Osborne later refers – see below) but no payment of tax. Further pressure was placed on Gower by another item that appeared in *The Times* on 18 July 1854. Under the heading of 'LORD HASTING'S HOSPITAL AT STOKE POGES', it was noted that: 'a meeting of the leading inhabitants of Stoke Poges was held a few days since at Stoke Park, the residence of the Rt Hon. Henry Labouchere, MP, when the following requisition was agreed to'.

This was a copy of a letter addressed to the Dean of Windsor and the Provost of Eton. There were seven signatories to this letter: John Shaw, Vicar of Stoke Poges; Henry Cantrell and William Cooper, his churchwardens; The Right Honourable Henry Labouchere MP, who, at the time was President of the Board of Trade and who occupied Stoke Park, the largest house in the district, built, as noted above, by a former benefactor of Stoke Hospital; Abraham Darby (of the ironmaster family); G.W. Dyson (Clerk to the House of Commons); and Major General Howard Vyse (famed for his exploration of the Pyramids, a sometime MP and High Sheriff of Buckinghamshire):

We, the undersigned, minister and churchwardens, and other inhabitants of Stoke Poges, have heard with great satisfaction that you propose to institute an inquiry into the state of the Hospital situated in this parish, of which you are the visitors. We have no doubt but that this investigation will be conducted in a manner to satisfy the just expectations of all who are interested in the condition and usefulness of this institution and we beg respectfully to offer such assistance and co-operation as it may be in our power to afford towards affecting these objects.

The news item continued: 'No reply has yet been received from the visitors, but it is expected that an early day will be fixed for the inquiry'.[33]

It is of some interest that whereas Osborne had appealed to the Charity Commissioners to institute an inquiry into the Hospital: 'the leading inhabitants of Stoke Poges' had directed their appeal to the traditional authority, the Visitors. In the event, the Charity Commissioners responded quickly by sending an inspector to conduct an inquiry: 'into the administration of the funds of the charity on Friday and Saturday, the 4th and 5th of August 1854'.[34]

The inquiry conducted by Inspector Skirrow took place in Gower's parlour and was attended by him; the Rev. Dr Hawtrey, Provost of Eton College and the Rev. G. Wellesley, Dean of Windsor ('for the time-being the ex-officio visitors of the charity'); the Rev. J Shaw, vicar of Stoke Poges and his curate, the Rev. Mr Franks, and his two churchwardens, Messrs Henry Cantwell and William Cooper; together with Colonel R H Vyse and the Rev. Mr Boultbee, the former master of the hospital.

According to the report of the meeting that appeared in *The Times*, the Provost of Eton opened the proceedings by reading the statutes under which the charity was constituted. It was recognised that some of these could no longer be complied with, but no obstacle stood in the way of others, yet they had not been carried out. For instance, 'prayers should be read daily in the chapel by the master in surplice, etc.'. Gower said he had done this for four to five years from 1836 (the year of his appointment) and at all other times in his own dining room. From May 1853 he appeared to have recommenced reading the prayers in the chapel.

According to the statutes, each Visitor was to receive 6s. 8d. and a pair of shoes once a year from the master. Hawtrey and Wellesley both pointed out that they had never received either, so that the charity was in 'large arrears to them upon that head.' The Commissioner (*sic*) – earlier referred to as the Inspector – then pointed out that Gower, for the last ten years, had absented himself for six weeks without appointing a *locum tenens*, and during that time had let his house for four guineas a week. He had also reduced the number of hospital inmates to four: 'for whose maintenance the same sum was charged as for the original number'. The inmates were provided with: 'seven half-quarters of bread and $1\frac{1}{2}$ quarters of flour every 14 days'. The vegetables were procured from the garden, which was cultivated by the inmates at their own expense. They were allowed a shilling a week each for meat, but they all complained that the quantity was insufficient, and that they would much prefer being allowed to provide for themselves. The master said that the average cost of the maintenance of each inmate was £16 a year.

Gower was then quizzed further by the members of the inquiry. In answer to the Inspector, he said that he had not 'performed in the chapel … because it was totally unfit for church service'. He admitted, however, that he had used it as a private apartment for the convenience of his family, carpeting and furnishing it for the use of his governess and children and also for keeping barrels of beer, sacks of beans and bran.

Two financial discrepancies were raised by the Vicar of Stoke Poges. He said that: 'he could only make out £45 17s. 6d. as the total expence of maintaining the inmates for one year, instead of £58 14s. 8³/4d., as had been stated by the master'. He then noted a charge for the Rector's tithes of £12 9s. 2d., 'whereas for the last five years he had received none'.

The Provost of Eton sought to defend the inaction of the visitors by deploring that: 'the master had not taken the necessary steps to inform the visitors of their duties'. He went on to say that the master had no right to appropriate to his own use the two best rooms in the house, and that if he had the sanction of the Provost for doing so, still it would not be legal. Similarly, he believed it was illegal for the master to let his house and, as regarded the chapel: 'it was quite clear that the building had been converted to other uses than those for which it was intended by the donor, and which could not have occurred, had the visitors been aware of their authority under [the] statutes'.

One bright note, so far as Gower was concerned, came when 'several of the inmates were called in and examined as to the treatment they received', for all 'admitted that they had no cause of complaint, except with regard to the deficiency of meat.' So far as the reporting of the inquiry was concerned, Gower had the last word. Returning to the issue of the chapel, he said that 'he had no hesitation in declaring that even now [it] was totally unsuited for any Christian man to hear prayers in or remain in it for 20 minutes'.

If Gower had hoped that, with the end of the inquiry, his public humiliation would cease, he was to be disappointed. For just a week after the report of it had appeared in *The Times*, another letter from S G Osborne appeared in that paper. Osborne was a formidable letter writer, especially to *The Times*. He wrote literally hundreds of letters, a large number of which were reprinted in two volumes edited by A White.[35]

The topics covered ranged widely from the Dorsetshire poor, Free Trade, famine in India, education, distress in Lancashire, emigration, disease, Ireland, crime – its origins and treatment – the Crimean War, religion and the Church and, as White notes in his introduction to Vol. 2, a series of letters dealing with the auditing of charitable accounts. 'Although making no definite suggestions to the audit of charitable accounts, SGO points not obscurely to the need for public audit of charitable funds subscribed by the public.' His onslaught against loose book-keeping brought on SGO the attack of 'a regiment of charities'.[36]

The letter reprinted below was typical of Osborne's mode of attack, although it does not appear in White's volumes as the latter had 'sought to exclude … all that could be justly distasteful to survivors'.[37] Osborne's final letter on the Stoke Poges' Hospital affair reads as follows:

> Sir, - The evidence lately given before the inspector sent by the Charity commissioners to inquire into the state of this charity [Stoke Hospital] will, I am sure, satisfy them that it was not without just cause I publicly sought their intervention.
>
> I have reason to hope that they are now themselves in possession of "the accounts" of the charity. I can easily conceive they may feel some delicacy in taking any exception to those accounts, on the grounds that they may have been already from time to time audited by the visitors. I, for one, shall not feel at all satisfied with the assumption that this sort of auditing is a ground to bar a renewed searching investigation.

A gentleman visitor of a neighbouring charity deals far too often with the reverend master's accounts as matters of mere form. He may glance at them as he rings the bell for the refreshment he offers the said master, but, as a rule, he is far too polite to ask for vouchers, to go into the nice questions, what repair is necessary? what is money spent, not in repair, but in additional buildings, such as verandahs, divisions of rooms, for further comfort or profit, not to the almspeople, but to the master and his pupils?

Nothing is so common in life as the civility with which one clergyman avoids going into the dry detail of accounts tendered to him officially by a brother reverend; it is not merely from the hate of "figures" natural to most men that this is the case, but because these audits, if narrowly carried out, might seem to imply that we really question the honesty of a neighbour we often perhaps ask to dinner or meet at dinner.

I trust, Sir, the commissioners, if it is true that their inspector carried off the accounts, will show no such delicacy – they are paid to be indelicate in such matters. Let me remind them that Mr. Gower published two accounts which differed; that he inserted a charge "for winding the clock" in one to in some measure balance the double income-tax he had not paid set forth in the other.

I know not what course the commissioners and the visitors may yet take in this matter, but from what I am credibly informed there never was a case which more deserved severe notice than this one. I unhesitatingly again aver that the founder's intentions have been frustrated; that the charity has been turned more and more to the profit of the master, while the interests of the almspeople have been most unjustly affected.

As to the nature of the "accounts," I reserve my observations until I know whether they are yet to undergo the dry ordeal of an official impartial investigation.[38]

The Context of the Attack on Gower

In assessing the culpability of Gower in his alleged maladministration of the Stoke Poges' Hospital one should, perhaps, see his case within a wider context. It has already been noted that Gower was on the margin, so to speak, as far as the Anglican clergy were concerned. As an ordained priest and Oxford MA he was expected to live as a gentleman, yet his income from the Hospital was derisory. Osborne, on the other hand, to take someone at the opposite extreme of clerical prosperity, had been appointed to the living of Stoke Poges by his father, Lord Godolphin, the patron, in 1831; a living valued some years later at £319 per annum.[39] Unlike many of his predecessors, including the Rev. Arthur Bold, his immediate one, Osborne did not take on what can only be described as the onerous mastership of Stoke Poges Hospital. The Rev. Richard Boultbee, who had held a curacy in Oxford from 1817-29, was in the post from 1831-36.[40] Osborne then, as noted above, engineered the appointment of Gower to the post. Osborne left Stoke Poges in 1841 for the even better living of Durweston, near Blandford Forum in Dorset, which, at that time, brought him an income of £538 a year.[41]

Osborne was not unsympathetic to the condition of the 'poor clergy', especially many curates. Indeed, no more than a year before Osborne's first letter on the Stoke Poges' Hospital affair appeared in *The Times*, Osborne had a long letter in that paper in which he quoted at length from letters of thanks sent to the *Poor Pious Clergyman Clothing Society*: 'My dear daughters are delighted; they know that they could not be clothed, year after year, as they are, without your kind help'; 'brown linen which makes up into waggoner's bibs for the boys'; 'the black cloth comes very seasonably'; 'the coat, trousers and waistcoats, ready-made, fit very nicely'; 'humiliating, as it is to the natural feelings to be the objects of such bounty, I cannot yet but feel that the association which you represent, is entitled to my gratitude and thanks' are just a handful of those quoted by Osborne. Here was yet another strand of the clergy's 'economy of makeshifts', although not one, so far as we know, John Alexander Gower made use of. Commenting on the letters from grateful clergy and their wives, Osborne notes: 'when I regard the "prizes" of the Church, and look on these "blanks" – when I turn from [Cathedral] chapter wealth, Episcopal luxury, pluralist indulgence, and see working clergymen grateful for old clothes – the alms-ventured men of chance benevolence – I own I am ashamed.'[42]

Osborne's shame was not so widely felt, or, at least dwelt upon, as the anger expressed at the perceived abuses of some Anglican clergy. Amongst these the most heinous and widely publicised was that associated with Earl Guildford, the master of St Cross Hospital near Winchester. The case against him was kick-started by Joseph Hume, the radical MP, who, in the summer of 1849 had asked in the House of Commons for a Royal Commission to inquire into the alleged mal-administration of the charity. In the event, the Government instructed the Attorney General to 'file an information in the Court of Chancery' against the master and brethren of St Cross Hospital.[43] The Earl Guildford had been appointed to the mastership in 1808 by his father, the then Bishop of Winchester. He had received the bulk of the income of the charity which, it was asserted, amounted to an average of £9,000 a year.[44] It was not only the size of the income that irked many people (judging by the virtually universal antagonism shown toward the Earl by most of the press that covered the case) but also the contrast with the relatively small amounts given to the thirteen brethren in the hospital. An example of this was given in April 1849 in *The Bradford Observer* under the headline: 'Eleven thousand pounds of charity money pocketed by the Rev. Earl Guilford'. The source of this was a fine levied on the granting of a lease on property owned by the St Cross Hospital. Of the £13,440 fine, each of the thirteen brethren received 2d. in the pound or £120 (*sic*), whilst the Earl got £1 6s. 10d. in the pound or £11,520 (*sic*).[45] The case continued until 1855, when Earl Guildford finally resigned the mastership (he was in his eighties), still not having surrendered his 'ill-gotten spoils'.[46]

Guildford was not the only almshouse master to be pilloried in the press. The case of the two Pretyman brothers, John and Richard, also aroused widespread condemnation. They were the sons of George Pretyman, who, having been tutor and secretary to William Pitt, became Bishop of Lincoln and then Bishop of Winchester. As such he was able to present his sons with numerous livings across the country (it was said that the name Pretyman was almost 'synonymous' with that of pluralist), of which two were almshouses in Lincolnshire at Mere and Spittall.[47] Unlike that at Stoke Poges, both were richly endowed with land and since, over time, the buildings had either disappeared entirely or fallen into disrepair and the number of almspeople fallen dramatically, the outgoings were minimal.[48]

The New Dispensation at the Stoke Poges' Hospital

Not until 1856 did the inquiry by the Charity Commissioners into the Stoke Poges' Hospital lead to a bill before Parliament for a new scheme of regulation. Despite going through three readings in both Houses of Parliament and being referred to a select committee, the bill ended its passage at the end of July 1856, when the House of Lords accepted the amendments put forward by the House of Commons, after a process of around two months.[49] The new scheme replaced the visitorial powers of the Dean of Windsor and the Provost of Eton with a board of ten trustees. Five of these were described as official trustees and included 'for the time being' the two former visitors; the vicar of Stoke Poges, 'unless he be master', and the two churchwardens of Stoke Poges. The remaining five trustees, termed non-official, were to live within ten miles of Stoke Poges. The first official trustees were the Right Hon. Henry Labouchere of Stoke Park, Abraham Darby of Stoke Court, Lt Col Richard Howard Vyse of Stoke House, Robert Harvey of Langley Park and the Rev. John Culling Evans of Stoke Poges who was to act as clerk, being remunerated with £10 a year and being responsible for drawing up annual accounts of the hospital.[50] The only change from the original Bill was the withdrawal of the 'Right Hon. George Augustus Frederick Louis Curzon, in favour of Robert Harvey'.[51] This was, indeed, a heavyweight body, more in keeping with the vast wealth of a St Cross Hospital, than its pauper cousin in Stoke Poges.

John Gower was to remain as master of the hospital and to be responsible for the 'maintenance, care, management and control' of its poor members. He was to 'occupy and enjoy residence in the hospital except such parts heretofore used by any poor members of the hospital'. This indicates a reduction in Gower's private space, a reduction made all the greater by his having 'to read prayers from the Book of Common Prayer in chapel every morning to the poor brethren and sisters', no more using the chapel as a store room.[52] As for his remuneration, what remained after management, repairs and insurance was to be divided between the inmates and the master in *equal* parts.[53] This was a major change from the original foundation, in which the master had always been remunerated with a greater sum than the brethren and sisters.

It is not, perhaps, surprising that Gower soon clashed with the trustees of the Hospital. After insisting, at their first meeting on 26 September 1856, that he should read morning prayers in the chapel in his canonicals, they said they were 'strongly inclined to disallow his salary of £30 in his accounts'. They maintained his salary should only be £23, that of former masters.[54] They also maintained that the master's house could only be let for the benefit of the charity. Finally, after inspecting the rooms occupied by the brethren and sisters, they expressed surprise at their 'squalor and desolate appearance'.[55]

At another meeting, a few days later (1 October 1856) the trustees returned to some of the issues raised at their first meeting. On the matter of Gower's salary, it was noted that the rise to £30 a year had first been made by the Rev. Boultbee (master 1831-36), arising from an item for fuel and the trustees could find no authority for this. On the accommodation issue, the trustees noted that:

> Large sums of money [had] been improperly expended on the master's use, done for his comfort and convenience to the injury of the inmates; whilst very little [was] laid out for several years [on those parts of the hospital belonging to the inmates] … and they were in a desolate and uncomfortable condition.[56]

The trustees now seemed to be in almost permanent session as, on 2 October, they minuted that a room used by the master as a scullery was in fact the brewhouse belonging to the inmates. On 8 October 1856, the trustees, in a letter to Gower, again raised the issue of the scullery/brewhouse, that he had bricked up a doorway and his right to the pigsties and barn and part of the garden. Gower replied that he would submit the trustees' letter to his legal advisor.[57]

The trustees, at their meeting on 22 October 1856 noted the receipt of a letter from Gower in which he admitted that he had not an 'exclusive right to the room called the brewhouse, the garden, the barn and pig-stys'. He offered to pay £1 a year 'by way of compensation for sole occupation'.[58] There is no information on whether these issues were subsequently resolved.

At their meeting on 6 November 1856, the trustees decided to ask the Charity Commissioners if the meaning of Clause 32 in the 1856 Act meant that, in effect, the master of the Hospital should be paid the same as each inmate. On 27 December the Charity Commissioners replied 'yes'. In fact the trustees had been doing this already. From 1858-62, Gower and each inmate received 6s. a week; from 1863-64, 6s. 6d. from 1865-81, 7s.[59]

From 1863 onwards, judging by the minutes, there seems to have been something of a thaw in relations with Gower. Thus, on 6 April 1863, the trustees wrote to the Charity Commissioners to seek permission to allow Gower to rent out his house: 'in view of the very small amount of the stipend' he received, and that the presence of a 'respectable family during his absence would be to the advantage of the inmates of the Hospital.' According to the minute of the trustees meeting on 18 April 1863, the Charity Commissioners agreed that Gower 'could let the house for three months for his own benefit and, furthermore, he could decide if prayers needed' to be read by a clergyman in his absence.[60]

A letter from the Charity Commissioners, minuted by the trustees at their meeting on 8 May 1865, made it clear that they were responsible for the upkeep of the master's house. Again, after consulting the Charity Commissioners, the trustees agreed to spend £20 on repairs to it.[61]

Gower's death in 1881 exposed the niggardliness of the trustees when it came to the condition of the master's house – although, as we have seen, they did not have much money to play with. When they came to consider his replacement, at their meeting on 10 November of that year, it was agreed that: 'no clergyman could be offered the appointment with the residence in its present state'. It was decided to ask a competent builder to submit an estimate of the cost of necessary repairs. An estimate of £87 was received and when it was decided to recommend that the vicar of Stoke Poges, the Rev. Vernon Blake, be the new master, the estimate was accepted.[62] In the event, Blake did not live in the house, but was given permission to let it as the residence of an assistant curate who might act as his deputy.[63]

Even in death Gower was a source of contention, for although his salary to Michaelmas (£9 2s., i.e. half a year) was paid to a Miss Gower (presumably one of the two unmarried daughters living with him at the time of the 1881 census), the claim by his executors for £68 12s. 6d. for fixtures was described as 'far too excessive' by the trustees, since it included 'many items' not 'coming under the Law of Fixtures'. In the event, Miss Gower was paid £22.[64]

CONCLUSION

The Rev. John Gower was born at an unfortunate time for the Church of England. Not only was it being assailed by the rapid rise of nonconformity, notably the Methodists, but in the early years of the 19th century, it was no longer recording in its parish registers between 26 and 32 per cent of births and between 20 and 33 per cent of deaths.[65] How much of this was due to the failings of the clergy, notably through non-residence and pluralism, and how much to the apathy of the population generally, it is difficult to say. It was not primarily a lack of manpower, as Oxford and Cambridge universities were producing far more clergy than the Church could satisfactorily employ. Almshouses, however, could offer employment to very few of them; only one other clerical appointment was located in Buckinghamshire (the master of Queen Ann's Hospital in Newport Pagnell) and he was, like some of Gower's predecessors, also the parish incumbent. Helen Caffrey, in her *Almshouses in the West Riding of Yorkshire 1600-1900*, found very few masters of almshouses, but this may be due to many of her almshouses being 19th-century foundations when the Charities Commission appeared to want institutions run by trustees. Many trustees, however, continued to be Church of England clergy, who often took a leading role in the day-to-day management of almshouses. One took his responsibilities so seriously that he was rebuked by the Charity Commission. This was the Rector of Quainton, who was one of the governors of the Winwood Almshouses (founded 1626) in Quainton, Buckinghamshire. As part of its endowment it had a 120-acre farm in the 'open and common fields'. Despite reducing the rent it failed to let it, so the Rector was told, by the governors, to borrow £500 'for the purpose of stocking and occupying it'. The Charity Commissioners criticised this 'mistaken sense of duty to incur such heavy responsibilities'.[66]

It is unlikely we shall ever know what induced John Gower to accept the mastership of the Hospital at Stoke Poges. That Sydney Godolphin Osborne, vicar of Stoke Poges at the time, did not take on the role, as many of his predecessors had, is also rather a mystery. John Gower managed to make a good living for himself in Stoke Poges by adopting a variety of stratagems. He continued undisturbed in this for almost twenty years (1836-54). When his actions were attacked publicly in 1854, the implication was that the hospital was mismanaged. Yet his misdeeds were small beer, compared to Earl Guildford at the Hospital of St Cross. A comparison of the press coverage of the latter's alleged misdeeds as against those of the former is evidence of this, with only two newspapers covering the case of John Gower, as against at least thirty commenting (often several times) on that of Lord Guildford.[67] There is much that we still do not know about the life of John Gower. Perhaps the time is ripe for a family historian to delve deeper into the Gower family. Where did Gower's father come from? Why does he make no appearance in the Church of England's clergy database? How did John Gower develop an Indian connection? Was there something about his personality that caused his sponsor (Sydney Godolphin) to turn against him and a prickly relationship with the Trustees appointed to manage the hospital from 1856 onwards? His case does, however, throw an interesting light on the problems of an under-endowed almshouse for both master and inhabitants.

Notes

1.   Knight, F. *The Nineteenth-century Church and English Society*, Cambridge University Press, Cambridge, 1995, p.107.

2.   King, S. & Tomkins, A. *The Poor in England, 1700-1850: an economy of makeshifts*, Manchester University Press, Manchester, 2003.

3.   URL: www.clergydatabase.org accessed 2007-11.

4.   The *Posse Comitatus* was a list of able-bodied men aged 15 to 60 years drawn up by the county sheriff with a view to repelling invasion from France. The entry for Great Marlow Borough reads: 'Revd H.H. Gower, clergyman.' Beckett, J.F. *The Buckinghamshire Posse Comitatus 1798*, Buckinghamshire Record Society, Aylesbury, 1985.

5.   *Parish Church Register of Great Marlow*, Microfilm in Milton Keynes Central Library.

6. The National Archives (TNA) PROB 11/1513/88. The will of the Reverend Henry Hesketh Gower, clerk.

7. Foster, J. *Alumnae Oxoniensis*, Nendeln/Liechtenstein, Kraus Reprint, 1968, vol.1, p. 547.

8. Ibid., p. 547.

9. *The Historical Register of the University of Oxford to 1900*, Clarendon Press, Oxford, 1900, p. 215.

10. Foster, p. 547.

11. TNA: The will of the Reverend Henry Hesketh Gower, clerk, op cit.

12. Census of 1841 enumerator's book Stoke Poges (Bucks), household of John Alexander Gower, www.ancestry.co.uk accessed 2007-2011.

13. *Twenty-fifth Report of the Commissioners of Inquiry into Charities in England and Wales, Buckinghamshire* (CC Bucks), XVIII, London, 1833, pp. 111-20; *Third Report of the Charity Commissioners of England and Wales*, XII, 1856, Appendix, p. 348.

14. Census of 1851 enumerator's book Stoke Poges (Bucks), household of John Alexander Gower, www.ancestry.co.uk accessed 2007-2011.

15. Census of 1861 enumerator's book, Stoke Poges (Bucks), household of John Alexander Gower, www.ancestry.co.uk accessed 2007-2011.

16. Census of 1871 enumerator's book, Stoke Poges (Bucks), household of John Alexander Gower, www.ancestry.co.uk accessed 2007-2011.

17. *The Pall Mall Gazette* (PMG), 6 Aug. 1874; *The Standard* (TS) 17 Sept. 1880.

18. TS, 21 March 1881. In John Murray's *New Army List of 1880,* John Murray, London, Gower was described as 'Squadron Commander 17th Bengal Cavalry'.

19. Census of 1881. The household of John Alexander Gower, Stoke Poges (Bucks) CEB, www.ancestry.co.uk accessed 2007-2011.

20. TS, 30 Aug. 1881.

21. *CC* Bucks, XVIII, 1833, p. 120.

22. Ibid.

23. Ibid.

24. Ibid.

25. Ibid., p. 119.

26. Ibid.

27. Ibid., p. 120.

28. Buckinghamshire Record Office (BRO) Ref. CH7/FA/4 Stoke Poges' Hospital Accounts.

29. Ibid.

30. *The Times*, 5 July 1854, p. 10, Letter from S G Osborne.

31. *The Times*, 11 July 1854, p. 7, Letter from John Alexander Gower.

32. *Daily News* (DN), 18 July 1854.

33. *The Times,* 18 July 1854, p. 11, Lord Hastings Hospital, Stoke Poges.

34. *The Times*, 7 August 1854.

35. White, A. *The letters of S.G.O.: a series of letters on public affairs written by the Rev. Lord Sydney Godolphin Osborne and published by The Times 1844-1888*. Griffin, Farrar, Okeden & Welsh, London, n.d.

36. Ibid., vol. 1, p. 386.

37. Ibid., vol 1, p. 102.

38. *The Times*, 12 August 1854, Letter from S G Osborne.

39. Colloms, B. 'The Rev. Sydney Godolphin Osborne, Parson and Crusader 1808-1889' in *Victorian Country Parsons*, Constable, London, 1977, p. 197; Matthew, N.C.G. & Harrison, B. *Dictionary of National Biography*, Oxford University Press, Oxford, 2004, vol. 42, pp. 23-4; *The Clergy List of 1852*, Cox, C., London, 1852, p. 193.

40. URL: www.theclergydatabase.org accessed 2007-11.

41. *The Clergy List of 1852* op. cit. p.66.

42. *The Times*, 12 April 1853, p. 7 col. d. Letter from S.G. Osborne.

43. *The Hampshire Telegraph and Sussex Chronicle (Portsmouth)* (HT and SC) 4 Aug. 1849, citing an article in the DN.

44. *The Era*, London, Sunday 7 Aug. 1853.

45.   *The Bradford Observer* (TBO) Thursday 19 April 1849; reprinted in *The Leicester Chronicle or Commercial and Agricultural Advertiser* (LCCAA), Saturday 28 April 1849.

46.   TBO, Thursday 26 April 1855.

47.   *The Times*, 9 February 1831

48.   I am grateful to Dr. D.R. Mills for drawing my attention to the Mere and Spital hospitals in White's *Directory of Lincolnshire 1850*.

49.   British Parliamentary Papers (hereafter BPP), BPP. 1856, VI pp.273-10. A bill entitled an act of the Charity Commissioners confirming a scheme for Stoke Poges

50.   DN, 11 June 1856; *Morning Post* (MP); *Morning Chronicle* (MC), 15 July 1856; TS, 16 July 1856; DN, 28 July 1856.

51.   BRO: CH7/G7.

52.   BPP. VI. pp.273-10, op.cit..

53.   BRO: CH7/G7, pp. 1070-74.

54.   Ibid., p. 1074.

55.   BRO: CH7/AM/2Q, Minutes of the trustees of Stoke Poges' Hospital, 1856-1986.

56.   Ibid.

57.   Ibid.

58.   Ibid.

59.   Ibid.

60.   BRO: CH7/FA5. Stoke Poges' Hospital Accounts.

61.   BRO: CH7/AM/2Q.

62.   Ibid.

63.   BRO: CH7/FA/5A.

64.   Ibid.

65.   Wrigley, E.A. & Scofield, R.S. *The Population History of England 1541-1871: a reconstruction*, Cambridge University Press, Cambridge, 1981, p. 561.

66.   *CC* Bucks, 25th report, 1833, pp. 21-3.

67.   URL: www.open.ac.uk/library/resources. 19th century British Newspapers are available online at British Universities, certain libraries and through subscription to various genealogical websites.

CHAPTER 14
ALMSPEOPLE AND THEIR POSSESSIONS: GLEANINGS FROM AN ADMISSIONS REGISTER, SHERBORNE, 1582-1866

Ann Clark

INTRODUCTION

Sherborne lies in the north-west of the county of Dorset, close to the border with Somerset and near the old main route from London to Exeter. The town grew up around its abbey. Its early cloth trade was lost after the Reformation, giving way to the making of buttons, haberdashery, and bone lace that provided occupation for many inhabitants. By the 18th century these manufacturing activities had declined and the town became reliant on its markets, fairs and passing trade from travellers on the London to Exeter road. The middle of that century saw the development of water mills for the manufacture of silk and, to a lesser extent, woollen and linen materials. When these industries also declined the mills were used for corn.[1] Sherborne is now a tranquil country town with narrow streets and an air of prosperous gentility.

One of the oldest surviving secular buildings is to be found in Half Moon Street. Founded in 1437 by license from Henry VI, the Almshouse of St John the Baptist and St John the Evangelist continues as an almshouse today.[2] The building follows the church-like form of a mediaeval hospital, the hall opening into the chapel at the east end, as found in some earlier almshouses, like Chichele's at Higham Ferrars. The Sherborne Almshouse differed slightly, the hall being two-storied with a roof pitched higher than that of the chapel and a gallery opening into the chapel from the upper floor, where less able residents accommodated there could participate in the services.[3] (*See* Illustration 14.a.)

The almshouse foundation deed decreed that:

> eury of the saide sixteyne pore men and wymmen … shall haue always …
> abedde and a beddeplace by hym selfe and that the men herborowe anyght
> [harbour of a night] by them selfe, and that there be a reasonable and sufficient
> closure by twixt them.[4]

The accounts for 1451-2 mentioned the making of wooden partitions in the house, suggesting cubicles for the almspeople.[5] Plans showing the 15th-century ground and first floor indicate individual sleeping accommodation, as at Chichele's, Higham Ferrars, St

Mary's, Chichester and St Giles in Norwich (Illustration 14.b.).[6] Hutchins, an 18th-century
Dorset historian, noted that: 'above stairs … the cells for the men remain in their antient [*sic*]
form'.[7]

Illustration 14.a. The Almshouse of St John the Baptist and St John the Evangelist,
Sherborne, *ca* 1800
*Reproduced by kind permission of Dorset History Centre
from Hutchins, 1904, plate 47.*[8]

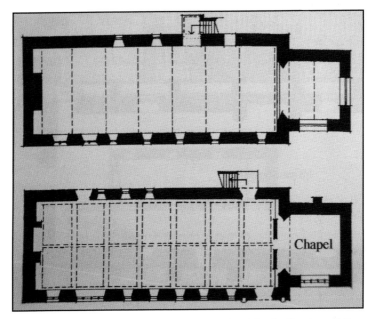

Illustration 14.b. Plan of the Almshouse of St John the Baptist and St
John the Evangelist, Sherborne, XVth Century
Reproduced by kind permission of Brian Howson.[9]

The foundation deed required the almshouse to provide shelter and care for 'pore feble
and ympotent' old men and women.[10] The Statute of Labourers of the 14th century had made

a distinction between those unwilling and those unable to work and writers over the centuries chronicled changing views of poverty. By 1500 this distinction between the 'deserving' (those poor 'against their will' or 'impotent') and the 'undeserving' (those poor 'by their will' or 'indigent') was well-established. With the Reformation in the 1530s and the subsequent dissolution of the monasteries, which ended their charity towards vagrants and beggars, came a hardening of attitudes. The Protestant view of the impotent as the 'true poor' and denigration of poverty or indigence as a conscious choice became entrenched.[11]

For many, advancing age resulted in poverty against their will. When they could no longer make shift through a combination of spasmodic work, cultivation, gleaning, fuel gathering, or other means they had to rely on help with food or loans from family or neighbours in the tradition of mutual help.[12] In 1598 parishes became responsible for poor relief, but only as a last resort, and 'lineal' kin – parents or children – were expected to contribute towards maintenance. This expectation became law in 1601.[13]

In Sherborne the Almshouse was considered to have been founded by the monarch and so was not directly affected by the Reformation's reduction in charitable options. However, Henry VIII's creation of the new Diocese of Bristol in 1542 divorced Sherborne people from the familiar Bishops of Salisbury, who then became absentee landlords, and local conditions deteriorated with the loss of their interest.[14]

As well as being poor, those entering Sherborne Almshouse had to be 'continual house-holders' or 'dwellers in the town or parish of Sherborne' and were 'required to bring into the house … their moveable goods and give or bequeath them to the Master and Brethren only and solely for the use of the house'.[15] The practice of requiring almspeople to surrender personal goods on admission derived from earlier times when this was expected of inmates of leper-hospitals but, as time went by, this rule of poverty was relaxed in some places. At St Nicholas in York it was abandoned completely in 1303 when compulsory surrender of goods was forbidden, although a voluntary gift would be accepted.[16] In Lichfield, the Hospital of St John the Baptist required goods to be left to the almshouse and in 1508 the property of one man was distributed amongst other residents and his money retained by the Master.[17] St Mary's Hospital in Chichester received property of intestate almsmen, provided nobody claimed it within a year.[18] Other hospitals and almshouses 'allowed their inhabitants to will their possessions away'.[19]

In the 16th century, Church Street Almshouses in Stratford-upon-Avon charged an admission fee of 6s. 8d.[20] In Coventry, Ford's Hospital received the residue of almspeople's estates after debts and funeral expenses and, in 1613, Bond's Hospital required an entrant to bring a pewter plate, a porringer and a pewter spoon for general use and 'a good flock mattress, a pair of sheets, a coverlet, a blanket and a bolster' for his own room, later expecting 'two pairs of sheets, two blankets and a chamberpot'.[21] Drapers' Almshouses in Shrewsbury, founded in 1444, required provision of 'a winding sheet with 4d. tied into one corner to pay for their burial', a salutary reminder that this would be the residents' final home.[22]

Trinity Hospital in Pontefract specifically required newcomers to bring:

> 8d worth of bread and ale, certain amounts of fuel, their bed: a towel in cloth,
> of eight-pence per yard or else two shillings in money … a pewter doubler of
> fourteen-pence, or fourteen-pence in money, and a porringer, or two-pence in
> money;

also to donate 'two-pence halfpenny in money'; to provide for eight-pence worth of bread and ale at their deaths; to bring in their own food at a certain time on Saturday mornings; and to provide 'one dozen horse loads of coal, every year, against winter'.[23] Also in Yorkshire, the 18th-century Tancred's Hospital for ex-servicemen and gentry expected specific items of bedding and clothing, an optional feather bed, a shoe brush and blacking.[24] In contrast to these entry conditions the flexible regime at Sherborne, requiring simply moveable goods, seems generous.

Distraint of possessions of the poor was not peculiar to charitable institutions but was also an interpretation of the old poor laws in some places. In Hertfordshire, old people who became 'bedes folk of the parish' at Little Gaddesden had to will all their possessions to be sold to supplement the poor rate. Some parishes in Kent and Essex inventoried paupers' possessions to ensure that none were sold or given away. A Northamptonshire parish branded paupers' goods with a parish mark.[25] No evidence suggests that inventories were made of applicants' possessions prior to entry to Sherborne Almshouse but their moveable goods *were* recorded on entry, a wealth of detail not mentioned elsewhere in this book. This chapter will consider what these possessions reveal about local almspeople and their level of poverty.

SOURCES

The ancient Sherborne Almshouse has a multitude of surviving records, many still in its possession, but a large number of copies, and some originals, are publicly accessible at the Dorset History Centre. Amongst these is a large vellum-bound volume of miscellaneous records, including the detailed admissions register, which spans nearly three hundred years and is the key source for this study; in this chapter much use is made of quotations from the register and any otherwise unattributed quotations come from this document.[26] A transcription has now been published.[27]

With some exceptions, register entries follow the same format from the 1590s until the 1760s, with minor changes, perhaps as one clerk succeeded another. A typical entry reads:

> 18 June 1635 The said day William Illery a poore man and an ancient inhabitante of this town was chosen into this house in the place of Brian Dew deceased and doth bring into this house a mattocke a spade one pottinger a dish and a spone and is sworne.

This highlights the entry criteria of poverty, long-time residence, surrendering possessions and requirement to take the oath of obedience. As time went by the word 'room' was increasingly substituted for 'place', but used synonymously, as it was in records of the election of the non-resident Brothers to the management of the house.[28] The consistency of recording is good, despite many changes of hand, although a few entries seem incomplete. Occasional notes slipped between the folios show three people nominated and one chosen for vacancies within the gift of either of two early benefactors or their heirs, one for a man and one for a woman. This word 'chosen' is used for each register entry although there is no evidence of several candidates for vacancies, which were unfunded by benefactions.

Since inventories of almspeople's possessions are rare, this detailed record over a period of 170 years is particularly interesting.[29] Unfortunately, possessions were no longer recorded in the register from the 1760s onwards, although other details, such as entrants' ages, from 1816, and ages of their predecessors, from 1820, were introduced. Three early inventories of residents' 'chambers' have been found in week books of Masters of the almshouse, enabling comparison of the contents of the rooms with the goods their occupants brought on admission.[30]

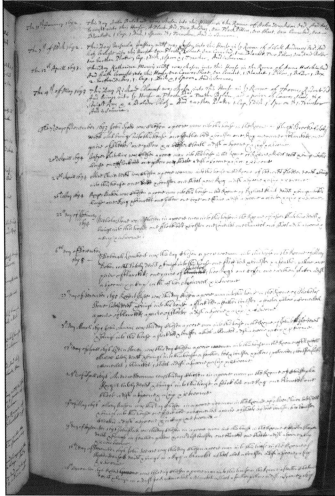

Illustration 14.c. A page from the Sherborne almshouse admissions register *Reproduced by kind permission of Dorset History Centre. DHC: D/SHA/D24*

In addition, three secondary sources concerning inventories have contributed either contemporary comparative information or, in one case, an extensive glossary giving details of possessions that are unfamiliar today and providing a picture of essentials for daily living.[31]

ALMSPEOPLE AND THEIR POSSESSIONS

The almshouse accommodated twelve men and four women, later increased by one for each gender, thanks to two benefactions during the reign of Elizabeth I.[32] The admissions register, starting in 1582, recorded few moveable goods in the first decade. This study therefore focuses on the 1590s to the 1750s, after which goods were noted in only three cases. Admissions ranged between twenty-one and forty per decade during that period, averaging three per year. During those 170 years, 499 were admitted: 344 men, 154 women and one whose gender was unclear because the page was torn.

The almspeople's possessions can be grouped into eight main categories: bedding; cooking/eating vessels/utensils; household items; furniture; clothing; money; and tools; the eighth category being those who brought nothing. This last is a mixture of fact and assumption. Some entries state categorically that nothing was brought. Elsewhere, without comment, no possessions were entered or the page has been damaged. Occasionally an entry seems incomplete, examples being: '...and brought with her...'(1591) and '...will bring with him...'(1608). Such entries are deemed nothing brought, although perhaps the clerk simply failed to complete the entry. The proportion of new entrants bringing goods in each category in each decade is shown in Table 14.I. The last column shows the percentage of people bringing goods of any kind. In none of these seventeen decades were items from all categories brought, and the variety reduced over time.

TABLE 14.I
Percentages of people bringing to the Almshouse goods in different categories, 1590-1759

Decade	Bedding	Cooking/ Eating	Household	Furniture	Clothing	Money	Tools	Nothing	Goods of any kind
1590s	68	68	39	0	39	23	0	10	90
1600s	81	67	33	0	14	14	5	10	90
1610s	68	49	16	0	14	8	3	16	84
1620s	95	81	10	5	5	0	24	5	95
1630s	67	73	3	13	0	0	13	13	87
1640s	75	86	4	0	0	4	4	4	96
1650s	75	86	7	4	0	0	0	11	89
1660s	88	94	3	3	0	3	0	3	97
1670s	100	97	16	0	0	0	0	0	100
1680s	96	100	0	0	0	0	0	0	100
1690s	92	94	14	3	0	0	3	6	94
1700s	80	68	8	0	3	0	3	5	95
1710s	90	83	3	3	0	0	0	3	97
1720s	87	67	17	7	0	0	0	10	90
1730s	88	4	0	0	0	0	0	8	92
1740s	56	0	0	0	0	0	0	44	56
1750s	27	0	0	0	0	0	0	73	27
Overall	78	66	10	2	4	3	3	13	87

Wrightson noted that possessions in poorer homes in the 16th century would be few, mainly: 'cooking and eating implements, bedding and provision for seating and storage'.[33] The register consistently recorded the majority having bedding until the 1740s. Most brought cooking/eating equipment until a sudden reduction in the 1730s. Household items and furniture were much less plentiful and reduced to zero in the 1720s. Clothing and money were rarely mentioned after the 1610s and tools rarely after the 1640s. Some could bring only one or two items but others brought several in more than one category. In the 1670s, for example, everybody brought at least one item of bedding and all but one brought cooking/eating items, while 20 per cent brought household goods. In that decade and the next, nobody was so poor as to bring nothing.

Historical research has revealed rising prices out-pacing wages for the lower paid from the 16th to at least the mid 17th century. Slack reported real hunger for the poor and Wrightson: 'massive distress in the textile districts of the west country' in the 1620s.[34] In Sherborne, the situation would have been exacerbated by the Civil War in the 1640s that included a siege of Sherborne Castle.[35] In 1647, the admissions register recorded that a room had been kept vacant because:

> provisions for the mayntenance of the pore people hath bin extraordinary deare and the rents [from land holdings] abated by reason of the late wares [*sic*].

Better times followed after 1650 when a general fall in food prices increased the purchasing power of labourers into the mid 18th century, except in the bad harvest years of the 1690s.[36]

Figure 14.A. compares the average volume of bedding, cooking/eating items and all other goods with the average total of items, per person per decade.

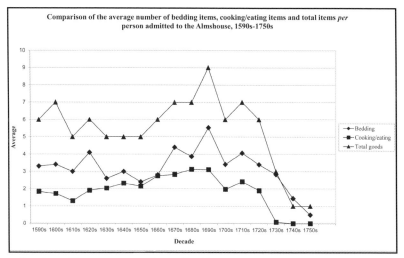

Fig. 14.A. The average numbers of bedding, cooking/eating items and goods in all other categories compared with average total per person per decade, 1590-1759.
Source: Compiled from information in the Admissions Register, DHC: D/SHA/D24.

The volume of all 'other goods' was negligible throughout. Bedding remained fairly consistent and cooking/eating utensils slightly increased till the 1650s, when both became more common, peaking in the 1690s. Both categories then fell steadily to almost zero at the end of the period. Although numbers are too small to be conclusive, the almshouse pattern shadows the national and local influences in a small way until the beginning of the 18th century. Despite the reported general continuation of low prices to mid century, almspeople's possessions reduced steadily after peaking in the 1690s and the sharp decline after the 1720s cannot be explained without further research.[37]

Bedding

Overall, more people, 390 or 78 per cent, brought items in this category than any other (Table 14.I). As elsewhere, in the register 'bed' meant 'mattress', filled with feathers, flock and feathers, flock, straw or dust. Flock comprised 'course tufts and refuse of wool', also used as a pillow and bolster stuffing. Dust, or chaff, was the residue of grain after threshing.[38] Almost half of the 497 entrants (242 or 49 per cent) brought beds. Flock was the most common filling, followed by feathers and then mixed flock and feather stuffing, leaving only 5 per cent with straw and dust, the poorest sort of beds. However, 52 per cent brought no bed at all.

Both the best types of bed, feather, and the poorer quality flock, featured from the 1590s to the 1740s, almost the whole period. Dust beds and the flock and feather mix were absent after the 1720s and straw beds were found only between the 1640s to the 1670s. The inventory studies provide some comparison. Machin found little evidence of dust and flock beds after 1720 in probate inventories for three villages near Sherborne, concluding that feather beds had become the norm; straw and mixed flock and feather beds were not mentioned.[39] It should be noted that probate inventories usually exclude poorer inhabitants, but the trend in the almshouse mirrored that found in local villages at a lower level. In Essex, to redress such bias, King compared probate and pauper inventories, 1658-1731 and 1710-1819, respectively, the latter contemporary only with the end of the register period. Flock, straw, and feather mattresses were used across the spectrum from paupers to yeomen, all groups having more feather than flock beds and more flock than straw, which was more often used by paupers. No group had dust or flock and feather mix beds. As in the almshouse, King's evidence that even paupers could have feather beds suggested that, for some, greater prosperity had preceded poverty but he also confirmed that flock beds lingered on, as they did in the almshouse.[40]

Over half the almspeople brought sheets compared with more than 60 per cent in King's later pauper sample. In the register, some sheets attracted comment, such as 'newe', 'old' or, in three cases, 'canvas'. In 1701 Elizabeth Hardy brought only a bed and half a sheet. Bolsters and pillows were common. King did not list these for paupers but the inventories for labourers to yeomen (1658-1731) indicated only 19 per cent of labourers having pillows. In contrast, over the same years, 43 per cent of almspeople had pillows, a further 31 per cent had bolsters, the total closely matching King's data, which showed over 70 per cent of artisans and tradesmen, yeomen and farmers having pillows.[41] Fifty-two per cent of almspeople had both a pillow and a bolster, seeming well-equipped in comparison with local paupers.

Other bedding included: blankets; coverleds, or coverlets, (an unquilted covering, sometimes of patchwork, to cover bedding); quilts; and rugs (coverings for beds). Unusual items included a bed cord, (woven across a bed frame to support a mattress), and a bed matt, (covering the bed cords to stop the mattress chafing on them), brought by John Okely in 1637; a bed tye brought by Mary Appleby in 1641; and Thomas Ladbroke's cadowe, 'a rough woollen covering', in 1596.[42] Pillowcases (listed as pillowberes or pillow tyes) and bolster cloths were seldom brought.[43] John Bealy's cushion (1632) was included in this category.

Cooking and Eating Vessels

In all, 329 people or 66 per cent, brought items in this category, a dish being brought by 87 per cent of those contributing to this group. Some were described as earthen (clay) or pewter. In 1656 Grace Lambe brought 'part of a dish'. In the Dorset villages, dishes were the most common tableware, followed by platters, (large flat dishes). The Almshouse received only fifty-six platters, recorded as earthen, pewter, wood or tin, those of tin before 1600 as in the local village inventories. Pottingers (small metal or pottery bowls for soup, stews or puddings) and trenchers (large wooden dishes) appeared less frequently.[44] Spoons, dishes and cups were the most common items but few had more than one. Machin found few cups and little mention of spoons, surmising the latter to be: 'probably wooden and so cheap as to be not worth listing'. The register noted thirteen 'sawsers' (shallow dishes for sauce or condiments), nine in the 16th century and another four by 1610. Machin found the last reference to sawcers in 1696.[45] Almspeople brought five 'brasse potts', all but one in the 17th century. A pot in 1592 was 'of three quarts' capacity. Another in 1606 was 'worthe 5s.', a valuable item compared with Essex weavers' daily wage of four to eight pence in 1603.[46] Richard Lane brought a treen (wooden) pot in 1691. Two skillets (cooking vessels with feet and a handle for boiling and stewing) and six kettles completed this category, which disappeared from the register in the 1730s.[47]

Household Items

Only 11 per cent brought household goods, mainly items for storage. In the 1590s, only coffers and chests were found in the local village inventories, becoming more numerous by the 1690s when half the houses also had one to three boxes or trunks.[48] The almspeople contributed twenty-one coffers (1590s-1720s) and nine boxes (1650s-1720s) but only three chests, all owned by women. Twenty-one candlesticks, five of brass, and a tin chamberpot were the only other household items.

Furniture

Throughout the period, just twelve people contributed furniture. Of eight bedsteads, two (in 1661 and 1673) were 'little' while in 1636, William Chafin's was 'newe' and John Bernard's was 'furnished for his lodging'. Henry Stone's was 'neawe for his continuall lodging' in 1642. Machin found a limited range of furniture in the 1590s, mainly tables, stools, chairs and bedsteads, with little change by the 1690s.[49] One stool was brought into the almshouse in 1710 and four chairs, two in the 17th century and two in the 18th. Only two women brought furniture of any kind. In contrast, King found that the range of household items owned by working people, including furniture, increased after 1700.[50]

Clothing

Clothing was mentioned only up until 1627, with one exception in 1704. Of ninety-seven admissions in that early period only twenty-two people (23 per cent) brought apparel of any kind. Ten brought unidentified apparel with various qualification, such as 'reasonable', 'some clothes to his body', 'apparell on his back' or 'double apparell of lynnen and woollen', possibly summer and winter wear. Of the remaining twelve people, three women and seven men brought gowns. In 1587 his white gown was the only garment recorded for William Poole but he brought ten other items falling into five different categories, making him by far the largest contributor of goods for that decade. Robert Blobell's 'white gowne newe of the livery of this house', for which 'Mr Ashbourne hath given his word … upon mistress Tillies promise', implies a benefactor funding or underwriting the making of the gown by a seamstress.

Shirts were the next most common garments, eight men each bringing more than one. Other male attire included two pairs of hose, a doublet and two coats (Thomas Ladbroke, 1596); Thomas Grayle's pair of shoes in 1610; cloaks brought by two others in 1611 and 1627; and Ambrose Chetmill's four shirt bands (a pair of strips of white fabric, worn round the neck, with the ends hanging down in front) in 1596.[51]

Four of the seven women brought clothing. Katheryn Symonds 'the newe wyffe of John Symonds', admitted with her husband's consent in 1596, had only one item, a 'peticote'. All her moveable goods would have become his on marriage.[52] Agnes Sansom brought one good gown and 'other apparell' in 1607. In contrast, the other two were well-clad. Agnes Baller (1603) had:

> 4d [four and one half] partlette [a woman's neckerchief, collar or ruff], 3 aprons, a nekkercheff, 2 hedd kercheffs [a cloth used to cover the head], 3 smoketes [or smoke, a loose chemise worn by women], a wastecoat, one gowne, 2 peticotes [and] one hatt'.[53]

Later that decade, in 1607, Anstye Freeman brought:

> 2 peticotes, a gowne, a good hatt and a worse [hatt] ... 3 smocks, 4 partletts good and two others, 2 apornes, 3 single heddclothes and a double kerchieffe.

Male wardrobes in the Dorset villages contained at least shirts, breeches, stockings and shoes, usually two sets. Occasional additions were coats and doublets (jerkins), an older type of outer wear. Female attire comprised gowns or coats, 'petticotes', waistcoats and aprons but no other items were mentioned.[54] Like the admissions register, the inventories rarely recorded clothing but the register gives greater insight into what poorer people wore.

Money

Fifteen people donated money before 1620, one in the 1640s and another in 1667. All but five brought other items too. Agnes Carpenter brought 24s. 8d. 'by the yeare' in December 1582, but she died in May 1583. In contrast, Agnes Lewes gave only 2s. 0d. 'a yeare during her liffe' but died a year later. Neither brought other goods. In the 1590s, Thomas Pouncefote brought 4d. and eleven other items, John Buckingham 4s. 6d. and six items, William Russell 18s. and two items and Robert Sexton thirteen items and money 'towards a newe gowne'. John Davis brought 20s. 'geven as a benevolence' and twelve possessions and John Dier brought 5s. 6d. with eleven other items. William Lockett's son pledged 10s. In 1606 John Luckes' son promised 20s. at the next Lady Day for a new gown for his father. Thomas Winchell's brother gifted 20s. in 1610 and in 1647 Peeter Freeman brought 20s., securing the room kept vacant since the Civil War. Anne Selby, widow, who brought only a sheet, dish, spoon and cup also gave in 1667: 'the rights in her house and garden at Horsecastle Well to buy her a bed and other necessaryes'. The amounts contributed varied considerably and higher amounts were not necessarily in lieu of goods. Promises of family and friends indicate their acceptance of responsibility for those who were poor against their will and imply the perception that contributions might secure a place.

Tools and Occupations

Men occasionally brought tools until 1700. In 1609, John Legost contributed 'an anvil, a paire of bellowes, and all his workinge tooles' and in 1617 Giles Stone brought 'sertayn carpenters toles'. Thomas Callowe had a 'pressinge iron and a paire of taylors sheears' in 1640. Henry Martyn brought only a blanket and a 'bittle' (a heavy wooden hammer for driving wedges, beating or flattening), possibly a weaver's tool.[55] Ten others had one or two of the following – spades, axes, hatchets, mattocks, hooks, sometimes 'woodhookes', and wedges. Machin associated hatchets and hooks with hedging, and mattocks and wedges with felling trees.[56]

Only one occupation is recorded in the entire register, in 1594, that of William Jervis, cardmaker - a maker of cards for carding wool in the cloth trade.[57] He brought nothing with him. Other sources show that in 1603/4, when 'he was eighty-eight years old and living in Sherborne Almshouse', John Dier was a deponent in a lawsuit concerning the right to fell trees in the churchyard. Witnesses testified that the wood was used to make a stage for the Corpus Christi play in the 1570s. John had an important role in the community, having been paid to oversee the designing and making of costumes for the play in 1571. He had also rented the church house for the performance of 'interludes' in 1567.[58] Robert Blobell, who brought ten items, including a feather bed and pillow in 1592, had been in a position to secure an education for his son, Walter, then rector of a nearby parish. The cost of Robert's new gown was underwritten, not by Walter but by a benefactor, as noted earlier. After Robert's death, Walter was to be chided in writing by the Almshouse Brethren for 'careless consideracon of his distressed mother', who was not an almshouse resident.[59]

In the 19th century, only the 1881 census recorded former occupations of almsmen, listing ten labourers, two carpenters, three masons, one sailor, one farmer and a tailor. This reflects the mix of skilled and unskilled workers hinted at in the tools and backgrounds mentioned above. It suggests little change in occupational status and mix of the almspeople over the centuries, compared with the focus on skilled craftsmen and traders in a Norwich almshouse and the preponderance of traders in a Rugby almshouse in 1881 compared with labourers in 1851.[60]

Those with Nothing

No goods were recorded for sixty-five people (13 per cent) who are assumed to have arrived with nothing. This was actually stated categorically for thirteen who, like Francis Bartlet in 1697, could 'bring nothing…by reason of his poverty'. Four of these thirteen were admitted in the seven decades between 1590 and 1659 and nobody was admitted empty-handed between 1661 and 1689. Two without possessions were admitted in the 1690s and the remaining seven entered the Almshouse before 1759. The latest nine impoverished entrants totalled more than twice as many as those admitted in the earlier period of seven decades. This pattern was repeated for the fifty-two whose lack of goods was recorded without comment and whose poverty was assumed: seventeen admitted between 1590 and 1659, one between 1661 and 1689 and thirty-four between 1690 and 1759.

Several entries recorded explanations for lack of possessions, suggesting that a surviving spouse required all, or most, goods at home. William Bennett (1593) brought fifteen items: 'and all other his goods if he survive his wyfe'; Margaret Browne (1615) brought: 'noe goods with the consent of her husband'; and Jeremiah Hebditch (1724): 'by reason of his wife's being aged and almost blind brings only …'. Marital status was not recorded for men, nor indeed for all women, and so there are only glimpses of the impact of their home situations on contributions to the Almshouse. It may be that policy with regard to almspeople bringing possessions into the Almshouse changed during the mid 18th century, since the recording of possessions on the admissions register ceased during the 1760s.

COMPARISON WITH ALMSHOUSE INVENTORIES

Three early inventories for the Almshouse include almspeople whose admissions were recorded in the register.[61] The first, for 1582/3, contains three relevant entries, for John Chapman and Agnes Stone, admitted in 1582 and Agnes Lewes, who brought money, in 1583. Despite such recent admissions, with no record of personal possessions, their rooms contained eleven, thirty-five and twenty-four items, respectively, in that inventory. All had bedding, the women possessed twenty articles of clothing each and Agnes Stone had a candlestick. Almshouse policy may not yet have required possessions to be recorded in the register. Only John Chapman survived to the next inventory in 1590 when his two blankets were not listed but he had gained two gowns and half a sheet. Table 14.II shows how many goods, in selected categories, brought on admission featured in both sources and how many were additional items.

Seven men brought items from categories not listed in Table 14.II, indicated by asterisks in the last column. None of the almspeople named in both register and inventories brought furniture and none was found in their rooms. The final two columns compare the number of items brought on entry with the number of possessions in the (final) inventory in which almspeople appeared. Only two, William Poole and Thomas Pouncefote, had fewer items than on arrival. Some had considerably more.

All bringing goods on admission had bedding. The 1590 inventory stated that Thomas Riall: 'brought a coverlet and blanket, a sawcer and had delivered him 2 gounes Michels bedd'. Another man was admitted 'in the roome of Mihell Berwick', whose bed was transferred to Riall. However, John Mogge, admitted before Riall, had no bed in his room in 1590. The one other such omission was found in the 1582/3 inventory. In the later inventories, those who brought nothing had been given bedding and most others had more items than originally.[62]

Of those who brought cooking/eating equipment, only Thomas Pouncefote had any such items in his room, a platter, a pottenger and a sawcer. It seems likely that these goods were usually diverted to communal use. Before 1590 nobody brought household goods, although the two men who survived from 1590 until the 1598/9 inventory had each by then acquired a bag, as had twelve others admitted during that decade. Nowhere was this item found in the admissions register. Candlesticks appear to have been surrendered since the inventories listed none in any of the rooms.[63]

The Almshouse allocated funding for clothing 'linen, woollen hose, shoes and other necessary things' and a Christmas gift of a white woollen gown and hood, the livery of the house at that time.[64] Two men admitted before 1590, and seven afterwards, brought clothing, but no women did. Not all had gowns, stockings or shoes in their rooms, especially in 1590, and not all men had breeches or hose (close-fitting breeches).[65] Possibly they were wearing them and had no spares.

In both inventories, the four women had between one and three smocks. Other items of attire included aprons, petticotes, partlettes (neckerchiefs, collars or ruffs), and head kercheffs, with occasional hats and 'wastcoats'.[66] Joanna Scope, Agnes Bartlet and Anne Chamberlayne had acquired twenty-six, nineteen and thirty garments, respectively, by 1598/9.[67]

All but two men, Greenwaie and Riall, had one to three shirts each by 1598/9. Poole and Pouncefote were without gowns, although Poole had brought one into the house. All had one to three gowns in the later inventory. In 1590 the only other items of male attire were breeches and a coat in John Mogge's room, but by 1598/9 the range included coats, doublets, hats, stockings and the occasional 'gerkene' or jerkin. As with the women, men often had many more articles of clothing than they did on entry. Shoes were rarely found in any of the rooms and may have been kept elsewhere in the almshouse.[68]

On the whole, it was not unusual for almspeople to have a good number of clothing items in those early years. In 1763, however, at the end of the period, another source recorded the Brethren's decision that:

every Man in this House shall have a new [Coate crossed out] Gowns [*sic*] the present condition of their clothing is such that they cannot appear decent into Church to be worn on Sundays only.[69]

Gowns and other clothing had been provided by the almshouse since its foundation, a practice which continued into the 20th century.[70] Further research might determine the reason for the poor state of the almspeople's attire at that time.

TABLE 14.II

Comparison of possessions of individuals listed in the register and in the inventories

Name	Entry date	Bedding Entry	Bedding 1590	Bedding 1598	Cooking/eating Entry	Cooking/eating 1590	Cooking/eating 1598	Household Entry	Household 1590	Household 1598	Clothing Entry	Clothing 1590	Clothing 1598	Total at entry	Total in room
John Chapman	1582	-	8	D	-	-	D	-	-	D	-	5	D	-	12
John Forte	1583	-	8	D	-	-	D	-	-	D	-	5	D	-	13
Katherine Elis	1584	-	6	D	-	-	D	-	-	D	-	4	D	-	10
Joanna Scope	1585	-	6	9	-	-	-	-	-	-	-	4	26	-	35
Thomas Camel	1587	-	5	N/A	-	N/A	N/A	-	-	N/A	-	4	N/A	-	9
William Poole	1587	4	7	N/A	5	-	N/A	-	-	N/A	1	3	N/A	11	10*
John Burgess	1588	-	11	12	-	-	-	-	-	1	-	3	4	-	17
Alice Lambert	1588	-	5	N/A	-	N/A	N/A	-	-	N/A	-	5	N/A	-	10
Agnes Bollyn	1589	-	5	D	-	-	D	-	-	D	-	5	D	-	10
Thomas Greenwaie	1589	-	7	7	-	-	-	-	-	1	-	2	12	-	20
John Mogge	1589	-	3	D	-	-	D	-	-	D	-	6	D	-	9
Thomas Pouncefote	1590	5	4	N/A	5	3	N/A	-	-	N/A	2	2	N/A	13	9*
Thomas Riall	1590	2	3	N/A	1	1	N/A	-	-	N/A	-	2	N/A	3	7
Alice Chamberlayne	1591	5	N/A	10	-	N/A	-	-	N/A	-	-	N/A	30	5	40
John Dier	1594	6	N/A	7	4	N/A	-	-	N/A	1	Yes	N/A	11	13	19**
Richard Roberts/Woodall	1595	9	N/A	10	1	N/A	-	-	N/A	2	Yes	N/A	14	12	26*
Robert Sexton	1596	9	N/A	9	1	N/A	-	1	N/A	2	Yes	N/A	13	17	24**
Thomas Ladbroke	1596	7	N/A	9	1	N/A	-	1	N/A	1	10	N/A	13	20	22*
Ambrose Chetmyll	1596	6	N/A	6	1	N/A	-	1	N/A	1	11	N/A	8	19	19*
John Davis	1597	6	N/A	5	3	N/A	-	2	N/A	2	1	N/A	2	15	20
John Rouswell	1598	2	N/A	2	2	N/A	-	1	N/A	1	2	N/A	13	7	21
Agnes Bartlet	1598	1	N/A	4	6	N/A	-	-	N/A	-	-	N/A	19	7	23
Elizabeth Hudd	1598	2	N/A	2	-	N/A	-	-	N/A	-	-	N/A	12	2	20
Thomas Lodge	1598	-	N/A	6	-	N/A	-	-	N/A	-	-	N/A	9	-	15
William Sansom	1599	-	N/A	6	1	N/A	-	1	N/A	-	-	N/A	10	2	16

CONCLUSION

It is very unusual to find a record of the possessions brought into an almshouse and so the admissions register for Sherbourne Almshouse provides rare glimpses into the lives of almspeople between 1590 and 1760. The detail of their possessions suggests an almshouse community comprising former artisans and tradesmen but also labourers and some who might possibly be described as paupers. Register entries reveal that, for some entrants, family circumstances meant that no possessions could be spared. However, because marital status was never recorded for men, and not always for women, it is rarely possible to identify when the needs of a surviving spouse limited an individual's ability to take goods into the Almshouse. The evidence from the register is, therefore, insufficient to gauge the level of poverty of newcomers to the Almshouse by their possessions alone. Nevertheless, the average decline in possessions in the first half of the 17th century does suggest an increase in poverty. It could reflect the 'real hunger of the poor' due to 'general impoverishment' and the 'massive distress… in the west country' because of reduction in export of cloth at that time.[71] Wars, at home and abroad, caused disruptions in trade not quickly resolved; military engagements were a feature of both this period and the first half of the 18th century, when the possessions brought by almspeople tapered to almost zero.[72]

It seems likely that the almshouse brethren endeavoured to choose those who were poor against their will. It is probable that some had seen better times earlier in their lives – those who brought feather beds and brass pots and candlesticks, for example. Others may have been very anxious not to appear empty-handed, even bringing items, such as half a sheet or a piece of a dish, thus demonstrating how important the achievement of a place at the Almshouse must have seemed.

Why, then, did the Brethren stop recording the possessions of new entrants in the 1760s, when the expectation that they would bring in their 'moveable goods' had been enshrined in the Almshouse foundation deed? A number of factors suggest three hypotheses: increasing local poverty meaning that eventually most people brought nothing; a decision by the Brethren that recording people's possessions was no longer necessary or useful; or successive scribes favouring brevity in record-keeping.

Looking at the evidence for each in turn, firstly the very few small luxuries seen in earlier times had disappeared by the 1670s and, over the seventy years from 1690, more than twice as many people brought nothing as in the previous hundred years. The range of goods reduced decade by decade until only bedding was recorded in the 1740s. Thereafter the number of items brought by individuals also plummeted, until only a few entries recorded one or two bedding items, interspersed with entries recording nothing. This circumstantial evidence would lend support to increasing levels of actual poverty in applicants to the Almshouse. Secondly, no administrative decision to stop recording possessions has yet been found, although extensive work on the Almshouse records might reveal evidence of such a decision, and this possibility cannot be entirely ruled out. Thirdly, transcribed into the same volume as the admissions register is a record of elections of the brethren of the Almshouse, covering the same period, 1582-1863. Throughout, these entries include the name of the brother whose place was being filled and the reason for the vacancy. Only during the 1790s was the entry truncated, omitting the circumstances of the vacancy. None of the evidence is conclusive, but the most likely explanation is that a decision was made, formally or informally, that detailed recording of almspeople's possessions in the register was unnecessary.

Not only does this admissions register give an exceptionally long and unbroken list of Sherborne residents who spent their final years in the safety and security of the Almshouse, but we can almost visualise some of the earlier entrants. We know the clothing they wore, and sometimes the condition of it. We know what bedding they had and, again, sometimes the condition of it. We know those who had nothing, except the clothes they wore; but we can be assured they would have received what was needful because provision was made for clothing from the foundation.

This record alone is a valuable source for studying various aspects of the Almshouse population: average duration of stay, for example. It is, however, only one item in the extensive Sherborne Almshouse collection at the Dorset History Centre. Collectively these documents reveal in detail both the internal functioning of the Almshouse and the much wider role it took in channelling private philanthropy into the community, both of which invite further study.

Notes

The source for all unattributed quotations is: Dorset History Centre (DHC): D/SHA/D24, Sherborne Almshouse Admissions Register, 1591-1866.

1. Hutchins, J. *The History and Antiquities of Dorset*, Vol. III. Wakefield, 1868, p. 209.

2. Fowler, J. *Mediaeval Sherborne*. Dorchester, 1951, p. 241.

3. Clay, R.M. *The Mediaeval Hospitals of England*. London, 1909, pp. 112-5. www.archive.org/stream/mediaevalhospita00clayuoft#page/112/mode/2up accessed January 2011.

4. Fowler, pp. 256-7.

5. Ibid., p. 256.

6. Clay, pp. 114-5; Howson, B. *Almshouses: a social & architectural history*. Stroud, 2008, pp. 77-82.

7. Hutchins, p. 144.

8. Hutchins J. *The Annals and Iconography of Dorsetshire and Dorset Worthies*. Extra Illustrated Edition, Vol. XI. London & Bridport, 1904, plate 47, facing p. 98.

9. Howson, p. 82.

10. Fowler, p. 242.

11. Slack, P. *Poverty and Policy in Tudor and Stuart England*. London, 1988, pp. 22-7.

12. Ibid., pp. 13, 20; Hindle, S. *On the Parish?: the micropolitics of poor relief in rural England ca 1550-1750*. Oxford, 2004, pp. 92-5.

13. Wrightson, K. *Earthly Necessities: economic lives in early modern Britain, 1470-1750*. London, 2002, p. 197; Hindle, 2004, pp.48-50.

14. Hutchins, p. 143; Slack, pp. 13, 20; Fowler, pp. 402-3.

15. Mayo, C.H. *A Historic Guide to the Almshouse of St John Baptist and St John the Evangelist*. Oxford, 1926, p. 38.

16. Clay, pp. 132, 134.

17. Greenslade, M. W. & Pugh, R. B. (eds) 'Hospitals: Lichfield, St John the Baptist', *A History of the County of Stafford*. Victoria County History (*VCH*, Staffs), Vol. 3, 1970, pp. 279-89. www.british-history.ac.uk/report.aspx?compid=37864&strquery=HOSPITALS LICHFIELD accessed January 2011.

18. Clay, pp. 133.

19. Tomkins, A. 'Retirement from the Noise and Hurry of the World?: the Experience of Almshouse Life 1650-1850' in McEwan, J. & Sharpe, P. *Accommodating Poverty: the housing and living arrangements of the English poor, ca 1600-1850*. Basingstoke, 2011, p. 268.

20. Langley, A. 'Warwickshire Almshouses, 1400 to 1900: "affording comfortable asylums to the aged and respectable poor"?', *Warwickshire History*, xiv/4, Winter 2009/10, p. 146.

21. Orton, M. & Cleary, J. *So Long as the World Shall Endure: the 500-year history of Ford's and Bond's Hospitals*. Coventry, 1991, pp. 46-8.

22.   Gaydon, A.T. & Pugh, R.B. (eds) *A History of the County of Shropshire*. Victoria County History, Vol. 2, 'Almshouses: Shrewsbury', 1973, pp.110-114, p.112. URL: www.british-history.ac.uk/report.aspx?compid=39945 accessed January 2011.

23.   Fox, G. *The History of Pontefract in Yorkshire*. (n.p., Pontefract, 1827), p. 323. URL: http://books.google.com/books?id=Gv9KsAakhbQC&printsec=frontcover&dq=the+history+of+pontefrac t+in+yorkshire&hl=en&ei=pGIjTebQAYGGhQfxsNmIAw&sa=X&oi=book_result&ct=book-preview-link&resnum=1&ved=0CCoQuwUwAA#v=onepage&q&f=false accessed January 2011.

24.   Source: Yorkshire Archaeological Society, YAS: DD160.

25.   King, P. 'Pauper Inventories and the Material Lives of the Poor in the Eighteenth and Early Nineteenth Centuries', in Hitchcock, T. *et. al.* (eds) *Chronicling Poverty: the voices and strategies of the English poor, 1640-1840*. Basingstoke, 1997, p. 159-60, 188 fn. 16.

26.   Dorset History Centre (DHC): D/SHA/D24, Register containing admissions to Sherborne Almshouse, 1437-1866 (the admissions register starts in 1582 and is transcribed in 27 below) pp. 62-134.

27.   Clark, A. (ed.) *Sherborne Almshouse Register*. Dorchester, 2013. This includes a transcript of all records in D/SHA/D24 (*see* note 26 above): election of brethren, pp. 41-61.

28.   Ibid., 2013.

29.   Tomkins, p. 268.

30.   DHC: D/SHA/A128, Almshouse Week Book of Henry Stephens, 1582-3, pp. 21-2; DHC: D/SHA/A141, Almshouse Week Book (Henry Stephens) 1589-90, pp. 21-2; DHC: D/SHA/A158, Week Book (John Thorne) 1598-9, pp. 31-33.

31.   King, 1997; Machin, R. *Probate Inventories and Manorial Exerpts of Chetnole, Leigh and Yetminster*. Bristol, 1976; Williams, L. & Thomson, S. (eds) *Marlborough Probate Inventories (1591-1775)*, Chippenham, 2007.

32.   DHC: D/SHA/D53, Notes concerning numbers of inmates of the Almshouse, 26 November 1836,

33.   Wrightson, p. 44.

34.   Slack, p. 47, Wrightson, pp. 199, 230.

35.   Underdown, D. *Revel, Riot and Rebellion: popular politics and culture in England 1603-1660*. Oxford, 1987, pp. 146-8, 172.

36.   Wrightson, pp. 230-1.

37.   Ibid., pp 230-1.

38.   Williams & Thomson, pp. 313-77.

39.   Machin, p.7.

40.   King, pp. 164, 172-7.

41.   Ibid., p. 164.

42.   Williams & Thomson, pp. 328; 360; 316; *The New Shorter Oxford English Dictionary*. Oxford, 1993, p. 315. Thanks to Graham Hoddinott, volunteer at Dorset History Centre, for reference for definition of 'cadowe'.

43.   Williams & Thomson, pp. 354-5.

44.   Machin, p. 7; Williams & Thomson, pp. 355-7.

45.   Williams & Thomson, p. 361; Machin, p. 7.

46.   Wrightson, p. 194.

47.   Williams & Thomson, pp. 371; 364.

48.   Machin, pp. 5-6.

49.   Ibid., pp. 5-6.

50.   King, p. 178.

51.   Williams & Thomson, p. 314.

52.   Wrightson, p. 43.

53.   Williams & Thomson, pp. 353, 344, 365.

54.   Machin, p. 8.

55.   Williams & Thomson, pp. 28, 317-8.

56.   Machin, p. 14.

57.   Wrightson, p. 310.

58. Hayes, R. C. *et. al.*, *Records of Early English Drama: Dorset/Cornwall*. Toronto, 1999, pp. 36, 360.

59. Fowler, p. 365; DHC: D/SHA/D1, Almshouse Minute Book, 1590-1756, 15 March 1602.

60. Census 1881, Sherborne, RG11/ 2117; fo. 11-12; p. 16-17; GSU roll: 1341512; Schedule: 80; Goose, N. 'Victorian and Edwardian Almspeople: Doughty's Hospital, Norwich, 1837-1911', *Local Population Studies*, 84, Spring 2010, pp. 79-80; Langley, p.149.

61. DHC: D/SHA/A128, Almshouse Week Book of Henry Stephens, 1582-3, pp. 21-2; DHC: D/SHA/A141, Week Book of Henry Stephens, 1589-90, pp. 21-2; DHC: D/SHA/A158, Week Book of John Thorne 1598-9, pp. 31-33.

62. DHC: D/SHA/A141, Week Book, 1589-90, pp. 21-2 and DHC: D/SHA/A158, Week Book, 1598-9, pp. 31-3.

63. Ibid.

64. Fowler, p. 242; Mayo, p. 48.

65. Williams & Thomson, p. 342.

66. Ibid., p. 353.

67. DHC: D/SHA/A158, Week Book, 1598-9, pp. 31-3.

68. Ibid.

69. DHC: D/SHA/D2, Almshouse Orders and Regulations, 1756-1813.

70. DHC: D/SHA/D24, Founders' Statutes; Mayo, 1926, pp. 48-9.

71. Slack, pp. 48-51.

72. Wrightson, p. 199.

ACKNOWLEDGEMENTS

I would like to thank:

Dr Mark Forrest, Archivist at the Dorset History Centre, for his patient help with reading the different hands in the admissions register and early inventories of Sherborne almshouse; Brian Howson for permission to reproduce his plan of the almshouse; and members of FACHRS Almshouse Project who provided relevant information and references.

CHAPTER 15
ALMSHOUSE CLOTHING

Brita Wood

'I'll give ... my gay apparel for an almsman's gown' said Shakespeare's King Richard II (Act III, iii, 131-133). An almsman's gown would have been a sober and practical garment, very different from that of a noble, thus recognisable as such to Shakespeare's contemporaries.

INTRODUCTION

In this chapter clothing of almshouse residents will be considered; that is clothing provided by an almshouse as part of their charitable support for residents. (Almshouses founded for former military personnel are not included.) Information about ninety-two almshouses that provided some form of clothing at some point in their history has been examined in this study. The almshouses are from nine different English counties plus London and Anglesey in Wales.

The proportion of almshouses where clothing was supplied at any point in time is relatively small; within Northamptonshire out of fifty-six almshouses investigated, only ten had any form of clothing provision. It may be that records concerning clothing have not been located and/or survived so that this 18 per cent may be a little low, but taking this study as a basis would suggest that less than a quarter of almshouses nationally had any form of clothing provision. What should also be considered is that in many cases once the almshouse itself had been built there was little money left from the original endowment to support the almspeople and, unless money was gifted to the almshouse by other benefactors, money for many of them remained in short supply.

THE PURPOSE OF ALMSHOUSE CLOTHING

'Clothing is never just clothing: it can carry with it a variety of social, economic, and even moral Implications'.[1]

The provision of clothing falls into two main categories: that aimed at advertising the generosity of the founder by way of a uniform, and that aimed at providing ordinary clothing or material to make clothes. The latter, while sensible and caring, would also ensure that poor residents did not disgrace their benefactor by their appearance. The boundaries between these two areas are not always distinct. Cunnington and Lucas suggest that:

When the community had a collegiate form, with its "tutor" or "master" a priest it seems natural that the inhabitants ... should be dressed according to a rule. But this uniformity applied in foundations of all kinds until the twentieth century. So indeed did the obligation to practise religion. This gave the old people an aim in life and a timetable – and for us the extra interest of comparing what they wore every day with the clothes they went to church in on Sundays.[2]

As this implies, some almshouses provided both a uniform and ordinary clothing for the residents.

A Uniform

'For thousands of years human beings have communicated with one another first in the language of dress'.[3] This communication happens in two distinct ways with regard to almshouse clothing. The first is the uniform style of clothing, setting the almshouse person apart from their fellows and to be worn in public to show off their attachment to the almshouse and its benefactor.

Almshouse founders were often wealthy merchants or aristocrats, who would have been used to displaying their wealth and privilege: they dressed their servants in livery; their carriages – particularly in the case of the nobility – would have advertised the status of the occupant by having the crest on the door. They continued this form of advertising in the ornate nature of the almshouse building and the clothing of the inhabitants. Another purpose of a uniform was to distinguish the wearer from others for the purpose of discipline, so that anyone who stepped out of line could be reported. Penalties for infringement of the rules could be as severe as losing a place in the almshouse.

Some of the London livery companies that had developed from the old guilds also provided almshouses. Over the years the Companies developed their own particular style of livery that was worn at special meetings and ceremonies and this concept was continued in their almshouse provision. At the Fishmongers' Guild's Newington Almshouse in south London the benefactor's will provided an 'out' brother with a gown that had the donor's arms with a dolphin above on it; this gown was to be worn when representing the almshouse.[4] Some uniforms therefore had a ceremonial function and had to be worn for attending church and special occasions. Ceremonial clothing was passed on from one recipient to the next — an almsperson who left the almshouse was required to hand their specially-designed clothes or hats to the next resident.

Everyday Clothing

In almshouses where everyday clothing was provided this was usually issued annually and allowed the almsperson to keep up a certain standard in dress:

Cleanliness may not always be next to godliness, but it is usually regarded as a sign of respectability or at least of self respect. It is also a sign of status, since to be clean and neat always involves the expense of time and money.[5]

At Parson Latham's Hospital, Oundle, in the 1870s each woman resident received a new gown at Whitsuntide and five shillings per quarter for washing.[6] St Thomas' Hospital, Northampton, was first endowed for twelve poor widows, each given an allowance of 1s. 11d. a week, together with clothing, firing and washing.[7] It can be inferred that it was important for these benefactors that, although not wearing a uniform, the residents were seen to be respectable and to reflect well on the almshouse and thus on the founder's generosity in providing for the 'deserving poor'. The actual clothing provided is discussed later in this chapter.

Status

The wearing of the civilian uniform of an almshouse defines the individual as a member of a group, giving them a status. How this status is viewed is dependent on the viewer and the point in time. When a uniform is first designed it is easy for the wearer's contemporaries to understand the symbols and interpret their meaning, but as time passes and the uniform remains frozen in the past, though worn in the present, the true meaning may be lost, but the concept of the wearer belonging to a specific group remains. The conspicuousness of a hat or gown conferred status on the wearer, so the idea that the almsperson might feel shame at being badged as poor and an object of charity is probably not correct. It is more likely that they were proud of their status when compared with their fellows as they had been chosen as deserving support. They were also upholding a tradition that confirmed their standing in the community as they maintained and took on the status of their predecessors.

Almspeople were generally older and usually over fifty years of age as a minimum. The majority of them, including women, would have worked and in the course of that work some of them would have worn either a formal uniform – for example, in domestic service – or an informal uniform of their particular trade, such as a butcher's apron. Working people had to show potential employers their occupation, particularly at hiring fairs that were regularly held throughout the country. The advertisement of their trade was done not only by carrying a symbol of their trade (such as a shepherd's crook) but also by the style of their dress and often the colour of the garment; identification could also be in the form of a badge worn on their clothing. As Helen Caffrey states, concerning almspeople: 'Residents should be respectable, orderly and deserving, appreciative of their good fortune and conformist as regards society's expectations of them'.[8]

THE SIGNIFICANCE OF COLOUR

There are two uses of colour in almshouse clothing; the colour of identification and the colour of practicality. Colour can play a major part in the 'advertising' side and a number of founders specified a particular colour be used. The choice of colour is also very important; the main colour chosen was blue. In the Middle Ages this colour symbolised the faithful servant; it stood for humility, devotion and faith and was associated with the Virgin Mary. Blue therefore proved popular with founders of almshouses, in part for its religious symbolism but also because in the medieval period blue was an expensive dye to produce and therefore showed that the benefactor was giving generously. In the 17th century, blue dye became cheaper to produce and therefore was viewed as a colour for servant's uniforms and less often worn by the higher classes. Blue dye became even cheaper with the invention of aniline dyes in the mid 1850s. It has always been a popular choice for work clothing — for example, gardeners' aprons have traditionally been blue.

Purple was originally the most expensive colour because it was produced from a rare shellfish and so was a colour worn by royalty. The invention of new dyes in the 19th century made purple dye cheaper and therefore the colour more accessible for clothing. In this sample, only four of the ninety-two almshouses had gowns of purple cloth. These were founded pre-19th century when the choice of purple demonstrated the wealth of the founder.

Black, brown, grey and white were colours originally associated with the religious life – the habits of friars, monks and nuns – and therefore also associated with humility. They were also sombre colours that were approved for charity clothing, whether for almshouses or charity schools. Brown has always been a cheap dye to produce; the colour is associated with strength and stability and has always been popular as a colour for country people's clothes. Very importantly:

> Drab, greyed browns are also the colours that show dirt least, and in a pre-laundromat age when soap was expensive and water for washing had to be hauled from a well or the town pump, then heated over a fire, this was an important recommendation.[9]

Red was a colour very rarely used for charity clothes; it was, however, commonly used for cloaks of working class women from the 17th to the 19th centuries. In this study of ninety-two almshouses that provided clothing or material, only two had red for a cloak and both were for women: Trinity Almshouse at Castle Rising; and the St John the Baptist and St John the Evangelist Almshouse at Sherborne. It is also worth noting that the red cloaks at Castle Rising were only introduced as ceremonial wear in the 19th century.

Distinctive clothing had the property of demonstrating the almshouse to which the wearer belonged. This advertisement was to show off the benefactor of the almshouse rather than a wish to brand the almsperson as receiving charity. Having given a large sum of money to set up and maintain the almshouse, the founder wanted to ensure that this charitable giving was noted not only by their social equals but by all members of society.

An interesting use of colour was that by two prosperous residents of Melbourne in Derbyshire: Henry Greene in his will of 1679 stipulated that the recipients of his charity should wear green; and Thomas Gray in his will of 1691 required that grey clothing should be purchased for the recipients of his.[10] At a time when few people were literate this was an ingenious way of linking their names with their charitable giving.

In the Rules and Orders of the Almshouse at Ravenstone in Buckinghamshire provision was made to provide clothing for the twelve inhabitants, six old men and six old women. In the Charity Commissioners *Report* of 1834 they are: 'old, unmarried, members of the Church of England, but not necessarily parishioners of Ravenstone'.[11] In 1827, £144 was being provided per year, £12 per person, from which a purple gown was to be purchased. The remaining monies were to be distributed to the old people. However, the rules go on:

> But because 3 shillings and 6 pence per week for each person, has been found to be sufficient which is but £109 4 shillings per annum this and the cost of the 12 gowns being deducted out of the £144. The residue shall not be given to them in money but be laid out for their use in buying wood and coals and utensils for each house as occasion requires.[12]

The Trustees wanted nothing to be wasted and they went on to say that all these materials must remain in the almshouse if the person died, presumably to be used by the next occupant of that house. The purple clothing supplied annually also had to be reused. Each almsperson 'was obliged every year, of their old gowns, to make such under habits, as are suitable to their sex and decent for them'.[13] Reusing the previous year's clothes was a common theme in almshouses and would have been usual practice for poor people outside the almshouse. When clothing could no longer be worn other uses would be found, such as being made into rag rugs for the floor. At the Holy Trinity Hospital at Clun in Shropshire, when the almsman's best blue gown was replaced after four years, the old one had to be dyed a more sombre colour and then cut up to make doublet and breeches to wear on a Sunday.[14]

Another instance of purple being used was at Doughty's Hospital in Norwich in 1687, where the founder, William Doughty, required that the inhabitants should have 'a gown or coat of purple cloth on their election to the almshouse and every two years thereafter'.[15] The wearing of these garments was compulsory and a resident would lose his place if he did not comply. By March 1727, the Mayor's Court was noting that the residents had not got adequate clothing, so the clothing provision may have lapsed. By 1841, however, the clothing allowance was more generous. Instead of the purple clothes 'the hospital was providing the male inmates with suits of clothes each year and thirty suits were produced by Brays at a cost of 26s. 6d. per suit'.[16] William White, writing in 1845, listed the annual clothing allowance for each resident as follows: 'one pair of shoes, blue clothing and linen for shirts and shifts. The return to provision of clothing on a biennial rather than an annual basis, therefore, effected a significant saving to the trust'.[17] There had been a colour change to blue, thus clothing was still being supplied but economy was also being practised in its provision. The clothing allowance was not stopped until the 1950s.

Where clothing of a specified colour was provided in mixed sex almshouses, the colour was usually the same for men and women. However, in two cases the men and women had different colours. At Revis's Almshouses at Newport Pagnell in Buckinghamshire the men had blue coats and the women black dresses.[18] At Calverhall Almshouses at Clun in Shropshire (founded in 1738) the dress/coat provision was in blue but in 1898 Mrs Heywood Lonsdale bequeathed black cardigans for the men and blue bed gowns or red jackets for the women.[19] These are the only examples of different colours found in the ninety-two almshouses in this study. The colour identification of the almshouse was still important in the provision of the clothing for all the residents: at Calverhall the different colours were only for indoor clothing.

Illustration 15.a. Cloaks with badges at Trinity Hospital, Castle Rising in Norfolk.
Photo © Brita Wood.

Illustration 15.b. Hats at Trinity Hospital, Castle Rising.
Photo © Brita Wood.

A Case Study: Trinity Hospital, Castle Rising, Norfolk

Trinity Hospital at Castle Rising was founded in 1614 by Henry Howard, Earl of Northampton, for twelve poor old women from three surrounding villages. The original clothing provision for the almswomen was:

> Blue fustian, lined with baize and with this was worn a high crowned hat, probably black, and most likely over a white cap. Living gowns are mentioned in the Hospital Account books in 1648 and 1749. Brown gowns are often mentioned and 1s. 6d. was paid for one in 1749 ... The baize for lining the gowns cost from 2s. 0d. to 2s. 4d. a yard.[20]

The Governess was provided with a gown made of sand-coloured cloth lined with baize; the material cost 13s. 0d. in 1620. By 1833 there were six almswomen and a Governess (the equivalent of a Master) resident in the almshouse. The Charity Commissioners' *Report* in 1833 shows that the women were being supplied not only with a uniform for Sunday use but also with everyday clothing. There is also evidence that the uniforms were expected to be recycled as women were given the old one for everyday use when they received the new one:

> The Governess ... with the help and advice of the assistants should buy as much black frieze or strong cloth or kersey of one sad colour as to make every one of the poor women a gown to wear on the weekdays each gown to cost 13/4 and to be delivered on St. Matthias' day the Founder's birthday [May 14th]: and should in like manner every seven years 30 yards of good blue broadcloth at 8/6 a yard to make every one of the poor women a livery gown for Sundays and festival days and 45 yards of blue baize at 5/- a yard for lining the same; and should on Trinity Sunday in every seventh year to each poor woman her gown readymade being of the same fashion as them then worn ...

a white lion embroidered and set on the breast of each gown – cost 40/-; and at the same time the Governess should deliver them a hat of the price of 4/- all of one fashion and at the delivery of the new she should give to each woman her old livery gown and hat for her own use.[21]

The distinctive scarlet cloaks first appear in the records in 1853:

These Cloaks are still worn on Sundays and are definitely the same shape and colour as the 18th- and 19th-century English and Lowland Scottish and some types of Welsh Cloaks. The present Trinity Hospital Cloak is made of scarlet serge with a deep hood edged with scarlet braid identical with those seen in the 18th- and 19th-century English paintings; the only difference being that the Hospital Cloak is made of scarlet and has the crest taken from the Earl of Northampton's Arms embroidered on the front.[22]

The design of the cloak is therefore no different from what their 19th-century rural contemporaries might have been wearing - what set them apart was the badge (*see* Illustration 15.a.). The gowns originally supplied would have been heavy to wear and very old-fashioned. By the mid 1850s a more modern style of lighter-weight dress had been introduced that would have needed a warm outer garment to go over it and thus the cloak was a good compromise for both the almshouse management and the almswomen.

The other distinctive element of the Castle Rising almshouse dress was the black conical hats looking not unlike a witch's hat or traditional Welsh hat (*see* Illustration 15.b.). However these hats are another survival of an earlier style as they are a modified version of the 17th-century 'sugarloaf' hat. These hats were still being worn by the residents in the late 20th century for church parades and important occasions. The Governess (later termed matron) although wearing a scarlet cloak, is set above the almswomen by the fact that her cloak is three-tiered and worn with a black three-cornered hat with a black ostrich feather (*see* Illustration 15.b.).

BADGING

Some founders advertised their generosity in the form of a badge. Badging by the wearing of the donor's initials or family emblem was more common in almshouses founded after the Reformation. Prior to this, coats of arms were occasionally used to form the basis of a badge, but this was not common. The badge could be made of metal, but more often it was embroidered directly on to the costume provided. Alternatively, a cloth badge that could be attached either to almshouse clothing or to residents' own clothes; a badge was usually worn on the sleeve or chest.

Some badges, whether of metal or embroidery, were highly ornamental and these have survived down the centuries as part of the ceremonial costume or 'Sunday best'. Besides initials, they may also contain coats of arms or similar devices. The badges were often passed on and as an almsperson died or left the almshouse they were given to the next entrant. This was particularly so for those made of silver. More utilitarian cloth badges and initials sewn onto garments had generally disappeared by the start of the 19th century.

Badging the Poor

Badging of the poor through the 16th to the early 19th century is a contentious subject. Under a 1697 Statute all poor people receiving a pension from the parish were required to wear a badge to indicate this fact. Prior to this badges were worn by the poor in many contexts to show their deserving status so that people were encouraged to give them alms. Hindle states:

'In early sixteenth-century English towns, badges were issued as a stamp of approval, a testimonial of the truth of the deserving or diseased status of those who wore them.'[23]

Following the introduction of the Statute it can be argued that the badge, instead of being a badge of honour, became one of shame. Attitudes within society to those seeking assistance had been changing prior to 1697 and continued afterwards. Hindle suggests: 'By the 1690s, however, the distinction between the undeserving and the deserving had come to seem less significant than that between the dependent and the labouring.'[24] To receive poor relief the recipients had to meet certain criteria, however Hindle also states:

In some respects, therefore, the parish badge was a testimonial of good behaviour, and many paupers evidently thought it worthwhile pleading for a pension, even though (possibly even because) it meant wearing one. That so many petitions (and, indeed, appeals), even in the years after the 1697 statute, were sent to magistrates by poor householders claiming that overseers had denied them relief is striking testimony to popular acceptance of the inevitability, possibly in some cases of the desirability, of badging, for without the badge there would be no collection.[25]

The badging of almshouse residents observed in this study would seem to follow the trend of the relevant period; the majority of almshouses where badges were worn were founded before 1697. The Hugh Perry Almshouses, Wotton-under-Edge, Gloucestershire were founded in the year of the Statute 1697:

It is agreed upon by the mayor of Wotton-under-Edge and his brethren, whose names are subscribed that the poor people of the new almshouse shall wear gowns, with the letters on them in remembrance of the donor and they shall begin this year and have new ones made once in 3 years and whoever of them shall refuse to wear them constantly to the church and prayers in the chapel or to come to the said prayers shall have no privilege of the gift - Dec 20th 1697.[26]

The 1697 Statute was repealed in 1810 and none of the almshouses in this study founded after 1810 had badges; indeed there is little evidence for any new badging during the 18th century, when it became less widespread.

Almshouse Badges

Of the ninety-two almshouses studied, records show only twenty-five having a badge for the almspeople and only five of these clearly specified a metal badge. The Shrewsbury Almshouse in Derby had a blue gown with a silver badge marked ES.[27] Archbishop Holgate's Hospital in Hemsworth originally had a white gown with a silver badge, whilst the Earl of Shrewsbury's Hospital in Sheffield stipulated purple with a silver badge.[28] The founder of Johnson's Almshouse at Blackwall in London willed that residents should have a blue gown with his coat of arms formed in a brass badge; no evidence has, however, been found to show that this provision was in fact carried out.[29] Residents of Berrington's Hospital at Bishopston in Herefordshire wore a brass or copper-plate badge on the right sleeve of their coat. This almshouse was founded in 1710 by Ann Berrington and the badge was described as having her coat of arms, which was 'Three greyhounds argent, stretched on a field of sable, and the words and figures (viz) "Mrs Anne Berrington, 1723" cut or engraved thereon, to denote the foundress of the said almshouse.'[30]

By far the most common form of badging was the initials of the founder, either embroidered or as letters sewn onto the almspersons' clothing, usually on the sleeve; examples of this are shown in Table 15.I.

The Fishmongers' Almshouse at Newington in London had a variation within the uniform in that: 'one 'out' brother to have 40 shillings a year and a gown bearing the donor's arms and a dolphin at the top of it to be worn when convenient'.[31] This was detailed under the founder's will, the almspeople receiving 'Each St. Thomas Day - a gown of good cloth of eight shillings a yard and six shillings for making up'.[32]

The Holy Trinity Hospital at Greenwich, like that at Clun, was founded by Henry Howard, Earl of Northampton; it was slightly larger, being for twenty poor men, whilst Clun was for twelve. The residents of both almshouses had a blue gown with an embroidered lion on the sleeve. The use of this embroidered badge at Greenwich had stopped by 1835, when the accounts of the Mercers' Court show a resolution that their Wardens and the Master should 'give directions for providing new Silver Badges for the Blue Gowns given to the Poor Men'.[33] This did not happen immediately, but within twenty years the silver badges were in existence and in use. This is the only example found in this study where a metal badge replaced an embroidered one and the only example found of a badge in any form being changed.

TABLE 15.I
Almshouses where clothing was badged with the initials of the founder

Almshouse	Badge	Reference
Allens Almshouses, Northleach, Glocs.	To wear an "A" on their clothing	Papers concerning review of local charities 1967-1975 Northleach. Northleach D3469/5/114
Almshouses, Bakewell, Derbyshire	Cloak/gown - small cross of blue and yellow on left side of chest	Bakewell-Reliquary vol 4, 1863, p. 119
Berwick Almshouses, Shropshire	Grey outer garment with SJ embroidered in green and white on the sleeves	R.R. James, Berwick Almshouses: the will of Sir Samuel Jones, Transactions of the Shropshire Archaeological Society, 4th Series, vol.3, 1921, p. 97
Bishop Wood's Almshouse, Clapton, London	The almswomen to wear gowns with the initials of the founder TW on the shoulder	Charity Commissioners' Report for London, BPP, Vol. 12, 1825, p. 136
Bradshaw Almshouse, Duffield, Derbyshire	Russet coloured coat with AB on the breast	Duffield-Reliquary vol. XX111 1882/3, p. 139
Duttons Almshouses, Northleach, Glocs	To wear a D on their clothing	Papers concerning review of local charities 1967-1975 Northleach. Northleach D3469/5/114
Fishmongers', Newington, South London	A gown with the donor's arms and a dolphin above	Herbert, 1836
Hugh Perry Almshouses Wotton-under-Edge, Glos.	Gowns with the initials of the founder	Account Book Gloucestershire Archives P379CH1
Lawrence Sheriff's Almshouses, Rugby, Warwickshire	A blue cloth coat with LS on it	White's Trade Directory for Warwickshire, 1874, p. 899

TABLE 15.I contd

Almshouse	Badge	Reference
Netherseal Almshouse, Derbyshire	Cloth gown with RJ on sleeve	Copy will of Richard Johnson 16/11/1697 – DRO: D810 A/PF 89
Lady Katherine Leveson's Hospital, Temple Balsall, Warks	Grey cloth gown with KL on in blue	Charity Commissioners' Report for Warks, p. 255
Oken's Almshouses, Warwick	Black cloth garment with TO in white cloth on it	Charity Commissioners' Report for Warks, p. 774
Reynardson's Almshouses, Tottenham, London	Black gown with the donor's initials on the left sleeve	Charity Commissioners Report for London, BPP 1826, Vol. 14, p. 162
Richard Read's Almshouse, Drax, West Riding	Grey coat or gown with a red R on the sleeve	Charity Commissioners' Report for the West Riding, 1897-99, Vol. 5, pp. 112-24
Roses Almshouse, Chesterfield, Derbyshire	Blue gown with SR on right sleeve	(1839) The History of Chesterfield with particulars of the Hamlets contiguous to the Town and Descriptive Accounts of Chatsworth, Hardwick and Bolsover, p. 228 (The Genealogist website)
St John the Baptist & St John the Evangelist Almshouses, Sherborne, Dorset	White woollen gown with a mitre on the right breast representing the Bishop of Salisbury and a shield with the arms of St George on the left. Later the mitre appeared on buttons.	Mayo, C.H. 1926, pp. 48-9
Stafford Almshouses, Shenley Church End, Bucks	A gown with a red cross on the left sleeve	Page W. (ed.) History of the County of Buckingham, Victoria County History, Vol 4, 1927, St Catherine Press, pp. 445-6
Trinity Hospital, Castle Rising, Norfolk	A blue gown with a white lion embroidered and attached to the breast. Later a scarlet cloak with crest embroidered on the front.	Trustees of the Almshouses of The Holy and Undivided Trinity, Castle Rising, 1998.
Trinity Hospital, Clun, Shropshire and Trinity Hospital, Greenwich	A blue gown with a silver lion rampant embroidered on the sleeve	Cunnington, & Lucas, pp. 242-244

Almshouses founded later on in the 18th and 19th centuries tended to have practical rather than ceremonial clothing and thus badges were not used as a means of identifying the donor. For example, the almshouses at Titchmarsh in Northamptonshire, founded in 1756, provided eight poor widows with a dress, cap, apron and handkerchief annually.[34] This clothing was still being received in the 1870s, but by the 1930s they received a monetary allowance of £25 10s. 6d. to buy their own clothing.

THE CLOTHING IN DETAIL

Cunnington and Lucas suggest:

Charity clothes would obviously as a rule be chosen with economy. If not the benefactors themselves, at least their trustees and/or management committees were generally business people, who were shrewd and would seek a good combination of cheapness and durability. [35]

Illustration 15.c. Almsmen outside Trinity Hospital in Clun
reproduced by kind permission of Shropshire Archives PC/C/22/13/6

Trinity Hospital Almshouse, in London's Mile End, had a uniform for the men but not for the women residents: the men wore blue suits with brass buttons.[36] The almshouse was open to ship's masters or their widows. Provision of clothing at an almshouse could vary in this way but was more often provided for both men and women.

Where clothing was supplied, even if not a uniform, it was usually set out what was to be purchased for the residents. Thus there would have been some conformity in the clothing worn in many almshouses even if it was not a ceremonial uniform. As discussed above, the colour of clothing was stipulated in some cases, but even where this was not the case, the material could be bought in bulk (which would be cheaper) and the same pattern used to make up the garments. At the French Protestant Hospital, Finsbury in London, all clothing was supplied as required but it was made by residents and issued from a central store.[37]

At Studley Almshouse at Chilton in Oxfordshire, in the 1820s, the provision varied in alternate years specifying: 'That there be allowed each [almsperson] at Christmas, every two years, a livery gown of russet broad cloth; and, in the alternate year, two shirts for each of the men, and two smocks for each of the women, ready made'.[38]

Where a master was appointed, he could receive a better quality cloth or garment to show his higher status within the almshouse community. This is evidenced at the Hospital of Stoke Poges, Buckinghamshire, where rule 6 instructed: 'all to have a livery of one colour: the master's to be of 4 yards of cloth at 6s. 8d. a yard, each brother and sister 3 yards of 5s. a yard'.[39]

Some almshouses also dictated what should not be worn. An early example of this comes from the 14th-century Hospital of St Mary at Great Yarmouth in Norfolk: 'Clothing, their upper garment or hose no other colour than dark russet or in part black. Vayles of silk they shall not ware'.[40] The avoidance of inappropriate dress or material was a common theme — the clothing provided for everyday wear was not to be obviously different from people of the same social class. Sumptuary laws, which restricted what people of lower status were allowed to wear, were enacted in England during the 16th century, and these attitudes would have influenced almshouse benefactors. The sumptuary laws were intended to maintain the distinction between the classes by restricting the use of more luxurious fabrics to the nobility, and were also sometimes used to protect local industry or stimulate trade.[41] In Tudor England: 'No man under the rank of lord could wear wool not made in England; no serving man could use more than 3 yards for a long gown'.[42] Most sumptuary laws in England were repealed during the early 17th century.

It could be argued that almspeople who received a regular reliable source of new clothing might be better dressed than many people of a similar age or position. In a number of the better-funded almshouses, provision was made for washing clothes: at Castle Rising the laundry is still there today, though it now has washing machines instead of wash tubs. In general, it was outer garments that were supplied to residents of almshouses and this did lead to problems in some places. Cunnington and Lucas state:

> A letter from the Warden of the Holy Trinity Hospital Greenwich, dated 1772, to an overseer of the poor in Bungay, concerning John Bass of Bungay, a resident in the almshouse, speaks for itself: "He has nothing but wrags about him, is a shame to the College and Swarms with vermin".[43]

The clothing provided for the residents of the Almshouses at Badminton in Gloucestershire are recorded in the Charity Commissioners *Report* of 1828: a gown, waistcoat, breeches and hat for the three elderly men and a gown, petticoat and hat for the three elderly women; clothes to the value of £3 were given to each person every three years.[44]

Shoes were rarely included in the clothing provision. Only four of the ninety-two almshouses provided shoes. Undergarments too were not often included: only ten of the ninety-two almshouses specifically supplied any form of undergarment, these being petticoats for women and shirts for men. As already mentioned, the residents of Ravenstone Almshouses were expected to cut up their old purple garments to make underwear.[45] At the Ironmongers' Almshouses at Hackney and Hoxton in London the almswomen were directed to make petticoats from their old dresses. Other places that provided new garments expected the old ones to be used as everyday wear and the new ones kept for best – for example, to attend church – thus ensuring the upkeep of appearances.

Cloaks are mentioned for ceremonial wear but for the most part the provision for women is of gowns rather than warm cloaks or shawls. Hosyer's Almshouses in Ludlow specified in 1862: 'a coat for men and a cloak for women of strong dark blue cloth lined with blue or black serge reaching the ankles and worth £1 15s.' but this was unusual.[46] Another exception is also Nicholas Chamberlaine's Hospital in Bedworth, which had an annual clothing provision in the 1830s

Illustration 15.e. Replica of clothing provided at Nicholas Chamberlaine's Hospital in the Parsonage display, 2007.
Photo © Anne Langley.

of 40-50s. for men and 20-30s. for women, with a red and black check shawl supplied for the women and especially-made buttons for men (*see* Illustration 15.e.).

THE COST OF CLOTHING

The cost of the clothing was usually itemised, sometimes as a total amount and at other times per garment. Where there is evidence of clothing or cloth being supplied, the provision was annual in thirty-five cases, biennial in twenty-eight and triennial in six. Particularly in the case of the triennial allocations, there is evidence that the provision conformed to what other almshouses in the locality were doing as in the case of those at Badminton, Northleach and Wotton-under-edge in Gloucestershire.

Calverhall Almshouses in Clun, founded in 1738, are interesting because they show a careful approach to the question of clothing provision. In her will the founder, the Honourable Katherine Kerr, provided £6 annually for the purchase of good blue cloth and the making of gowns for the four male and four female residents of the almshouse. In 1898, material was still bought for the gowns but money for making them up was only given on inspection of the completed garments.[47]

The eight widows in the Almshouse in Titchmarsh, Northampton, were given a gown, apron, cap and handkerchief annually and 4s. 6d. a week in 1874. By 1924:

> The Almshouses are managed by a body of Trustees consisting of the Rector and 5 others. The full number of almswomen is 12 and during the year ended 30 June 1924, £134 15s. was applied in stipends, £33 0s. 4d. in firing, £25 10s. 4d. in clothing, £9 10s. in nursing and medical attendance for inmates.[48]

Other Providers of Clothing for the Poor

Almshouses were not the only type of charity providing clothing for the poor. Mackinnon states: 'Testators could also leave either clothing, or cloth of a specified value and quality to be made up into suitable clothes, for the poor'.[49] She also notes that:

> Female wills make social and material cultural distinctions regarding charity clothing. The quality of the fabric is often indicated and distinctions between new and old clothes are made even indicating colours such as a "northern russet or other suitable cloth".[50]

In the 19th century clothing might be given by employers where wages were very low, particularly to the families of agricultural workers. 'The village schoolmaster, too, would sometimes organise a coal and clothing club for the parents of his pupils'.[51] Working class self-help movements, such as Clothing Clubs also developed during the 19th century. Almspeople were therefore not singled out from this perspective; where they did stand out was if the clothing formed a uniform to advertise their relationship to the almshouse.

There is some evidence of different charities helping one another in the provision of clothing; Cunnington and Lucas note:

> The Red Maids' School Bristol, helped, from 1780 on, by the almswomen of Fry's House of Mercy, had to make shirts for the boys of the neighbouring but quite separate charity school of Queen Elizabeth's Hospital.[52]

Almspeople were not the only ones having to wear clothes that they had not chosen for themselves. Many people, particularly as children, have worn hand-me-downs from older siblings. Others in various levels of society may have been the grateful or ungrateful recipient of clothing that they had not chosen but had no choice but to accept. The poor did not have a lot of options and therefore the gift of clothing to almspeople, whether it was as a uniform or just as a clothing allowance, may well have been gratefully received and not seen as a badge of shame. Instead it would have allowed the wearer to maintain respectability and raised their status above their fellows who could not afford new clothing.

CHANGES OVER TIME

The style of the garments worn for ceremonial occasions remained very similar through the centuries. Ceremonial clothing helped to advertise the almshouse; this was particularly evident when the wearers were parading to church. This may have been a way of charming wealthy citizens into giving monies to help support the almshouse. The old-fashioned style of the clothing emphasised the historic nature of the almshouse, provided a link to the founder and also, where appropriate, the religious origin of the almshouse. The design of ceremonial clothing remained largely unaltered from centuries earlier, typically for men an ankle-length loose black gown with the badge of the almshouse, a design dating back to the 16th century. This ceremonial clothing is still worn for Founder's Day and church or civil ceremonies.

The adherence to tradition and an absence of change in design is found in other settings, including the ceremonial garb of mayors and the working clothes of barristers. Mansfield suggests:

> Workers having the same calling obviously cling to common custom for a number of subtle reasons. When new conditions have made their traditional costume quite inappropriate in a utilitarian sense it may be preserved by a laudable solidarity within the group and a vague loyalty to generations past.[53]

Not surprisingly, everyday wear in almshouses changed more than ceremonial wear. In 1439 at St John the Baptist and St John the Evangelist Almshouses in Sherborne a new resident was 'provided that eight marks (£5 6s. 8d.) per ann. should be spent on "clothes, lynnen and woollen, hoses and shoes, and other necessary thynges," inclusive of the gowns and hoods.'[54] The gowns and hoods were white and badged (for detail see Table 15.I). They were still in use on 1 March 1592-3 when Robert Blobell entered the almshouse and 'brought with him "a white gowne newe of the livery of this house"'.[55] By 1926, however, the almsmen at Sherborne on entry received two dark navy blue suits, two hats and two overcoats; one set of these clothes was for formal use on Sundays. After two years a new Sunday set of clothes was issued with the previous set then being used for everyday wear. Though the original provision included both ceremonial and everyday wear, by the 20th century it had evolved into practical provision that could be used for both.

By the 19th century clothing or provision of cloth became less common. The need to advertise the generosity of the benefactor through the provision of distinctive clothing or badges was no longer seen as so important; most benefactors were long dead and therefore more practical and financial considerations could prevail. Money originally provided for clothing was often diverted into other benefits, particularly fuel; in some cases this may have been because the endowed funds of the almshouse proved inadequate. The Almshouses at Chaddesden in Derbyshire are an example of this: in 1712, the almspeople were supplied with a black gown with red facings and three yards of linen to make shirts, but by 1827 they received 10 shillings in place of the gown and 3 shillings in place of the linen.[56]

In other places provision remained very similar through the 19th and into the 20th century; for example, at the King's Almshouse at Worminghall in Buckinghamshire the provision in both 1834 and 1895 was of a great coat for the male residents and a gown every two years for the women; indeed a clothing allowance was still being provided in 1925.[57] At John Baker's (Brewers' Company) Almshouse at Whitechapel in London the Charities Commissioners *Report* of 1897 states:

> To each of the 8 female inmates Founder specified one camlet or stuff gown, 2 shifts, 1 flannel petticoat, 2 prs worsted stockings & 2 prs shoes on 10 Oct. (Still received a gown annually in 1897.)[58]

An example from Derbyshire of the uniform style being replaced by practical everyday clothing is at the Bakewell Almshouses, where originally a cloak or gown with a small blue and yellow cross on the left breast was given every two years. By 1826 this had been replaced with a suit of clothes and hat, as needed.[59] Colour also has not remained static: as already discussed, individual almshouses sometimes changed the colour of their clothing to be more impressive or for pragmatic reasons of economy.

Thus almshouse clothing provision varied over time, to a greater or lesser degree, but was often made up of styles retained from earlier times. There is also evidence that where clothing was not originally provided by the founder it could be introduced later by another benefactor. An example of this is the Church Street Almshouses in Stratford-upon-Avon. These were founded in the 15th century with no clothing allowance, but in 1732 Sir Hugh Clopton (a local landowner) left a:

> Gift to pay for blue coats and gowns (worth 20s. each) every other year; payment to vicar and clerk and 12d. each to the almspeople, and the residue to provide straw hats and aprons for the almswomen and hats for the men every other year.[60]

The red cloaks and conical hats make it seem as though the residents of Trinity Almshouses in Castle Rising were wearing Welsh costume. There is, however, nothing Welsh in this costume, which is actually based on original English 17th-century dress. Welsh costume arises out of a similar source; an example of a pastiche of this costume can be seen in Chapter 10 on Anglesey almshouses. The same tradition may be seen in the red winter cloaks that the women at Sherborne wore, exchanging them for red cashmere shawls in the summer.

Cunnington and Lucas noted that the first example they had come across of almspeople being asked for their views as to what should be worn was in 1962 when the Holy Trinity Hospital at Greenwich consulted the men on whether their brown and black cloaks should be replaced (the decision was that the brown cloaks should go and the black cloaks should be kept but with no lining in the future).[61] The women residents at Castle Rising successfully lobbied the management to change their uniform dresses in the mid 19th century and, though no other evidence was discovered in this research, it is possible that residents at other almshouses may have been involved with changes to the provision of clothing to a greater or lesser degree.

As already mentioned, badging had in the main died out by the start of the 19th century. The reduction in the number of badges on almshouse clothing by this time can in part be attributed to the fact that the number of almshouses supplying clothing fell, clothing being replaced by a different benefit or an allowance to purchase clothing individually. For example, at Bakewell by 1826 a suit of clothes and a hat were supplied as needed. At the Bishop Wood's Almshouses in London by 1824 the women received 9 shillings every other year instead of the gown.[62] At Oken's Almshouse in Warwick by 1874 the women received a drapery ticket every three years instead of a gown.[63] Where the ceremonial uniform was maintained, as at Castle Rising and Clun, the badge remained as part of that uniform; however, it is worth noting that these badges bear the coats of arms rather than the initials of the donor.[64]

CONCLUSION

This study shows that the allocation of clothing was not a primary concern of the majority of benefactors of almshouses throughout the full time frame of this study, perhaps only one in four almshouses having some such form of provision. Where clothing was provided, there is evidence of this being more important for those founded prior to the 19th century. Two distinct forms of provision were noted: clothing for ceremonial occasions; and that for everyday use. A number of almshouses provided both, but the majority were giving either ceremonial or everyday clothing. The foundation date of the almshouse played a significant part in the type of clothing issued, early almshouses being more likely to provide ceremonial clothing and badges.

There does not appear to be a correlation between the size of the almshouse and the provision of clothing. Within this study the almshouses providing clothing had from four to fifty or more residents, the average number being eight. Instead it appears to have been the individual decision of the founder, or subsequent benefactors, as to whether clothing was supplied and of what type. This decision was determined in part by whether the prime motive had been one of advertising the benefactor's generosity, which tended to result in ceremonial clothing, or simple care for the old people that resulted in everyday clothing (and in a few cases, a combination of both).

It could be concluded that another important motive of the founders in providing clothing was the outer look of respectability; it maintained the status of their almshouse and thus themselves. This is discussed in more detail in Chapter 18. The replacement of the clothing at regular intervals was an important part of this maintaining of standards.

It is not possible to confirm, in most cases, exactly when the provision of clothing was phased out, but in the majority of cases it had been replaced by other benefits, such as money or fuel, by the end of the 19th century. Clothing was still provided in a few almshouses during the 20th century but in the main this was limited to the provision of ceremonial wear and indeed this continues to the present day in such places as Castle Rising in Norfolk.

There is little direct evidence of the attitudes of almspeople to the clothing and badges provided. Hindle points out, however, that:

> Badged coats and gowns of this kind were much more elaborate than the badges worn by beggars or paupers, and effectively functioned as liveries, publicly representing the munificence of the benefactor and the gratitude of those who were proud to accept it.[65]

Thus it may be reasonable to conclude that most almspeople did not feel shame in the outward and visible signs of their charitable status but were proud to be seen as the 'deserving' poor, no matter at what time period they resided in the almshouse.

Notes

1. Hartman, R. Sometimes a Codpiece Is Just a Codpiece: the meanings of medieval clothes, 22 October 2001, URL: www.strangehorizons.com/2001/20011022/medieval_clothing.shtml. accessed February 2015.

2. Cunnington, P. & Lucas, C. *Charity Costumes*, London, 1978, p. 228.

3. Lurie, A. *The Language of Clothes*, London, 1992, p. 3.

4. Herbert, W. *1836 History of the 12 Great Livery Companies,* London. An 'out' brother was non-resident.

5. Lurie, p. 13.

6. Whellan's *History, Topography and Directory of Northampton,* 2nd Edn, London, 1874, p. 715.

7. Wetton's *Guide to Northampton and its Vicinity*, Wakefield, original edition 1849, republished 1969, p. 81.

8. Caffrey, H. *Almshouses in the West Riding of Yorkshire: 1600 -1900*, Kings Lynn, 2006, p. 67.

9. Lurie, p. 203.

10. White F. & Co. *History, Gazetteer and Directory of Derbyshire*, 1857, Sheffield, p. 366.

11. *Twenty-seventh Report of Commissioner of Inquiry into charities of England and Wales, Buckinghamshire* (*CC* Bucks), BPP, 1834, xxi, p. 183.

12. Northants Records Office (NRO): FM4466, Rules and Orders appointed by the Trustees for the Alms-House at Ravenstone according to the Power given to them by the 15th Article of the Lord Chancellor Nottingham's Instructions.

13. Ibid. Purple garment use is also mentioned in the Charity Commissioners' Report for Buckinghamshire, BPP 1834, xxi, p. 180.

14. Cunnington & Lucas, p. 10.

15. Goose, N. & Moden, L. *A History of Doughty's Hospital Norwich 1687-2009*, Hatfield, 2010 p. 31.

16. Ibid., pp. 72-3.

17. Ibid., p. 73.

18. *CC* Bucks, 1834, p. 162.

19. Trustees' Minutes of Trinity Hospital Clun, Shropshire Archives P52/Q/1/2.

20. Trustees of the Almshouses of The Holy and Undivided Trinity, Castle Rising, Norfolk. *Information Regarding Cloaks and Hats.* Crome & Alker Ltd, 1998.

21. *Charity Commissioners' Report for Norfolk*, 1815-35, p. 321.

22. Trustees of Castle Rising, 1998.

23. Hindle, S. 'Dependency, Shame and Belonging: badging the deserving poor, c. 1550-1750', *Cultural and Social History*, 2004; 1;6-35, p. 11.

24. Ibid., p. 16.

25. Ibid., p. 29.

26. Gloucestershire Archives: P379CH1, Account Book.

27. Glover, C. & Riden, P. (eds) W*illiam Woolley's History of Derbyshire*, Vol 6, Chesterfield, 1981, pp. 27-8.

28. Caffrey, pp. 23 and 96.

29. The National Archives (TNA): PROB 11/392 83-130.

30. *Charity Commissioners' Report for Herefordshire*, 1834, pp. 123-6.

31. *Charity Commissioners' Report for London*, Vol. I, HMSO, 1897, p. 106.

32. Herbert, W. 1836.

33. Cunnington & Lucas, pp. 243-244.

34. Whellan, p. 737.

35. Cunnington & Lucas, p. 5.

36. Ashbee, C. R. *The Trinity Hospital in Mile End: the Guild and School of Handicraft*, London, 1896.

37. URL: www.frenchhospital.org.uk, accessed February 2010.

38. *Twelfth Report of the Commissioners of Inquiry into the Charities of England and Wales*, Oxfordshire, BPP 1825 x: p. 223.

39. *CC* Bucks, pp. 111-5.

40. Rawcliff, C. 'Cartullary of St Mary's Hospital Great Yarmouth', *Norfolk Record Society*, Norwich, Vol. 71, 2007, p. 184.

41. Hartman, 2001.

42. Castle A. *Honoured in the Breach: sumptuary laws*. Historical Fiction ebooks posted Nov 3, 2014 in 16th Century England, Historical Research, Historical Tidbits, Japan. URL: http://hfebooks.com, accessed February 2015.

43. Cunnington & Lucas, p. 16.

44. *Report of the Commissioners on Charities for Gloucestershire*, 1828, p. 289.

45. *CC* Bucks, 1834, p. 180.

46. *A History of the County of Shropshire*, Victoria County History, Vol. 2, London, 1839, p. 109.

47. Trustees' minutes, Shropshire Archives P52/Q/1/2.

48. Page, W. (ed) *A History of the County of Northamptonshire*, Victoria County History, Vol. 3, FSA, London, 1930, p. 149.

49. Mackinnon, D. '"Charity is really worth it when it looks that good" Rural women and bequests of clothing in early modern England', in Tarbin, S. & Broomhall, S. (eds) *Women, Identities and Community in Early Modern Europe*, Farnham, 2008, p. 91.

50. Ibid., p. 86.

51. Horn, P. *Labouring Life in the Victorian Countryside*, Stroud, 1976, p. 34.

52. Cunnington & Lucas, p. 6.

53. Mansfield, A. Rationale of Irrational Clothes, in Cunnington, P. & Lucas, C. (eds) *Occupational Costume in England from the Eleventh Century to 1914*, London, 1967, p. 392.

54. Mayo, C.H. *A Historic Guide to the Almshouse of St John Baptist and St John the Evangelist Sherborne*, Oxford, 1926, pp. 48-9.

55. Ibid., p. 48.

56. Glover, & Riden, p. 85.

57. *CC* Bucks, 1834, p. 38; Kelly's *Post Office Directory of Berkshire, Buckinghamshire and Oxfordshire*, 1895, London, p. 186.

58. CCEC, Vol. I, HMSO, 1897, p. 106.

59. Bakewell-Reliquary, Vol. 4, 1863, p. 119.

60. White, F. & Co. *History, Gazetteer and Directory of Warwickshire*, Sheffield, 1874, p. 1246.

61. Cunnington & Lucas, p. 245.

62. *CC* London, BPP, 1825, Vol. 12, p. 136.

63. Whites *Trade Directory*, 1874, p. 237.

64. Crome & Alker, 1998, *Information Regarding Cloaks and Hats*.

65. Hindle, p. 13.

CHAPTER 16
'A COMFORTABLE LODGING AND ONE SHILLING AND FOURPENCE A DAY': THE MATERIAL BENEFITS OF AN ALMSHOUSE PLACE.[1]

Angela Nicholls

The early 19th-century Charity Commissioners for County Durham were dismayed to find Thomas Cooper's Almshouse in Sedgefield (*see* Illustration 16.a.) so impoverished that: 'old persons have been known to leave it to reside in the workhouse'.[2] The suggestion that poor people might ever have been better off in the workhouse than in an endowed almshouse challenges all our preconceptions about almshouses as institutions of genteel poverty for the relatively well-off and deserving poor, in stark contrast to the brutalised, stigmatising subsistence of the union workhouse. In reality, the experience of almshouse life and the benefits that occupants received was surprisingly variable. Some almshouses provided residents with comfortable accommodation, a regular allowance, clothing and fuel. Other foundations, with modest or non-existent endowments, provided little more than rent-free accommodation. Some establishments, although founded with adequate endowments, had their income misappropriated, or suffered long-term decline through an inability to keep pace with inflation. The result was a range of institutions providing greatly varying material benefits.

Illustration 16.a. Cooper's
Almshouses, Sedgefield,
County Durham
Durham County Record Office
D/Cl 27/278/ packet 86
*Image reproduced by
permission of Durham County
Record Office*

Much of the literature to date has focused on almshouse buildings, particularly on those well-known and better-off foundations with interesting architecture; less is known about poorer foundations or about the lives of the mostly elderly and sometimes disabled people who lived in these almshouses. This examination of the material benefits of an almshouse place will attempt to uncover how well-off almspeople really were, and what position they were able to occupy in the socio-economic hierarchy of their local communities. It will focus on the stipends, or financial allowances, granted to almspeople, and will outline some of the additional benefits provided, such as food, fuel, rent-free accommodation and practical help, with examples drawn from the late 15th to the 19th centuries.

ALMSHOUSE STIPENDS

Medieval hospitals, the earliest forms of almshouse, were generally modelled on monastic institutions. They had a strong corporate identity and communal life, and all the occupants' needs – including food, drink, warmth, clothing, companionship, and, when necessary, nursing and care – were met within the institution. The 12th-century charter of St Cross Hospital, Winchester, for instance, specified that thirteen poor men were to be provided with:

> necessary clothing … and beds fit for their infirmities; and daily a good loaf
> of wheaten bread of the weight of five measures, three dishes at dinner, and
> one for supper, and drink in sufficient quantity.[3]

During the 15th century, however, there was an observable shift away from communal living in almshouses and hospitals, with the construction of individual chambers for the almspeople, as at St Cross, refounded by Cardinal Beaufort in 1445 as the House of Noble Poverty.[4] This development reflected the desire for greater privacy and comfort observed in domestic architecture from the 15th and 16th centuries onwards. The retreat from communal life was mirrored by the introduction of monetary allowances in almshouses in lieu of the provision of food.

The change was gradual. Even where individual accommodation was provided for the almspeople, as at St Cross, the brethren were still expected to dine in the communal hall. The guild almshouses at Stratford-upon-Avon were rebuilt in 1427 to provide individual rooms for the twenty-four almspeople, yet in 1442 the regulations still required the occupants to eat and drink together.[5] Over time, however, the financial allowance became an increasingly important element in the offer of an almshouse place, to the extent that it became almost universal, and seems to have been considered an integral part of what makes a 'proper' almshouse. The payment of money with which an almsperson could purchase the necessities of life not only freed these recipients of charity from want and the need to make shift for themselves but also enabled them to retain a degree of autonomy and status. Rexroth has suggested that the introduction of individual rooms, each with its own fireplace, which became a standard feature of many of the almshouses built by the London guilds and livery companies in the 15th century, enabled poor guild members to retain the status of householders, even when reduced to a position of economic dependence; it is likely that the provision of an independent income performed the same function.[6]

Typical payments to almspeople in the 15th century were a penny (1d.) a day (that is £1 10s. 5d. per annum). For instance, the new statutes of St John's Hospital in Lichfield (refounded by the Bishop of Lichfield and Coventry in 1495) specified that each almsperson was to receive 7d. a week: 'with which seven-pence, thus weekly paid, the poor men are to remain contented, nor must they presume to beg'.[7] In other words, the expectation was that the stipend represented an adequate, though by no means generous, amount to live on. According to Christopher Dyer, seven pence a week at that time would have given an individual: 'a decent but sparse living'.[8] A particularly well-endowed and high-status establishment, such as God's House at Ewelme in Oxfordshire, paid the twelve almsmen two pence a day, but they were also expected to undertake an onerous regime of prayer.[9] Despite rapid inflation from the 1540s, some 16th-century foundations, such as the Lawrence Sherriff Almshouse at Rugby in Warwickshire (founded in 1567), still specified a penny a day, but some paid considerably less. Thomas Oken's and Nicholas Eyffler's Almshouses in Warwick (founded in 1571 and 1597, respectively) paid each of the almswomen only one shilling (twelve pence) a quarter. This would not have been sufficient to sustain even the most meagre existence, and, unsurprisingly, Oken's almswomen are recorded as receiving parish relief in 1582 and 1587.[10] At the other end of the scale, the master and twelve brethren of Lord Leycester's Hospital in Warwick, also founded in 1571, had an annual income of about £200 to share amongst themselves.

These extreme variations in benefits are typical, and occur across the country.[11] Some of the variation in payments reflects the differing wealth and status of foundations, but there also seems to be evidence of regional variation. In his study of 18th-century poor relief, Steven King identified a difference in the amounts paid in poor relief between the parishes of the north and west of the country from those of the south and east, notwithstanding individual differences between parishes. He ascribed this to a more ingrained culture of independence and 'making do' in the north and west, and to harsher attitudes exhibited by magistrates and overseers towards the poor. On the other hand, he suggests that in the south and east there was greater generosity and readiness to assist the poor.[12] In this case, charitable giving was likely to have reflected these same differences in cultural attitudes towards the poor.

In his study of the charities of rural England, W K Jordan averaged the almshouse stipends for particular counties across the years 1480–1660. Thus the average annual stipend from his fourteen Buckinghamshire examples (which ranged from £1 to £7 10s. a year) was £4 8s. 7d., which he suggests 'was sufficient to provide: 'a maintenance probably not much less straitened than that of an agricultural labourer'.[13] Across the same period, he calculated that the average for London foundations was similar, at £4 4s. per annum.[14] But in Yorkshire the average was much lower, as was the range (from 10s. to £5 a year). Only a third of the eighteen Yorkshire almshouses he mentions paid stipends of £4 to £5 a year, and none paid more than this. The remaining twelve paid sums ranging from 10s. to £3 a year, and a further seven paid no allowances at all after the death of the founder. Jordan remarks that: 'the life afforded in these institutions must, save for about a score of exceptions, have been hard and meagre'.[15]

Not only were there differences between establishments, but occasionally *within* them. Sometimes there were differential rates for men and women within an institution, although this was rare. An example is Sir John Constable's Almshouse in Halsham, Yorkshire, where eight almsmen each received £4 a year but the two women only received £2.[16] Ford's Hospital in Coventry, founded in 1509 for five married couples and a nurse, initially gave each couple a weekly allowance of 7½d. If the wife died before her husband he was able to keep the whole allowance, but if he died first her allowance was reduced to 3¾d. and she was expected to share her room with another widow (*see* Illustration 16.b.).[17] Although elderly widows were often expected to share rooms in almshouses, this sort of financial discrimination was rare, and in 1609 Coventry City Corporation, which administered Ford's Hospital by then, discontinued the practice.[18] Occasionally one or two of the almspeople would receive additional payments for undertaking particular duties, such as reading the daily prayers, or assisting with nursing older residents, but generally the occupants of an almshouse were treated equally. Unlike poor relief, the amounts of which were based on assessed need, an almshouse stipend was a guaranteed income to those who had been accepted for admission.[19]

Illustration 16.b. Ford's Hospital, Coventry
Photo © Anne Langley

The Charity Commissioners' reports of the early 19th century provide an opportunity to see what happened to almshouse allowances over time. The amount of allowance paid at the foundation of the almshouse was generally determined by the wealth of the benefactor and by prevailing ideas about what was an adequate allowance for the poor, but over time this could change. The almshouse at Houghton-le-Spring in Durham (founded in 1666) provides an interesting example. Its two wings were built and endowed by separate founders, George Lilburne and Rev. George Davenport, Rector of Houghton-le-Spring. Lilburne and Davenport each built three rooms and provided £10 annually to be divided between their three almspeople. By the 19th century, further endowments by subsequent rectors of Houghton for 'Davenport's wing' had maintained an adequate income for those three occupants, but fewer additional endowments to the other part of the almshouse had resulted in the relative poverty of the occupants of Lilburne's wing.[20] Many almshouses received further endowments after the initial foundation, and for most this was an essential factor in their long term survival.[21] The terminology of the founder's will, and the way in which the almshouse was funded, left many establishments impoverished within a few generations. A common method of providing permanent funding was for the benefactor to place a specific rent charge on lands bequeathed to their heirs to maintain an almshouse. The rent charge remained in perpetuity, to be paid by whoever subsequently owned the land, but with inflation it declined in value over time, as happened with the £10 rent charges specified by Davenport and Lilburne at Houghton. The generous allowance of 3s. 4d. a week (£8 13s. 4d. a year) provided by Sir Baptist Hicks in 1612 for his almspeople in Chipping Campden was still the amount being paid at the end of the 19th century, by which time its purchasing power was significantly reduced.

On the other hand, testators might leave property to the almshouse itself, in which case the income could maintain the almspeople and building in perpetuity, ensuring the survival of their foundation. It was often a matter of chance how foundations prospered. In 1567, Lawrence Sherriff, a London grocer, endowed the school and almshouse he founded in his home town of Rugby with property in Lambs Conduit Street, London, which became valuable beyond his imaginings.[22] The wealth attached to property, however, was always at risk of misappropriation, and heirs and executors could, and often did, neglect the testators' wishes. Sherriff's descendents, for instance, battled unsuccessfully for more than a century in an endeavour to wrest possession of this valuable property from the charitable institution he had founded.[23] Even without misappropriation there could be abuse. If the amount of the allowance to be paid to the almspeople was specified in the testator's will, it could be difficult to increase maintenance payments in line with inflation, even though the income of the establishment increased.

This was, famously, the situation described in Trollope's novel, *The Warden*, where the fictitious Hiram's Hospital was still paying the almsmen 1s. 4d. a day (£24 6s. 8d. a year) while the Master, the Rev. Septimus Harding, received the rest of the income for himself, a sum which by the mid 19th century amounted to £800 per year.[24] Trollope supposedly based his novel on the notorious case of St Cross in Winchester, but there were many other examples he could have chosen. At the supposedly impoverished St John's Hospital in Barnard Castle, where two almswomen housed together in a single, thatched room each received £3 a year plus gowns and coal in the early 19th century, the number of almswomen had been reduced from three to two in order to increase the pitiful stipends. Yet the Charity Commissioners reported that the Master of the Hospital, the Rev. William Lipscomb of Yorkshire, who had 'no duties to perform', received — between 1790 and 1796 — £461 in emoluments arising from granting leases of the hospital's property in the town.[25]

The contrast between these valuable clerical sinecures and the subsistence allowances paid to the almspeople seems to have given few churchmen any qualms of conscience. Trollope's honourable and well-intentioned Master of Hiram's Hospital had been enjoying his comfortable livelihood for more than ten years before the interfering John Bold raised questions about whether this situation reflected the true intentions of the founder's will. At Greatham Hospital, County Durham, the income from the hospital lands in 1593 supported not only the poor brethren but the master, his family and a large household, including a minister to take services twice a day, a clerk, a doctor, a bailiff, a porter, stewards, two serving men, five women servants, a cook, under cook, butler, laundress, sixteen labouring servants in husbandry, a shepherd, cowherd, swine herd, slaughterman, horse boy, a baker, brewer and two millers. The total wages bill came to £82 4s. Only £13 18s. 8d. of this was paid in allowances to the nine poor brethren. The Master claimed, somewhat disingenuously, that after necessary charges, stipends and repairs 'there doeth not any thinge of moment remaine'.[26] Another case is discussed in detail in Chapter 13.

Many almshouses struggled to manage their resources so that they could provide an adequate allowance for their almspeople. For instance the trustees of the Leamington Hastings Almshouse debated in 1696 how to get more rental income from the almshouse's lands; with careful management and an additional endowment from the widow of the lord of the manor they were able to increase allowances to twenty pence a week (£4 6s. 8d. a year) in 1698.[27] Meanwhile, there were wealthy establishments like Greatham Hospital and St John's, in Barnard Castle, where it was considered acceptable to dedicate little of the foundation's income to the benefit of the very people it was there to support. This evidently reflects how the poor were viewed, and what was considered an appropriate standard of living for poor people in receipt of alms. On the one hand they needed to be adequately housed and supported, and visibly so; anything less would reflect badly on the founder and trustees. But, equally, allowances that were too generous were considered to be unsuitable for poor people, and even dangerous. Caffrey refers to the 19th-century debates around the appropriate level of stipend at the wealthy Archbishop Holgate's Hospital in Hemsworth, where concerns were expressed that if the allowance were raised, the almspeople might spend lavishly or hoard their allowance and pass it on to others. The Reverend Joseph Hunter, reporting in 1831 that the stipends of the poor at Hemsworth had been raised to £90 a year, opined that it did not appear: 'that the sudden removal from a state of poverty to the affluence of the hospital is always favourable to the real happiness of the benefitted'.[28] Trollope's bishop refers to the 'propriety of maintaining the due difference in rank and income between a beneficed clergyman and certain poor old men who were dependent on charity'; almsman Bunce clearly agrees, declaring: 'Was it to make gentlemen of us we were brought in here?'.[29]

It seems, then, that founders and those who were responsible for administering almshouses, expected recipients to be privileged, because such prestige reflected well on them, but there were, nonetheless, clear limits as to how well-off almspeople were allowed to be. For those foundations with sufficient resources, it seems that the intention was to give almspeople a basic, subsistence existence. Abbot's Hospital in Guildford, founded in 1622 by George Abbot, Archbishop of Canterbury, provided the twenty almsmen and women with a weekly allowance of 2s. 6d. (£6 10s. a year), a gown every two years, and also firewood and coal. In the first half of the 17th century, this allowance would have enabled the almspeople to buy three candles a week and daily rations of a loaf of bread, half a pound of cheese, peas pottage, and four pints of beer, typical of the diet of an agricultural worker.[30] The provision of rent-free accommodation maintained in good repair, plus clothing and fuel, were valuable additions to this fairly basic standard of living. Yet even so, the allowances at many almshouses fell far short of this example, reducing their occupants to a meagre existence.

OTHER MATERIAL BENEFITS

A very few traditional foundations continued to provide food for their residents in addition to a monetary allowance. After its refounding, for instance, Sherburn Hospital in Durham continued to feed and clothe the fifteen in-brethren, but it is unlikely that this was to a lavish standard. Bishop Chandler's visitation in 1735 established the diet of the Sherburn brethren, possibly as a result of complaints, and ordered that all who were not sick should eat together in the common hall. The prescribed diet was nutritious, though monotonous, consisting of one pound of boiled or roasted meat daily for each man, a quart of beer, and a weekly allowance of bread and cheese. On Fridays and fast days the meat was replaced by a pudding.[31]

At Greatham Hospital the early 19th-century diet was more varied, with meat (either mutton, beef, pork or veal) for dinner on Sundays, Tuesdays and Thursdays, with porridge and eggs for supper. On Mondays, Wednesdays and Saturdays, dinner consisted of milk porridge, with a quart of milk and half of pound of cheese for supper, and pudding on Friday. In addition, each man had an allowance of bread, butter and ale. There were special diets for religious festivals, with no cheese or milk on Wednesdays in Lent, while on Christmas Day the men had a roasted goose and two large plum puddings between them.[32] The arrangement at Greatham Hospital at the time of the Charity Commissioners' inquiry was that the food was provided and cooked by the tenant of the Hospital Farm, who brought the food up to the common hall where one of the brethren divided it into portions for the men to take back to their own apartments to eat. Complaints must have been anticipated, for the Commissioners reported: 'the chaplain or his deputy is always ready to attend to any complaints that may be made as to the quantity and quality of the provisions.' The farm tenant, Mrs Stonehouse, was allowed £22 per head a year for the men's food. The Commissioners commented: 'The allowances to the brethren seem to be amply sufficient for their comforts'.[33]

The quantities specified at both Greatham and Sherburn Hospitals seem generous, and would certainly be more than many poor labourers could have expected. The dietary approved for the aged and infirm in the workhouse of the Berkhamsted Union in 1836 was not dissimilar, but the quantities were much less, and the food was probably designed to be unappetising (for instance by omitting salt). The aged and infirm at Berkhamsted Workhouse were allowed 10oz. of bread and a pint and a half of gruel every morning; 5oz. of beef or mutton and 1lb. of potatoes for dinner on Mondays, Wednesdays and Saturdays, with broth for supper; only soup and 2oz. of cheese on Tuesdays, Thursdays and Sundays; and rice pudding and cheese on Fridays.[34] At Belper Workhouse in Derbyshire, meat was only provided on Sundays and Wednesdays in 1841.[35] Prescribing diets for workhouse inmates did not prevent the scandal at Andover Workhouse in 1845, where: 'starving paupers were discovered eating rotting marrow from the bones they were meant to be crushing'.[36]

The impracticality of the arrangement at Greatham and the potential for abuse may be a reason why the provision of food in almshouses was generally so rare; and, even in a traditional institution such as this, the men seem to have preferred to eat in their own rooms rather than communally, despite the Hospital's rules. A 19th-century commentator on the London Charterhouse considered that it was good discipline for the men to have a compulsory meal together, preventing them from dropping into: 'semi-piggish habits, living on scraps of food, and perhaps spending the balance of their pensions on gin'.[37] Yet earlier in the 18th century it was recognised that: 'the number of Brothers who failed to attend meals reflected the unsuitability of the food; some of them just could not "bear with the usual Diet of the Hospitall"'.[38] Prescott describes how the men of the 15th-century Higham Ferrers Bede House used their 7d. a week allowance to buy their own meat, which they each gave to the nurse to cook for them in the communal pot.[39] This may well have been the arrangement at the Lord Leycester Hospital in Warwick. Here the 17th-century stewards' accounts list payments to a nurse, the purchase of vegetable seeds and nets, and a woman and boy to weed the gardens and scare away the birds. No food items appear in the accounts other than the celebration wassail cake at Christmas, indicating that the men usually provided their own food; but the communal vegetable plot suggests that the nurse may have cooked up a communal vegetable stew (pottage) to which she added the men's individual portions of meat, as at Higham Ferrers.[40] Many almshouses had gardens for residents to grow their own food. How practical this was for many elderly almspeople is debatable, but, along with the domestic architecture of many almshouse buildings, it reflects an idealised representation of almspeople as sturdily independent poor cottagers.[41] Gardens are discussed in detail in Chapter 17 of this book.

Some almshouses gave their residents basic provisions. For instance, the foundation document for Coningsby Hospital in Hereford (founded in 1617), specified a regular supply of bread, ale, cheese, butter and firewood for the men, and cows to be kept to supply them with milk. Over and above their weekly allowance, they also had a dinner of roast beef and supper of mutton and broth served in the common hall on the main festivals.[42] Lady Leveson's Hospital at Temple Balsall provided the almswomen with a weekly allowance of 8lb. of bread, which they collected from the nearby Hall using a path known as 'the

Breadwalk'. It seems, however, that the bread was not always of a quality acceptable to the almswomen; some of them were reported in 1887 to be selling on their bread supply at reduced rates to poor neighbours, and using their own money to buy better bread for themselves. In 1801, because of the high price of food, a cow was purchased to provide the almswomen with milk.[43] In the Gascoigne Almshouses at Aberford in Yorkshire, meals were provided for the almspeople in the dining hall, although they took breakfast in their own rooms. The 1888 rules stated that: 'the week's supply of Coffee, Tea, Sugar, Soap, Candles, together with Sixpence in money shall be given out by Matron every Monday morning to each inmate'.[44]

The majority of almspeople would have purchased their own food from their allowance and cooked it themselves, particularly the women. Most almshouse rooms had their own fireplace, and there is evidence of cooking implements included in the furnishings of some rooms. For instance, the 1597 building accounts for Eyffler's Almshouse in Warwick include expenditure on four pot hangings in the chimneys: 'to hang on their potts', indicating that the women would be cooking in their rooms.[45] The inventory of the Stratford almswoman Joan Patrick in 1597 included a brass pot, four kettles, a skillet, chafing dish and platters, and also bellows, pot hooks and a fire shovel.[46] Cooking implements also appear in the surviving inventories of some of the 18th-century almswomen at Temple Balsall. Among their possessions Bridget Phipps left a large frying pan, chafing dish, spit and hanging iron; while Ann Evetts left a fire shovel, tongs, warming pan, bellows, flesh fork and pot hooks.[47]

Some almshouses, like the 16th-century Eyffler's, provided basic furnishings, such as bedsteads, which would have been necessary for poor women coming to the almshouse from service or a relative's home.[48] Similarly at Greatham Hospital the men were provided with beds, while at Sherburn Hospital they were provided with bed linen and bedding as well. A petition in 1777 to the governors of the London Charterhouse alleged that the men's rooms and beds were 'in exceeding bad condition'; and a magazine article in 1855 claimed they were provided with 'less bedding than is to be had in gaols'.[49] Mostly, however, almspeople had to supply their own furnishings, and in many almshouses residents had to agree to leave their possessions to the almshouse on their death, to be either sold for the benefit of the establishment or passed on to the next resident. At Eyffler's Almshouse, although the level of allowance was extremely low, the women were provided with beds and a table board. In a nice touch of domestic comfort, the fitting out of the almshouse also included sixteen yards of painted cloth, a cheaper alternative to tapestry wall hangings.[50]

Individual fireplaces required fuel for heating and cooking, and many almshouse charities specified a fuel allowance, in either wood or coal or both. It would certainly have been more economical to provide one fire around which all the residents could huddle, and this would have been the norm in early almshouses, such as Browne's Hospital in Stamford, where the dormitory-hall had only one fireplace. Prior to the 17th-century insertion of individual fireplaces and chimneys in the medieval hall of St Mary's Chichester, the only heating appears to have been from a swinging brazier, as can be inferred from the deep groove worn into one of the overhead beams. Having one's own fireplace was, however, typical of the autonomous living arrangements that pertained in most almshouses. The frequency with which fuel allowances occur indicates how fundamental a benefit this was considered. Fuel was costly, particularly when there was no access to firewood, perhaps because of urbanisation or enclosure of commons, or because the almshouse residents were too frail to go out gathering firewood themselves. Many almshouses provided a 'chaldron' or wagonload of coals to be delivered to each person to see them through the winter. Like the provision of clothing (described in Chapter 15 of this book) this was a valuable resource. The coal allowance for each almswoman at Temple Balsall was assessed to be worth £4 10s. in 1908, on top of the annual stipend of £15 12s. and greatly exceeding the £2 12s. rental value of the room.[51] In 1777, amongst their numerous other complaints, the men of the London Charterhouse alleged that they were not allowed fires in their own rooms, and there was only space for twenty-six around the fireplaces in the two halls (the almshouse was supposed to accommodate eighty men).[52] According to the 19th-century *Durham Chronicle*, at Sir John Duck's Almshouse in Chester-le-Street, the poor residents regularly suffered the indignity of having their coal store raided by uncharitable neighbours.[53]

Free accommodation maintained in good repair was a considerable financial benefit for almshouse residents. Most almshouses provided one – or occasionally two – rooms rent free for each resident, or for two sharing. This was a valuable asset in itself, regardless of the level of comfort provided. Examination of 17th- and 18th-century poor law records indicates that where parishes paid rent for paupers, rents could be anything from 4s. or 5s. up to £2 or £3 a year. Jeremy Boulton quotes estimates that working class families in London spent an average of 10% of their income on rent in the 18th century, and 13% in the 19th.[54] The proportion for non-wage earners was likely to be greater, and demonstrates the value of rent-free accommodation provided by almshouse charities. The cost of repairs could also be considerable. Where parishes owned their own accommodation for paupers, repairs could constitute a heavy expenditure. For instance, the Warwickshire parish of Leamington Hastings spent £6 3s. 6d. on repairs to Widow Anne Tarsey's house between 1661 and 1669, and a further £5 9s. 5d. on Nicholas Jelley's house in 1672.[55] Broad has shown that poor relief expenditure on housing costs for the year 1776 was as much as £64,341 in Norfolk, whilst the proportion of poor relief expenditure spent on housing costs that year ranged from 3% (Bedfordshire) to an astonishing 14% in Lancashire.[56] Almshouse charities similarly had to dedicate a considerable proportion of their income to keeping their buildings in good repair. The Charity Commissioners reported that the £5 annual income of Bowes Almshouse for twelve poor women in Bishop Wearmouth was used to provide an annual gift of 5s. to each of the almswomen at Christmas, and the remaining £2 was put towards repairs to the building.[57] At the neighbouring Gibson's Almshouse, a repairs fund was maintained by making each new resident forego their stipend for the first six months.[58]

With a population of mainly elderly and often disabled residents, practical help was required in many almshouses. Some 16th- and 17th-century almshouses provided for a 'nurse', but this was principally a domestic role. The stewards' accounts at the Lord Leycester Hospital show regular payments for 'ashes' (for washing clothes) and besoms (brooms) for the nurse, payments to her for scouring the pewter, and only occasional payments for taking care of an almsman when sick.[59] Some almshouses allowed relatives to live in the person's room in order to take care of them, but in other cases the almsperson went to stay with relatives if they were ill. At Temple Balsall in 1704 the trustees were prompted to appoint someone to attend to the women, as 'some almswomen are absent from the Hospital with their relations upon pretence of want of health, to take care of them'. The trustees resolved to appoint two of the younger women to care for the sick, each with a salary of 40s. There was a complaint against one of these nurses, Widow Truelove, in 1724, for behaving 'in a turbulent manner, scolding and swearing'. As Gooder remarks: 'hers cannot have been the most soothing hand for the fevered brow'. A full-time Matron was not appointed until 1774. She supervised the nurses and perhaps as a result of her recommendation an apothecary was hired in 1776 on an annual contract of £5 per year to attend the women and provide medicines.[60]

Most almshouses were not well provided for in this way, however, and in the absence of proper care, many almspeople had to leave the almshouse when they become increasingly infirm or perhaps mentally ill. In the early years of the 18th century, Susanna Isaacson, one of the Leamington Hastings almswomen, was being boarded out at the charity's expense with Griffin Fennel, although the nature of the care she was receiving was not specified.[61] One of the 19th-century inmates of Kepier Almshouse in County Durham was less fortunate; she became insane and was removed to the county asylum as a pauper lunatic.[62] Similarly Mrs Foulsham was removed from Doughty's Hospital in Norwich in 1907 and placed in the workhouse infirmary because of her delusions and the fear she would burn down the building.[63]

The poverty of many almshouses raises the question of how almspeople lived, when stipends were low and additional benefits so variable. Alannah Tomkins concludes: 'For every ancient pensioner maintained comfortably there was at least one almsperson whose entitlements and receipts were thin indeed'.[64] According to the 19th-century Charity Commissioners' reports, many occupants of almshouses received parish poor relief.[65] With the increasing stigmatisation of parish paupers from the 18th century, later almshouses often stipulated that only people who had never been in receipt of parish poor relief could be admitted.[66] Realistically, however, stipends were often so low or non-existent that almshouse residents were forced to apply for relief if they did not have independent means or families to support them. Other residents probably worked. The 19th-century *Durham Chronicle*, in a series of articles on local charities, reported that many of the poor women at Sir John Duck's Hospital in Chester-le-Street were compelled: 'not only to seek assistance from the parish but to execute such work for the inhabitants of the village as will enable them to get the common necessaries of life'.[67] Until the advent of old age pensions in the 20th century, it was usual for older people to work for as long as they were capable, and parish relief was often only a contribution towards poor people's living costs. The pre-Reformation almshouses in Stratford-upon-Avon and Gloucester, both of which previously paid the usual 7d. a week allowance, *reduced* payments to 4d. a week in the mid 16th century. This retrenchment was probably driven by economic necessity, as town corporations that had newly taken on responsibility for almshouses struggled to maintain endowments; but it might also have reflected a harsher view of what was appropriate for poor recipients of charity, and an expectation that even almspeople contributed to their own keep.

One of the survival strategies frequently adopted by the poor has always been co-residence with other poor people.[68] This seems to have been adopted by almspeople as well, a number of whom appear to have had friends or family members living in their rooms.[69] In some cases this would have been to provide care in the absence of formal nursing provision, but in many other cases a family member would have been sharing the benefit of the rent-free room while contributing something in wages. In 1867 the Charity Commissioners even found residents of the almshouse in Llanfaes, Anglesey, taking in 'persons to board and lodge for profit'.[70] From the frequent prohibitions against lodgers in almshouse regulations, and periodic orders to clear almshouses of 'hangers-on', it is clear that this was not approved. Almshouses were expected to represent order and respectability, however poor their occupants.

Their visible presence in the community, representing the deserving poor, enabled them also, however, to be the recipients of informal gifts and donations in addition to their regular allowance. Almspeople were not normally allowed to beg, since that would be demeaning to the founder's reputation. But the location of many almshouses, beside the churchyard, or next to the entrance to the guildhall, was calculated to solicit casual almsgiving. Abbot's

Hospital (founded in 1622) on the High Street in Guildford had an alms box in the main entrance. The one at Sandes Hospital in Kendal (founded in 1659) was inscribed: 'Remember the Poor Widows' (*see* Illustration 16.c.).[71] Almspeople were frequently remembered in wills, or were included in funeral doles. At a time when donors were anxious about the deservingness of the recipients of their largesse, almspeople represented a safe, pre-selected group of 'approved' poor. It is likely, then, that the allowances of many almspeople were enhanced by additional, occasional, payments.

The allowance itself, however, even if small, remained significant. The lives of the poor were generally characterised by chronic insecurity as well as grinding poverty. Perhaps the most important feature of an almshouse stipend, no matter how small, was the fact that, unlike parish relief, it was a permanent, guaranteed income. Once accepted into an almshouse, the recipient had an income for life, although breaches of the rules might lead to fines, and flagrant and persistent breaches of the rules could occasionally result in expulsion. The guaranteed nature of the stipend, however, was generally accepted, giving it the nature of an annuity, to the extent that the Poor Law Guardians attempted to claim the former almswoman's stipend from Kepier Almshouse when she was admitted to the county asylum.[72] For some almspeople, the stipend was undoubtedly more valuable than the accommodation. A few early almshouse charities, such as the Hospitals of St Cross, Kepier, Greatham and Sherburn, provided out-relief to people in the community, providing money or food to people who were not

Illustration 16.c. Collecting box in the entrance of Sandes Hospital, Kendal. *Photo © Anne Langley*

resident. These were legally sanctioned out-payments. Elsewhere, the frequent almshouse rules against non-residence suggest that many more almspeople would have preferred to take the money without the accommodation, if the opportunity arose. Where rules were non-existent, or not enforced, some almspeople might actually be non-resident, as at St Bartholomews Hospital at Oxford in the 18th century.[73] When the Bishop of Durham increased the accommodation at Sherburn Hospital in 1819 by building an additional fifteen rooms for the out-brethren, only six of the men took up the offer.[74] Perhaps in recognition of this reluctance, as well as for reasons of economy, a number of almshouse charities used their increased revenues in the 19th century to provide for additional pensioners in the community, rather than to extend their accommodation to increase resident numbers.

CONCLUSION

Over the long historical time frame covered in this chapter, the changing balance between private philanthropy and statutory assistance within the mixed economy of welfare inevitably affected the role and contribution of almshouses. The extensive use of parish housing and, later, workhouses for the aged and infirm by the poor law authorities, might suggest that almshouses over time tended to become the preserve of the 'better off' poor. This chapter, however, identifies the great variation found in the material benefits associated with an almshouse place. This demonstrates that, while some almspeople would have achieved a reasonable standard of living in comparison with other poor people, not all almspeople would have been living comfortably or could be regarded as amongst the pauper elite. Even residents of wealthier establishments may not have benefited in the way that the founder intended, as the many problems and abuses uncovered over the centuries attest. Tomkins concludes that only for some residents did almshouse life represent a genuinely secure retirement.[75] Yet even for those with small or non-existent stipends, rent-free accommodation was a valuable resource, and the often overlooked additional benefits could make an important contribution to a resident's standard of living. The security provided by the guaranteed nature of even a modest stipend was in marked contrast to the chronic insecurity experienced by the majority of poor people. Moreover, the physical representation of almshouse residents as the idealised, deserving poor gave them a rank and status above that of the ordinary poor, despite their economic dependence. This in turn presented many of them with further opportunities to enhance their financial position through the receipt of gifts and informal donations. Status and respectability may have been their own reward, but they also brought more tangible benefits in their wake. The paucity of some of these in the more impoverished almshouses indicates how miserable was the alternative for many of the aged poor.

Notes

1.   Trollope, A. *The Warden*. 1855, reprinted Oxford, 1998, p. 4.

2.   *Charity Commissioners' Report for County Durham* (*CC* Durham), Further Report. 30 Jan. 1830, London, p. 102.

3.   McIlwain, J. *The Hospital of St Cross and St Cross Church*. Andover, 1993.

4.   Prescott, E. *The English Medieval Hospital 1050-1640*. Melksham, 1992, p. 56.

5.   Ibid. pp. 66-7.

6.   Rexroth F. (Selwyn, P E trans.), *Deviance and Power in Late Medieval London*. Cambridge, 2007, p. 254.

7.   *Charity Commissioners' Report, Staffordshire*. 1839, p. 387.

8.   Dyer, C. *Standards of Living in the Later Middle Ages: social change in England ca 1200-1520*. Cambridge, 1989, p. 253.

9.   Founded in 1437 by William and Alice de la Pole, Earl (later Duke) and Countess of Suffolk; Goodall, J.A.A. *God's House at Ewelme: life, devotion and architecture in a fifteenth-century almshouse*. Aldershot, 2001, pp. 231, 232-7.

10.   Kemp, T. (ed.), *The Book of John Fisher, Town Clerk and Deputy Recorder of Warwick 1580-1588*. Warwick, 1900, pp. 93, 169.

11.   *See*, for instance, Caffrey, H. *Almshouses in the West Riding of Yorkshire 1600-1900*. King's Lynn, 2006, p. 62.

12.   King, S. *Poverty and Welfare in England 1700-1850*. A Regional Perspective. Manchester, 2000.

13.   Jordan, W.K. *The Charities of Rural England 1480-1660*. London, 1961, pp. 48-9.

14.   Jordan, W.K. *The Charities of London 1480-1660*. London, 1960, p. 165.

15.   Jordan, 1961, pp. 252-81. For further discussion on local and regional differences in almshouse foundations, *see* Goose, N. 'The English Almshouse and the Mixed Economy of Welfare: medieval to modern', *The Local Historian*, Vol. 40, 1, 2010, pp. 8, 13-4.

16.   Jordan, 1961, p. 263.

17.   Cleary, J. & Orton, M. *So Long as the World Shall Endure: the 500-year history of Ford's and Bond's Hospitals, Coventry*. Coventry, 1991, p. 45.

18.   Coventry History Centre: BA/H/3/17/1, Council Minute Book 1557-1640, entry for 25 Oct. 1609.

19.   According to the 1582 Warwick census, the women in Okens and the Westgate almshouses received sums in poor relief of 2d, 4d, 6d or 8d a week. The reasons for the variations are not given, but it is possible that some of the women had earnings from employment; Kemp, p. 93.

20. Davenport's beneficiaries were receiving £15 13s. 4d. each per year in 1878 while Lilburne's three only received £9 6s. 8d. Durham Record Office (DRO), Ep/Ho 280.

21. Goose, N. & Moden, L. *A History of Doughty's Hospital Norwich, 1687-2009*. Hatfield, 2010, pp. 35-8.

22. The foundation prospered, and became Rugby School.

23. Rouse, W.H.D. *A History of Rugby School*. London, 1898, pp. 44-82.

24. Trollope, pp. 4, 6.

25. *CC* Durham. 1818 -1837, pp. 333-5.

26. Replies of Henry Dethicke, Master of Greatham Hospital, to Elizabeth I's inquiry into colleges, hospitals and almshouses, Durham University Library Special Collections, DCD/T/YB f.119v.

27. Warwickshire County Record Office (WCRO): DR43a/195.

28. Caffrey, p. 63; Hunter, J. *South Yorkshire*. Vol. II, London, 1831, p. 434.

29. Trollope, pp. 39, 53.

30. Information from Matthew Alexander, former Curator of Guildford Museum.

31. *CC* Durham, p. 128 (494).

32. DRO: D/Gre 105.

33. *CC* Durham, p. 767 (535).

34. May, T. *The Victorian Workhouse*. Oxford, 1997, pp. 23-4.

35. Fowler, S. *Workhouse: the people, the places, the life behind doors*. The National Archives, 2007, p. 193.

36. Ibid., p. 7.

37. *The Daily Graphic* 23 Feb. 1893. Quoted in Porter, S. *The London Charterhouse*. Chalford, 2009, p. 111.

38. Porter, p. 69.

39. Prescott, p. 68.

40. WCRO: CR 1600/42.

41. *See* Lloyd, S. 'Cottage Conversations: poverty and manly independence in eighteenth-century England', *Past and Present*, Vol. 184, 2004, pp. 78, 82-5.

42. *CC* Hereford, p. 54.

43. Gooder, E. *Temple Balsall: from hospitallers to a caring community, 1322 to modern times*. Chichester, 1999, pp. 79, 128, 63.

44. Quoted in Hallett, A. *Almshouses*. Princes Risborough, 2004, p. 43.

45. WCRO: CR1618/WA12/36/13.

46. Jones J. (ed.), *Stratford-upon-Avon Inventories Vol. I, 1538-1625*. Warwick, 2002, p. 171.

47. WCRO: CR112/Ba65/47, 67.

48. The reference to four beds between the eight women makes it clear that the women were expected to share.

49. Porter, pp. 84, 104.

50. WCRO: CR1618/WA12/36/13.

51. Gooder, p. 130.

52. Porter, p. 84.

53. DRO: Du 6/1/9 (6).

54. Boulton, J. ' "Turned into the Street with My Children Destitute of Every Thing"; The Payment of Rent and the London Poor, 1600 - 1850', in McEwan, J. & Sharpe, P. (eds), *Accommodating Poverty: the housing and living arrangements of the English poor, ca 1600-1850*. Basingstoke, 2011, p. 33.

55. WCRO: DR43a/19.

56. Broad, J. 'The Parish Poor House in the Long Eighteenth Century', in McEwan & Sharpe, p. 248.

57. DRO: Du 6/1/6, CC, Further Report 30 Jan. 1830.

58. *CC* Durham, p. 434 (68).

59. WCRO: CR 1600/31.

60. Gooder, pp. 60-3.

61. WCRO: DR43a/195.

62. DRO: Ep/Ho 280.

63. Goose & Moden, p. 160.

64. Tomkins, A. 'Retirement from the Noise and Hurry of the World?: the experience of almshouse life', in McEwan & Sharpe, p. 264.

65. For instance, the women of Forster's Almshouses, Darlington.

66. For instance, Penrhos, Anglesey (founded 1859); Whitehead, Tanworth-in-Arden (founded 1871).

67. DRO: Du 6/1/9 (6), Chester-le-Street Charities.

68. A.L. Beier calculated that in 1587 in Warwick, 45% of the poor were either inmates (lodgers) themselves or lived in households with inmates; 'The Social Problems of an Elizabethan Country Town: Warwick, 1580-90', in Clark P. (ed.) *Country Towns in Pre-Industrial England*. Leicester, 1981, p. 61.

69. This is shown most clearly in 19th-century census data, for example, in Goose, N. & Basten, S. 'Almshouse Residency in Nineteenth-century England: an interim report', *Family and Community History*, Vol 12 no. 1, May 2009, p. 71.

70. Charity Commission Inquiry under Mr Skirrow, quoted in the *Charity Commissioners' Report for Anglesey*. London, 1897, p. 44.

71. Hallett, pp. 29, 57.

72. DRO: Ep/Ho 280.

73. Tomkins, A. *The Experience of Urban Poverty 1723-82: parish, charity and credit*. Manchester, 2006, p. 93.

74. DRO: Du 6/1/6.

75. Tomkins, in McEwan & Sharpe, p. 277.

CHAPTER 17
ALMSHOUSE GARDENS WITH PARTICULAR REFERENCE TO SOMERSET

Sarah Hare

If the published knowledge of almshouses is small, that of almshouse gardens is minimal, but as an intrinsic part of the almshouse they form an area worthy of closer study. An examination of almshouse gardens, past and present, adds to the overall picture of the lifestyle of the almspeople, the motivation of the benefactors and the relation of the gardens to the buildings themselves. It is significant that 'garden/s' does not rate an entry in the index of many published books about almshouses even though in most of these books gardens are mentioned and photographs of almshouse gardens are included.[1] Helen Caffrey's book on the almshouses of the West Riding does, however, discuss the importance of gardens and also includes an illustration of a plan for a central communal garden drawn up in 1880 for Joseph Crossley's Almshouses in Halifax.[2]

The current chapter focuses on the gardens found in Somerset (based on research for an MA dissertation on this topic). An initial look at the almshouses studied for this nationwide project, however, reveals certain similarities and I am very grateful to all the researchers who provided information about almshouse gardens. As in Somerset, very few detailed descriptions of the gardens survive. The majority of almshouses, however, did have gardens, and mention of the provision of gardens is made in some of the founding trusts; for example, at Thomas Seckford's Almshouse at Woodbridge in Suffolk:

> I ordain, that the poor of the said Almes-House, shall, in avoidance of idleness, each of them according to their ability and strength of body, labour and be occupied, either in digging, planting or setting the gardens and grounds allotted to them.[3]

A brief look at the architecture, intentions of the benefactors, the almspeople, the accounts and rules will set the context for a chronological study of Somerset almshouse gardens including a more detailed look at four of them.

THE ARCHITECTURE

As has been mentioned in Chapter 2 on almshouse buildings, the style and materials used depended initially on local builders rather than architects, who were not generally involved until the 18th century. The style and layout of the almshouses give the best indication as to the size and shape of the gardens as most have retained their original plot of land, whilst adjacent buildings that pre-dated the houses help to establish the boundaries. As the style of buildings changed over the centuries, so did the site and use of the gardens.

THE BENEFACTORS, ALMSPEOPLE, RULES AND ACCOUNTS

No description of early almshouse gardens has been found but the benefactor usually endowed the house with a certain amount of land although the use of this land was rarely stated. Looking at the rules attached to the various foundations is helpful in defining the role of the garden, more perhaps in what they do not say rather than what is said. Most aspects of the residents' lives were subject to stricture, whether of their spiritual or bodily purity, cleanliness of their surroundings, sobriety or socialising. However, apart from the occasional mention that gardens must be kept tidy, rules regarding the gardens are absent. The residents are not ordered to weed, or grow vegetables and herbs, or to grow produce for sale, or to labour in the gardens. It is one of the few areas of their lives that seemed to be free of regulation, which would imply that the benefactor intended the garden to be a source of food, fresh air, exercise and possibly even pleasure.

The almspeople themselves might provide further clues as to what went on in the gardens. In Somerset, the labouring poor were generally agricultural workers and, as such, used to growing their own vegetables and herbs, so their inclination would be to tend the almshouse garden as they had their own. Another indication that the garden was considered the responsibility of the individual almsperson is to be found in the almshouse account books. With very few exceptions, the account books of the almshouses give details of bills for such items as carpenters, wheelwrights, surgeon, apothecaries, the occasional funeral, new hats, gowns and shoes, pensions for the residents, but no mention of any item connected to the garden. There is very seldom any purchase of seeds, plants or garden implements, which would imply that the residents bought or acquired these things themselves. That being the case, the gardens would replicate the farm or cottage gardens they had worked in before entering the almshouse. The examples of garden items included in the accounts for Bubwith House and Sexey's Hospital (mentioned below) are the exception rather than the rule.

FIFTEENTH, SIXTEENTH AND SEVENTEENTH CENTURIES

Despite local differences in building materials and styles, a common theme existed throughout Somerset. The almshouses were built in a row or terrace on the edge of the road, with the gardens behind the house, as shown in Illustration 17.a.

To understand how they might have been used, it is necessary to examine contemporary accounts of cottage or kitchen gardens. This is not straight forward, as Edward Hyams points out when writing about early cottage gardens: 'we have only hints and fragments; it rarely occurred to garden writers, diarists or economists to notice the poor man's garden.'.[4] Prior to the Reformation, the gardens of the farm labourer or cottager would have been heavily influenced by monastic gardens and the need to supplement their diets, as well as to produce medicinal cures. According to Colin Platt, Alexander Neckam, a noted 12th-century scholar and teacher, advised that:

> The garden should be adorned with roses and lilies, the turnsole or heliotrope, parsley, cost, fennel southernwood coriander, sage, savery, hysop, mint, rue ... lettuce, garden cress ... onions, leeks, garlic, pumpkins, shallots, cucumber

This shows a good range of plants and herbs; Neckam also advocated growth of medicinal herbs.[5]

Illustration. 17.a. Garden of Alexander Avery Almshouse in Broadway,
founded in 1588.
Photo © Sarah Hare.

The 16th century saw the beginning of publications like William Turner's *A New Herball* printed between 1551 and 1568 in three volumes.[6] The notable feature of Turner's *Herball* was that it was printed in English with detailed illustrations of all the plants for medicinal use and whilst it would have been unlikely that almspeople would have access to it, information from it would have been disseminated by word of mouth. Another source of information would have been Thomas Hill's *The Gardener's Labyrinth* of 1577, which was full of practical advice to the gardener, from methods of irrigation to the benefits of manure and removal of garden pests.[7] This book was aimed at the woman of the house and, once again, information would have been passed on to her servants and labourers. After the Reformation, the gardeners of the big estates were looked to for advice and the odd gift of seeds. According to Lesley Gordon, the cottage gardener could also turn to the local church where 'help and advice, and a cutting or two were given by the parson, or his wife, to their worthy parishioners, and the spread of good cottage gardening was insured'.[8] For the most part, Hyams says: 'The cottage garden continued unaffected by change manifest in such great Tudor creations as Hampton Court'.[9] He goes on to say that the new interest in style and science of gardening during the Elizabethan and Jacobean periods 'had little or no influence on the cottage garden'.[10] Two interesting and well-documented examples of almshouses from this period are the Bubwith Almshouse in Wells and Sexey's Hospital in Bruton.

Bubwith Almshouse in Wells, Built in 1436

The Wells City Almshouses, as they are now known, consist of a conglomeration of buildings, the earliest of which was the Bubwith Almshouse, built in 1436. Later additions followed with endowments from Bishop Still in 1616, Walter Brickes in 1636 and Bishop

Willes in 1777. However the Bubwith Almshouse lies at the heart of the complex and when it was originally built consisted of a long hall to accommodate twenty-four poor people, with a chapel at the east end and a guildhall for use by the City Corporation at the west end.

Illustration 17.b. Bubwith Almshouse in Wells.
Photo © Sarah Hare.

Illustration 17.c. Bubwith Almshouse: south-facing view of garden.
Photo © Sarah Hare.

The Bubwith Almshouse, which has since been converted to eight flats, was built on the edge of the road, with the chapel and the guildhall flanking the original hall. Built with local stone rubble and Doulting stone dressings, with Welsh slate roofs, the situation is typical of earlier almshouses in Somerset, and so it can be assumed that in a similar style, the gardens lay to the back and would have run the length of the almshouse before the other wings were added. By 1626, the garden had been divided by the additional buildings, which is mentioned in the accounts of that year when the almspeople were paid 'for carrying some 30 loads of dung out of the street into the great garden 18d.' and 'given the men to drink for gardening in the little garden'.[11]

Following the usual pattern, mentions of the garden in the rules are not found. The Rules, Ordinances and Statutes dated 15 November 1446 required the almspeople to attend mass to 'pray for the souls of all benefactors, keep peace and agree with one another' but no instructions were included regarding the garden.[12] The account books reveal a little more information that helps to build up a picture of how the garden was being used. An entry in 1501, 'repair for keeping bees in the house', informs us that bees were kept at that time but as there is no later reference perhaps the beekeeping did not continue beyond the 16th century.[13]

In 1625 there was an entry for: 'Forks to prop up the vine tree' that is repeated in 1636.[14] There was also expenditure for: 'Forks and poles to prop up the vine 12d. Propping up the vine tree 6d.'.[15] Thus the vine appears to have survived for at least ten years. Another entry in 1628 for: 'Hundred cabbage plants 6d.' would support the use of the garden for growing vegetables and fruit.[16] Between 1750 and 1778, a quarterly payment was made for 'seeds and plants as usual 3/4d.' without giving details of what seeds and plants.[17] The Governor would not be able to justify spending the Bubwith Trust money on frivolous items like flowers, so it was in all likelihood for vegetables and herbs. After this date, for some reason the accounts become more haphazard with no mention of any items connected with the garden. The regular supply for seeds and plants has been stopped, which could mean that the almspeople had been made responsible for replenishing garden stocks themselves.

The passing of the Municipal Corporations Act in 1835 resulted in the City Council taking responsibility for running the almshouses (by 1840) and the Governor was replaced with a matron. By coincidence, a major upheaval in the garden was recorded in the Trustees Minute Book:

> 7 October 1846 garden to be turned into "airing" yard: trees to be cut down, earth removed to level of ground floor of almshouse, covered with gravel, benches fixed for use of inmates instead of having to go beyond the precincts of the almshouse when they required air and exercise.[18]

This certainly has echoes of the paternalistic approach of the 19th century. It is likely that this proved to be both unpopular with the residents and a mistaken use of the area, because the garden was subsequently reinstated. The exact date that this happened is uncertain but various items in the accounts between 1865 and 1872 indicate that the 'airing yard' had been replaced with a lawn, beds and paths:

1865	5/-	to Betty Small, keeping lawns walks & borders in order
1866	10/-	to John George for keeping lawns walks & borders in order
	1/-	for clover seed for lawn
1870	10/4	to Stephen Fenatt, taking care of garden and broom
	2/6	to Jacob Machin, cleaning garden
1872	£2.1.9	Re-gravelling walks
	5/-	Philip Hardwick attending garden[19]

An Ordnance Survey Map of 1886 shows details of borders and paths, as well as delineating the beds of the Little Garden to the west of Still's wing. The garden would almost certainly have been used for growing vegetables during the First World War, if not before, and it is still in use at the time of writing. One of today's residents complains that if he digs too deeply in the garden he hits a stony base, which is probably the remnant of the foundations for the 1846 gravelled yard. Today, although surrounded by busy roads, the garden provides a secluded and peaceful spot for the residents' enjoyment. They are enormously proud of the garden, which is open to the public several times a year, and participates in the 'Wells in Bloom' competition.

Hugh Sexey's Hospital in Bruton, Built in 1638

Hugh Sexey's Hospital was built in 1638 to provide a home for twelve poor people, seven men and five women. In addition, Hugh Sexey, a local man who had risen to become an Auditor of the Exchequer from 1559 to 1619, provided a school for twelve orphaned boys and the school remained there until it was moved to new premises in 1891. The Hospital was more grandiose than the usual Somerset almshouse, having a chapel, a hall and a school. As can be seen in the plans of Illustration 17.d., the second court was initially used as the children's playground until the school moved and it was turned into the Master's garden. The privacy of the Master's garden was protected by forbidding entry to the almspeople, which is not the case today. When it was converted from a playground, it was the only place where flowers were grown and it is still a charming courtyard garden.

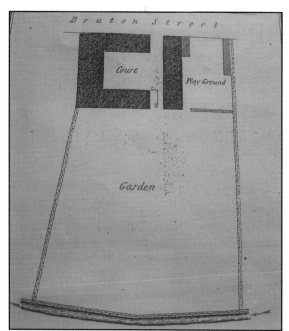

Illustration 17.d. Sexey's Hospital: 1824 plan of garden *reproduced by kind permission of the current Master.*[20]

With regard to the main garden, this almshouse is one of the very rare cases in Somerset when the benefactor made his intentions for the garden absolutely clear. In the original statute, it was clearly set down what was due to the 'objects of the charity. The allowance to each of the Men and Women consists of a Room in the Hospital, in which is a Bedstead, a small piece of Garden Ground of about 12 feet square'.[21] The garden consists of a south-facing, two-acre, walled plot of land, which would have been divided into small plots for each almsperson to grow their vegetables and fruit.

The account books of the Hospital reveal very little of what might have been grown in the garden. Payments were made for plumbers, masons, apothecary, sacramental bread and wine in 1825. A new introduction in 1843 was 'Gas Light' and in 1873 the rather charming entry for 'cricket bat and balls'.[22] It is not until 1876 that there is a purchase for the garden:

'1876 Eatons - Seeds and Manure £4-3-10' and '1879 C. Pocock Apple Trees for Hospital Garden 18/-'.[23]

Illustration 17.e. Sexey's Hospital: the main garden.
Photo © Sarah Hare.

From 1888 until 1894 regular payments were made for thorn plants and apple trees, such as:

June 1888	for 300 Thorn plants - 9/-
June 1889	Kelway and Sons for apple Trees £1-5-0
	And Edwin Marsh for Apple Trees £1-8-0.
June 1892	June First instalment towards cost of Implement shed £2-10-0
Dec. 1892	G. Rice for Thorn plants - 5/-
	And Second instalment for shed £2-10-0.
June 1893	300 thorn plants - 6/-
	Peter Fry Seed Merchant £2-17-0
	And Apple Trees £2-0-0
June 1894	Thorn plants 14/-
	Thorn plants and apple trees £1-6-0
Dec 1894	Apple trees and Thorn Plants 17/-[24]

It would seem there was trouble with the thorn hedge and the number and frequency of apple trees being bought could indicate that the old fruit trees were dying off. Whatever the reasons, these were obviously expensive items, intended for communal use in the garden and well beyond the purse of the almspeople. With no mention of seeds or plants in the accounts, it seems that, as other almspeople had to do, they were required to purchase their own seeds and plants or, more likely, rely on gifts to fill their vegetable plot. It is probable that the garden continued to be maintained in this fashion until the early 20th century.

One of the current residents was able to provide a detailed picture of the garden during and since the Second World War. For obvious reasons, during the war the main garden was used solely for vegetables, fruit trees and soft fruit and a full-time gardener was employed who lived on the premises. When his services were dispensed with after the war, the residents' individual patches had disappeared, so they began to garden communally. A pump at the bottom of the garden, which took water from the river, kept the garden well-watered. Today the tradition of producing vegetables is continued and the sight of the well-tended and fully stocked garden, with flowers and trees in amongst the plants, is one of great pleasure. A gardener is employed specifically to provide fruit and vegetables for the residents and these are his priority, although he may carry out other general garden duties. The fruit and vegetables in season are put out in an allocated area in the Hospital for the residents to help themselves. The present gardener carries out a system of crop rotation and companion planting in the very productive soil. As most residents are usually people who have had gardening experience, they still help when physically able.

The role of the garden today is very plainly set out in the Residents' Handbook:

> Gardens are laid out for the use and benefit of all residents. The Gardener is responsible for their maintenance and upkeep. After consultation with the Master, some residents assist him at intervals on a purely voluntary basis. The vegetables which are grown in the garden are made available to the residents and placed in the area provided for that purpose.[25]

Apart from providing a wide range of salads, herbs, vegetables and fruit, the garden is also a source of great pride amongst the residents, as well as the Master and staff. It seems likely that they will continue tending it in the way that had originally been intended by Hugh Sexey.

EIGHTEENTH CENTURY

The 18th century saw a refinement in the style of almshouses, which showed that the changes taking place in architecture at the national level were gradually filtering down, through the gentry, to the counties. A major change, as far as Somerset almshouses were concerned, was the involvement of architects, notably in the case of St John's Hospital in Bath, where the well-known John Wood the elder was the architect. However, whilst the almshouses became more sophisticated, the gardens remained at the less stylistic level of cottage gardens. The great plant collectors, like the Tradescants, father and son, in the 17th century, followed by Sir Joseph Banks and others during the 18th century, had greatly increased the variety of plants available to gardeners. Whether any of these new plants would have reached the gardens of cottages, much less almshouses, is debatable.

During this period the fate of the country cottage garden was dependent upon the generosity of the lord of the manor as well as the aspirations of the local landowner. The fashion for creating sweeping landscapes during the period of Lancelot Brown (1716-1783) and his followers, might well affect the injudiciously placed cottage, which could be swept away if it stood in the way of creating the desired effect. As far as records show, nothing as draconian as this occurred in Somerset and the almshouses remained untouched, whilst in all likelihood cottage and almshouse gardens continued in much the same way without interference.

NINETEENTH CENTURY

During this period of great philanthropic works, Somerset benefited from a large increase in endowments for almhouses and these 19th-century houses reflected the substantial flavour of the Victorian building style. The gardens were varied, depending on the size and shape of the almshouse plot of land, and there was a very noticeable move away from terraced almshouses with gardens behind them.

By contrast with previous centuries, there is a wealth of information about cottage gardens in the 19th century. One of the major changes that the new century brought was the great number of publications on gardening that were available to the general population. One of the earliest was *Cottage Gardening* written in 1817 by William Salisbury 'for the industrious cottager'.[26] *The Gardeners' Chronicle* was started in 1841 by a group of men led by Joseph Paxton, to be followed by William Robinson's *The Garden* magazine in 1871; both offered useful additions to the list of gardening publications. However, the real champion of the less wealthy gardener was John Claudius Loudon who produced *The Gardener's Magazine*, from 1826-1844, as a quarterly magazine, at an affordable price.

For a first-hand account of what was happening in cottage gardens during the latter part of the 19th century, one of the best sources is Flora Thompson's trilogy *Lark Rise to Candleford*. From her we learn that 'all vegetables, including potatoes, were home-grown in abundance. Fat green peas, broad beans, cauliflowers, runner beans, cabbage, kale, lettuce, radishes and young onions' were all grown in the cottage vegetable patch.[27] Whilst the vegetable garden was the domain of the men, women were permitted 'to cultivate a flower garden, and most of the houses had at least a narrow border beside the pathway'.[28] There was still no money available for the luxury of flower seeds and so 'they had to depend upon roots and cuttings give by their neighbours; and there was little variety'.[29] Flora Thompson lists the flowers grown in spring as pinks, sweet williams, love-in-a-mist, wallflowers, forget-me-nots, 'holly-hocks and Michelmas daisies in autumn. Then there were lavender and sweetbriar bushes' and an ubiquitous white rose.[30] Women:

> cultivated a herb corner, stocked with thyme, parsley and sage for cooking, rosemary to flavour the home-made lard, lavender to scent the best clothes, and peppermint, pennyroyal, horehound, camomile, tansy, balm and rue for physic.[31]

Blackberries, sloes and wild crab apples were used to make wine and 'the garden provided rhubarb, currants, gooseberries and parsnips'.[32]

Edmund Blunden's poem *Almswomen* adds another valuable insight with his description of the almshouse garden in the late 19th century:

> How happy go the rich fair-weather days
> When on the roadside folk stare in amaze
> At such a honeycomb of fruit and flowers
> As mellows round their threshold; what long hours
> They gloat upon their steepling hollyhocks,
> Bee's balsams, feathery southernwood, and stocks,
> Fiery dragon's-mouths, great mallow leaves
> For salves, and lemon-plants in bushy sheaves,
> Shagged Esau's-hands with five green finger-tips.[33]

Poetic licence aside, the poem helps to confirm the translation of the cottage garden plants into almshouse gardens. The country men and women in Somerset would have been more than familiar with all these plants and it is reasonable to assume that when moved to an almshouse, if they were strong enough, they would continue to garden their allocated plot in the same way. However, there were exceptions to the rule of cottage gardens and Partis College in Bath is one of them.

Partis College in Bath, Founded in 1826

Illustration 17.f. Partis College in Bath.
Photo © Sarah Hare.

The elegant Partis College was founded in 1826 by Mrs Anne Partis and stands out from the average almshouse in Somerset for its size and style. The almspeople for whom it was intended were also in a completely different class from the usual impotent poor. Mrs Partis and her husband had been deeply moved by the situation of many widows and daughters who suffered a loss of income and station in life because their husbands or fathers had been killed during the Napoleonic Wars. The Indenture for the purchase of land on 30 January 1824 describes: 'Mrs. Partis's intention of founding a College for the residence of thirty Females, to be called "Partis's College for decayed Gentlewomen"'.[34] The reference to the residents as 'Gentlewomen' is a far cry from the 'objects' of Sexey's Hospital. The Rules and Regulations stated that each gentlewoman should 'be possessed of a certain Income, not less than Twenty pounds nor exceeding Thirty pounds per annum' and should be able to support a maidservant to look after her.[35] In addition, the ladies had to be widows or:

> unmarried daughters of Clergymen, Officers of the Army or Navy, Professional men in Law, Physic or Divinity or of Merchants, who should be of irreproachable characters and Members of the Church of England, and such as have seen better days.[36]

Mrs Partis was obviously a lady of taste as well as considerable wealth, and the building is testament to that. Partis College is a Grade I listed building, laid out on three sides of a rectangle, with a chapel at its centre. According to Historic England: 'The Chapel was built first and the architect was reputed to be "H.E. Goodridge"'.[37]

The first mention of the garden is in a clause in the 1824 Indenture that the Trust is: 'To permit the residue of the land to be allotted into gardens, or walks, or terraces'.[38] The residue consisted of three acres of land, on a hill overlooking Bath. By the time the gardens of Partis

College were being laid out in 1826, there had been a move away from the picturesque style: 'and some designers urged a return to formality' that is reflected in the mention of walks or terraces.[39] Originally a clerk or porter was employed, amongst whose duties it was stipulated that: 'He shall keep the Gravel Walks and Lawn in neat order'.[40] In the Petty Disbursements book, evidence of this work is shown by various references to payments for labour and garden equipment:

1846	Clover and grass seeds
1847	Mowing, and walks, weed docker, weeding, hedge cutting, digging all shrubberies
1887	Extra labour in shrubberies
1899	Garden barrow, garden shears
1893 - 1900	Mowing lawn, hedging and ditching, weekly mowing in summer [41]

There was no doubt that the appearance of the garden was of utmost importance and it was not only the public areas of the garden that were to be kept immaculate. The long-suffering wife of the clerk was required to be of good character, a member of the Church of England, to clean the chapel and 'find Brushes and Dusters for that purpose at her own expense'; it was further ordered that: 'She must not hang out any clothes to dry in view of the College'.[42] Even the residents were under the same stricture. Rule 6 of the Rules and Regulations states: 'No Clothes will be permitted to hang out in view either at the front or back of the College'.[43] No lines with flapping clothes were to be allowed to impinge on the overall view of the garden, and to this day the same rule applies.

On entering Partis College, the first impression is of the magnificent building, with the lawns, trees and shrubs, but slight disappointment that there appears to be no additional garden. It comes as a delightful surprise, therefore, to discover the individual gardens of the residents at the rear of the building. Mrs Partis's intention had been that they should be pleasure gardens for the enjoyment of the residents, and to provide somewhere cool from the sun (see Illustration 17.g. Partis College in Bath, colour Plate XI).

These gardens are not the cottage gardens (with rows of cabbages, lettuce, tomatoes and fruit trees) that are seen at the majority of almshouses. Even the garden ornaments are more likely to be replicas of Italian statuary than the garden centre variety seen in most almshouse gardens. The only thing they have in common is that the residents are responsible for the upkeep of their own garden.

It might be supposed that, unlike the poorer almspeople, the 'Gentlewomen' would have had sufficient funds to buy their own seeds and plants, without being dependent on gifts. However, these 'irreproachable' ladies were not above a bit of skulduggery when it came to replenishing their gardens. The admonition issued by the Trustees in June 1884, would imply that a little bit of underhand 'borrowing' had been carried out, whenever a house had been left vacant: 'The Trustees wish it to be understood that during the times a house is vacant, the garden thereto attached is in their occupation; and that on no account should flowers, plants or anything whatsoever be removed from it, except by direction of the Chaplain'.[44]

Albeit an almshouse, the style of the gardens reflects the architecture of the building, and the purpose for which they were intended was influenced by the residents who were, uniquely in Somerset, of a genteel class rather than the 'deserving' poor of contemporary almshouses. Today the gardens are more reminiscent of the small show gardens at the

Chelsea Flower Show than an almshouse garden, but this would very likely have greatly pleased Mrs Partis.

Illustration 17.h. Partis College in Bath: resident's garden.
Photo © Sarah Hare.

TWENTIETH CENTURY

The result of two world wars and the introduction of custom-built housing for the elderly in the public and private sector had an effect on almshouses. Those that were less well-endowed fell into disrepair, whilst some were sold off, demolished or converted. At this stage local town and district councils stepped in to take over the running of almshouses in many cases. In Somerset, however, a few new almshouses were built but there was no architectural homogeneity about the almshouses, each one reflecting the taste, and possibly the purse, of the benefactor. The plethora of published books and journals on style in the house and garden, enabled people to follow their own inclination without slavishly copying the fashion of the moment, with the result that the new almshouses and their gardens could not be more different.

The Bartholomew Thomas Almshouses, designed by a local architect, were described as having 'a distinctive late William Morris feel' and it certainly looks as if the architect had been strongly influenced by the Arts and Crafts movement.[45] Whilst there is a common entrance at the front of the building, the gardens are to the rear of the houses and are allocated to each resident although without formal demarcation. By complete contrast, the Davis Homes in Wincanton are purely functional, built of red brick with no decorative features at all. The two attached houses were set in the middle of the garden, the front section of which has now been turned into a drive with parking bays. The garden in the rear runs across both houses without any division at all. Historic England describes Welch Almshouse in Lamyatt as being 'Gothic' and, with its grey 'central ashlar stack' and 'gothic' lettering in the cartouche, it certainly has a forbidding look.[46] The site of the almshouse on a slope makes the front impractical to garden, therefore the majority of the garden lies to the side and the rear.

At the back of the house the garden is divided between the two apartments, but the larger section to the side is shared by the two occupants.

The Sidney Hill Wesleyan Cottage Homes in Churchill, built in 1907

An almshouse that gives a very precise picture of what was going on in the gardens at this time, is the Sidney Hill Wesleyan Cottage Homes. Sidney Hill was a local philanthropist who built the Victorian Jubilee Cottages at Langford as well as the Sidney Hill Wesleyan Cottage Homes in Churchill. The Grade II listed building was designed by Silcock and Reay in the 'Arts and Crafts vernacular style'.[47] The twelve Cottages are one-storied houses with an attic window, built in a 'U' shape of red brick, with plain roof tiles. The south-facing garden consists of a sunken garden, divided into four grassed quadrants, with a sundial on a pillar in the centre.

Illustration 17.i. Sidney Hill Wesleyan Cottages in Churchill: sunken garden. *Photo © Sarah Hare.*

A terraced walk with flower borders surrounds the sunken garden, and through the wrought iron gate at the far end, is the vegetable garden. A contemporary print of the garden shows that very little has changed from its original inception. There is a thoroughness and practicality in the planning of the garden, as well as the materials used, which implies the influence of the Arts and Crafts Movement. Whilst the sunken garden is attractive, it is the vegetable garden that delights the onlooker, with the same attention to detail evident in the way it is arranged (*see* Illustration 17.j. colour Plate XII).

Each resident was allotted a vegetable plot and they were numbered accordingly. Miraculously, these iron numbers, together with the boot scrapers and edging, have all survived, and continue to serve their original purpose.

Not only were the residents responsible for their own vegetable plot, but they also had to maintain the area of garden in front of each house. This is organisation of an almshouse

Illustration 17.k. Vegetable plots at the Sidney Hill Wesleyan Cottages, showing number and bootscraper.
Photo © Sarah Hare.

garden on a scale not seen elsewhere in Somerset. Sidney Hill's intention was for the residents to lead an upright and industrious life, attending the Wesleyan chapel at least once a week, remaining sober, clean and tidy. Although the almshouse was run on strict Methodist lines, he was a benevolent founder and provided the almspeople with two summer houses at the end of each wing, facing south, where the residents could sit and enjoy the garden, sheltered from rain or sun. As has been shown, the garden is used today in much the same way as was originally intended, with the addition of a gardener to help with cutting the grass and hedge trimming. An extensive renovation programme was carried out in the 1990s to bring the interiors of the houses up to modern standards so that, combined with their beautiful garden, the Sidney Hill Almshouses are much sought after.

TWENTY-FIRST CENTURY

When looking at the new almshouses built since 2000, it can be seen that a completely different approach has been taken to the gardens. When it became too expensive for the Almshouse Trust to restore the Jubilee Cottage Almshouses in Chard, they sold the buildings and used the funds to build two brand new almshouses on a different site, taking the opportunity to employ an ecological approach to building methods. The houses, completed in 2005, each with its own bicycle store, are set amongst a group of local authority-owned housing, around a communal grassed lawn. There are only small flower beds in front of each house, but residents still manage to grow pots of herbs and flowers in them.

The St John's Hospital Almshouse built at Combe Park in Bath in 2003 presents a strikingly different approach to almshouses for the future. For the first time in Somerset, current garden design concepts are used in an almshouse garden. The garden has been designed in the centre of the building with all the apartments surrounding it. This garden is far removed from the traditional almshouse gardens, but although the element of growing produce is removed, the whole design is aimed at providing pleasure for the residents. Elements, such as the raised beds, different textures and the water feature, produce a peaceful but interesting atmosphere that can be easily used by all the residents.

New approaches to design are not restricted to brand new buildings but are also employed where older almshouse gardens have been redesigned as part of a renovation programme. A good example of this can be seen in Taunton. As part of a general upgrading programme being carried out on the flats in the Huish Almshouses (founded in 1615), a new community room was built in the grounds and the gardens were redesigned at the same time. Again the pattern of a communal space is followed, with different areas for sitting out in, raised beds, but no individual gardens. In the middle of a big town like Taunton, the garden provides the residents with a peaceful haven in which to relax. Another change is that gardeners are now employed to work in the almshouse gardens, as in the case of Sexey's Hospital in Bruton and The Blue House in Frome. An example from outside Somerset shows gardener Geoffrey Beck clearly playing an important part in the life of Doughty's Hospital in Norwich.[48]

Illustration 17.1. Courtyard garden at St John's Hospital, Bath.
Photo © Sarah Hare.

CONCLUSION

There can be little doubt that almshouse gardens have always played a significant role in the overall life of almshouses and their occupants, from the vegetable plots of the early centuries to the more sophisticated communal gardens of the 21st century. The changes in style and usage of the gardens over the years reflect altering attitudes to poverty and the recipients of almshouse charity, from authoritarian discipline and condescending benevolence to the partnership of today. The changing role from practical usage to pastime and leisure is underlined by the employment of garden designers when creating new almshouse gardens, as in the case of St John's Hospital at Combe Park in Bath.

Bryson and Ford's report for the Nuffield Foundation on almshouses (published in 2000) found that: 'Gardens are the most common extra-feature provided beyond basic rooms', thus emphasising the importance placed on the provision of gardens for almspeople.[49] The examples of the new or restored almshouse buildings discussed above show that gardens are still at the centre of almshouse living in the 21st century.

Notes

1. *See* for example: Bailey, B. *Almshouses*, London, 1988; Hallet, A. *Almshouses*, Princes Risborough, 2004; Howson, B. *Houses of Noble Poverty*, Sunbury-on-Thames, 1993; Howson, B. *Almshouses: a social & architectural history*, Stroud, 2008.

2. Caffrey, H. *Almshouses in the West Riding of Yorkshire, 1600-1900*. Kings Lynn, 2006, pp. 42-3.

3. Weaver, C & M. *The Seckford Foundation: four hundred years of a Tudor charity*. Woodbridge, 1987, p.16.

4. Hyams, E. *English Cottage Gardens*. London, 1970, p. 1.

5. Platt, C. *Medieval England*. London, 1978, p. 190.

6. Turner, W. *A New Herball*, Part I. 1551; Chapman, G.T.L. & Tweddle, M.N. (eds); *A New Herball*, Parts II and III. 1562; Chapman, G.T.L., McCombie, F. & Wesencraft, A (eds), 2 vols. Cambridge, 1955.

7. Hill, T. *The Gardener's Labyrinth*, 1577, Mabey, R. (ed.). Oxford, 1987.

8. Gordon, L. *Poorman's Nosegay*. London, 1973, p. 34.

9. Hyams, p. 8.

10. Ibid., p. 11.

11. Wells Cathedral Archive (WCA): 453.

12. Parker, J. *Architectural Antiquities of the City of Wells*. Oxford & London, 1860, p. 60.

13. WCA: AH289.

14. WCA: AH452.

15. WCA: AH467.

16. WCA: AH455.

17. WCA: ADD/1697(a).

18. WCA: AH555, p. 142.

19. WCA: AH559.

20. Sexey's Hospital archive (not numbered).

21. Somerset Heritage Centre (SHC): DD/BT 7/4.

22. SHC: DD/BT 7/1.

23. Ibid.

24. SHC: DD/BT 7/6.

25. *The Residents' Handbook*, Sexey's Hospital, Bruton.

26. Salisbury, W. *Cottage Gardening*. London, 1817, p. vi.

27. Thompson, F. *Lark Rise to Candleford*. Harmondsworth, 1945, p. 27.

28. Ibid., p. 115.

29. Ibid.

30. Ibid.

31. Ibid.

32. Ibid., p. 116.

33. Blunden, E. *An Anthology of Modern Verse*. London, 1930, pp. 10-11.

34. Bath Record Office (BRO): 035/4.

35. Ibid.

36. Ibid.

37. Historic England (HE): URL: www.imagesofengland.org.uk accessed 22 Oct. 2007.

38. BRO: 0354/4.

39. Bond, J. *Somerset Parks and Gardens*. Tiverton, 1998, p. 112.

40. BRO: 0354/4.

41. BRO: 0423/1/6/13.

42. BRO: 0354/4.

43. Ibid.

44. Binding, H. *West Somerset Free Press Newspaper*. 15 April 2005, p. 10.

45. HE: URL: www.imagesofengland.org.uk accessed 22 Oct. 2007.

46.   Ibid.

47.   HE: URL: www.imagesofengland.org.uk accessed 22 Oct. 2007.

48.   Goose, N. & Moden, L. *A History of Doughty's Hospital Norwich, 1687-2009*. Hatfield, 2010.

49.   Bryson, J.R. & Ford, R.G. *The Almshouse Renaissance and the Care of the Elderly and Poor in Urban and Rural Britain*, Final Report for the Nuffield Foundation. Birmingham, Aug. 2000, p. 18.

CHAPTER 18
THE SOCIAL STATUS OF ALMSPEOPLE

Judith Ellis

INTRODUCTION

In 1875, following their inspection of the French Hospital in Hackney, the Charity Commissioners observed:

> The Hospital, including the Chapel, is a handsome building, too handsome indeed for the purpose for which it was designed, viz the board and lodging of aged weavers and weaveresses, ordinary labourers and domestic servants ... it appears that this Institution ... is eminently adapted to aged and decayed French governesses who ... have been accustomed to more care, better accommodation and greater consideration than were ever dreamt of in the wretched hovels of Spitalfields.[1]

The Charity Commissioners, reflecting the views of the time, were making their own judgement about the relative status of people who might qualify for a place in an almshouse (or hospital as this one was called). The almshouses founded over the centuries conferred a status on their 'inmates' (not a word we would use now) that demonstrated how those in the community were regarded at the time.

Status can be inferred from a number of related aspects of life in the almshouses compared to the life of poor older people in the community and there are questions to ask that enable these contrasts to be explored. Was a place in the almshouses appealing or a last resort? Was it a privilege or were the people objects of pity? How significant were the previous occupations and standing of the applicants for places? Were there considerable pressures to conform, reflecting the intentions of the benefactors who built the almshouses? Were they accorded status within the community, participating in public life? Did the material benefits – clothing, money, fuel – compensate for the more restrictive life of subservience to the rules of a charitable institution, or is this a modern view that was not a consideration for the old people who 'knew their place' centuries ago? How did almshouse life contrast with that of older people living on poor relief in the community? And did attitudes towards maintaining almshouses and almspeople change over time? This chapter examines the social status of almspeople through a case study of the Sir Baptist Hicks Almshouses at Chipping Campden in Gloucestershire (hereafter referred to as Campden Almshouses) with comparisons from other almshouses that, in their variety, may have other distinguishing features.

MOTIVES OF FOUNDERS

An enquiry into the status of almspeople starts with a view of the intentions, motives and ambitions of the founders of almshouses. These were many and varied and have changed over time: guilds established places of refuge for their aged members, as did churches, and much later philanthropic industrialists provided for their retired workpeople. Individual local benefactors had more complex reasons, demonstrating their charity, perhaps hoping that such an act would store up goodwill in this life and the next, combined with a genuine wish to help the poor. Whatever the reasons, those who lived in almshouses reflected the good name of the benefactor. The buildings, nearly always specially designed for the purpose, may be large edifices or a row of cottages, but in themselves they give significance and status to those who live there, as well as reflecting the intentions of the founders. Sir Baptist Hicks was perhaps an outstanding example of an almshouse founder who wished to demonstrate his wealth and power in the town that he had effectively taken over.

Illustration 18.a. Sir Baptist Hicks Almshouses in Chipping Campden, *ca* 1920
photograph by Jesse Taylor, reproduced courtesy of Chipping Campden History Society

The Chipping Campden Almshouses are notable, even in a town famous for its Cotswold stone buildings (*see* Illustration 18.a.). The single building comprises twelve dwellings built in 1612, possibly on the site of a former 'hospital', by Sir Baptist Hicks, a very wealthy London mercer and moneylender to King James I.[2] He was not local to Chipping Campden, but came from a Gloucestershire family. He had formally acquired the manor of Campden in 1608 and planned substantial developments to his property. In 1612 he was building Campden House on land adjacent to the church, and his almshouses on the opposite side of the lane complemented the design, even benefiting from the estate's new piped water supply from Westington Hill, which contrasted with the town's communal supply from brooks and wells. The building was perfectly sited so that his London visitors, having travelled along the main street of the town, passed the substantial almshouses before entering his gates. The almshouse residents themselves were part of this display of grandeur and patronage. In his will, proved in 1629, Sir Baptist Hicks endowed the almshouses with

£140 per annum, the income from his lands in Charingworth, to provide accommodation and a pension for six poor men and six poor women from Campden and Berrington.[3] The almshouse residents were individually named in the will and must have been very carefully chosen to ensure that they did not spoil his show of beneficence to the town, thus confirming the importance of their status. Sir Baptist Hicks had no surviving son, so the title of Viscount Campden, bestowed on him a year before his death, passed to Lord Edward Noel, husband of his eldest daughter, Juliana. It was their grandson, Edward Noel, who became the 1st Earl of Gainsborough in 1682.[4]

At this time, almshouses were also established in other towns and villages by London merchants, many of whom wished to benefit their birthplace and at the same time impress local people. Nicholas and Ellis Crispe came from Marshfield, Gloucestershire, and had found success as skinners at the same time as Hicks, Nicholas being an alderman in London. Together they endowed an almshouse in 1625 for 'the perpetual harbouring and relief of eight poor householders of the town and parish'.[5] Another 'local man made good', Lawrence Sheriff, was born in Rugby and became a wealthy London grocer, providing spices to Princess Elizabeth who, when Queen, granted him the title of Esquire with a coat of arms. Although married he had no children and when he died in 1567 he left money for a school and almshouses in Rugby.

In later centuries, individual founders appear to have been less concerned about their own status and there are many examples of men and women who wished to benefit the poor people around them without such an ostentatious display of wealth through their buildings. Their name, however, or that of their family, was usually attached to the bequest. In 1851 Mrs Mary Jones erected cottages in Winterbourne, Gloucestershire: 'The 10 cottages are by the desire of Mrs. Jones to be called 'The Perry Almshouses' out of respect to her family and dearest relatives'.[6] The Widows and Old Maids Almshouses, Nantwich, Cheshire, were founded in 1676-7 by Roger Wilbraham in memory of his wife: 'to devote something of this nature to the Honor of God and to her memory that had been mindfull to lay something by, to be distributed to poor widows in her own street'.[7]

In the 19th century a proportion of almshouses, such as Sir Titus Salt's Almshouses in Saltaire, and the Bradford Tradesmen's Homes Charity in Bradford, were built for retired workmen and tradesmen. As in earlier times, the conditions for entering and remaining in the almshouses were strict, but with these went an acknowledgement on the part of the patrons that the almspeople had earned a right to be looked after when they had ceased work. This philanthropic attitude was perhaps associated with a sense of valuing the contribution made by workers, rather than a sense of self-worth that prompted benefactors in earlier centuries to set up homes for the poor. Helen Caffrey suggests that the development of almshouses at this time was partly due to a greater understanding of the problem generally through investigations into poverty and deprivation.[8]

Having put their names to their almshouses, it is not surprising that the benefactors wanted to ensure that the inhabitants did not bring disgrace to them and so they often set out conditions for entry and behaviour (as described in Chapter 12). Thus almshouses were intended for those seen as the 'deserving' rather than the 'undeserving' poor. People aspiring to be admitted to Winterbourne Almshouses had to plan well ahead of time:

> who not being let by sickness or some other urgent cause have attended Divine Service at the Church … for the time being every Sunday for the last 5 years and been partakers of the Holy Communion and lived a righteous and sober life to the glory of God's holy name.[9]

Many almshouses required entrants to be demonstrably sober, respectable and God-fearing, the founders being anxious that their name should not be brought into disrepute. Only the most suitable people were selected, immediately giving them a status above that of their neighbours. Trustees – initially appointed by the founders but subsequently self-appointed from within their circles of gentry, clergy, churchwardens, elite members of the vestry and town or parish officials – would know the applicants and make their judgements.

The Campden Almshouses were managed in a different manner; Sir Baptist Hicks' will stated that: 'the said poor people shall be from time to time placed in the said almshouses by the nomination and appointment of my Heirs and their successors' and this continued, nominally, until a Trust was formed in 1962.[10] This example of a family's sole patronage for over 350 years may be unique and it certainly created a different and quite special relationship with the almspeople, although the daily management was by the absentee Earl's local agent, a man of great influence in the town.[11] The places in the Campden Almshouses were therefore awarded by the Earl of Gainsborough on the recommendation of the Vicar and Vestry; a letter from the Earl to his Campden agent in 1824 states:

> Mr Leland Noel [brother of the Earl and Vicar at St. James's Church, Chipping Campden] has given me 21 petitions for the vacant place in the Almshouse. I shall award to Thomas Paine who Mr Leland Noel is recommended by Mr Spooner and yourself.[12]

And again in 1830: 'Pray let James Allen have the vacant Almshouse. I enclose you a letter from Mr. Leland Noel'.[13]

Competition was also fierce in Stratford-upon-Avon where the Corporation held ballots for places in the 19th century.[14] It could be said that places awarded by patronage conferred more status on the almspeople than those awarded by a vote, in that the judgement of the trustees or patron placed more value on the person and their potential contribution to the life of the almshouse. A vote could be influenced by external considerations; Alannah Tomkins gives the example of the almswomen living at Jackenetts Almshouse in Cambridge, who were chosen by rate-payers:

> And in the early nineteenth century the elections gave rise to some closely-fought battles; however, this might speak more reliably to the energies and interests of ratepayers than to the enthusiasm of the women.[15]

The demand for places confirms the view that the almshouse was a desirable place to live and conferred status on the residents. Applicants might have some time to wait for a place, perhaps because life in the almshouses was fairly comfortable and residents long-lived.

OCCUPATIONS

Status is significantly suggested by people's background and occupation and a number of almshouses were established for retired people from specific backgrounds or occupations, such as the military, weavers, miners or the clergy. These occupational almshouses often draw applicants from all over the country and have a specific role and status that is discussed elsewhere (particularly in Chapters 9 and 19). Almshouses, like those in Campden, that specified a local connection or residential qualification, contained people from a greater variety of occupations.

The censuses from 1841-1901 give some information about the previous occupations of people in the Campden Almshouses, but accurate comparisons between the decennial censuses are difficult because the instructions for describing occupations varied over the years, and were open to interpretation by the local enumerators. There were no instructions in 1841 for people who were retired or unemployed and in many census records they were all listed as 'Ind' (independent means) bracketing almspeople with those who had private funds, other pensioners and those on poor relief. The 1851 census provides a better indication as: 'Almspeople, and persons in receipt of parish relief should, after being described as such, have their previous occupations inserted'.[16] In the Campden Almshouses, of the ten pensioners in residence in 1851, there were three male agricultural labourers, two gardeners, a shoemaker, a schoolmistress and three tradesmen's widows, indicating perhaps residents of higher status than other old people receiving poor relief.[17] In subsequent censuses the words 'late' and 'formerly' (in relation to occupations) were used but there was great variation across the country, some merely putting 'Occupant of Almshouse'. In 1861, the Richardson Almshouses in Tewkesbury housed a woman who 'of late kept cows', as well as a 'late' seamstress, laundress, gardener, brewer and bricklayer.[18] Previous occupations can sometimes be traced through earlier censuses that record the person's work when they were living in the community. Further study and analysis would help in defining any distinctions between the perceived status of almshouse residents and retired people living in the community.

Nigel Goose and Stuart Basten, in their preliminary study of the Project's census data, found only 2,804 out of 8,048 cases analysed provided information about occupations.[19] The many and varied occupations were standardised, initially into 546 categories, and those that occurred most frequently are set out in a table.[20] In their study, agricultural labourers and labourers formed a substantial proportion of the men's occupations (40 per cent), with a variety of skilled workmen and tradesmen making up the balance. The picture for women was more complicated. Thirty-five per cent were listed as 'Nurse', 'Domestic servant' and 'Servant', but the analysis of ages suggests that there were servants living in the almshouses as well as almspeople, so there is not yet a clear view about the social profile of the almswomen. Ongoing research will provide much more information about the occupational and social profile of the residents and their status in the community.

BEHAVIOUR IN ALMSHOUSES

Significant indicators of the status of almspeople were the rules for their behaviour, with the consequences of non conformity being the threatened loss of the regular allowance or ejection back into the community, which would have caused a considerable loss of face (*see* Chapter 12).

The Campden Almshouse Admissions Book 1739-1916 contains signed (or marked) statements from each entrant. All of the 118 men and women admitted to the almshouses between 1739 and 1820 were illiterate; they put their mark against the admission statement. The educational status of entrants then rose. The first signature appeared in 1820, with nine out of thirty people able to write their name over the next twenty years. The literate proportion rose to 50 per cent amongst the sixty-three entrants between 1840 and 1885, with a further slight improvement (thirteen out of twenty-three) of those who entered from then until 1900. The lack of literacy confirms the low status of early entrants, and the rise during the 19th century reflects that of the general population as national provision of elementary education increased. Here is the statement that entrants signed:

Be it remembered that I .... being put into the Almshouse at Campden
in the room and place of .... Deceased for one year and so from year
to year so long as I shall behave myself well Do hereby promise and agree with
The Rt. Honourable The Lord of Gainsborough to submit to obey and abide by
the rules, orders and constitutions of the said Almshouse and not to keep or
entertain any dweller or dwellers in my apartment of the said Almshouse
without a licence obtained from the said Earl of Gainsborough or his steward
for the time being for so doing upon pain of forfeiting my weekly allowance
to the Poor of Chipping Campden for every and each weeks offence contrary
to the above-mentioned agreement.[21]

This was, therefore, a licence for one year initially, but there is no evidence that anyone
forfeited their place or lost their allowance at the end of their first year. As in other
almshouses, the conditions appear to have been a deterrent rather than a real threat, but they
strengthen the argument that a place in an almshouse conferred status above that of older
poor people living elsewhere in the community.

Another condition made by some founders was that the resident would remain single,
which may have been to prevent families moving in. In 1744 the then Earl of Gainsborough
reaffirmed the order of his ancestor, Sir Baptist Hicks, and set out the conditions for living
in the Campden Almshouses, which every pensioner had to abide by:

I do order and appoint that none of the said poor pensioners either men or
women shall marry after they are admitted into the same House, should any
such marriage be contracted the place of such man or woman shall
immediately be void.[22]

Other almshouses had similar conditions: Wright's Almshouses in Nantwich, (founded
in 1638) had numerous rules that governed the behaviour of the charity recipients with
threats of fines, suspension or even expulsion for breaking them. Twice-daily prayers and
(for the able-bodied), regular attendance at church services were required, while the rules
prohibited marriage, 'swearing, Drunkenness, and all such scandalous Vices [and] keeping
any Woman as an Harlot'.[23]

Although the rules specify single people, the censuses show that by the mid 1800s,
couples were living in the Campden Almshouses, a not uncommon trend nationally.
However, the listed occupant was the husband and on his death his widow had no right to
remain. Richard Petty (and his wife Sarah) entered the Campden Almshouses in 1845 and
lived there until his death twenty years later, at the age of 72 years. Within a month of his
death a new resident was admitted and as there was no vacant place in the women's end of
the block Sarah had to leave. The 1871 census shows her as a pauper, living with her son and
daughter-in-law in High Street. Not only did she lose the material benefits of her husband's
pension and fuel but she was also reduced to applying to the Union for relief, with a
significant change to her status. In other almshouses, too, wives were ejected on the death of
their husbands.[24]

As in the Campden admission statement, it was not uncommon for the rules of an
almshouse to specify that in event of misbehaviour an almsperson's benefits should be given
to someone in the community. The rules of Perry's Almshouses in Wotton-under-Edge,
Gloucestershire (founded in 1630), included the provision that:

If any persons in this almshouse shall behave themselves in carriage or in
conversation as to be thought unfit and unworthy of the charity of this gift,

then their part and portion of apparel, fuel and money, shall be given to such persons as the mayor and his brethren [the feoffees] think fit.[25]

People in the community were, therefore, chance recipients, an indication of their lesser status.

The Campden Almshouses Admissions Register shows only one resident who left ahead of death but not to be cared for elsewhere. William Hughes left within two months of his entry into the almshouses in December 1866: 'finding that the almshouses did not suit him returned to his former residence'.[26] He is listed in the 1871 census as a pauper living on his own aged 95; it seems likely that he found the pressure of conforming to life in the almshouse too restricting, though it is possible that it was not his choice to return to a poorer life, but one made by the agent acting for the Earl.

MATERIAL BENEFITS

The material benefits to almshouse people, described in detail in other chapters, demonstrated their status within in the community. Once in an almshouse, the pensioner did not have to make new appeals for money or clothing; this compares favourably with those receiving occasional poor relief (who had to return to the Vestry for help) and even those on regular poor relief, who could have the payment taken away from them. The almshouse pensioners did not have to apply to the Vestry and be subject to their judgement — this must surely have added to a sense of advantage over the poor in the local community. The value of the almshouse pension was, however, dependent on the continuing income from the original bequest and in some cases the good intentions of the trustees. In the Campden Almshouses, the pensioners received a ton of coals yearly and a weekly pension of 3s. 4d., which in 1614 must have made the position very desirable indeed compared to scraping an existence in the local community. According to the Receipts and Payments Book, in 1884 the pension was still the same, which – as a result of inflation – drastically reduced its value in real terms.[27] In addition, by this time married couples and families were permitted and they had to share this amount, because only the head of the household qualified for the allowance.[28] The pension was supposed to be still being given in 1898, according to a letter printed in the *Evesham Journal*:

> Sir, - Can any person answer the following? How is it that the old people living in the Almshouses of this town did not obtain, or rather receive, which is by law theirs, viz. – their weekly allowance for four weeks during the spring time? If so, I should be glad and many others. Also why it is that they do not receive it regularly, and at the proper time, now? Here is a distinct case for the Charity Commissioners and the sooner an enquiry is made the better for all concerned. Why it has been so quietly passed over I cannot understand; surely some light can be cast on the affair and let us know the reason. I should be glad of an answer if any one can bring any reasonable and lawful excuse, if not, then let the case go before a proper authority. Campden, August 15, 1898.   ANON.[29]

The Campden almspeople were clearly held in some regard, for a protest to be made in the press on their behalf. No further information is available about how this particular issue was resolved, but it is known that the allowance and free accommodation continued until just before World War II. The Campden Almshouses were by this time severely underfunded;

even as early as 1835 the Charity Commissioners recorded that the original bequest had lost value and the Gainsborough estate was subsidising the costs of running the almshouses.[30]

A number of almshouses received additional bequests or endowments over the years, possibly from donors who wished to be associated with such visible good works, and this could be seen as an indication that the almshouses and their inhabitants were held in high regard. The Hugh Perry Hospital in Wotton-under-Edge benefited from three additional bequests up to the 1830s, providing money and bread annually: 'in addition to what they should otherwise receive and be entitled to'.[31] In 1871 Stephen Sylvester, a local merchant in Chipping Campden, invested £360, with the proceeds to be used to purchase coal annually for the Campden Almshouse residents; this must have been a useful addition to the declining value of the pension.[32] Similar almshouse examples compare well with the individual local charities that provided benefits for the poor in the community. These local charities, such as the 'Charities composing a Consolidated Fund' in Wotton, provided bread, clothes or money, which were sometimes handed out on Sunday after church, ensuring that the beneficiaries were demonstrating a godly life.[33] Although some distributions were weekly, they were mainly on the quarter-days or Christmas Day, and therefore could not be regarded as a significant or reliable addition to the life of the poor.

CLOTHING

Almshouse clothing is described in detail in Chapter 15, but it is important to recognise the significance of 'uniforms' in demonstrating the social status of the almspeople and the importance of the founders.

> December 20th 1697
> It is agreed upon by the mayor of Wotton-under-Edge, and his brethren, whose names are subscribed, that the poor people of the new almshouse shall wear gowns, with the letters on them, in remembrance of the donor, and they shall begin this year, and have new ones made once in three years, and whoever of them shall refuse to wear them constantly to the church, and prayers in the chapel, or to come to the said prayers, shall have no privilege of the gift.[34]

However, by the 1830s: 'It has not for many years been thought expedient to carry the above resolution respecting the dress of the poor people into practice, but the rule enjoining a regular attendance at prayers appears to be enforced'.[35] This is not the only example of stated penalties for refusal to wear the given clothes in public. It is interesting to speculate why it was thought necessary to insist. Was there a feeling amongst older people that they did not want to be singled out in this way? This seems to argue against a sense of privilege being felt by the almspeople concerning their clothing.

In Wotton, as in many other almshouses, a set of clothes had to last at least two years, but Sir Baptist Hicks specified 'a frieze gown and a hat' to be given annually to the Campden almspeople.[36] This custom was retained, even though the income to support these almshouses had declined by the 19th century — Margaret Smith charged £2 for twelve Alms hats 'for the year 1820' and in 1848 the Earl of Gainsborough paid for:

72 yds. of Almshouse cloth @ 2/8d.	£9. 12s.
12 Men's and Women's Hats 3/4d.	£2. 0s.
Paid making 12 gowns and coats	£1. 4s.
	£12. 16s.[37]

A surviving Receipts and Payments Book for 1870-84 shows payments being made to the drapers, Roberts, of £6 a year for women's clothing and to T. Brace of £5 19s. a year for men's clothing, which indicates that they still received a fresh set of clothes annually.[38] By comparison, the Accounts of the Overseers to the Poor in Campden show workhouse payments in the early part of the 19th century to local farmers for flax and to a thread manufacturer for thread and ashes, presumably for the making of rough cloth for clothes for the poor.[39] These clothes would have been very poor quality compared to those of the almspeople, who would have been very distinctive as they walked around the local town in their almshouse clothes.

'Badging the poor' has a contentious history, being interpreted variously according to the viewpoint of those examining the issues. Steve Hindle argues that by the end of the 17th century 'the shame of poverty was inscribed in a physical emblem which was applied to all paupers including those in almshouses'.[40] The 1697 statute, that insisted that those on parish relief wore badges, was seen as separating the 'deserving' and 'undeserving' poor, but the badges worn by almspeople can be interpreted differently because many almshouse founders stipulated that their own distinguishing marks were to be incorporated into the clothes they provided (just as logos today advertise the wealth and beneficence of sponsors).

ALMSHOUSE PORTRAITS

In 1849 Canon Charles Edward Kennaway, the Vicar of Campden, commissioned an unknown artist to paint some watercolour portraits that remained in the Vicarage until their recent removal to Gloucestershire Archives. They were of eight Campden Almshouse residents, with their name, age and date of the painting. Canon Kennaway became Vicar in 1832 and for the next forty years was a significant and influential figure in Campden life. His first wife, Emma, was the niece of the Earl of Gainsborough and doubtless this connection ensured that he was given the living as his predecessor was her uncle the Revd Leland Noel.

Canon Kennaway personally initiated and subscribed to a number of developments and services in Campden, including the infant and National Schools, internal changes to the parish church and support for the poor. He built six model cottages for his staff. He led the decisions of the Vestry and interested himself in the welfare of the almspeople.[41] The Vicar may well have been sympathetic to the growing philanthropic movement that encouraged the building of many new almshouses,

Illustration 18.d. Portrait of Sarah Penson deposited at Gloucester Archives *(GA ref P81 MI 1/6) and reproduced courtesy of St James' Parochial Church Council, Chipping Campden.*

Sarah Penson was born in Blockley and was listed as a schoolmistress in the 1841 census. Her unmarried daughter, also a schoolmistress, was living in the Almshouses in 1851, but Sarah, head of the household, is not there. She was 74, and a widow, when the portrait was painted in 1849.

particularly in the north of England. This point of view may have prompted Canon Kennaway to commission the portraits, which would not have been put on public display and have only been recently recognised for what they are. Four of them are reproduced in this book, together with pen portraits of the individuals concerned: Illustrations 18.b. and c. as colour plates (*see* colour Plates XIII and XIV) and Illustrations 18.d. and 18.e. in this chapter.

Illustration 18.e. Portrait of Margaret Emms deposited at Gloucester Archives *(GA ref P81 MI 1/6) and reproduced courtesy of St James' Parochial Church Council, Chipping Campden.*

Margaret Emms is listed in the 1851 census as the widow of a butcher, aged 67. She was born in Evesham and there are no records of any family in Campden who might have supported her. In the 1841 census she was living in Vicarage Cottages, newly built for the Vicar's employees, although she is listed as having 'Independent Means'. She was accepted into the Almshouses in 1842.

Eight portraits have come to light, namely of Margaret Emms, Martha Nobes, Mary Sandford, Richard Chamberlayne, Richard Cooper, William Wilson (misnamed Richard on the portrait), Sarah Penson and William Gardner. It is not known whether the other four residents were also painted. It is to be hoped that the residents themselves saw their pictures, which are remarkable for showing what must have been recognisable faces, although the unknown artist's skills did not extend to portraying feet accurately. The news must have circulated in the town through the sitters and this would certainly have added to their status.

The portraits show the seemingly well-satisfied pensioners, wearing clothes of the period with the remarkable brooch that was presumably handed down to each new resident. A description was given in the *Evesham Journal* in 1888:

> The dress of these almshouse people is very quaint, the men wearing thick black overcoats with capes attached to them, and both men and women carrying silver ornaments, dating from the time of the foundress, Juliana Viscountess Campden, daughter of Sir Baptist Hicks. The ornaments consist of the coronet and stag's head in the form of large brooches, beautiful in design and of great solidity.[42]

One of these 'brooches' has been found recently (*see* Illustration 18.f.); it is made of low-grade silver, pressed from a mould, with five rings on the back that show that it

Illustration 18.f. Brooch worn in the Campden almshouses (private collection). *Photograph by kind permission of the owners*

was designed to be sewn on the outer garment, and possibly only seen on special occasions. As the pensioners were given a new set of clothes every year, it is possible that they used their older clothes as everyday wear. An assessment of the clothes in the portraits concludes that the women's costumes are in the fashion of those a little earlier in the century but that their bonnets were very modern, which must have added considerably to their status. No other portraits like these have been found so far, although almspeople have been commemorated by statues, for example in Kirkleatham, Yorkshire, and — more recently — at Clun in Shropshire.[43]

COMPARISON OF LIFE IN ALMSHOUSES WITH THAT IN THE LOCAL COMMUNITY

In the 1851 census, Campden had 2,352 inhabitants, of whom 110 were aged 60-69 years, and seventy-five were over 70 years old. Of these 185 older people, thirty-six were listed as 'Paupers' or on 'Parish relief', and of these eighteen were also listed as labourers (mainly in agriculture) including three men over 80. The Almshouse pensioners were listed as 'Occupants of Almshouse' and not as 'Paupers', so there was a clear distinction in status as well as monetary support between those on a pension and those who claimed poor relief. There are no records showing the amount of money given to individual claimants on outdoor relief in the Shipston Union at this time but Campden Vestry accounts show that in 1834 the usual amount awarded to a single older person was 2s. a week.

The 1841-1901 censuses show that not only married couples but also a range of relatives occupied the almshouses, with the younger members of the family bringing in wages. According to the 1851 census just four occupants were living alone; one dwelling was empty and three contained married couples. Of the remaining four almshouses, William Wilson's brother, aged sixty-nine and working as a flax dresser was present; Richard Cooper's son, Francis, was an agricultural labourer; Sarah Penson's daughter was a schoolmistress and one dwelling had no head of household present but two granddaughters aged nineteen and twelve, the elder being a shoe binder.[44] These supplements from wage-earning relatives may have been seen by the Earl of Gainsborough as a way of supplementing the weekly pension at a viable level, given that the income for maintenance of the Almshouse was by then so low.

A similar situation was to be found in the local community at that time: of the thirty-six older people living on parish relief, three were living alone and thirteen were with a spouse, three were living in a household headed by an unrelated person and eight were head of the household with sons and daughters and their families. In addition, four of the older paupers had only grandchildren with them, ranging in age from three to sixteen years old.[45] The caring situation could work both ways and the Board of Guardians may have seen this outdoor relief as a way of keeping both old and young out of the workhouse. It may be inferred that outdoor relief was still seen as preferable for maintaining older people in the community. It appears, therefore, that many almshouse residents, like the paupers in the local community, were relying on family support at this time. Combining the 1851 census with the parish registers for family details it can be seen that only three of the almshouse pensioners had other adult children living in Campden and the lack of family support for the remainder may have been a contributory factor in their admission.

The pensioners who had their portraits painted in 1849-51 included two gardeners (one of whom is listed in an earlier census as a botanist), a shoemaker, a schoolmistress and the widows of a butcher and a basketmaker. The other six were agricultural labourers or their widows, giving an equal mix of skilled and unskilled people. Two of the former labourers were well-known to the Vestrymen. Richard Cooper was a regular applicant for poor relief in the years prior to his entry into the Almshouses in 1839. The 1822 Vestry Minutes detail applications for a sheet and an amount of 1s a week for his son Charles, indicating that the family was already on a regular allowance.[46] In April 1835 he applied for a pair of shoes for himself and a smock for his son Francis, but was only allowed the smock. He followed up in December with a successful request for shoes for Francis.[47] The decisions for poor relief then passed to the Shipston Union Board of Guardians but the Campden Vestrymen may have felt that such a long-standing petitioner deserved a recommendation for an almshouse place. It is interesting to consider what the views of the community might have been about a man who could have ended up in the workhouse but instead had his portrait painted. William Wilson was another almshouse resident who had previously applied for support: in 1835 he unsuccessfully asked for relief for time lost from work due to the hard weather and later he applied for 'labour'.[48] Further study that compares applicants for poor relief with almshouse pensioners might reveal more about the attitudes of those making decisions about the poor people in their community.

NOTABLE CHARACTERS

Poor though they may have been, there were some notable characters who entered almshouses and by their renown added to the publicity and high regard for the institutions. The 'Poet of the Peak', Joseph Waterfall, was a resident in the Bakewell Almshouses from 1892 until his sad death by fire in 1902. He was disabled from birth and could not write, instead cutting and pasting letters to create his poems and 'Information Broad Sheets' about the locality that he sold for a penny. He was visited by members of the British Archaeological Association in 1899 when they held their conference in Buxton and 'his collection of curios and acknowledgements from Royalty and other distinguished people to whom he had sent literary contributions were among his most treasured possessions'.[49] Doughty's Hospital, Norwich, also had residents who were well-known in the wider world. Blyth Hancock was a schoolmaster and mathematician who, when he was admitted to the hospital in 1791, had already published two books of calculations. Hancock had been given free admission, due to his poverty, to a Norwich fraternity that promoted science and learning and this led to his place at Doughty's. He continued to write mathematical papers until his death at Doughty's in 1796 and was well-regarded by local society. Elizabeth Bentley was another local celebrity, already a published poet and contributor to the *Norfolk Chronicle,* when she was admitted to Doughty's Hospital in 1835.[50] Almshouses in villages and small towns were less likely to have residents who were well-known in the wider world. There was possibly some reluctance on the part of lettered or 'genteel' people to share accommodation with the poor people of the community. In larger towns and cities there may have been less stigma and the almshouses for those with a specific background, such as military men and clergy, may well have attracted people who had fallen on hard times. St Cross Almshouses in Winchester distinguished between the forty poor men who wore black and the four 'purple brethren' who were 'decayed gentry' and wore purple gowns.[51] It is difficult today, with different attitudes to the distinctions between classes, to decide how the two groups regarded each other.

PUBLIC LIFE

The rules of many almshouses were prescriptive about the role of the almspeople in church life, in particular ensuring that they were seen to participate as a group in church services as described in Chapter 12. The rules of St Edith's Home in Emscote, Warwick (founded in 1868) included the statement that:

> All the inmates accompanied by the Superintendent shall attend Divine Service at All Saints Church, Emscote, on every Sunday in the year both in the morning and evening unless prevented by illness or other sufficient cause and on all Holy Days and other days on which prayer is said.[52]

A photograph of the Brethren of Holy Trinity Hospital, Long Melford, Suffolk returning from church shows that they walked in procession and this appears to have been the custom for many almshouses, demonstrating their institutional role in the community. Similarly, some almspeople were accorded their own group pews, giving the institution recognition amongst the congregation. The Brethren of the Lord Leycester Hospital, Warwick: 'were settled in two seates in ye middle Isle being the 4th and 5th forms'; in other words they were in a prime position in the centre of the nave.[53] In contrast, the almspeople of Leamington Hastings had the back pews on either side of the nave.[54] A memory was recorded in 1932 about Coningsby Hospital Chapel, Hereford, which had speaking tubes running from the reading desk to the worshippers' pews for residents who were hard-of-hearing. The pipes were removed in the late 1800s, but could be thought of as an early 'loop system' endeavouring to provide equal opportunities for the elderly.[55]

Even in death, recognition was given to some almspeople (*see* Illustration 3.h.). According to local memory, the residents of Campden Almshouses were accorded the distinction of the church bell tolling on their death, a custom which was not revived after World War II, to the disappointment of current almspeople who feel the loss of this sign of status.[56] Another form of recognition was the presence of the almshouse residents at public events, although this was more marked in the hospitals associated with cathedrals and large institutions, or those for retired military men such as the Chelsea Hospital in London.

From 1784, inhabitants of Bond's Hospital in Coventry were treated to an annual visit by the Corporation, and Ford's Hospital was viewed by the King of Saxony in 1844, as part of his visit to Coventry, demonstrating the Corporation's pride in their almshouses.[57] As local newspapers became more widespread, almshouse events were reported and the descriptions, in the style of the times, demonstrate attitudes about the residents and their benefactors. For example, the local paper for Campden reported in 1862:

> Our alms houses, which were built and endowed by one of the Noel family, and which are sure to gain the admiration of all who see them, not more for the beauty of the buildings than the pleasantness of their situation, were visited by Viscountess Campden and her daughter the Hon Miss Noel on Christmas Day, when the inmates, twelve in number, were each presented with 1 lb tea, 1 lb sugar and 2s 6d in cash – gifts which excited the most grateful feelings in the hearts of the recipients.[58]

And in 1888:

> TREAT TO ALMSHOUSE INMATES – On Tuesday week Mr. and Lady Constance Bellingham, who have been passing the summer at Campden House, entertained all those inmates of the almshouses that were able to come, with a substantial dinner. After the dinner they went over the house and grounds. They were brought up to the house in brakes, provided at the Noel Arms Hotel, and seemed to have enjoyed themselves greatly in spite of the

weather, which was somewhat damp and cheerless. After a good tea, they were all re-conveyed in the same manner to their homes.[59]

The tone of these newspaper reports gives some indication of the view held by the public in the 19th century: that almspeople had status in the community and deserved some attention, with an expectation that gratitude would be displayed in return. A modern view might be that just as the term 'inmate' would not be used now, an expectation of subservient gratitude is also inappropriate. The perception of the attitudes determining the treatment of almspeople and older people in the community has changed over the past hundred years but in fact it appears that the founding rules of the majority of almshouses had not been strictly observed for far longer. The examples given show that life in the almshouses was a privilege and demand for a place was high, with few people being ejected for breaking the rules. Conformity may have been more a matter of pride than fear of returning to a poorer and less noteworthy life in the community.

CONCLUSION

The evidence discussed here from the history of the Campden Almshouses demonstrates the high status given to the residents through the centuries — from individuals being named in the foundation charter in 1629, through the long-term patronage by the Earls of Gainsborough, culminating in the portraits of individuals made in the mid 19th century. Study of censuses for Campden and other almshouses shows that almspeople came from a variety of backgrounds and suggests that, although relatively poor, most of them enjoyed a better quality of life than similar people living in the community, who had to apply regularly for poor relief and other benefits and might have to work until they died or were admitted to the workhouse.

The advantage of the almshouse allowance, fuel and clothing was that it did not have to be reapplied for, as did poor relief, although conversely, almspeople suffered if these benefits were misappropriated and they had no form of appeal. Alannah Tomkins writes that:

> One plausible conclusion is that election to an almshouse could confer a measure of status substantially out of proportion to its material benefits. Indications of esteem are most clear where almspeople became embedded in community activity such as the election to charity itself, ecclesiastical celebrations or parliamentary elections. Such occasions might carry material perquisites but these were probably secondary in importance to the marks of inclusion and respect that they carried.[60]

Participation in public events and being entertained by patrons provides more evidence of the particular status given to almspeople. Future research may uncover personal recollections that indicate how almspeople regarded their position in the community whilst recognising that individual almspeople would have had differing views, though set in the context of the prevailing beliefs of their day. Given the importance now placed on recording people's memories and views, it is hoped that there will be projects around the country to archive the current experience of almshouse residents for future studies. Looking at the evidence from various almshouses it seems that the relatively high status of almspeople came, in the past, at the cost of obligation and conformity to the expectations of their patrons.

Notes

1. Murdoch, T & Vigne, R. *The French Hospital in England.* John Adamson, Cambridge, 2009, p. 64.

2. Leicester, Leicestershire and Rutland Record Office (LLRRO): DE3214/3015, 10 Oct 1590, 'Lease for 81 years; Sir Thomas Smith leases to W, Edwardes a house & building on the cawsey Way in Berrington adjoining the alms house with barns and backsides; consid. £105'.

3. National Archives (TNA): prob/11/156, Will of Sir Baptist Hicks, Viscount Campden, 1629. Berrington was the original parish in which the almshouses were built, now part of Chipping Campden.

4. Noel, G. Sir Gerard Noel MP and the Noels of Chipping Campden and Exton. *Campden and District Historical & Archaeological Society*, 2004 Appendix VI. The title Viscount Campden was subsequently used by the eldest son of the Earl of Gainsborough.

5. *Charity Commissioners' Report for Gloucester (CC* Glos.), 1819-1837, p. 370.

6. Ibid, p. 462.

7. Hall J. *A History of the Town and Parish of Nantwich, or Wich Malbank, in the County Palatine of Chester*, Didsbury, (2nd edn) 1972, pp. 428-35, 437-8.
   http://en.wikipedia.org/wiki/Special:BookSources/0901598240

8. Caffrey, H. *Almshouses in the West Riding of Yorkshire 1600-1900*, Heritage, Kings Lynn, 2006, p. 12.

9. *CC* Glos., p. 462.

10. TNA: prob/11/156 Will of Sir Baptist Hicks, Viscount Campden.

11. Noel, G. chap. 3. Exton, in Rutland, was the home of the early Noel family and after Campden House was burned down in 1645 Lady Elizabeth Hicks, widow of Sir Baptist, moved there to join her daughter and family. It is still the seat of the Earls of Gainsborough.

12. LLRRO: Gainsborough Papers, DE 3214/9205.

13. Ibid.

14. *The Reports of the Commissioners on Charities for Warwickshire*, 1819-35, p. 47.

15. Tomkins, A. *Retirement From the Noise and Hurry of the World?: the experience of almshouse life 1650-1850.* Paper presented at Voluntary Action History Society Seminar 22 April 2008, p. 22.

16. Higgs, E. *Making Sense of the Census Revisited.* London Institute of Historical Research, The National Archives of the UK, London, 2005, p. 113.

17. Censuses: 1851 HO 107/2076, fo. 140; 1861 RG 9/2237, fo. 119.

18. 1861 census RG 09/1806/96, p. 15.

19. Goose, N. & Basten, S. 'Almshouse Residency in Nineteenth-century England: an interim report'. *Family and Community History,* Vol. 12, 1, 2009. pp. 65-75.

20. Ibid. p. 74.

21. Sir Baptist Hicks Almshouses Trust (BHAT): Admissions Book 1739-1916.

22. Ibid. Order made by the Rt. Hon Baptist Earl of Gainsborough, June 1744.

23. Hall, pp. 365-7.

24. Aliberti, M. *Aspects of the Past III*, Rugby Local History Research Group, Rugby, 2001, p. 64.

25. CC Glos., p. 352.

26. BHAT: Admissions register 1739-1916.

27. BHAT: Receipts and Payments Book, 1870-1874.

28. This was not necessarily the case in other almshouses.

29. Evesham Library (EL): *Evesham Journal*, 20 Aug. 1898.

30. *CC* Glos., p. 462.

31. Ibid. p. 355-64.

32. BHAT: Declaration of Trust, Stephen Sylvester's Charity 13 October 1871.

33. *CC* Glos., p. 141.

34. Ibid, p. 150.

35. Ibid., p. 352.

36. TNA: prob/11/16 Will of Sir Baptist Hicks, Viscount Campden.

37. LLRRO: Gainsborough Papers, DE 3214/6303.

38. BHAT: Receipts and Payments book, 1870-84.

39. Wood ash was dissolved in water to create 'lye', an alkalized potassium-rich solution in which cloth woven with thread from flax or hemp was bleached; Gloucestershire Archives (GA): Accounts of the Overseers to the Poor, 1805, P81 O/V 2/3.

40. Hindle, S. *Dependency, Shame and Belonging: Badging the Deserving Poor, ca 1550-1750*. University of Warwick, 2004.

41. In 1838 Rev. F.E. Witts wrote a description of Canon Kennaway: 'Mr. Kennaway, Vicar of Campden, who is apparently a very amiable pious man, bred up among the evangelical clergy, but moderate, and now disposed I should say to keep a middle course between the party and the High Church section owing Pusey and Newman as their leaders, at present exercising no small influence – probably to good – in the Church'. *Reverend F.E. Witts, Diary of a Cotswold Parson*, ed. D. Verey. 1986, Alan Sutton, p. 43.

42. EL: *Evesham Journal* 29 Sept. 1888.

43. Sir William Turner's Almshouses, Kirkleatham. There are two figures, probably lifesize, in white stone, each in an alcove or niche, at first floor level, at either end of the building. One is male, the other female, shown in the ordinary dress and with the genuine stance of an elderly person. The figures probably date to the mid 1700's, when the almshouses were developed by the great-nephew of William Turner. (Personal communication, Helen Caffrey, 2.9.2011. The statues at Clun can be seen at www.clun.org.uk/trinity.htm, accessed April 2012).

44. Census: 1851 HO107/2076, fo. 140.

45. Ibid.

46. GA: Campden Vestry Minutes, P81 VE 2/1.

47. Ibid., P81 VE 2/5.

48. Ibid.

49. Joseph Waterfall published his poems in 1896. They are now available in Trutt, D. (ed), *Haddon Hall's Poems: an afterword,* Los Angeles, 2007, (based on material at the Local Studies Library, County Hall, Matlock, Derbyshire), URL: *www.haddon-hall.com* accessed in 2014.

50. Goose, N. and Moden, L. *A History of Doughty's Hospital, Norwich, 1687-2009*. University of Hertfordshire Press, Hatfield, 2010, pp. 43-4.

51. Cunnington, P. & Lucas, C. *Charity Costumes*. A & C Black Ltd. 1978, p. 235.

52. Warwickshire County Record Office (WCRO): DR 395/19/8.

53. WCRO: CR 1600/31. House Book of the Lord Leicester Hospital, 10th April 1664.

54. WCRO: B.Lea.Wig. Wigram, G.E. History of Leamington Hastings, 1948, p. 8.

55. Bettington, E. J. *Transactions of the Woolhope Naturalists Field Club*, 1930. p. c.

56. Personal communication from John Nicholls, Captain of the Bell Tower, St. James' Church, Chipping Campden, 2011.

57. Tomkins, A. p. 24; Cleary, J. & Orton, M. *So Long as the World Shall Endure: the 500-year history of Ford's and Bond's Hospitals*. Coventry Church Charities, Coventry, 1991, pp. 56, 130-1.

58. EL: *Evesham Journal*, 11 January 1862.

59. Ibid, 29 Sept. 1888.

60. Tomkins, A., p. 26.

CHAPTER 19
THE DERBYSHIRE ALMSHOUSES
FOR CLERGY WIDOWS

Clive Leivers

INTRODUCTION

In March 1836, a year or so after her admission to the Clergy Widows' Almshouse in Ashbourne, Derbyshire, Sarah Edwards addressed a petition for assistance to the trustees of the Beloved Wilkes' Charity based in Gloucestershire, which provided funds for the distressed widows of clergymen. Sarah was the thirty-two year old, childless widow of David Edwards, a former curate of Mucklestone and Woore in Staffordshire who had died in 1829. Her late husband had gone to Bermuda in 1822, appointed to the rectory of Warwick and Paget, but had contracted an almost fatal illness and was consequently compelled to return to England in 1825. He had remained in poor health until his death. Sarah was herself an invalid as a result of 'that peculiar affliction called a stroke of the sun' contracted during her time in the West Indies. Her only income was £13 10s. yearly received from the Almshouse trustees and a donation of £10 from another charity for the relief of poor widows and children of clergymen. She received no financial assistance from the Church, since her husband had not been a licensed curate. Sarah's petition was supported by a letter from the vicar of Ashbourne who reported that his parishioner was usually confined to her bed and, because of her illness, was frequently in need of proper food and clothing. She needed a resident servant as she was incapable of looking after herself and had no close relatives to offer assistance. Her yearly income was not quite £25. Sarah was granted £10 by the Wilkes' trustees and made a further application ten years later, the result of which was not recorded. She remained a resident at Ashbourne until her death in 1866 when her personal effects were assessed for probate at under £100.[1]

    Sarah's pitiable story illustrates several features about admission to, and life in, the clergy widows' almshouses: admission at an early age; the absence of any prior link to the locality; the co-residence of a servant; and the length of her stay in the establishment.

    These features distinguish these establishments from the generality of almshouses, where provision was concerned with the relief of the poor and aged, often of the parish or town in which the establishment lay. No such conditions applied to the three clergy widows' establishments in Derbyshire and this chapter will further explore the differences between these foundations and other almshouses. After a brief description of the foundation of the three almshouses and the criteria for admission, the overall situation regarding their inmates as set out in the decennial censuses from 1841 to 1901 will be examined. Thereafter specific aspects of the widows' lives, both before and after admission, will be reviewed: age at admission; length of residence; the interval between widowhood and admission; prior links to Derbyshire; stipends; and life in the community after admission.

Illustration 19.a. Ashbourne Clergy Widows Almshouse.
Photo © Clive Leivers

Since no admission registers survive for these three Derbyshire almshouses, the review will primarily use the 19th-century census returns, supplemented by records of birth/baptism, marriage and death, trade directories and local newspapers, to determine the facts relating to these topics. The other main sources used are those providing information on the career of the widows' husbands: their benefices, from *Crockford's Clerical Directories* and the Clergy of the Church of England database; and – in a few cases – the provision they were able to make for their relicts, taken from probate records. Where appropriate and possible, comparisons will be drawn with similar establishments for clergy widows in other areas and with the more general almshouse provision in Derbyshire.

THE DERBYSHIRE FOUNDATIONS

The three Derbyshire establishments devoted to providing accommodation for the widows of Anglican clergymen were Large's Hospital in Friar Gate, Derby, the house on Church Street, Ashbourne founded by Nicholas Spalden (in which Sarah Edwards resided) and the nearby establishment at Mapleton founded by Sir Rowland Okeover.

All three were foundations of the early 18th century although this seems to be simply coincidental since establishments for clergy widows had been founded in other locations from 1610 onwards. In his will, dated 6 April 1710, Nicholas Spalden directed the building of 'four neat and pretty houses for entertaining the widows of four clergymen of the Church of England' to each of whom he bequeathed £10 per year. Appointments were to be made without any restriction as to the place of residence of the deceased husband. Because of disputes over the endowment, it was not until 1752 that land was purchased and surviving building accounts suggest that it was a further fifteen years or so before the building work was completed. By 1857 the annual stipend had increased by dint of three further endowments to £35 10s.[2]

Edward Large, in his will of 1709, bequeathed funds for the erection of 'five small almshouses for the habitation of five poor parsons or vicars widows' near Nuns Green in Derby, with each resident receiving a stipend of £17 per annum. The establishment had been built by 1721 when one of the first residents, Mary Broom, left her property to the almshouse trustees. The original foundation was rebuilt in 1880, by which time the annual stipend had increased to £30.[3]

The third benefactor was Rowland Okeover of Okeover Hall, just over the River Dove in Staffordshire. In an indenture of 1727 he directed the building, after his death, of 'a neat and convenient house … for three such widows of clergymen of the Church of England as the trustees should think most proper' with an annual stipend of £10. Okeover died in 1729 and the almshouse in Mapleton seems to have been built within a year or so of his death. Appointments were made without any limitation as to the county or diocese in which the deceased husbands may have resided. By the time of the Charity Commission enquiry of 1827-30 the stipend had been increased to £30.[4]

These Derbyshire benefactors were not, of course, unique in their concern for the welfare of clergy widows, but their foundations were somewhat unusual in the absence of any age or residential restrictions on admittance. The three individuals were laymen, as were the majority of the founders of clergy widows' almshouses, exceptions being the establishments at: Bromley, founded by the Bishop of Rochester in 1666; Salisbury, founded by the Bishop of that diocese in 1685; Winchester, similarly founded by the diocesan bishop in 1673; and Wigton, founded by the Rector of Rothbury in 1723.[5]

TABLE 19.I
The almshouse households 1841-1901[6]

| Year | Almswomen | Relatives | Servants | Age of Almswomen | | |
				Average	Range	Median
1841	7	4	2	54	37-75	45
1851	11	14	3	58	38-72	59
1861	12*	7	6	56	40-79	55
1871	11*	9	8	60	47-71	63
1881	9	8	8	66	57-81	62
1891	10	12	8	67	45-88	67
1901	10	12	9	68	46-86	70

* includes almshouse residents visiting elsewhere

Table 19.I shows the ages and co-residents of the women in the three almshouses, as recorded in the seven decennial census returns from 1841 to 1901. There were a total of twelve places available for the clergy widows (five in Derby, four in Ashbourne and three in Mapleton); as the table shows, only in 1861 were all places filled. The 1841 census enumerators' books, particularly for Ashbourne, are not clearly legible, but one residence seems to be indicated as uninhabited in all three locations. There was one uninhabited residence recorded in Mapleton in both 1851 and 1871, and two in Ashbourne in 1881. From that year onwards, there are only one or two residents recorded in Mapleton, suggesting some decline in its popularity or a deterioration in conditions, although vacancies were advertised in 1880 and 1886.

On only three occasions were co-resident relatives absent from the almshouses: at Mapleton in 1841 and 1891, and at Ashbourne in 1881. Of the sixty-six co-residents enumerated, the vast majority were children of the almswomen, with twelve sons and thirty-eight daughters living with their widowed mothers. The remainder were seven grandchildren, three sisters, three presumably unrelated visitors, an aunt, a niece and a boarder. Thirty-four of the daughters were unmarried, and in some cases their co-residency was long term. In Ashbourne, Harriett Grover lived with her mother in both 1841 and 1851; Alice Gibson was resident in 1871 and from 1891 to 1901; and Elizabeth Edwards from 1891 to 1901. Sybil Oliver had joined her mother in Mapleton by 1901 and was still living there ten years later. Mary Garton was recorded in three successive censuses – 1861 to 1881 – living with her mother in Derby and almost certainly stayed until her mother's death in 1888 since she was heading her own household in Derby in 1891 at the age of sixty-three.

The number of servants in the almshouses steadily increased over the 60 years. In 1841 and 1851 only the Ashbourne widows had resident servants: three of the four residents in 1851 having this assistance. From 1861 onwards the Derby widows increasingly came to employ resident servants: two of the five widows in 1861; four of the five residents in the following two census years; and all four residents in 1901. It was not until 1881 that servants came to reside in Mapleton but from then on each widow had a resident servant apart from one 1901 resident. Each widow had just the one servant except for Mary Smith of Ashbourne in 1871 and Mary Spencer of Derby in 1881, both of whom employed two. The only servant found in successive census returns was Ann Allen, who is recorded as serving the invalid Sarah Edwards (who began this narrative) from 1841 to 1861 and may perhaps have been with her mistress throughout her thirty years in the almshouse. Of the forty-two individual servants named, twenty-nine were born in Derbyshire with another eight native to the adjacent counties of Staffordshire, Leicestershire and Nottinghamshire. All were described as general/domestic servants except for two housemaids, one cook and one lady's help.

The presence of servants in the general run of almshouses was a rare event. In the other Ashbourne establishments, of which there were four, one blind widow aged seventy-five had a resident servant in 1881, as did a pair of sisters in their seventies. This absence of servants is not unexpected, as most almshouse residents came from the level of society that would be unlikely to have employed servants in their own homes and their income and accommodation in the almshouse would probably not have allowed for the payment or housing of a servant. In contrast, the accommodation occupied by the clergy widows provided room for resident servants: the 1911 census returns show that there were five or six rooms at Mapleton; six in Ashbourne and six or seven in Derby. Moreover, the financial situation of the clergy widows (discussed in a later section) was markedly better than that of most other almshouse residents. In some other clergy widows' establishments servants were found as often as in the Derbyshire examples. The 1881 census records that in the establishment in South Cerney, Gloucestershire, all the almswomen had servants, as did six of the seven widows enumerated at an establishment in Winchester. Their incidence varied: at Bromley College, the largest of the clergy widows' establishments with forty places, twenty-three of the thirty-seven residents had servants; but they were kept by only five of the twenty-four residents in the Duchess of Somerset's Hospital at Froxfield in Wiltshire.[7]

AGE AT ADMISSION

Some establishments for clergy widows, such as those at Salisbury, Lichfield, Wigton and Cambridge, imposed a minimum age of admission. This was forty at Cambridge, forty-six at Wigton and fifty at both Lichfield and Salisbury. However, there was no such criterion for admission to the three Derbyshire houses.[8]

TABLE 19.II

Age of residents on admission to Derbyshire almshouses

Age on entry	Ashbourne	Derby	Mapleton
30-40	1	5	Nil
41-50	4	3	2
51-60	4	3	4
61-70	1	2	1
Over 70	Nil	3	1
TOTAL	**10**	**16**	**8**

Notes

Date of admission taken as first reference traced in census, trade directory or newspaper report.

Excludes individuals where only one piece of evidence available, e.g. 1841 census.

Year of birth derived from census returns, verified in some cases by reference to baptismal dates

Sarah Edwards was the youngest widow in being admitted at the age of thirty-two but there were three other admissions of widows in their thirties and over 40 per cent of the admissions recorded in Table 19.II were of widows admitted to the Derbyshire almshouses by the time they reached the age of fifty.

Whilst Sarah Edwards was childless, some of the other younger widows brought their children into the almshouse. One such was Mary Francis, a resident in Large's Hospital from 1851 to her death in 1873. Her husband James had been incumbent at St Paul's in Newport, Monmouthshire, until his death in 1843. Mary was then aged thirty, had six children under the age of ten, and was again pregnant. The 1851 census records Mary as a widow aged thirty-eight with two of her children, aged nine and seven, living with her in the almshouse, with others in boarding schools, including a boy and girl in the Clergy Orphans School in Marylebone. The two youngest children had also left their mother for other institutions by 1861: son Albert to Oundle grammar school and daughter Georgina to the Adult Orphans Institution in Regent's Park, London, which had been established in 1820 to educate as governesses the orphan daughters of clergymen and military officers.[9] At the other end of the age spectrum were Jane Slight, Sarah Jane Groves and Ellen Milward: respectively, seventy-six, seventy-five and seventy-five at the time of their admission. All three had Derbyshire connections with their husbands having livings in the county.

Whilst the husbands of Mrs Slight and Mrs Milward had been long-serving clergymen in Derbyshire (both for about forty years) by contrast Sarah Groves and her husband had lived a relatively short time in Derbyshire prior to her admission to the Mapleton Almshouse.

William Kynaston Groves had spent thirty years as minister of the British church in Boulogne from 1842 to 1872. On his return to England he was appointed as rector of Thorpe in Derbyshire, the parish adjacent to Mapleton. He died in 1878 and his widow had moved into the almshouse by 1881 together with her daughter Josephine. Their stay was relatively brief. Sarah is recorded as resident in Mapleton in a trade directory of 1888, but by the census of 1891 Josephine and her mother (then described as blind) were living in Uttoxeter where Sarah died a year later at the age of eighty-seven.[10]

LENGTH OF RESIDENCE

As shown in Table 19.III, for the majority of the clergy widows their residence in the almshouse was a long-term affair. Over two-thirds of the women were resident for over ten years, with three spending more than thirty years in their institution. These three, all Ashbourne residents, were Caroline Gibson, Elizabeth Hough and Jessy Lammin.

TABLE 19.III
Length of residence of clergy widows in almshouses

Residence In Years	Ashbourne	Almshouse Derby	Mapleton
5-10	1	6	4
11-20	2	2	3
21-30	4	8	1
Over 30	3	Nil	Nil
TOTAL	**10**	**16**	**8**

Notes
Cessation of residence derived from records of death (newspaper reports or Free BMD) or last recorded entry in census or trade directory.
Length of stay ranges from 6 to 36 years, with the average being 18.3 and the median 20 years.

The longest residence – of thirty-six years – was that of Elizabeth Hough. She had been widowed at the age of forty-six when her husband George, then the chaplain at the Westminster house of correction, died in 1878. At the time of the 1881 census, Elizabeth was a visitor in a household in Burton upon Trent but is listed as resident in Ashbourne in a directory of that year, presumably moving in after the date of the census. Her two daughters were then in school in London, the younger, Rose, at the Clergy Orphans Asylum in Marylebone. In 1890 Elizabeth petitioned the Beloved Wilkes charity for assistance. Her income was said to be £53 per annum: £33 from the almshouse trustees, £10 from the diocesan fund, and a further £10 from two other charities. Elizabeth spent the rest of her life in Ashbourne, dying in 1917 at the age of eighty-six.[11] Age at admission was clearly a factor in the number of years of residence and this relationship is shown by the chart in Fig. 19.A.

The only Derbyshire almshouse for which a list of residents survives is the establishment for three poor women at Newbold on the outskirts of Chesterfield. This gives dates of admission and discharge (in all but three cases on death) but not ages, although census returns show all the almswomen to be over sixty years old.[12] Of the twenty-seven women whose records can be used, two stayed less than a year, another six less than five years, eight between five and ten years, nine from eleven to twenty years and two over twenty years. The average length of stay was just over nine and a half years, about half the average for the clergy widows.

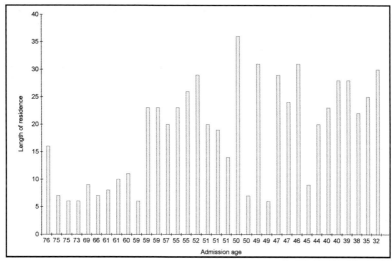

Fig. 19.A. Relationship between age of admission and length of residence in an almshouse

As at Newbold, the clergy widows usually stayed in the almshouse until death, with a few instances where widows appear to have been resident shortly before their death, but moving to spend their last days with relatives. This was certainly so with Anne Hayden, who died in her daughter's home in Derby after seven years' residence in Large's Hospital. Sarah Groves' relatively short stay in Mapleton has already been noted and the case of one other widow was out of the normal run of long-term, continuous residence. Elizabeth Nicholls was resident in Mapleton in 1841, then aged forty. Ten years later she had moved to the Derby establishment, where again her residence was relatively short-term, for by the following census she was to be found in Newton's College, Lichfield, another almshouse for the widows of clergy. Here she remained until her death in 1886, so Elizabeth had spent at least forty-five of her eighty-five years as an almshouse resident.[13] It has not proved possible to identify her husband, but Elizabeth was a native of Staffordshire and may possibly have been waiting for a vacancy in her home county, although a higher stipend – £50 in 1834 compared to the £30 in Derby and Mapleton later in the century – may have been an added attraction!

LIFE BEFORE ADMISSION

One other factor determining length of residence was the interval between widowhood and admission to the almshouse. Table 19.IV shows the situation for those widows where the date of their husband's death has been established. Twenty-one of the thirty listed had entered an almshouse in the first ten years of widowhood.

Of those individuals admitted within five years of widowhood, we have already detailed the case histories of Sarah Groves and Elizabeth Hough. The other two widows in this category were Eliza Flesher and Elizabeth Snowden. Mrs Flesher was admitted to Derby in 1856 at the age of fifty; she had been widowed four years earlier when her husband, John Thomas, died in his rectory at Tiffield, Northants, a benefice he had held for twenty years in succession to his father. Eliza was to remain in the almshouse for twenty-nine years until her death in January 1885, when she left an estate worth over £2,500.[14]

TABLE 19.IV
Interval between widowhood and admission

Interval (in years)	Ashbourne	Derby	Mapleton
Under 5 years	1	1	2
5-10	5	11	1
11-20	3	Nil	2
21-30	1	Nil	2
Over 30	1	Nil	Nil
TOTAL	**11**	**12**	**7**

But, as Table 19.IV demonstrates, several widows made a life outside the almshouse for a good number of years following widowhood. Mary Spencer had been widowed for thirty-one years before she became resident in Derby in 1874. Her husband John had been appointed as chaplain in the East India Company in Bengal in 1840. Two daughters had been born in Oxford before the family went to India, and Martha Ann was born in India shortly before her father died there in 1843 at the early age of thirty-three. The widow and her daughters returned to England and the 1851 census records Mary and her youngest daughter living with her married sister in Belper, Derbyshire with the two eldest girls in the Clergy Daughters' School at Casterton in Westmorland. By 1861 Mary had set up house in Prestbury, in Gloucestershire, with her three daughters (none shown as employed), a cook and housemaid. This situation had ended by 1871 when Mary and her youngest daughter were lodging with a carpenter in Weymouth; three years later Mary had been admitted to the almshouse, still accompanied by her youngest daughter. It may be that Mary's changing circumstances indicate a declining income until she was compelled to seek admission to a charitable institution, although she was still able to employ two resident servants in the almshouse. She died suddenly there in 1884 at the age of seventy-three.[15]

One of the other women who spent over twenty years of her widowhood before admission to the almshouse was Frances Oliver. She was the second wife of Samuel, who was the vicar of Calverton, in Nottinghamshire, for some forty-seven years. They were married in 1863 soon after the death of Samuel's first wife, who was alive in 1861 when the census of that year recorded Frances as the twenty-one year old housemaid in the vicarage. By 1871 Frances had borne four children and was widowed three years later when Samuel died at the age of seventy-four; his estate was worth less than £200. The 1881 census lists Frances as a nurse in the household of a surgeon in Nottingham, with two of her sons in schools for sons of the clergy at Leatherhead and Canterbury, and a daughter lodging with a farm labourer in Southwell, Nottinghamshire. Ten years later Frances was running a lodging house in Skegness, but is listed as resident in Mapleton in a directory of 1895. She had been joined in the almshouse by her daughter Sybil when the 1901 census was taken and this remained the situation ten years later. Frances lived another ten years before dying in 1921, aged eighty-two, having spent twenty-six years as an almshouse resident.[16]

STIPENDS

Some information about the stipends payable to the Derbyshire widows has been given earlier. Over the period covered by this review, payments had increased and continued to rise during the latter half of the 19th century. By 1857, the Ashbourne residents were receiving £35 10s. per year and by 1912 this had risen to around £43. In 1860, payment to the widows in Derby was £30 and this sum had doubled by 1908. Mapleton widows were in receipt of £30 per year by 1830 but this increased only slightly to £35 in 1884.[17] These figures were in the middle range of the payments identified in other clergy widows' establishments. These ranged from a meagre £2 a year at Wragby, Lincolnshire in 1861, through £10 at Newton Abbot (in 1850) to £50 at Lichfield (in 1834), £70 at the establishment at Osgathorpe, Leicestershire (in 1878) and £80 at Winchester in 1895.[18] They were, however, generally higher than the annual payments to residents in other Derbyshire almshouses at the time of the Charity Commission enquiry of 1827-30 when the range was from £2 – paid to the widows at Cromford – to the £20 received by the male residents at nearby Wirksworth. The average annual pension paid to almshouse residents in the West Riding of Yorkshire over the second half of the 19th century was between ten and fifteen pounds.[19]

So the Derbyshire clergy widows were relatively well off: sufficient at least to be able to employ servants, as we have noted previously. Their situations clearly varied and whilst some – like Sarah Edwards and Elizabeth Hough – were dependent on periodic charitable grants, others were certainly quite wealthy women. We have already seen that Eliza Flesher left an estate of more that £2,500; when Annie Burn died in Derby in 1928 her effects were valued at over £2,000; Jane Slight left £1,704 in 1907; and Rebecca Edwards £5,279 in 1914.[20]

LOCALITIES

As mentioned in the introduction, there was no residential qualification for admission to the three Derbyshire almshouses. This was unusual since most similar establishments were provided for the widows of clergy from a specified area. For example, the Duchess of Somerset's Hospital at Froxfield in Wiltshire, founded in 1686, provided thirty places for widows from Wiltshire, Somerset and Berkshire, one third of whom were to be clergy widows. The Matron's College in Salisbury restricted admission to widows of clergy ordained in that diocese. The College of Matrons at Wigton in Cumberland provided six places for the widows of clergymen in the diocese of Carlisle, that part of the diocese of Chester that included parishes in Cumberland, and two specified parishes in Northumberland and County Durham. The Winchester almshouse was for widows of clergy within the diocese and the parish of Taunton Deane and Newton's College in Lichfield gave priority to the widows and daughters of clergy who had served in the cathedral.[21] Table 19.V analyses by county the place of birth of the widows and the location of their husbands' last benefice where this is known.

This table indicates that the widows came from locations across England and Wales, but that there was apparently some preference to remain in, or return to Derbyshire in around 15 per cent of cases. Three of the five widows whose husbands had been Derbyshire clergymen have already been noted: Mesdames Slight, Groves and Milward. The others were Mary Pearman and Caroline Gibson. James Pearman had held three positions in the county:

as curate of North Wingfield, vicar of Pilsley, and finally rector of Tansley and vicar of Crich. Mary was widowed in 1890 at the age of forty and had entered the Derby almshouse by 1900 after initially setting up house in Matlock with three children. Mrs Gibson's husband had been perpetual curate at Stanley for nine years before his death in 1866; she had entered the Ashbourne Almshouse by 1871 and was resident for thirty-one years until her death in 1902 at the age of eighty.[22]

TABLE 19.V
County of widow's birthplace and husband's benefice

Widow's Birthplace

4 instances:	Derbyshire, London
3 instances:	Nottinghamshire, Staffordshire
2 instances:	Cheshire, Lancashire, Oxfordshire, Shropshire, Warwickshire
1 instance:	Cardiganshire, Cumberland, Devonshire, Gloucestershire, Herefordshire, Leicestershire, Lincolnshire, Suffolk, Yorkshire, Ireland, Channel Islands
Total	**35**

Husband's Benefice

5 instances :	Derbyshire
4 instances :	Staffordshire
3 instances :	Northamptonshire, Nottinghamshire
2 instances :	Cumberland, Surrey, Yorkshire
1 instance:	Hampshire, Herefordshire, Huntingdon, Lancashire, Lincolnshire, London, Middlesex, Monmouth, Rutland, India
Total	**31**

It is readily understandable that widows like these should have a preference for a local establishment but, as Table 19.V shows, in another four cases widows sought a return to their native county, probably because of continuing family ties.

Mary Spencer (born in Belper in 1812) has already been discussed. Her first residence on return to England from India was with her sister at her birthplace and she eventually ended her days in the Derby establishment. The other three Derbyshire natives were Frances Fayrer (born and married in Tissington), Eliza Flesher (born in Duffield) and Mary Ann Smith. Mrs Smith's husband, Benjamin, had been master at the grammar school at Drax in Yorkshire from 1828 until his death in 1842. Mary was a native of Ockbrook near Derby but the couple married at Kellington in Yorkshire in 1828. Mary moved to the Ashbourne Almshouse between 1851, when she was visiting in a surgeon's household in County Durham (with a daughter in the Clergy Orphans' School in Marylebone) and 1857 when she is listed in a directory. The Smiths' eldest daughter, Amelia Ann, had died in Ashbourne at the age of twelve in 1841 and this was probably another reason why Mary wished to return to the county of her birth. In 1871 she was visiting her brother in Stoke-on-Trent and died in Ashbourne in 1876 aged seventy.[23]

Two other widows also had previous links to Derbyshire. The benefices of Priscilla Crowther's husband at the time of his death in 1881 were parishes abutting Derbyshire – Alstonefield and Longnor – but he had previously held a curacy in Derbyshire at Taddington for a few years. Agatha Eldrid had married in Derby in 1869 when her husband Edwin had been curate of St Peter's in the town. After his death in 1893 the widow had entered Large's

Almshouse by 1900 (probably accompanied by the three adult children recorded in the census of the following year). Her eldest daughter married in Derby in 1906 but by the census of 1911 Agatha had left the almshouse to live with her sister in Gloucester.[24]

Illustration 19.b. Large's Hospital for Clergy Widows
from Hutton's *The History of Derby*, 1817, p. 45

The cluster of four widows from Staffordshire benefices can probably be explained by the fact that Derbyshire was at this time within the diocese of Lichfield; the three from Nottinghamshire simply by dint of proximity, but the group from Northamptonshire is less explicable. All three benefices were in the same part of that county – at Towcester, Tiffield and Patishall – and all the widows entered Large's Hospital: Eliza Flesher in 1856, Mary Garton in 1860 and Laura Welch by 1891. This suggests perhaps some personal recommendation or a particular relationship between the trustees of the almshouse and the clergy of that specific part of Northamptonshire.

RELATIONSHIPS OUTSIDE THE ALMSHOUSE

We have already seen that several of the widows had co-resident relatives at various times during their stay in the almshouses. But it was not just within the almshouse doors that the widows maintained ongoing contact with relatives. Jessy Lammin had settled in Ashbourne by 1848, and by 1851 three of her daughters had joined her in the town and were running a girls' boarding academy on Church Street near to the almshouse in which their mother lived. This continued to be the case for at least twenty-five years and during that time the sisters were regularly featured in the parish magazine as contributors to various good causes – including the National and Sunday schools – with the eldest daughter being a Sunday school teacher. Jessy herself is listed as a subscriber to the National school fund in 1875. The family left Ashbourne in 1879 and moved to Croydon where Jessy died a year later.[25] The same situation was found with Lydia Grover, who had entered Ashbourne by 1829, five years after the death of her husband, the curate of Finningley in north Nottinghamshire. Like the Lammin daughters, two of the Grover girls became pupils at the Clergy Daughters' School in Westmorland, being contemporaries of the Brontë sisters there. By 1842 all three daughters had also established a boarding academy on Church Street, which continued until at least 1857, some five years after the mother's death. These three spinsters themselves became resident in a clergy widows' almshouse – the establishment at South Cerney, in Gloucestershire, which also admitted the dependents of clergy as well as their widows – where they are listed in the 1881 census.[26]

Establishing a girls' school seemed a popular career choice – or perhaps one from the limited options open to the daughters of clergymen – particularly after education at one of the charitable schools for the daughters of clergymen. Indeed, the admission registers of the establishment at Cowan Bridge/Casterton specifically record both the Grover and Lammin daughters as being educated for governesses and grants were available from the Cholmondeley Charity for the education of daughters of clergy for teaching.[27] In Osmaston Road in Derby, the daughter of Anne Hayden was running a ladies' day and boarding school in 1855 when Anne was supposedly resident in Large's Hospital. A Charity Commission enquiry of 1860, two years after Anne's death at her daughter's address, was told that: 'Mrs Hayden for a long time lodged with her daughter in the town and had a lodger in the almshouse who paid rent to her'.[28] One of the almswomen may have been running a school herself — a directory of 1874 listed Caroline Gibson, who was resident in the Ashbourne almshouse from 1871 to 1902, as running a boarding and day school in the town but this may have referred to her co-resident daughter, who had the same christian name.[29]

As well as having relatives nearby, other widows kept in touch with kin some distance away. In 1871 Mary Smith had made the journey from the Ashbourne Almshouse to visit her brother in Stoke-on-Trent and Emma Hutton had made the longer journey from Derby to see her sister at Penge, in Surrey. Emma's husband had been a curate at Norwood, in Surrey, and her daughter was a pupil at the school in Marylebone in 1861. There may have been stronger links with London because the 1860 Charity Commission enquiry was told that Mrs Hutton 'was to all intents a non-resident as she keeps a lodging house in London and is seldom seen in the hospital'. The Commissioner recommended that the matter needed resolution and since Emma remained in the almshouse until her death in 1888 it seems as if she did subsequently comply with the requirement for regular residence.[30] In 1881, three years before her death in Ashbourne at the age of seventy-six, Frances Fayrer travelled to visit her married daughter on the Isle of Wight.

Other widows had clearly established friendships outside the almshouse. In both the 1851 and 1861 census Elizabeth Parsons, resident in Mapleton from 1841, was a visitor in the household of Thomas Maskery, a farmer in nearby Okeover, accompanied in 1861 by her granddaughter Anne Williams; and in 1861 Mary Francis, who had been resident in the Derby Almshouse from 1851, was visiting an iron founder in the town.

There is one reported example of a widow being active in charitable works herself. Rebecca Edwards was a resident in Ashbourne by 1878; when she died in 1914, at the age of ninety-five, she had been living for a few years with her daughter in Buxton but was buried in Ashbourne cemetery. The newspaper report of her funeral reminded readers that she had spent thirty-three years as an Ashbourne resident and had lived under six sovereigns. More pertinently she had served as secretary and treasurer of the Orphans' Association (from 1878 onwards) and was a constant help to the vicar of the town.[31]

Rebecca was surely typical of many of the widows: used to helping their husbands in their parochial duties, and spending a good part of their active years in the almshouse, it seems highly likely that many of them would continue to have an involvement in the church and charitable life in the neighbourhood.

OTHER CHARITABLE PROVISION

The death of any husband creates stress and difficulty for his widow, particularly those with young children, but 'clergy wives and families were in a particularly vulnerable position … they were immediately homeless and without income'.[32] They were, of course, not unique in this. The widows of agricultural labourers living in tied cottages were similarly placed. However, the impact of this sudden change in circumstances is illustrated by the case of Jessy Lammin. Within two months of the death of her husband in March 1837 the widow had returned to her native parish of Moresby in Cumberland and two of her daughters had been admitted to the Clergy Daughters' School in Casterton.[33]

In a couple of cases we can gauge the degree of the financial difficulties facing the widow through the value of their husbands' estates given in the national probate calendars. That of James Pearman was assessed at £131 13s. on his death in 1890, leaving his wife to cope with two children of school age; Henry Welch's estate was valued at less than £100 in 1883 though his widow had just one child to bring up.[34]

The parishioners and friends of the deceased clergyman were, in some cases, quick to recognise the need for prompt action to help the widow. In the sermon preached at the 1864 funeral of William Chettle, late chaplain at Nottingham workhouse, Reverend Cope pointed out that the widow and her child were 'unprovided for' and he hoped that 'this would not be lost sight of'.[35] In the event, the widowed Hannah found a home in Large's hospital by 1871 when her daughter was yet another pupil at the Clergy Orphans' School in Marylebone. Henrietta had joined her mother in the almshouse in 1881, employed as a school governess.

The financial help given to Anne Fenton, after the death of her husband in 1846, can be more readily quantified. An appeal headed 'Distressed Clergyman's Family' appeared in the *Morning Post* on at least two occasions in 1847. This stated that Richard Fenton had died after a few days illness 'leaving a widow entirely destitute and eight children, none of whom are in a condition to render her the smallest pecuniary assistance', with six of them totally dependent on her (the 1841 census records five children residing with their parents, with ages ranging from one to thirteen). A list of 159 donations already received was appended, ranging from £5 from the Bishop of Lincoln, £30 from the owner of Cockerington Hall (the parish in which Richard had been vicar), £10 each from two MPs, £10 from the fellows of Magdalen College, Oxford to 10s from the landlord of the Masons Arms, Louth who had also collected £1 in 'sundry sums' at his public house.[36] Anne had moved into the Mapleton Almshouse by 1851 accompanied by three children between the ages of fifteen and nineteen, the youngest of whom was the only one with an occupation.

A similar public appeal was made in 1843 for Mary Francis and her 'six infant children' who had been left in 'a state of dependency' by the sudden death of her husband. It was confidently hoped that those who 'delight in the Christian obligation of succouring the fatherless and distressed' would respond to the call for contributions to the trust fund for which £900 had already been raised in the first three weeks of Mary's widowhood.[37]

A more spontaneous collection was held for Frances Fayrer when her husband died in 1850. Robert Fayrer had been curate of Emmanuel Church in Camberwell since 1842 and within a fortnight of his death, his parishioners had collected £500, including a donation of £20 from the Bishop of Winchester, in aid of the widow and her three children.[38] As already noted, Frances quite soon made the return to her native Derbyshire, having secured admission to the Ashbourne Almshouse by 1855.

Most widows, however, had recourse to a range of national and diocesan charities if needed. We have already seen that Elizabeth Hough received £10 annually from a diocesan fund and £5 from the Cholmondeley Charity and there were associations for the relief of the widows and orphans of clergymen operating nationally and in most counties.

The national organisation of the Sons of the Clergy was founded in 1655 to meet a pressing need among clergy families for charitable help and continues to operate today. One of the Derbyshire widows was a beneficiary, with the charity supporting the education of the daughter of Sarah Tate at Cowan Bridge in 1826. A society for the relief of the families of distressed clergymen within the deaneries of Derby, Ashbourne, Repington and Castillery had been instituted in 1721 and in 1836 it was reported that the Clergy Widows & Orphans Society for the Archdeaconry of Stafford had distributed the sum of £520 to a number of applicants in amounts varying from £10 to £45 each.[39]

Throughout this chapter several examples have been quoted where the children of the widows were receiving education in schools for the children of the clergy, some specifically for orphans. In total, fourteen of the widows had secured places for their children at the establishments at Cowan Bridge/Casterton (nine daughters), Marylebone (seven daughters and one son), Canterbury (four sons) and Leatherhead (two sons), and this was a constant feature throughout the period under review. The annual fees at Casterton were £14 in 1848 but the education at Leatherhead was free for the sons of poor clergymen.[40]

CONCLUSION

The provision of almshouse places for clergy widows was part of a comprehensive system for the care of the widows and children of deceased clergymen. Although the rationale behind the establishment of such almshouses was essentially the same as for all other foundations – to provide residential accommodation for people in need through poverty or old age – this review has identified distinctive features of the clergy widows' establishments, which in some respects were specific to the three Derbyshire houses.

In broad terms, in Derbyshire admission was not restricted to the elderly, whilst two foundations elsewhere imposed a lower age limit of fifty. Most of the establishments elsewhere required that the applicants were widows of clergymen from a specified area, usually a diocese or county in which the almshouse lay, but again no such restriction applied in Derbyshire. The founders of some houses specified that the clergy widows should be 'poor' or 'indigent', as was the case for Canterbury, Exeter, Wigton and the Derby almshouses, but this was not a requirement at Ashbourne and Mapleton.

The stipends received by the clergy widows were generally higher than those received in other almshouses, enabling them to retain residential servants and in many cases to have relatives residing with them and therefore probably living a more comfortable life than other almsmen and women. Because of the lower or non-existent age limits for admission, several of the widows spent a good part of their lives in the almshouse; most stayed in the house until death and no case of remarriage has been found among the Derbyshire clergy widows, perhaps underlining the assumption that life in the almshouse was reasonably comfortable and congenial, with fellow residents sharing values and expectations, and support provided throughout by a range of charitable provision sponsored by the Anglican church.

Notes

1.   Bristol Record Office (BRO): 33792/49/3 and 11; Derbyshire Record Office (DRO): Will of Sarah
         Edwards, proved 1867.

2. *Charity Commissioners' Report for Derby* (*CC* Derbys), London, 1815-35; Henstock, A. *A Georgian Country Town. Ashbourne,* Vol 2., Ashbourne, 1991, p. 61-4; F White, *History, Gazetteer and Directory of Derbyshire and Sheffield.* Sheffield, 1857, pp. 400-1.

3. Hutton, W. *The History of Derby.* Derby, 1817, p. 44; Kemp, H. L. *Derby Charities,* Derby, 1861, pp. 15-6.

4. CC Derbys, 1815-35, pp. 69-71.

5. URL: www.bromleycollege.org/history accessed 14 June 2010; Lysons, D. & S., *Magna Britannia,* Vol. 4. Cumberland. London, 1816, pp. 159-75. URL: www.british-history.ac.uk/report.aspx?compid=50694, accessed 13 Aug. 2010; 'Winchester: Charities', in *A History of the County of Hampshire,* Vol. 5. 1912, pp. 76-80. URL: www.british-history.ac.uk/report.aspx?compid=42053, accessed 8 Aug. 2010; 'Salisbury: Charities', in *A History of the County of Wiltshire:* Vol. 6. 1962, pp. 168-78. URL: www.british-history.ac.uk/report.aspx?compid=41807 accessed 9 June 2010.

6. Census Enumerators Books, the National Archives, Kew: 1841, HO107 197/1,198/4, 199/17; 1851, HO107/2143, 2146; 1861, RG9 2503, 2521-2; 1871, RG10 3571, 3598, 3600; 1881, RG11 3398.3423-4; 1891, RG13 2731, 2753-4; 1901, RG13 3221, 3236, 3239.

7. Information supplied by John Loosley (South Cerney) and Noel Grimmett (Winchester); Census 1881, RG11/853 (Bromley), RG12/75 (Froxfield).

8. Gardner, R. *History, Gazetteer & Directory of Cambridge.* Peterborough, 1851, p. 161; White, W. *History, Gazetteer & Directory of Staffordshire.* Sheffield, 1834, pp. 98-9; Mannix & Whellan, *History Gazetteer and Directory of Cumberland.* Beverly, 1847, p. 497; Salisbury Charities, 1962.

9. *The Standard,* 7 and 14 June 1843; Thornbury, G.W. *'The Regent's Park' Old and New London,* Vol. 5. London, 1878, pp. 262-86. URL: http://www.british-history.ac.uk/report.aspx?compid=45236, accessed 24 Aug. 2011.

10. Venn, J.A. *Alumni Cantabrigenses.* London, 1922-54; Kelly & Co *Derbyshire Directory.* London, 1888, p. 233; Census 1891 RG13 2193.

11. *The Times,* 21 Jan. 1878; Kelly & Co *Derbys.* 1881, p. 903; BRO: 33792/49/29.

12. DRO: D 2398 A/PF 2.

13. Census 1861, RG9 1973; 1881, RG11 2773.

14. Foster, J. *Alumni Oxonienses.* Oxford, 1888-92; DRO: Will of Elizabeth Flesher, proved Feb. 1886.

15. Venn, 1922-54; Cumbria Record Office (CRO): Kendal, WDS 38/39.

16. Crockford's *Clerical Directory,* 1874; *Nottinghamshire Guardian,* 24 April 1863; Probate calendar 1874, Samuel Oliver.

17. *CC* Derbys.,1815-35; White, *Derbys,* 1857, pp. 400-1; *Derby Mercury* 22 Aug. 1960 and 23 June 1884; Kelly & Co, *Derbys.* 1908, p. 140 and 1912 p. 30.

18. Kelly & Co, *Post Office Directory of Lincolnshire.* London, 1861, p. 299; W White, *History, Gazetteer & Directory of Devonshire.* Sheffield, 1850, p. 457; White, *Derbys,* 1834, pp. 98-9; Wright, C.N. *Directory of Leicestershire.* Leicester, 1888, p. 532; Warren, *Directory of Winchester and District.* Winchester, 1895, p. 16.

19. Caffrey, H. 'The Almshouse Experience in the Nineteenth century West Riding' in *Yorkshire Archaeological Journal,* Vol. 76, 2004.

20. Probate calendars: 1907, 1914, 1928.

21. URL: www.duchessofsomerset.co.uk/history accessed 14 June 2010; URL: www.british-history.ac.uk accessed 9 June 2010; Mannix 1847; Warren, 1895; *'Lichfield: The cathedral close',* A History of the County of Stafford, Vol. 14. Lichfield, 1990, pp. 57-67. URL: www.british-history.ac.uk/report.aspx?compid=42343, accessed 8 Aug. 2010; Salisbury Charities, 1962.

22. Crockford's *Clerical Directory,* London, 1868; Kelly, *Derbys.* 1881, p. 1118, 1899, p. 29; *Bristol Mercury,* 21 July 1888.

23. Venn, 1922-54; White, *Derbys,* 1857, p. 402.

24. Census 1861. RG9 2539; *Derby Mercury,* 7 October 1868, 8 September 1869; Cook, W.J. *Directory of Derby and District.* Derby, 1900, p. 81.

25. Census 1851, HO107/2146; DRO: D662 A/PI 14/1-7, Ashbourne Parish magazines 1873-79.

26. Pigot J. & Co *National and Commercial Directories of Derbyshire.* London, 1828/9, p. 108, 1842 p. 5; White, *Derbys,* 1857, p. 403; Census 1881, RG11/2555.

27. CRO: WDS 38/3 and 38/7-8; London Metropolitan Archives: A/CHM.

28. *Derby Mercury,* 22 August 1960; Kelly & Co, *Post Office Directory of Derbyshire and Nottinghamshire,* 1855, p. 60.

29.   Wright, C.N. *Directory of South Derbyshire*. Derby, 1874, p. 154.

30.   *Derby Mercury*, 22 August 1960.

31.   *Ashbourne Telegraph*, 27 March 1914; DRO: D662 A/PI 14/6-8, Ashbourne Parish magazine, March 1878, October 1889.

32.   Jacob. W. M. *The Clerical Profession in the Long Eighteenth Century 1680-1840*, Oxford, 2007, p. 159.

33.   CRO: WDS 38/7-8.

34.   Probate calendars 1890 James Pearman; 1887 Henry Welch.

35.   *Nottinghamshire Guardian*, 29 January 1864.

36.   *The Morning Post*, 4 April and 17 September 1847.

37.   *The Standard*, 14 June 1843.

38.   *The Morning Post*, 25 April 1850.

39.   URL: www.sonsoftheclergy.org.uk accessed 14 Aug. 2010; CRO, WDS 38/3; Glover, S. *History and Directory of the Borough of Derby*. Derby, 1849, p. 39; *Observer*, 18 July 1836.

40.   Lewis, S. *A Topographical Dictionary of England*. London, 1848, pp. 526-31; URL: www.british-history.ac.uk/report.aspx?compid=50860, accessed 1 April 2010; URL: www.stjohnsleatherhead.co.uk/stjohnshistory, accessed 5 April 2010.

CHAPTER 20
CATHOLIC ALMSHOUSES
IN LONDON[1]

Carmen M. Mangion

INTRODUCTION

Catholic institutional care for the elderly in 19th-century England and Wales developed in two separate, but interwoven strands. The first was shelter for the aged offered by communities of female and male religious. Though numerous religious communities provided some temporal and medical provision for the elderly, it was often *ad hoc*. The exception to this was the network of thirty-five homes for the elderly managed by two religious congregations, the Sisters of Nazareth and the Little Sisters of the Poor.[2] The second form of institutional care for the elderly, which is the primary focus of this essay, was almshouse provision. Six Catholic almshouses existed in England and Wales in the 19th century and this chapter will focus on the development of five of the six, all located in London.[3] First it notes the various motivations behind Catholic almshouse provision. Next, it analyses criteria for entrance into Catholic almshouses and argues that almshouse accommodation was not necessarily occupied by the 'most destitute', but by those who had some alternate sources of income. Finally, it looks at the Catholic almshouse as a component of the mixed economy of Catholic welfare and examines the integration between almshouses and the homes managed by religious institutes. As noted by Nigel Goose and others, almshouses, as a form of philanthropy, were an important component of the 'mixed economy of welfare' that allowed the elderly poor to reside in some sort of material comfort and independence in Victorian London.[4] London's Catholic philanthropists supported a flexible, and integrated, network of care for the elderly that provided for the physical and medical needs of the Catholic elderly.

Philanthropy, according to Frank Prochaska, was on the ascendant in the 19th century.[5] Though published works, including Prochaska's, rarely mention Catholic charities, they were, in fact, developing in large numbers, as was visible, year by year, in the thickening section of the annual *Catholic Directory*, entitled 'Charitable Institutions', which went from nine pages in 1850 to fifty-two in 1900.[6] *The Handbook of Catholic Charitable and Social Works* published in 1905 included 673 charitable activities, approximately 70 per cent of which were managed by religious communities, the remaining by the Catholic laity.[7] Catholic philanthropic institutions and their managers developed a more vocal and public religious identity – in line with what scholar Mary Heimann refers to as the late 19th-century trend towards 'denominational distinctiveness'.[8] Yet histories of these charities, their objectives, contributions, benefactors and recipients, are barely acknowledged in historical works on philanthropy.[9] Such research is important as it charts the changing nature of Catholic identity, Catholic involvement (or not) with civil society and the journey from a religion in the shadows to a faith assertively defended. My own work has examined Catholic women religious and their contributions to the medical marketplace as well as provision for the aged.[10] There were numerous endowed and unendowed charities run by Catholics, lay and religious, often (but not always) exclusively addressing the needs of Catholics. This chapter adds to this small body of research through its examination of Catholic almshouse provision.

The survival of Catholic almshouse records has been haphazard. St John's Hospice, endowed by William Harrison (1802-1876), has virtually no extant sources that identify its almspeople; it is not even listed in *The Catholic Directory*. We know of its presence from Elizabeth Harrison's (1798-1867) obituary in *The Tablet* and through the will of her brother, William Harrison. By contrast, the records of the Aged Poor Society that managed St Joseph's Almshouse in Hammersmith include most annual reports from 1851 and minute books from 1850, although little correspondence. Documentary evidence of the remaining Catholic almshouse records falls in between these two poles. The Hoxton Almshouse sources consist of excerpts in the minutes of the Benevolent Society from 1857-1891, a letter book dated 1895-1900 and a typescript history of the Benevolent Society written in 1927. There are no extant almshouse rules, register or annual reports (though they are mentioned in the minutes so they did exist at one time). The 19th-century records of St Joseph's Almshouse, which still exists in the heart of Chelsea, have not been located. St Scholastica's Retreat records survived somewhat patchily but include an almshouse register as well as some correspondence, minute books, grant books and financial ledgers. As with institutional structures more broadly, the public face of these institutions, recorded in annual reports and in the Catholic press, reflected the usual characteristics: they promoted their charitable objectives and the deservedness of their recipients, and they contained endless pleas for benefactors and donations. They also offer the researcher a deeper understanding of the politics of philanthropic institutions. The institutional records, including registers, minutes, regulations and correspondence, are management focused, recording and often summarising events and situations. The paucity of personal documents is disappointing; diaries and correspondence from almspeople have not been found despite extensive searches. Notwithstanding these drawbacks, however, extant documents give us a sense of the individual within the confines of the institution. Individual circumstances, though refracted through benefactors and administrators, hint at the almsperson's own character and agenda.

This chapter is consciously microhistorical and seeks to develop connections between these five Catholic almshouses with respect to the almspeople that resided in them. It will begin first by identifying the motivations behind creating Catholic almshouses.

MOTIVATIONS

Of the five Catholic almshouses in London, all of which were founded in the 19th century, two were managed by subscription-based philanthropic institutions, one by the parish and the remaining two were endowed foundations.[11] The philanthropic bodies, the Benevolent Society for the Relief of the Aged and Infirm Poor (henceforth Benevolent Society) and the Aged Poor Society, offered outdoor relief and later extended their charitable support to almshouses. The Benevolent Society was founded in 1761 by Richard Challoner (1691-1781) and was sustained in the early years by tradesmen who granted aid to the 'most destitute of aged poor' to 'preserve them from destitution and death'.[12] Those eligible for outdoor relief were men and women over the age of sixty and residing in London.[13] The aid, normally a weekly cash payment, totalled 1s. per week in 1788; by 1871, the amount had increased to 3s.[14] Lump sums were sometimes distributed for temporary emergencies, such as illness and accidents; these ranged from 5s. to £2. The number of pensioners provided for rose from approximately seventy-five in 1827 to 190 in 1898. The second philanthropic body, the Aged Poor Society, founded in 1708, supported 106 pensioners in 1900 with a pension of 4s. a week for men and 3s. a week for women.[15] These small pensions, like those of the Benevolent Society, were expected to supplement other resources available to the pensioners.

Illustration 20.a. St Joseph's Almshouse, Chelsea.
Photo © Carmen Mangion

The Benevolent Society opened St Joseph's Almshouse, located on Cadogan Street in Chelsea in 1849 and it is still occupied today. The ground for the almshouse was donated by benefactor Joseph Knight (*ca* 1781-1855), a retired horticulturist who owned a successful nursery on the King's Road, Chelsea. The Benevolent Society funded the building of the almshouses and managed St Joseph's for a short time. Probably sometime after 1855 the almshouses became 'partly diocesan, partly parochial in their management'. The day-to-day activities were managed by the nearby Sisters of Mercy. It was originally intended to accommodate twenty-four elderly women, but building works stopped at accommodation for eighteen when funding dried up.[16] The second almshouse, also named St Joseph's, was managed by the Aged Poor Society. In 1851, the respected architect William Wilkinson Wardell (1823-1899), convert and student of Augustus Welby Pugin, was hired to design this almshouse in Hammersmith for the Catholic elderly that is also still in use. This almshouse held sixteen occupants in 1853 and twenty-eight in 1901. The third almshouse was founded by the Benevolent Society in a more *ad hoc* manner. The *Catholic Directory* in 1864 records an interest in opening an almshouse in Hoxton but it wasn't until 1870 that we read of the acceptance of pensioners for the Hoxton Square Almshouse.[17] Census records indicate that six to eleven almspeople were housed next to St Monica's Catholic Church, built in 1863 to serve the Irish community and managed by the Augustinian Friars. This almshouse was not purpose-built but appears to be part of the terraced housing surrounding St Monica's. Though no register is extant, a list of almspeople recreated from meeting minutes and census returns indicates at least forty-two almspeople were accepted into the almshouse. In addition to lodging, almspeople received pensions of five shillings a week plus an extra three shillings for coals at Christmas.[18] In 1883, the Benevolent Society discussed selling this property and rebuilding elsewhere, but these discussions came to naught.[19] In 1896, the property was sold to the Augustinians and the almspeople were asked to leave; the Benevolent Society returned to providing only out-relief to the elderly poor.[20]

The next two London almshouses were endowed by Hackney-born siblings William (1802-1876) and Elizabeth Harrison (1798-1867). St John's Hospice, founded around 1861, housed four elderly poor persons of Hackney and was probably managed by William Harrison, a retired timber merchant, until his death.[21] It was located on Warburton Street near St John the Baptist church in Hackney. At William's death, he left a legacy of, at most, £450, which was invested in order to pay almshouse inhabitants 7s. 6d. a week.[22] Four trustees, including the mission priest of St John the Baptist, were named to manage what appears to have been a purpose-built structure. This almshouse remained open until around 1971. Elizabeth Harrison used the legacy from her elder brother, Robert, and his wife Scholastica to build the forty-person almshouse, St Scholastica's Retreat, on Kennington Road in Clapton, for the 'ranks of the gentry, or of the professional or wholesale commercial classes'.[23] She administered it personally from its opening in 1861 until her death in 1867. Afterwards, five trustees, along with a warden (from 1874) and porter (from 1884) managed the almshouse. Almspeople after 1867 were given a stipend that varied according to their guaranteed annuity but never exceeded £25 per annum. This was, as will be discussed later in this chapter, a middle-class almshouse that maintained its class identity.[24]

Though only one inmate register is extant, using the census, along with lists of almspeople and meeting minutes, the minimum number of elderly Catholics residing in these five Catholic almshouses during the period 1861-1901 can be calculated (*see* Table 20.I) at 379.[25] At its most populous, in the 1891 census (*see* Table 20.III), these almshouses held ninety-eight persons at one time.

TABLE 20.I
Almspeople resident in Catholic almshouses from 1849-1901

Almshouse	Managed by	Funding	Numbers of almspeople
St Joseph's, Chelsea (1849-today)	Benevolent Society/parish and diocese	parish charity	71
St Joseph's, Hammersmith (1851-today)	Aged Poor Society	subscribers	133
St John's Hospice, Hackney (1861-1971?)	William Harrison/trustees	endowment	16
St Scholastica's Retreat, Clapton (1861-today)	Elizabeth Harrison/trustees	endowment	117
Hoxton Almshouse (1871?-1896?)	Benevolent Society	subscribers	42
TOTAL			**379**

Sources: Census; APS: Annual reports; SSR: St Scholastica's Retreat Register;
            SMM: Benevolent Society Minute-Book 1857-1891

There was a variety of reasons for the development of these Catholic almshouses. Firstly, there existed a 'duty of almsgiving'.[26] Catholic charity was linked to personal salvation, thus beneficial to the giver as well as the receiver.[27] Archbishop of Westminster

Henry E. Manning (1808-1892) noted it was well known that 'the Catholic religion is the religion of charity, and that the Catholic Church is the Church of the poor'.[28] Social investigator Charles Booth (1840-1916) acknowledged that 'The ministrations of these churches [Roman Catholic] touch the poorest, and to give freely in charity is the rule of their religion.'[29] There was also a humanitarianism, a concern for the alleviation of suffering, in the charitable responses to the needs of the elderly. The Benevolent Society aided those who, due to 'sickness or infirmities', were 'rendered incapable of obtaining anything approaching an adequate subsistence'. In addition to these altruistic aims, the desire to support or encourage the practice of the Catholic faith was an important motivation. The Catholic almshouse could be seen as one antidote against acts of anti-Catholicism. In 1855, the Benevolent Society advertisement noted that:

> Those on our lists are widows, - the infirm and decrepit scattered over the vast metropolis, - whose attachment to religion makes them turn in fear from the confinement of the poor-houses; who seek in vain for relief from those of a different creed, where often the only condition of support is a practical denial of their belief; and who therefore come back to us, having the strongest and most urgent claims on those of the household of the faith.[30]

As reflected in this excerpt, poor-law workhouses were problematic, because the Benevolent Society saw them as Protestant institutions, which promoted the national church, the Church of England, and discouraged Catholics from practicing their faith.[31]

Some almshouses too, within their rules, incorporated an intolerance of specific religious denominations. There were, of course, denominational almshouses, including Catholic almshouses, which would often have excluded those of other faiths.[32] Almspeople from the Sidney Hill Wesleyan Cottages, Bristol, were expected to attend Methodist chapel weekly.[33] The Victoria Jubilee Homes founded in 1887 in Langford, Somerset required almspeople to be protestant.[34] Many almshouses implied, though perhaps did not specifically detail in the rules, a Church of England ethos. If the local Church of England vicar was a trustee or chaplain, this might lead to an expectation that complying with Church of England faith practices was obligatory. Some almshouses specifically excluded Catholics and others: the Blythe & Davis Homes in Wincanton, founded in 1909, disallowed Catholics.[35] Some benefactors made abundantly clear the depth of their anti-Catholicism: siblings Thomas and Sarah Ridley founded Ridley's Almshouses in Bristol in 1739 for ten almspeople who 'are not nor ever have been Roman Catholics or inclinable to be such'.[36] The Wyndham Cottle Almshouses, Shanklin, IOW, founded in 1921 required: 'English or Scotch by nationality of parentage and are not Roman Catholic or Jews'.[37] Even stranger yet were the foundation documents of Charles Edward Sugden's Almshouses, Bradford, opened in 1916, which insisted residents 'not to be members or supporters of the Roman Catholic church, the Socialist Party or the Labour Party'.[38] Non-believers would have also found almshouse living problematic, as church-going was often an integral part of almshouse rules and regulations. Many, like the Ellen Cottages founded in 1860 in Burnham-on-Sea, required church attendance though they did not specify a particular denomination.[39] The regulations, however, are not the final word on the topic; whether these regulations were followed is open to question and requires further research.

Potential exclusion was not the only reason for creating Catholic-run almshouses. The workhouse climate was seen to inhibit the 'good death', or more particularly, the 'good Catholic death'. The Aged Poor Society noted that:

Although the Catholic in our workhouses is now at liberty to follow his own religion, still, when affliction and decrepit old age steal upon him, and he sinks to the borders of the grave, his latter moments are pre-eminently embittered by the scoffs and taunts of his companions in age and misery.[40]

St Joseph's Almshouse in Chelsea was described as a Catholic space where 'poor Catholics' could 'retire in old age from a world of care, to spend the evening of life in peace, preparing for eternity'.[41] This preparation for death was perceived as an important benefit of almshouse living, all five almshouses were located near a Catholic church and nearby Catholic clergy were readily available to administer the last sacraments, especially that of extreme unction.[42] This sacrament was believed to not only prepare for death but also to give grace and patience during times of sickness.[43] The author of *How to Help the Sick and Dying* noted the last sacraments (penance, holy viaticum and extreme unction) were 'given to us by God in His goodness to comfort and strengthen us in our Last Agony, and they help us wonderfully to die a happy death'.[44]

Catholic almshouse inhabitants were expected to regularly attend to their religious duties; it was often the parish priest who vouched for an almshouse candidate's respectability and deservedness, so we can presume that almshouse inhabitants would have been practising their faith before their entry into the almshouse.[45] The Rules and Regulations of St Scholastica's Retreat, endowed by Elizabeth Harrison, mandated that all inmates and co-inmates were Catholic. Forty-one-year-old Mary Jane Richardson, the daughter of Joseph Richardson, a retired master builder, was named as an attendant to her father but was asked to leave St Scholastica's Retreat when: 'It having come to the knowledge of the Warden that Mr Richardson's daughter was not living in the practise of the Roman Catholic religion'.[46] Practising the Catholic faith was taken seriously, noted and commented upon. Trustee John Haly wrote to Warden Henry Lewinton noting that, although he understood that Mrs Kirkby could not attend chapel for health reasons, he was 'at a loss to account for M M Fialon and Andrews'.[47] No recourse was suggested so it appears this transgression was not acted upon. The Aged Poor Society also required that their pensioners were Catholic, and the almspeople residing at St Joseph's Almshouse in Hammersmith were reminded in the Rules and Regulations of the almshouse of their duty 'to offer up prayers for the welfare of their benefactors'.[48]

That said, being a Catholic was not essential to receive relief from the Benevolent Society. The Society's secretary, James McAdam, replied to Miss A M Clarke's nomination of George Street of Chelsea with: 'The fact of his not being a Catholic will make no difference whatever — as you rightly conclude, the benefits of the Benevolent Society are open to all without distinction of creed'.[49] It is not known whether they accepted non-Catholic pensioners into the Hoxton Almshouse but it seems likely that they did. There were no discussions of the creed of pensioners noted in the minute books, though this does not mean the issue was not discussed. It is likely that, as subscribers could be Catholic and non-Catholic, the Benevolent Society did not feel they could limit their pensions or almshouse places to Catholics only. Benevolent Society notices in *The Catholic Directory* and *The Tablet* did not indicate that almspeople were required to be Catholic. In 1896, Secretary of the Benevolent Society James McAdam explained to a subscriber:

With reference to your enquiry, I have to say that the pensioners of this Society are not selected from the Catholic poor only. In fact we do not ask of candidates any questions as to their faith. They must be recommended by a subscriber, must be over 60, and of course very poor.[50]

The reliance on subscribers of all creeds, which was certainly the case with the Benevolent Society, influenced their decision to accept all nominated pensioners without asking questions about religion. Unfortunately, that means we have no way of knowing if any of the almspeople were, in fact, non-Catholic. It would seem, though, that Catholics would be favoured. The Benevolent Society noted in 1855 that: 'those having the strongest and most urgent claims on those of the household of the faith', which would imply Catholics would have some sort of preference.[51] That said, openness to non-Catholics was not uncommon amongst Catholic philanthropies. The homes for the aged poor of the Little Sisters of Charity and the Sisters of Nazareth as well as the majority of the hospitals managed by women religious were open to those of all creeds.[52] Catholic doctrine on charity encouraged a denominational blindness with regards to charity, though how this played out practically speaking is more difficult to ascertain.[53]

Religion has played a role in almshouse history from the very first almshouses.[54] The practice of the faith was an important aspect of the educational and charitable institution-building of the 19th century and almshouses were part of this network of Catholic institutional care. The motives behind developing these Catholic almshouses were complicated but reflected primarily the need to relieve the poverty of elderly Catholics as well as to allow or encourage them to practise their faith. Deservedness was often (though not always) related to the practice of the Catholic faith. Another aspect of deservedness and motivations was related to questions of class as the next section will explore.

CRITERIA AND CLASS

There was fierce competition for almshouse places. Once residents met the basic criteria, listed in Table 20.II, potential candidates for St Joseph's Almshouse (Hammersmith), St Scholastica's Retreat and the Hoxton Almshouse were visited and interviewed by trustees or administrators, often in their home environments, before they were eligible to join the waiting list for almshouses.[55] It seems likely that St Joseph's Almshouse (Chelsea) and St John's Hospice were managed at the parish level and almshouse inhabitants would come from the surrounding parish and would be known to the parish priest or religious sister, so such formal investigations may not have occurred.

TABLE 20.II
Requirements for candidates for almshouse places, 1894

Almshouse	Creed	Age	Location	Class	Nominators
St Joseph's (Chelsea)	likely Catholic		likely local parish	no information available	likely parish priest or Sister of Mercy
St Joseph's (Hammersmith)	Catholic	60	no location noted	'old and destitute catholic'	subscriber
St John's Hospice (Hackney)	likely Catholic		likely local parish	no information available	likely parish priest
St Scholastica's Retreat (Clapton)	Catholic	60	Great Britain	'middle and upper classes'	likely clergy, bishops
Hoxton Almshouse	all creeds	60	10 miles from GPO	'aged and infirm poor'	member of Benevolent Society

Source: *Handbook of Catholic Charities, Associations, etc., in Great Britain* (London: Catholic Truth Society, 1894), pp. 52-4; APS: Annual reports

Competition for donors and subscribers was fierce in the philanthropic marketplace, and charities needed to be seen as discriminating between the deserving and undeserving.

Many applicants nominated by subscribers or clergy were rejected; there were far fewer places available than there were applicants, which attests to the desirability of almshouse living.[56] The interview or home visit was crucial to acceptance into the almshouse. The Committee of the Benevolent Society, which managed the Hoxton Almshouse and for a short time St Joseph's in Chelsea, was keen to remind subscribers and donors that they distributed the funds received 'with prudence and discretion'; committee members would verify that nominated pensioners met their criteria through initial visits by at least two members of the committee.[57] James McAdam visited the home of Mr D J Flanagan, aged sixty-two, recommended as a pensioner by the Earl of Denbigh in 1895. McAdam noted: 'the house presented a poverty-stricken aspect, though there was a somewhat pathetic attempt to save appearances'. Canon Pycke, of St John's Islington, who had known Flanagan for fifteen years, indicated that he was 'a very pious good man; nearly a daily communicant; has served our 7 o'clock mass for years'; however, he was 'a most unfortunate man in business'.[58] After interviewing Flanagan, McAdam remarked to the Earl of Denbigh: 'I feel sure he is deserving. Twenty years ago he had a good business, but has been struggling against adversity ever since that failed him'.[59] The Benevolent Society gave Flanagan a pension of 3s. a week though expected him to continue looking for employment.[60] To assure themselves of pensioners' continued deservedness, pensions were distributed through a series of almoners, often, but not always, Catholic clergy.[61]

Unfortunately, only one almshouse register is extant for the five almshouses (that of St Scholastica's Retreat) so the census must be relied upon, along with data from other sources, to develop a demographic profile of Catholic almshouse inhabitants.[62] As can be seen in Table 20.III, almspeople were overwhelmingly female (91 per cent). This preponderance of women in almshouses was not unusual.[63] Historians continue to debate the numerous reasons for this.[64] One in four almspeople had a co-resident, though it was rarely a spouse and more often a family member (and typically a daughter: six of the nineteen co-residents were daughters). Occupants of St Scholastica's Retreat were more likely to have residential companions than any of the other almshouses, in part because their almshouse accommodations included a separate room for a servant or co-resident.[65]

TABLE 20.III
Catholic almspeople and co-residents, 1891

Almshouse	TOTAL	Number of almspeople			Residential Companions			
		Male	Female	Total	Husband	Wife	Other	Total
St Joseph's (Chelsea)	19	0	18	18	0	0	1	1
St Joseph's (Hammersmith)	27	2	22	24	0	2	1	3
St John's Hospice (Hackney)	4	0	4	4	0	0	0	0
St Scholastica's Retreat (Clapton)	38	3	24	27	0	2	9	11
Hoxton Almshouse	10	2	4	6	0	1	3	4
TOTALS	**98**	**7**	**72**	**79**	**0**	**5**	**14**	**19**
%		8.9%	91.1%		0.0%	6.3%	17.7%	

Source: 1891 Census

The majority of Catholic almshouse occupants were widowed (53 per cent), as noted in Table 20.IV, and ranged in age from fifty-one to eighty-nine years of age, though the average age in the 1891 census was seventy-two (with the median age of seventy-one and the modal age of seventy).[66] The place of birth of the majority of almspeople was England (65 per cent) and the remaining occupants were typically Irish-born.

TABLE 20.IV
Demographic profile of Catholic almspeople, 1891

Almshouse	Total	Marital Status			Place of birth			Age	
		Married	Widowed	Single	England	Ireland	Other	Average	Range
St Joseph's (Chelsea)	18	0	11	7	7	10	1	70	58-80
St Joseph's (Hammersmith)	24	2	10	12	16	7	1	72	64-89
St John's Hospice	4	0	2	2	2	2	0	76	68-82
St Scholastica's Retreat	27	3	14	10	24	2	1	73	62-85
Hoxton Almshouse	6	1	5	0	2	4	0	70	51-82
TOTALS	**79**	**6**	**42**	**31**	**51**	**25**	**3**	**72**	**51-89**
%		7.6%	53.2%	39.2%	65.4%	32.1%	3.8%		

Source: 1891 Census

Determining the social class of almshouse inhabitants given incomplete census data proves to be somewhat problematic on a number of levels, but it still allows us to explore the links between poverty and deservedness in almshouses.[67] As expected, St Scholastica's Retreat featured a higher social class of almsperson. Founder Elizabeth Harrison was explicit in her aims regarding the social class of the occupants of St Scholastica's Retreat and built these almshouses for the 'decayed members of the middle and upper classes of society'.[68] Their living quarters were generous and included a suite of five rooms with one of these rooms designated for a servant or co-resident. Few female inhabitants reported waged occupations but those that did were governesses, teachers and authors. Their middle-class status was confirmed not only through their own occupations (or lack thereof) but by those of their husbands or fathers. Male residents, and male relations of female residents, often worked as merchants or were 'gentlemen'. This class status was important to the institutional identity of the almshouse.[69] In many ways this reflects what Patrick Joyce concludes in his examination of Morden College, an almshouse for 'decayed' merchants: 'in poverty as in wealth two worlds were maintained in distinction and separation'.[70]

Yet this conclusion does not hold true in the four remaining Catholic almshouses. An examination of almshouse residents' occupations, as recorded in the decennial censuses, confirms that the majority of residents had working-class occupations. However, curiously, we find a mix of social classes living together in these four almshouse complexes. Sixteen of the seventy-five almspeople with recorded occupations in St Joseph's Almshouse in Hammersmith from 1861 to 1901 lived on their own means or were annuitants. Eleven had occupations in education; these included a former governess, private teacher, school master, school mistress and a proprietor of a ladies boarding school. More residents however, twenty-nine, had working class occupations: they were charwomen, domestic servants, cooks, housekeepers, ladies' maids, needlewomen, dressmakers, glovemakers, hatmakers and lacemakers. Though calculating statistics on such a partial sample would be misleading, the presence of such diverse occupations implies that St Joseph's Almshouse in Hammersmith was a place where a charwoman lived next door to a governess and that the 'two worlds' did indeed co-exist in this location.[71]

Illustration 20.b. St Joseph's Almshouse, Hammersmith.
Reproduced with permission of the Trustees of St Joseph's Society
(formally The Aged Poor Society)

The records of the Aged Poor Society divulge some explanations of this range of social classes. Its original intent was to care for the 'old and destitute Catholic'.[72] While this was probably the case with out-relief pensioners, the definition of 'destitute' was stretched when it came to almshouse candidates. From the beginning, almshouse residents at St Joseph's, Hammersmith, were meant to be a cut above the ordinary poor that were given outdoor relief. In the 1857 annual report, the Aged Poor Society described the 'deserving poor' that would occupy the almshouse:

> How frequently does it happen, that persons brought up in every comfort, with cheerful homes, are, from fortuitous circumstances, reduced in their advanced age to almost abject poverty, and sometimes compelled to seek the shelter of the workhouse, in which to end their days? Now, these Alms-Houses are especially suited to such, and what a comfort it will be to any who may have the misfortune to be so reduced, to reflect that when in good circumstances, they contributed to such Alms-Houses, thus giving them a claim for admission.[73]

This excerpt highlights the precariousness of financial security, even for the middle classes, suggesting, rather provocatively, that subscribers and donors could, through 'misfortune', find themselves in an almshouse.[74] The Molineux bequest of 1851 initially supported two additional almspeople with £20 per annum, but required their applicants to have held 'a respectable position, have become reduced to distress in their old age'.[75] Annual reports asserted that those who had lived comfortable lives, but had fallen on bad times upon ageing, were more deserving of support:

> Sad as is the case of the poorest of the poor, from among whom the greater part of our ordinary pensioners are taken, perhaps that of the class a little above

them who have been reduced by misfortune in their old age from affluence to want is still more so. The very poor have been familiar with poverty through their lives and by that familiarity their present sufferings, severe as they are, are in some degree lessened; at any rate they are not increased by that feeling of degradation which renders the receiving of alms from public or private sources so painful. Not so with the broken merchant or his widow, and the poor governess, old and past work, but striving with decent pride to keep up appearances, and hide their want from those with whom they lived in better days as friends and equals.[76]

Though it would appear that the managers of the Aged Poor Society were motivated by self-interest in the easing of the financial difficulties of members of their own social class; their continual requests for more subscribers, more donations and more legacies reflected an awareness that they were meant to serve the 'old and destitute Catholic'. Annual reports consistently noted the disappointment that:

> The want of sufficient funds greatly limits the class from which the Directors have to admit candidates for election...it has happened that candidates otherwise eligible have been rejected for the very reason which would have rendered their election most desirable, viz., their great poverty and want of friends to assist them.[77]

Directors wished to build an endowment fund that would allow pensions for all almspeople including those without friends or funds.[78] But, until that time arrived, almshouse inhabitants of St Joseph's Hammersmith needed to 'possess sufficient means of support', which, by 1867, was confirmed by a guarantee form, signed by family, friends or former employers.[79] By 1900, their efforts had met with some success: the endowment fund contained enough to allow pensions of £20 a year to ten pensioners. These pensions had no social class requirements.

Despite this apparent emphasis on providing for those who had drifted from 'affluence to want', an examination of occupations listed on the decennial censuses (1861-1901) for St Joseph's Almshouse in Hammersmith suggests, as noted above, a less cohesive picture of class status within the almshouse. St Joseph's in Chelsea shows a similar disparate occupational profile. Here were twenty-five almspeople who could live on their own means or had annuities; they lived alongside at least eleven charwomen, cooks, housekeepers, domestic servants and dressmakers. The Hoxton almspeople appeared more unified in terms of class; the census records no annuitants or those living on their own means.[80] The majority of the almspeople were bricklayers, charwomen, nurses and servants. However, their minute books offer additional evidence that reflects, on occasion, a higher class of almshouse occupant. The managers of the Hoxton Almshouses accepted, at the request of the Archbishop of Westminster HE Manning, Edward Deavis (d 1873), aged seventy and 'a Gentleman by birth, reduced to such poverty as to be compelled to go to the Workhouse'.[81] Another almsperson, Mrs Ellen Connolly, made a £100 donation to the Benevolent Society in order to be admitted as a resident of the Hoxton Almshouses. This was considered 'exceptional circumstances' as she was admitted without a recommendation.[82] The Aged Poor Society made similar 'exceptions'. In 1853, one of the former Directors of the Aged Poor Society was given temporary use of one of the vacant rooms.[83] Benjamin Ball paid £200 to obtain a residence at St Joseph's Almshouse in Hammersmith.[84] The minute books give additional evidence of the financial pressures faced by these charitable institutions:

'exceptions' were made by committee members to the usual 'subscriber democracy' of nominating almspeople.[85]

Patrick Joyce, using the case of Morden College and noting other occupational almshouses, argues that social status was maintained through the exclusiveness of charitable institutions for the middle classes.[86] An examination of Catholic almshouses, however, indicates that this was not always the case. Almspeople of different social classes lived together in the almshouse complexes in rooms that were identical, other than in terms of location, within the complex and perhaps variations in normal wear and tear.[87] The Aged Poor Society and the Benevolent Society did not choose to explicitly limit almshouse inhabitants by social class as did St Scholastica's Retreat. Though the Aged Poor Society insisted on 'sufficient means of support', this criterion did not eliminate working-class occupants as family, friends or employers provided the support needed for working-class pensioners.[88] Secondly, it is useful to consider how poverty was regarded in Catholic teaching. Poverty was meant to be exalted as a 'higher state' and, as one Catholic writer opined: 'this implies that poverty itself be not considered as a disgrace'; the same writer reminded readers that 'the poor are higher in the spiritual order than the rich, and have a quicker and clearer insight into the truths of religion'.[89] Perhaps this ideology, coupled with financial straits, moved these charitable societies away from a model of almshouse living that insisted on social class 'distinction and separation'.[90]

A MIXED ECONOMY OF WELFARE

Frank Prochaska has argued that almshouses were 'likely to be a last resort' for 'genteel' residents.[91] While this may be true for some residents, Catholic almshouse records reflect a more flexible community, which suggests that those who entered almshouses had other options and the almshouse was just one alternative in their mixed economy of welfare. Even those who applied for entry into almshouses sometimes rejected their place; Bridget Ryan, Maria Cullen and Maria Dennis all declined rooms in the Hoxton almshouse. Mary Cullen indicated the room assigned to her was not 'suitable'; Maria Dennis rejected the upper floor room offered to her as her health ('weakness of the heart') made it difficult for her to climb stairs.[92] Similar responses occurred in St Scholastica's Retreat where four residents did not take up their places in the almshouse.[93] Almshouse residents, like Timothy Buckley and Mary Izod, left the Hoxton Almshouse to go elsewhere though no reasons were given for their departure.[94] This suggests that almshouse residents had other options available that were more suitable for their needs.

In most instances, however, the primary reason for an almsperson's departure from the almshouse was related to health. Chronic illness or incurable conditions made independent almshouse living difficult, and such almspeople often relocated to live with family or friends, or entered workhouse infirmaries, Catholic hospitals or Catholic homes for the aged when in need of medical care. From 1883 to 1897 at least ten almspeople from the Hoxton Almshouse were admitted to one of the thirty-five homes for the aged run by the Little Sisters of the Poor or the Sisters of Nazareth. These homes allowed some independent living, but were often used by those who needed some sort of medical as well as temporal care.[95] Once Elizabeth Sullivan became 'too infirm to continue living alone in the almshouse', she was transferred to the Sisters of Nazareth in Hammersmith where she died soon afterwards.[96] Other almshouse inhabitants, such as Elizabeth O'Connor and Honora Dryer, became residents of the homes managed by the Little Sisters of the Poor.[97] Miss O'Reilly was one of twenty-three almspersons who left St Joseph's Almshouse in Hammersmith to enter the home of the Little

Sisters of the Poor.[98] Ten occupants of St Scholastica's Retreat left for reasons of health, some entering homes for the aged poor run by women's religious communities but others leaving to reside with family members.[99] However, it was not always the case that almshouse inhabitants entered the homes of religious communities. Almspeople were also taken in by family and friends when they became ill. Mr Treacy, after a severe fall whilst in St Joseph's Almshouse in Hammersmith, went to live with his son who was financially 'now in better circumstances'.[100] Mrs Christian was withdrawn by her relatives as she was acting 'childish [and the] necessity of her condition rendering special care and attention desirable'.[101] This reflects also what Pat Thane has noted as the 'English experience' of old age; the 'pull towards autonomy' meant ageing parents maintained their independence for as long as they were able.[102] When long-term illness struck, then family or friends took responsibility for them if they could; otherwise they found a place in other Catholic institutions or in poor law infirmaries.[103]

Illustration 20.c. St Scholastica's Retreat, *postcard 'St Scholastica's Retreat' by 'sludgegulper' on flickr.com, used under the Creative Commons license CC By SA 2.0* https://www.flickr.com/search/?l=commderiv&q=st%20scholastica's%20retreat *accessed 20 August 2014*

When acute care was needed, Hoxton Almshouse residents often went to the local workhouse infirmary. Margaret McCarthy left for the parish infirmary during her illness but retained her place in the almshouse. Mary Clancy was elected into the Hoxton Almshouse on 18 March 1875 and went into the workhouse infirmary in late 1877; she returned to the Hoxton Almshouse the next year.[104] In rare exceptions, almshouse inhabitants received some nursing care in the almshouse. Ann Briars was nursed by fellow almshouse occupant Margaret White for two weeks in 1885. Two years later, Briars left the almshouse for the workhouse infirmary but her place was saved and she later re-occupied her room in the Hoxton Almshouse. She became ill again and was nursed by Margaret White for two to three months. In 1888, she entered the workhouse again but returned to the almshouse after a time. The Benevolent Society committee displayed some flexibility in allowing Ann Briars to return to the almshouse once her health had improved by both saving her room and by paying Margaret White for her nursing care.[105] Similarly, in St Joseph's Almshouse in Hammersmith, Mrs Esner's son paid for her to be nursed in the almshouse.[106] However, this was more the exception than the rule with regards to almshouse living, and none of the Catholic almshouses provided long-term medical care in the 19th century.

While many almspeople remained in almshouses until their death, others came and went according to their needs and the preferability and availability of other options. Catholic almshouses were part of the web of agencies and institutions that comprised a Catholic 'mixed economy of welfare'.

CONCLUSION

As has been noted by other researchers, the geography of charity remains largely unexplored and in need of further investigation.[107] The FACHRS almshouse research project, and this volume, have taken the initiative in developing our understanding of almshouse spaces and their occupants. This particular chapter points to the significance of religion in almshouse living in the 19th century. Although the motivations for developing Catholic almshouses were complex, Catholic benefactors believed that the faith needs for the Catholic aged were not being met in either public institutions or existing charitable almshouses. Five London almshouses opened in the latter half of the 19th century to meet the needs of 'deserving' Catholics. It is important to note that this denominational almshouse accommodation was not always held by the 'most destitute', as some almspeople were required to have alternative sources of support. The social class of almshouse residents varied; they could be members of the working-class poor as well as the middle classes. The reliance of three of the Catholic almshouses on the precarious nature of philanthropic giving meant that separation by social class was not rigid; a charwoman could be found living side by side with a governess. Catholic almshouse living was only one form of accommodation for the elderly poor. It allowed the elderly to live independent lives, but if such autonomy was not possible because of ill health, there were other alternatives to family and friends or the workhouse: Catholic institutions managed by religious provided another form of institutional care offering temporal and physical care as well as the requirements of the Catholic faith. Almshouse accommodation provided an important component of the 'mixed economy of welfare' that allowed the elderly poor (and indeed some of the not so poor) to subsist in Victorian London.

Notes

1. This has been an intensely collaborative effort as the records of some of these almshouses proved very difficult to locate. Thanks are due to Sister Clare Veronica Wyman, ra, Fr David Lannon and Sister Catherine Ryan who answered queries and provided suggestions for sources. Special acknowledgement should go to R A Kidd who generously shared with me the fruits of his meticulous research on the history of St Scholastica's Retreat. In addition, I owe a debt of gratitude to the archivists who obtained permission to access these private archives including Nicholas Schofield of the Archives of the Archdiocese of Westminster, Father Peter Newby of St Mary Moorsfield, Simon Dolan of St Joseph's Society and Reverend Seán Duffy of St Scholastica's Retreat. Special thanks to Helen Caffrey, Janet Cumner, Sarah Hare, Anne Langley, Sylvia Pinches and Robert Ruegg who responded to my plea regarding almshouses and religious restrictions. I am also grateful for the detailed feedback from various reviewers of this chapter including Caroline Bowden, Helen Caffrey, Anne Langley and Nigel Goose. All errors, of course, remain my own.

2. Both congregations offered homes for the elderly without payment. For more on the Sisters of Nazareth homes for the aged poor *see* Mangion, C.M., 'Faith, Philanthropy and the Aged Poor', *European Review of History* 19: 4, 2012, pp. 515-30. Calculation of number of homes of the Little Sisters of the Poor from Leroy, A., *History of the Little Sisters of the Poor*, London, Burns, Oates & Washbourne, 1925, p. 537.

3. There is a sixth Catholic almshouse located in Ingatestone, Essex endowed by Sir William Petre in 1557 and rebuilt by another Lord Petre in 1840, which housed eight women and four men. *Handbook of Catholic Charities, Associations, etc., in Great Britain*. London, Catholic Truth Society, 1894, p. 54.

4. The 'mixed economy of welfare' refers to the provision of welfare that existed in the 19th century that ranged from help from friends and family to charitable efforts, friendly societies and the poor law. The elderly would have cobbled resources together through negotiating the requirements of not one, but numerous sources. *See* Goose, N. 'The English Almshouse and the Mixed Economy of Welfare: medieval to modern', *Local Historian* 40: 1, 2010, pp. 3-19.

5. Prochaska, F.K. *Women and Philanthropy in Nineteenth-Century England*. Oxford, Clarendon Press, 1980, pp. 22-3.

6. *The Catholic Directory*, London, 1850, 'Charitable and other Institutions in London and its Environs', pp. 137-145; *The Catholic Directory*, 1900, 'Religious and Charitable Institutions, Societies, etc.' pp. 498-549.

7. *The Handbook of Catholic Charitable and Social Works*. London, Catholic Truth Society, 1905. Author's own calculation.

8. Heimann, M. *Catholic Devotion in Victorian England*, Oxford, Clarendon Press, 1995, p. 123.

9. The historiography on Catholic charity includes: Carter, B. 'Catholic Charitable Endeavour in London. 1810-1840. Part I', *Recusant History*, 25: 3, 2001, pp. 487-510; Carter, B. 'Catholic Charitable Endeavour in London. 1810-1840, Part II', *Recusant History*, 25: 4, 2001, pp. 648-69; Gilley, S. 'English Catholic Charity and the Irish Poor in London: Part I, 1700-1840', *Recusant History*, 11: 4, 1972, pp. 179-95; Gilley, S. 'English Catholic Charity and the Irish Poor in London: Part II, (1840-1870)', *Recusant History*, 11: 5, 1972, pp. 253-69; Gilley, S. 'Heretic London, Holy Poverty and the Irish Poor, 1830-1870', *The Downside Review*, 89: 294, 1971, pp. 64-89; Kanya-Forstner, M. 'The Politics of Survival: Irish Women in Outcast Liverpool, 1850-1890' (Ph.D., University of Liverpool, 1997); Moretti, C. 'The Aged Poor Society and Saint Joseph's Almshouses', *Catholic Ancestor*, 10:3, 2004, pp. 89-97; Pearce, L.R. 'Catholic Philanthropy in Mid Nineteenth-century Britain: the reformatory work of the female congregations' (PhD thesis, University of Kent, 2003); Pinches, S. 'Roman Catholic Charities and Voluntary Societies in the Diocese of Birmingham, 1834-1945', (MA dissertation, University of Leicester, 1997).

10. Mangion, C.M. 'Developing Alliances: Faith, Philanthropy and Fundraising in Nineteenth-century England' in *The Economics of Providence: management, finances and patrimony of religious orders and congregations in Europe 1773 to ca 1930*, Maarten Van Dijck, *et al.* (eds), Leuven, Leuven University Press, 2013, pp. 205-26; Mangion, C.M. 'Medical Philanthropy and Civic Culture: Protestants and Catholics united by a 'common christianity" in *Proceedings - First Danish History of Nursing Conference*, ed. Dietz, S.M. Aarhus, Faculty of Health Sciences, 2009, pp. 107-22.

11. The Relief Act of 1791, the repeal of the Test and Corporation Acts in 1828 and the Catholic Emancipation Act of 1829 gave some civil rights to Catholics in the United Kingdom of Great Britain and Ireland and signaled a growing acceptance of Catholic institutions.

12. St Mary Moorfields Archives (SMM): 'A Short History of the Benevolent Society for the Relief of the Aged and Infirm Poor', *ca* 1927; *The Catholic Directory*, 1851, p. 143.

13. SMM: Benevolent Society letter book 1895-1900. Letter from James McAdams to Frederick A. Hoare, Esq dated 25 April 1896, p. 45.

14. *The Catholic Directory*, 1871, pp. 347; SMM: 'A Short History', p. 3.

15. London Metropolitan Archives (LMA): 4439/02/001, *Aged Poor Society and St Joseph's Almshouses Annual Report,* 1901, p. 3. The difference in provision between men and women is unexplained in the existing documents. In 1910, a suggestion was mooted in the minutes to equalise the amounts but was firmly rejected by the trustees with no stated explanation.

16. Anderson, W.J. *A History of the Catholic Parish of St Mary's, Chelsea*. Hinckley, Leicestershire, Samuel Walker, 1938, pp. 57-9; *The Catholic Directory*, 1860, p. 244.

17. *The Catholic Directory*, 1864, p. 226; SMM: Benevolent Society Minute-Book 1857-1891, 17 Feb. 1870.

18. *The Catholic Directory*, 1880, p. 388; SMM: Benevolent Society Minute-Book 1857-1891, 16 Dec. 1880.

19. SMM: Benevolent Society Minute-Book 1857-1891, 13 Dec. 1883, 21 Feb. 1884.

20. SMM: Benevolent Society letter book 1895-1900, Letter from James McAdams to Dr Kelly dated 22 May 1896, p. 58.

21. Archives of St Scholastica's Retreat (SSR): R.A. Kidd, 'St John's Hospice'.

22. SSR: 'The Will of William Harrison of The Triangle Mare Street Hackney', Oct. 1875; R.A. Kidd, 'The Harrison Family of Hackney 1792-1876'.

23. 'St Scholastica's Retreat, Clapton, and the adjoining new mission of the Fathers of Charity', *The Tablet*, 27 Sept. 1862, p. 613.

24. Mangion, C.M. 'Housing the "Decayed Members" of the Middle Classes: social class and St Scholastica's Retreat, 1861-1900', *Continuity and Change*, 29:3, 2014, pp. 373-98.

25. This is only a rough, and minimal, estimate. The list of almshouse occupants from St Joseph's, Hammersmith was calculated from Annual Reports and may not include all residents. The Hoxton almshouse occupants were derived from the Hoxton minutes which did not list all elected almspeople. All that was available to calculate the list of St John's Hospice and St Joseph's, Chelsea almspeople was the decennial censuses. Only St Scholastica's Retreat archives contained an inmate register which appears to be complete for the 19th century.

26. Anon. 'Christian Charity and Political Economy', *The Dublin Review* 21X New Series: 1877, pp. 360-86, pp. 380-1.

27. Gilley, 1971, pp. 64-89, 67.

28. Guy, R.E. O.S.B., (ed.), *The Synods in English: being the text of the four Synods of Westminster. Stratford-on-Avon*, St Gregory's Press, 1886, p. 298. This synodal letter from Archbishop of Westminster H.E. Manning was published after the Fourth Synod dated 12 Aug. 1873.

29. Booth, C. *Life and Labour of the People in London Third Series: religious influences.* Vol. 2. London, Macmillan, 1902, p. 38.

30. *The Catholic Directory*, 1855, p. 197.

31. Louisa Twining, in her report to the Select Committee on Poor Relief noted that the Women's Visiting Society was not allowed to visit some workhouses because 'admission of visitors involves the admission of Roman Catholics' and the 'jealousy' of workhouse officials who were suspicious of inspection by outsiders who had befriended inmates. British Parliamentary Papers (BPP): Reports from Committees, Fourth Report from the Select committee on Poor Relief (England) 1861, Vol IX, paragraph 11405; 11455-11477.

32. Though, as will be discussed later, the Hoxton Almshouse was open to all creeds.

33. Personal communication from Sarah Hare 13 September 2011.

34. Ibid.

35. Ibid.

36. St John O'Neil, B.H. 'Ridley's Almshouses Bristol', *Transactions of the Bristol & Gloucestershire Archaeological Society* 70, 1951, pp. 54-63, p. 55.

37. Charity Commission website URL: www.charity-commission.gov.uk, accessed 22 Jan. 2012. Charity 205293. Thanks to Sylvia Pinches for alerting me to this almshouse.

38. Charity Commission website URL: www.charity-commission.gov.uk, accessed 8 Aug. 2011. Charity 243833.

39. Personal communication from Sarah Hare 13 September 2011.

40. *The Catholic Directory*, 1850, pp. 143-4.

41. *The Catholic Directory*, 1851, p. 143.

42. This is only partially true for St Scholastica's Retreat. A church adjacent to St Scholastica's Retreat was planned but a mass centre was not built until 1882. There was a priest resident at St Scholastic's Retreat from 1861 to 1873; but from 1873 to 1882 the almshouse was served by the priest from Homerton parish. SSR: 'St Scholastica's Retreat: a short historical record' compiled by the Warden, Gilmore, H., 1966, pp. 20-2 and 'History of St Scholastica's', 1987, p. 2.

43. Egger, J. *Consolations of the sick-room; and the Christian Nurse's Guide.* London, Burns & Oates, 1900, p. 14.

44. Catholic Truth Society, *How to help the Sick and Dying.* London, Catholic Truth Society, London, ca. 1890, p. 24.

45. *The Catholic Directory*, 1855, p. 198.

46. SSR: St Scholastica's Retreat Register, inmate 107. Mary Jane was received into the Roman Catholic Church eight years later and in 1895 returned to live with her father as a co-inmate.

47. AAW: Box AIE, 'Correspondence Copy Book 1873-1874', Letter from John Haly to Henry Lewinton dated 11 June 1874, p. 41.

48. LMA: 4439/02/001, *Aged Poor Society and St Joseph's Almshouses Annual Report*, 1853, p. 10.

49. SMM: Benevolent Society letter book (1895-1900), Letter from James McAdams to Miss A.M. Clerke dated 18 Nov. 1896, p. 150.

50. SMM: Benevolent Society letter book (1895-1900), Letter from James McAdams to Cecil Clarke, Esq dated 7 Dec. 1897, p. 321.

51. *The Catholic Directory*, 1855, p. 197.

52. Mangion, C.M. '"Meeting a well-known want": Catholic Specialist Hospitals for Long-Term Medical Care in Late Nineteenth-Century England and Wales' in *Hospitals and Communities, 1100-1960*, Bonfield, C.,

Huguet-Termes, T. & Reinarz, J. (eds), Oxford, 2013, pp. 239-62; Mangion, C.M. 'Faith, Philanthropy and the Aged Poor', 2012. Brian Carter notes a similar pattern of philanthropic giving in the period 1810-1840: Carter, 2001, pp. 648-69, & 666-7.

53.   Pearce, p. 60.

54.   Goose, N. & Moden, L. *A History of Doughty's Hospital Norwich, 1687–2009*. Hatfield, Hertfordshire, 2010, pp. 4-8.

55.   Information was not available for all almshouses.

56.   Both the Aged Poor Society and the Benevolent Society operated as 'subscriber democracies' where subscribers nominated pensioners that met the specified criteria in Table 20.II. St Scholastica's Retreat nomination policies were more opaque, though it appears as though clergy, bishops and the trustees suggested potential pensioners. Morris, R.J. 'Voluntary Societies and British Urban Elites, 1780-1850: an analysis', *The Historical Journal* 26: 1, 1983, pp. 95-118, p. 101.

57.   *The Catholic Directory*, 1855, p. 197.

58.   SMM: Benevolent Society letter book (1895-1900), Letter from James McAdam to the Earl of Denbigh 27 Dec. 1895; Letter from James McAdam to the Earl of Denbigh 27 Dec. 1895, pp. 1-2.

59.   SMM: Benevolent Society letter book (1895-1900), Letter from James McAdam to the Earl of Denbigh 27 Dec. 1895; Letter from James McAdam to the Earl of Denbigh 31 Dec. 1895, p. 3.

60.   SMM: Benevolent Society letter book (1895-1900), Letter from James McAdam to The very Revd L. Canon Pycke 17 Jan. 1896; Letter from James McAdam to D.J. Flanagan 17 Jan. 1896, p. 11.

61.   SMM: Benevolent Society letter book (1895-1900), Letter from James McAdam to Hon H. Thomas Preston 25 April 1896, p. 47.

62.   I have used 1891 for this discussion as this is the latest census year where all five almshouse were operating. I have analysed almshouse residents using each of the decennial censuses from 1861 to 1901 and there is no significant variance from the demographic profile that I am discussing.

63.   Goose, N. & Basten, S. 'Almshouse Residency in Nineteenth-century England: an interim report', *Family & Community History* 12: 1, 2009, pp. 65-76, p. 69. This closely aligns to Goose and Basten's preliminary findings of 82.65% female occupants in Middlesex almshouses.

64.   Goose, N. 'Poverty, Old Age and Gender in Nineteenth-century England: the case of Hertfordshire', *Continuity and Change* 20: 3, 2005, pp. 351-84, pp. 351-2.

65.   Mangion, C. 'Housing the "Decayed Members of the Middle and Upper Classes"', 2014.

66.   Goose and Basten's statistics on the ages of almshouse residents point to similar results with a median and mode of 70 years, a mean of 64 and a 60 to 90 age range. Their figures include all almshouse occupants, whereas mine include only elected residents. Goose & Basten, 2009, pp. 65-76, p. 70.

67.   Census enumerators unfortunately did not consistently report occupation on the census worksheets. In addition, translating the 'rank, profession, or occupation' column in the census into social class is difficult. For example, 'living on own means' can reflect the means of a servant or a gentlemen. This essay has used occupational categories very broadly in order to suggest social class.

68.   'Death of Miss Harrison', *The Tablet*, 26 Oct. 1867, pp. 675-6.

69.   Calculated by the author from SSR: St Scholastic's Register and the census. For more on waged occupations of St Scholastica Retreat residents see Mangion, C.M. 'Housing the "Decayed Members of the Middle and Upper Classes"', 2014.

70.   Joyce, P. *Patronage and Poverty in Merchant Society: the history of Morden College, Blackheath 1695 to the present*. Henley-On-Thames, Gresham Books, 1982, pp. 1, 23. Anne Shepherd, in her examination of mental health care for the middle classes, also notes that the middles classes were seen as needing separate institutions. Shepherd, A.C. 'Mental Health Care and Charity for the Middling Sort: Holloway Sanatorium 1885-1900', in *Medicine, Charity and Mutual Aid: the consumption of health and welfare in Britain, ca 1550-1950*, Borsay A. & Shapely P. (eds). Aldershot, Hampshire, Ashgate, 2007, pp. 163-82, p.182.

71.   Unfortunately, I have found no extant documented evidence of voluntary or involuntary interactions in common areas of the almshouses.

72.   *The Catholic Directory*, 1850, pp. 143-4.

73.   LMA: Aged Poor Society *Annual Report*, 1857, 2nd page.

74.   Lester argues that bankruptcies were on the increase in the nineteenth century. Lester, V.M. *Victorian Insolvency: Bankruptcy, Imprisonment for Debt, and Company Winding-up in Nineteenth-Century England*. Oxford, Clarendon Press, 1995, pp. 163-7, 299.

75.   LMA: Aged Poor Society *Annual Report*, 1862, p. 5, *also* Aged Poor Society *Annual Report*, 1900, pp. 3-4. Upon her death in 1851, Miss Theresa Molineux, a 'very old subscriber' of the Aged Poor Society left the residue of her estate, (which amounted to £560 annually) to the Society. This was used to increase the

number of out-relief pensioners from seventy to one hundred, and to nominate two almshouse inmates who received £20 a year from the Molineux Fund.

76.   LMA: Aged Poor Society *Annual Report*, 1864, pp. 5-6.

77.   LMA: Aged Poor Society *Annual Report*, 1864, p. 67.

78.   LMA: 4439/01/002, Almshouse Committee Minute Book, 1850-1869 'Rules and Regulations of St Joseph's Alms Houses' after 30 May 1853 entry.

79.   LMA: Aged Poor Society *Annual Report,* 1867, p. 43. The guarantee form appears first in the 1867 annual report. By 1900 the pension amount was quantified at 7s. per week. LMA: Aged Poor Society *Annual Report*, 1901, pp. 49, 56-7.

80.   This data was gathered from the 1851 to 1901 censuses of the St Joseph's Almshouse (Chelsea) and Hoxton Almshouse. As mentioned about, this data is incomplete because not all residents' occupations were listed in the census.

81.   SMM: Benevolent Society Minute-Book 1857-1891, 15 Dec. 1870.

82.   SMM: Benevolent Society Minute-Book 1857-1891, 16 Feb. 1871, 16 March 1871.

83.   LMA: Aged Poor Society *Annual Report*, 1853, p. 8.

84.   St Joseph's Society Archives (APS): Minute Book, 1887-1885, 24 Nov. 1877.

85.   For more on how subscriber democracies operate *see* Waddington, K. 'Subscribing to a Democracy?: management and the voluntary ideology of the London Hospitals, 1850-1900', *English Historical Review* cxviii: 476, 2003, pp. 357-79.

86.   Joyce, P. *Patronage and Poverty in Merchant Society: the history of Morden College, Blackheath 1695 to the present*. Henley-On-Thames, Gresham Books, 1982, p. 23.

87.   This begs the question of how well the different social classes got along together. While minutes do record some friction between almshouse occupants, there is no explicit suggestion that frictions were because of the social class of the almspeople.

88.   LMA: Aged Poor Society *Annual Report*, 1867, p. 43.

89.   'Christian Charity and Political Economy', *The Dublin Review* 21X New Series: 1877, pp. 360-86, pp.377-9.

90.   This Catholic ideology was not consistently adhered to in other institutions, numerous examples exist where schools separated students by social class.

91.   Prochaska, F.K. 'Philanthropy' in *The Cambridge Social History of Britain 1750-1950: social agencies and institutions*, F. M. L. Thompson, (ed.). Cambridge, Cambridge University Press, 1990, pp. 357-93, p. 375.

92.   SMM: Benevolent Society Minute-Book 1857-1891, 14 Dec. 1876; 16 Feb. 1888; 18 June 1891.

93.   SSR: St Scholastica's Retreat Register, inmates 180, 184, 189 and 191. There were no reasons noted for their refusal of the almshouse place.

94.   SMM: Benevolent Society Minute-Book 1857-1891, 14 Sept. 1882,154 Feb. 1883.

95.   Author's calculations made from SMM: Benevolent Society Minute-Book 1857-1891. Mangion, C.M. 'Faith, Philanthropy and the Aged Poor', 2012.

96.   SMM: Benevolent Society Minute-Book 1857-1891, Aug. 1882.

97.   SMM: Benevolent Society Minute-Book 1857-1891, 18 Dec. 1885.

98.   LMA: St Joseph's Almshouses*, Annual Report*, 1878, p. 4.

99.   SSR: Calculated from St Scholastica's Retreat Register.

100.   APS: St Joseph's Alms Houses Brook Green Minute Book 1866-77, Aug. 1868.

101.   LMA: St Joseph's Almshouses*, Annual Report*, 1880, p. 4.

102.   Thane, P. *Old Age in English History: past experiences, present issues*. Oxford, Oxford University Press, 2000, p. 302; Botelho L. & Thane P. (eds) *Women and Ageing in British Society since 1500*. London, Longman, 2001, p. 215.

103.   These networks of Catholic care, especially the links between religious and lay institutions, need to be researched in more detail.

104.   SMM: Benevolent Society Minute-Book 1857-1891, 13 Jan. 1874, 18 Mar. 1875, 15 Nov. 1877, 14 Mar. 1878.

105.   SMM: Benevolent Society Minute-Book 1857-1891, 18 June 1885, 14 April 1887, 27 Oct. 1887 and 12 July 1888.

106.   APS: St Joseph's Alms Houses Brook Green Minute Book 1866-77, 9 Nov. 1868.

107.   Bryson, J.R., McGuiness, M. & Ford, R.G. 'Chasing a 'loose and baggy monster': almshouses and the geography of charity'. *Area* 34: 1, 2002, pp. 48-58; Goose & Basten, 2009, pp. 65-76.

BIBLIOGRAPHY

Alcock, N. *People at Home: living in a Warwickshire village 1500-1800*. Phillimore, Chichester, 1993.

Aliberti, M., 'The Lawrence Sheriff Almshouses', *Aspects of the Past III*. Rugby Local History Research Group, Rugby, 2001.

Anderson, W.J. *A History of the Catholic Parish of St Mary's, Chelsea*. Samuel Walker, Hinckley, Leicestershire, 1938.

Anon. *A Short History for the 125th Anniversary*. Trustees of the Cuckfield Cottage Homes Trust, Cuckfield, Sussex, 2007.

Anon. 'Christian Charity and Political Economy', *The Dublin Review,* 21X New Series: 1877.

Anon. 'Robert Stiles, Merchant, of Amsterdam', *Wiltshire Notes and Queries*, Dec. 1914.

Anon. 'St Scholastica's Retreat, Clapton, and the adjoining new mission of the Fathers of Charity', *The Tablet*, 27 Sept. 1862.

Archer, I.W. 'Hospitals in sixteenth- and seventeenth-century England', in Europäisches Spitalswesen. Institutionelle Fürsorge in Mittelalter und Früher Neuzeit: Hospital and Institutional Care in Medieval and Early Modern Europe, M. Scheutz, *et al.* (eds) *Mitteilungen des Instituts für österreichische Geschichtsforschung*, 51, 2008.

Archer-Thompson W. *Drapers' Company: History of the Company's Properties and Trusts*. London, 1940.

Ashbee, CR. *The Trinity Hospital in Mile End*. The Guild and School of Handicraft, London, 1896.

Ashmole, E., *The Antiquities of Berkshire Vol. I: With a Large Appendix of Original Papers, Pedigrees of Families in the Said County, and a Particular Account of the Castle and Town of Windsor*. William Carnan, Reading, 1736.

Athinson, T., *Elizabethan Winchester*. Faber & Faber, London, 1963.

Baigent, F. & Millard, J. *History of Basingstoke*. Jacob, Basingstoke, 1889.

Bailey, B. *Almshouses*. Robert Hale Ltd, London, 1988.

Bakewell-Reliquary, Vol. 4, 1863.

Ballantyne, A. 'First Principles and Ancient Errors: Soane at Dulwich', *Architectural History,* 37, 1994.

Batho, G.R. (ed.). *Household Papers of Henry Percy, 9th Earl of Northumberland (1564-1632)*. Royal Historical Society, London, Camden Series 3.

Beckett, J.F. *The Buckinghamshire Posse Comitatus 1798*. Buckinghamshire Record Society, Aylesbury, 1985.

Belfield, G. 'Cardinal Beaufort's almshouse of noble poverty at St Cross, Winchester', *Proceedings of the Hampshire Field Club*, 38, 1982.

Ben-Amos, I.K. *The Culture of Giving. Informal Support and Gift-Exchange in Early Modern England*. Cambridge University Press, Cambridge, 2008.

Bettington, E. J. *Transactions of the Woolhope Naturalists Field Club*, 1930.

Binding, H. *West Somerset Free Press Newspaper*. 15 April 2005.

Black, D. *History of Brechin to 1864*. William Paterson, Edinburgh, 1867.

Blandy, W.E.M. *History of the Reading Municipal Charities: including Allen's Charity and the Green Girls' Foundation*. Greenslade and Co., Reading, 1962.

Blunden, E. *An Anthology of Modern Verse*. Methuen & Co. Ltd, London, 1930.

Bolitho, P. *Warwick's Most Famous Son*. The Charity of Thomas Oken and Nicholas Eyffler. Warwick, 2003.

Bond, J. *Somerset Parks and Gardens*. Somerset Books, Tiverton, 1998.

Booth, C. *Life and Labour of the People in London Third Series: Religious Influences*. Vol. 2. Macmillan, London, 1902.

Botelho L. & Thane P. (eds). *Women and Ageing in British Society since 1500*. Longman, London, 2001.

Bretton, R. 'Crossleys of Dean Clough', *Halifax Antiquarian Society Transactions,* i-iv, 1950-54.

Bridge, M. *Waddington Village Life in the Nineteenth Century*. Hudson, Settle, 1994.

British Parliamentary Papers: Reports from Committees, Fourth Report from the Select Committee on Poor Relief (England), Vol. IX, 1861.

Broad, J. 'Parish Economies of Welfare, 1650-1834', *Historical Journal,* 42, no. 4, 1999.

Broad, J. 'Housing the Rural Poor in Southern England, 1650-1850', *The Agricultural History Review*, 48, 2000.

Brown, A. *The Whiteley Homes Trust 1907-77*. Phillimore, Chichester, 1992.

Brunskill, E. *Some Yorkshire Almshouses*. York Georgian Society, York, 1960.

Bryson, J.R. & Ford, R.G. *The Almshouse Renaissance and the Care of the Elderly and Poor in Urban and Rural Britain, Final Report for the Nuffield Foundation*. University of Birmingham, Birmingham, 2000.

Bryson, J.R., McGuiness, M. & Ford, R.G. 'Chasing a 'loose and baggy monster': almshouses and the geography of charity'. *Area*, 34: 1, 2002.

Bullen, M., Crook, J. *et al*. *The Buildings of England: Hampshire: Winchester and The North*. Yale, New Haven & London, 2010.

Caffrey, H. *Almshouses in the West Riding of Yorkshire: 1600 -1900*. Heritage Marketing & Publications Ltd, Kings Lynn, 2006.

Caffrey, H. 'Durham Aged Miners' Homes: unique provision for retired workers', *Journal of the Durham County Local History Society*, 80, 2015.

Caffrey, H. 'Faith, Penitence and Charity: Pugin, Myers and Sibthorp at St. Anne's Bedehouses, Lincoln', *True Principles* (Journal of the Pugin Society), vol. iv no. iv, 2014.

Caffrey, H. Housing the Elderly Poor: from philanthropist to local authority, *Yorkshire Archaeological Journal*, 87, 2015.

Caffrey, H. 'The Almshouse Experience in the Nineteenth-century West Riding'. *Yorkshire Archaeological Journal*, Vol. 76, 2004.

Caird, J. *English Agriculture in 1850-51*. Longmans, London, 1852.

Carpenter-Turner, B. *St John's Almshouse Charity*. Phillimore, Chichester, 1992.

Carr, A. 'An Introduction to the Endowed Charities of Anglesey', *Transactions of the Anglesey Antiquarian Society*, 1966.

Carter, B. 'Catholic Charitable Endeavour in London. 1810-1840. Part I', *Recusant History*, 25: 3, 2001.

Carter, B. 'Catholic Charitable Endeavour in London. 1810-1840, Part II', *Recusant History*, 25: 4, 2001.

Catholic Truth Society, *Handbook of Catholic Charities, Associations, etc., in Great Britain*. Catholic Truth Society, London, 1894.

Catholic Truth Society, *How to help the Sick and Dying*. Catholic Truth Society, London, *ca* 1890.

Chapman, G.T.L., McCombie, F. & Wesencraft, A. (Eds). *A New Herball, Parts II and III. 1562*, 2 vols. Cambridge University Press, Cambridge, 1955.

Charity Commissioners' Report for Anglesey. BPP, London, 1833.

Charity Commissioners' Report for Anglesey. BPP, London, 1897.

Charity Commissioners' Report for Buckinghamshire, XVIII. BPP, London, 1833.

Charity Commissioners' Report for Buckinghamshire, XXI. BPP, London, 1834.

Charity Commissioners' Report for Buckinghamshire, XII. BPP, London, 1856.

Charity Commissioners' Report on City of London Livery Companies, Vol. 4. BPP, London, 1884.

Charity Commissioners' Report for County Durham. BPP, London, 1830.

Charity Commissioners' Report for Derbyshire. BPP, London, 1815-35.

Charity Commissioners' Report for Gloucestershire. BPP, London, 1828.

Charity Commissioners' Report for Gloucestershire. BPP, London, 1819-1837.

Charity Commissioners' Report for Hampshire 1819-1837. BPP, London, 1890.

Charity Commissioners' Report for Hampshire and the Isle of Wight, 1837-38. BPP, London, 1837.

Charity Commissioners' Report for Herefordshire. BPP, London.

Charity Commissioners' Report for London, Vol. 1. BPP, London, 1897.

Charity Commissioners' Report for London, Vol. 12. BPP, London, 1825.

Charity Commissioners' Report for Norfolk. BPP, London, 1815-35.

Charity Commissioners' Report for Oxfordshire. BPP, London, 1825.

Charity Commissioners' Report for Staffordshire. BPP, London, 1839.

Charity Commissioners' Report for Warwickshire. BPP, London, 1819-35.

Charity Commissioners' Report for the West Riding, Vol. 4. BPP, London, 1897-9.

City of London Livery Companies Commission 'Report on the Charities of the Drapers' Company: Appendix', Vol. 4, 1884.

Clark, A. (ed.). *Sherborne Almshouse Register*. Dorset Record Society, Vol. 17, Dorchester, 2013.

Clark, P. (ed.). *Country Towns in Pre-Industrial England*. Leicester University Press, Leicester, 1981.

Clay, R. M. *The Mediaeval Hospitals of England*. Methuen & Co., London, 1909.

Cleary, J. & Orton, M. *So long as the world shall endure: the 500 year history of Ford's and Bond's Hospitals*. Coventry Church Charities, Coventry, 1991.

Clifford, D. J. H. (ed.). *The Diaries of Lady Anne Clifford*. Sutton, Stroud, 1990.

Cockburn, E. O. *The Almshouses of Dorset*. The Friary Press, Dorchester, 1970.

Colloms, B. 'The Rev. Sydney Godolphin Osborne, Parson and Crusader 1808-1889' in Victorian Country Parsons. Constable, London, 1977.

Cook's *Directory of Derby and district*. W.J. Cook, Derby, 1900.

Cooper, A. T. P. *Wimborne St Giles Church 'A Ninian Comper Restoration'*. St Giles Church booklet, Wimborne, (undated).

Coss, P. *The origins of the English gentry*. Cambridge University Press, Cambridge, 2003.

Coull, W.W. & Johns, T.W. *Dorward House, An Anniversary History 1838-1988*. Angus Council, Angus, 1988.

Cox, C. *The clergy list of 1852*. C. Cox, London, 1852.

Cox, J. *London's East End*. Weidenfeld & Nicolson, London, 1994.

Crawford, A. *The Vintners' Company*. Constable, London, 1977.

Crockford's Clerical Directory. J. Crockford, London. 1868, 1874.

Crust, L. *Lincolnshire Almshouses: nine centuries of charitable housing*. Heritage Lincolnshire, Sleaford, 2002

Cunnington, P. & Lucas, C. *Charity Costumes*. A. & C. Black Limited, London, 1978.

D. & S. Lysons, *Magna Britannia*. Vol. 4. Cumberland. T. Cadell & W. Davies, London, 1816.

Darby, H.C. & Campbell, E.M.J. (eds). *The Domesday Geography of South-East England*. Cambridge University Press, Cambridge, 1962.

Darby, H.C. (ed.). *An Historical Geography of England before 1800*. Cambridge University Press, Cambridge, 1936.

Darley, G. *Villages of Vision*. Architectural Press, London, 1975.

Davies, J. *A History of Southampton*. Gilbert & Co, Winchester, 1883.

Dickens, C. *The Uncommercial Traveller*. Oxford University Press reprint, Oxford, 1964.

Dickens, C. *The Uncommercial Traveller*. Mandarin Paperbacks, London, 1991.

Donachie, I. & Hewitt, G. *A Companion to Scottish History from the Reformation to the Present*. Batsford, London, 1989.

Draisey, D. *Women in Welsh History*. Draisey Publishing, Swansea, 2004.

Durston, C.G. 'London and the Provinces: the association between the capital and the Berkshire county gentry of the early 17th Century', *Southern History*, Vol. 3, 1981.

Dyer, C. *Standards of living in the Later Middle Ages: social change in England ca 1200-1520*. Cambridge University Press, Cambridge, 1989.

Dyson, T. *The History of Christchurch*. Henbest, Bournemouth, 1954.

Eason, A.H. *The Story of the Fishmongers' and Poulterers' Institution 1827-1927*. Whitefriars Press, London, 1930.

Egger, J. *Consolations of the sick-room; and the Christian Nurse's Guide*. Burns & Oates, London, 1900.

Englander, D. *Poverty and poor law reform in 19th century Britain, 1834-1914: from Chadwick to Booth*. Longman, London, 1998.

Fairfax-Lucy, A. (ed.). *Mistress of Charlecote: the memoirs of Mary Elizabeth Lucy*. Gollancz, London, 1983.

Farr, M. 'Nicholas Eyffeler of Warwick, glazier: executors' accounts and other documents concerning the foundation of his almshouse charity', 1592-1621 in Bearman, R. (ed.) *Miscellany*. Dugdale Society Publication 31, Stratford-upon-Avon, 1977.

Farrington, A.J. *A Biographical Index of East India Company Service Officers 1600-1834*. British Library, London, 1999.

Finch, J. 'Twyford almshouses', *Journal of the Twyford & Ruscombe Local History Society*, Vol. 34, 1993.

Fissell, M.F. 'Charity universal? Institutions and moral reform in eighteenth-century Bristol', in *Stilling the Grumbling Hive. The Responses to Social and Economic Problems in England, 1689-1750*. Davidson, L. *et al.*, (eds), Alan Sutton, Stroud, 1992.

Fordyce, W. *The History & Antiquities of the County Palatine of Durham*. Vol. 2. Nichols & Son, London, 1857.

Foster, J. *Alumnae Oxoniensis*. Oxford, 1888-92, Nendeln/Liechtenstein, Kraus Reprint,1968.

Fowler, J. *Mediaeval Sherborne*. Longmans (Dorchester) Ltd., Dorchester, 1951.

Fowler, J. *Richard Waldo Sibthorp: a Biography*. Skeffington, London, 1880.

Fowler, S. *Workhouse: The People, The Places, The Life Behind Doors*. The National Archives, Richmond, 2007.

Fox, G. *The History of Pontefract in Yorkshire*. J. Fox, Pontefract, 1827.

Freeman, M. & Wannell, L. 'The family and community lives of older people after the Second World War: new evidence from York', *Local Population Studies*, 2009.

Gardner's *History, Gazetteer & Directory of Cambridge*. R. Gardner, Peterborough, 1851.

Garlick, V.F.M. *Newbury Charities and Gifts*. V.F.M. Garlick, Newbury, 1972.

Gillet, M. *Talbot Village: a Unique Village in Dorset 1850-1989*. Bournemouth Local Studies, Bournemouth, 1989.

Gilley, S. 'English Catholic Charity and the Irish Poor in London: Part I, 1700-1840', *Recusant History*, 11: 4, 1972.

Gilley, S. 'English Catholic Charity and the Irish Poor in London: Part II, (1840-1870)', *Recusant History*, 11: 5, 1972.

Gilley, S. 'Heretic London, Holy Poverty and the Irish Poor, 1830-1870', *The Downside Review*, 89: 294, 1971.

Glover, C. & Riden, P. (eds). *William Woolley's History of Derbyshire*. Derbyshire Records Society, Chesterfield, 1981.

Glover's *History and Directory of the Borough of Derby*. S. Glover, Derby, 1849.

Godfrey, W.H. *The English almshouse with some account of its predecessor the medieval hospital*. Faber and Faber, London, 1955.

Gommersall, M. & Whinney, R. 'The Hospital of St John Baptist, Winchester', *Hampshire Studies*. 2007.

Goodall, J.A.A. *God's House at Ewelme: life, devotion and architecture in a fifteenth-century almshouse*. Ashgate Publishing Ltd, Aldershot, 2001.

Gooder, E. *Temple Balsall from Hospitallers to a Caring Community, 1322 to modern times*. Phillimore, Chichester, 1999.

Goose, N. 'Decay and Regeneration in 17th Century Reading: a study in a changing economy', *Southern History*, Vol. VI, 1984.

Goose, N. 'Poverty, old age and gender in nineteenth-century England: the case of Hertfordshire', *Continuity and Change*, Vol. 20.3, 2005.

Goose, N. 'The English almshouse and the mixed economy of welfare: medieval to modern', *The Local Historian*, Vol. 40, 1, 2010.

Goose, N. 'The rise and decline of philanthropy in early modern Colchester: the unacceptable face of mercantilism?' *Social History,* 31, no. 4, 2006.

Goose, N. 'Victorian and Edwardian Almspeople: Doughty's Hospital, Norwich, 1837-1911', *Local Population Studies*, 84, Spring 2010.

Goose, N. 'Workhouse populations in the mid-nineteenth century; the case of Hertfordshire', *Local Population Studies*, Vol. 62, 1999.

Goose, N. & Basten, S. 'Almshouse residency in nineteenth century England: an interim report', *Family and Community History*, Vol. 12 no. 1, May 2009.

Goose, N. & Looijsteijn, H. 'Almshouses in England and the Dutch Republic circa 1350-1800: a comparative perspective', *Journal of Social History,* 45, no. 4, 2012.

Goose, N. & Moden, L. *A History of Doughty's Hospital Norwich, 1687-2009*. University of Hertfordshire Press, Hatfield, 2010.

Gordon, L. *Poorman's Nosegay*. Collins & Harvill Press, London, 1973.

Gorsky, M. *Patterns of philanthropy. Charity and society in nineteenth-century Bristol*. The Boydell Press, Woodbridge, 1999.

Gray, E.W. *History and Antiquities of Newbury and its Environs*. Hall and Marsh, Speenhamland, 1839.

Green, K. 'The Hospital of St. Mary, Chichester', *Otter Memorial Papers,* 34, University of Chichester, Chichester, 2013.

Gretton, *The Burford Record*. Oxford University Press, Oxford, 1920.

Griffith, W.P. 'Addysg a Chymdeithas ym Môn, 1540-1640' ['Learning and Community in Anglesey, 1540-1640'], *Transactions of the Anglesey Antiquarian Society*, 1985.

Griffiths, J.E. *Pedigrees of Anglesey and Caernarvonshire Families*. Privately printed, London, 1914.

Guilding, J.M. (ed.). *Reading Records: Diary of the Corporation Vol. II James I to Charles I (1603/4-1629)*. J. Parker and Co., London, 1895.

Guy, J. *Tudor England*. Oxford University Press, Oxford, 1988.

Guy, R.E. O.S.B. (ed.). *The Synods in English: Being the Text of the Four Synods of Westminster*. St Gregory's Press, Stratford-upon-Avon, 1886.

Hall, D. 'Unto yone hospital at the tounis end': the Scottish medieval hospital, *Tayside and Fife Archeological Journal*, 12, 2006.

Hall, D & Cachart, R. *Gazetteer of medieval hospital sites in Angus, Perth and Kinross and East, West and Midlothian council areas*. (Report prepared for Historic Scotland), Scottish Urban Archaeological Trust, Perth, 1997.

Hall, J. *A History of the Town and Parish of Nantwich, or Wich Malbank, in the County Palatine of Chester*. 2nd edn, E.J. Morton, Didsbury, 1972.

Hallett, A. *Almshouses*. Shire Publications Ltd, Princes Risborough, 2004.

Hargrove, W. *A History of York*. William Alexander, York, 1818.

Harriss, G.L. *Cardinal Beaufort: A Study in Lancastrian Ascendancy and Decline*. Clarendon Press, Oxford, 1988.

Hayes, R.C. *et al*. *Records of Early English Drama: Dorset/Cornwall*. University of Toronto Press, Toronto, 1999.

Haynes, N. *Perth and Kinross, An Illustrated Architectural Guide*. Rutland Press, Edinburgh, 2000.

Heather, P. *Andrew Windsor's Almshouses in Farnham*. Farnham & District Museum Society, Farnham, 2008.

Heimann, M. *Catholic Devotion in Victorian England*. Clarendon Press, Oxford, 1995.

Henstock, A. *A Georgian Country Town; Ashbourne*. Vol 2, Ashbourne Local History Group, Ashbourne, 1991.

Herbert, W. *History of the 12 Great Livery Companies*. W. Herbert, London, 1836.

Hey, D. *Derbyshire - a history*. Carnegie, Lancaster, 2008.

Higgs, E. *Making Sense of the Census Revisited*. London Institute of Historical Research, The National Archives, London, 2005.

Highmore, A. *Pietas Londinensis: the history, design and present state of the various public charities in and near London*. Phillips, London, 1810.

Hill, T. *The Gardener's Labyrinth, 1577*, Mabey, R. (ed.). Oxford University Press, Oxford, 1987.

Hillier, B. & Hanson, J. *The Social Logic of Space*. Cambridge University Press, Cambridge, 1984.

Hinde, A. & Turnbull, F. 'The Population of Two Hampshire Workhouses 1851-1861', *Local Population Studies*, Vol. 61, 1998.

Hindle S. 'Dependency, Shame and Belonging: Badging the Deserving Poor, c. 1550-1750', *Cultural and Social History*, Vol 1, 2004.

Hindle, S. *Dependency, Shame and Belonging: Badging the Deserving Poor, c. 1550-1750*. University of Warwick, Warwick, 2004.

Hindle, S. *On the Parish? The Micropolitics of Poor Relief in Rural England c.1550-1750*. Clarendon Press, Oxford, 2004.

Hindle, S. *The Birthpangs of Welfare: Poor Relief and Parish Governance in Seventeenth-Century Warwickshire*. Dugdale Society Occasional Paper 40, Stratford-upon-Avon, 2000.

Hitchcock, T. *et al*. (eds). *Chronicling Poverty: the Voices and Strategies of the English Poor, 1640-1840*. Macmillan Press Ltd, Basingstoke, 1997.

Hopewell, P. *Saint Cross England's Oldest Almshouse*. Phillimore, Chichester, 1995.

Horn, P. *Labouring Life in the Victorian Countryside*. Alan Sutton Publishing Ltd., Stroud, 1976.

Howson, B. *Almshouses. A Social and architectural history*. The History Press, Chalford, 2008.

Howson, B. *Houses of noble poverty: a history of the English almshouse*. Bellevue Books, Sunbury-on-Thames, 1993.

Hughes, D.L. & Williams, D.M. *Holyhead: The Story of a Port*. Hughes and Williams, Holyhead, 1981.

Hughes, M. *The Small Towns of Hampshire, Southampton*. Hampshire Archaeological Committee, 1976.

Humphreys, R. *Sin, Organised Charity and the Poor Law in Victorian England*. Macmillan, Basingstoke, 1995.

Hunt, T. F. *Designs for Parsonage Houses, Almshouses, etc., with examples of Gables and Other Curious Remains of Old English Architecture*. Longman, Rees, Orme, Brown & Green, London, 1827.

Hunter, J. *South Yorkshire*. Vol.II, London, 1831. Reprinted by EP Publishing, Wakefield, for Sheffield City Libraries, 1974.

Hutchins, J. *History and Antiquities of Dorset*. Bower & Nichols, London, 1774.

Hutchins, J. *The Annals and Iconography of Dorsetshire and Dorset Worthies, Extra Illustrated Edition*. Vol. XI. Collected and arranged by Broadley, A.M. Printed by W.V. Daniel, London & W. Frost, Bridport, 1954.

Hutchins, J. *The History and Antiquities of Dorset*. 3rd Edn, Vol. III. EP Publishing Ltd. in collaboration with Dorset County Council, Wakefield, 1868.

Hutton, W. *The History of Derby*. Nichols, Son & Bentley, Derby, 1817.

Hyams, E. *English Cottage Gardens*. Coln Het Books, London, 1970.

Jacob, W. M. *The Clerical profession in the long Eighteenth century 1680-1840*. Oxford University Press, Oxford, 2007.

James, J. *Wimborne Minster The History of a County Town*. Dovecote Press, Wimborne, 1982.

James, T.B. *Winchester*. Batsford, London, 1997.

Jenkins, J.G. *The Welsh Woollen Industry*. National Museum of Wales, Cardiff, 1969.

Johnstone, R. *The Thomas Huntbach Charity of the School and Almshouses – Shustoke*. Privately printed, Shustoke, 2006.

Jones, A. *A History of Dedham*. Wiles and Son, Colchester, 1907.

Jones, E. (ed.). *The Welsh in London, 1500-2000*. University of Wales Press on behalf of the Honourable Society of Cymmrodorion, Cardiff, 2001.

Jones, J. *Family Life in Shakespeare's England, Stratford-upon-Avon 1570-1630*. Sutton Publishing, Stroud, 1996.

Jones, J. (ed.). *Stratford-upon-Avon Inventories Vol. I, 1538-1625*. Dugdale Society, Stratford-upon-Avon, 2002.

Jordan, W.K. *Philanthropy in England 1480-1660. A study of the changing pattern of English social aspirations*. Russell Sage Foundation, New York, 1959.

Jordan, W.K. *The Charities of London, 1480-1660: the Aspirations and Achievements of the Urban Society*. Allen & Unwin, London, 1960.

Jordan, W.K. *The Charities of Rural England, 1480-1660: the Aspirations and Achievements of the Rural Society*. Allen & Unwin, London, 1961.

Joyce, P. *Patronage and Poverty in Merchant Society: The History of Morden College, Blackheath 1695 to the present*. Gresham Books, Henley-on-Thames, 1982.

Kaye, J. *The Cartulary of God's House Southampton*. Vol. 1, Southampton Record Series, Southampton, 1976.

Kelly's Post Office Directory of Berkshire, Buckinghamshire and Oxfordshire. Kelly & Co., London, 1895.

Kelly's Post Office Directory of Derbyshire. Kelly & Co., London, 1888.

Kelly's Post Office Directory of Derbyshire and Nottinghamshire. Kelly & Co., London, 1855.

Kelly's Post Office Directory of Hampshire including the Isle of Wight. Kelly & Co., London, 1875.

Kelly's Post Office Directory of Lincolnshire. Kelly & Co., London, 1861.

Kelly's Post Office Directory of Warwickshire. Kelly, E.R. & Co., London, 1882.

Kemp, H. L. *Derby Charities*. Bemrose, Derby, 1861.

Kemp, T. (ed.). *The Book of John Fisher, Town Clerk and Deputy Recorder of Warwick 1580-1588*. HT Cole & Son, Warwick, 1900.

Kidd, A. *State, society and the poor in nineteenth-century England*. Macmillan, Basingstoke, 1999.

King, A. D. *The Bungalow: the production of a global culture*. Routledge and Kegan Paul, London, 1984.

King, S. *Poverty and Welfare in England 1700-1850: a regional perspective*. Manchester University Press, Manchester, 2000.

King, S. & Tomkins, A. *The poor in England, 1700-1850: an economy of makeshifts*. Manchester University Press, Manchester, 2003.

Knight, B. *Voluntary Action*. Centris, London, 1993.

Knight, F. *The nineteenth-century church and English society*. Cambridge University Press, Cambridge, 1995.

Langley, A. 'Warwickshire Almshouses 1400-1914, Part II: Founders, buildings and residents', *FACHRS Newsletter*, Vol. 10, Feb. 2009.

Langley, A. 'Warwickshire Almshouses, 1400 to 1900: "Affording comfortable asylums to the aged and respectable poor"?', *Warwickshire History*, xiv/4, Winter 2009/10.

Langley, A. 'The Promised Land: Allotments in Nineteenth-Century Warwickshire', *Warwickshire History*, 8, ii, 2005-6.

Leivers, C. 'Housing the elderly in nineteenth-century Derbyshire: a comparison of almshouse and workhouse provision', *Local Population Studies*, 83, 2009.

Leroy, A. *History of the Little Sisters of the Poor*. Burns, Oates & Washbourne, London, 1925.

Lester, V.M. *Victorian Insolvency: Bankruptcy, Imprisonment for Debt, and Company Winding-up in Nineteenth-Century England*. Clarendon Press, Oxford, 1995.

Levack, B.P. *The Civil Lawyers in England, 1603-1641: a Political Study*. Clarendon Press, Oxford, 1973.

Lewis, S. (ed.). *A Topographical Dictionary of England*. Samuel Lewis, London, 1848.

Lloyd, J.E. & Jenkins, R.T. *Dictionary of Welsh Biography down to 1940*. Honourable Society of Cymmrodorion, London, 1959.

Lloyd, S. 'Cottage conversations: poverty and manly independence in eighteenth-century England', *Past and Present*, Vol. 184, 2004.

Longley, D. 'Tudor Rose, Castle Street, Beaumaris', *Transactions of the Anglesey Archaeological Society*, 2010.

Lurie, A. *The Language of Clothes*. Bloomsbury, London, revised edition 1992.

MacFarquhar, G. *Leamington Hastings Almshouses and Poor's Plots*. Trustees of Leamington Hastings Consolidated Charities, Rugby, 1984.

Mackinnon, D. '"Charity is really worth it when it looks that good" Rural women and bequests of clothing in early modern England', in Tarbin, S. & Broomhall, S. (eds) *Women, Identities and Community in Early Modern Europe*. Ashgate Publishing Ltd., Farnham, 2008.

Macpherson, E. & Fitchet, J.M. *Brechin through the Ages*. Angus District Libraries Museum Service, Angus, 1984.

Magilton, J., Lee, F. & Boylston, A. *"Lepers outside the gate" Excavations at the cemetery of the Hospital of St. James and St. Mary Magdalen, Chichester, 1986-87 & 1993*. Chichester Excavations Vol. 10, Research Report 158, Chichester, 2008.

Mangion, C.M. 'Developing Alliances: Faith, Philanthropy and Fundraising in nineteenth-century England' in *The Economics of Providence: Management, Finances and Patrimony of Religious Orders and Congregations in Europe 1773 to ca.1930*. Maarten Van Dijck, *et al.* (eds), Leuven University Press, Leuven, 2013.

Mangion, C.M. 'Housing the "decayed members" of the middle classes: social class and St Scholastica's Retreat, 1861-1900', *Continuity and Change*, 29:3, 2014.

Mangion, C.M., 'Faith, Philanthropy and the Aged Poor', *European Review of History,* 19: 4, 2012.

Mangion, C.M. 'Medical philanthropy and civic culture: Protestants and Catholics united by a 'common christianity'' in *Proceedings - First Danish History of Nursing Conference*, ed. Dietz, S.M. Faculty of Health Sciences, Aarhus, 2009.

Mangion, C.M. '"Meeting a well-known want": Catholic Specialist Hospitals for Long-Term Medical Care in Late Nineteenth-Century England and Wales' in *Hospitals and Communities, 1100-1960*. Bonfield, C., Reinarz, J. & Huguet-Termes, T. (eds), Peter Lang, Oxford, 2013.

Mannix & Whellan. *History Gazetteer and Directory of Cumberland*. Mannix & Whellan, Beverly, 1847.

Mansfield, A. Rationale of Irrational Clothes, in *Occupational Costume in England from the Eleventh Century to 1914*. Cunnington, P. & Lucas, C. (eds), A & C Black Limited, London, 1967.

Marsh, R.H. 'Presidential Address', *Journal of the Friends History Society*, Vol. 14, 4, 1917.

Matthew, N.C.G. & Harrison, B. *Dictionary of National Biography*. Oxford University Press, Oxford, 2004.

Matz B.W. 'Through Whitechapel with Dickens', *The Dickensian*, I, 9, Sept. 1905.

May, T. *The Victorian Workhouse*. Shire, Oxford, 1997.

Mayo, C.H. *A Historic Guide to the Almshouse of St John Baptist and St John the Evangelist Sherborne*. Oxford University Press, Oxford, 1926.

Mayo, C.H. *An Historic Guide to the Almshouse of St John the Baptist and St John the Evangelist, Sherborne*. Oxford University Press, Oxford, 1933.

McCombie, G. *Newcastle and Gateshead*. Yale University Press, New Haven, 2009.

McEwan, J. & Sharpe, P. (eds). *Accommodating Poverty: The Housing and Living Arrangements of the English Poor, c. 1600-1850*. Palgrave Macmillan, Basingstoke, 2011.

McIlwain, J. *The Hospital of St Cross and St Cross Church*. Pitkin, Andover, 1993.

McIntosh, M. 'Local responses to the poor in late medieval and Tudor England', *Community and Change*, 3 (2), 1988.

McIntosh, M.K. *Autonomy and community. The Royal Manor of Havering, 1200-1500*. Cambridge University Press, Cambridge, 1986.

McIntosh, M.K. *Controlling Misbehavior in England, 1370-1600*. Cambridge University Press, Cambridge, 2002.

McIntosh, M.K. *Poor Relief in England 1350-1600*. Cambridge University Press, Cambridge, 2012.

Milburn, G.E. & Miller, S.T. (eds). *Sunderland River, Town and People: a history from the 1780s*. Sunderland Borough Council, Sunderland, 1988.

Milne, R. *Rental Books of King James VI Hospital, Perth*. Wood & Son, Perth, 1891.

Mitchison, R. *The Old Poor Law in Scotland, 1574-1845*. Edinburgh University Press, Edinburgh, 2000.

Morant, P. *The History and Antiquities of Colchester, 1748*. Phillimore, Chichester, reprinted 1970.

Moretti, C. 'The Aged Poor Society and Saint Joseph's Almshouses', *Catholic Ancestor*, 10:3, 2004.

Morris, D. *Mile End Old Town 1740-1780: a social history of an early modern London suburb*. The East London History Society, London, 2002.

Morris, R.J. 'Voluntary Societies and British Urban Elites, 1780-1850: an analysis', *The Historical Journal*, 26: 1, 1983.

Morris, W.A.D. *A History of the Parish of Shaw-cum-Donnington*. W.A.D. Morris, Newbury, 1969.

Murdoch, T. & Vigne, R. *The French Hospital in England*. John Adamson, Cambridge, 2009.

Murray, J. *New Army List*. J. Murray, London, 1880.

Noel, G. *Sir Gerard Noel MP and the Noels of Chipping Campden and Exton*. Campden and District Historical & Archaeological Society, 2004.

Noorthouk, J. *A New History of London: Including Westminster and Southwark*. R. Baldwin, London, 1773.

Official Guide Book, *Eastbridge Hospital: the Hospital of St. Thomas the Martyr*.

Official Guide Book, *The Royal Hospital Chelsea*. Jarrold, Norwich, 2002.

Orme, N. & Webster, M. *The English Hospital 1070-1570*. Yale University Press, New Haven and London, 1995.

Owen, D. *English Philanthropy, 1660-1960*. Harvard University Press, Cambridge MA., 1965.

Pannell, J. & Thomas, C. *Almshouses into the next Millennium: paternalism, partnership, progress?* Policy Press, Bristol, 1999.

Parker, J. *Architectural Antiquities of the City of Wells*. Parker & Co, Oxford & London, 1860.

Pearson, E. *Ripon: some Aspects of History*. Dalesman, Clapham, 1972.

Pevsner, N. *The Buildings of England, Yorkshire: The North Riding*. Penguin Books, Harmondsworth, 1966.

Pevsner, N. *The Buildings of England, Yorkshire: York and the East Riding*. Penguin Books, Harmondsworth, 1972.

Pevsner, N. & Grundy, J. *The Buildings of England, Northumberland*. Penguin, London, 2nd edn, 1992.

Pevsner, N. & Lloyd, D. *The Buildings of England: Hampshire and the Isle of Wight*. Penguin, Harmondsworth, 1967.

Pigot, J. *Directory of Warwickshire*. J. Pigot & Co., London & Manchester, 1821.

Pigot's *National and Commercial Directories of Derbyshire*. J. Pigot & Co., London, 1828/9, 1842.

Platt, C. *Medieval England*. Routledge & Kegan Paul Ltd, London, 1978.

Porter, S. *The London Charterhouse*. Amberley, Chalford, 2009.

Potts, R. *Dame Sarah's Legacy: a history of the Lady Hewley Trust*. The Lady Hewley Trust, York, 2005.

Pountney, E.R. *Cleave's Almshouses 300th Anniversary*. Cleave's Almshouses, Kingston-upon-Thames, 1969.

Prescott, E. *The English Medieval Hospital: 1050-1640*. Seaby, London, 1992.

Prichard Jones Institute. *Catalogue of Books and Rules of the Institute*. Trustees of Prichard Jones Institute, London, 1905.

Prochaska, F.K. 'Philanthropy' in *The Cambridge Social History of Britain 1750-1950: Social Agencies and Institutions*. Thompson, F.M.L. (ed.), Cambridge University Press, Cambridge, 1990.

Prochaska, F.K. *The voluntary impulse. Philanthropy in modern Britain*. Faber and Faber, London, 1988.

Prochaska, F.K. *Women and Philanthropy in Nineteenth-Century England*. Clarendon Press, Oxford, 1980.

Pugin, A.W.N. *Contrasts, or, a parallel between the noble edifices of the fourteenth and fifteenth century and similar buildings of the present day; shewing the present decay of taste*. Contrasted Residences of the Poor, repr. Leicester University Press, Leicester, 1973.

Raphael, M. *The Romance of English Almshouses*. Mills and Boon, London, 1926.

Rawcliffe, C. 'Cartullary of St Mary's Hospital Great Yarmouth'. *Norfolk Record Society*, Norwich, Vol. 71, 2007.

Rawcliffe, C. *Leprosy in medieval England*. Boydell Press, Woodbridge, 2006.

Rawcliffe, C. *Medicine for the Soul. The Life, Death and Resurrection of an English Medieval Hospital*. Sutton Publishing, Stroud, 1997.

Rexroth, F. (trans. Selwyn P.E.). *Deviance and Power in Late Medieval London*. Cambridge University Press, Cambridge, 2007.

Reynolds, J. *The Great Paternalist*. Temple Smith, London, 1983.

Riden, P. & Fowkes, D. *Bolsover: castle, town and colliery*. Phillimore, Chichester, 2008.

Rodger, N.A.M. *The Safeguard of the Sea*. Penguin, London, 2004.

Roffey, S. *Chantry Chapels and Medieval Strategies for the Afterlife*. Tempus, Stroud, 2008.

Roffey, S. 'Medieval Leper Hospitals in England: an Archaeological Perspective', *Medieval Archaeology*, 56, 2012.

Rooke, J. *Reminiscences of Woburn by a ninety year old*. Drakeloe Press, Woburn, 1982.

Rose, M.E. *The Relief of Poverty, 1834-1914*. Macmillan Press, Basingstoke, 1972.

Rouse, W.H.D. *A History of Rugby School*. Duckworth, London, 1898.

Rubin, M. *Charity and community in Medieval Cambridge*. Cambridge University Press, Cambridge, 1987.

Rugby Local History Research Group. *Aspects of the Past III*. Rugby, 2001.

Salisbury, W. *Cottage Gardening*. Longman & Co, London, 1817.

Shepherd, A.C. 'Mental health care and charity for the middling sort: Holloway Sanatorium 1885-1900' in *Medicine, Charity and Mutual Aid: The Consumption of Health and Welfare in Britain, c 1550-1950*. Borsay A. & Shapely P. (eds), Ashgate, Aldershot, 2007.

Sinclair, Sir John (ed.). *The Statistical Account of Scotland, 1791-1799*. Vol XIII. E.P. Publishing, Wakefield, 1976.

Slack, P. *Poverty and Policy in Tudor and Stuart England*. Longman, London, 1988.

Slack, P. *The English Poor Law*. Macmillan, Basingstoke, 1990.

Smith, A.D. *The Derbyshire Economy in 1851*. Derbyshire County Council, Derby, 1977.

Solar, P.M. 'Poor Relief and English Economic Development Before the Industrial Revolution'. *Economic History Review*, XLVIII, I, 1995.

Sotheran, P. *Sir William Turner's Almshouses, Kirkleatham*. The Trustees of Sir William Turner's Hospital, Redcar, 2008.

Spaul, J. *Andover an Historical Portrait*. Andover History & Archaeology Society, Andover, 1977.

St John O'Neil, B.H. 'Ridley's Almshouses Bristol', *Transactions of the Bristol & Gloucestershire Archaeological Society*, 70, 1951.

Stanford, G. M. 'Old Charities' in *The Dorset Year Book*. Society of Dorset Men, Weymouth, 1961-2.

Statham, M. (ed.). *Accounts of the Feoffees of the Town Lands of Bury St Edmunds,1569-1622*. The Boydell Press, Woodbridge, 2003.

Stone, B.J. *A Record of England National Photographic Record Association*. Dewi Lewis Publishing, Stockport, 2006.

Stroud, D. *Sir John Soane Architect*. Faber, London, 1984.

Sweetinburgh, S. *The role of the Hospital in medieval England. Gift-giving and the spiritual economy*. Four Courts Press, Dublin, 2004.

Tames, R. *East End Past*. Historical Publications, London, 2004.

Taylor, B. *Abbot's Hospital, Guildford*. St Thomas's Trust, Guildford, 1999.

Thane, P. *Old Age in English History: Past Experiences, Present Issues*. Oxford University Press, Oxford, 2000.

The Catholic Directory, 'Charitable and other Institutions in London and its Environs'. Battersby, London, 1850, 1851, 1855, 1860, 1864, 1871, 1880, 1900.

The Handbook of Catholic Charitable and Social Works. Catholic Truth Society, London, 1905.

The Historical Register of the University of Oxford to 1900. Clarendon Press, Oxford, 1900.

The New Shorter Oxford English Dictionary. Oxford University Press, Oxford, 1993.

The New Statistical Account of Scotland. Vol XI, Blackwood & Sons, Edinburgh & London, 1845.

Thompson, F. *Lark Rise to Candleford*. Penguin Books Ltd, Harmondsworth, 1945.

Thornbury, G.W. 'The Regent's Park' in *Old and New London*. Cassell, Petter & Galpin, London, Vol. 5. 1878.

Tiffany, M.N.E. *The History of the Rev. Mr. William Stone and his Hospital*. The City of Oxford Charities, Oxford, 2000.

Tighe, R.R. & Davis, J.E. *Annals of Windsor being a history of the castle and town with some account of Eton and places adjacent*. Vol. II, Longman and Co., London, 1858.

Tompkins, A. 'Almshouse versus Poorhouse: Residential Welfare in Eighteenth-century Oxford', *Family and Community History*, Vol. 7.1, 2004.

Tomkins, A. *The Experience of Urban Poverty 1723-82. Parish, Charity and Credit*. Manchester University Press, Manchester, 2006.

Trollope, A. *The Warden, 1855*. Reprinted Oxford University Press, Oxford, 1998.

Trustees of the Almshouses of The Holy and Undivided Trinity, Castle Rising, Norfolk, Information Regarding Cloaks and Hats. Crome & Alker Ltd, [no place given], 1998.

Trutt, D. (ed). *Haddon Hall's Poems: an afterword*. David Trutt, Los Angeles, 2007.

Turner, W. *A New Herball, Part I*. 1551, Chapman, G.T.L. & Tweddle, M.N. (eds).

Underdown, D. *Revel, Riot and Rebellion: Popular Politics and Culture in England 1603-1660*. Oxford Paperback, Oxford, 1987.

Venn, J.A. *Alumni Cantabrigenses*. London, 1922-54.

Victoria County History, *A History of the County of Durham*, Vol. 2. Constable & Co., London, 1907.

Victoria County History, *A History of the County of Essex*, Vol 9. Oxford University Press, Oxford, 1994.

Victoria County History, *A History of Hampshire and the Isle of Wight*, Vol 2. Constable & Co, London, 1903.

Victoria County History, *A History of the County of Hampshire*, Vol. 5. Constable & Co., London, 1912.

Victoria County History, *A History of the County of Northamptonshire*, Vol. 3. St Catherine Press, London, 1930.

Victoria County History, *A History of the County of Shropshire*, Vol. 2. Oxford University Press, Oxford, 1973.

Victoria County History, *A History of the County of Stafford*, Vol. 3. Oxford University Press, Oxford, 1970.

Victoria County History, *A History of the County of Stafford*, Vol. 14. Oxford University Press, Oxford, 1990.

Victoria County History, *A History of the County of Warwickshire*, Vol. 2. Constable & Co., London, 1908.

Victoria County History, *A History of the County of Warwickshire*. Oxford University Press, London, 1945.

Victoria County History, *A History of the County of Wiltshire*, Vol. 6. Oxford University Press, Oxford, 1962

Waddington, K. 'Subscribing to a Democracy? Management and the Voluntary Ideology of the London Hospitals, 1850-1900', *English Historical Review*, cxviii: 476, 2003.

Wadmore, T.F. *Some Account of the Skinners' Company*. Blades, East & Blades, London, 1902.

Warren's *Directory of Winchester and District*. Warren, Winchester, 1895.

Watson, H. 'William Dorward Esquire', *Journal of the Tay Valley Family History Society*, June 2004.

Watson, W R. *The Illustrated History of Duffield*. Chevin Books, Otley, 1986.

Watts, S. *Shropshire Almshouses*. Logaston Press, Logaston, 2010.

Weaver, C & M. *The Seckford Foundation: four hundred years of a Tudor charity*. The Seckford Foundation, Woodbridge, 1987.

Webb, C. *Index of Vintners' Company Apprenticeships*. Society of Genealogists, London, 2004.

Wetton's *Guide to Northampton and its Vicinity*. SR Publishers, Wakefield, 1849, reprint 1969.

Whellan's *History, Topography and Directory of Northampton*. 2nd Edn, Francis Whellan & Co, London, 1874.

White, A. *The letters of S.G.O. A series of letters on public affairs written by the Rev. Lord Sydney Godolphin Osborne and published by The Times 1844-1888*. Griffin, Farrar, Okeden & Welsh, London, undated.

White's *Directory of Lincolnshire*. F. White & Co., Sheffield, 1850.

White's *History, Gazetteer and Directory of Derbyshire and Sheffield*. F. White & Co., Sheffield, 1857.

White's *History, Gazetteer & Directory of Devonshire*. W. White, Sheffield, 1850.

White's *History, Gazetteer & Directory of Staffordshire*. W. White, Sheffield, 1834.

White's *History, Gazetteer and Directory of Warwickshire*. F. White & Co., Sheffield, 1850.

White's *History, Gazetteer and Directory of Warwickshire*. F. White & Co., Sheffield, 1874.

White, W. & Co. *Directory of Northumberland and Durham*, E. Baines & Son, Leeds, 1827.

Wigmore, E. *Holy Trinity Hospital, Long Melford: a 16th century almshouse*. AP3 Imaging Services, Long Melford, 1995.

Williams, E.A. (trans. Gwynne Griffith, G.), *The Day before Yesterday. Anglesey in the Nineteenth Century*. G. Gwynne Griffith, Beaumaris, 1988.

Williams, K. *From Pauperism to Poverty*. Routledge and Kegan Paul, London, 1981.

Williams, L. & Thomson, S. (eds). *Marlborough Probate Inventories (1591-1775)*. Wiltshire Record Society, 59, Chippenham, 2007.

Williams, R.T. *(Trebor Môn), Nodion o Gaergybi, sef cyfres a lythyrau hynafiaithol, hanesol a chofianol am Ynys Cybi*, ['Notes from Holyhead, i.e. collections and letters ancient, historical and reminiscent about Holy Island'], H. Evans, Bala, 1879.

Wilson, J. *A History of the Durham Miners Association 1870-1904*. Veitch & Sons, Durham, 1907.

Wing, K.R. *A History of Bancroft's School, 1737-1987*. Bancroft's School, Woodford, 1987.

Witts, F.E. *Diary of a Cotswold Parson*. D. Verey (ed.), Alan Sutton, Stroud, 1986.

Woodfield, C. & Woodfield, P. *Lyddington Bedehouse*. English Heritage, London, 1988.

Wright's *Directory of Leicestershire*. C.N. Wright, Leicester, 1888.

Wright's *Directory of South Derbyshire*. C.N. Wright, Derby, 1874.

Wrightson, K. *Earthly Necessities: Economic Lives in Early Modern Britain, 1470-1750*. Penguin Books Ltd, London, 2002.

Wrigley, E.A. & Schofield, R.S. *The population history of England 1541-1871: a reconstruction*. Cambridge University Press, Cambridge, 1981.

Wrigley, E.A. *et al. English Population History from Family Reconstitution 1580-1837*. Cambridge University Press, Cambridge, 1997.

Young, S. *Annals of the Barber-Surgeons*. Blades, East & Blades, London, 1890.

Unpublished theses and papers

Blackmore, Son & Co. *Durham Aged Mineworkers' Homes Association Feasibility Study*. Hull, 1980. Unpublished report.

Caffrey, H. 'Charity at both ends of Life: schools and almshouses', (unpublished conference paper Open University) 2010.

Durston, C.G. 'Berkshire and its County Gentry, 1625-1649', unpublished PhD thesis, University of Reading, 1977.

Goose, N.R. 'Economic and social aspects of provincial towns: a comparative study of Cambridge, Colchester and Reading, c1500-1700', unpublished PhD thesis, University of Cambridge, 1984.

Griffith, W.P. 'Welsh Students at Oxford, Cambridge and the Inns of Court c.1540-1640', (unpublished PhD thesis, University of Wales, 1982), cited in Griffiths, W.P. 'Addysg a Chymdeithas ym Môn, 1540-1640' ['Learning and Community in Anglesey, 1540-1640'], *TAAS*, 1985.

Hunnyball, P. M. 'Status, Display and Dissemination: social expression and stylistic change in the architecture of seventeenth-century Hertfordshire', (unpublished DPhil. thesis, University of Oxford 1994).

Kanya-Forstner, M. 'The politics of survival: Irish women in outcast Liverpool, 1850-1890', (unpublished PhDThesis, University of Liverpool, 1997).

Lambert, S. '17th Century Berkshire Almshouses', (unpublished MPhil thesis, University of Reading, 1997).

Machin R. Probate Inventories and Manorial Excerpts of Chetnole, Leigh and Yetminster, (unpublished, Bristol, 1976).

Nicholls, A., 'The Relief of the elderly poor in early modern almshouses: a Warwickshire case study', unpublished MA dissertation, Warwick University, 2007 (WCRO library: C 362.6 Nic).

Pearce, L.R. 'Catholic Philanthropy in Mid-Nineteenth Century Britain: The Reformatory Work of the Female Congregations' (unpublished PhD thesis, University of Kent, 2003).

Pinches, S. 'Roman Catholic Charities and Voluntary Societies in the Diocese of Birmingham, 1834-1945' (unpublished MA dissertation, University of Leicester, 1997).

Tomkins, A. *Retirement from the noise and hurry of the world?: the experience of almshouse life 1650-1850*. Paper presented at Voluntary Action History Society Seminar 22 April 2008.

Websites

Roffey, S. & Marter, P. *2008, Excavations of St Mary Magdalen Leper Hospital, Winchester: 1st Interim web report.*

Chapter 1
URL: www.almshouses.info/, 'What are almshouses?' accessed 13th Jun. 2012.
Chapter 2
URL: www.imagesofengland.org.uk, accessed Oct. 2014.
URL: www.bristolcharities.org.uk, accessed Oct. 2014.
URL: www.leylandhistoricalsociety.co.uk, Fox Lane, accessed Oct. 2014.
URL: www.herefordcityheritage.info, Hereford's Almshouses: Coningsby's Hospital, accessed Oct. 2014.
URL: www.whiteleyvillage.org.uk, *Surrey County Magazine*, vol. 25, no 5, accessed Oct 2014.
URL: www.lentontimes.co.uk, The Lenton Listener, Albert Ball V.C., accessed Oct. 2014.
URL: www.chelseapensioners.org.uk, accessed Oct. 2014.
Chapter 3
URL: http://genuki.cs.ncl.ac.uk/DEV/WithycombeRaleigh/ALaRonde, accessed Dec. 2010.
URL: www.heritageopendays.org.uk, accessed Aug. 2011.
URL: http://en.wikipedia.org/wiki/A_La_Ronde, accessed Dec. 2010.
URL: www.imagesofengland.org.uk, entry 217087, accessed 2007.
Chapter 4
URL: www.winchester.ac.uk/academicdepartments/archaeology/Research/MHARP/Documents/MHARPREPO
RT_2010%20with%20copyright%20statement.pdf, accessed Apr. 2011.
URL: www.hants.gov.uk/an_overview_of_the_hampshire_landscape-2.pdf, p.31, accessed May 2011.
URL: www.winchester.ac.uk/archaeology/Leper.htm, accessed Apr. 2011.
Chapter 5
URL: www.oxforddnb.com/view/article/18167, accessed 12 Mar. 2010.
URL: www.oxforddnb.com/view/article/17128, accessed 12 Mar. 2010.
Chapter 6
URL: www.hrionline.ac.uk, accessed Sep. 2013.
URL: www.mercers.co.uk, accessed Sep. 2013.
URL: www.vintnershall.co.uk, accessed Sep. 2013.
URL: www.skinnershall.co.uk, accessed Sep. 2013.
URL: www.british-history.ac.uk, City of London Livery Companies Commission Report, Vol. 4, 1884, accessed
Sep. 2013.
URL: www.thedrapers.co.uk, Francis Bancroft, accessed Mar. 2011.
URL: www.thedrapers.co.uk, Fullers almshouses, accessed Sep. 2013.
URL: www.portcities.org, accessed Sep. 2013.
URL: www.ads.ahds.ac.uk/catalogue/adsdata/arch-457-1/dissemination/pdf/vol09/vol09_01/09_01_006_015.pdf,
accessed Sep. 2013.
URL: www.gihs.gold.ac.uk/gihs11.html, accessed Sep. 2013.
URL: www.trinityhouse.co.uk, Captains' Houses Mile End, accessed Sep. 2013.
URL: www.findmypast.co.uk, accessed Sep. 2013.
URL: www.cracroftspeerage.co.uk.online/content/AbdyBa1660, accessed Sep. 2013.
URL: www.mernick.org.uk/thhol/whitechapel, accessed Sep. 2013.
URL: www.newhamstory.com/node/1127, accessed Sep. 2013.
URL: books.google.co.uk/books?id=EiAFAAAAQAAJ, accessed Sep. 2013.
URL: www.oxforddnb.com, Michael Yoakley, accessed Sep. 2013.
URL: www.stokenewingtonquakers.org.uk, accessed Sep. 2013.
URL: www.michaelyoakley.com, accessed Sep. 2013.
URL: www.ucl.ac.uk/bloomsbury-project/institutions, accessed Aug. 2011.

URL: www.kouroo.info/kouroo/transclusions/18/80S/84/1884_ElizabethFry.pdf, accessed Sep. 2013.

URL: www,bevismarks.org.uk, accessed Sep. 2013.

URL: www.britishlistedbuildings.co.uk, German Jews' Hospital Mile End, accessed Sep. 2013.

URL: www.housingcare.org/housing-care/facility-info-129157, accessed Sep. 2013.

URL: www.lse.ac.uk/geographyAndEnvironment/theimpactofrecentimmigrationonthelondoneconomy.pdf, accessed Sep. 2013.

URL: www.jhse.org/book/export/article/15356, accessed Sep. 2013.

URL: www.jewishgen.org/JCR-UK/susser/roth/chfifteen.htm, accessed Sep. 2013.

Chapter 7

URL: http//www.vahs.org.uk, accessed Aug. 2011.

Chapter 9

URL: www.englandsnortheast.co.uk, accessed 20 Feb. 2012.

URL: http://en.wikipedia.org/wiki/keelmen, accessed 20 Feb. 2012.

URL: www.southtyneside.info/applications/2/listedbuildings, accessed 20 Jan. 2011.

URL: www.british-history.ac.uk, A Topographical Dictionary of England.

URL: www.ramsdale.org/scarboro.htm, accessed 2 Mar. 2011.

URL: www.trinityhouse.co.uk, Trinity Houses in the North East, accessed 20 Feb. 2012.

URL: www.bbc.co.uk/northyorkshire, accessed 20 Feb. 2012.

URL: www.british-history.ac.uk, A History of the County of York East Riding.

URL: www.trinityhousenewcastle.org.uk/history.asp.

URL: http://irenaus.net/how/ahnen12.html, accessed 20 Feb. 2012.

URL: www.sunderland.gov.uk, Listed Building Entry.

URL: www.durhamhomes.org.uk/theminersheritage.

URL: http://www3.northumberland.gov.uk/catalogue, NRO 08303/18.

URL: http://www.houghtonlespring.org.uk/articles/dedication_stones_in_houghton.htm, accessed 8 Feb. 2012.

URL: http://ushawmoor.awardspace.info/history/aged.htm, accessed 8 Feb. 2012.

URL: www.durhamhomes.org.uk, accessed 20 Feb. 2012.

Chapter 10

URL: www.visionofbritain.org.uk/data_theme_page.jsp?u_id=10134754&c_id=10001043&data_theme=T_POP, accessed 28 Aug. 2011.

URL: www.archive.org/details/annalsofbarbersu00youn.

URL: www.penmon.org/page83.htm, accessed 17 Apr. 2010.

URL: www.llgc.org.uk/fileadmin/fileadmin/docs_gwefan/amdanom_ni/cyfeillion/darlithoedd/cyfn_dar_CStevens_000916S.pdf, accessed 13 Dec. 2010.

URL: www.findmypast.co.uk/RG14/34/4, accessed 7 Aug. 2013.

Chapter 12

URL: www.british-history.ac.uk/report.aspx?compid=69711, accessed 31 Mar. 2009.

URL: www.frenchhospital.org.uk.

Chapter 13

URL: www.clergydatabase.org, accessed 2007-11.

URL: www.bl.uk/reshelp/findhelprestype/news/newspdigproj/database/.

Chapter 14

URL: www.archive.org/stream/mediaevalhospita00clayuoft#page/112/mode/2up, accessed Jan. 2011.

URL: www.british-history.ac.uk report.aspx?compid=39945, accessed Jan. 2011.

Chapter 15

URL: www.strangehorizons.com/2001/20011022/medieval_clothing.shtml, accessed Feb. 2015.

URL: www.frenchhospital.org.uk, accessed Feb. 2010.

URL: http://hfebooks.com, accessed Feb. 2015.

Chapter 17

URL: www.imagesofengland.org.uk, Bartholomew Thomas Almshouses, Partis College and Sidney Hill Wesleyan Cottage Homes, accessed 22 Oct. 2007.

Chapter 18

URL: www.clun.org.uk/trinity.htm, accessed Feb. 2015.

URL: www.haddon-hall.com, The Poet of the Peak, accessed Feb. 2015.

Chapter 19

URL: www.bromleycollege.org/history, accessed 14 June 2010.

URL: www.british-history.ac.uk/report.aspx?compid=50694, accessed 13 Aug. 2010.

URL: www.british-history.ac.uk/report.aspx?compid=42053, accessed 8 Aug. 2010.

URL: www.british-history.ac.uk/report.aspx?compid=41807.

URL: www.duchessofsomerset.co.uk/history, accessed 14 June 2010.

URL: www.sonsoftheclergy.org.uk, accessed 14 Aug. 2010.

URL: www.british-history.ac.uk/report.aspx?compid=45236, accessed 24 Aug. 2011.

URL: www.stjohnsleatherhead.co.uk/stjohnshistory, accessed 5 April 2010.

Chapter 20

URL: www.charity-commission.gov.uk, Charity 205293, accessed 22 Jan. 2012.

SUBJECT INDEX

The index is alphabetised in word-by-word order, e.g. *West Ham* is filed before *Westcott.*
Page numbers are given in short form, i.e. 133-5.
Page numbers shown as 133....135 indicate sporadic, often unrelated, references throughout the range.
References to illustrations, maps and figures are given in **bold**. Those for tables are given as 133T, those for appendices as 133A.

SWING UNMASKED
the agricultural riots of 1830 to 1832 and their wider implications

edited by

Michael Holland

ISBN: 0954818088 ppbk

The Captain Swing Riots of 1830 to 1832 alarmed all levels of society at a critical time in British history. This was the last mass rising of the agricultural workers protesting against their pay and conditions – a period when men (and women) flew in the face of authority, disregarding the Draconian sentences that awaited them if they were caught, in a desperate bid to improve their lot. Never again was there to be what almost amounted to insurrection on this scale. This was the last, desperate attempt by the agricultural work force to rid itself of the threat of mechanisation, from the threshing machine, the mole plough, and the winnowing machine.

This new study examines this three-year period of social history, focussing upon unrest amongst ordinary men and women in the pre-trade-union countryside. In addition to nine original essays on the Swing Riots themselves, it offers new work on the transportation of prisoners and fresh material on the cholera riots and other disturbances of the time. Its pages (and the CD-ROM available separately) are packed with newly discovered data, the outcome of a unique national research project undertaken by members of the Family & Community Historical Research Society (FACHRS) using local sources across the country. The result is the discovery that Swing covered a larger geographical area with outbreaks of violence on a scale far wider than had previously been imagined.

Further details and information on this book and benefits of membership of FACHRS can be found on the Society's website

www.fachrs.com

BREAKING NEW GROUND
nineteenth century allotments from local sources

edited by
Jeremy Burchardt and Jacqueline Cooper

ISBN: 978-0-0548189-1-2 ppbk

This book offers important new evidence about the history of 19th century allotments, and shows how deeply embedded they were in rural society. Based on a nationwide research project, Breaking New Ground reveals that allotments were numerous and wide-spread, cherished not only by agricultural labourers, but also by tradesmen, artisans and industrial workers. They were not just a means of alleviating poverty, but a major institution of Victorian village life.

The fifteen chapters include detailed local studies of how allotments developed all over England – in East Anglia, the West Country, northern England, the Midlands and elsewhere. Aspects of allotment history, little explored before, come under the spotlight: the moral dimension of allotment rules, the link between allotments and riots, the intervention of paternalistic employers and the people's desire for allotments to replace lost rights of common.

Accompanying the book is a CD containing a database of over 3,000 allotment sites, by far the most comprehensive yet published, and nearly 1,000 allotment tenants, of particular interest to local and family historians. This important book, the outcome of work by the Family & Community Historical Research Society (FACHRS), will change the way we look at 19th century allotments..

Further details and information on this book and benefits of membership of FACHRS can be found on the Society's website

www.fachrs.com